Praise for *Edison's Environment*

"George Hill's new book introduces an angle to our understanding of the 'Wizard of Menlo Park' that is utterly new: his impact on the environment. Every school child knows that Thomas Edison invented the electric light; and a long parade of historians have acquainted us with Edison the industrialist and employer, the husband and father. But as Hill demonstrates, Edison also had an 'environmental footprint.' That imprint loomed as large as his inventor's persona. It could prove as destructive as it was creative, with ravages sometimes rivaling those very accomplishments for which his life is so often celebrated. The edges of this footprint ranged far and wide, from cities of Newark and New York to rural New Jersey, across topics we usually consider separate: from Edison's and his family's personal health to those of his employees, to his laboratory and factory building; and even to the establishment of an iron mine.

"Along the way, Hill proves a genial guide, with an infectious passion for digging out what remains, be it in documents or photos or on the land itself, of places Edison knew or altered. We learn, in visits to overgrown laboratories, sheds, and mines, that nature has powerful inexorable ways of covering over even the most far-reaching of human tracks. Some sourer legacies of the great inventor nevertheless stand out: a scarred mountainside, numerous factory fires, tons of wastes dumped into rivers, a future Superfund site. For our own age, when new industries and technologies seem once again to be reworking the limits of human endeavor and possibility, George Hill has brought out a side to Thomas Edison that urgently bears remembering."

— *Christopher Sellers, M.D., Ph.D.*
Associate Professor of History
State University of New York, Stonybrook, N.Y.

"This scrupulously researched and carefully documented work illuminates a hitherto little-known area of Edison's life and work. While it is a thoroughly scholarly book, *Edison's Environment* also incorporates the author's reflections regarding resemblances between the details of his own life and that of Edison lending it the charm of a memoir. The observations reveal the strong appeal of the subject to the author, which undoubtedly transformed the exhaustive research required into an enjoyable exploration of a fascinating and complex life. The author has also captured information about sites that no longer exist, making the work a valuable document for both the serious researcher and the Edison enthusiast for years to come."

— *Laura Barrett, M.L.S.*
University of Medicine and Dentistry of New Jersey

"Overall, a great tour de force – a really monumental study. Should become part of the Edison canon. I really liked the mixture of travelogue, scientific history, historical reassessment, biography, ecology, geography ... The use of the first person and the sense of a personal journey works well."

– Sandra Moss, M.D., M.A.
Past President
Medical History Society of New Jersey

"Thomas Edison is acclaimed as the 'Wizard of Menlo Park,' and as *Time* magazine's 'Man of the Century.' Edison saw himself as a benefactor of humanity. But in this startling new look at Edison, Dr. George J. Hill suggests that the price of invention was serious industrial pollution and other environmental costs. Meadows, ponds, and forest disappeared to make way for Edison's laboratories, factories, and mining operation; water and soil pollution were rife, and the health consequences for workers and residents were severe.

"Dr. Hill is the first author to offer a comprehensive look at Edison's impact on the environment. *Edison's Environment* examines the inventor's interactions – as expressed in his life, thought and career – with the natural world, and traces the development of environmental consciousness in the views of Edison and his contemporaries. He explores the fundamental debate about how we should judge the actions and ethics of past generations. In so doing, George Hill has written one of the most novel and original works on Edison to appear in a generation."

– Mark Edward Lender, Ph.D.
Chairman, History Department
Kean University, Union, N.J.

"The wanton dumping of mercury and carbolic acid into a brook, a lawsuit for environmental damages, and angry Italian families marching on a factory carrying dead dogs and cats are not part of the popular image of Thomas Alva Edison. The environmental destruction of Silver Lake is just one of the previously unexplored aspects of Edison's life that Dr. George Hill uncovers in *Edison's Environment* . . . The indifferent attitude of Edison toward the health and safety of workers and neighbors at his Silver Lake plant, which Dr. Hill documents through court papers and through the recollections of plant manager William Hand, is a theme that weaves throughout Edison's manufacturing career."

– Mark J. Magyar
Editor, New Jersey Reporter
Introduction to the First Edition of Edison's Environment

EDISON'S ENVIRONMENT

PHOTO COURTESY OF NATIONAL PARK SERVICE

EDISON'S ENVIRONMENT

The Great Inventor Was Also a Great Polluter

By

George J. Hill, M.D., M.A., D.Litt.

HERITAGE BOOKS
2017

HERITAGE BOOKS
AN IMPRINT OF HERITAGE BOOKS, INC.

Books, CDs, and more—Worldwide

For our listing of thousands of titles see our website
at
www.HeritageBooks.com

Published 2017 by
HERITAGE BOOKS, INC.
Publishing Division
5810 Ruatan Street
Berwyn Heights, Md. 20740

Copyright © 2007, 2017 George J. Hill, M.D., M.A., D.Litt.

Publication history:
First edition published by New Jersey Heritage Press, 2007
Second edition published by Independent Books, 2011

Photos courtesy of National Park Service: Cover photo, Frontispiece, and pages 62, 77, 80, 82, 83, 96, 101, 108, 123, 134, 139, 143, 145, 146, 148, 152, 154, 175, 177, 182, 187, 195, 205, 233, 244, 249, 254, 256, 275, 282, and 285.

Maps on pages vi and 65, and Edison's Family Tree, page 6, were drawn by Axiam Printing Co., Union, N.J., © George J. Hill.

Image courtesy of Newark Public Library on page 15.

Image courtesy of Newark Museum on page 20.

Edison's handwritten map and note, pages 230 and 243, courtesy of Professor Margaret Pierce.

Images courtesy of George F. Smith Library of the Health Sciences on pages 287 and 289.

All other photos were taken by the author.

All rights reserved. No part of this book may be reproduced or transmitted in any form or by any means, electronic or mechanical, including photocopying, recording or by any information storage and retrieval system without written permission from the author, except for the inclusion of brief quotations in a review.

International Standard Book Number: 978-0-7884-5765-4

In Memory of

Thomas D. Hill, Ph.D.

Lieutenant Colonel, USAF, DFC

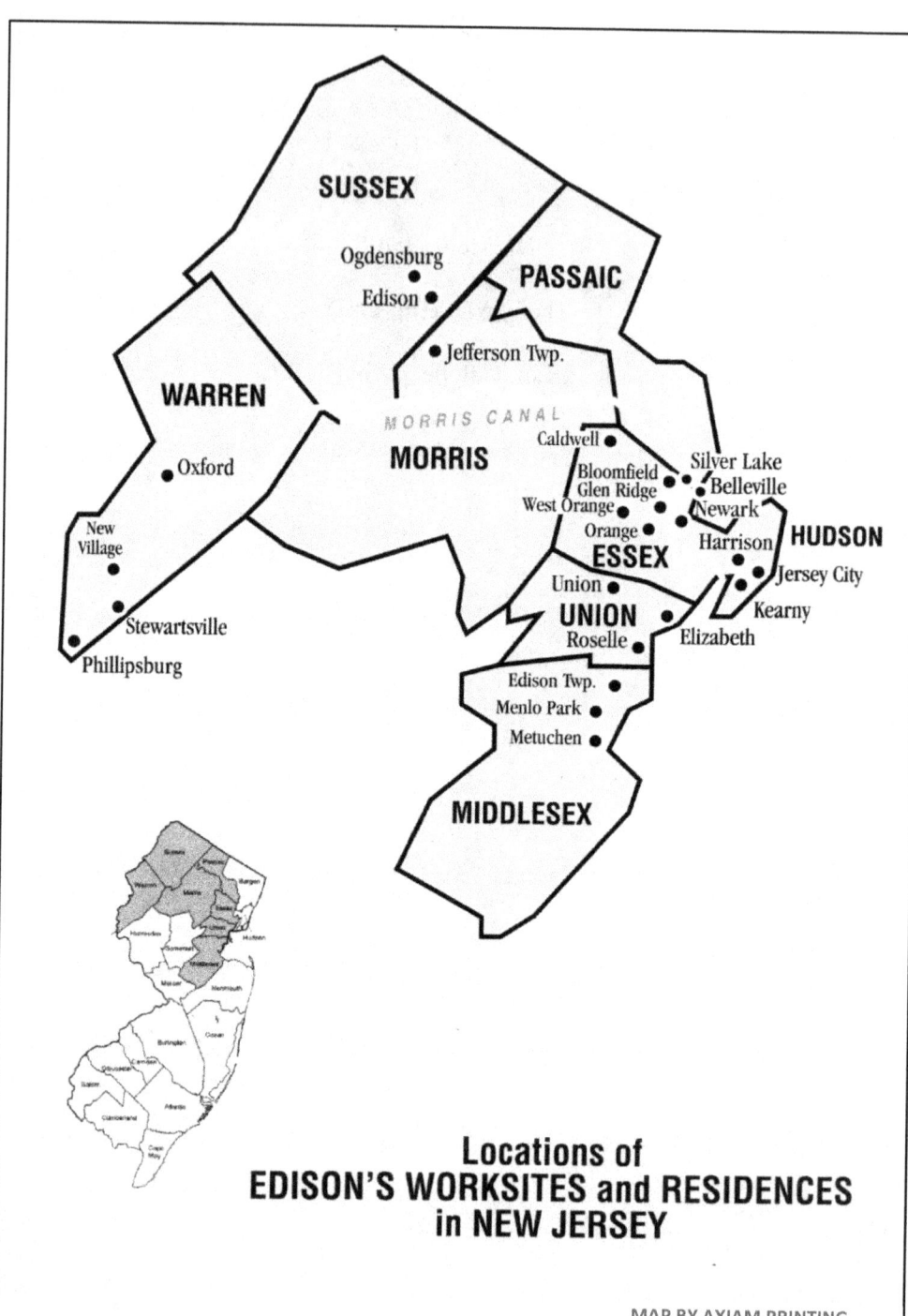

Locations of EDISON'S WORKSITES and RESIDENCES in NEW JERSEY

MAP BY AXIAM PRINTING

Table of Contents

List of Illustrations   vii
Foreword by Mark Lender   xi
Preface   xiii
Introduction   xxi

Part I: Edison's Environment, 1869-1931: The Life of Thomas Alva Edison

Chapter 1. Family and Footprints   3
    The Edeson/Edison Family   4
    Synopsis of Edison's Life, 1847-1886   7
    Edison's Mature Years, 1886-1831   9
    History and Geography of Edison's Footprints in New Jersey   12

Chapter 2. History of the Environment in Orange Valley to 1886   13

Chapter 3. In the Valley   29

Part II: Edison's Environment, 1869-1931 Case Studies of Edison's Impact on the Environment

Chapter 4. The Early Days in New Jersey, 1869-1875
    Elizabeth, N.J., 1869-1870   47
    Jersey City, N.J., 1869-1870   55
    Newark, N.J., 1870-1875   59

Chapter 5. The Wizard in Menlo Park, N.J., 1869-1931   75

Chapter 6. Harrison, Roselle, and Winthrop: Lampworks, Light and Nature, 1882-1892
    Harrison, N.J., 1882-1892   105
    Roselle, N.J., 1883   111
    Winthrop, Mass., 1885   114

Chapter 7. Edison's Glenmont: At Home in Llewellyn Park
    West Orange, N.J., 1886-1931   117
    A Lively Place: Glenmont and Llewellyn Park   119

Chapter 8. Edison in West Orange: The Laboratory and Factories, 1886-1931   137

Chapter 9. The Destruction of Silver Lake: Bloomfield, Belleville and Glen Ridge, 1887-1931   151

Chapter 10. Iron Mining: Ogdensburg, Sparta Mountain, and Lake Hopatcong, 1889-1900   189

Chapter 11. Cement: Limestone Quarries, Roads, and Houses: Warren, Union, and Essex Counties, 1899-1931   221

Chapter 12. Kearny: Battery Factory and the Model A Ford, 1927-1931   267

Chapter 13. Edison and the *milieu interieur*: Health, Hygiene, X-Rays, and Radium   277

Part III. Edison's Environment, 1869-1931: Denouement

Chapter 14. Epilogue: Edison's 'Footsteps' Revisited   295

Chapter 15. Judging Edison: The Issue of Accountability   312

Chapter 16. Conclusion: Environmental Legacy of Edison   361

Appendix – Site Visits   365

Endnotes   371

Bibliography   447

Index   471

About the Author   499

EDISON'S ENVIRONMENT

List of Illustrations

Edison in his laboratory, West Orange, N.J. (1906)	Frontispiece
Map of Edison's Worksites and Residences in New Jersey	iv
Family Tree of Thomas A. Edison (1847-1931)	6
Eagle Rock – 19th Century, Seen from the Base	15
Eagle Rock Crest	16
Eagle Rock Today	17
The Orange Valley in the Late 19th Century	20
The Orange Valley in the Late 20th Century	21
View Toward the Oranges from Eagle Rock	22
Elizabeth Home, 559 Morris Ave., Elizabeth, N.J.	49
Itinerant Boarder, 235 Morris Ave., Elizabeth, N.J.	52
Railroad Access, Railroad station, Elizabeth, N.J.	53
Jersey City Shop, Exchange Place, Jersey City, N.J.	56
Edison in Newark: "Edison Park Fast," Edison Place	60
First Year Site, 15 New Jersey Railroad Avenue	62
Largest Factory in Newark, Ward Street	62
Ward Street Site Today, McCarter Highway at Edison Place	63
Map of Edison's Worksites and Residences in Newark	65
Last Bachelor Quarters, 854 Broad Street	66
Newlyweds, Wright Street	67
Railroad Avenue, Penn Station by Morris Canal	68
Sites of Subsidiaries: 155 N.J R.R. Avenue; 39 Oliver Street	71
The Wizard and His Men, Menlo Park Laboratory	77
Menlo Park Marker: Boulder on Route 27 with Plaque	78
Edison Tower, built in 1937	79
Outcault's Perspective: R. F. Outcault's painting – 1881	80
Outcault's Perspective from Alfieri building – 1998	80
Menlo Park Laboratory Exterior, with Workmen	82
Edison and His "Muckers" in the Laboratory	83
Orientation Map: Sketch Map of Menlo Park	89
Menlo Park Museum on site of the Machine Shop	93
In Edison's Time: Menlo Park – 1880, by Theodore Davis	96
The View Today: Cellar hole at Edison's house lot	97
Edison's Electric Train "Trucks" in West Orange	99
Ghosts of Menlo Park	101
The Edison Lamp Works in Harrison, N.J.	108

Edison's Environment

The Last Vestige of Edison in Harrison	109
Proud Memory: Monument in Roselle, N.J.	111
Edison's Electrolier at Roselle Presbyterian Church	113
The Edison Home, Glenmont, in Llewellyn Park	119
Inside Glenmont: Master Bedroom and Trophy Room	121
Edison at Glenmont: Reading on the Lawn, 1917	123
Cooking with Gas: Gas stove in Glenmont kitchen	124
Gardener's Cottage: Concrete Greenhouse, house, shed	126
Concrete two-story garage at Glenmont, built in 1908	127
Remains of swimming pool and pond at Glenmont	128
Thomas and Mina Edison, and their graves at Glenmont	134
Mausoleum: Charles Edison's tomb, Rosedale Cemetery	135
The West Orange Plant: Building 5 and other buildings	138
Chemist at Work: Edison in his laboratory, West Orange	139
Crook's Pond, and the site today	143
During and after the Great Fire on December 9, 1914	145
"Edison Effect": Edison and an "Edison Effect" light bulb	146
Catnap: Edison asleep on a workbench in West Orange	148
Aerial view of Edison's Silver Lake Plant	152
"Something's Happening in the Silver Lake District" sign	153
Alva Street in Bloomfield, 1912 and 1997	154
Silver Lake, before July 30, 1889	158
The River That Tries to Come Back: Second River's wall	159
Present site of Ink Factory in Glen Ridge (two views)	169
Battery Factory site in Glen Ridge is now Hurrell Field	171
Bloomfield Avenue location of Edison's battery factory	171
Edison's Chemical Works at Silver Lake, 1911 and 1971	175
Settling tanks for crude phenol at Silver Lake in 1915	177
Heckel Street pollution site in Belleville	179
Railroad and rubble at Silver Lake (2 views)	182-83
Silver Lake factory site, now supermarket at Belmont Ave.	184
Fence lining Belmont Avenue in Silver Lake today	185
Silver Lake Chemical Works, 1938	187
Schoolhouse for families of miners at Edison Iron Mine	190
Edison's Iron Mine Company on Sparta Mountain	191
The Iron Miner: Edison at his Ogden/Edison Mine	195
The Lyons House in Ogdensburg	199
General store made from 2 Edison miners' homes	200
Miner's home on Main Street in Ogdensburg	201

Edison's Environment

Sparta Mountain Wildlife Management Area	202
Edison's Iron Ore Separating Plant site on Sparta Mountain	203
The "Horseshoe Cut" in 1997, and when Edison mined it	204
Stone-lined trough on Sparta Mountain	208
Pohatcong Creek near Edison Cement Company site	225
In Edison's own hand: Edison's plan for New Village	230
Darling's house, where Edison stayed	231
First Concrete Road: Route 57 in Warren County	233
Edison's Handwritten note of June 22, 1900	243
Francis Upton and the Upton home	244
From a Crater to Edison Lake	249
Edison's Cement Works: A 1906 factory building in 1997	250
Edison's reputed laboratory in New Village	251
Towering silos once used to store cement	252
Interior view of Edison Cement Works	254
Prefabricated cement houses in Union, 1912	256
Cement house at 983 Ingersoll Terrace	257
A mansion of concrete in Upper Montclair	259
Concrete home at 740 McLaughlin Place, Orange	259
Edison Quarry, now Oxford Quarry	263
"Edison Quarry" name adorns truck door	264
First Factory in Kearny Meadowlands: E-Mark Factory	271
Edison's E-Mark Battery Plant in 1930	275
Edison and his famous traveling companions	282
Gatehouse to the Edison Plant in West Orange	284
First Martyr: Clarence Dally and the fluoroscope	285
Radium Girls: Watch painters at U.S. Radium Corporation	287
Radioactive plume from U.S. Radium Corporation	289
Wigwam Brook: From Edison plant to U.S. Radium Corp.	290

Edison's Environment

Foreword

THOMAS Edison is acclaimed as the "Wizard of Menlo Park," and as *Time* magazine's "Man of the Century." Edison saw himself as a benefactor of humanity. But in this startling new look at Edison, Dr. George J. Hill suggests that the price of invention was serious industrial pollution and other environmental costs. Meadows, ponds, and forest disappeared to make way for Edison's laboratories, factories, and mining operations; water and soil pollution were rife, and the health consequences for workers and residents were severe.

Dr. Hill is the first author to offer a comprehensive look at Edison's impact on the environment. *Edison's Environment* examines the inventor's interactions – as expressed in his life, thought, and career – with the natural world, and traces the development of environmental consciousness in the views of Edison and his contemporaries. He explores the fundamental debate about how we should judge the actions and ethics of past generations. In so doing, George Hill has written one of the most novel and original works on Edison to appear in a generation.

— Mark Edward Lender, Ph.D.
Chairman, History Department
Kean University, Union, N.J.

Edison's Environment

Preface to the Third Edition

THIS project spans two lifetimes, a total of about 170 years. It begins with the birth of Thomas Edison in February 1847 and it continues until his death at age 84 in October 1931. My life nearly overlaps with Edison's. I was born in October 1932, and I am now age 84. I mention this coincidence, because in so many ways, Thomas Edison has profoundly affected my own life.

Thomas Edison was, more than any other individual, the Great Inventor of the modern world. His inventions made possible the phonograph, the long-lasting electric light, and motion pictures. The phonograph was a unique discovery, his alone, although others were more skillful than he was in making improvements in it and in sales of recordings. And although he was not the only person to work on the development of electric lights and movies, his inventions were coupled with an uncanny ability to market them. Edison invented many other products, some of which are no longer in use, but nearly all found a market at the time, and some are still used today. He invented important safety devices such as the miner's lamp and battery-operated signals for train crossings in remote locations. Edison also invented the fluoroscope, although it was not one of his patents. Ahead of his time, he developed the electric automobile and the electric train. Electricity now powers many of the trains in use today, and the electric car now appears to be the car of the future.

His restless mind was always at work. Edison foresaw the use of atomic power and solar power. He also understood the uses of carbon-based polymers better than anyone else in America. He was a pioneer in the separation of metals, and of manufacturing high quality concrete. In the 1930s, Henry Ford and Harvey Firestone persuaded Edison to search for an alternate source of rubber, believing – correctly – that another world war would soon break out, and that rubber would become the most important strategic commodity in that conflict. Shortly before he died, Edison found a good source of latex for rubber in goldenrod.

More than seventy years ago — like many of my contemporaries — I began to do experiments with the wonderful powders and liquids that came in my first A. C. Gilbert Chemistry Set. This was in the fall of 1943, and the chemistry set was a gift for my eleventh birthday. Our house in rural Iowa had no gas (although we had electricity, our house was heated by a coal furnace in the basement and by a coal stove in the kitchen), so I used the flame of a candle for boiling my chemicals. A marvelous little

EDISON'S ENVIRONMENT

alcohol lamp was a later addition to my laboratory. I recall having been given a choice. Would it be a chemistry set, or an electrical set (which included, I think, a small crystal radio), or an erector set? Without hesitation, I chose the chemistry set, because I already knew that I wanted to experiment with chemicals. Was this because of Thomas Edison? I don't know, but I do know that Edison was often referred to in my home and in my classrooms when I was a boy.[1]

The "Wizard of Menlo Park" died less than a year before I was born, and the legends of his life were told and retold to schoolboys throughout the Midwest — where Edison was born, and where I too, was born and grew up. His first experiments, we were told, were done in chemistry laboratories that he put together in his home and on the train where he worked as a newspaper and food salesman. How natural it was, then, for many boys in the 1930s and 1940s to begin to emulate Edison by doing experiments of their own, in their own home chemistry laboratories. My mother, who had taught geology at Cornell College in Mt. Vernon, Iowa, before I was born, encouraged me to develop a small chemistry laboratory in our home. I later learned that young Thomas Edison was encouraged in a similar way by his mother, in rural Michigan, nearly a century earlier. I suspect that my mother had Edison in mind when she gave me the chemistry set for my birthday. Having returned to Cornell College to teach navigation to naval aviation candidates while my father was in the service, Mother encouraged me to expand my little laboratory with cast-off glassware from the college chemistry lab. I was also encouraged by my mother's younger brother, a chemical engineer who later became vice president of Nalgene, a large scientific glassware company.

I later learned that when he was a boy, Edison had bought chemicals from a pharmacist in his home town, and that he enjoyed mixing up explosive mixtures in his laboratory. Like many other youngsters since Edison's time, I followed the same route to obtain pyrotechnic chemicals. Sulfur and powdered charcoal (two of Edison's favorite chemicals) were in my Gilbert Chemistry Set, and the formula for black powder (gunpowder) was in my high school's *Encyclopedia Americana*. All I had to do to make gunpowder was to mix sulfur and charcoal with sodium or potassium nitrate, which I could buy at the local drugstore. With money earned from selling newspapers (once again, like the young Thomas Edison) and delivering laundry in my neighborhood, I eventually bought the druggist's entire supply of these items. Also, in unconscious imitation of the Great Inventor, I intensified my explosive mixtures with potassium perchlorate, which I read would (and in the event, did) enhance the ignition of the three elements of black powder. I used homemade fuses and electricity from dry cell batteries that I borrowed from our doorbell to blow up tin cans in my back yard with black powder. For a time, I even considered making dynamite (the method was right there in the encyclopedia, for every boy to read), but I decided that I didn't want to make, in my bathroom laboratory, the nitroglycerine that had to be made first, in order to make dynamite. I also thought of making guncotton and trinitrotoluene, but the descriptions of these explosives in the encyclopedia were clearly too vague to be recipes, and I finally decided that other types of experiments would be more likely to keep me out of trouble, and in good health.

No adult ever said "No" to any of my questions about chemistry, nor did anyone discourage me from proceeding with these hazardous experiments, before I was even twelve years old. I think many people believed that I was going to be another Tom Edison, and they just hoped that I wouldn't burn our house down or blow myself up while I was finding my way. In fact, both the president of Cornell College and the head of the Navy unit encouraged me to learn Morse code — a skill that Edison, too, learned when he was about the same age as I was then. I was given a seat in a class for a small group of "special" students, including the Navy unit's skipper, Lieutenant Commander Totten P. Heffelfinger, a scion of the Pillsbury family of Minneapolis.

I later learned of other similarities between my background and that of Thomas Edison. Like Edison, I, too, have ancestral roots in Canada. When I was a boy, one of our "family secrets" was that my mother's paternal grandparents had emigrated in the nineteenth century to eastern Iowa from Nova Scotia, where their families had lived as the descendants of Tories who were expelled from Massachusetts during the Revolutionary War. (My mother's ancestors actually migrated from Massachusetts to Nova Scotia before the Revolution, but the legend that they were Loyalists persisted. It was instead my father who had Tory ancestors from New York and Vermont who went to Canada.) Thomas Edison's great-grandfather, John Edison, was expelled to Nova Scotia after the Revolutionary War. During the Revolutionary War, "Tory John" Edison was then living in Essex County, New Jersey, and it was there that his son, Thomas Edison's grandfather, Samuel Ogden Edison, Sr., was born. Later, as an old man, John Edison migrated to western Ontario with his family. Thomas's father, Samuel Ogden Edison, Jr., was also rebellious, and he fled for his life to the United States after participating in an abortive insurrection in Canada. After a childhood spent in Ohio and Michigan,

EDISON'S ENVIRONMENT

and after a variety of jobs throughout the Midwest, in Boston, and New York, it was to Essex County, N.J., where his grandfather was born, that Thomas Edison returned at the age of twenty-three. Edison moved away for a while, but he returned again to Essex County when he was thirty-nine and lived there for the last forty-five years of his life.[2]

My long-standing but dormant interest in Thomas Edison was renewed when I moved to New Jersey in 1981 and bought a home in West Orange, less than three miles from Edison's Laboratory, some of his factories, and his home. In the course of getting acquainted with my new neighborhood, I enjoyed taking a tour of Edison's Laboratory, which is maintained as a museum by the National Park Service. The Laboratory and his home, Glenmont, are now collectively called the Thomas Edison National Historic Park (TENHP). In 1997-8, the park was called the Thomas A. Edison National Historic Site (ENHS), and the acronyms TAENHS or ENHS therefore appear throughout the book. I also saw Glenmont on many occasions when visiting friends in the private, gated community where it is located, known as Llewellyn Park. I was fortunate to have a chance to take a closer look at the Edison Laboratory during a field trip with my fellow graduate students in Professor Richard Sher's course on the History of Technology in the fall of 1996, and to read Matthew Josephson's thoughtful biography of Edison under Professor Sher's guidance.[3]

Many accounts of Edison's life and his great achievements appeared in 1997, the sesquicentennial year of his birth. Praise for Edison was, however, offset to some extent by comments in local newspapers from individuals in West Orange who bemoaned the deterioration of the valley in which Edison's Laboratory and factories were built. And some of the older residents had bitter recollections of Edison's unpaid bills, and of his thoughtless or capricious ways with his workers. Everyone in the community seems to have a favorite Edison story. Most of them are pleasant, but there is an edge to some of these stories that suggests a less-than-mythical appreciation for Edison, the man, and for Edison, the businessman. I therefore decided to take a close look at Thomas Edison, to try to place him in perspective with respect to the environment in which he lived, and upon which he had such a profound effect.[4]

I am pleased to acknowledge the encouragement and assistance that I received from many individuals during the planning and preparation of this book, including, alphabetically: Marie Acceturo, Bill Anderson, Mr. and Mrs. John L. "Jack" and Augusta Baum, Helen Beckert, Brian Bilby, Bill Boland, Charles Boll, Carl J. Brown, Dr. Ronald C. Brown,

Edison's Environment

George Campbell, Dr. Bohdan Chudio, Dr. Fred Cohen, Mrs. Anne Connell and her sons Roger and Dennis, Ms. Christine Connor; Rev. Dr. J. Max Creswell, Kathy Craig, Mrs. Lester Daugherty, Lois Densky-Wolf, William C. "Doley" Dolan, Rich and Marlene Dutton, Betty Frolich Edwards, Arthur Ellenberger, Professor George Erikson, Nancy E. Felter, Joseph Fonzia, Bill and Ruth Frolich, Barbara Fuller, Bill Graff, Claire Griese, Elmer Gustafson, the Rev. Abigail Hamilton, Jim and Bob Hauk, Charles E. Hill, Dr. Helene Z. "Lanie" Hill, Paul F. Hill, Dr. Sarah Hill, Dr. Thomas D. Hill, Wasco and Sylvia Hadonowetz, Bill Hamilton, Dr. E. Denman Hammond, Charles Hummel, Barbara Irwin, Professor Paul Israel, Ms. Dorothy Johnson, Dr. Robert and Mrs. Janet Johnson, Jim Kellogg, Linda Kimler, Joseph Knapp, Leo Koncher, Dr. John Laszlo, Carl Kantrowitz, Dr. Fred Kilgour, Jeffrey Kirk, David Koenig, Jim and Mary Lee, John Lender, Professor Mark Lender, Frederick Lewis, Professor Jan Ellen Lewis, Professor Jacob Lindenthal, Clifford Lindholm III, Professor George Lovell, Mark J. Magyar, Harry B. and Betty Mahler, Professor Peter Masseri, Helen (Mrs. Ronald) McGuirk, LaChone McKenzie, Gary Meddaugh, Steve Misiur, Bill Mogilski, Dr. Mirseyed A. Mohit-Tabatabai, Dr. Robert O'Driscoll, Mrs. Evelyn "Betty" Naomi Olson, Joe Penkara, Tony Petrangelo, Professor Peggy Pierce, Sheldon Pincus, Professor Clement Alexander Price, Rabeya Rahman, Mrs. Robert U. (Nancy) Redpath, Robert M. "Bob" Reed, Keith Robbins, Margaret "Peggy" (Shippen) Robbins, George Rogers, Professor Bob Rosenberg, Ms. Lucy Sant'Ambrogio, Professor Christopher Sellers, Charles Shallcross, Professor Richard Sher, Bob Shubert, Mrs. Skok, Dr. David Edison Sloane, Jack Stanley, Doug Tarr, Dr. George Tselos, Richard Volkert, George K. Warne, Joan White, Lee B. Williams, Dr. Arthur Winter, George Wise, and Dr. Robert "Bob" Woolsey.

I thank all the people who added interesting information about Edison and his family after reading the first edition of this book., and although I cannot thank them all, I mention a few who were especially helpful: Chris Bobbins, Joe Bolster, Theodore "Ted" Brewer, Stan and Leanna Brown, Governor Brendan Byrne, Bernard J. D'Avella Jr., Richard Dutton, Maureen Edelson, Doug Smith Governor Christie Whitman, Frank Williams, and Frank Zupa.

I also thank the following institutions and organizations: Charles Edison Fund, East Orange, N.J.; Dana and Alexander Libraries of Rutgers University; Belleville, N.J., Public Library and its Silver Lake Branch; Bloomfield, N.J., Public Library; Boxwood Hall State Historic Site, Elizabeth, N.J.; Church of the Holy Innocents, West Orange, N.J.;

Edison's Environment

Caldwell, N.J., Public Library; Thomas Edison - Henry Ford Estates Museum, Fort Myers, Fla.; Thomas A. Edison National Historic Site (TAENHS, or ENHS) [now Thomas Edison National Historic Park], West Orange, N.J.; Edison Tower/Edison State Park, Edison Township, Middlesex County, N.J.; Elizabeth, N.J., Public Library; Essex County Medical Society; Fairmount Cemetery, Newark, N.J.; First Presbyterian Church of Caldwell, N.J.; First Presbyterian Church of Orange, N.J.; First Presbyterian Church of Roselle, N.J.; Franklin Mineral Museum, Franklin Township, Sussex County, N.J.; Franklin Township Branch Library, Warren County, N.J.; Friends of Edison; Glen Ridge, N.J., Public Library; Harrison, N.J., Fire Department; Henry Ford Museum at Greenfield Village, Dearborn, Mich.; The Historical Society of Bloomfield, N.J.; Harrison, N.J., Public Library; Kearny Museum and Kearny Public Library, Kearny, N.J.; Montclair, N.J., Historical Society; Montclair State University; Mount Pleasant Cemetery, Newark, N.J.; New Jersey Department of Environmental Protection, Fish Game and Wildlife Service, and New Jersey Geological Survey; New Jersey Department of Labor; New Jersey Historical Society; Newark Museum; Newark Public Library, Newark Stamp and Coin Shop, Ogdensburg Historical Society, and Old Firehouse and Old Schoolhouse Museum of Ogdensburg, N.J.; The Old Guard of Princeton; Orange Public Library; Oxford Quarry, Oxford, N.J.; Rosedale Cemetery, Orange, N.J.; Roselle, N.J., Historical Society and Roselle Public Library; publishing advice from Rutgers University Press; Health Sciences Library, Saint Barnabas Medical Center, Livingston, N.J.; Sterling Hill Mining Museum, Ogdensburg, N.J; Triart Graphics; Union County Cultural and Heritage Advisory Board; Union County Historical Society; University of Medicine and Dentistry of New Jersey (now Rutgers University) - George F. Smith Library; Upland Press, Union, N.J.; Victaulic Company of America, New Village, N.J.; Village Camera, Inc., South Orange, N.J.; Warren County Cultural and Heritage Commission, Oxford and Belvidere, N.J.; West Orange, N.J., Health Department; West Orange Public Library; and Yale Club of Central New Jersey.

My first book on this subject was *Edison's Environment: Invention and Pollution in the Career of Thomas Edison* (2007). It was a lightly edited revision of the thesis that I submitted in January 1999 for the M.A. in history at the Graduate School-Newark of Rutgers, The State University of New Jersey. After I completed the thesis, and before and after the book was published, I began to respond to requests to lecture on Edison. Over the last fifteen years I have given more than twenty-five lectures on

EDISON'S ENVIRONMENT

various topics related to the Great Inventor, including his genealogy, his inventions, and his impact various communities in New Jersey. I have been amazed at what I have learned from people in my audience. At almost every lecture, at least one or two people, sometime more, have wanted to tell their own stories about Edison, his companies, or his family. Some of the older ones had worked for one or another of the Edison companies, and others recalled stories told by older relatives who had worked for Edison when he was alive. A few members of my audience actually had personal recollections of Edison. Others had recollections of Edison's immediate family, especially his widow, and her children. They usually referred respectfully to "Mr. Edison," or to "Mrs. Edison." Although I don't believe any of my listeners have challenged my findings, their comments have helped me to appreciate the complexity of Edison, the man, and of his work. Several of my listeners and readers of my book have used it as a guide to follow the path of Edison as he lived and worked in New Jersey, and thus to find his "footsteps." Many changes have already occurred in these sites during the past two decades, and more will surely occur in the future.

Four books were published after I wrote *Edison's Environment* in which other aspects of the troubled legacy of the Great Inventor are mentioned. Jill Jonnes discussed his questionable business practices in *Empire of Light* and Mark Essig showed his dissimulation in *Edison and the Electric Chair*. Edison and his involvement with electrocution are also discussed by Thom Metzger, in *Blood & Volts: Edison, Tesla and the Invention of the Electric Chair*, and by Michael Daly, in *Topsy: The Starling Story of the Crooked Tail Elephant*.[5]

The first and second editions of *Edison's Environment* are now out of print. Many people have asked me how to find a copy to buy, but I have only a few left for my family. Used copies are sometimes available from second-hand dealers, but they are usually offered for sale at prices that are beyond the range of most readers. In response to requests from potential readers, I have decided to publish another edition of *Edison's Environment*. The subtitle of this edition was first expressed by one of the history professors at Rutgers-Newark in 1999. He said, after reading my thesis, George, "You have shown that the Great Inventor was also a Great Polluter." A knowledgeable New Jersey politician heard me say this and said, to my surprise, that "He also wasn't a very nice man."

Edison's Environment

Introduction

Cook's pond, where ducks sported in the summer months, was at the back door of the laboratory, and meadowland stretched in every direction.

— David Lawrence Pierson, 1922[6]

AT the age of seventy-four, Thomas Alva Edison was not just the most famous citizen of the town of West Orange, New Jersey, where he had lived for the past thirty-five years; he was arguably "The Most Notable Man in the World." He was thus described in 1922 by David Lawrence Pierson, historian of the Oranges, who wrote a lyrical description of the site that Edison had chosen in 1887 for his laboratory and factory. Cook's pond, Pierson continued, was "a small body of water, the delight of the boys in the decade immediately preceding." Pierson hardly needed to add that by 1921 Cook's pond was long gone. The aerial photograph that accompanied Pierson's biographical sketch of Edison showed that the pond had been buried under the massive buildings of the Edison plant, its former location marked by the chimney of the Laboratory's powerhouse on Lakeside Avenue. With quiet understatement, Pierson wrote an obituary and epitaph for Cook's pond, and for the meadowland of West Orange. It was fitting for Pierson to refer obliquely to the disappearance of Cooks's pond and the meadows around it, for in 1922 Thomas Alva Edison owned this area. Edison was the most famous and probably also the richest man in West Orange, and he was a man who did not enjoy being criticized.[7]

Thomas Edison achieved prominence as an inventor while he was still a young man, and he achieved a near-mythical status before he was forty, as the "Wizard of Menlo Park." Born in 1847, this hard-working, insightful, ambitious, and clever man had, before his death in 1931, invented or co-invented and manufactured a wide range of new products that made his name and face familiar to millions of people throughout the world. His insatiable curiosity led him to make important discoveries that were later exploited by others, and he continued to perform scientific research until the last weeks of his long life. In his own lifetime, Edison was credited by the public with the invention of the incandescent electrical light and the phonograph, of motion pictures, of many useful electrical appliances, and of the alkaline storage battery. He was recognized by contemporary academic scientists, other inventors, and businessmen for his seminal observations and discoveries in fields as diverse as telegraphy, the telephone, electricity, radio, organic chemistry, metallurgy, cement manufacturing, and botany. He pioneered the development of the industrial laboratory, and many of his business methods were employed as models by his admirers and his competitors. Edison was acutely aware of his public image, and he assiduously courted the press to enhance and maintain his reputation. He was a master at responding with "one-liners" that would become eminently quotable. He was widely believed to be a genius, a selfless humanitarian who worked indefatigably and successfully to make the world a better place in which to live. The myth of "Thomas Edison," which he helped to create, eventually became larger than the man.[8]

Even now, a century and a half after Edison's birth and more than six decades after his death, Americans still rank him as one of the most admired figures in the history of the world. Only a few years ago, a Gallup Poll showed that Edison ranked sixth, after Jesus Christ, George Washington, Abraham Lincoln, Franklin Delano Roosevelt, and Douglas MacArthur. Edison was featured in the "The Inventors' Specials" series on the HBO television network that premiered on 8 July 1997, along with "Einstein: Light to the Power of 2"; subsequent specials were presented on Leonardo, Galileo, the Curies, Edison, and Isaac Newton.[9]

During Edison's lifetime, rumblings occasionally surfaced regarding his companies' problems with labor relations and industrial pollution, issues that would now be called "environmental" concerns. These concerns are recalled even now, especially by residents of the communities in which Edison's factories were located, and by some scholars. But the image of the white-haired, folksy, humble philosopher made it difficult to criticize him personally when he was alive. And even now, long after his death, the impact of Edison on the environment has not been subjected to an in-depth appraisal, in which his contributions to the environment are assessed in detail, along with whatever negative aspects are also present. This was, however, my task, although I must admit that I embarked on it with mixed feelings. My misgivings arise because I appreciate Edison's admirable characteristics, as they were described by his contemporaries and by historians and biographers, and for many of his contributions to the world that we now inhabit. Nevertheless, I believe that the environmental effects that resulted from Edison's life and work must be drawn together, so we may view them comprehensively, and learn whatever lessons they may tell us.

Edison's Environment

For this book, "environment" refers to that which "surrounds," and "all the conditions, circumstances and influences surrounding and affecting the development of an organism or group of organisms." The environment thus defined includes the nature and quality of human life, the biotic ecosystems of non-human flora and fauna, and the landscape of earth, air, and water. In this book, I will examine the aspects of Edison's life, thought and career that relate to the development of human values regarding the natural world. I also intend to study the views of Edison and his contemporaries regarding the nature of life and of the human body, as reflected in concepts of health, wellness, illness, safety, and medicine. I plan to determine how the environmental perspectives of Edison and his contemporaries were developed, and see how well the actions of Edison and others conformed to their own beliefs.

The main body of the book is divided into three parts. Part I is an introduction to the geography of the Orange Valley in eastern New Jersey, where Edison lived for five years (1870-1875), and to which he returned for the last forty-five years of his life (1886-1931). During the latter period, Edison's Laboratory and many of his factories were located in the Orange Valley. This part also provides a brief synopsis of Edison's life, focusing on the aspects of his life which relate to the environment. Part II is a case study of Edison's environmental impact in New Jersey, based on site visits, a review of archival documents, other primary and secondary sources, and current observations. Part III, "Denouement," is composed of an Epilogue, Discussion, and Conclusion.

Part III examines the changes that are associated with Edison's activities in seven counties of New Jersey: Essex County (where he lived in Newark and later in West Orange, and where he had factories in the towns of Newark, West Orange, Glen Ridge, Bloomfield, and Belleville); Hudson County (where he had a shop in Jersey City and where two of his factories were located, in Harrison and Kearny; Middlesex County (where he lived from 1876 to 1881 at Menlo Park, and where he built a laboratory and factory); Sussex County (where he conducted a major iron ore mining operation); Morris County (where his iron ore was transported en route to the marketplace); Warren County (where his Portland cement factory was located); and Union County (where he lived briefly in 1869-1870, and where he later built a small municipal electric power system and several pre-fabricated cement houses). The principal focus of Part II is on the latter half of Edison's life (1886-1931), during which he lived and had his main laboratory in West Orange. This was not only the longest period of

Edison's residence in one place; it was, as we shall see, the period during which Edison had his greatest personal impact on the environment.

Part III, "Denouement," discusses the environmental transformations that are associated with Edison, especially those that are studied in depth in this book. I begin this part with an Epilogue that is based on my personal observations and on comments by others, to bring the reader forward by seven decades, from 1931 – when Edison died – to when this first edition was being written in 1998. Many more changes have occurred since then, but they are beyond the scope of this book. The environment is always changing. The Epilogue is followed by a Discussion, in which Edison's environmental impact is assessed, and in which Edison's impact is contrasted and compared with other significant contributions to the environment (through either change or preservation) that occurred during and after his lifetime. The facts, speculations, and arguments of the book are then drawn together and summarized in a Conclusion.

This book does not review or discuss in depth the technical details or the history of development of all his inventions and of his 1,093 patents, although many of these inventions will be referred to as part of the outline of Edison's work. Also, this book does not, in general, engage in a discussion of the controversies regarding whether Edison invented, or co-invented, or "stole" this or that invention from someone else, or whether a given invention represented a major breakthrough or was simply a part of the evolution of a field. I have excluded these topics from extended discussion because Edison's leadership in various fields of invention and manufacturing is a matter of historical record, and has been thoroughly discussed by biographers of Edison and his colleagues and competitors. The validity of these claims is, nevertheless, important with respect to the degree of responsibility for environmental impact that may reasonably be assessed to Edison for the many inventions, discoveries, products, business practices, and other actions that he claimed, or that have been attributed to him.

Throughout this book, unless otherwise indicated or modified, the proper name Edison refers to Thomas Alva Edison, not to other members of the Edison family or to the various uses of the Edison name in Thomas A. Edison's partnerships and corporations. Also, unless otherwise indicated, the chronology of Edison's life that has been prepared by the Edison Papers Project is considered to be definitive.[10]

In summary, this book examines the environmental impact and the environmental legacy of Thomas Alva Edison, the industrialist and Great

Edison's Environment

Inventor who was one of the most famous men of his era, and who is still a legendary figure more than eighty-five years after his death. The book will show that the Great Inventor was also a Great Polluter; and that Edison's adverse impact on the environment was sometimes – although not always – the result of conscious actions taken by him or at his direction, knowing the risks, and proceeding to take them anyway, and to shield them from public view.

Part I

EDISON'S ENVIRONMENT, 1869-1931

The Life of Thomas Alva Edison

THIS chapter of the study of "Edison's Environment" provides a synopsis of the life and work of Thomas Alva Edison. This chapter also reviews the geography and environmental history of the Orange Valley of eastern New Jersey, where Edison spent most of the latter part of his life. This chapter begins with a brief review of the existing literature on the Great Inventor.

* * * * *

The vast amount of material written about Edison and the enormous mass of documents that he left to posterity give pause to the scholar. Assessment of previous scholarship and review of the archival material on Edison is a formidable, but not hopeless, task, because the strong, continuing interest in Edison by scholars and the public has led to the publication of a fine array of currently in-print, well-documented biographies and focused monographs. Furthermore, teams of scholars are now hard at work on the preservation, cataloguing, description, assessment, and publication of the papers, notebooks and other artifacts that were left by Edison.

The archivists of the Edison National Historic Site (now called the Thomas Edison National Historic Park) in West Orange and the historians of the Edison Papers Project of Rutgers University, New Brunswick, are leaders in the ongoing scholarship on Edison. Other teams of scholars are at work at locations as distant as Fort Myers, Florida; Dearborn, Michigan; Milan, Ohio; and Port Huron, Michigan. Oral reports and recently published work from all of these sources provide invaluable assistance to a student of Edison's environment. The perspective that is presented in this book is, nevertheless, not that of any one of the scholars or groups of scholars whose work is cited. There are differences of opinion regarding the validity of some information related to Edison, inasmuch as distinguishing "fact" from "fiction" or "myth" is often difficult, and this is certainly true in the case of Thomas Edison. In addition, some of the stories and legends that relate to the topic of Edison and the environment appear in only one or two of the published monographs.

Chapter 1

Thomas Alva Edison:
Family and Footprints

THE principal sources that I utilized for information regarding the life and work of Thomas Alva Edison are five full-length, in-print scholarly biographies (listed in order of publication) by Matthew Josephson (1959, reprinted in 1992), Robert Conot (1979), Martin V. Melosi (1990), André Millard (1990), and Neil Baldwin (1995); and eight focused scholarly monographs (listed alphabetically by first author or editor): Robert Friedel and Paul Israel, with Bernard S. Finn; Paul Israel; Charles Musser; William S. Pretzer (ed.); George Tselos; Byron M. Vanderbilt; Wyn Wachhorst; and Raymond R. Wile (ed. Ronald Dethlefson). All of the focused monographs except those by Tselos and Wachhorst are currently in print, and those two are readily available from major libraries. Paul Israel's biography of Edison was published in 1998.[11]

Six other monographs that are currently in-print provide useful information regarding Thomas Edison and the environment. Valuable information was also obtained from presentations and in conversations with participants at the "Interpreting Edison" Conference, held in Newark and West Orange, New Jersey, 25-27 June 1997. In addition, the first three volumes of the Edison Papers Project and the microfilm index of the unpublished papers were referred to in hard copy and were accessed through the Edison Papers' world wide web home page.[12]

The history and geography of the areas surrounding Edison's homes, laboratories and factories in New Jersey during the period 1886-1931 were summarized from information in the aforementioned monographs, plus histories of the Oranges by Stephen Wickes and David Lawrence Pierson, and the history of Essex County by John T. Cunningham and Charles F. Cummings. Additional information was derived from three bound reports and a Master's thesis, and from maps that were obtained from governmental and commercial sources. Ephemera and periodicals, principally newspapers, provided details that were lacking in the larger publications.[13]

Thomas Edison has been the subject of a great number of books, pamphlets, scholarly papers, and articles in periodicals for the general public. Many of these appeared before he died in 1931, and were either written by his associates and friends, or authorized by him. These early publications provide interesting background information, and they serve as loci for efforts made by later scholars to develop a chronological record of Edison's life. They thus provide clues that help to distinguish between facts and legends or myths regarding Edison. However, with one exception, publications that appeared before Edison's death have not been reviewed for general background information in the preparation of this book, since they have not been thoroughly vetted for accuracy. The single exception to this general rule is Francis Jehl's *Menlo Park Reminiscences* (1937), which was reprinted in 1990 by the Henry Ford Museum, with an Introduction by the curator of the museum. We will return to Jehl's work in due time, after discussion of recent biographies, focused scholarly works, and other sources that are used in this book.[14]

My summary of the history of Edison's family and of his childhood and early years as an inventor is a composite of information drawn from four biographies of Edison that are listed above, and of the outline of his life that has been prepared by the Edison Papers Project.[15]

The Edeson/Edison Family:
Thomas Edison's Ancestors and Siblings, 1727-1896

Thomas Alva Edison (1847-1931) was the fourth son and the seventh and youngest child of Samuel Ogden Edison, Jr., and Nancy (Elliott) Edison. His father was the grandson of John Edeson, who was born in the Netherlands in about 1727 and came to New Jersey with his widowed mother in 1730, when he was about three years old.

As an only child, John Edeson inherited an estate that was substantial enough to enable him to own a seventy-five acre farm near the Passaic River in what is now the town of Caldwell, in the western part of Essex County, west of Newark, New Jersey. In 1765, John Edeson married Sarah Ogden, who was a daughter of Samuel Ogden; the Ogdens were early settlers in northern New Jersey, and were a prominent family at that time. John and Sarah Edeson had ten children, of whom the eldest son, Samuel Ogden Edeson, (the spelling was later changed to

Edison) was born at the family home in Caldwell. John Edeson was a Loyalist in the Revolutionary War, and in 1783 he and his family, including Sarah and their seven children, were forced to emigrate to Nova Scotia along with British troops and thousands of other Tories.

While living in Digby, Nova Scotia, Samuel Edison met and in 1792 married Nancy Stimson. The sixth of their eight children was a son, Samuel Ogden Edison, Jr., who was born in Digby in 1804. In 1811, John Edeson led his family, including many of his children, their spouses, and his grandchildren, into the area north of the Great Lakes that was then known as Upper Canada, in the search for better land and greater opportunities for the future. His son, Samuel, was a captain in the British forces in the War of 1812. The community that the Edeson/Edison clan and others from Digby founded is now known as Vienna, Ontario. The patriarch, John Edeson, died there at the age of 87. Samuel, Sr., widowed at the age of 60, remarried and had five more children before he died at the age of 98. It was in Vienna, Ontario, in 1828, that Samuel, Jr., then 21, met and married 17-year-old Nancy Elliott, daughter of the Rev. John Elliott and granddaughter of Capt. Ebenezer Elliott, of Massachusetts. Samuel and Nancy (Elliott) Edison had seven children, of whom the first four were born in Ontario. In the winter of 1837, Samuel Edison, Jr., was involved in a rebellion against the Canadian government and fled across 80 miles of frozen woods and lakes to safety in the United States.

Sam Edison settled in Milan, Ohio, and was later joined there by his wife and children. They had three more children in Milan, including the youngest, who was named Thomas for his father's uncle and his brother, and Alva for his father's friend, Captain Alva Bradley. Three of the children died at Milan in infancy or childhood, leaving only four survivors: The eldest, Marion (born in 1829, for whom Thomas would name his own eldest daughter); William Pitt (born in 1832, for whom Thomas would name his second son); Harriet Ann (born in 1833); and Thomas Alva (born in 1847). In 1854, when Thomas was seven years old, the family moved to Port Huron, Michigan. Marion married a man who was a farmer near Milan; later, as a widow, she lived in the Edison family house in Milan. The ancestral Edison house had by then been purchased by Marion's younger brother, the now-famous inventor, to become a museum. William Pitt, Thomas' older brother, remained in Port Huron; his son, Charles, worked for his uncle, Thomas Alva Edison, in New Jersey and in Europe. Thomas Edison later named his youngest child for Charley, who died of peritonitis in Paris at the age of 19.[16] Nancy Elliott Edison died in 1871 in Port Huron, and Sam had

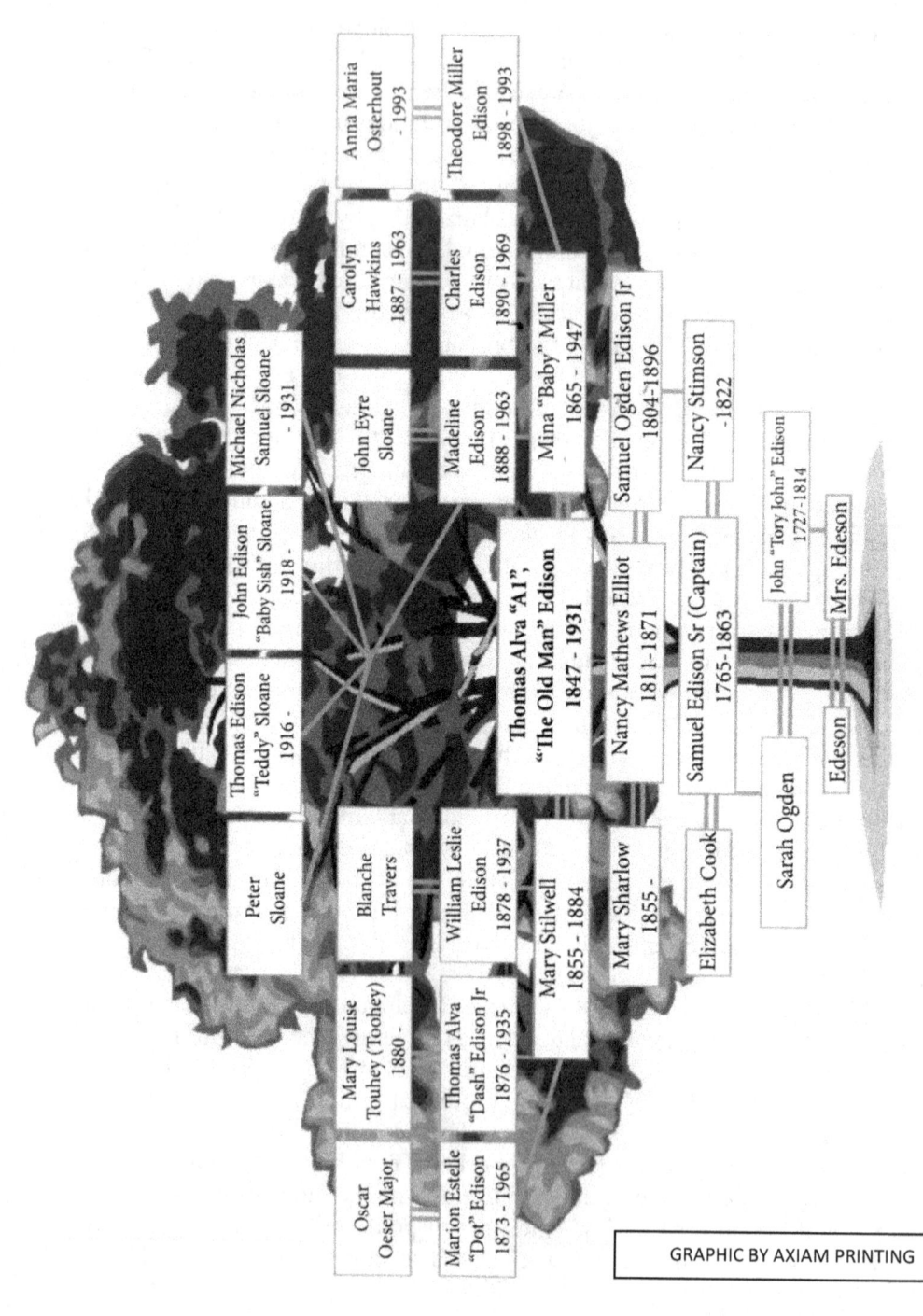

three more children by Mary Sharlow. Miss Sharlow was a sixteen-year old servant girl in Sam's house when Nancy Edison died, and Thomas Edison apparently never accepted her three daughters as relatives of his, although they were his half-siblings. Thomas Edison asked his father to supervise the construction of his laboratory and other buildings at Menlo Park, and he later supported his father's travels with a friend, Jim Symington. Samuel Edison, Sr., died at the age of 92 in 1896 while returning to his home in Port Huron.

It is not entirely clear how much of this family history was known to Thomas Edison, but he was familiar with the general outline, including the fact that some of his ancestors and relatives were soldiers in the Revolutionary War, and that the Edisons had migrated across Canada and down to Ohio. When he was a boy, he visited his relatives in Ontario on many occasions, where he met his very elderly grandfather, Samuel Edison, Sr. What he knew of the Ogdens of New Jersey is not clear, but he presumably knew of his connection to the Ogden family, since his grandfather, father, and his deceased baby brother all bore the same name: Samuel Ogden Edison. Thomas Edison also believed that his ancestors were long lived; indeed, having apparently misplaced a generation, he thought his grandfather was 102 when he saw him as an old man in Canada. Whether or not Edison was conscious of this aspect of his heritage, it is interesting that over a span of three generations, Thomas Edison, his father, and his paternal grandfather remarried and had second families after the deaths of their first wives. Furthermore, in the same year—1871—both Thomas (in New Jersey) and his father (in Michigan) married sixteen-year old women who worked for them.

Synopsis of Edison's Life
from 1847 to 1886

The happiest time in my life was when I was twelve years old.[17]

It was my good fortune to encounter Thomas Paine's works when I was thirteen. . . . I recall thinking, "What a pity these works are not today the school-books for all children!"[18]

—Thomas A. Edison

Thomas Alva Edison was born in Milan, Ohio, on 11 February 1847. At the time of his birth, this last child of Sam and Nancy Edison had two older sisters, Marion (18) and Harriet Ann "Tannie" (14), and a brother,

William Pitt (5). Two brothers and a sister who were born after Tannie had already died, and young Thomas Edison (who was called "Al") was thus the only survivor of his parents' last four children. Al Edison's childhood was interrupted by his family's move to Port Huron, Michigan, when he was seven years old. Edison had a few months of classroom education at Port Huron, but he received most of his education at home from his mother, who had been a schoolteacher before she was married. Following a series of childhood illnesses, including scarlet fever, he developed a serious, progressive loss in his hearing; as we shall later see, Edison's deafness had a profound effect on his relationship to the environment, and on his life's work.[19]

At the age of twelve, Thomas Edison began to work as a salesman of snacks (a "candy butcher") and newspapers on the railroad that ran from Port Huron to Detroit, and he eventually began to print his own newspaper for sale on the train. Throughout his years as a boy and young adult, Edison experimented with chemicals, batteries, and telegraphy. Although he was somewhat of a "loner," Edison was involved in many mischievous activities and so-called "practical jokes," and he developed a reputation for both impudence and independence.

In 1862, at the age of fifteen, Edison began to study telegraphy under the guidance of a railroad stationmaster who was an acquaintance of his father. He was soon able to find work as a telegrapher, and he qualified as an expert by the age of eighteen. Between 1863 and 1867 Edison was an itinerant telegraph operator. During this period, he continued to perform experiments in telegraphy, including improved methods of transmission, and on the batteries that were used for telegraphy. His career as an inventor is traceable to his early experiments with the telegraph, and with the chemical reactions that produced direct current electricity for telegraphy and other communications, such as the stock ticker and the telephone.

Edison accommodated well to the boisterous, semi-vagrant life of the young men who worked as itinerant telegraphers in the Midwest and upper Southern states during the Civil War, and some of his acquaintances from those early days were a part of his personal environment in later years. During the late fall and early winter of 1867-1868, near the end of his twentieth year, Edison became seriously ill and spent several months recovering at his home in Michigan. In the spring of 1868, at the age of 21, he left the Midwest and landed a job with Western Union as a telegrapher in Boston. It was then said of him that "Mr. Thomas A. Edison is a man of genius ... of the highest order of mechanical talent, [whose] mode of transmissions both ways on a single wire [is] interesting, simple and ingenious."[20]

In 1869 Edison moved to New York City to continue his work on telegraphy and electrical devices, while boarding in New York and then in Elizabeth, New Jersey. The next year he established a shop in Newark, New Jersey. A year later he wrote to his parents that "I am now what you Democrats call a 'Bloated Eastern Manufacturer'"[21] In 1871 Edison married one of his young employees, Mary Stilwell, and purchased a home in Newark. Their first child, a daughter, was born there in 1873, followed by a son in 1876. In the meantime, Edison worked successfully as an independent inventor while also collaborating (and alternatively, contending) with a wide range of companies and individuals, including Western Union and the financier, Jay Gould.

In 1876 Edison moved his family and his base of operations to Menlo Park, New Jersey. His stated plan was to create "a minor invention every ten days and a big thing every six months or so." A second son was born at Menlo Park in 1878. Between 1876 and 1884, when Mary Edison died, Edison conceived and directed the construction of a wide range of new inventions and products, including the first phonograph and an important improvement in the telephone, known as the carbon button transmitter. In October 1879 Edison conducted "the first successful experiment with a high-resistance carbon filament" for the electric light, and he held the "first successful demonstration of his incandescent electric lighting system" on 31 December of the same year. In 1881 Edison moved his residence and business operations to New York City, followed in the next year by his laboratory, after the successful opening of his Pearl Street central station for electrification of the Wall Street district. In 1882 Edison had reached a pinnacle in his life, and he wrote that "I have accomplished all that I have promised."[22]

Edison's Mature Years: 1886-1931

I will have the best equipped & largest Laboratory extant.

—Edison, 1886[23]

In 1885, during the year following the death of his first wife, Edison purchased land for a winter home in the village of Fort Myers, Florida. In the same year, Edison met and proposed marriage to Mina Miller, daughter of a prominent Ohio industrialist; he married Mina in 1886. They moved into Glenmont, a mansion in Llewellyn Park, West Orange, New Jersey, which was their home until his death forty-five years later, and where their three children — a daughter and two sons — were born in 1888, 1890 and 1898.[24]

In 1887, Edison constructed a laboratory on fourteen acres of land near Glenmont. He then resumed work on the phonograph and perfected it for the marketplace, as well as a motion picture camera, projector, and movies that had great commercial public success. He formed and later sold Edison General Electric, the predecessor of the present General Electric Corporation. He then reorganized and consolidated his laboratory and businesses under his own name, as Thomas A. Edison, Inc., which operated factories in West Orange and several other locations in New Jersey, and elsewhere. In the latter part of the nineteenth and in the early twentieth centuries, Edison developed new techniques and large industrial operations for magnetic ore separation and for the manufacture of Portland cement. He served the U.S. Navy as a civilian consultant during World War I, and he later developed a successful nickel-iron-alkaline storage battery. In the last years of his life, Edison conducted extensive research at his property in Florida, on alternative sources of latex for production of rubber. By the time of his death, Edison had transformed his previous image as the young "Wizard of Menlo Park" into that of the "Old Man," a practical philosopher, whose passing was widely mourned.[25]

In January 1886, Thomas Edison purchased Glenmont, which was to be his new home in Llewellyn Park, West Orange, and on 24 February he and Mina Miller were married at her parents' home in Akron, Ohio. They moved into Glenmont in the spring, following a honeymoon at Fort Myers, Florida. The following winter he purchased land near Glenmont on which to build a new laboratory, which opened in December 1887. Mina Edison's first child, and Thomas Edison's second daughter, Madeline, was born on 31 May 1888; Madeline later married and had four children, who were Thomas Edison's only grandchildren. Thomas and Mina's next child, Charles, was born on 3 August 1890. Their third child, and Thomas's sixth, Theodore Miller Edison, was born on 10 July 1898. Mina Edison was the "home executive," in charge of the family affairs at Glenmont and Fort Myers. She was also active in civic affairs and oversaw the education of the children and the organization of her husband's life to a greater extent than his first wife had done. William Pitt Edison, Thomas's brother, died in Michigan, in 1890, and his father, Samuel, died in Ohio on 26 February 1896; Thomas attended these funerals. In 1916 Edison took the first of several annual camping trips with Harvey Firestone and other famous men, including John Burroughs and Henry Ford.

Following a strike at the Edison Machine Works in 1886, Edison relocated his machine works to Schenectady, New York, and in 1888 he began to discuss the business consolidation that became the Edison General Electric Company in 1892; he later withdrew from General Electric and invested his proceeds in his other businesses. In the same year, Edison began to construct his Phonograph Works in West Orange, and electrocution experiments with dogs and other animals were conducted in his laboratory. Also, in 1888, he organized the New Jersey and Pennsylvania Concentrating Works to develop his ideas for mining iron ore. In May-August 1890, ore separation tests were begun at the Ogden mine that he purchased in Sussex County, New Jersey. He was soon conducting large scale surface mining and ore concentration activities at Ogden, which he renamed as "Edison" in 1892.

Thomas Edison was personally involved in the iron ore operations for much of the time until he shut down the ore milling plant in December 1898. He subsequently moved much of his equipment from the iron mine and mill to Warren County, New Jersey, where it was used for cement mining and manufacturing. In 1890 Edison purchased property at Silver Lake, in the Bloomfield-Belleville area in New Jersey, on which he located the Edison Manufacturing Company. In the following year, he demonstrated his kinetoscope for the Federation of Women's Clubs, and in 1894 he copyrighted his first motion picture. In the same year, the first commercial viewing of the peephole kinetoscope was held in New York City, and he produced seventy-five movies. In 1896 Edison experimented with Roentgen's discoveries in x-rays and produced an x-ray fluoroscope.

In 1898 Edison began to study the production of Portland cement, and in the following year he began work on storage batteries. By 1907 he had produced poured concrete houses for sale, and in 1909 he marketed his successful alkaline storage batteries. His many industries were consolidated as Thomas A. Edison, Inc., in 1911, and in 1926 he turned this organization over to his son, Charles, as president. He introduced his popular Diamond Disc phonograph in 1912, but two years later, on 9 December 1914, the Edison Phonograph works and his other factories in West Orange were destroyed by fire. However, the laboratory was spared, and he soon rebuilt and resumed his manufacturing operations in West Orange. The following year he was appointed head of the Naval Consulting Board, and Naval research continued to occupy much of his attention until the end of World War I. In 1927 Edison organized a corporation to develop a means to produce rubber from plants that were indigenous to the United States, and he experimented with commercial sources of latex up to the end of his life.

Thomas Edison was showered with awards during the last years of his life, including many honorary degrees and a medal from Congress in 1928. His laboratory at Menlo Park, New Jersey, was reconstructed as a museum by Henry Ford at Dearborn, Michigan; this museum was officially opened for the Golden Jubilee celebration of the electric light on 21 October 1929. Edison executed the application for the last of his 1,093 patents in January 1931 and he died at Glenmont at the age of 84 on October 18 of the same year.

The History and Geography of Edison's "Footprints," His Principal Locations in New Jersey

"Tate! See that valley?" "Yes, beautiful, isn't it!" Tate replied. "I'm going to make it more beautiful. I'm going to dot it with factories."

—**Edison to Alfred O. Tate, about 1887**[26]

We do not know if this anecdote of a conversation between Thomas Edison and his personal secretary is an accurate record of Edison's beliefs and plans, but it is consistent with the history that subsequently evolved in Essex County, New Jersey. As we will see, Edison did indeed "dot" the valley with factories. However, it has been said that beauty is in the eye of the beholder, and it remains to be seen whether Edison and others considered that the valley was "more beautiful" after the factories were built.

In the next chapter, I examine the early history and geography of some of the places in New Jersey where Edison lived and worked during the last half of his life. These are the places that I call the "footprints" of Edison.

Chapter 2

History of the Environment in the Orange Valley of Essex County to 1886

> *[A] spring, less constant in its flow, trickles down the gully and descends the mountain through the southern limits of Llewellyn Park.*
>
> —*Stephen Wickes, 1892*[27]

IN 1892, Llewellyn Park had been Thomas Edison's terrain, his habitat, for six years. This book explores some of the changes that have occurred in the past century to the mountain that Stephen Wickes wrote about, to its springs and gullies, and to Llewellyn Park itself. Although the focus of this portion of the book is on the period from 1886-1931, our study is framed by the history of this region prior to Edison's arrival, and by what has happened since his death. Let us, therefore, begin in the present, and work our way back into the distant past.

The Unseen Valley

"A marvelous view," exclaims the young man from Colorado on this warm summer day, as he looks at Manhattan Island from the Eagle Rock Reservation in Essex County, New Jersey. He sees New York City, but he pays no attention to the valley that sweeps toward the horizon, or to the hillside below him, where Llewellyn Park is located. One hundred years ago, a spring-fed brook, "less constant in its flow," entered the Park from this summit ridge. The changes in landscape that have subsequently diverted this brook away from Llewellyn Park will concern us, but are of no interest to the tourist. Like countless others who stand here whenever the skies are clear, the tourist is struck by the awesome sight of the Empire State Building and the Twin Towers of the World Trade Center in New York City, fifteen miles to the east, as they appear from this vantage point in West Orange, some 580 feet above sea level. (n.b.: The Twin Towers were destroyed on 11 September, 2001. The tourist is not at all curious about the valley, how it was formed, and what is in it. For him, the eastern valley of Essex County is just a dark green sea of leafy treetops, a pleasing foreground for the skyscrapers on the horizon. This valley is unseen by most of the visitors who come here to get a view of New York City, it is the valley, not the city, that is the focus of our interest.[28]

The tourist leans on a low retaining wall, hardly aware of the twenty foot cliff that falls away into the trees before him. Below the cliff — although he cannot see this at all — the ground continues to drop steeply through the trees for another 200 feet over a distance of less than an eighth of a mile. The ground soon levels off, and a dense forest then appears in the middle distance, that stretches nearly to the horizon. At first glance, it appears to be an ancient forest — primeval, ageless. But on closer inspection, the tops of a few tall buildings can be seen above the trees. And in the southeast, what appears at first to be a miniature white cylinder on stilts, is a water tower. With binoculars, the word "EDISON" in black capital letters can be read on its north side. This is the water tower of the Edison laboratory and factory, now the Edison National Historic Site; the water tower is four hundred feet down and a mile and a quarter away. Thomas Edison's home in Llewellyn Park is also down there and about the same distance from us, further around to the south, hidden in the trees.

There are, indeed, thousands of homes and factories and offices in the eastern valley of Essex County. They are largely hidden by the trees that, in the aggregate, comprise the mass of greenery which frames the lower portion of the view to the east from this point. We begin to see that this is not a primeval forest after all, but it is instead a densely-populated valley that is covered with large trees. The tourist from Colorado is riveted on his study of Manhattan, which appears to be treeless and covered with buildings from end to end. He does not see that Essex County, New Jersey, where he is standing, is also covered with buildings, roads and highways, for these are, in this season of the year, obscured by

COURTESY OF THE NEWARK PUBLIC LIBRARY

EAGLE ROCK IN THE 19TH CENTURY: This undated drawing by Harry Fenn shows an artist painting Eagle Rock from its base.

PHOTO BY GEORGE J. HILL, M.D.

EAGLE ROCK CREST: An American flag whips at the peak of Eagle Rock during a visit in 1997.

vegetation. A third of a million people live and work in the valley, but they cannot be seen or heard from this point, an outlook that has been known for many decades as Eagle Rock. The tourist from the Far West makes no connection between this view of Manhattan and Thomas Edison who lived and worked, died, and was buried in the valley below him. Nor does he consider the impact that Edison had on this valley, and on the cities and towns that lie within and beyond it. In order to understand Edison's role in this environmental transformation, we need to step back in time to consider the region's geology, geography, and environmental history, prior to Edison's arrival in 1886.

    The place where we are standing gives us a good vantage point to begin this study of Edison's effect on the environment in Essex County, New Jersey. Our study begins with an anomaly. Although we are in the Eagle Rock Reservation, it is strange that there is apparently no specific place here that we can locate that is called "Eagle Rock." "Where is Eagle Rock?" I ask two elderly women from South Orange, who have picnicked on these grounds since they were children; they are baffled by the question. So, too, is a middle-aged man who strolls by. He lives in Livingston, over the mountain, to the west. He hikes here frequently, looking for dinosaur fossils, and he knows all the trails on this wooded summit. I have come to the Reservation with a nineteenth century artist's sketch of Eagle Rock in my mind's eye. Eagle Rock was then a craggy peak, 630 feet above sea level. No one can tell me where it is.[29]

Never mind, I finally say to myself. For the time being I will assume that the nineteenth century painter of Eagle Rock used a lot of artistic license. I decide that the term "Eagle Rock" may refer to a place near where we are standing, where the edge of the cliff rises slightly and is covered with small, loose rocks. This rocky point, which I have decided is as good as any to call Eagle Rock, is rimmed by a short wrought iron fence. The gate is unlocked, and I step inside. I approach the edge of the cliff cautiously, for it would not be wise to stumble here. Inside the enclosure is a sturdy but windblown oak tree with wide spreading branches, and a flagpole with an American flag whipping at its peak in a brisk southern wind. There is also a granite marker that is inscribed in memory of an Essex County freeholder, one

PHOTO BY GEORGE J. HILL, M.D.

EAGLE ROCK TODAY: The regrowth of dense vegetation at the base of Eagle Rock has hidden the face of the cliff, which was so striking in the 19th Century perspective provided by artist Harry Fenn. (See drawing on page 15).

Michael Leo Delahunty (1928-1990). This point at the edge of the cliff, which I have decided to call Eagle Rock, is midway between the north end of the retaining wall against which the tourist lounges, and the Highlawn Pavilion, a five-star restaurant located about 30 yards further to the north.[30]

The *Orange, N.J.* quadrangle map shows that the point that I have decided to call Eagle Rock is on the east loop of Crest Drive at about 40°48'30"N and 74°14'W. The height of land in the Eagle Rock Reservation, about 650 feet above sea level, is 300 yards or so to the west of us. The quadrangle map shows that we are on a long ridge called "First Watchung Mountain." The full length of the mountain becomes apparent only when we inspect the adjacent *Caldwell* and *Roselle* quadrangle maps, and the map of Essex County. We then see that this mountain arises in Passaic County to the north and extends for the full length of Essex County — a distance of nine miles — into Union County, where it appears again as the Watchung Reservation, east of the town of Summit. First Watchung Mountain, or "First Mountain" as it is often called, is crossed by many important roads, some of which we will soon examine in detail. First Mountain is also familiar to travelers, who have seen its innards where it is pierced by Interstate 280 in West Orange and Interstate 78 in Union County.

First Mountain runs generally from northeast to southwest, with a long, relatively flat summit that is relieved by gentle depressions through which paths and roads have crossed the mountain for hundreds of years. First Mountain's highest points are located in Eagle Rock Reservation, on a mile-long ridge that is between 600 and 650 feet in elevation. Somewhere on this ridge in the woods near Eagle Rock is the true summit of the mountain. The specific summit point is not marked on our map, and it is not apparent in the dense woods. The trails along the summit ridge go over at least three places that exceed 640 feet, and one of these locations is presumably the highest point. How this mountain came to be called First Mountain will soon become apparent, as will the sequence of changes that have occurred on the mountain, along its slopes, and in the valley east of it since the first English settlers arrived here in 1666.

In ancient geological times, the place called Eagle Rock has not always been 580 feet above the "line of mean high water," nor has the Atlantic Ocean always been fifteen miles or so to the east of this point. In the context of geological time, the transformations of First Mountain and of the valley to the east of it during the past few centuries are, in fact, trivial, compared to the Metazoic metamorphosis that created the two great mountains of Essex County. In order to understand these changes, we need to step far back in time. More than half a billion years ago, beginning in the Precambrian era and continuing through much of the Paleozoic, the mountains that we call the Appalachians began to rise to the west of what is now Essex County, New Jersey. The Appalachians rose to immense height, as high as the Rocky Mountains of western America are today. The Highlands of western New Jersey are included in the Appalachian uplift, but First Mountain, on which we are standing, is not. Some 280 million years ago, in the Pennsylvanian period, the rise of the Appalachian fold was complete, and the Appalachians have since been worn down to their present height. The Watchung Mountains then began to form.[31]

The Watchung Mountains, including First Mountain, where Eagle Rock is located, were formed later than the Appalachians, and in a distinctly different way. The three ridges of the Watchungs, which cover some 500 square miles of New Jersey, were created beginning about 230 million years ago, in the Mesozoic Era. The Watchungs were formed as the result of forces that developed at the close of the Triassic Period and continued through the Jurassic, when the supercontinent known as Pangea began to break apart, creating the Atlantic Ocean. The crustal rupture caused by the separation of Europe from North America opened crevices, called dikes, in the Earth's mantle, through which molten rock, known as magma or lava, hundreds of feet thick flowed onto large areas of the Earth's surface, and then solidified. When the magma cooled, it became a form of very hard, dark gray rock that is known as basalt, which then was covered with sediment that washed down from the western Highlands. The process of extrusion of magma onto the surface was repeated two more times over a period of some 20 million years. The three layers of extruded magma resulted in the production of three distinct layers of basalt.

About 180 million years ago, the western supports of these three thick layers of basalt began to drop and the layers tilted, becoming higher in the east than in the west. The exposure of the eastern edges of the three tilted layers of basalt, and the erosion of the sediment between the basaltic layers, produced three ridges, which are called First, Second, and Third Mountain. These three mountains are collectively known as the Watchungs, meaning "High Hills" in the language of the Lenni Lenape Indians. The Watchungs and their intermontane valleys comprise the Piedmont of eastern New Jersey, while the western New Jersey Highlands are foothills of the Appalachians.

COURTESY OF THE NEWARK MUSEUM

THE ORANGE VALLEY IN THE LATE 19TH CENTURY: Carl August Sommer painted this view of the Orange Valley from First Mountain.

    The Watchungs were thus not formed by being driven upward above the earth's surface, as was the case with the older Appalachians and the younger Rocky Mountains in the west. Rather than being thrust above the earth's surface, the Watchungs were instead revealed by erosion and disappearance of the softer and looser rocks that lay around and between them. The first of the three ridges that one encounters when proceeding west from Newark was also the first of these ridges to be formed. It is known as First Mountain.

    The English Puritans who came to this area in 1666 bought a tract of land from the Lenni Lenape Indians that ran from the west bank of the Passaic River to the base of First Mountain. Their little settlement on the river eventually became known as Newark. Twelve years later, the colonists purchased an additional tract which included the eastern slope of First Mountain from its base to the ridgeline, thus completing their acquisition of the eastern valley of Essex County. This valley is part of an even larger geologic depression known as the Newark Basin that extends from northern Bergen County in the north to the Raritan River in Middlesex County in the south.

PHOTO BY GEORGE J. HILL, M.D.

THE ORANGE VALLEY IN THE LATE 20TH CENTURY: The unbroken expanse of trees seen by Carl August Sommer in the 19th Century is now dotted with houses and factories stretching all the way to Manhattan.

The Newark Basin encompasses the eastern lowlands of Passaic, Essex, Union counties. The valley that was purchased by the English in the seventeenth century spreads out before us, as we stand on the edge of the cliff at Eagle Rock on First Mountain. As we look ahead to the horizon, and down into the forest, we can see why the colonists needed to secure the ridgeline. The early English settlers must have soon discovered that the base of this mountain, deep in the woods below us, was totally vulnerable to those who controlled the *defilade* where we are standing, and the summit ridge of the First Watchung Mountain that lies behind us.[32]

We will soon descend into the valley, to examine more closely the area where Edison lived and worked in West Orange. Before we do that, however, there is more for us to see from Eagle Rock. From this point, it is possible to view, or at least to imagine, the location of nearly all of Edison's "footprints" in New Jersey. We spread out the *Orange, N.J.* quadrangle map, to see the foreground, and roadmaps of Essex County and of New Jersey, which provide a distant perspective. We first decide to simplify our examination by accepting a convenient bit of shorthand: We

PHOTO BY GEORGE J. HILL, M.D.

THE VIEW TOWARD THE ORANGES FROM EAGLE ROCK: The water tower of the Edison complex in West Orange and the gold steeple of Our Lady of Mount Carmel Church in Orange are seen through the trees in the valley below Eagle Rock.

will refer to this mountain as running in a north-south direction, and we will continue to say that Newark and New York City are to the east of us, although these are not precisely correct statements.[33]

Somewhere in the woods directly in front of us, below Eagle Rock, is the town of Glen Ridge, where Edison had at least one of his factories. Beyond this, further to the east, is the area known as Silver Lake, on the border between Bloomfield and Belleville, where Edison had a large factory complex; this area, too, is now hidden in the woods. Glen Ridge and Silver Lake are about on the line of sight between Eagle Rock and the Empire State Building. One can also imagine the course of Bloomfield Avenue, as it runs from Newark through Silver Lake and Glen Ridge, and then proceeds on the west. Bloomfield Avenue crosses First Mountain in Montclair, where one of Edison's cement houses is located. Thomas' grandfather Edison was born in 1765 in a farmhouse just north of Bloomfield Avenue in Caldwell, two miles to the west of First Mountain. This ancestral Edison farmhouse is still standing, at 71 Elm Road, near the present location of Caldwell College and the birthplace of President Grover Cleveland.[34]

By turning a bit more to the right, to the southeast, (although the map shows that it is nearly due south), we see again, down in the valley, the water tower that marks the location of the Edison laboratory and factory complex. Beyond this, in the same direction, but somewhat farther away (about a mile, in fact), the gold steeple of Our Lady of Mount Carmel Roman Catholic Church in Orange rises through the trees. Mount Carmel Church is at South Center Street and Freeway Drive East, adjacent to Interstate 280. The church is close to Parrow Street, near the geographic center of the town of Orange.

We need to mark the location of these two structures — the Edison water tower and Mt. Carmel Church — in our mind's eye, because between them is the height of land that divides the watershed of the Passaic River from that of the Elizabeth River and the Rahway River. This watershed passes along an imaginary line running from center of Newark to the summit ridgeline of First Mountain. To our left (to the east and north, as we look east from Eagle Rock), the water flows to the Passaic, while to our right (southeast and south), water flows into the Elizabeth and Rahway Rivers. The thoroughfare known as Park Avenue runs from Newark to West Orange on the north side of this watershed, while a few blocks south of Park Avenue, Main Street (known by various names in Newark and the Oranges) runs roughly parallel to Park Avenue on the south side of the watershed. The watershed or "divide" (as in "Continental divide") between Park Avenue and Main Street is such a gentle elevation that few residents of the Oranges realize that it exists.

Along the entire length of the base of First Mountain in Essex County a street or road can still be found that is identified, in various ways, with the valley that we have been examining from Eagle Rock. It is called, at different places, by such names as Valley Street, or Valley Avenue, or Valley Road, or South Valley Road. This street is a very old thoroughfare, and we shall learn more about it in due time. For now, suffice it to say that when Edison moved to West Orange in 1886, the street known as Valley Street or Valley Avenue was the principal north-south route through West Orange. This street ran from South Orange on the south, to Montclair on the north. Indeed, to this day, Valley Street runs along the east bank of the East Branch of the Rahway River from South Orange Avenue in the township of South Orange, through Maplewood (which was once part of South Orange), and thence to the southern border of Essex County in Millburn. To the north, although there is no river beside it (the Passaic is far away at this point), Valley Road runs along the eastern base of First Mountain from Bloomfield Avenue in Montclair to the northern border of Essex County, and on into Passaic County. Valley Avenue once formed the eastern boundary of Llewellyn Park, where Edison lived, and it was also the western boundary of the property that he bought on which to construct his laboratory.

Valley Street or Valley Avenue (which is now called Main Street) thus served as the interface between Park Avenue, which joined West Orange to Newark, and Mt. Pleasant Avenue, which proceeded west over First Mountain from a point only one hundred yards south of Park Avenue. Mt. Pleasant Avenue was once the southern border of Llewellyn Park. Valley Street or Valley Avenue was at one time the western terminus of Main Street, which ended at St. Mark's Church in Orange (now West Orange). From this point Northfield Avenue arose and continued across First Mountain to the town of Livingston. Valley Street, by its various names, is thus an important landmark for us, as we consider the geography that Edison encountered and which he transformed. We must, however, imagine its location in our mind's eye, for it is hidden in the trees below Eagle Rock.

When we descend into the woods below Eagle Rock, our focus will principally be on the northern part of the eastern valley of Essex County, the part that is drained by the Passaic River, where Edison's home and factories were located. But we will also be concerned with the upper reaches of the Rahway River, because the history of land use and industrial development in Essex County that preceded Edison's arrival includes major changes in the towns now known as the Oranges. These towns were originally part of one large town, known as Orange. The town of Orange once included most of the enormous wooded valley that we have been looking at below Eagle Rock (and, indeed, also most of First and Second Mountain and the valley, known as Pleasant Valley, that lies between these mountains). We therefore need to examine the history of the towns of Orange and West Orange to understand what Thomas Edison found when he moved here. To this end, we now descend, in our mind's eye, to the area of the Edison water tower, at the base of First Mountain. Our descent will be circuitous, for we have two more "footprints" of Edison to see before we leave First Mountain.

In order to find the other two locations of Edison's activities in New Jersey that can be visualized from First Mountain, we must travel five miles to the south, to another lookout point, known locally as Washington Rock, in South Mountain Reservation. From this place, we can see, or at least imagine (for it is usually too hazy in the valley to make out distinct landmarks) the location of the cement houses that Edison built in Union, New Jersey. We can also visualize the location of Menlo Park, where Edison worked so productively in the years before he moved to West Orange. To find Washington Rock, we now leave Eagle Rock Reservation and proceed south along Prospect Avenue to where it ends in about two miles, at Northfield Avenue. Prospect Avenue follows the ridgeline, but is just to the west of it. While most of the ridge is now occupied by homes and business locations, and is bristling with telecommunication towers, we should observe several important landmarks that recall what this area was like when Edison arrived here. The first of these landmarks is in an area called the Crystal Lake Woods.

Crystal Lake is located a few hundred yards south of Eagle Rock Road. At this point the ridgeline is covered for a tenth of a mile or so, not with buildings, but with grass and trees, enclosed within a chain link fence. In 1997, this was believed to be the last remaining undeveloped land on First Mountain in West Orange. Still privately owned, this piece of property surrounds Crystal Lake, and was originally part of Llewellyn Park. Further to the south, Prospect Avenue crosses over Interstate 280, which runs through an enormous gash in the mountain. I-280 slices through West Orange, cutting off what was once the southwest corner of Llewellyn Park and dividing the township into two parts. A half mile south of I-280, we cross Mt. Pleasant Avenue; this intersection once marked the southwestern corner of Llewellyn Park. Across the street, to the southwest, is the Essex County Country Club. This private club was established in 1887, the same year that Edison built his laboratory on the other side of First Mountain, in the valley below the Park. Prospect Avenue ends at Northfield another mile to the south.

It is theoretically possible to hike from here directly to our destination, but to go on foot we would have to pass through private land (including the golf course of the Rock Spring Club) for the next mile. So instead, we descend to the east and skirt the ridgeline by driving south along Gregory Avenue in West Orange and its extension, Wyoming Avenue, in South Orange, to South Orange Avenue. Turning west on South Orange Avenue, we ascend the mountain again for a half mile, and enter South Mountain Reservation. This reservation is more than three square miles in size. Like the Eagle Rock Reservation, it is part of the Essex County Park System, which was created in 1895, eight years after Thomas Edison built his laboratory at the base of First Mountain.[35]

In the South Mountain Reservation, we drive or walk south for about one and one-half miles along a paved road that is — like the road that we were on at Eagle Rock — named Crest Drive. We soon pass a fine lookout with a view to the east that is similar to the one that we had at Eagle Rock, and then, about a half-mile from South Orange Avenue, we encounter a horizontal metal pole that closes the southern extension of Crest Drive to vehicular traffic. On any clear day there will usually be others who are also walking along the road that continues to the south for another mile. The road ends at a lookout that is called Washington Rock.

Washington Rock is a boulder at the end of the loop at the southern point of Crest Drive on Essex County maps, and on the *Roselle* quadrangle. The boulder bears a plaque that tells of the battle that was fought in the valley below here in June 1780; an American flag flies from a pole nearby. Legend has it that George Washington stood here to watch his troops turn back the British at the East Branch of the Rahway River. The site of the battle is marked on the bridge over the river on Vauxhall Avenue, near its intersection with Millburn Avenue, a short distance from Valley Road, of which we spoke previously. The location of the battle is no longer visible from Washington Rock, because the trees have regrown to obscure the base of the mountain. But our purpose for being here is to visualize Edison's footprints, not a battle that was fought a century earlier, and this spot suits our needs very well.[36]

We begin by orienting ourselves, using the Empire State Building as a land-mark if the day is clear, or with a compass if it is not. The Empire State Building is on 34th Street, which is just north of east from our vantage point, while 10th Street in New York City is due east of us. Turning to the southeast, we can see airplanes descending into Newark airport in the middle distance. Closer than that, in the valley below us, in the same line of sight, is the sprawling intersection of Interstate 78 and the Garden State Parkway. The large billboard erected by the town of Hillside helps us to identify I-78 just east of this intersection. Unseen, the Elizabeth River passes under this mass of concrete (the Parkway occupies the valley of the Elizabeth just north of I-78), and then turns east. The West Branch of the Elizabeth joins the main river about a mile to the southeast of this point, below Kawameeh Park, which is on the east side of the Parkway near Exit 140. On the west side of the Parkway, near Exit 140, opposite Kawameeh Park, is a short street in the town of Union that is called Ingersoll Terrace. This is where, in 1917, Edison built eleven prefabricated houses of poured cement; later, we shall find ten of these houses, which now serve as family homes.

    Let us now take another quarter-turn to the right, and face the southern horizon as it appears from our position along the low retaining wall on the east loop of Crest Drive. Recall, if you will, that we are in the South Orange Reservation in Millburn, near Washington Rock. We can now visualize, at least in our mind's eye, the location of Edison's laboratory, home, and factory at Menlo Park. The Edison Memorial Tower, marking the site of the laboratory at Menlo Park, is eleven miles away, almost due south of this point in Millburn; in fact, it is due south of Short Hills, which is the western part of Millburn. For a comparison of distances, our New Jersey roadmap shows that the Edison Memorial Tower is about the same distance to the south as Jersey City is to the east. The Empire State building, which can be seen on a clear day by moving a bit to the left, is four miles further to the east, about 15 miles away. I have never had a powerful enough telescope to be able to search for the Edison Memorial Tower, to see if it can be located, rising above the trees in Middlesex County. However, the tower in Edison Township might be visible, when the leaves are off of the trees, given the distance and the contour of the ground between South Mountain and the northern limit of the town of Metuchen, which is less than a mile beyond the tower.

    The village of Menlo Park as it was in Edison's day no longer exists, for the buildings that remained there were moved to Greenfield Village at Dearborn, Michigan, in 1928. However, the location of Menlo Park is marked by the Edison Memorial Tower, in what is now Edison township, across the Amtrak railroad tracks from the Metro Park station in Iselin, New Jersey. (We will see in the next chapter that the new building in which the Menlo Park post office is now located is in a shopping center about a mile south of the Edison Memorial Tower.) In the 1870s the village of Menlo Park was in what was then farmland at the southern extremity of the watershed of the Rahway River. This is the same river that receives some of its northernmost waters from the south side of Mt. Pleasant Avenue and from the south side of the gentle height of land along Main Street in West Orange. The height of land that defines the northern limit of the East Branch of the Rahway River is located only two hundred yards south of the Edison water tower, which seen above from Eagle Rock.[37]

    Our map shows that the South Branch of the Rahway River arises near the Metro Park railway station in Iselin, which is across Route 27 from the small state park where the Edison Memorial Tower is located. Route 27, which follows the route of the ancient road known as the

Essex-Middlesex Turnpike, later known as the Lincoln Highway, continues to rise for a few hundred yards to the south of the Edison Tower. Just south of the next main intersection, a hundred yards or so beyond Parsonage Road, Route 27 reaches the crest of a small hill and passes down into Metuchen. This hill marks the divide in the watershed between the Rahway River on the north, and the Raritan River on the south. This hill, just south of Edison's "footprint" at Menlo Park, also marks the southern limit of the Newark Basin, which we read about in the discussion of the geology of northern New Jersey. Thus, perchance, Edison's "footprints" mark the limits of the entire valley of the Rahway River, from north to south, from West Orange to Metuchen. This may be coincidental, but I am skeptical of coincidences, and I leave it to the reader to wonder if this may not be a sign of Edison's attraction for the central valley of Essex County. The valley of the Rahway River is the valley of Edison.

In any event, the Rahway passes from our area of interest for the time being, as did the Elizabeth River. We shall now focus on the valley of the Passaic River, where Edison's home, his laboratory, and his factories in Essex County were located. It is time to descend into the valley of the Passaic — the northern part of the Orange Valley of Essex County.

We turn away from Washington Rock and return to South Orange Avenue at the entrance of South Mountain Reservation. Proceeding down the mountain to the east, we soon reach South Orange Village, where we turn north along Ridgewood Avenue, one of the valley's oldest roads, now nicely paved and straightened. We are, at this point, about two and a half miles south of the Edison water tower in West Orange. Ridgewood Avenue becomes South Valley Road as it passes into West Orange, and South Valley Road becomes Valley Road shortly after it crosses a culvert that marks the official origin of the East Branch of the Rahway River. Valley Road changes its name to Main Street at St. Mark's Square in West Orange, four blocks south of the Edison water tower that rises above the Edison National Historic Site. We pause at St. Mark's Church to reorient ourselves, and to resume our review of the history of this valley.

Chapter 3

In The Valley

*At the union of the stream from the springs,
north of St. Mark's Church, with Wigwam Brook,
the remains of a beaver dam were apparent to the early settlers.*

—Stephen Wickes, 1892[38]

IN 1885, when Thomas Edison and Mina Miller decided to buy Glenmont and move to West Orange, St. Mark's Episcopal Church was already located at the corner of Valley Road and Main Street, as it had been for nearly sixty years. But the springs, stream and beaver dam north of St. Mark's Church had long been gone, and Wigwam Brook would largely disappear in the years to come.[39]

Before St. Mark's was built at this corner in 1827, the intersection had been known as "Wheeler's," named for an early resident of Newark. Nathaniel Wheeler had moved to the base of First Mountain in the seventeenth century to establish a farm in what later became the town of Orange. Before Wheeler arrived, this had been hunting country for the Indians, and before that, in geological times, the valley had been covered for very long periods with ice and water. In order to understand the topography that Edison found when he came to West Orange, and what became of this land after Edison arrived, we need to appreciate the geology of this part of Essex County. Let us therefore continue the story of the formation of the valley, which we previously saw from Eagle Rock, four hundred feet up and a mile northwest of St. Mark's Square.[40]

Geologists tell us that "the geologic history of [this] area since the beginning of Triassic time is relatively simple." First Watchung Mountain, which dominates the western side of the valley, was, as we previously learned, formed during the Triassic and Jurassic Periods. The Jurassic was the age of the dinosaurs, the largest land animals in the history of the planet, and fossils and footprints of these great creatures can be found in the mountain above this valley. During the Jurassic, the Earth was warm and moist, and even the poles were free of ice.[41]

Following the Jurassic, the Cretaceous Period (named for chalk, as in the white cliffs of Dover), lasting 70 million years, was a time of large scale marine inundation, when the sediments of fossil fuels were created that have been so important in the modern era. The eastern valley of Essex County was eroded and flattened as the sea advanced to the base of the mountains during the Cretaceous Period, which concluded the Mesozoic era. The sea continued to cover the valley throughout the first part — the Tertiary Period — of the current era (the Cenozoic), which began 65 million years ago and ended about 2.5 million years before the present. During this period, much of the rest of the world experienced extensive volcanism, and the biota of modern life forms developed, including the mammals. The Tertiary was followed by the Quaternary Period, which is the most recent period in geological history. During this period, the sea withdrew from the surface of Essex County, and the valley was repeatedly compacted and rearranged by successive waves of glaciation in what is called the Pleistocene epoch.[42]

The Pleistocene began about 2.5 million years ago, and it closed with the end of the last ice age, some 10,000 years before the present time. During the Pleistocene, the low hills that existed within the valley to the east of First Mountain were scraped and smoothed, and much rock and sand—called "sedimentary drift" — was deposited in the valley. This glacial drift filled the previously existing streambeds and considerably altered drainage patterns in the valley. In the Pleistocene era, this material, also called "stratified drift, was deposited in a well-defined strip that begins near Silver Lake, on the Bloomfield-Belleville border, where Edison's factory was later located.[43]

The strip of glacial drift now traverses the southern portion of Glen Ridge, where Edison had another factory, and then passes down through Montclair and along the border between West Orange and Orange, where Edison built his laboratory and his main factory complex. From there, the strip of sedimentary drift follows quite precisely the bed of the East Branch of the Rahway River between West Orange and Orange, and then travels through the center of South Orange to the northern border of Maplewood. This strip of sedimentary drift, extending for about eight miles from Belleville to Maplewood, has been a splendid water resource. No less than twenty-seven major wells were drilled along this strip in the present century, including two that are beneath or near the site of the Edison laboratory and factory in West Orange. The access to well water in this basin was even better when Edison arrived here in the nineteenth century, before extensive mining of groundwater aquifers caused the water table to fall. During the twentieth century, the wells of Essex County have become deeper, the salt concentration of well water has increased, and deep groundwater has been polluted by surface wastes.[44]

After the most recent ice age, a general rise in the level of the sea flooded the lower coastal areas, creating Newark Bay. After the recession of the last glaciers, the surface of the valley and of the meadows along the bay was altered through the formation of soil by the erosion of rocks and by the accumulation of successive layers of biomass. The eastern valley may have been scoured with glaciers in the last period of glaciation, ending 10,000 years ago, or it may have last been glaciated some 25,000 years ago. In any event, it is believed that migration of humans from Asia occurred across a land bridge from Siberia to America about 12,000 years ago, during the last ice age, following which the new immigrants spread rapidly throughout North and South America.[45]

In May 1666, when Puritans from the New Haven Colony sailed up Newark Bay and arrived on the west bank of the Passaic River, they found that this area of New Jersey was peopled by Native Americans called the Lenni Lenape, a confederation of Algonkian-speaking Indians who then occupied the Atlantic Seaboard from Cape Henlopen, Delaware, to western Long Island. The Lenape, also known as the Delaware Indians, depended primarily on agriculture, with hunting and fishing as important additions to their economy. By the late seventeenth century the Lenni Lenape knew about the manufactured goods of Europe. In 1665 they had agreed with Governor Carteret to treat with the colonists who were expected to arrive from New Haven. They then sold their land to Robert Treat and his fellow Puritans for such goods as "forty double hands of powder, one hundred barrs of lead, twenty Axes, twenty Coates, ten Guns, twenty pistolls, ten kettles, ten Swords, four blankets," and so forth.[46]

The land purchased by the Puritans was bounded by the Passaic River on the east, the base of First Mountain on the west, the Yountakah (Third) River on the north, and Bound Brook (the border of Elizabethtown) on the south. As we previously saw, the Indians later allowed the English to extend their boundary to the top of "the Great Mountain Watchung," for the additional small price of "two Guns, three Coates, and thirteen kans of Rum." Perhaps by then the English had already seized the mountain top, and the guns, coats, and rum were accepted in acknowledgment of a *fait accompli*, although the historical record is silent on this subject. By 1678-1679 Newark consisted of some sixty square miles of territory, stretching from what is now Clifton to Hillside; it included Belleville, Bloomfield, much of Montclair, Glen Ridge, most of the Oranges, Maplewood, Irvington, and some of Millburn. When the boundaries of Essex County were formed in 1683, the county included all of modern Essex, Union, and Passaic Counties, and most of today's Bergen and Somerset Counties.[47]

The Lenape/Delaware Indians were more sedentary than the Indians of the Great Plains, and while living on the East Coast, they were grouped in clans and lived in longhouses. During their years in New Jersey, the Lenape or Delawares "stayed in the hills during the winter to hunt meat, collect nuts and take sanctuary in the many rock shelters." After selling what is now the area covered by several counties in eastern New Jersey to the Puritans, they were gradually pushed away from the coast. After 1690, the Delawares were dominated by the Iroquois and they drifted west along the path of the Susquehanna and Allegheny Rivers into Ohio. The Delaware Indians appear in the record of the European colonial wars: They defeated the British in the French and Indian War, and they later sided with the Americans against the British in the Revolutionary War. The Delawares were displaced from Ohio in 1795 and had were in Kansas by 1835; they were pushed on into Oklahoma in 1867, but later were dispersed and numbered only about 3,000 by the late twentieth century.[48]

Many of the stories and practices of the Lenni Lenape/Delaware Indians have been incorporated into legends that are remembered by Boy Scouts in New Jersey and elsewhere in America, but there are only a few memorials of their long presence in the Orange Valley. The valley of the Oranges has been dramatically altered since the Indians left, so it is perhaps appropriate, although ironic, that there is little in the valley that recalls them. A few of the places that were close to Edison's properties have Indian names: A short street known as Old Indian Road at the top of First Mountain; Wigwam Brook, which flows down the mountain near Glenmont and later passes by Edison's laboratory; Nishuane Park, and Nishuane River in Montclair; Watsessing Avenue and Watsessing Park in East Orange and Montclair, where Wigwam Brook joins Toney's Brook to become Second River; and Watchung Avenue, the boundary between West Orange and Orange at the eastern end of the Edison plant.

When Edison moved to West Orange, he found a town that perfectly suited his needs. West Orange was then quiet and pastoral, with world-class elegance in a rural setting. And while it was sparsely populated and private, West Orange was also close to major population centers that provided a source of labor, access to financial power, and markets for consumer products. There was also a splendid network of roads, railroads, and trolley lines in the Orange Valley, as well as the last vestiges of the Morris Canal in Bloomfield. However, as we have begun to see, this area was remarkably different when the first English farmers penetrated the woods west of Newark to the base of First Mountain, two hundred years earlier.

In the mid-seventeenth century, the valley at the base of First Mountain was a vast, dark, swampy forest. "Being densely wooded, it was the abode of wild beasts" such as otters and bears, reported the historian of the Oranges in 1892. The area of the Oranges was a mass of pools and streams that were fed by countless springs and retained by beaver dams at critical points. The Nishuane River was so broad that it was crossed by a ferry which was accessed from what is now Dodd Street in Orange, and Wigwam Brook was large enough to power a mill in Montclair. The high points in the valley were connected by paths, but major roads could not be built until the land was cleared, the beavers were trapped, and the streams were bridged and channeled. The Nishuane River is gone; it is now just a pleasant park in Montclair. Some of the high points or "Islands" can still be found in the Oranges, such as the hilltop where Berkeley Street crosses Tremont Street. Another prominent height of land in Orange is a few blocks southeast of the Edison plant, at the intersection of White and Ridge Streets. This summit is easily recognized from miles away, for it is marked by the lofty spire of St. John's Catholic Church, and by the outstretched arms of the statue of Jesus on the roof of St. John's School at the same intersection. Other hills in Orange have been removed, such as the "great mound of earth twenty feet or more in height" at the corner of Center Street and Henry Street; this "fine viewing point" was leveled in January 1886 to construct four new streets.[49]

The existence of twelve major roads in the valley was made a matter of record in 1705, although some were probably usable only in the dry season. One of these roads — the portion of Valley Road that ran from St. Mark's Church to what later became known as Tory Corner, about half a mile to the north of the Edison plant — was described in 1705, but this road was not "made" until after 1750, because "there was then a big swamp there that interfered with roadmaking." By 1886, when Edison arrived, the great swamp along Valley Road had shrunk to be just a pond, albeit a beautiful one: "Cook's pond [was] a small body of water, the delight of the boys in the decade immediately preceding."[50]

The southern portion of Valley Road — the part that ran between St. Mark's Church and South Orange Avenue in South Orange — followed an equally challenging course. It still appears to be, as it was in 1705, "a Road . . . as streight as the Ground will allow." Large as the swamp was to the north of St. Mark's Church, a swamp "of much greater extent than that just described occupied a district south of the 'highway to the mountain,' now Main Street." This immense swamp, on the south side of Main Street, began between Scotland Road and Center Street in Orange and extended to the south for several miles, across South Orange Avenue to Irvington. From here, the ill-fated Parrow Brook (of which we will soon have more to say) flowed north, ultimately to Second River, while the headwaters of the Elizabeth River originated in springs in the same swamp, flowing to the south. St. Mark's Church stood on the divide between the Passaic and Rahway Rivers: "The south-west roof of St. Mark's Church sheds its rainfall into the Staten Island Sound; its north-east shed into the Passaic River and Newark Bay."[51]

During the eighteenth and nineteenth centuries, the valley of the Oranges was converted from woods and swamps to farmland, and what would today be called light industry, began to appear in the valley. John Dod, for whom Dodd Street is named (he spelled his name with only one "d"), opened a copper mine on his 500-acre farm in Orange in 1719; the mine extended underground for 700-800 feet. Hat manufacturing, which eventually became the principal industry of Orange, began in about 1790, and by 1892 there were 21 factories that made soft hats, employing 3,722 operatives. By the first part of the nineteenth century there were more than twelve distilleries in the Oranges, and by mid-century the valley was traversed by both the Morris Canal, along Bloomfield Avenue, and the Morris and Essex Railway. This rail line, later known as the Erie and Lackawana, and now as the Morris and Essex branch of New Jersey Transit, passed from Newark to Orange, and then, as now, turned south into Millburn, from whence it proceeded on to Morristown.[52]

The rise in population and in the workforce, coupled with pollution from factories and excrement from privies, barns, and horses, was producing an increasingly intolerable situation in Orange. When Edison arrived in the Oranges, Parrow Brook was in serious trouble. As we saw previously, Parrow Brook arose near the center of Orange, just north of the junction of Center Street and Harrison Street (where the Charles Edison Foundation is now located). It flowed north, receiving a tributary from the ridge that is now marked by Scotland Road, and then merged into Wigwam Brook at the corner of Day and Washington Streets. By 1890,

"Black dyestuff from the factories, house drainage and general refuse, found a handy depository in [its] 'murky depths'," and a sewer system was proposed to conduct its waters to the Passaic River. When the sewer system from Orange, West Orange, Montclair, Bloomfield and Belleville was finally completed in 1897, a historian wrote that "Parrow Brook was now of the past."[53]

From our perspective, Parrow Brook may be gone, but it is not quite forgotten; its former location is marked by Parrow Street, two blocks long. The western end of Parrow Street faces the Church of Our Lady of Mt. Carmel, at the south side of Interstate 280 — the church whose gold spire we previously saw from Eagle Rock. And, perhaps more important for the residents of the Oranges, a sixteen-acre swampy area that once was the origin of Parrow Brook, between Harrison and Center Streets and Central Avenue, was purchased by Orange in 1895 to be a park; now known as Orange Park.[54]

On his arrival in 1886, Thomas Edison was not only the successor to George Brinton McClelland as the most famous citizen of the Oranges, he was arguably "The Most Notable Man in the World." McClelland, it may be noted in passing, had commanded the Union Army from July 1861 until November 1862, when an impatient President Abraham Lincoln relieved him for what he believed to be excessive caution. After retiring to West Orange, McClelland ran on a peace platform against Lincoln, but he carried only New Jersey and two other states against the President. McClelland was governor of New Jersey from January 1878 to January 1881, a position that was later held by Thomas Edison's son, Charles. The general's property was a few hundred yards south of Llewellyn Park, on the ridgeline of First Mountain. He died in 1885, the year before Thomas and Mina Edison moved to West Orange. Llewellyn Park, which was established in 1857, and the area on the ridgeline to the south of the Park, was a residence location for the rich and famous well before the Edisons arrived. It is therefore pertinent to our study of Edison's relationship to the valley to review the story of the unique housing development that Llewellyn Haskell laid out, and where Glenmont — Thomas and Mina's home — was located.[55]

In order to understand Llewellyn Park, and to prepare to explore the complex relationship that Thomas Edison had with the valley in which he was to spend most of the last half of his life, we must digress briefly to review the early political history of West Orange, where the Park is now located, and of the town of Orange, in which Llewellyn Park was located when it was created. Our focus will later be drawn to the much smaller area within the valley where Edison's home was located and where he built his laboratory and factory complex.

As we have seen, this area was originally part of the town of Newark. The laboratory and factory complex that Edison built along Valley Road (now the northern extension of Main Street) were part of the first purchase, in 1666, while Glenmont is in the land purchased in 1678-1679. As settlers moved west from Newark, they formed several towns, such as Montclair (founded as Cranetown in 1694) and Horse Neck (now Caldwell), where Thomas Edison's ancestor, "Tory John" Edeson, was one of the early settlers. Hamlets also developed in the central part of the valley, such as Doddtown (now East Orange), and Williamstown and Freemantown (now part of West Orange).[56]

In the first decade of the nineteenth century, the various villages and towns that now comprise the four Oranges and Maplewood were brought together as the town of Orange, which was formed in 1807. These five towns later separated again, and Orange, once the grandest, became by far the smallest of them all; it is barely two square miles in size, 2.2 square miles to be exact, while West Orange, at 12.1 square miles, is half as large as Newark. West Orange became an independent city in 1863, ten years after Llewellyn Haskell moved to Orange and began to develop the first planned suburban community, or villa park, in the United States, so Llewellyn Park was originally a part of Orange, New Jersey. West Orange was a large town, rising in the valley to the west of Orange, sprawling across First Mountain and the valley of the West Branch of the Rahway, and then up the slope to the ridgeline of Second Mountain. But the rugged, wooded slopes of West Orange were thinly settled, and its population had grown to only 4,358 residents by 1890, four years after the Edisons arrived. As we shall soon see, West Orange began to change, and to grow steadily in population, in the decades after Thomas Edison built his laboratory and factories in the valley below Llewellyn Park.[57]

Llewellyn Park is now a quintessential West Orange subdivision, for Orange has become but a shadow of its former state. Although its people are friendly and its history is proud, many of the fine public buildings and mansions of Orange, built in the late nineteenth century, are beset by urban blight. And—as we shall later study in more detail—Orange, New Jersey, is the location of one of the nation's most notorious sites of industrial pollution. This is the site once occupied by the U.S. Radium Corporation, which is situated, sad to say, on the edge of Wigwam Brook, hardly a stone's throw from the eastern border of the Edison plant. But we are getting ahead of our story. When West Orange separated from

Orange in 1863, Orange was still prosperous, so Edison would list Orange as his business address, even though his laboratory and manufacturing plants were always located in West Orange.

Following the political separation of Orange and West Orange, these two communities both continued to grow and prosper for the next several decades, with West Orange hardly being thought of as a separate town by the historian who wrote of the Oranges in 1921. The arrival of the Edisons in this community was, indeed, but a minor event in what was, thirty or forty years later, described as "Orange's Most Eventful Decade" —the period from 1880-1890. Only four years previously, a group of wealthy citizens of Orange had formed the Essex County Hunt, to hunt wild foxes in the Orange Mountains. They believed (incorrectly, as it turned out) that their purchase of a twenty-eight acre tract including the "ravine up to Gregory Avenue . . . saved for all time a rugged and beautiful section of the Orange Mountain." This area was then so wild that Charles Delmonico, owner of the New York restaurant that was one of Edison's favorite places, died of exposure in the snow along Northfield road in January 1884. I suspect that Delmonico died near the land that was owned by the Hunt Club, less than a mile from Llewellyn Park.[58]

The Orange Lawn Tennis Club was founded in 1880, providing the community's wealthy residents with some of the nation's first and best grass tennis courts; it is still in the same place, on North Ridgewood Avenue, in South Orange. First Mountain was then the playground of the Essex County Toboggan Club, which was organized "for sliding . . . one thousand feet down the eastern slope of Orange Mountain." We previously saw that the Essex County Country Club was created on the western slope of Orange Mountain in 1887, the same year that Edison was building his laboratory at the base of the eastern slope of the mountain.

Orange Mountain was also a place of dreams in 1887 for the organizers of the Orange Mountain Cable Company. This company constructed a cable carline for tourists from Valley Road at the base of the eastern slope to a point near the St. Cloud Presbyterian Church, on Old Indian Road, at the ridgeline of the First (Orange) Mountain. By 1896 the cable company had failed. The cable railway is recalled only by those who happen to know that the base station still exists, now serving as a restaurant known as Suzy Que's on South Valley Road. The cable carline began less than one hundred yards from the East Branch of the Rahway River in West Orange. The cable railway ascended the mountain along the route now occupied by Orange Heights Avenue, Winding Way, and Walker Road. The route winds over the crest of the mountain, passing through the golf course of the Rock Spring Club and along the side of South Mountain Reservation to enter Northfield Avenue near the St. Cloud shopping center. We can thus see that West Orange, and parts of Orange and South Orange, were delightful places in which wealthy members of society could live and play, without peril to happiness or health.[59]

For the working class, life was not as pleasant. By the 1880s, strikes or lockouts were frequently occurring in the hat factories, and a total walkout occurred in 1882. By 1908-1909 the hat workers had become organized, and a long strike, from 15 January 1909 until 8 November of the same year, was settled only after management accepted mediation by the United Hatter's Association of North America. Horse-drawn trolleys were gradually replaced by street railways and electric trolleys, although not without opposition from the gentry, who opposed the Sunday trolley schedules that were popular with the working class.[60]

Llewellyn Park, where the large frame mansion known as Glenmont was completed in 1880, is on the eastern slope of First Mountain in West Orange. Although considerably reduced in size from what it was when Thomas and Mina Edison moved there in 1886, Llewellyn Park is still an impressive, somewhat mysterious place that occupies a unique niche in American history and in the history of the environment. We had previously glimpsed the approximate location, if not the trees and homes in Llewellyn Park, from our perch at Eagle Rock. This was, in fact, the same outlook that in 1853 captivated Llewellyn Haskell, a native of Maine, and a wealthy thirty-seven-year old pharmaceutical manufacturer in New York City. Haskell suffered from rheumatism and was concerned about diseases such as cholera and tuberculosis that were thought to be caused by the foul air of the cities. He sought to find a rural environment that would be esthetically pleasing and at the same time would maintain and improve his health.[61]

Haskell was apparently familiar with the villa parks of England, and he was influenced by others in America who sought a similar healthy, pleasing environment near the city. One such person was Matthias Ogden Halsted, a wealthy New York merchant, who had acquired one hundred acres of land in Orange in the wake of the financial crash of 1837. Halsted constructed on this land a beautiful house and a depot on the Morris and Essex Railroad, to be able to commute from his property in Orange to New York City, less than an hour away. In 1853, Halsted sold Haskell forty acres and an old farmhouse, which Haskell remodeled with the help of Alexander Davis, an architect from Orange. Davis also built Haskell a tower on the nearby cliff—at Eagle Rock—from which he could enjoy the view that we and thousands of other visitors have had. Davis was so enchanted by the location that he bought twenty-five acres of land from Haskell, on which he built a house of his own.

Over the next four years, between 1853 and 1857, Llewellyn Haskell acquired 350 acres on the slope below Eagle Rock on which he would build a villa park that offered "country homes for city people." To his initial holdings, Haskell added an additional 400 acres of land. With the help of Davis and other landscape architects he created a private park as large as New York City's Central Park, which was being constructed at about the same time (1858-1865) by Frederick Law Olmsted.[62]

The "1858 Prospectus Map" of Llewellyn Park shows Haskell's property at the summit of First Mountain on the north side of Eagle Rock Road, surrounding Eagle Rock. Haskell's "Tower" is located just to the northwest of "The Rock," where we were standing or perhaps where the Highlawn Pavilion restaurant is now located. On the south side of Eagle Rock Road, immediately across the road from Haskell, is Davis' property, which appears to extend far enough to the south to include Crystal Lake, although the lake is not identified on the 1858 map of Llewellyn Park.

In 1858 Llewellyn Park thus encompassed the entire area between the ridge line of First Mountain on the west (identified by what was then called Cliff Walk, part of which is retained as Ridge Road), Mt. Pleasant Avenue (then called Newark & Mt. Pleasant Turnpike) on the south, Valley Road (now the northern extension of Main Street) on the east, and Eagle Rock Road (now Eagle Rock Avenue) on the north. Additional properties owned by Haskell were shown on the 1858 map to extend far to the north of Eagle Rock Road, for about the same distance to the north as Mt. Pleasant Avenue is to the south. The northern border of Llewellyn Park was then presumably somewhere in Montclair (called Eagleton or West Bloomfield on Haskell's map). The streets on the northern portion of the 1858 map were either not drawn to scale or have been considerably altered in the past century. The property of "L. S. Haskell" is shown to extend about as far north as Bloomfield Avenue, although that street is not shown on his map. Instead, the drawing of a building called "Eyrie Eagle Rock" dominates the northern portion of his map. Haskell's "1858 Prospectus Map" of Llewellyn Park is vague, for Bloomfield Avenue had been in existence since the last half of the eighteenth century.

One of the most interesting features of Llewellyn Park in 1858 was "The Ramble," a 50-acre area of woods, in a ravine high in the western portion of the Park. Haskell deeded this to the association of landowners, establishing a precedent of a "commons" that has been followed in later gated developments. This wooded area is clearly visible on modern maps of Essex County and on the *Orange* quadrangle map, west of the street known as Oak Bend. We shall later see that The Ramble passes by Glenmont, and its waters flow into Wigwam Brook.[63]

Another important geographic feature that appears on Haskell's "1858 Prospectus Map" that has largely disappeared during the past century is Wigwam Brook, which we saw was a tributary of Second River that ultimately passes into the Passaic River, draining this part of First Mountain and the valley below it. Haskell's map shows that in 1858 Wigwam Brook arose at the height of First Mountain in the Davis property on the south side of Eagle Rock Road. It then plunged over a cataract and descended along Eagle Rock Road (now Eagle Rock Avenue). The brook then passed under the intersection of Eagle Rock, Valley Road (now Main Street), and Park Avenue (now Harrison Avenue) to form a pond (now gone) on the lower side of this intersection, just east of where Our Lady of Lourdes Church is now located. From this corner, the brook flowed along the east side of Valley Road to its intersection with Washington Street, known as Tory Corner. The valley to the east of Tory Corner was, in Haskell's day, called Wigwam Valley.[64]

The eastern slope of First Mountain and the valley to the east of it are much drier than they were in the nineteenth century. The brook (unnamed) that is now shown at Tory Corner on the Orange quadrangle map no longer arises at the top of First Mountain, since presumably the springs there have dried up to some extent, as they have at the summit near Mt. Pleasant Avenue. The large pond that once was located at the lower end of Eagle Rock Avenue, at the northeastern corner of Llewellyn Park, has been drained sometime in the past century. The approximate location of this pond on Wigwam Brook is now occupied by a group of buildings, one of which is, ironically, the Thomas A. Edison Junior High School. The stream reappears south of the school and passes under Washington Street to disappear again at Alden Street, which was the northern border of the Edison company property. The building occupied by Barton Press and a large parking lot to the south of it now occupies this site; the Edison water tower, which we saw from Eagle Rock, stands over it.

In the 1870s Wigwam Brook probably formed another lake or pond as it passed through the property that Edison bought for his laboratory. This was the body of water known as Cook's pond, of which Pierson wrote appreciatively in 1921, and for which Lakeside Avenue was named. This pond was located beside Edison's laboratory when it was built in 1887, and it was later buried or dried up in the course of reclaiming land to build the Edison Phonograph Works to the east of the laboratory. As we shall later see in more detail, the unfortunate Wigwam Brook reappears at the eastern edge of the former Edison property, whereupon it crosses into Orange, and courses along the south side of the property once owned by the U.S. Radium Corporation. Further downstream, near Dodd Street, the Wigwam once received the waters of the "ill-fated" Parrow Brook; this polluted brook was diverted into the sanitary sewer system that was created in the Orange Valley between 1890 and 1897.

The intentions of Llewellyn Haskell, and the topography, size, and scope of his plan were dominant influences on the character of Llewellyn Park when it was first settled in the late 1850s. The first generation of residents of the Park created an environment that was remarkably enduring, and which has been subjected to both criticism and praise. The Edisons became members of what might be called the second generation of residents of the Park when they arrived in 1886. The Park already had developed many of its traditions, such as the annual May Festival. However, the Edisons lived there for so long (Thomas for forty-five years and Mina for sixty-one years) that it would not be surprising to find that their presence had an impact on the culture of the Park, and that the Park had an important impact on the Edisons. This book examines, among other things, the reciprocal interactions between the Edison family and the other residents of the Park. Let us therefore begin by seeing what is known and what has been said of the culture of Llewellyn Park, at the time that Thomas and Mina Edison arrived in 1886.

The plan developed by Llewellyn Haskell called for homesites ranging in size from one to twenty acres, linked by carriage roads that opened out onto attractive scenes or magnificent views. The architecture was eclectic, and although the initial "cottages" that Davis designed were in the "romantic" style, many of the later and larger houses were distinctly avant-garde. Haskell would sell land to anyone who could afford to buy and wanted to live in the Park, and the development "quickly acquired a reputation for housing almost scandalous modernists, 'long-haired men and short-haired women'." Residents of the Park were individualistic, practicing Swedenborgianism, atheism, spiritualism, and even nature worship, but they had in common the fact that they were financially successful and were generally of Anglo-European ancestry. Most of all, "they valued their privacy." Haskell spent more than one hundred thousand dollars landscaping the Park, which he transformed with tens of thousands of imported trees and shrubs. We will later see how

Edison followed Haskell's example, perhaps unknowingly, on property that he owned, and on adjacent areas that he wished to beautify.[65]

The mansion called Glenmont, which was the home of Thomas and Mina Edison from the time of their marriage in 1886 until his death in 1931, and of Mina until her death in 1947, was one of most imposing houses in Llewellyn Park. It was designed by a prominent architect, Henry Hudson Holly (1843-1892), for a New York department store executive named Henry C. Pedder, who was forced to put the house and its furnishings on the market when he was found guilty of embezzlement. The twenty-three or twenty-six or twenty-nine room house (accounts vary), located on fourteen acres of land, was a stunning wedding gift from Thomas to Mina, who became its "home executive." Glenmont was the archetype of the Queen Anne style of American Victorian houses, exhibiting all the characteristic features of this style: a steeply pitched roof of irregular shape, with a front-facing gable; textured shingles on the facade between the uppermost windows and the peak of the roof; an asymmetrical one-story high porch, extending on one or both side walls; and an asymmetrical facade. Glenmont was spectacularly decorated and furnished, based on the concepts that Holly had expressed in his book, *Modern Dwellings in Town and Country* (1878).[66]

The Edisons thus moved into a highly visible yet private, exclusive, and imposing setting, which provided endless opportunities for them to enjoy their own unique home and the transformed landscape that surrounded their property. They must have felt pride, and perhaps awe, at their good fortune. In the case study which appears in the next chapter, I shall examine what happened during the next four and one half decades to the environment of Glenmont and Llewellyn Park, to the Orange Valley of Essex County, and of other areas in New Jersey which were touched by Edison.

Part II

EDISON'S ENVIRONMENT, 1869-1931

Case Study of Edison's Impact on the Environment

Built an air castle or two.

—Thomas A. Edison, 1885[67]

IN this section, I present my case study of the impact of Thomas Edison on the environment. Edison's biographers have shown us that 1885 was a crucial year in Edison's life. At age thirty-eight, he was dreaming about the future — building "an air castle or two." Recently widowed, the inventor was planning to marry again, and his "air castle" included dreams of Mina Miller, as well as plans to expand his laboratory and business operations. The next forty-five years, from 1886 to 1931, will be the major focus of this case study, for it was during this period that Edison had his greatest impact on the environment. The case study will, however, begin by examining Edison's environment and his environmental impact in the years before 1886, starting with his arrival in Elizabeth, New Jersey, in 1869 when he was twenty-two years old.

The purpose of the case study is to enable me to develop a clear picture of the environmental impact of the Great Inventor. My final assessment of Edison, which appears in Part III, is based on the scholarship of others — which I have reviewed in the preceding chapters — and on my own research, which I present in this section. I conducted my research during the last half of 1997 and the first half of 1998. At the risk of being redundant, let me recall at this point that my principal focus is on Edison's environmental impact in New Jersey, and my greatest interest is on the period when his impact was at its height, from 1886 until his death in 1931. However, to understand the environmental effects of Edison's work during the years from 1886-1931, we must not lose sight of his earlier interactions with the environment, particularly during the first years of his residence in New Jersey, from 1869 to the end of 1885. This case study of Edison is composed of a group of individual case studies. Some of these studies were designed to answer questions that were posed as the result of discrepancies that I identified in the "facts" that were presented in recent biographies and focused monographs. Other case studies were initiated to explore gaps in the historical record, while some investigations were conducted because I believed that several of Edison's recent biographers had erred, even though they agreed with each other.[68]

In each of these case studies, I examine in depth several of the locations and projects that Edison was involved with in New Jersey during the period from 1869 to 1931. In each case study, I attempt to determine the characteristics of the local environment at the time that Edison began to work at a specific location, or on a new subject. I then study the impact that Edison had on the environment of that site or subject during his lifetime, and what has happened subsequently to the environment there, up to the present time. Additional information regarding the present status of Edison's "footprints" appears in the Epilogue, Part III. As we have seen in the Introduction and Part I, I have defined the word "environment" rather broadly, and I have retained this broad definition in Part II. To restate the essence of the definition, the environment is what surrounds us, and it includes aspects of both landscape and life; it also includes the "internal environment," within the human body.

Some of the case studies in this section were conducted to answer specific questions that arose in my review of the existing literature. For example, I previously observed that there were differences in quotations, citations, recollections, and "facts" in various monographs and legends about Edison. Differences in opinions and conclusions regarding Edison's impact on the environment have thus been derived from variations in objective information, as well as from differences in philosophy and perspective. In conducting these case studies, I endeavored to approach each site or problem objectively, although I recognize that it is impossible to be completely free of opinion or prejudice. Nevertheless, I attempt to report the facts in each case as clearly as possible, before I draw conclusions and state my opinions. In the end, I try to determine in each of the case studies what Edison and his contemporaries thought that the impact of his life and work had on the environment. In many cases, I will add my own opinion regarding Edison's environmental impact — particularly if it now appears that the conclusions of Edison and his contemporaries were incorrect.

In addition to the case studies of specific locations that are the principal focus of Part II, some of the investigations were conducted to clarify and to document statements and opinions that were either unsubstantiated (and therefore must be classified as myths and legends), or were attributed to questionable sources such as the older — hagiographic — biographies, and recollections and reminiscences. The case studies in Part II are intended to be focused and selective, rather than to encompass all aspects of Edison's life. The Great Inventor generated a rich legacy of archival material, artifacts, and stories, which is still incompletely catalogued, and more information about Edison is continually being discovered. I have been offered generous assistance by scores of knowledgeable people who have access to Edisonia, and who have wanted to help me in my research. Tempting as it is to look at each new piece of information that is proffered, I have concentrated my attention on Edison and the environment in New Jersey — particularly in the Orange Valley of Essex County, the Newark Bay area, Sussex County and Warren County, and Menlo Park. I will also refer to environmental issues related to Edison's "footprints" in Ohio, Michigan, and Florida, when they offer insights into his work in New Jersey. By examining Edison's activities and his heritage in these places, I expect to discover the pattern of his impact on the environment.

Each of these case studies can be considered from a geographic, a topical, or a chronological perspective. The studies were principally initiated on a geographical basis (e.g., to look at Edison's impact on West Orange, or at his business locations in Newark), and in connection with specific topics (e.g., iron ore, cement, and storage batteries). However, it gradually became apparent to me that the case studies can best be understood by placing them in a chronological context. I have summarized the site visits in an Appendix so the reader can see their geographic orientation, but I have chosen to organize the presentation of the case studies in an order that is more or less chronological. The reader can thus follow the "footprints" of Edison from his arrival in Elizabeth,

New Jersey, in 1869 until his death in West Orange in 1931. Some antecedents and digressions in Edison's own life are replicated in the case studies.[69]

Chapter 4

The Early Days: Elizabeth, Jersey City, and Newark (1869-1875)

Thomas Alva Edison ... resided with his business partner, Franklin A. Pope, at 235 Morris Avenue, Elizabeth, from September 12, 1869, to April 23, 1870 ...

— Charles L. Aquilina, *Elizabethtown and Union County: A Pictorial History*[70]

Elizabeth, New Jersey, 1869-1870

WELL, maybe he did, and maybe he didn't. We sometimes pick up important clues from local history, but it is important to remain skeptical about new information until it is confirmed. For example, Aquilina, Koles, and Turner continue: "while he was operating a factory on Edison Place, Newark, [i]t was during this period that he met and married his first wife, Mary Stilwell [sic], one of his employees." Although the date when Edison opened his first shop in Newark is still uncertain, the statement that he operated "a factory on Edison Place" in Newark in the spring of 1870 cannot be substantiated, even if we modernize the name of the street from Mechanic Street (which is now called Edison Place) or Ward Street (which then intersected with Mechanic Street). Furthermore, it is believed that Edison first employed Mary Stilwell in October 1871, and it is a matter of record that he married her in December 1871. With problems like this, I wondered how much use Aquilina, Koles, and Turner would be in my study of the environment of Edison. It was therefore a pleasant surprise to find that there were, indeed, some interesting clues regarding Edison in Aquilina, Koles, and Turner, as will soon become apparent.[71]

My research on Edison's environment in Elizabeth revealed the following facts and beliefs:

- There is no longer a building at 235 Morris Avenue; this address is now either a parking lot just east of 249 Morris Avenue, or it is further to the east of the parking lot, in the pavement of the wide intersection where Morris Avenue begins at the railroad.[72]

- Local residents and historians of Union County have long believed that Edison boarded at a house on Morris Avenue that is several blocks west of the railroad. This house is now number 559 Morris Avenue. These residents and historians were aware of the statement by Aquilina, Koles, and Turner regarding 235 Morris Avenue, but they believed that number 235 Morris Avenue was not the address of the house that Edison lived in. They also believed that Edison lived near the city limits, not near the railroad, or that he may have lived at a house near the railroad, i.e., 235, but that he also lived for some time at the house that is now numbered 559 Morris Avenue.[73]

- The following addresses for residents named Pope appear in the *Elizabeth Directory for 1870*:
    Pope, Ebenezer, h 235 Morris av
    Pope, Frank L., telegraph operator, b 235 Morris av
    Pope, Henry, telegraph operator, b 235 Morris av
    Pope Ralph, telegraph operator, h Salem rd n limits [74]

- In 1870, Morris Avenue ran from "Broad and the R.R. Depot to the City Limits," according to the *Elizabeth Directory for 1870*.[75]

- In the *Elizabeth Directory for 1870* Morris Avenue had many addresses with numbers lower than 235, e.g.:

PHOTO BY GEORGE J. HILL, M.D.

ELIZABETH HOME: Local historians believe Thomas Edison boarded at this house at 559 Morris Avenue when he first moved to New Jersey in 1869. Edison left Elizabeth for Newark the following year.

> Ayars Barzilla, blacksmith, 56 Morris
> av, h do Walter Armitage, mason, h r, 60
> Morris av
>   Edwin S. Belknap, h 111 Morris av
>   Edward L. Bouton, clerk, h 141 Morris av

The oldest maps of Elizabeth at the Elizabeth Public Library that show street addresses are dated 1909 and 1922, respectively. Both of these maps show a house at 559 Morris Avenue that is essentially the same as the house that is now located at that street address. In 1902 and 1922 the lowest number on Morris Avenue was 245, which was a short distance west of the origin of Morris Avenue, at the railroad. In 1902, 245 Morris Avenue was the address of Regge & Co. The 1902 map shows the names of many of the residents, as well as the outline of their houses. At 559 Morris Avenue, there is a house, with no name. This house is located in the first address that is to the west of the Elizabeth-Union city line, although the rear of its lot is crossed by the city line. The adjacent property to the east is 551-557, of Fred Hegemeyer. The city line passes through his house, which is at 557, although his barn is entirely within the city of Elizabeth.

Immediately across the intersection from 559 Morris Avenue on the 1922 map is the unnumbered house on Cherry Street of R. W. Pope. [n.b.: We saw above that a Ralph Pope, telegraph operator, lived near the Elizabeth city limits in 1870.] The street numbers on Cherry Street end at the western border of Elizabeth, which is five house lots east of the Pope house. The R. W. Pope house is similar to the house at 559 Morris Avenue, but is smaller and stands on a smaller lot.[76]

- The oldest maps of Elizabeth that show street numbers that I have located are in the possession of Charles Shallcross, Past President of the Union County Historical Society. Mr. Shallcross says that both the 1882 and 1872 atlases of Elizabeth show Morris Avenue, starting at the train station, and that the first house is 247 Morris Avenue.[77]

- The 1995 version of the computerized map of Elizabeth in the DeLorme atlas shows that Morris Avenue, at its origin, has a short course that is parallel to the railroad. It then turns sharply to the west and proceeds to the city limits. Low numbers appear on this short section, which is roughly where Julian Place (on the west side of the tracks) or Railroad Place (on the east side of the tracks) are located at present. This short segment of Morris Avenue that appears in the 1995 DeLorme atlas would account for the low numbers on Morris Avenue in the Elizabeth *Directory for 1870*.[78]

- In 1889 the Board of Trade the Board of Trade of the City of Elizabeth – which was the forerunner of the Chamber of Commerce – included in its list of Officers and Board members the names of Henry W. Pope (on the Committee of Railroads) and Frank L. Pope (member of the Board of Trade).[79]

In order to be able to interpret these fragments of information that relate to Edison's living arrangements in Elizabeth, we need first to see what changes occurred in Elizabeth between the Revolutionary War and the time Edison arrived.

*****

Dramatic changes occurred in Elizabeth in the nine decades between 1780 and 1869, the first year of Edison's residence there. In 1780, Elizabeth was a small town, which was largely divided up into farms. It was also a regional business center and a port of transit between New York City and its hinterland in what was then the southern part of Essex County, New Jersey. Shops and businesses such as the ferries were located along the waterfront in Elizabeth Port, and other shops, churches, and government buildings were clustered a mile west in Elizabeth Town, along Broad Street where it crossed the river. A tavern was then standing beside the mill where John Ogden's mill was located in the 1660s, and a series of dams and mills then extended upriver towards the residence of Governor Livingston, which is now just beyond North Street on Morris Avenue.[80] Most of the area of Elizabeth was still divided into farms, and nearly all of the roads were unnamed paths that led from one farm to another, or to adjacent villages. By 1780, the Industrial Age had begun to transform Great Britain, but not yet to Elizabeth, New Jersey.[81]

During the nineteenth century, the open land that once stretched from Broad Street down to Elizabeth Point was criss-crossed with streets. Rows of houses were built where once there were farms, and the water-mills along the river were rendered obsolete by factories that were powered by coal-driven steam engines. By 1869 Elizabeth had joined the Industrial Revolution in America and two great railroads had been built through Elizabeth: The Pennsylvania Railroad swept through t site for industry, that in 1873 Isaac Singer decided to build his sewing machine factory in Elizabeth. Singer's great five-story plant, located on thirty-two acres where Crane's Ferry had once been berthed, became the largest factory in Elizabeth. Singer's firm was said by a local historian to have become the largest manufacturing company in the world. The three-story he city from north to south, following the route that is now called Amtrak. The Central Railroad of New Jersey also passed through Elizabeth. It crossed the Pennsylvania Railroad at the busy intersection from which Broad Street, North Broad Street, Morris Avenue, and several other streets issued. This was the intersection where the Pope family lived and had its telegraph business, at 235 Morris Avenue.[82]

East of the railroad tracks, downtown Elizabeth in the 1870s was solidly built up with three- and four-story office buildings of brick and

PHOTO BY GEORGE J. HILL, M.D.

ITINERANT BOARDER: The vacant lot to the right of the row of buildings is the location of the Pope family home at 235 Morris Avenue. Edison, who had formed a partnership with Frank Pope to develop electrical devices related to telegraphy, accepted Pope's invitation to move into his mother's home. Edison did not live there long before moving up the street to 559 Morris Avenue.

stone. The handsome building of the First National Bank that was present in 1869 at 233 Broad Street was destroyed by fire in 1890, but other similar buildings can still be seen on the north side of Broad Street, close to the tracks.[83] The city was then prosperous, and a good brick building of the Elizabethtown Water Company at 92 Broad Street, built in the 1880s, was typical of many that exist to this day near the railroad tracks on the east side of town. This building had large plate-glass windows on the ground floor, shuttered windows on the two upper floors, and a decorative brickwork balcony across the front of the roof.[84]

In contrast to the fine buildings to the east of the tracks, on the west side of the railroad tracks — where the Popes lived — the shops and residences were more modest in size and height. Judging by the buildings

PHOTO BY GEORGE J. HILL, M.D.

RAILROAD ACCESS: Edison, who began his career as a telegrapher on the railroad in Michigan, always lived and built his factories near railroads. In Elizabeth, Edison's first home at 235 Morris Avenue was located within one hundred yards of the railroad station at the intersection of the north-south Pennsylvania Railroad and the east-west Central Railroad of New Jersey.

that remain at 249-253 Morris Avenue, the Popes' home and business building at 235 Morris Avenue was a relatively plain brick structure, three stories high, with a plate glass window on the ground floor. The Popes' building would have been fifty or sixty feet long, extending to the back of its lot. The Popes' residential areas would have been at the rear of the first floor, and in the upper two floors. The Popes' building would have been shorter than those a block to the east on Broad Street — the older buildings on Morris Avenue lack the decorative pediments of the nineteenth century office buildings on Broad Street.

As Elizabeth became more prosperous and more populous, it began to break up and to shrink in size. Elizabeth became a city in 1855, and Union County was formed in 1857. Linden separated from Elizabeth in 1861 and Clark split off in 1869. In 1868, farmland only four miles northwest of the beginning of Morris Avenue at the railroad tracks was being developed into the planned village known as Roselle. Within two decades, Edison would transform the environment of Roselle by electric lighting of several streets and houses, and a church. In the twentieth century Elizabeth began to grow again. With the creation of new land for the seaport and the airport, Elizabeth now totals 11.7 square miles, about half the size of Newark.[85]

The Pennsylvania and Central Jersey Railroads passed through Elizabeth at grade level in the 1870s, for the great stone arch and underpass at the origin of Broad Street and Morris Avenue was not built until 1891. The crossing of several roads and the two railroads must have made this a busy and dangerous intersection. One can easily see why telegraphy was needed at this point, for coordination of the railroad switches. Many buildings were removed in 1890-1891, and roads near the tracks were relocated, to construct the stone foundations on which the railroad lines now pass through Elizabeth. The elevated roadbeds and two large train stations still exist within a hundred yards of this point, which is almost exactly where 235 Morris Avenue was located in 1869-1870 — if the numbering system is similar to what it is today.[86]

Can we make some sense out of this disjointed information, and visualize Thomas Edison's environment during the period that he lived in Elizabeth? And was Edison's environment in Elizabeth of any significance in his later life? The answer to both of these questions, I would argue, is "Yes." A reasonable scenario that accepts and unifies the apparently disparate fragments of information regarding Edison and Elizabeth, N.J., in 1869-1870, goes as follows:

Edison gladly accepted Frank Pope's invitation to form a partnership for inventing and producing electrical devices related to telegraphy. Pope was already well-known in this field in the New York-New Jersey area, and he was a rising leader in the business community of his home town, Elizabeth. Edison was also delighted to room and board with Pope at his mother's home, for that would make it easier to communicate with his partner and mentor (remember that the partnership was Pope & Edison, not Edison & Pope), and this plan provided Edison with a family environment — something that was largely missing in his life since the time he became an itinerant telegrapher. While living at the Popes' house, Edison would have seen that it was possible to have both a comfortable home and a business at or near the same location in the city, and that such a mixed-use building could be located close to a major railroad. This lesson was, as we already know, learned well by Edison, who later created a similar environment on many other occasions.

The area around the Popes' house was busy, vibrant, and noisy, and Edison had to adjust to the rules that were established by Mrs. Pope for a large family that included at least three adult males. There were undoubtedly many children and young adults in the neighborhood as well, if not in the Popes' house.

Into the Pope household came a brash young man named Thomas Edison, who we already know could be boisterous and eccentric in his behavior. He kept odd hours, and his dietary preferences were, well, unusual. Edison was often charming and interesting, but he could also be egocentric and selfish. His personal habits were, so to speak, not particularly refined. Like many other men of his era, Edison did not bathe frequently and he chewed tobacco. In later years, he did not like to use a spittoon, but preferred a broader area, such as the floor. His deafness interfered with making "small talk" at the dining table, and it would have impaired his table manners as well. This would hardly be a problem in an impersonal boarding house, but in this case, he was living with a family of some substance. He did not have a steady income, and he was notoriously slow in paying his bills. Edison also had an eye for young women, as had been reported from his days in Boston. A roomer like this could rapidly become tiresome.

In addition, we know from later events that Edison and his partner drifted apart, and within only a few years Frank Pope became cynical and sarcastic about Edison. We do not know whether the strains in their relationship began at Pope's home, or in their work together. However, tensions at home could certainly affect harmony at the workplace. It would not be surprising, therefore, that Edison might look for another place to live. 559 Morris Avenue was just down the street, near the house of another member of the Pope family. It was on the trolley line, and it was within walking distance of the railroad station, if Edison got back late at night.

At 559 Morris Avenue, Edison would have had a room or bed-sitter in a quieter neighborhood, at the end of the trolley line, near the city limits. This house was a two-story dwelling with a large living room that had a bay window at the left front, and a one-story kitchen that extended to the right rear. Roomers usually stayed at the rear of the second floor in such houses, and in this case his window would have looked out onto a two-hundred-foot lot with a large barn at the far end of the lot next to it. This was more like what Edison was used to in Michigan, in contrast to the side-by-side, lot-filling brick buildings in downtown Elizabeth. The house at 559 Morris Avenue wasn't the grandest on the block, nor did it have the largest lot, but it was comfortable and detached. Since the owner is unknown, we can speculate that 559 Morris Avenue may have also given Edison a chance to regain some measure of independence.[87]

Whether Edison lived at one or both addresses on Morris Avenue, and whether the scenario that I have proposed has any connection with reality is unknown at present. I have been told that newspaper stories have been published in Elizabeth from time to time over the past several decades regarding Edison and 559 Morris Avenue. I have been unable to locate any trace of these articles thus far, so I simply present what I have learned, in the hope that it may be helpful for another student, sometime in the future. We do know, however, that while Edison was living in Elizabeth, he was working in Jersey City, and that at some time — for reasons still unknown — he decided sometime in 1870 to leave both Elizabeth and Jersey City, and move to Newark. Before we follow Edison to his new environment in Newark, let us see what he would have experienced while working in Hudson County, New Jersey.[88]

Jersey City, New Jersey, 1869-1870

Pope, Edison & Co. established a workshop in an old building at 7-9 Exchange Place, Jersey City, across the street from the Pennsylvania Railroad Terminal and a minute's walk to the New York ferry.

—J. Maurice Hicks, 1979[89]

From the northeast corner of Liberty State Park in Jersey City, I had a magnificent view of the entire area where Thomas Edison had worked more than a century ago. It was a cool, sunny Sunday afternoon in January, and I had this part of the park to myself. In front of me, on the north side of the park, lay the Great Basin of the Morris Canal. Beyond the canal, a mile further north, rose the gleaming, glassy skyscrapers of Exchange Place in Jersey City. I knew that at the foot of these tall buildings lay the Port Authority of New York and New Jersey's railroad terminal — the easternmost PATH station on this line in New Jersey — and the waterfront from which countless ferry boats once shuttled back and forth across the Hudson River. The environment that I saw was a remarkable combination of the natural world and the built world: an environment of water, land and

PHOTO BY GEORGE J. HILL, M.D.

JERSEY CITY SHOP: This modern bank building at Exchange Place, located across the street from the current PATH Railroad Station, occupies the site where Edison's workshop was located in 1869. The site would have been convenient to the railroad station, to the Morris Canal, and to ferry service to New York City.

grass, with clear air, and (today) silence, yet it also was filled with buildings, ships, motor vehicles, and — I knew, but could not see or smell — industrial waste. This was the environment that was developing when Edison came here in 1869, and that has continued to evolve since he left. "How many of these changes," I wondered, "may be said to be due to the inventions of Thomas Edison?"[90]

There was no river traffic on this weekend afternoon, and no wind, so I was not distracted as I shifted my gaze to the right, towards Manhattan. I focused first on the Empire State Building, and then turned further to the right to study the Twin Towers of the World Trade Center. Directly behind me was the magnificent, massive brick Victorian building that once was the terminal of the Central Railroad of New Jersey. This great station, I saw, was now restored enough to serve as the terminal for tourist boats that travel to Liberty Island and Ellis Island. Like a good Jerseyan, I thought, "These islands are surely close to New Jersey.

Closer than they are to New York, and Staten Island is, too. Saw it last month, only two hundred yards across the Arthur Kill from Elizabeth." I wondered if Thomas Edison had stood here in 1869 and paused to reflect, and to look at the Hudson River, when he came from his apartment in Elizabeth to his shop in Jersey City. His apartment in Elizabeth, I knew, was close to the stations of both the "Jersey Central" and the Pennsylvania Railroad; he could have taken either one to Jersey City.

Historians and biographers agree that Edison operated a shop in Jersey City in the fall of 1869, so I wanted to attempt to visualize the environment that he encountered there. However, I had not known where to look for the inventor's "footprints" in Jersey City, since the references had been rather non-specific. For example, it has been written that his shop in Jersey City was "near the Pennsylvania Railroad yards," or "in the electrical instrument factory of Leverett Bradley."[91] A breakthrough of sorts occurred in January 1998, when I accidentally encountered Hicks' reference to the Exchange Place address, given in the epigraph to this section, in my case study of Roselle (which appears later, following my study of Menlo Park). Hicks' statement was not referenced, and I have not attempted to confirm it by a study of the city directories or maps of Jersey City, as I did for Elizabeth. The reason that I have not pursued proof of Hicks's statement is that having walked through the area in Jersey City near where the Pennsylvania Railroad yard was once located, and where the ferries once berthed at Exchange Place, I have no reason to believe that the building where Edison worked is still standing. The precise spot where his shop was located is, therefore, less important to me than to reconstruct, in my mind's eye, what the environment was like in this part of Jersey City in 1869-1870.

Jersey City is built on a promontory that has long been known as Paulus Hook, which juts into the Hudson River from New Jersey. "Paulus Hook," not "Jersey City," appears on the map of New Jersey at the time of the Revolutionary War, and the strategic importance of Paulus Hook is described on the plaques and the twenty-foot obelisk in a small park at the intersection of Washington Street and Grand Avenue. The Paulus Hook Battle Site Park is only four blocks south-west of the Exchange Place PATH Station where Edison's shop was once located. The events at Paulus Hook during the Revolutionary War were important in local history, and for those whose lives were immediately affected by them, but Paulus Hook is not one of the great historic sites of that war.[92]

We can thus see that at the time that Edison worked in Jersey City, it was a city with a long and interesting history. How much of this the inventor knew about is unknown, and there is no need to speculate about the impact of this "historical environment" on Edison. What is clear, however, is that the streets that led in all directions from the Paulus Hook monument were lined with rows of handsome homes of brick and stone that were built side by side. Many fine town-houses that clearly date to the mid-nineteenth century, if not earlier, still stretch from this corner for many blocks to the west, down Grand Street, and intermittently for shorter distances in the other three directions. When Edison worked at Exchange Place, he surely would have walked a block or so to the west for lunch from time to time. A half-block long row of fine three- to five-story brick buildings, half a block long, is still standing along Greene Street, three blocks from Exchange Place. A restaurant at the corner of York and Greene Streets occupies the ground floor of a three-story building with a roof garden that is edged by a row of small evergreen trees. Edison would also have seen the elegant homes on Grand Street, only two blocks further to the west, even if he paid no attention to the Paulus Hook battle site monument and its reminder of the bitter war between the Tories and their Revolutionary cousins a century earlier. Exchange Place is only one block long, but it is so important that it has its own U.S. Postal Service zip code — 07303. Exchange Place is the eastern extension of Montgomery Street; it runs from Hudson Street to the river. The east end of Exchange Place is marked by the dramatic sculpture of a dying Polish soldier — the "Katyn 1970" monument. East of Exchange Place, extending onto a pier and along the riverfront, is a New Jersey "Green Acres" park that in 1986 was named for one J. Owen Grundy. Exchange Place now is a vibrant transit point for thousands of commuters on weekdays, and it is lined on both sides by tall commercial buildings.

Only one building on this street, now occupied by Fleet Bank, shows an address that we can associate with Edison's shop: "One Exchange Place," built in 1920, is located on the south side of the street at its western end. We may imagine that Edison's little shop at 7-9 Exchange Place — where Leverett Bradley's factory was located — would have been in the middle of this block, on the south side of the street. This spot is now occupied by newer buildings, and Edison's environment here is gone. But the Hudson River is just a few steps away, and the Small Basin of the Morris Canal is only six blocks to the south. The land under our feet is still Paulus Hook, and this is where in New Jersey Thomas Edison began to forge a new career as an inventor and as a businessman. Jersey City provided the venue that Edison needed for a business partnership. What Edison saw and learned in the environment of Jersey City and Hudson County would be carried forward into the next phase of his life, as he emerged in Newark as a successful inventor, manufacturer, and salesman, and as he also attempted to create a successful family environment.

Newark, New Jersey, 1870-1875

In 1870, nearly seventy-five percent of all county residents lived in the city. . . . By then, Essex County had gained national attention for its industrial prominence, particularly Newark.

— John Cunningham and Charles F. Cummings, *Remembering Essex*[93]

WITH his move to Newark from Elizabeth – where he was then living – and from Jersey City – where he worked – Edison came into an environment that was more challenging, yet it also provided him with greater opportunities for personal growth, fame, and fortune. Newark was only a few miles from where he had recently lived and worked, but it was a larger and more impersonal city than was either Elizabeth of Jersey City. For then Newark was – as it is now – the largest city in New Jersey. Edison had no mentors or family to live with when he moved to Newark, as he had when he boarded with his partner, Frank Pope. He came to Newark alone. But Newark was the hub of New Jersey's industry, and it was potentially a congenial environment for a young man like Edison.

Newark's most famous inventor, the prolific genius Seth Boyden (1788- 1870), was then in the last year of his long and productive life. Among his many inventions, Boyden had been the first to produce malleable iron, and he was the first to make what is called "patent leather" (which he didn't patent, by the way). Boyden was also a gifted horticulturist who bred giant strawberries on his farm west of Newark. Edison deeply respected Boyden and was later said to have called Boyden the greatest inventor in the history of Newark. It is interesting to observe that both Boyden's and Edison's inventions were important for the railroad industry. Boyden devised methods to enable locomotives to climb steep grades, while Edison was a pioneer in the development of the electric propulsion system for railroad engines. And Edison, like Boyden, was an avid horticulturist, as was seen during the long search that led

Edison to Japanese bamboo as a filament for the incandescent lamp, and in his later studies of latex-bearing plants. Like Boyden, Edison also lived into his ninth decade. Both men were somewhat similar in appearance. The description of the aged Boyden ("tousle-haired, strong, sad-faced, homely, and dignified") would have applied equally well to Edison, in his later years.[94]

In the 1870s, when Edison worked and made his home in Newark, the city was already two centuries old, and it had matured into a major center of commerce and industry. Photographs and narrative descriptions of Newark at this time reveal a city that was bustling with activity, a city that was covered with two to three-story brick buildings and was crossed by countless streets paved with bricks, cut stones, and cobblestones. In 1867 the ten-story high flour mill of Fagin & Company on the Passaic River in Newark produced 2,400 barrels of flour daily; it was said to be the largest of its kind in the world.

By 1870, Newark was a center of the leather and tanning industries, and ninety per cent of all patent leather in America was made in Newark. From 1870 to 1910 leather products were the leading manufactures of Newark, but Newark was also famous for its breweries — particularly Peter Ballantine & Sons — and for its production of fertilizer, zinc, jewelry, and thread. The Clark Thread Works employed more than one thousand men and women by 1870, and Clark later opened additional

PHOTO BY GEORGE J. HILL, M.D.

EDISON IN NEWARK: The "Edison Park Fast" lots that dot Newark are constant reminders of the famous inventor's presence in New Jersey's largest city. The brick building behind this sign on what is now Edison Place was the location of Edison's shop on Mechanic Place.

PHOTO BY GEORGE J. HILL, M.D.

FIRST YEAR SITE: The grassy park in the foreground is the location of Edison's first workshop in Newark, at 15 New Jersey Railroad Avenue.

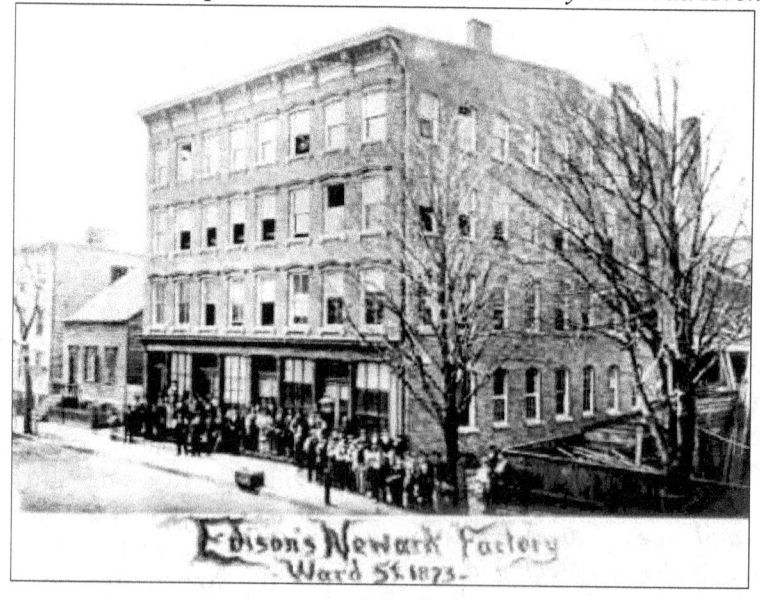

PHOTO COURTESY OF NATIONAL PARK SERVICE

PHOTO BY GEORGE J. HILL, M.D.

WARD STREET SITE TODAY: Edison's brick factory on Ward Street has been replaced by a concrete warehouse that is two stories taller and occupies a much larger footprint than the original building. The south-west corner of Ward Street and Mechanic Street, facing Ward Street, where Edison's factory was located, is now McCarter Highway and Edison Place.

buildings in East Newark, Harrison, and Kearny, employing thousands more workers. Edward Weston, "whose inventive genius rivaled Edison's," came to Newark in 1875, and in 1877 — the year after Edison moved his own operations to Menlo Park — Weston "established the nation's first electrical machinery plant" in Newark. In the following year, Military Park in Newark was electrified with Weston's arc lamps. Weston's enormous factory complex at the corner of Plane and Orange Streets dwarfed the smaller plant that Edison had operated a half mile south on Ward Street. By 1882, Weston had built a three-story building on Mechanic Street as his central station for street lamps in Newark. "Celluloid," which has been called the "first commercially successful synthetic plastic," was made by its inventor, John Wesley Hyatt, in a five-story plant on Mechanic Street. We will soon see that Edison also selected Mechanic Street and the areas immediately adjacent to it as the location for several of his shops.[95]

The Morris Canal, which had initially begun in Newark and extended over the ranges of hills and mountains to the west, had by 1831 connected Newark to the Delaware River, ninety-two miles to the west, and by 1836 the canal had connected the Delaware River to the Hudson at Jersey City, ten miles to the east. The Morris Canal passed through Newark just to the north of the Pennsylvania Railroad station, its course now marked through downtown Newark by Raymond Boulevard, which terminates at Lock Street on the hillside above the New Jersey Institute of Technology. Lock Street is, of course, named for the function of this place on the canal, and the environment of the canal, and of Newark, in the mid-nineteenth century can be visualized by studying the brick buildings along the west side of Lock Street. Edison would, in his long career, later operate several shops, plants, businesses, and quarries along the course of the Morris Canal, which he had first encountered a few blocks south of his shop in Jersey City.[96] During Edison's half-decade of residence in Newark, the city was the epitome of risk and opportunity for a young man. A drawing made of the city in 1874 shows innumerable tall smokestacks rising from factories in the downtown area, along with the spires of at least sixteen churches. The Morris Canal was by 1874 no longer a continuous watercourse as it passed through the city, but the Passaic River was then teeming with sailboats and side-wheelers, and the river was crossed by at least three railroad bridges and a swivel bridge for horse-drawn vehicles. The Central Railroad of New Jersey crossed the Pennsylvania Railroad near Mechanic Street, now called Edison Place. The ruins of the abutments of the old CRRNJ can still be seen on both sides of McCarter Highway near Penn Station, and also to the east of the Amtrak lines in the "Ironbound" section of Newark. The CRRNJ station was then located on Broad Street, a few blocks west of Market Street..[97]

EDISON'S WORKSITES AND RESIDENCES IN NEWARK

1. *First Apartment, Raymond Park West.* **2.** *Last Bachelor Quarters, 854 Broad St.* **3.** *First House, 53 Wright St.* **4.** *15 N.J.RR. Ave.* **5.** *4-6 Ward St.* **6.** *24 Mechanic St.* **7.** *103-109 N.J. RR Ave.* **8.** *788 Broad St.* **9.** *"White's Building" on Morris Canal.* **10.** *115 N.J. RR Ave.* **11.** *39 Oliver St.* **12.** *Apt., 65 Bank St.* **13.** *Second House, 89 So. Orange Ave.*

MAP BY AXIAM PRINTING

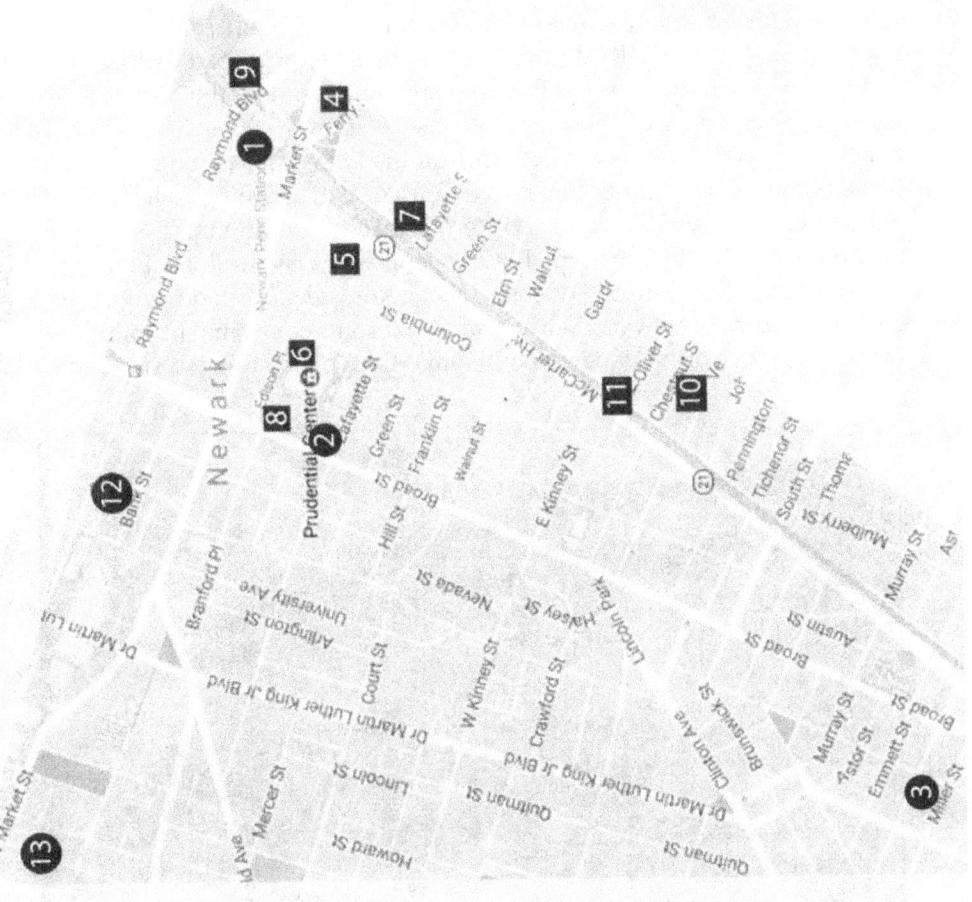

Locations in Newark

1. First Apartment, Raymond Park West.
2. Last Bachelor Quarters, 854 Broad St.
3. First House, 53 Wright St.
4. 15 N.J.RR. Ave.
5. 4-6 Ward St.
6. 24 Mechanic St.
7. 103-109 N.J. RR Ave.
8. 788 Broad St.
9. "White's Building" on Morris Canal.
10. 115 N.J. RR Ave.
11. 39 Oliver St.
12. Apt, 65 Bank St.
13. Second House, 89 So. Orange Ave.

In 1874 Pennsylvania Station was — as it is now — located where Market Street crossed the tracks of the railroad which is now Amtrak, although the present stone terminal building was not yet constructed. This was a familiar environment for Edison, who had lived near the intersection of the CRRNJ and the Pennsylvania Railroad in Elizabeth, and who had worked near the Pennsylvania Railroad and the Morris Canal in Jersey City. All of these great transportation systems were within a hundred yards of the place where Edison made his first home in Newark. It may have been a "dingy apartment," as one of his biographers put it, but we can see that it was also "ground zero" for an ambitious young industrialist. In this section, I will reconstruct, as well as I can, the environment that Edison selected for his residences and workplaces during his years in Newark. We will study Edison's environment in Newark as part of our effort to understand his intentions and actions in succeeding

PHOTO BY GEORGE J. HILL, M.D.

LAST BACHELOR QUARTERS: Edison was boarding in a house at 854 Broad Street at the time of his marriage to Mary Stilwell in December 1871. That address is now part of the Renaissance Mall, a major downtown development that was never completed.

decades, as he created and transformed the environment in other places in New Jersey, and in the world. In this case study, I shall show that there was a clear pattern to Edison's choices of workplaces and residences in Newark: Edison's shops, factories, and apartments were all located close to either the railroad or to the major commercial thoroughfare — Market Street — that crossed the railroad, while his homes were located in neighborhoods that were quieter, yet were within a short ride or walking distance from his business locations.

Thirteen sites where Edison had businesses and residences in Newark between 1870 and 1876 have been identified and are shown on maps in the *Edison Papers*. Edison had eight businesses and five residence locations in Newark during this period. At first glance, the sites appear to be a random, scattershot array of locations throughout the downtown area. However, when his residences and business locations are examined individually, a pattern becomes clear. We can see that his shops and businesses were all

PHOTO BY GEORGE J. HILL, M.D.

NEWLYWEDS: Edison and his bride, Mary Stilwell, moved into a house on Wright Street, adjacent to the house shown in this picture. Edison's house has been torn down, but it probably was similar to this three-story residence, with a mansard roof and dormer windows. A modern garage occupies the site of Edison's house.

PHOTO BY GEORGE J. HILL, M.D.

RAILROAD AVENUE: In 1871-72, Edison had a small experimental workshop in White's Building on the Morris Canal, at a site which is now occupied by the two tall buildings on Raymond Boulevard seen at the rear of this photo. The workshop was located immediately east of the railroad tracks across from the current Penn Station, which was built after Edison's time.

located within a one-half mile square in the downtown area, along a T, in which the vertical aspect was represented by the city's principal east-west thoroughfare, Market Street, and the cross-bar was represented by the Pennsylvania Railroad. For Edison, the inventor *cum* businessman, the key location in Newark was the point where Market Street met the railroad, even though the main business intersection in Newark was some five blocks west, at Market and Broad Streets. Proximity of his industrial sites to railroads was vital for Edison at this time, and would continue to be important for the rest of his life.

While his businesses were located close to the railroad, Edison's residences moved progressively further away from the T that identified the business sites. His first rooms in Newark, when he was a bachelor, were within the T, while his two houses were well away from it. For a few months in 1874-1875, when the inventor and his family lived in an apartment, they returned closer to the T, but this was a temporary location. The places that can be identified with Edison during the period from 1870 through the end of 1875 are shown on two maps in the *Edison Papers*. The first map shows eleven sites, and the second map shows an additional two sites. These are the thirteen places that I call the "footprints of Edison" in Newark during the years 1870-1875.

The eleven sites that Edison occupied between 1870-1873 are shown on an 1875 map of Newark in *Edison Papers*, in which, for clarity, I have indicated the location of his residences with a circular dot and his businesses with a square dot (see map on page 65)[98]:

1. This is the block where the Gateway Hilton Hotel and the Gateway office building are now located, across Raymond Plaza West from Newark's Pennsylvania Station. Edison boarded at this site when he arrived Newark in 1870, and he lived here until some time in 1871. His "dingy apartment" was at this location, north of Market Street and just west of the Pennsylvania Railroad.

2. 854 Broad Street, where Edison was boarding at the time of his marriage in December 1871. This location is near the corner of Broad and William (which enters Broad from the west) or Broad and Lafayette (Lafayette, which enters Broad from the east, was known as Farr Street in Edison's day) and is now occupied by the shell of what was to be the Renaissance Mall.

3. 53 Wright Street, later renumbered 97 Wright Street, was the first house that Edison ever purchased. Edison bought this house in December 1871 and he lived here with his wife and his first child, Marion (who was born in February 1873), until November 1874. Wright Street is about 6 blocks south of Lincoln Park. The Edison house was on the south side of the street, about one and one half blocks west of Broad Street, about one-half block west of Pennsylvania Avenue, and one-half block east of Frelinghuysen Avenue. There is now no building located at 97 Wright Street. This location is now a vacant lot, and the house which was once located at #97 has been replaced by a low, flat roofed, two-car, cement block garage that is attached to #99.

It is likely that this was a row of at least four — probably six — houses that were built according to the same plan. I hesitate to use the word "identical," for if they were built before the mid-1870s, they would probably have been individually finished to satisfy the prospective owner(s).[99]

By examining the three houses that exist of this group on Wright Street, we can easily visualize what the house was like that Edison purchased for his young wife, and where they lived with their first child and members of his wife's family. These houses were (and still are) attractive and sturdy, although they are not particularly elegant. They would, however, have been more than large enough for a family of two young adults and a small child (Thomas and Mary Edison and their baby, Marion.

4. 15 New Jersey Railroad Avenue, which is at the southeast corner of the intersection of New Jersey Railroad Avenue and Ferry Street. This address is just across the street to the east of Pennsylvania Station in Newark. Edison's first Newark shop was located here; it was the Newark Telegraph Works, which he operated with William Unger in February 1870. The "Edison Park Fast" parking lot across Edison Place from this park is said to be the first "Edison Park Fast" parking lot.

5. 4-6 Ward Street, renumbered 10-12 Ward Street. The Edison and Murray shop was in a handsome building that appears at this address in many photographs. Ward Street was a short street that was replaced by McCarter Highway, and the Edison shop was at the southwest corner of what is now Edison Place and McCarter Highway. The present Newark Warehouse Co. building is the antithesis, architecturally, of the interesting factory building that had once occupied this location, when it was 10-12 Ward St.[100]

Edison Place extends west from Ferry Street (on the east side of the railroad) to Broad Street, about six blocks. Edison Place memorializes not only Edison's Ward Street shop, but also three other Edison sites that were located near it (See #2, #6, and #8). In Edison's time, the thoroughfare that is now named for him was called Mechanic Street; it is parallel to, and one block south of, Market Street in downtown Newark.

6. 24 Mechanic Street; Edison used this as an annex to his Ward Street shop in the fall of 1871. #24 would be on the south side of Edison Place, one-half block east of Broad Street. The location that was once known as 24 Mechanic Street may now be occupied by a two story brick industrial building that is vacant, unnumbered, and marked "For Sale/Lease" by "Prime Network Realtors (201) 378-9100," on behalf of the owner, W. V. Egbert, Inc."[101]

PHOTOS BY GEORGE J. HILL, M.D.

SITES OF SUBSIDIARY: Murray and Company, an Edison subsidiary, occupied this building at the corner of New Jersey Railroad Avenue and Green Street in 1872 (above). The firm moved to 39 Oliver Street later that year. The foundation, sill and bricks (below) can still be seen near the intersection of New Jersey Railroad Avenue.

7. 103-109 New Jersey Railroad Avenue, which in October 1870 was the location of the American Telegraph works, one of Edison's companies. This address occupies part of a short city block that is situated between Railroad Avenue and Bruen Street, one block north of Elm Street, just east of the Amtrak railroad in the area known as "the Ironbound." (See also site #10, below, which is adjacent to this location). The American Telegraph Company building at 103-109 Railroad Avenue is gone, and this corner is now the parking lot for "Lafayette Auto Parts."

8. 788 Broad St., where in 1871 Edison had a short-lived enterprise, the News Reporting Telegraph Co. Edison's company occupied space in the *Daily Advertiser* Building, which was located at the southeast corner of Broad and Market Streets, Newark's principal business intersection. Mary Stilwell was employed in this company of Edison's when she first met him. This building, like those in locations #2, 5, and 6, is within one block of what is now Edison Place (known as Mechanic Street in Edison's day). The southeast corner of this intersection is now occupied by the Kinney Building, which was completed in 1912; it is also the corner on which Newark's founder, Robert Treat, was said to have built his home.[102]

9. "White's Building," on the Morris Canal (now Raymond Boulevard), immediately east of Penn Station, where the canal (no longer functioning as a commercial waterway through Newark in 1871) crossed the Pennsylvania Railroad. Edison had a small experimental shop in this building in 1871-72. The location is easily identified, but the building is long gone.

10. 115 New Jersey Railroad Ave. This building is shown in the map in *Edison Papers* as being at the corner of Railroad Avenue and Elm Street in "the Ironbound" district, in the short block between Railroad Avenue and Bruen Street (see site #7, above, that was adjacent to it). Edison established a small shop in this building for Murray and Co. in February 1872. The original entrance to the building that is now located at the corner of Railroad Avenue and Green Street was almost certainly known as 115 New Jersey Railroad Avenue in earlier days. It is the only one of the thirteen business and residence buildings that Edison used in Newark during the period from 1870 to 1876 that I am reasonably certain is still standing.

11. 39 Oliver St., in the Ironbound section, to which Murray and Co. moved in May 1872. The present building at 39 Oliver Street cannot be identified with certainty, but it is probably a side entrance to a garage-type annex which occupies approximately half of a city block. The building that Edison used is now gone, but the original doorsteps and sill

for 39 Oliver Street are still present. Between 1873 and 1876 Edison had two additional residences in Newark, in addition to his continued use of the Ward Street shop and, until November 1874, his home on Wright Street. His new locations are shown on another 1875 map of Newark in *Edison Papers*[103]:

    12. 65 Bank St, where the Edisons lived over a pharmacy for about five months in 1874-1875. This location is at the northeast corner of the intersection of Bank Street and Washington Street, in downtown Newark, now occupied by the New Jersey Superior Court.

    13. 89 South Orange Avenue, at the northeast corner of Boston Street and South Orange Avenue, two streets east of Norfolk Avenue. The Edison family moved to their house at 89 South Orange Avenue in the spring of 1875, and their second child, Thomas, Jr., was born there. The Edisons remained at this house until they moved to Menlo Park in March 1876.[104]

* * * * *

    In summary, of the thirteen buildings that Thomas Edison used as residences and businesses in Newark during the period 1870-1876, One or two may still exist, more or less as they were in the 1870s, and traces of two or three others may still be found. The "footprints" of Edison during this period that may still be seen are (numbers refer to the list on the preceding pages):

    (6) A building at 30-42 Edison Place on the south side of the street, which is now owned by the Egbert Company, about one-half block east of Broad Street."[105]

    (10) A building at the southeast corner of New Jersey Railroad Avenue at Green Street, which is probably 113-119 New Jersey Railroad Avenue, and which had its original entrance at 115. This was the building used in 1872 by Edison's subsidiary, Murray and Co.

    (11) The foundation bricks, sill, and steps for 39 Oliver Street, where Murray and Co. moved later in 1872.

    (3) The only other site in Newark that bears any resemblance to the time of Edison's presence is 99 Wright Street. This house is in the middle of the block on Wright Street between Pennsylvania and Frelinghuysen Avenues, near the southern end of Broad Street.[106]

    Of the other nine sites that Edison used in Newark during this period, one is a small but attractive park in the Ironbound, located just a stone's throw from Penn Station. Of the others, one (89 South Orange Avenue) is gone, but has been replaced with an attractive Society Hill townhouse that has an address on Boston Street. Another Edison "footprint" (where he roomed in a "dingy boardinghouse" when he arrived in Newark) is now the site of the Gateway Hilton Hotel and the Gateway One tower, and the rest are occupied by office buildings (such as the Kinney Building at Broad and Market Streets), industrial buildings, or parking lots.

While the commercial environment in Newark was important and attractive for Edison as he was building up his manufacturing operations, we can see that the natural environment of Newark was being seriously degraded. By 1900,

Industry had created problems undreamed of in 1870. The sweet Passaic River had turned sour and filthy, despoiled by man. The creeks and marshes were redolent with sewerage. Water became nearly as precious as gold — and often as tainted and foul as the sewage-infested Passaic. Streets were often nightmares of congestion and confusion, clogged with wagons and horse-drawn street cars. Dimly lit streets were not always known for quiet, peace or general safety.[107]

We know from Edison's comments, in his biographies, that he was aware of these problems, and in his own way he was working to address them. We will see, in the case studies that examine the later years of his life, to what extent was successful, and in what ways his inventions and his factories contributed to pollution and destruction of natural habitat — the very problems that he deplored.

* * * * *

We shall now follow Edison as he moves his family and his laboratory to Menlo Park, in the farmland of Middlesex County, a dozen miles south of Newark. We have seen the accretion of a variety of environmental influences on the young inventor and father, some of which he was surely aware of, and others which were subtle, but were embedded in his character. In the next decade, Edison achieved fame, fortune, and a measure of happiness. In the death of his wife, Edison also suffered a loss that permanently transformed him, and which had a significant impact on the environment of Menlo Park.[108]

Chapter 5

The Wizard in Menlo Park
(1876-1931)

"There's nothing there anymore."

—A Rutgers University historian, 1997[109]

IN spite of this comment from a professor of history, it should be remembered that to a student of the environment, and to an environmental historian, "nothing" is not an adequate description of any place on earth. Indeed, "Nature abhors a vacuum." My goal, which was realized in due time, was to see what I could learn about the environment at Menlo Park when Edison and his family lived there, and what happened to the environment of Menlo Park during the rest of his life. I was also concerned with the evolution of the environment at Menlo Park prior to Edison's arrival, and with what has happened there following his death.

It was apparent from Edison's biographers and from other writers — especially Jehl and Pretzer — that Edison and/or members of his family continued to own or control some or all of the Menlo Park property for the duration of his life. The published details were sketchy and contradictory. Much as I wished that I could study Menlo Park in depth, I knew that I would not be able to conduct the types of title searches that had been commissioned by the National Park Service to study the ownership of the Edison properties in West Orange. Instead, I planned simply to go to the place known in the 1870s as Menlo Park and ask people in this area what they had heard about the history of this property during Edison's lifetime, and since his death.

I knew from previous trips down State Route 27 from the Garden State Parkway to Metuchen that there was a monument to Edison along Route 27, near the Metro Park Amtrak station in Iselin, and that the area around the monument was called Edison Township. The Edison Tower was the monument that would orient me to the place where Edison's house had once been located. My next job was to talk with the curator at the Edison Tower Museum, located at the base of the tower, and ask for his help in locating the ruins of the Edison house — if they still existed. My task here, as elsewhere in my search for the "footprints of Edison," was to visualize the environment where the inventor lived and worked, whether it was urban or rural, and to figure out what he had done with or done to this environment. In the end, I was more successful than I had expected to be, in my rambles through the old Menlo Park property, and in my roaming in the valley below Menlo Park and on the hillside to the south of it. By the time, I was done, I had a clear image of the environment at Menlo Park when Edison arrived in 1876, and of the changes that have occurred in the environment there during the ensuing 120 years. In contrast to what I had been told by the professional historian whom I quoted above, much is still there at Menlo Park, but a lot of work will be needed to bring it to light.

* * * * *

The area between Metuchen, in Middlesex County, and Westfield, in Essex (now Union) County, was terra incognita to the mapmaker, William Faden, in 1778. Indeed, the Rahway River and its valley are completely missing from this map. The Rahway River, we have previously learned, originates just south of Metuchen (in its southern branch) and on the slopes of First Mountain in Orange and West Orange (in its northern branches), and it drains a long, narrow territory between the Passaic and the Elizabeth Rivers. The Rahway valley, where Thomas Edison worked for the next fifty-five years, was readily apparent to local residents in the late eighteenth century. But by 1876, in the late nineteenth century, the valley of the Rahway had been extensively developed, and it was no longer easy to visualize its course, its tributaries, and its valley of drainage.

By the time Edison arrived at Menlo Park, on the hillside just north of Metuchen, the valley of the South Branch of the Rahway River had been logged off and converted to farmland. The Rahway valley in Raritan Township was by then traversed from north to south by the

COURTESY OF NATIONAL PARK SERVICE

THE WIZARD AND HIS MEN: Thomas Edison (center, holding a hat) and his "muckers," who worked and played together while creating the phonograph, the incandescent lamp, and the other electrical devices that drew crowds of curious admirers to Menlo Park.

arrow-straight path of the portion of the Middlesex-Essex Turnpike that was known locally as the Lincoln Highway, and by the gentle curves of the nearly-straight Pennsylvania Railroad which crossed the Turnpike just south of the intersection of Thornall Avenue and Christie Street.

This is where the Menlo Park Land Company built its office and anchored its development of eighty to 120 acres of farmland on the hillside above the railroad. A Post Office and Railroad station at this corner took the name of Menlo Park, which had been the name of a successful development in — of all places — California. The Menlo Park Land

Company had built a handsome three-story house which served as its office building. This house became the Edisons' home from March 1876 until March 1881, when they moved to New York City. The house at Menlo Park continued to be used by the Edison family from time to time, and Mary Stilwell Edison died there in 1884. The Menlo Park house was abandoned by Edison after Mary's death, and it was accidentally destroyed by fire about thirty years later.[110] Others have previously discussed and speculated on the reasons for Edison's decision to leave Newark, and for his choice of Menlo Park as the venue for his new industrial village. I have nothing new to add in this regard. I focus instead on the environment that Edison encountered at Menlo Park and in the area around it when he arrived, and what has happened there in the years that followed. This was America's first "industrial village," a nineteenth century counterpart to the "Silicon Valley" that developed not too far from Menlo Park, California, in the Twentieth Century. To see what it was like in Edison's day, and now, is a window through which we can examine the values that we assign to our historical environment.

* * * * *

MENLO PARK MARKER: A plaque erected by the Edison Pioneers stands in the front yard of the property where Edison's house once stood. The house, into which Edison moved in 1876, burned down about 40 years later in a fire reportedly caused by sparks from a passing locomotive.[111]

PHOTO BY GEORGE J. HILL, M.D.

We approach Edison's Menlo Park by car, as do most of today's visitors; we are proceeding southwest on State Route 27 from Exit 131 on the Garden State Parkway. Yes, the road runs from northeast to southeast here. Technically speaking, it is incorrect to say that one goes "south" or "north" on Route 27 or Amtrak at this point, as is the convention at present, nor was it correct to say that the Pennsylvania Railroad ran "east" and "west" from here, as was the custom in Edison's day. We pass the Metro Park railroad station on our left as we approach the busy intersection of Wood Avenue and Route 27, and then — watching carefully to avoid being rear-ended as we slow down — we pass two streets that proceed to the right. In the middle of the next block, on our right, is a boulder on which is affixed a bronze plaque, darkened with patina. We see the words "Thomas Alva Edison" on it as we pass, but we dare not pause to read more. We do not see the flagpole in the woods above the boulder, for the pole is bare these days. In a few moments we reach the next corner, and turn right, uphill, on Christie Street. There are woods along the entire block to our right, and on the left, too, at the next intersection — where Christie Street is crossed by Monmouth Avenue. There are one-story houses in view on the side streets, and on the right side in the first half of the second block. But there are woods, too, along most of the left side of the street as we approach the next intersection — with Tower Road — which on our 1876 map is called Woodbridge Avenue.

At this point, we see the only other structures that are visible in this area that

PHOTO BY GEORGE J. HILL, M.D.

EDISON TOWER: Built in 1937 on the site where Edison developed the first successful incandescent light bulb, this 131-foot concrete obelisk towers over the memorial to the "Wizard of Menlo Park."

COURTESY OF NATIONAL PARK SERVICE

OUTCAULT'S PERSPECTIVE: In 1881, R. F. Outcault created an image of the Edison laboratory complex (above) from a perspective that was not then obtainable except from a balloon. Visitors to the sixth floor of the Alfieri Building 300 yards south of the Metropark station can see the view imagined by Outcault.

PHOTO BY GEORGE J. HILL, M.D.

connect us with Thomas Edison: the magnificent Edison Tower, 131 feet high; and the low, one-story modern cement museum building to the right rear. We pause at this point and day-dream a bit, imagining what it was like here in the winter of 1880-1881, when R. F. Outcault painted the laboratory complex as it existed then. Outcault's perspective, we can see, was as if he had been in a balloon or on a tall structure of some kind, located just behind us, looking up Christie Street toward the laboratory building (where the cement Edison Tower is now located) and the brick machine shop (where the museum building is now standing). To the right, along the third block of Christie Street, woods have grown up where there were open fields in Edison's day. At the next intersection — at Middlesex Avenue — across the street from the museum building, there was once a small shed. And off to the right from the shed, towards the top of the hill, led the tracks for Edison's electric train. We see the train — an engine and two cars — in Outcault's painting, and we recall that the "trucks" for this engine are now on display at the Edison National Historic Site in West Orange. In Edison's day, there were woods along the top of the hill. The woods extend all across the background of the Outcault painting. There are woods here now, too, although there are not as many trees as were shown by Outcault. And the "Skating Lake" in the "Public Park" across Middlesex Avenue from the electric train tracks is gone now.

We have now driven or walked past almost all of the places that were used by Edison and his associates at Menlo Park. Edison and his associates used only two other pieces of land here: the Upton house, a block south-west, at Monmouth and Frederick; and the Lamp Factory, which was one block in the opposite direction, and on the other side of the railroad tracks, at the foot of Park Street (now Philips Street). We can see that Edison's buildings occupied only a small part of this planned housing development, not more than two to three blocks of the proposed sixteen-block development, and both the maps and the illustrations show that they were closely and cohesively grouped. Yet because there were so few others living here, Edison and his colleagues and his family had abundant outdoor space in which to move, and to seek the silence or solace that rural farmland and woods can provide. There was also a brook that wound its way down from the top of the hill, that then — as now — ran along the street that was then called Courier Street, which we know as Wood Avenue. This stream, which drains into the South Branch of the Rahway on the other side of the railroad, has a very steep right bank. The

COURTESY OF NATIONAL PARK SERVICE

MENLO PARK LABORATORY: This sturdy, two-story frame building was designed by Thomas Edison and was constructed by workmen who were supervised by his father, Samuel Ogden Edison Jr. After Edison moved to West Orange, the building fell into disrepair. What remained was transported to Dearborn, Mich., in 1928 and reassembled by Henry Ford.

gently sloping left bank of the brook was then known as Serpentine Park which may have taken its name from the winding nature of the stream, or from the local fauna. Marion Edison, Thomas and Mary's first child, recalled learning to jump over blacksnakes that lay in the paths, during her childhood at Menlo Park.[112]

A young man who was growing up in Metuchen, sixteen miles from Newark and two miles south of Menlo Park, recalled that,

When I was a boy there wasn't a paved road in Metuchen and few paved sidewalks. The sticky red mud was everywhere. What is now the Lincoln Highway [State Route 27] was in the spring just a quagmire of liquid red mud. The railroad cut at Metuchen was made through red shale, a kind of soft, red, fine-grained rock which one could cut with a

COURTESY OF NATIONAL PARK SERVICE

EDISON AND HIS "MUCKERS" IN THE LABORATORY: The second-floor lab in Menlo Park, one year after Edison and his researchers developed the first long-lasting incandescent lamp here.

knife. *When this rock is exposed to the air it crumbles and makes the characteristic red Jersey mud about which the New Yorkers are so fond of joshing the Jerseyites.*[113]

The young man from Metuchen was David Trumbull Marshall, the son of a schoolteacher who lived with his wife and seven children in the Presbyterian parsonage. Four of the boys eventually graduated from Rutgers and one of the girls graduated from Wellesley College. Born in 1865, David Marshall was eleven years old when Edison moved to Menlo Park. The stories that he told in 1929, at the age of sixty-four, provide a clear and often amusing description of small town life in New Jersey in the 1870s and 1880s. "Country," he wrote, was a "proper place for children." As a boy, Marshall had — like Edison — gotten into mischief, including making batteries out of copper, zinc, and sulfuric acid in jars made of cut-off wine bottles.

He worked for Edison for ten years and later graduated from medical school. His stories about Edison and Menlo Park validate some of the undocumented statements that have appeared in various stories about Menlo Park. David Marshall recalled that,

> *My earliest recollections of Menlo Park date back to 1876, before Edison came out there and put the place on the map. My father used to conduct a Sunday school in the Pennsylvania Railroad Station at Menlo Park. . . . Later the Sunday School was located in the office of the Edison Laboratory. . . . Some of the Edison outfit might have been benefited by the reforming influence of a Sunday school.*[114]

Marshall admired Edison, and he later worked for Edison in what he called "the Laboratory at Orange, N.J." One of David Marshall's brothers worked at the Edison Lamp Factory from 1881 (when it was located in Menlo Park) until 1910, by which time the Lamp Factory was in Harrison, New Jersey. Marshall describes Edison as a kindly but sometimes mischievous person, who often acted like a child:

> *Like most country churches our church was always giving entertainments to raise money. . . . My father went to Menlo Park where he was very courteously received by Mr. Edison, who showed him the phonograph and loaned him one for use at our church.*
>
> *It used to be said that Mr. Edison, in order to induce his wife to move out to Menlo Park, had told her that there was a lake out in front of the house. That there was a lake about 800 yards in front of the house was strictly true and just so at times. In the spring the low land way down in the valley in front of the Edison house was sometimes flooded, but the lake never lasted many days at a time.*
>
> *One day, in 1877, [William] Bogen was fishing in a little pond near where the old office on the Laboratory grounds at Menlo Park stood later. Mr. Edison came along and asked Bogen to lend him his hook and line to see if he could catch anything. . . . Mr. Edison started to fish and became so absorbed that he forgot to go home to dinner. He caught two catfish and Bogen says he was as pleased as a little boy.*[115]

When Edison arrived at Menlo Park in 1876 the valley below him had largely been converted from woods and swamps into farmland. Photographs show that the trees were gone in the valley and on the hillside of Menlo Park, although woods remained at the summit of the hill, if Outcault's painting can be believed. There was more standing water in those days, with a pond existing where swamps and sewers now exist on the other side of the tracks, draining into the South Branch of the Rahway River. And when Edison arrived, there was a small body of water marked "Lake" on Christie Street, between the street and the place where his laboratory building was soon built. (This was presumably the "little pond" where Edison caught two catfish with William Bogen.) No doubt, therefore, that it was a wise decision to set the lab back from the street. There were no other buildings near the areas that Edison selected for his use, except for a large Thornall house across Christie Street from Edison's, and a large Thornall Estate House at the corner of Monmouth and Frederick, which Francis Upton later occupied. Only three other houses were then present in the entire development, if the 1876 map is correct: the Andrus house on Jersey Avenue adjacent to the Skating Lake; the Hoyt house on a large piece of land at the opposite corner of the development from Edison, a third of a mile to the north; and the small Moffit house, which sat on two lots another block beyond the Skating Lake on Jersey Avenue.

We do not see on the 1876 map of Menlo Park the buildings that were identified on the 1925 map as Mr. Dean's house, and Mrs. Sarah Jordan's boarding-house, at Woodbridge (now Tower) and Christie Streets, and the home of Batchelor and Kruesi at Monmouth Avenue and Christie. The board walks that were built to connect the houses do not appear in the pictures, although we know about the board walk from Marion Edison's recollections.

Much has been written about the work environment, and the business environment, at Menlo Park, but relatively little about the family environment. Hear, then, what Edison's oldest child recalled about those days. In 1956, when she was eighty-three, here is Marion Edison Oser, speaking into a Voicewriter from her home in Wilton, Conn.:

Looking back . . . one of the highlights was my childhood days at Menlo Park. That was the time my father invented the phonograph and the electric light, and they were exciting days indeed.

Menlo Park was a tiny village on the Pennsylvania Railroad . . There were about a dozen houses and a store. The landscape was unusually pretty but it was marred by the closeness of the railroad. As the old homestead was too near the railroad tracks, my father later bought Carmen's Pond, or so it was called, and property behind it, on which he intended to build a secluded home. Had my mother not died, he would have done so.

> *Mother was not very happy in Menlo Park, as my father neglected her for his work, or so it seemed to her. He never would come to her parties and he would often skip meals and very often would not come home until early morning or not at all. . . .*
>
> *This happy life came to an abrupt close when my mother died of typhoid fever at Menlo Park in August 1884. I found my father shaking with grief, weeping and sobbing so he could hardly tell me that mother had died in the night. . . . It seems that my father took a dislike to Menlo Park after my mother's death and while he kept the homestead, he lived there only a short time.*[116]

In 1956, Marion Edison recalled that their home at Menlo Park was:

> *. . . a three story Victorian house run by three servants either all black or all white. In addition, there was a coachman who lived in an apartment over the stable. . . . Many years later sparks from the railroad ignited the roof and it burned to the ground.*
>
> *I've always wondered why the first electric lights were not put in our house first; instead they were put in Mrs. Jordan's boarding house, known as "Aunt Sally's," the home of many of father's bachelor's assistants. . . . I later came to the conclusion that father was not quite sure of its safety and thought of his two small children sleeping on the third floor of our home, while at Mrs. Jordan's there were only adults.*[117]

Edison's daughter provided information regarding the length of the electric railroad at Menlo Park, and spoke of her father's relative disinterest in it, in comparison with his intense activity on the phonograph and the incandescent light. She remembered that she was

> *Very happy when riding on his electric railway which was narrow gauge and led from the laboratory grounds to an abandoned copper mine, a distance of two or three miles. As a matter of fact, I never saw him show the slightest interest in it.*[118]

Marion Oser's recollection may have been incorrect regarding her father's interest in the railroad, for she was only seven years old in 1880 when Edison built his railroad to the old copper mine at Mine Gully, about a mile north of the laboratory.[119]

Marion Edison recalled going to a "beach" somewhere near their home at Menlo Park. Although we do not know exactly where the beach was located that Marion Edison refers to, it was presumably somewhere in the valley below their home at Menlo Park, for she was able to drive there in a pony cart. The body of water must have been more substantial than the transient swampy area that Marshall said formed in wet seasons near the railroad tracks, about 800 feet below their house. In any event, Marion recalled the effects of industrial pollution on the charmed environment that she had enjoyed as a child. We wonder if the factories that she referred to were, indeed, her father's, and whether or not she intended for us to draw this conclusion:

Among my father's diversions were our trips to Boynton Beach. . . . As I had two ponies and a surrey, it was an easy drive from Menlo Park and we children were often allowed to go alone. . . . When I returned many years later to this haunt, I was horrified to see the hotel where we had always had our dinner in ruins and all the bath houses blown over. I found out that the factories had polluted the water and the beach had been closed to the public for many years.[120]

In the end, Marion Edison provides an epitaph for her father's effect on Menlo Park. In her "Early Recollections," Marion Edison Oser said, "The natives resented his leaving [Menlo Park] and coined the phrase that Menlo Park was dead and Thomas A. Edison had killed it."

Thomas Edison moved to New York City before his wife, Mary, died at Menlo Park in 1884. As his daughter, Marion, and others have observed, he abandoned Menlo Park thereafter. Her suggestion, that Menlo Park reminded him of his grief, appears to be a sufficient explanation for his withdrawal, but the effect of his departure on the environment of Menlo Park was devastating, nevertheless. The illustrations in Pretzer's and Marshall's books show vividly the deterioration of the neglected and abandoned buildings, and his former home there was lost to fire within twenty years. It is therefore easy to see why Edison showed little or no reluctance to allow Henry Ford to remove whatever he could find at Menlo Park and move it to the museum that he was creating in Dearborn, Michigan.

I have been able to locate a record of only one other visit by Edison to Menlo Park. It occurred in 1925, on the occasion of the dedication of the memorial plaque on the boulder that stands at the base of the hill on State Route 27, in front of where the front yard for his house had been some fifty years earlier. The photograph taken of Edison at this location in 1925 shows that the hillside behind the boulder was bare of trees, although other photographs taken within another year or two show the dolorous state of the buildings and a few scraggy trees here and there.

The deterioration in the appearance of Menlo Park from the late 1880s through the 1920s must have been heart-breaking to Edison. The progression of trees and brush over the foundations and cellars of the homes of Edison and his co-workers at Menlo Park for the subsequent seventy-five years has protected whatever remains there, and it has also restored the environment in those areas of Menlo Park to a semblance of nature, although it is, of course, second growth. It is, in short, surely more attractive now at Menlo Park than it was before the dilapidated buildings were removed to create the Henry Ford Museum and Greenfield Village. All is not lost at the former Menlo Park site in New Jersey, however, as we shall soon see. Let us now take a close look at what remains of the Edison site at Menlo Park, New Jersey, and see what might be done about it, from the perspective of environmental history.

* * * * *

In order to probe beneath the surface at Menlo Park, we need to outfit ourselves with a set of photographs, and to prepare a composite map that shows the present geography and street names in the development once known as Menlo Park, as well as the location of buildings and street names that were used there in the 1880s. It is easiest to examine the terrain at Menlo Park in the fall and winter, after the leaves are off of the trees and shrubs. It is also necessary to wear sturdy boots, heavy trousers, and thick gloves, for the brambles and thornbushes are formidable, and the woods are full of perils, such as broken glass and other trash, in addition to the cellar holes and foundation stones that we are seeking.

Our composite field map (see illustration at right) is constructed from the map of Menlo Park in 1876, maps of Menlo Park in 1925 and 1931, and current maps of Middlesex County and the U.S. Geological Survey's Perth Amboy quadrangle. We have made copies of photographs of the houses and terrain at Menlo Park as they appeared in the monographs that we have reviewed, and we have indicated on our field map the probable location of the photographer and the camera angle used to take each photograph. We have at our disposal more than a dozen photographic views of Edison's Menlo Park, plus Outcault's painting of the laboratory complex, an artist's sketch of several of the homes and laboratory buildings, and an engraving of a sketch of Edison's home. Together, these constitute an excellent representation of the entire property as it existed in Edison's lifetime, and the images enable us to determine exactly what exists at each photographic site at the present time.[121]

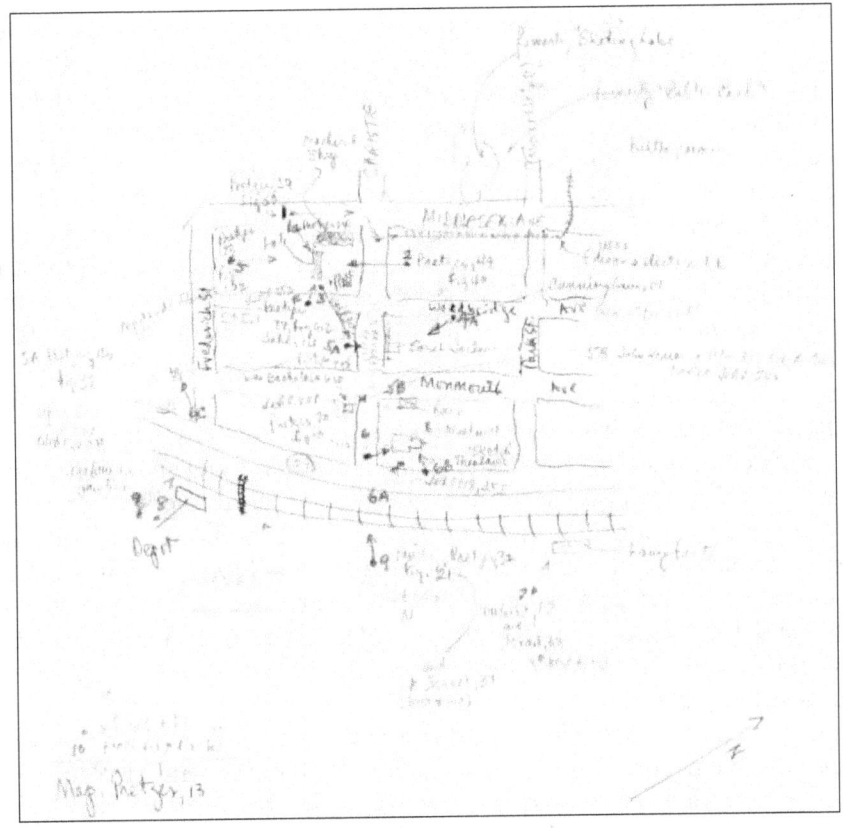

MAP BY GEORGE J. HILL, M.D.

ORIENTATION MAP: This sketch of Menlo Park, adapted from a map in a book by William S. Pretzer, shows the old and present street names, the locations of buildings during Edison's era, and the present status of those lots; it also shows the locations and perspectives of photographers who recorded buildings and community life in Menlo Park from the 1870s to the present.

Before we begin this trip back into the period from 1876 to 1929, it should be observed that although the Menlo Park site is referred to on the current map of Middlesex County as "Edison State Park," it is, in fact, not a state park. The curator of the Edison Tower museum is employed by Edison Township, which is administratively responsible for the Edison Tower and the grounds that surround it. This is an area of mowed grass that is one block long and a half block wide, facing Christie Street between Tower Avenue and Middlesex Avenue. The area under observation and management of the curator is partially enclosed by a chain-link fence that surrounds the base of the tower itself. The state of New Jersey, I was told, owns a substantial part of the land that I have come to regard as the Edison sites near the Edison Tower. The management by the state of New Jersey is administratively under the jurisdiction of the Superintendent of the Cheesequake State Park. However, the Superintendent at Cheesequake has neither a map nor a physical description of the state-owned property near the Edison Tower, so it is not clear what is owned by the state. (I was told by the Cheesequake administration that I could look this up on the real estate tax records.) There are no fences, except at the base of the tower, and no signs that indicate that any of this area is owned by the state of New Jersey.

There is also — in addition to the areas that I have mentioned and which I will soon describe in more detail — a larger piece of property that is densely wooded, pathless (as far as I can determine), unsigned, and largely unfenced, that abuts the site of the Edison Tower, which is called "Edison State Park" on the map of Middlesex County. This property is trapezoidal in shape, bounded on two sides by State Route 27 and by Frederick Street, and on the other two sides by Dellwood Road, which bends around it on the south and west. Except for its proximity to the various properties occupied by Edison and his associates, I can find no particular connection with Edison's Menlo Park to the wild piece of land between Frederick Street and Dellwood Road on Route 27. This property would, however, be suitable for recreational development as an adjunct to the historical sites along Christie Street.

* * * * *

I now ask the reader to join me on a journey through space and time, to study the "Footprints of Edison" at Menlo Park, New Jersey, as they were recorded by the camera or in the art work of illustrators during Edison's lifetime, and to see the traces of these "footprints" as they exist at the present time. Imagine, if you will, that you are walking through the countryside in Edison's day, even though what now exists on the surface in many places is quite different than it was at that time.[122]

We will begin our tour by viewing Edison's Menlo Park from the ridgeline across the valley of the South Branch of the Rahway, where now stands the New Jersey Home for Disabled Soldiers, the shopping center known as the Menlo Park Mall, and the Roosevelt Hospital. After locating the Edison Tower as a point of reference in the distance, we then move down into the valley, toward the Tower. Our next vantage point is from an upper floor of the Alfieri Building, on the south or east side of the railroad tracks at the foot of Christie Street. From this location we can look down onto the area of the laboratory, from the perspective that R. F. Outcault imagined in his painting during the winter of 1880-1881. We then cross the tracks, in our imagination, at the place where once the Menlo Park station, post office, and store were located, across the railroad from the foot of Christie Street. There is no longer a crossing at this point, so in reality we would have to detour along the tracks to Wood Avenue, and then return to Christie Street. We will then leap in our imagination to the upper end of Christie Street, to the intersection of Christie and Middlesex Avenue, and then work our way back down Christie again to the tracks, looking for the "ghosts" of buildings along both sides of the street. Our little trip will end by crossing the tracks once again to look at the site of the Lamp Factory.

Let us now begin by turning from Route 27 onto Parsonage Road, a half mile southwest of the Edison Tower, and then proceed for another half mile to our first viewpoint at the height of land where the Roosevelt Hospital is located. These are the views that we see on our tour:

- A distant view of Menlo Park from across the valley to the south appears in Pretzer, *Menlo Park*. This view shows open farmland studded here and there with trees, dirt roads and a pond in the foreground. There is a gentle, treeless hillside in the background, which is said to be the location of the Menlo Park Laboratory. The photograph in Pretzer was probably taken from the ridgeline where we are now standing, near the Roosevelt Hospital.[123] We might also imagine this distant view of the Laboratory at night, as it was when David Trumbull Marshall's brother was walking along the railroad from Metuchen to Menlo Park:

He fell into conversation with an old tramp and as they came out of the cut and rounded the curve just before you get to Menlo Park the old tramp stopped and exclaimed, "What is that place? I have traveled this road for thirty years but I never saw that place before." There before them was the whole round hill on which Menlo Park is built dotted all over with brilliant lights.[124]

- The Laboratory complex, with Christie Street running from front to back along its right side, is seen in the painting by R. F. Outcault. This was an imaginary view in 1880-1881, but the same location from the same perspective can now actually be seen from the tenth floor of the Alfieri office building, across the railroad tracks from Christie Street. The laboratory buildings are dispersed over an area that is approximately three hundred feet by three hundred feet in size, although the artist elongates the perspective, suggesting that it is a long rectangle. This would be approximately two acres, of which the buildings occupied about 7,500 square feet of space.[125]

- Edison's electric train was loaded with passengers and proceeded along Middlesex Avenue from Christie Street.[126] As David Trumbull Marshall recalled it in 1929,

In 1880 Mr. Edison built his first electric railroad. The ties were laid over some pretty rough ground. The track ran down a slope in or near Mine Gully.

Mr. Edison later in 1881 built another electric railroad which ran about two miles out to Dark Lane, northwest of the Laboratory. The track was laid more carefully. The ties consisted of square-sawed lumber about five inches by five. Each tie had to be dipped in asphalt to render it non-conducting when wet.[127]

- The west or back end of the laboratory building, and its rear corner, can be seen in the dilapidated building in the photograph in Pretzer, *Menlo Park*.[128]

- The long side of the laboratory building that faces Christie Street also appears in Pretzer.[129]

- A view of the Charles Dean house appears in Jehl, *Reminiscences*. This picture also shows the barn, windmill and rear of the Edison home; the edge of the brick office building appears at the left side of the photograph.[130]

- Photographs of the front of the laboratory building have been reproduced on many occasions, often with a group of Edison's fellow workers — the "muckers" — standing or sitting around on the porch.[131]

PHOTO BY GEORGE J. HILL, M.D.

MENLO PARK MUSEUM: A small Edison museum is located in the one-story concrete building (right), which was built on the site of Edison's Machine Shop. The Laboratory Building was located where the Edison Tower now stands (left).

- The dilapidated laboratory buildings that appear in Pretzer were viewed from a stance near Frederick Street, looking toward Christie Street.[132]

- Sarah Jordan's boardinghouse stood on Christie Street in the middle of the block between Monmouth Avenue and Woodbridge Avenue (now Tower Road). Sarah Jordan's boardinghouse is now at Dearborn, Michigan.[133]

- Upton's home was located at the corner of Monmouth Avenue and Frederick Street; it was apparently at one time the Thornall Estate house.[134]

- The locations of several buildings in Menlo Park, from Kruesi and Bachelor's on the north to Upton's on the south, including the back of Sarah Jordan's boarding house and the north side of the brick office building and the main laboratory building, can be seen by looking south toward the corner of Frederick Street and the Lincoln Highway from a stance on Woodbridge Avenue (now Tower Road) between Christie Street and Park Street (now Philip Street).[135]

- Edison's house at the corner of Christie Street and the Lincoln Highway (now Route 27) is shown in a photograph that is reproduced by Pretzer. To gain this perspective, stand in Christie Street near the corner and look north into the woods.[136]

- A sketch of Edison's house that was converted into an engraving in 1880 was made by looking uphill toward the present location of the flagpole and memorial boulder on Route 27.[137]

- Views of the memorial boulder at the time it was dedicated in 1925 can be obtained by standing (if you have the nerve to do it) in Route 27 and looking up the hill. Edison was standing there, at the north side of the boulder, on 16 May 1925.[138]

- Edison's lamp factory was on the other side of the tracks, with its long axis parallel to the railroad.[139]

* * * * *

Let us now return to the Edison Tower, and examine more closely some of the places that we have seen, but which we passed by rather quickly in our initial survey of Menlo Park. Some additional opportunities await us in our examination of the environment of this area in the lifetime of the Great Inventor.

In the first place, it should by now be obvious that virtually all of the places that are identified with Edison and his associates are now covered with trees and brush. Although all of the buildings that were here in Edison's lifetime are gone (moved to Dearborn, Michigan, destroyed, or moved elsewhere), the places where they stood are still undeveloped. The Menlo Park housing development as it was laid out in 1876 has finally been built up with many houses.

However, houses or other buildings have not yet been built on the sites of the Edison house (which was on "Property held by Edison Pioneers" in 1925), or of the Sarah Jordan Boardinghouse, and of the homes of Mr. Dean, of Batchelor and Kruesi, and (probably) of Mr. Upton. All of these house sites are at present covered with trees and brush (and some trash, sad to say). The roadbed of the first fifty yards or so of the experimental electric railroad is also on land that is still undeveloped, and which has returned to woods and shrubs. The only construction that exists where Edison's buildings had stood is the memorial tower and the museum building.

The half block on which the laboratory complex was built, as it appeared in the Outcault painting, is now covered with mowed grass except for the tower and the museum building. The close-cropped grass around the tower makes it possible to see that the stone foundations for Edison's brick office building are still in place at the corner of Tower Road (formerly Woodbridge Avenue) and Christie Street. We can thus see that the transportation of buildings and excavation of dirt that Edison authorized in 1928, and that Henry Ford's men performed, did not result in a complete removal of everything connected with Edison at this site. In addition to the foundations of the office building, the curator of the Edison Tower museum says that there are countless shards still present in the ground near the tower: "Wherever you dig, you find old bottles and things like that." This would suggest that there might be more to find than just shards, important as they may be to an archaeologist — and I will return to that point shortly.

The Edison Tower, sometimes called the Edison Memorial Tower, is a unique and impressive monument. Since it was built in 1937, six years after the inventor's death, the tower would presumably be important in this study of Edison and the environment only insofar as it serves as a useful reference point for identification of the location of the laboratory building. However, the tower actually connects the inventor's life with ours in a most remarkable way, if the oral history associated with it is correct. The legend goes as follows:

When the scraps and boards and bricks that remained of Edison's buildings were removed in 1928 and shipped by train to Dearborn, Michigan, a steel tower was erected over the place that — in the laboratory building — the final work was completed on the incandescent lamp in October 1879. Fifty years later, in October 1929, when the Golden Jubilee ceremony took place in the reconstructed laboratory complex in Dearborn, Edison threw a switch that was linked

LITHOGRAPH BY THEODORE DAVIS, 1880

THE VIEW IN EDISON'S TIME: This lithograph by Theodore Davis shows Edison's home in Menlo Park as it appeared in 1880

electronically to the base of the steel tower at Menlo Park, New Jersey, and thus lighted up an incandescent bulb. The bulb was small — about two inches in diameter — and it was made of a bluish-green translucent glass. It was not transparent, so the filament could not be seen, and because of its small candlepower, the bulb glowed rather than illuminating its environment.

A few years after the steel tower was built at Menlo Park, the tower was struck by lightning and destroyed. Ordinarily, one would expect that the little blue-green incandescent light at its base would have been destroyed, too, but it was not. And because several back-up sources of electricity had been connected with it, the bulb was also not extinguished. The legend goes on to say that the rubble of the steel tower was removed, all the while protecting the little bulb and keeping it electrified and glowing.

Over the next few years, arrangements were made with Corning Glass, RCA-Victor (Edison's former competitor), Public Service Electric and Gas, and the Edison Pioneers to build and electrify a new

PHOTO BY GEORGE J. HILL, M.D.

THE VIEW TODAY: Edison's house lot is completely overgrown with trees and brush, and no visible structures remain above the ground. A depression in the woods clearly marks the location of the cellar hole, which apparently has not been disturbed since the house burned down between 1913 and 1917.

memorial tower. The tower was designed by Massena & DuPont and was built by Walter Kiddie, Inc., as a gift of William Slocum Barstow to the Thomas Alva Edison Foundation. It was constructed out of 1,200 barrels of Edison Portland Cement (which must have been about the last of that company's cement, for the company was discontinued soon thereafter), and some fifty tons of steel. The new tower consisted of 117 feet of concrete on a twenty-four-foot base, 131 feet in all. It was surmounted by a replica of an incandescent light, thirteen feet in diameter, and weighing three tons, that generated 9,500 watts of light. The new concrete tower was dedicated on what would have been the inventor's ninety-first birthday, 11 February 1938. It originally was outfitted with twelve heavy duty loud speakers that broadcast all sorts of Edison recordings, and the base was surrounded with great bronze plaques that provide details about the inventor's life and work.

With the passage of time, the concrete began to crumble, and the loudspeakers have failed. The tower is now closed to the public. It is no longer considered safe to climb the stairs to the top, or even to approach the base without some degree of caution. But a little blue-green light still glows steadily in the center of a small room at ground level in the base of the Edison Tower — the same light, I was told, that was electrified by the hand of Edison himself in October 1929 and that has glowed constantly ever since.[140]

Having seen the foundation for the brick office building that once stood at the corner of Woodbridge and Christie, I was encouraged to believe that other building foundations might still exist at Menlo Park. In November 1997, I had also seen that the lot where the Edison house had stood was covered with trees and brush. It was not yet the site of a new house and yard. It was still too early in the fall to study the Edison house lot in detail, however. In order to do that I needed to wait until winter, when the leaves were all down, and the branches and brambles were as dry and brittle as they would get. I therefore returned with camera and notebook in January 1998, on a clear, cold day, when there was no snow on the ground. I was dressed in several layers of heavy clothing, with sturdy boots and heavy gloves. I found what I was looking for.[141]

The Edison house lot runs the full depth of the block from Route 27 to Monmouth Avenue. At the front of the lot, immediately behind the flagpole and a row of tall trees, is a narrow strip of grass that has been mowed by someone who wants to have access to the flat, solid ground that was once Edison's front yard. The front yard was much larger in Edison's day. It has been foreshortened by a deep excavation that was made to bring Route 27 down to a lower and more level grade, sometime since Edison lived here. Behind the narrow strip of grass is the cellar hole for the Edison house, exactly where it appears on all of the maps of this area. I could not tell if the sides of the house had been aligned parallel to Christie Street and the Lincoln Highway, as it appears on some maps, or if they were canted at an angle, as it appears on the 1925 map of Menlo Park, for the sides of the cellar hole slope gently down and the foundation stones are either gone or are completely buried.

The cellar hole is about four feet below grade level at its deepest point, and it is about twenty to thirty feet in width and breadth. There are many large trees that grow out of it and adjacent to it, as would be expected for a piece of land that has remained vacant and more or less untended for six or seven decades. The cellar hole is overgrown with much brush and small trees, and a formidable mass of thornbushes which are

PHOTO BY GEORGE J. HILL, M.D.

"TRUCKS" FOR EDISON'S ELECTRIC TRAIN: Edison designed and built a train at Menlo Park that was self-propelled by a "dynamo" generating direct current. The train and its engine are long-gone, but the engine's massive wheels, called "trucks," are now on display at the Edison National Historic Site in West Orange.

probably blackberries. The stems of these brutes are a centimeter in diameter and they are covered with razor-sharp spines. There are at least two hummocks that rise from the bottom of the cellar hole that are undoubtedly the bases of fireplaces. These would be formed from piles of rip-rap, cut stones, or bricks. The bases of the fireplaces would at one time have been covered with a flat surface of bricks, and they are now covered with layers of earth. The cellar hole was probably originally filled in with debris from the burned house and was then covered with dirt, to protect against accidental falls and injuries, especially at night. This is what makes such a hole an archaeologists' dream house.

The surface of the base of the cellar hole is now a layer of earth, leaves, and trash, the result of years of accumulation of nature's compost and "midnight dumpers." Poking around a bit in the deepest places, I found some items that may or may not be from the original house, such as a ten-inch diameter ceramic pipe that was (and still is) deeply embedded in the dirt, and some rough old bricks or cement building blocks about four to five inches across. There were also a few old milled boards, partially buried in the dirt and leaves, which appeared to be pieces of wood that were used in construction many years earlier. Whether or not these objects are from the Edison house, or from later accretions, remains to be seen after the site is properly excavated.

I did not find, in my brief trek through the Edison house lot, the foundations for his barn, which I understand from the museum curator was still standing long after his house was gone. Nor did I find (or fall into) Edison's well or his privy. It is, however, clear that the cellar hole and the rest of this property would be an interesting site to excavate, and that it should be protected until time, money, interest, and expertise converge to make this possible. This is apparently beyond the capabilities of Edison Township, and it should be undertaken by the state of New Jersey. At present, it is not clear who owns and who is responsible for the Edison house lot, and the other undeveloped lots that are scattered throughout Menlo Park. For example: the area along Middlesex Avenue where the experimental train once ran; the house lots of the Dean, Jordan, Bachelor and Kruesi, and Upton houses; and many other lots and larger areas near the Edison Tower that are presently covered with brush and trees.

* * * * *

As we prepare to leave Menlo Park, let us reflect for a moment on what this case study has added to our understanding of Edison's relationship to the environment. We have again seen the importance of a railroad, good roadways, and proximity to water in Edison's working environment, as we had in Elizabeth, Jersey City, and Newark. We also learned more about the personal environment of Edison and his family, and we saw the first hints of Edison's impact on the environment: On the one hand, his lighting of houses and of the streets in his section of Menlo Park turned dark night into something magical. On the other hand, the people of Menlo Park, who relied on him, were bitter about the environmental impact of his departure. There is also a hint, just a suggestion, that his factory may have been a polluter of a bathing beach somewhere in the valley.

In Menlo Park, Edison's home was so close to the tracks that it eventually burned down with sparks from a locomotive. His factory was immediately adjacent to the railroad, and his laboratory was less than three hundred yards away. The railroad was essential for transportation for Edison and his family, for his senior associates and his workmen, and for transportation of the raw materials and products of his laboratory and factory. We have also seen that although Edison moved

COURTESY OF NATIONAL PARK SERVICE

GHOSTS OF MENLO PARK: Edison's Menlo Park laboratory is in the center and the machine shop is at right in the top photo, which was taken before the buildings deteriorated. Below, the laboratory building was in ruins before it was taken to Dearborn, Michigan, to become part of Henry Ford's Greenfield Village museum.

to a rural environment at Menlo Park, he did not stray at all from a major roadway — the Lincoln Highway. Menlo Park was, in fact, within walking distance of Princeton, Metuchen, New Brunswick, Elizabeth, Newark, and Jersey City, so even if the workmen that he needed for his factory had not the means to take the train, or were unable to "hitch" a ride on a wagon, it would have been an easy day's walk from the Hudson River to his employment office. It was only ten miles from Jersey City to Newark, and thirteen miles from Newark to Menlo Park, on level roads with bridges over all of the waterways.[142]

Edison needed water for industry, for his residence, and for recreation. He built his laboratory at Menlo Park beside a small lake (which disappeared thereafter, perhaps becoming a water well for the lab), and he was only two blocks from a large lake. His laboratory was about a half mile from a stream to the northeast (which he had to pump water from at least once), and he was only a little farther from the South Branch of the Rahway River to the southeast. His daughter Marion says that he purchased Carmen's Pond nearby, where he planned to build a house, and that she drove a pony cart to Boynton Beach at another lake near their home.

In Marion's recollections, Edison appears to be a relentless worker in his laboratory, who neglected his wife. Marion Edison thus confirms what others have written about Thomas and Mary Stilwell Edison during this period. Yet Marion also recalls that Edison doted on his children, and their years at Menlo Park were happy ones. The rural environment and her easy access to Father in his laboratory were pleasant for her. Mary Edison's death appears, in Marion's recollection, to have been more sudden and unexpected than it is portrayed in Edison's biographies. Marion's account is substantiated by her descriptions of Edison's reactions after Mary's death: his grief and tears, his decision not to build a new house at Carmen Pond, and finally his abandonment of Menlo Park. We might say that the "ghosts" of the buildings that we saw in our mind's eye while walking through Menlo Park are not the only "ghosts" that inhabit this place. There is also the ghost of a failed marriage, and of a young wife who died in a house that is now only a depressed area in a wild patch of woods and brambles. Finally, we can see that Edison, at Menlo Park, was for the first time personally beginning to transform the environment, not simply to be impacted upon by it. His invention of the incandescent lamp at Menlo Park introduced what Roger Rosenblatt lyrically calls "Winter Lights": Edison's goal, says Rosenblatt, citing Neil Baldwin, was "to find an incandescent light that glowed at a steady rate, a clean, pure force." And it was here, at Menlo Park, that he "created the world's first showplace for electric light . . . on lampposts, set 50 ft. apart and crowned with helmet-shaped glass bulbs, [which] cast light over bare trees and snow-dusted fields." Incandescent lights now, says Rosenblatt, make "necklaces of lights along the coasts."[143]

We also know that at Menlo Park, prior to perfecting the incandescent light and the lighting system that made it a practical reality, Edison had invented the phonograph, which charmed his daughter, Marion, and also changed the world forever. We have had little to say in this case study about either Edison's invention of the electric light or the phonograph at Menlo Park, because others have analyzed the history and the impact of both of these inventions. I have, however, pointed out the less interesting (to Edison), yet vital (for us) contribution that he made to the development of the electric train. It is difficult today to imagine the soot and smoke that accompanied the passage of coal- and diesel-powered locomotives for many decades, until the electrified railways of the eastern seaboard essentially banished the pollution associated with energy generation to less-populated areas of the country. Without attempting at this point, to summarize — much less to judge — the environmental impacts of nuclear power, hydro-electric power, and power from fossil fuels, it is nevertheless appropriate to point out that an enormous shift occurred in the environmental impact of rail transportation with the implementation of electric railways. In America, this change began at Menlo Park, with Edison's little electric train — the trucks (wheels and axles) of which were salvaged for historical purposes by his son, Charles, and rest today on the grass beside Edison's laboratory in West Orange. Of the many thousands of commuters who pass by the Edison Tower on a typical workday, there are undoubtedly only a few who realize that this massive impact on their environment began near the base of that tower in Menlo Park.

*****

The reader will recall that for about five years before Edison remarried and moved to West Orange, he lived and worked in New York, while retaining ownership of property at Menlo Park, and acquiring real estate in Florida. To be specific, in March 1881 Edison moved his residence and business operations to New York City. He began laying conductors for the Pearl Street central station in the Wall Street area in the spring of 1881, while his business office was located at 65 Fifth Avenue. The station at 255-257 Pearl Street became operational on 4 September 1882. Two months later, he closed his Menlo Park laboratory and established a laboratory in the factory of the Bergman Company in New York City. Mary Edison died at Menlo Park in August 1884. In March 1885 Edison purchased land in Fort Myers, Florida, on which he later built a residence and a small laboratory.[144]

These simple facts belie the presence of an extremely complicated existence for Edison and his family during the period from 1881-1886, in which his environment was largely urban and peripatetic, and his life was frenetic. Several of Edison's residences in New York City were mentioned in his biographies, and Marion alludes to some in her recollections. At this point in Edison's life, he needed the business environment of New York City as a marketplace for his products, and he needed to be close to his factory, laboratory, and market. I have recently seen some of these places as they exist today, and I have previously driven by others. The environment in the places that Edison lived and worked in New York City has been greatly altered during the past 120 years. What Edison found when he arrived at the existing, built environment of the city, and what he did to the environment in New York City, would be appropriate for an in-depth study that would delve into the archives of the city and its newspapers. I leave this opportunity for others to seize. Edison's biographers had found reports that noise and smoke were produced by his generators, fires were caused by his electric lines and light bulbs, streets were accidentally electrified by inadequately insulated mains under the surface, and even some accidental deaths were recorded.[145]

There were many other events in Edison's life during the period 1881-1886 that relate to the environment, which might be explored. I have selected three of these for analysis. The first is the movement of Edison's Lamp Works in 1882 from Menlo Park to Harrison, across the Passaic River from Newark; this has previously been neglected by historians. The second — which is more an activity than a single event — shows that Edison was increasingly able to work within an existing environment to make changes that were desired, to evaluate the impact, and to carry forward what he learned to make large-scale alterations of the environment. By this, I refer to Edison's electrification of the village of Roselle, New Jersey, in 1883. In the third example, Edison's vacation at Winthrop, Massachusetts, in 1885, the inventor shows us his deep interest in the environment of nature.

Chapter 6

Harrison, Roselle and Winthrop: Lampworks, Light and Nature (1882-1892)

September 4, 1882 – [Edison] moved the first commercial incandescent lamp factory from Menlo Park to Harrison, New Jersey.

— **James G. Cook, 1976**[146]

Harrison, New Jersey, 1882-1892

IT'S getting easier, I thought — easier to figure out where Edison would set up shop. It would likely be near a railroad. And so it was: I was standing at the corner of Essex Street at Fifth Street in the southern part of the town of Harrison, two blocks from Interstate 280 and three blocks from the drawbridge that travelers often curse as they pass west into Newark on I-280. This intersection was a block up a gentle hill from the old railroad tracks that once brought trains to Edison's Lamp Works. It was February 1998, one hundred and sixteen years since Edison relocated his lamp works to this place, and I had now accomplished the first part of my task. I had come to Harrison to learn why Edison came here, and to study the environmental effects of his tenure in Harrison. As I have demonstrated in other case studies, and as I will show in those which are still ahead, I discovered more than I expected about Edison and the environment in Harrison, although some aspects of his presence here are still clouded in the mists of history that are not yet revealed.

Only a few references to Edison's shop in Harrison appear in standard biographies and histories. For instance, Conot says that:

> *At the electric-light factory in East Newark, Upton was able to hire all the girls he needed at fifty to seventy cents a day. Everyone was paid on a piecework basis, the price set according to the output of the fastest and the most skilled.*[147]

The point that Conot made was not particularly related to East Newark (which we will soon see is within, but is not, strictly speaking, a part of Harrison); he was referring to the management techniques used at this plant. Conot continues by saying that:

> *— though the efficiency engineer was not to become fashionable for another generation, Upton was one in everything but name. Demand, however continued to be comparatively low, so that the factory was losing eight cents on each of the 200,000 lamps it turned out annually.*

Neither the movement of the Lamp Works to Harrison, New Jersey, nor its termination as an Edison company, are recorded in the *Chronology* of the Edison Papers Project. The "Harrison Lamp Works," as this operation is called in common parlance, is not mentioned in the index of the biographies of Edison by Josephson, Melosi, Baldwin, and Millard — or in the texts of these books, as far as I can determine. Nor is the transfer of the Lamp Works from Menlo Park to Harrison or East Newark mentioned by Friedel and Israel, in *Electric Light*, or by Pretzer, in *Menlo Park*. In June 1997, the location of this plant was unknown to the ENHS archivists or to Professors Rosenberg or Israel. One of the staff at the ENHS speculated to me that the Harrison Lamp Works was not included in the Index of the Edison Papers Project because it was not a major activity of Thomas Edison personally, and because it was transferred to the General Electric Company by 1892. However, it was reported at the "Interpreting Edison" Conference that Edison was commuting to the Lamp Works in Harrison from his home, Glenmont, until he built the Laboratory at Lakeside Avenue and Valley Road/Street (now Main Street) in West Orange. I therefore decided to look for the site of Edison's Lamp Works in Harrison, to see what the environment was like when Edison arrived, and to determine what has happened since then to the environment in that location. What I read, what I saw, and what I was told about Edison's activities in Harrison provided me with a new window into the environment of the Great Inventor.[148]

* * * * *

Harrison, New Jersey, lies on the left (east) bank of the Passaic River, immediately upstream from the river's sharp bend to the east that gives a characteristic contour to the portion of Newark called "the Ironbound." We have previously encountered the portion of Newark that is across the Passaic from the southern part of Harrison: Edison's factory at Ward Place and his shops along New Jersey Railroad Avenue were across the river and within a mile to the south of this location in Harrison. In fact, one of the major bridges across the river at that time, and now, is the Bridge Street bridge. Bridge Street in Newark becomes Harrison Avenue in Harrison, which was only four blocks north of the main building of Edison's Lamp Works. Within the town of Harrison, there is a small borough called East Newark, which was created in 1892, but it is very small, and it does not include the area of Harrison where the Lamp Works buildings were located.[149]

Harrison was settled soon after the Puritans landed in Newark in 1666. Historians say that the first settlement was two years later. When Edison arrived in 1882, Harrison was a busy industrial center with breweries and factories, looking very much like Newark. The Pennsylvania Railroad ran through it, one stop north of Newark's Pennsylvania Station, and there was abundant water from the river. The sloping land from north to south toward the delta of the river at Newark bay meant good drainage, and there were many laborers in these cities who were ready to work for the scanty wages that Edison could afford to pay. Indeed, there was already a factory waiting for Edison. On Bergen Street, between Fourth Street and Fifth Street, the Peters Manufacturing Company had built their works for manufacturing oil cloth in 1877, but "Owing to frequent fires they abandoned their plant." The Peters plant, which Edison took over, occupied the entire block between Bergen and Essex Streets, and Fourth and Fifth Streets.[150]

The "Edison Lamp Works," as it was called in Harrison, "initially employed only 150 people." After three years or so, the Lamp Works became a component of the Edison General Electric Company: "In 1885 the interests of the Edison Lamp Company were purchased by the General Electric Company," although the Lamp Works were still supervised by Edison and his designated representatives. Edison described the history of the early years of the Lamp Works, as follows:

> When we first started the electric light we had to have a factory for manufacturing lamps. As the Edison light company did not seem disposed to go into manufacturing, we started a small lamp factory at Menlo Park.

. . We then bought at a receiver's sale at Harrison, New Jersey, a very large brick factory building which had been used as an oil-cloth works. We got it at a great bargain. . . . We then moved the lamp works from Menlo Park to Harrison. The first year the lamps cost us about one dollar and ten cents each. We sold them for forty cents. . . The fourth year I got it down to thirty-seven cents, and I made all the money in one year that I had lost previously. I finally got it down to twenty-two cents . . . Whereupon the Wall Street people . . . bought us out.[151]

FROM HENRY A. MUTZ, *HARRISON: THE HISTORY OF A NEW JERSY TOWN*, 29.

THE EDISON LAMP WORKS IN HARRISON: Edison's operation in Harrison began when he purchased an existing factory complex (left foreground). He then constructed a four-story factory that occupied the block between fourth and Fifth Streets, facing Bergen Street, and another building across Fifth Street (right foreground) which is still standing.

In 1887, Francis R. Upton was the manager of the works of the Edison Lamp Company in Harrison. When Upton "went abroad for a prolonged vacation," Alfred O. Tate was appointed acting manager. Tate served as manager of the Lamp Company until the Laboratory opened in West Orange later in 1887, at which time Upton returned to take charge in Harrison. Tate then moved to West Orange as Edison's Private Secretary, succeeding Samuel Insull.

The office of the Lamp Works must have been handsomely appointed, for Edison received a number of distinguished visitors there in comfort, including the Duke of Marlborough in 1887, and later a group of four representatives of Alexander Graham Bell who were led by his cousin, Chichester Bell. By 1890, Edison had expanded his operations in Harrison by construction of a new four story building that occupied the entire block to the north of the Peters building. The new building, which had "Lamp Works" on its Bergen Street pediment, occupied the block between Bergen and Sussex Streets, and Fourth and Fifth Streets. The Edison Chronology and Edison's biographers are agreed that on 15 April 1892 the General Electric Company was organized as the successor to Edison General Electric. During General Electric's period

PHOTO BY GEORGE J. HILL, M.D.

LAST VESTIGE OF EDISON IN HARRISON: This factory building at the corner of Bergen and Fifth Streets is the last remaining structure of Edison's Lamp Works in Harrison. The three-story brick structure is painted a cream color, and it is now used for light industry.

of ownership, the block to the east, between Bergen and Sussex Streets and Fifth and Sixth Streets, was added to the complex. The pediment on Bergen Street then proclaimed: "General Electric Company — Edison Lamp Works." Edison was invited back to a formal Reunion Luncheon at the plant in 1900, and by 1912 nearly 4,000 workers were employed at the General Electric Lamp Works in Harrison. In 1925, Edison still proudly said that "the first lamp factory in the world — the Edison Lamp Works — now located at Harrison, N.J. — was not started until 1880, and I was told it would never pay."[152]

The Lamp Works buildings in the two city blocks between Sussex and Essex, and between Fourth and Fifth Streets, were used by R.C.A. from 1930 until they were demolished in 1975. These two blocks are now filled by one-story buildings and parking lots: "Wendy's," "R & S," "Radio Shack," and other familiar names now face Bergen Street, where once the "Lamp Works" sign dominated the street. Only one narrow strip of grass from the earlier days still exists; it is along the Essex Street curb just west of Fifth Street. If you look carefully there, you can see a few small scraps of metal, some flat slate stones, and some pieces of brick and cement — all that remain of the first building that housed Edison's Lamp Works in Harrison. One of the large Lamp Works factory buildings is also still standing, and is still in use. This building appears in the picture of the Lamp Works during the General Electric period, at the corner of Bergen and Fifth Streets. This three-story brick building is now painted an attractive cream color; it is well-maintained and is used for light industry.[153]

One final puzzle remains: Why did Edison select Harrison when he moved his Lamp Works out of Menlo Park in 1882? I suggest that Edison needed to move out of Menlo Park, which was too far from his main base of operations in New York City, and he had already learned that real estate was less dear in New Jersey than in New York. Conot would have us believe that the low wages he paid to women in Harrison was an important consideration, and we now know that there was also a factory ready for him to move into in Harrison. There was a railroad adjacent to the factory, and water nearby. And he was familiar with the area, having lived across the river in Newark from 1870 to 1875. But the firemen in Harrison had a different answer, when they asked me what I was looking for, and I replied: "Why did Edison come to Harrison?" Their answer stopped me dead in my tracks.

The firemen said, "Didn't you know about his lady friend? Mrs. Border or whatever her name was . . . the eel lady.'" I replied that Edison had many faults (and I named a few, like spitting on the floor, not bathing very often, and paying bills as late as he could get away with), but "playing around" with women wasn't in the books that I had read about him. It is clear, however, that five generations later, Edison-the-man is still revered in Harrison, not just because he was a Great Inventor and a man whose Lamp Works provided employment for much of the town. He was (and is) also believed to be a clever fellow who operated a factory where he could be close to a lady friend, who lived "just over the walking bridge that used to connect Harrison with Newark, by the Bridge Street bridge." That is an environmental influence that I hadn't even considered, and which I have no way to investigate at this time.[154]

Roselle, New Jersey, 1883

Edison's first village electric lighting system using overhead wires begins operation in Roselle, New Jersey.
— *Edison Chronology*, **1883**[155]

THIS straightforward statement in the Edison Chronology introduces a fascinating episode in Edison's life, which had an environmental impact that is still appreciated in the small town of Roselle, New Jersey. In his development of an electric lighting system for Roselle, Edison again showed that he kept in mind the desires of potential customers (i.e., the public) and their ability to pay for what he produced. He also wished to deliver a high quality, safe product, and to provide continuing service for it, as needed. In this regard, at Roselle as in Menlo Park, the desires of potential customers (i.e., the public) and their ability

PHOTO BY GEORGE J. HILL, M.D.

PROUD MEMORY: This plaque on a boulder next to a monument of coal symbolizes the energy source used by Edison in 1883 to make Roselle the nation's first electrified village.

to pay for what he produced. He also wished to deliver a high quality, safe product, and to provide continuing service for it, as needed. In this regard, at Roselle as in Menlo Park, the environment included a railroad and an adjacent area of fine houses that was planned by a Land Company, with well-to-do families in mind.[156]

As in Menlo Park, excellent roads already were in existence in Roselle, and the land was well-watered, yet also well-drained. Coal and water were thus readily available for Edison's boilers, and the affluent residents of this new area had only kerosene lanterns and candles for light. Gas lines had not yet reached Roselle from Elizabeth, five miles away. The Central Railroad of New Jersey and Westfield Avenue ran along the north side of Roselle, and St. George Avenue (which was the northern extension of the Lincoln Highway) ran across the opposite side of town. Edison undoubtedly knew something of Roselle, for the streets in this new village were being laid out in 1868-1869 when he was living in Elizabeth — one stop away on the CRRNJ — and one of his senior managers was living in a newly constructed house in Roselle. The environment was right, in all respects, for the first village in America to be lighted with incandescent lamps. Edison's power plant was built in space that he leased from the Roselle Land Company in its building adjacent to the railroad, and poles were placed around a circuit five blocks long and one block wide, bearing the wires for street lights and lights for thirty-five houses, the railroad station, several stores, and a church. Most of the houses were handsome three-story Victorian dwellings with mansard roofs, and some were crowned with cupolas, as had been seen on Upton's house at Menlo Park. The First Presbyterian Church in Roselle thus became the first church in America to be wired with electricity, and the vestibule of this church is still lighted by the thirty-bulb Edison "Electrolier" that was first turned on in 1883. The church building where the Edison Electrolier was originally installed was destroyed by fire in December 1949 (from a faulty chimney, not electricity), and the Electrolier was badly damaged. The Electrolier was, however, preserved, restored, and placed back in service again, although it was installed a few feet from its original location. It is now suspended from the ceiling in the entry hallway between the sanctuary and the parish house that was built on the site of the original, smaller, church building.[157]

The Edison Company for Isolated Lighting gained the experience in Roselle that it needed to be able to develop proposals for other communities, and soon many small towns in America had been electrified. Roselle is no longer thought of as an affluent country town

EDISON'S ELECTROLIER:
The 1883 electric chandelier, or "electrolier" (right) was badly damaged in a 1949 fire, but was subsequently restored. It still lights the hallway between the church and the parish hall of the First Presbyterian Church of Roselle (above).

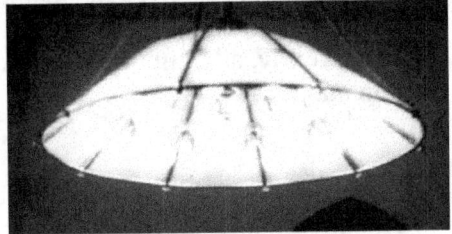

PHOTOS BY GEORGE J. HILL, M.D.

or suburb; central New Jersey's wealthy retirees and commuters now live further to the west. Trains no longer pass through Roselle along Westfield Avenue. The CRRNJ, that once brought hundreds of commuters past Roselle on their way to and from New York, is no longer in existence. But in contrast to Menlo Park, the older residents of Roselle prize their connection with Edison. They are proud to have been the venue for his experiment in 1883, and they do not attribute any of the negative changes that have occurred in their environment in the past century to either Edison's work in Roselle, or to the departure of his company from their village.

One may ask, why do the residents of Roselle have a fond recollection of Edison, and speak with pride of their connection with him, in contrast to most New Yorkers, who have no knowledge of Edison's work at Pearl Street, and to the embittered residents of Menlo Park that Marion Edison Oser spoke of? The answer, of course, is that Edison's environmental impact on Roselle was very different than it was in New York City and at Menlo Park. New Yorkers, sad to say, have a short "corporate memory" for past events, and most residents of that great city are unaware of their historical environment. At Menlo Park, Edison constructed many buildings, and he filled the community with activity and hope. Whatever negative impacts might have been observed on the environment would have been mitigated by new opportunities, new income, and the aura of success. When Edison abandoned Menlo Park, many years passed before the community saw the last of the dilapidated laboratory buildings that were an eyesore and a safety hazard. And to this day, neither the non-profit foundations that are associated with the Edison name, nor the government agencies that are responsible for property at Menlo Park have found a way to repair the legacy of environmental damage that was wrought in the inventor's lifetime. At Roselle, in contrast, Edison's environmental effect was small but positive; it was, shall we say, a "light" impact, and when he was gone, the magic of light remained.

* * * * *

Edison, while grieving after Mary's death, began to search for female companionship, and he needed to reconstruct a family environment for his children. He was introduced to Mina Miller by his associate and friend, Ezra Gilliland, whose wife was a friend of the Millers. Edison was invited to join the Gillilands at their country place in Massachusetts in the summer of 1885. While vacationing at "Woodside," the Gillilands' rental cottage near the Cottage Park resort in Winthrop, Massachusetts, Edison kept a diary, which provides an opportunity for us to study his thoughts regarding the natural environment, and the human body.[158]

Winthrop, Massachusetts, 1885

Arose before anyone else – came down and went out to look at Mama Earth and her green clothes.

— Thomas Alva Edison, 20 July 1885[159]

THE cottage in which Edison stayed has not been located, but photographs of country houses of the late nineteenth century that remain near Winthrop, Massachusetts, appear in the background for the facsimile reproduction of his diary of July 1885, which Kathleen McGuirk compiled and edited in 1971. The small white wooden cottages with bric-a-brac trim were rural yet civilized. They epitomize the environment of the New England country vacation homes of well-to-do Americans in the Victorian era.[160]

Edison was an early riser in Winthrop, and he enjoyed getting his nose into nature. On 12 July, he was "awakened at 5:15 a.m. My eyes were embarrassed by the sunbeams ..." And on 20 July, we have already read that he "went out to look at Mama Earth and her green clothes." His description of himself as a patient observer of nature shows his sense of humor, and recalls stories of his curiosity as a child on his sister's farm in Ohio:

Been hunting around for some ant nests, so I can have a good watch of them laying on the grass — Don't seem to be any around — don't think an ant could make a decent living in a land where a Yankee has to emigrate from to survive.

Edison's concept of the conscious and subconscious minds, which others have commented upon without providing a reference, appears in this diary. He says that his new, tight shoes are:

Small and look nice. No. 2 mind (acquired mind) has succeeded in convincing my No. 1 mind (primal mind or heart) that it is pure vanity conceit and folly to suffer bodily pains.[161]

Into his descriptions of nature and of his activities while he was on vacation, Edison interjects comments about other topics, such as religion and health. Consistent with some (although not all) comments that he made elsewhere about tobacco, Edison here condemns smoking, writing that "Smoking too much makes me nervous . . . The roots of tobacco plants must go clear through to hell." And he makes use of a metaphor from the rural environment to poke fun at those who fear Hell: "Satan is the scarecrow in the religious cornfield."[162]

Edison's nine days of diary entries were so carefully composed and so neatly written that it appears likely that he expected that the diary would be read by others — or at least that he would share it with Mina, who had already captured his heart. Even if he was not entirely forthright, the comments made by Edison still warrant our consideration, for they represent his position at that time on a number of environmental topics. Taken as a whole, the comments made by Edison in this diary show his philosophical connection with the late transcendental movement, with which some of his biographers have associated him because of other aspects of his writing and thought. Transcendental and Deist connections appear in Edison's admiration for Thomas Paine, and because of his comments that recall aspects of the philosophy of men such as Thomas Jefferson, Benjamin Franklin, Ethan Allen, Henry David Thoreau, and Walt Whitman. As Edison enters the next phase of his life, which we already know was long and interesting, we will see in what ways his childlike curiosity and admiration for Nature persists, and in what ways he changes. As our next case study begins, six months have passed; Edison and Mina have married, and they have moved into Glenmont, in Llewellyn Park, West Orange, New Jersey.

Chapter 7

Edison's Glenmont: At Home in Llewellyn Park

West Orange has numerous connections to Thomas Edison. It was the site of his home and plant from the late 1880s until his death in 1931. . . . Llewellyn Park (the "Park" to residents) has existed as an independent community within the local municipality for 140 years.

—Ethnographic Overview, 1997[163]

West Orange, New Jersey, 1886-1931

THE National Park Service (NPS) commissioned two studies related to the Edison National Historic Site (ENHS) that were completed in 1997. The reports of these studies provide a wealth of information regarding the environmental history of Edison's laboratory and factory buildings in West Orange, and about his home in Llewellyn Park. The National Park Service's *Ethnographic Overview*, from which two sentences were quoted to introduce this section, is focused principally on the demography and ethnography of West Orange, including Llewellyn Park, whereas the NPS's *Cultural Landscape Report* focuses mainly on the Laboratory and factories, which are often collectively called "the West Orange Plant."

The other principal source for my case study of Edison and West Orange is an oral history collection that was kindly loaned to me in January 1998 by Jack Stanley of Newark, N.J. I call these documents the

Jack Stanley Papers (JSP). In addition, I have utilized documents provided for my inspection by archivists at the ENHS and other materials that are on display there, as well as maps and documents in several libraries in this region. The Museum of The Historical Society of Bloomfield was an unexpectedly fine source of information regarding Edison's impact on the environment in the northern part of the Orange Valley. Some of my sources were copies of previously unpublished letters and notes of Edison that were provided to me by Professor Margaret Pierce of Knoxville, Tenn.; these are referred to as the Pierce Papers. Since I live in West Orange, I have had ample opportunity to draw upon my personal observations of the interiors and exteriors of several buildings in the Edison National Historic Site and in surrounding areas of West Orange and Orange. I also reviewed relevant documents regarding this period in the archives of the University of Medicine and Dentistry of New Jersey's George F. Smith Library of the Health Sciences (now Rutgers University), particularly the archives of the Essex County Medical Society, and the vertical files of information at the Smith Library regarding the U.S. Radium Corporation site in Orange, N.J.[164]

The reader should recall that at its peak, the Edison Plant in West Orange was situated between Main Street (on the west) and Watchung Street (on the east), and between Alden Street (on the north) and Lakeside Avenue (on the south). The Edison Plant also occupied much of the adjacent block to the south, bounded by Lakeside Avenue (on the north), Main Street (on the west), Charles Street (on the south) and Ashland Street (on the east), where the Edison Battery Factory was located. And as we shall soon see, Edison also owned some property on the east side of Ashland Street, near the railroad spur that existed at the time, between Ashland Street and Standish Street. The precise limits and the history of acquisition of these sites of the Edison Plant have recently been confirmed by the National Park Service.

In describing Edison's various properties, I continue to use the simplified reference to the cardinal bearings of the compass that is conventional at this time in the Orange Valley. That is to say, in West Orange, Main Street is commonly said to run east and west as it passes from West Orange into Newark, and it is referred to as a north-south running street as it goes from St. Mark's Square in West Orange towards Montclair, passing Llewellyn Park (on the "west") and the Edison Plant (on the "east"). In truth, the Watchung Mountains actually run from northeast to southwest, and Main Street therefore actually runs along the base of the mountain in a northeast-southwest direction.

PHOTO BY GEORGE J. HILL, M.D.

THE EDISON HOME: Thomas and Mina Edison moved to Glenmont, their estate in Llewellyn Park, in 1886. Thomas Edison lived there until his death in 1931, and Mina remained there until her death in 1947.

A Lively Place: Glenmont and Llewellyn Park

We had a couple of cows, and the lower part of what is now Glenmont was all in hay, most of the time, and we used to go haying in the summer, and support the cows, and Mother had to manage all that because Father never bothered.

—Madeline Edison Sloane, 1972[165]

BORN in 1888, Madeline Edison was the first of Thomas and Mina's three children. The recollections of Madeline when she was interviewed in 1972 and 1973, in her eighty-fifth and eighty-sixth years, provide valuable insights into the environment at Glenmont when the Edison family lived there. Madeline also tells of other aspects of the environment as she saw it — especially the family and social environment that was created by her parents, her brothers, and her chums from school and college.[166]

Llewellyn Park is now a hidden and remote enclave on the wooded hillside of Orange Mountain in West Orange, protected from casual entry by a guard and a gatehouse at the western end of Park Avenue, and isolated from the observation of those who pass by on Main Street. Glenmont has been an important feature of the Park from the time of its construction in 1880 to the present. It has been said that "Glenmont functions as an important 'witness' to the history of the Park, to the values and ideals of historic preservation, and to the general condition of the Park."[167]

In our case studies, we have attempted to recreate the environment that existed when Edison came to each of the places where he lived or worked, and to study the changes in the environment during the period that he was there. For Glenmont and Llewellyn Park, this is a long time, some forty-five years, from February 1886 until October 1931. As we roll back the years from 1998 to 1886, we can see many changes that have occurred in the environment along Main Street, and we can imagine enough of the changes that occurred in the Park to be able to visualize what it was like there when Mina and Thomas Edison moved into Glenmont. For example, in 1886 there were dramatic differences in the trees, buildings, and traffic patterns in and around Llewellyn Park from what we see today. Llewellyn Haskell had planted hundreds of trees and shrubs throughout his Park, but they had been growing for only thirty years by the time the Edisons arrived. We have previously mentioned the barren nature of the hillside as it appeared in drawings and photographs of the 1850s and 1860s. However, the residents of the Park continued to plant trees, and this second growth forest has flourished for one hundred and ten years since Thomas and Mina arrived.

In 1877, three years before Glenmont was built, and eight years before Glenmont was selected by Thomas Edison and Mina Miller to be their home, the perimeter of Llewellyn Park was bounded by Mt. Pleasant Avenue on the south, Prospect Avenue on the west, Eagle Rock Avenue on the north, and Valley Road (now Main Street) on the east. The extensions to the north side of Eagle Rock Avenue, onto Eagle Rock and as far north as Nishuane Park in Montclair had been eliminated from the plan for Llewellyn Park that was shown on maps drawn in 1857 and 1858. In 1877, the property on Glen Avenue on which Glenmont was soon constructed had been divided into six lots, of which five had owners designated, the largest being a "C. Harrison." Llewellyn Park, in 1877, consisted of 750 acres, of which 50 acres had been set aside as "The Ramble," which extended from Cliff Avenue, just east of the ridge line, to Valley Road.[168]

PHOTOS BY GEORGE J. HILL, M.D.

INSIDE GLENMONT: Thomas and Mina Edison's bedroom (above) features a dresser with a mirror and writing table. The sunny first floor den (below), which tour guides refer to as the "Trophy Room," was completed by the Edison to showcase his books, gifts, and awards.

"The Ramble," down which one of the northern branches of Wigwam Brook tumbled through Llewellyn Park, was a deep, wooded gulch that ran along the south side of the Edisons' property. The Ramble was separated from the grounds of Glenmont by only a narrow road, Park Way, leading to the entrance to the Park. Trees in The Ramble blocked the Edisons' view to the south. But when they moved into Glenmont, the hayfield that Madeline described must have provided a nearly clear field of view to the valley immediately below Glenmont, across what was then called Valley Street to Cook's Pond. This is where Edison would soon purchase a piece of farmland and begin to construct his laboratory. The pond would then disappear, as we previously learned. The view from Glenmont would have continued on across several low hills in the Orange Valley that Park Avenue traversed to reach Mount Pleasant on the west bank of the Passaic River in Newark.

The Edisons might have had to climb a bit higher in the Park in order to identify each of the hills along the route of Park Avenue: The first hill that they would see was the gentle ridge on High Street, just into Orange, which diverted Wigwam Brook toward the north. The Wigwam Brook, which Edison would later bury under his battery factory, soon turned east again, flowing along Dodd Street into East Orange. At this point, the brook was near the southeast corner of Rosedale Cemetery, where Thomas and Mina were originally buried. Wigwam Brook then flowed north again along Glenwood Avenue into the center of Bloomfield. We will return again to Bloomfield when we examine Edison's factory operations there, but at this time a small pond known as Silver Lake shimmered in the light along the north side of Bloomfield Avenue. The route of Wigwam Brook was easy to identify, because by 1877 the lower course of this brook was already the path of the Orange Branch of the Erie Railroad. Coal smoke from the locomotives marked the route of this line as it passed on to the east through Bloomfield and the district known as Silver Lake before entering Belleville and Newark. The Orange Branch's depot at Ashland Avenue and Park Avenue, which later was known as the Llewellyn Station, was less than a block from the corner where Edison built his Laboratory on Lakeside Avenue.

As the Edisons looked to the east from Llewellyn Park, the second hill that Park Avenue crossed as it made its way from the Park to Newark was the low summit marked by Prospect Street and Glenwood Avenue — the same avenue that we previously followed north into Bloomfield. Indeed, Wigwam Brook crossed under Glenwood Avenue in Bloomfield

COURTESY OF NATIONAL PARK SERVICE

EDISON AT GLENMONT: The Great Inventor, reading on his front lawn in Llewellyn Park in 1917. His chair faces his laboratory and factory complex on Main Street.

where it picked up water from the Toney Brook and became Second River, a major tributary of the Passaic. In the nineteenth century, this junction occurred in a handsome body of water known as Watsessing Lake, but this lake — like so many others in the Orange Valley — has since dried up. The lakebed is now known as Watsessing Park. Second River and the Morris Canal ran side-by-side for a half mile in Bloomfield, between Franklin Street and Montgomery Street, and the stone-lined remains of the canal can still be seen at this point. In its heyday, the Morris Canal actually crossed Second River in Bloomfield on a stone aqueduct. After the canal and the river diverged at the Bloomfield-Belleville border, Second River ran east into the Passaic. We have already read in Part I that Second River was the convenient route for the great sewage system that drains the entire valley north of the "ill-fated Parrow Brook" in Orange. The fate of the Morris Canal, on the other hand, was to become the bed of the Newark City Subway, which now winds along the west side of Branch Brook Park to Raymond Boulevard in Newark.[169]

PHOTO BY GEORGE J. HILL, M.D.

COOKING WITH GAS: Edison's kitchen featured this gas stove, a minor irony for the inventor who made his name with electricity.

The Edisons could, in those days, have easily seen the next two hills that Park Avenue crosses before it ends at Broadway in Newark. The low summit at Arlington Street is familiar even today, for it is here that Park Avenue crosses the Garden State Parkway. Park Avenue continues to the east, descending into the wide valley of Branch Brook, which is now a splendid county park. After crossing the brook, Park Avenue then rises to its fourth summit on Clifton Street. This height is now crowned by the largest church building in Newark, the Sacred Heart Cathedral. Edison's first wife was buried at Mount Pleasant Cemetery, just northeast of the termination of Park Avenue. His eye must surely have been drawn to that hilltop as he looked east across the valley of farms and small factories from his new residence in Llewellyn Park. The great regrowth of trees in Llewellyn Park and in the valley, which we observed previously from Eagle Rock, now makes it difficult to visualize what the Edisons saw. Nor can an ordinary citizen stand in the windows on the third floor of Glenmont to study the valley below, or peer out of the attic window on the fourth floor, or climb from the attic up to the "widow's walk" — five floors above the ground — as the Edisons and their and servants could. But we can see it all in our mind's eye, if we simply let our imagination do the work. The view of the valley from the widow's walk must have been spectacular.

My research in this case study has not revealed a definitive answer to the question of why Edison decided to purchase Glenmont. That is to say, it is still moot, whether Thomas and Mina bought Glenmont because they wanted to live there, and the fact that land was available nearby for a laboratory and factories was secondary; or the reverse: the availability of land for his work was the primary factor, and the existence of Glenmont was important, but secondary. The oral histories in the Jack Stanley Papers, the 1997 study of the site by the National Park Service, and the 1877 map of Llewellyn Park suggest that both reasons were important, and that both arguments are valid.

One puzzling feature regarding the oral histories is, however, the failure of the reporter, Milton Marmor, to discuss the acquisition of Glenmont in his interview with Mina Edison. In January 1974, Mina was then eighty-one years old, and although she was frail — she was to die seven months later — her recollections were clear, and she was willing to commit herself to many points. She discussed her courtship with Thomas Edison at some length, albeit politely declining to elaborate in answer to the question, "I heard he proposed to you by Morse Code," saying only, "Yes. I think that is a little sacred."[170]

Madeline Edison Sloane appears to concur in part with her interviewer's suggestion that Mina picked Glenmont because it was a country place, and that Mina wanted to live in the country rather than in the city. However, Madeline emphasizes her belief that her father was going to build his laboratory in the valley, and that her mother knew this. This implies that the decision to build the laboratory in the Orange Valley took precedence, and that the availability of Glenmont made it a good choice. In any event, Madeline recalls the environment at Glenmont as busy, and happy.[171]

I have wondered for some time if Edison used the library that he acquired with his purchase of the fully-furnished Glenmont. In this regard, I applied — without success — to review the titles for topics related to philosophy and to what we now call "the environment." If any of the titles in the libraries at Glenmont were within the scope of my book, such as works by Thomas Jefferson, Benjamin Franklin, Ethan Allen, Thomas Paine, Robert Owen, Henry David Thoreau, Ralph Waldo Emerson, or Walt Whitman, I intended to ask for the opportunity to look in these books for marginalia by Edison. I was told by the NPS that there is no list available of the books at Glenmont, and I was not granted permission to examine the spines of the books in the Glenmont libraries to look for authors that I was interested in.[172] Nevertheless, although her answer is not definitive on this subject, Madeline implied in 1972 that her father did indeed make use of the library of the first owner of Glenmont, on the first floor, that is said by the National Park Service tour guides to be decorative, unread, and largely uncut.

PHOTO BY GEORGE J. HILL, M.D.

GARDENER'S COTTAGE: *The Gardener's Cottage, which also served as the Greenhouse and Potter's Shed, was built out of concrete made from Edison Portland Cement in 1909. The Cottage was furnished to match the Garage (photo at right).*

Let us now take a closer look at Glenmont, by examining some of the documents assembled by the National Park Service in 1997, and oral histories in the Jack Stanley Collection. We shall endeavor to probe for additional information regarding the nature of Glenmont and its surrounding environment in 1886, and for insights into changes at Glenmont and in Llewellyn Park during the inventor's lifetime.

In 1978, the Edison National Historic Site was nominated by the National Park Service for inclusion in the National Register of Historic Places. At that time, Glenmont was situated on 15.67 acres of land in Llewellyn Park; the Laboratory unit occupied 5.69 acres. At a later point in time, the property in Llewellyn Park was said to consist of "thirteen and one-half acres of landscaped grounds on which are situated the Edisons' twenty-three room house, a Gardener's Cottage and Potting Shed, Greenhouse, Garage, Barn, Pump House, and Hose House."[173]

The den was incomplete when Edison purchased Glenmont in 1886 and it was completed between then and 1890. A ceiling was added to the

PHOTO BY GEORGE J. HILL, M.D.

AN IMPOSING GARAGE: This handsome building, constructed in 1908 from Edison Portland Cement, currently houses three of Edison's unique automobiles – far fewer than it undoubtedly did in Edison's day.

den in 1935 to reduce drafts, but this false ceiling was removed in 1966. The second floor included five large rooms that opened onto a broad hallway, as well as a family living room built by the Edisons over the *porte cochère*, and a sun porch on the south side. The servants' quarters on the third floor were not described at all. The application states that Glenmont was originally lighted with gas, and that it was electrified by Edison in 1889.

The fact that the kitchen range was still a gas stove was not mentioned in the nomination form (and I was therefore surprised to see that this use of gas persisted at Glenmont), nor was Edison's laboratory near the kitchen mentioned.[174]

The Gardener's Cottage and Potting Shed was described in the nomination form as a 3,283 square foot, flat-roofed "two-story reinforced concrete structure with basement," built in 1890. The Garage was described as a 4,404 square foot two story building with a partial basement. This building was built in 1908, one of the first examples of monolithic poured concrete construction. An electric turntable was set

PHOTOS BY GEORGE J. HILL, M.D.

POOL AND POND: Edison's Glenmont estate featured a swimming pool and a skating pond that are small by modern standards. Today, slight depressions in the ground show the locations of the pool (top) and the pond (below). The estate's garage can be seen through the trees in the top photo.

into the floor of the garage, and the second floor originally contained eight rooms and a bath for a chauffeur's quarters. It has since been renovated into employees' quarters for the NPS. The eloquent language of the nomination form emphasizes the importance of this building in architectural history.[175]

The Barn was an L-shaped, 2,135 square foot, wood frame Victorian style building that was one story high, with a loft. Its original date of construction was unknown, but it was moved to its present location east of the Greenhouse in 1908. The 114-square foot Pump House was built between 1882 and 1886 to provide potable water for Glenmont, with a pump powered by an Edison bi-polar motor. The wood-sided, shingled Hose House was built in 1904 and was reconstructed in 1964. Its twenty-nine square feet of floor space were used to store fire hose.[176]

Three small but important bodies of water on the grounds of Glenmont during the Edison period are now gone: the swimming pool, the skating pond, and the cistern. The swimming pool was small, by current standards, so most tourists would not realize the purpose of the rectangle formed by the low concrete wall that now stands near the barn and the greenhouse. The filled-in skating pond was also small by present standards. The pond appears to have been about fifteen to twenty feet in diameter, although its original depth cannot be judged from its present surface appearance in the wooded area, west of the garage. The cistern was recalled by the Edisons' gardener, W. I. Halstrom, in 1965. At some point in time, the cistern at Glenmont was permanently closed by filling it with a year's worth of ashes, and its location is unknown.[177]

It was noted in the nomination form that twenty or more specimen trees had died or blown down since Edison's death, and that some of the flower and vegetable gardens that had been converted to lawn and footpaths had been partly overgrown with shrubbery. These and other changes in the grounds and out-buildings at Glenmont were described in some detail in comments by one of the Edisons' last gardeners, W. I. Halstrom, in 1973. Mr. Halstrom apparently began work at Glenmont when he was a young man in about 1921 or 1922, and he continued working there for some time after the death of Mina Edison in 1947. Through his recollections, we gain insight into the environment of the Edison family and their employees in Llewellyn Park, and into the interactions that occurred between humans and Nature in this setting. We also can see the difficulty that historians face in trying to reconstruct the environment of a historic site, if the changes were not recorded contemporaneously, after memories fade.[178]

Weeds

Halstrom tells of the type of work that he and the other employees performed, and of the marginalized life that was typical at that time for manual laborers:

Fabio Definis, he was the grass man. . . . When Edison was living, see, they had two cows here, and Fabio was the cow man. . . . He told me for nine years he never had a day off. . . . The old man [Atkinson, not Edison] couldn't milk a cow. So like on Sundays and holidays, he'd come up in the morning, milk the cows, clean the barn, take the milk over to the house. Then he'd go home. Then he'd come back in the afternoon again, same thing.

Then the second year, we had an Irishman here, Finnigan, and — well, what we used to do in the springtime when Mr. Edison came back from Florida, he put on an extra man for the springtime, to get the planting done and things like that. Then in the summer when there wasn't no more planting, well, then he let him go. That's what they used to do in those days, you know. They didn't hire them year round.[179]

The construction of the swimming pool, the greenhouse, the barn, the pond, and a wall at Glenmont were recalled by the gardener, in answer to probing questions from the Park Historian.

Q: Could you tell me when the swimming pool was built?
<u>Halstrom:</u> *No, that I don't know. Because I know another Irishman that had worked here, back in the nineties, and he said that the swimming pool was there at that time. . . .*

Q: I guess he started making cement about 1900 or a little later.
<u>Halstrom:</u> *That doesn't say that that's his cement, you know. He could have bought it. . . . Well, it could be around the turn of the century that was built, then. . . . Of course, it was built before they moved the barn.*[180]

Halstrom then spoke with his interviewer during a walking tour of the grounds, beginning near the greenhouse. In this conversation, we see a kaleidoscope of forty to fifty years of history of the grounds and gardens at Glenmont, ending on a sad note:

<u>Halstrom:</u> *There was nothing seeded down here till Mrs. Edison died. . . . When Mrs. Edison died they cut down to two men. I had an old man here who had a stroke, wasn't able to even run a lawn mower.*

. . . And we just forgot about it, forgot about the greenhouse, because I had to take care of the grounds first.

. . . as soon as Mrs. Edison died . . . the days the cows left, that was the 1st of October, the man that took care of the cows died at the same time. [Mina Miller Edison died 24 August 1947]. . . Greenhouses is gone, everything is gone there, Italian garden is just grown over, weeds.[181]

And so, for the gardener, it was a sad trip back to Glenmont: "Mrs. Edison died . . . the cows left . . . everything is gone there . . . weeds."

* * * * *

The streets that surround Llewellyn Park are now closely built up with houses and business buildings. We have previously observed that the Park was, at the time the Edisons arrived in 1886, bounded by Valley Street on the east (now known as Main Street), Mt. Pleasant Avenue on the south, Eagle Rock Avenue on the north, and Prospect Avenue on the west. At that time, in 1886, the perimeter of the Park was largely open. This can be surmised by looking at the age of the buildings that now are located on these four thoroughfares, as well as by inspection of the 1877 map of the Park and examination of the background of early photographs of the Laboratory buildings built by Edison. It was then protected by its rural location and the imposing nature of the houses on it. It is now protected by the nearly continuous wall of houses and businesses that surround it, backed up by a chain-link and board fence between the houses in the Park and those outside of it (and the great canyon of Interstate 280 which cuts off what was once the southern part of the Park).[182]

When Edison moved into Llewellyn Park, he could have walked directly down the hill from his house to Valley Street. It was just a quarter of a mile, down what is now called Honeysuckle Avenue, which runs along the north side of Glenmont, onto what is now called Edisonia Terrace, where the parking lot for the Edison National Historic Site is located. Few people now would think of trying to enter Llewellyn Park by ascending Edisonia Terrace from Main Street, for the way is presently blocked by a fence at the west end of Edisonia Terrace, but for residents of Glenmont in the 1880s and 1890s, this would have been the most convenient route. Edison's sons would certainly have gone directly back and forth between their home and the Laboratory, and it is likely that their adventurous older sister, Madeline, would have shown them the way.[183]

The environment in and around Llewellyn Park in 1886 was different in many other ways from that in 1998: It was much quieter, in general, and the pace of life was vastly slower then, than now. The sounds of 1886 were the occasional neighing of horses, lowing of cattle, and cackling of chickens. Dogs barked at each other, and at strangers — except perhaps at Glenmont, where dogs were not mentioned by the Edison children and former employees. It was usually silent then, at night. Daybreak was signaled by the crowing of a rooster, rather than the first roar of jet engines crossing the valley from Newark International Airport. Church bells then, as now, marked the passing hours except in the middle of the night, but the most prominent noises of traffic came from chugs, bells and whistles of coal-fired, steam-driven locomotives, instead of the perpetual hum of traffic and engines that is always in the background today. Ninety thousand cars a week now pass along Northfield Avenue, less than half a mile south of Glenmont.[184]

In 1886, as it is today, the prevailing winds in this part of Essex County blow down the mountain and across the valley towards Newark, so whatever sounds and smells rose from factories along Main Street in Orange, and along the Passaic River in Newark, were carried on to the east; they did not disturb the residents of Llewellyn Park. Everyone, however, had to contend with the pervasive aroma of horse manure, and the problems associated with its collection and disposal. Photographs of Newark and of the towns in the Orange Valley from this period until well into the second decade of the twentieth century remind us that horses were everywhere in the streets, pulling buggies, carts, and wagons. Edison needed horses at Glenmont, and we have read that he had them. However, he knew that they could be dangerous, and he detested the refuse that they produced. His goal, often expressed, was to eliminate the horse as a form of transportation. We already know that Edison's work with batteries and the electric railway made a significant impact on the elimination of this form of pollution, while at the same time producing a new set of environmental problems.[185]

Silent Springs

We shall soon study Edison's impact on the environment in West Orange in some detail. In my next case study, I will show that the changes that occurred in the environment of Glenmont and in Llewellyn Park during Edison's lifetime were relatively small compared with the dramatic changes that occurred elsewhere in West Orange and in the Orange Valley during the same period of time. Many of those changes in the environment were directly due to actions that were taken — or were not taken — by Thomas Edison. However, before we cross Main Street to the "superblock" where Edison built his Laboratory and factories, let us consider what we have learned about the stream that passes through Edison's property, the watercourse known as Wigwam Brook. This brook was once a system of springs, streams, wetlands, ponds, and lakes along the north-eastern slope and base of First Mountain.

In the eighteenth and early nineteenth centuries, Wigwam Brook had several origins, high on the side of First Mountain, and it had a winding route in the Orange Valley. There is no single map that shows Wigwam Brook as it existed before the English farmers arrived in the Orange Valley, nor do any of our sources describe its status fully and accurately at the time Edison arrived in 1886-1887. Enough information is now available to us, however, to construct a composite story of the geography and history of Wigwam Brook, and to compare and contrast Wigwam Brook with the "ill-fated" Parrow Brook — the other stream that originally drained a portion of this part of the Orange Valley. It should be recalled that Parrow Brook became so badly polluted by farms, mines, houses, breweries, and hat factories that it was converted to a sewer at about the time that Edison arrived in the Orange Valley. The worst of the "stinking mess" of Parrow Brook came from the hat factories, some of which were owned by Edison's distant kinsmen — although Edison was undoubtedly unaware of his connections with the Stetson family when he moved into Glenmont.[186]

In contrast to Parrow Brook, Wigwam Brook — although seriously abused — still exists. It has been narrowed, its sources dried up and diverted, channeled and polluted, but it still continues to drain much of the northeastern slope of First Mountain, at least the portion that is in the valley of Second River, from West Orange to Montclair. The southernmost source of the Wigwam, which arose in springs where Mt. Pleasant Avenue crossed First Mountain, has been amputated from the Wigwam by the construction of Interstate 280. Rather than draining into the Passaic, these now-seasonal springs bubble up through the asphalt surface of the parking lot behind the Gatehouse Restaurant on Prospect Avenue, where the water eventually evaporates, lacking an outflow channel. After heavy rains, these obstructed springs also weep (the metaphor is appropriate) from the raw southern edge of the cleft in First Mountain that was blasted out to accommodate Interstate 280. In winter, the springs that once fed into the Wigwam from the southwestern corner of Llewellyn Park now produce sheets of ice on the face of the unnatural cliff on the south side of the interstate highway. This water is now channeled along the ditch by the highway until it passes into the concrete

COURTESY OF THE NATIONAL PARK SERVICE

FINAL RESTING PLACE: Thomas and Mina Edison originally were buried in a section of Rosedale Cemetery in West Orange, about a mile from Glenmont. Their son, Charles, moved their graves to Glenmont (below). Charles Edison then built a magnificent mausoleum for himself and his wife in Rosedale (right).

trough that is the beginning of the East Branch of the Rahway River in West Orange.

The tributary of the Wigwam that drains the southern portion of what is left of Llewellyn Park is the only tributary that is still intact. Although the ridgeline of First Mountain, along Prospect Avenue, is no longer in the Park, the regrowth of forest along The Ramble within the Park provides enough ground cover and roots for some degree of water retention. Unfortunately, the slope in this part of the Park is so steep that heavy rains cannot be accommodated, and the tributary of the Wigwam in The Ramble has carved out a rather deep canyon. This branch of the Wigwam disappears into a storm sewer as it leaves the Park and crosses Main Street, and — as we shall shortly see — it does not reappear until it exits from the land that was once occupied by the Edison Plant.

There were once two northern tributaries of the Wigwam. One arose in springs east of Crystal Lake at the summit of First Mountain and passed down the steep valley that is now occupied by Eagle Rock Avenue, forming a small pond where the Thomas A. Edison Middle School is now located, and then passing on down to Tory Corner. At this

PHOTOS AT LOWER LEFT AND ABOVE BY GEORGE J. HILL, M.D.

point it was joined by the most northern of the branches of the Wigwam, which arose in a body of water that, in its day, was also called Crystal Lake or Crystal Springs. This area is now occupied by the Montclair Community Hospital, and the flow of water from these springs has been both reduced and restricted. In colonial days, this was the source of the stream called the Nishuane River. The Nishuane drained the south side of the ridge that is now surmounted by the Mountainside Hospital, while the north side of this ridge drained into the tributary of the Passaic known as Third River. The Nishuane River at the northern border of West Orange is now a fenced-off U.S. Environmental Protection Agency Superfund Site. Although there are no signs that indicate what pollutant is being removed carefully from the Nishuane site, local residents believe that it is radium-contaminated fill that was dumped there from the U.S. Radium Corporation factory in Orange, New Jersey. As we shall later see, the U.S. Radium Corporation Superfund Site is adjacent to Wigwam Brook, just downstream from the former location of the Edison plant.[187]

The mighty Nishuane River, which once was so large that it was crossed by ferry boats, is now just a ditch that conveys water into the Wigwam from this part of the Orange Valley. The Nishuane ditch is now principally notable as a long-standing obstruction to traffic near the northern border of West Orange. This most northerly branch of the Wigwam conveys whatever water is left in it south along the east side of Rosedale Cemetery, whereupon it quietly suffers permanent burial as it passes into storm sewers before joining, underground, with other branches of the Wigwam. Other storm sewers convey additional water into the Wigwam from along Franklin Street to the underground pool at Tory Corner. An unnamed lake that was once located at Tory Corner — the northwest corner of the "superblock" that is apparent on the 1877 map of the Park — is covered with closely-spaced business buildings and houses.

We have previously read in Pierson's *History of Orange* that Cook's Pond, at the southwest corner of the same "superblock," was drained by Edison soon after he built his Laboratory on its western edge. Our next case study reveals more of the details of Edison's land acquisitions and environmental transformations that began in 1887. The Laboratory and factories built by Edison buried the Wigwam Brook down to the eastern border of West Orange under twenty-six acres of brick and cement buildings, wooden sheds, sidewalks, railroad spurs, grass, and trash.[188]

Chapter 8

Edison in West Orange: The Laboratory and Factories (1886-1931)

The West Orange Plant experienced a tremendous physical growth between 1899 and 1914, expanding from 7.5 acres to 26.26 acres . . . more than ten times larger than at its beginning.

— David L. Uschold and George W. Curry, 1997[189]

"A Very Pleasant Old Gent"[190]

THE defining moment in my study of the impact of Thomas Edison on the environment actually occurred long before I began my study of his life and his "footprints" for this book. The critical instant in my study of Edison was the time, several years ago, when I stood on the sidewalk at the corner of Lakeside Avenue and Main Street in West Orange and contemplated the exterior of his Laboratory building, thinking "So this is actually where he worked!" With the

PHOTO BY GEORGE J. HILL, M.D.

THE WEST ORANGE PLANT: Building 5, Edison's famous library and office building, is in the foreground at the corner of Lakeside Avenue and Main Street, dwarfed by the long three-story brick Machine Shop that stretches behind it. Edison's concrete Battery Factory building is at the right.

passage of time, and as the result of my studies, I now realize that this corner was, yes, where Edison worked, but the environment at this spot is nevertheless vastly different than it was when the Great Inventor arrived, when he lived and worked in West Orange, and when he died.

In this case study, I will draw upon some of the ethnographic and environmental research that has recently been conducted, but not yet published, by scholars of Edison's operations in West Orange, and oral histories that were conducted several decades ago. The oral histories provide human insight into the environment of the Laboratory, the factories, and of West Orange during the latter years of the inventor's life. Along the way, I will intersperse some of my personal observations regarding the Laboratory buildings and other aspects of what was once Edison's West Orange Plant, as well as information from a few documents in the vast but still largely inaccessible archives at the Edison National Historic Site.[191]

COURTESY OF NATIONAL PARK SERVICE

CHEMIST AT WORK: Edison pours chemicals in his West Orange laboratory in this undated photograph.

In their recent study of the "cultural landscape" of the areas associated with Edison in West Orange, Uschold and Curry provided useful definitions of "the environment" of a historic landscape, and of the characteristics of "a historic setting" itself. Since I will be quoting extensively from Uschold and Curry, I wish to indicate at this point the extent to which I concur with their concepts, and to what extent my definition of the environment differs from theirs. For Uschold and Curry, "the environment" consists of "the general external influences affecting the historic landscape, the off-site larger physical and visual context which contains or encompasses the historic landscape." This consists of two components, the "natural," and the "social/cultural." For Uschold and Curry, the "historic setting" is located within "the environment," as defined above. The "historic setting" includes eight elements: landscape, natural systems, topography, buildings, vegetation, views and vistas, water features, and furnishings and objects. For example, a "historic setting" such as an important house would include its furniture and its grounds, which might include fences and a pond. The surrounding area, beyond the fences, would be "the environment" of the "historic setting."

In contrast to Uschold and Curry, when I refer to "the environment" of my subject, Thomas Edison, I consider that the elements of the "historic setting," as defined by them, are not separate from "the environment." Instead, for me, "the environment" of Edison in West Orange consists of the eight elements of the "historic setting," plus the natural and social/cultural aspects of the surrounding area.[192]

Uschold and Curry also provide a useful method to assess "the integrity" of a historic setting, which is defined by them as having seven qualities: location, design, setting, materials, workmanship, feeling, and association. I shall later return to this definition of "the integrity" of a historic setting, to review and comment on the assessment by Uschold and Curry of Edison's West Orange Plant as it now exists.[193]

* * * * *

Uschold and Curry discussed the reasons for Edison's decision to move to West Orange, giving consideration to information and opinions previously published by other scholars, to which they added their own research, which was principally that of the sequence of Edison's acquisitions of property. They concluded that the decision to purchase Glenmont was foremost in Edison's mind, and that the meadows below Llewellyn Park were an added attraction, since they were available and accessible as a place on which he could build his Laboratory.[194]

Uschold and Curry summarize the history of the West Orange Plant from its inception in 1887 to the completion of their report in 1997 in a succinct and useful outline of a complex subject. The first part of the 110 years of history begins at the time that:

The Edison Laboratories began operating in 1887, initiating their evolution into a unique industrial empire. Edison managed the site for 44 years, during which it experienced continuous and extensive physical changes. . . . By 1899 these combined facilities were commonly known as the "West Orange Plant." At the end of this period the Edison Laboratories' 2 acres combined with the Edison Phonograph Works 5.5 acres making the West Orange Plant approximately 7.5 acres.

[During the period 1899-1914] the Plant expanded aggressively into a business empire. . . . [with] physical transformation of the West Orange Plant into the "Edison District" consisting of several square

blocks of manufacturing, industry and research facilities. . . . The end of this period was marked by a devastating fire which nearly destroyed the entire West Orange Plant.

The third time period (1914-1931) began after the 1914 fire with the rebuilding of the West Orange Plant. . . . The Edison Laboratories fundamentally changed from an experimental laboratory to a support facility for the manufacturing functions of the West Orange Plant. . . . Edison handed the reins of the company over to his son Charles. Shortly afterward, in 1931, Edison passed away at his home.[195]

The final phase of the history of the West Orange Plant began after Edison's death, when:

In 1939 TAE Inc. began efforts to turn the Laboratories into a museum. . . . In 1955 the TAE Inc. donated the site to the National Park Service (NPS). . . . In the 1960s, Urban Renewal plans were developed and resulted in the demolition of all of the West Orange Plant except the Laboratories and the Storage Battery Complex. . . . Today the . . . Laboratory Unit is comprised of a 5.78-acre parcel of land, the majority of which is part of what once was the West Orange Plant. Within this parcel is the original 2-acre Edison Laboratories site and the six lab buildings originally erected in 1887, as well as seven subsequently added structures. Edison's home, Glenmont, was donated to the NPS in 1962.[196]

* * * * *

The environmental changes in the meadows at Lakeside Avenue and Valley Street began in the mind of the Great Inventor:

In 1886 Edison had sketched preliminary designs for a West Orange laboratory. His plans were a three-story, rectangular laboratory building with a central courtyard and mansard roof. . . . The building's tower and courtyard were common features in the nearby Newark textile mills and also gave the design the dignity of an important building.[197]

As we now know, within less than a year, Edison changed his plans. In 1887 he built instead a Laboratory complex that consisted of six buildings rather than the single large building that he originally sketched, and by October 1887 the "Laboratories began to take shape. . . . The Main Laboratory, constructed in 1887, was a three-story brick building measuring 200 by 50 feet." The following year, Edison acquired a 5.5 acre parcel that "was a meadow and agricultural field separated by Crooks Pond. . . . After Edison purchased the site the pond was filled in."[198]

We can visualize the environmental changes in the meadows and in the esthetic environment of the buildings through the description in Uschold and Curry: "Prior to construction of the Edison Laboratories the site was an open meadow with a few scattered trees. Most of the vegetation was removed during the construction of the Laboratories and what little vegetation remained was removed as the Laboratories' work force used the site." The still-existing Gate House was constructed in 1890, and the original Black Maria, constructed in February 1893 to be "the world's first structure specifically built as a motion picture studio," was located near the open side of the property on Alden Street.[199]

Most of the physical growth of the West Orange Plant occurred between 1899 and 1914. During this time the plant grew from 7.5 to 26.26 acres. It included vacant lots as well as residential lots that had to be cleared for construction. Between 1899 and 1903, Edison purchased "ten out of the thirteen remaining lots that existed between the block containing the Edison Laboratories and Edison Phonograph Works," which then occupied nine and one-half acres within the ten-acre block.

Between 1904 and early 1905, he acquired thirteen more properties along the northeast side of Alden Street, adding another three acres to his holdings. During a three year period beginning in 1905, the Edison companies expanded to the northeast, and by 1908 the West Orange Plant occupied the entire block between Valley Road, Lakeside Avenue, Alden Street and Watchung Avenue. In addition, properties were added to the southwest, including a two acre, L-shaped parcel that occupied more than half of the block to the south, which was purchased by the Edison Phonograph Company. This property is easily recognized today as the site of the Edison battery factory. Other properties purchased during the period 1905-1908 included several parcels between Ashland Avenue and the Erie Railroad tracks, across Ashland Avenue from the battery factory. These acquisitions included residential lots as well as vacant land. Some were held open, others were rented out, and yet others were used for garages and storage facilities. Dramatic changes occurred in the environment of West Orange during this period, which were largely the result of the growth of the Edison Plant, including the employment of many more workers, and the need for water service and sewage disposal.[200]

PHOTO BY DICKSON, EDISON NATIONAL HISTORIC SITE

THE POND IS GONE: Crooks Pond (above) gave its name to Lakeside Avenue, where Edison began building laboratory buildings in 1887. The pond was later drained, and Edison built a water tower and a complex of factory buildings on the site. Today, the factory buildings are gone, replaced by a parking lot (below), but the water tower remains. The brick smokestack, just to the left of the water tower in the photo below, is in the center of the photo above, which was taken from the same direction across what was then Crooks Pond.

PHOTO BY GEORGE J. HILL, M.D.

Uschold and Curry now shift gears. Their pejorative language calls attention to the environmental degradation that the development of the Plant produced in the meadows near Lakeside Avenue: A "building spree" in the "superblock" produced a "fortress-like" Plant and channeled Wigwam Brook along the railroad tracks. The number of laboratory employees rose steadily during this period, and the environment was busy, even chaotic.[201]

In an often-quoted article that he wrote in 1932, M. A. Rosanoff described the Laboratory in 1903 from the perspective of a new employee. It is remarkable that more than one-fifth, some 316 half-lines, of Rosanoff's fifteen-page paper consisted of direct quotations of Edison's statements, bracketed with quotation marks, yet Rosanoff said very little about the physical environment of the Laboratory. In other words, the environment at the Laboratory was Edison himself. For Rosanoff, the environment was the "Great Inventor." Rosanoff says not a word about Edison's factories or the outdoor environment at the Plant, or elsewhere in West Orange. His description of Edison is warm and admiring, and it is all the more credible because he sees that the Old Man is not without his flaws. For example, Rosanoff said that Edison did not have "a receptive mind. . . . What I could have taught any average college bozo, I could not teach to this, one of the most brilliant men of the century." Rosanoff balances his criticism of the inventor with praise: He writes that "Edison had a prodigious memory, and his mind was an immense junk yard of heterogeneous information," but "He was master of his mental junk yard." However, except for a description of the long hours of work that Edison expected of his employees and the mucker's atmosphere ("the floor itself was the surest spittoon because you never missed"), Rosanoff's article does not describe what we would call "the environment" of the Laboratory.[202]

A view of the Edison Laboratories in 1912 shows that there were only a few scattered houses along Main Street/Valley Road, over the top of the Phonograph Works. However, the Plant itself became increasingly crowded and cluttered. Within two years it became apparent that this was scene of an environmental disaster in the making. "Lumber, wooden crates, surplus material and testing apparatus. . . gave the site a cluttered appearance." The intense level of activity in experimentation and manufacturing continued to rise. "The turning point came in 1914 when a tremendous fire swept through the site. . . . The flash . . . in the ironclad film inspection building No. 41 . . . led to the great fire that destroyed nearly all of the buildings at the West Orange Plant."[203]

PHOTOS COURTESY OF NATIONAL PARK SERVICE

THE GREAT FIRE: The December 9, 1914, fire (above) that began in ironclad inspection building 41 destroyed most of Edison's West Orange factory complex (below), although the laboratory and the battery factory were spared. Snow and ice slowed the blaze, and none of the nearby residences were damaged. Nevertheless, one employee was killed.

COURTESY OF NATIONAL PARK SERVICE

"EDISON EFFECT" Edison poses in Building 1 of the West Orange plant with an "Edison Effect" light bulb in this undated photo.

The fire of December 9, 1914, was one of the most disastrous events in the history of West Orange up to that time, but its environmental effects were mitigated by the low loss of life (only one death), the few casualties (although the exact number is unknown), and the containment of the fire to only some of the factory buildings (sparing the Laboratory buildings, the power plant, and the Storage Battery Factory). The snow and ice present in December interfered with firefighting but also impeded the spread of the fire to the adjacent small residential houses. Although the wind direction was not mentioned in the reports, since the prevailing winds are from the west and sweep down through Llewellyn Park, the woods and homes in the Park were also spared. The noxious and dangerous smoke was soon dissipated, and the pollution of earth and water by the chemicals released in the fire was not recognized then as being worthy of comment.

I endeavored without much success to determine whether the environmental effects of the fire were commented upon by those who observed it, or those who analyzed the fire afterwards. I was also interested to see how many casualties had occurred, and what their causes were, since my definition of the environment includes aspects of safety and health. In my search for information regarding the fire I looked in two sets of archives: the Minutes of the Essex County Medical Society, and the archives at the Edison National Historic Site. The fire at the Edison Plant on 9 December 1914 was not mentioned in the minutes of the Essex County Medical Society at its next meeting, on 17 February 1915, or at its 100th Annual Meeting, on 5 October 1915. As far as I can determine, the Essex County Medical Society never expressed an official opinion regarding health or safety hazards associated with any of Edison's plants or products.[204]

A slim but succinct report was prepared on 30 January 1915 by the National Fire Protection Association and the National Board of Fire Underwriters. The report stated that the fire started at 5:17 p.m., on Wednesday, 9 December 1914, and that it destroyed fifteen of the twenty-two buildings of Thomas A. Edison, Inc., principally those of the Edison Phonograph Works. The buildings occupied a ground surface area of 40,000 square feet. This fire, says the report, "adds another disaster to the credit of the nitrocellulose material used in this case as a base for motion picture film." The report goes on to say that all of the 5,500 employees escaped safely, and that the only loss of life occurred when "one of the male employees went back into the film inspection department, supposedly to make a rescue or recover some personal property" and was overcome by smoke and heat.[205]

A young man who came to work for Edison soon after the fire described, many years later, the cleanup and rebuilding of the plant and his subsequent work for Edison, first as a chemist and then as an accountant. The work environment and the physical environment in the Orange Valley at this time are visible in the recollections of Edward J. Daly, who in 1973, when he was in his ninth decade, said that "in 1915 when they rebuilt . . . the hours in those days were 55 hours a week. . . . The starting lowest pay was 10 cents an hour — that would be a dollar a day." Daly added: "The working conditions in the early days were not good, but they were the same as in any other factory. . . . Factory workers — if you didn't work you didn't get paid."[206]

Although the plant was more cohesive and attractive, in a muscular way, after it was rebuilt, the environment in this part of the Orange Valley

COURTESY OF NATIONAL PARK SERVICE

CATNAP: Thomas Edison asleep in his West Orange plant in 1911.

continued to be marginalized and has never fully recovered, to the present day. By 1921 it was estimated that less than 2,000 workers remained in Edison's factories at West Orange. "The Laboratories' 65 employees in September 1923 gradually decreased to a low of seven in 1930. . . . In 1926 Edison's son, Charles, became president of TAE Inc. On May 1, 1930, Edison sold the laboratory buildings to the TAE Inc. for $165,000."[207]

Edison's operations contributed to the environmental problems in West Orange:

> *Besides labor problems, the surrounding community was continually concerned with the pollution from the West Orange Plant, specifically from the spray basins. Between 1919 and 1924, complaints had been registered with the Board of Health regarding the pollution. Complaints against the plant continued until November 1924 when the Board of Health visited the plant and the complaints were not pursued.*[208]

The environment in the laboratory and in the community of West Orange at this time was recalled many years later by one of Edison's employees. Ernest Stevens remembered that in 1925, "I always looked up to him and thought he was the world's greatest man." When asked what West Orange was like at that time, Stevens replied: "It hasn't progressed very much. . . . Edison was the main institute, the plant, and since they've gone out of business with the phonograph, that took away a lot of the population too."[209]

One of Edison's senior employees who was still alive in 1973 described the environment at the West Orange Plant in the late 1920s and thereafter. Edward Cary came to work for Edison at the age of twenty-three after graduating with a degree in chemistry from Cornell, when the inventor was eighty years old. Cary lost his sense of smell from exposure to carbolic acid (phenol) fumes in the plant at Silver Lake. In 1927 he obtained an accounting position at the Orange plant, which he held for the next twenty-eight years. "As long as you played fair by him [Edison], he'd do all right. . . . [but] he never was a good businessman. . . . After the Depression . . . they were lucky to get 14 or 16 million dollars a year. . . . [and] They weren't very generous.[210]

The present built environment of the Edison Plant, while superficially resembling the environment at the time that Edison was alive, is actually quite different. Uschold and Curry remind us that "The site is now surrounded by undeveloped land on the northeast, light industrial on the southeast, the Storage Battery Factory on the southwest, and Main Street on the northwest. . . . Today the site's manicured appearance greatly contrasts [with] its historic cluttered appearance." On the other hand, in spite of the dramatic changes in the buildings and in the level and type of activity in the environment at the Edison Plant over the past sixty years, the terrain underlying the Laboratory buildings has remained relatively unchanged since Edison died.[211]

* * * * *

We have traced the Wigwam Brook into the meadows where the Plant was built, and we know that the brook eventually exits at Watchung Street, at the eastern boundary of the Plant. Later in this book, we will see the Wigwam Brook again, as it receives a new and peculiarly ominous form of pollution less than one hundred yards downstream from the Edison Plant. But let us now put the Wigwam Brook and the West Orange Plant aside in our thoughts, and turn instead to a major environmental catastrophe: Silver Lake, New Jersey.[212]

Chapter 9

The Destruction of Silver Lake: Bloomfield, Belleville, and Glen Ridge, N.J. (1887-1931)

Out at the dump there was a shelter and when I went around in front of the shelter I saw a man who was a skeleton . . . He said, "I was working in the foundry."

—Chemist William Hand, describing Silver Lake, c. 1926[213]

"Something's Happening in the Silver Lake District"

HISTORY is timeless, though it is rooted in time. It has neither a beginning nor an end. And so it is that the environmental history of Silver Lake did not begin with the arrival of Thomas Edison in 1888, nor did it end when Edison died in 1931.[214]

This case study is, however, focused on the period of Edison's presence at Silver Lake, New Jersey, and in other areas near it. This study can be thought of as one chapter — perhaps the most dramatic episode — in the larger history of Silver Lake, which ought someday to be written. My study of Silver Lake began rather late in the course of my search for Edison's "footprints" in New Jersey, because initially I believed that there would be little to see there. Silver Lake, Bloomfield, and Glen Ridge, N.J., were mentioned in some of Edison's biographies, but I had been told by various people at the "Interpreting Edison" Conference in Newark in

May 1997 that Edison didn't do anything important there. Yes, he had some factories in Silver Lake or Bloomfield, but he didn't "invent" anything there, and a study of that aspect of Edison's life would not be very interesting.

There was, in the summer of 1997, nothing related to Silver Lake in the *Edison Chronology* on the web page of the Rutgers-NPS Edison Papers Project except a statement that he purchased land at Silver Lake in 1890 for the Edison Manufacturing Company. Nothing was yet published by the Rutgers group on this period in Edison's life. At about this time I learned that Edison began to purchase property on which to build factories at Silver Lake in 1888, and that he owned 47 acres of land there by 1889. This was more land than he ever owned in West Orange.[215]

COURTESY OF NATIONAL PARK SERVICE

A FORGOTTEN TIME: Edison's huge industrial complex in the Silver Lake section of Bloomfield caused major pollution on the Belleville side of what once had been Silver Lake. Today, few residents remember that Edison was ever there. (See text, page 178)

I was told at the Edison National Historic Site that there were "no pictures of Silver Lake" in the archives. However, in late March 1998 I finally located a photograph of the lake that was called Silver Lake. By this time, it had become apparent to me that Edison's operations in this area probably extended over the entire period of his work in West Orange (1887-1931). Furthermore, by March 1998 it was clear to me that Edison had been engaged in short-term and long-term projects in separate areas in three adjacent towns (Glen Ridge, Bloomfield, and Belleville). I was by then certain that Edison's largest project in this part of Essex County was his Plant in an ill-defined area known as the Silver Lake District, which appeared to be in the borderland that was shared by Bloomfield and Belleville.[216]

APT SLOGAN: "Something's Happening in the Silver Lake District" is the slogan used to tout economic growth today. Business leaders were equally enthusiastic in the 1880s when Edison decided to build a factory there, but what happened was an environmental disaster.

PHOTO BY GEORGE J. HILL, M.D.

In February 1998, at about the time that I began a serious search for material related to Silver Lake, I was fortunate to receive, by coincidence, copies of several oral history interviews with former Edison employees that mentioned Silver Lake. I was also given copies of two old articles from the *New York Times* that provided a few details which were consistent with the comments made by one of Edison's biographers regarding hazardous events at Sliver Lake. The comments in the oral histories – especially in one of them – suggested that the environment in the Edison factories at Silver Lake was dangerous, potentially lethal, or perhaps even worse than that. Therefore, by the time I actually began to search for the terrain on which the Edison factories had been located, and for more information about Edison's operations in Bloomfield and Silver

PHOTO BY GEORGE J. HILL, M.D.

TRACES OF EDISON: Signs proclaiming "Alva Street" and "Edison Street" were easy clues to the location of Edison's long-forgotten factory on the Bloomfield side of the Silver Lake district. Some of the older brick buildings on Alva Street (above) could date back to Edison's time. The photograph below depicts Alva Street as it appeared on January 3, 1912 -- 25 years after Edison arrived.

COURTESY OF NATIONAL PARK SERVICE

Lake, I expected to find the residue of wrecked factories and perhaps to meet some older local residents who had memories of Edison's impact on this part of Essex County.[217]

As was the case with my previous visits in Newark, Elizabeth, Menlo Park, Harrison, and West Orange, I did indeed find traces of Edison's presence at Silver Lake, and I was able to talk with a local resident who remembered those days. Nevertheless, I was astonished to find that Edison's enormous factories at Silver Lake are apparently entirely gone, as is the lake once known as Silver Lake, and that the physical pollution and social degradation which the factories produced is no longer spoken of ("disremembered," I would say).

"Something's Happening in the Silver Lake District" is now cheerfully proclaimed on dozens of handsome banners in the Belleville part of this district. It was my task to learn what happened at Silver Lake from 1887 to 1931, and in this case study I will describe what I have read, seen, and heard about this period in the Silver Lake District. My sources are remarkably consistent, although some are more vivid than others, and they suggest that I have, so to speak, only scratched the surface of the environmental disaster that occurred at Silver Lake between the late 1880s and the late-1920s.[218]

The biggest challenge that I faced was to determine where the lake that was known as Silver Lake was located, and what became of it. After I pieced together the story of this lake, I saw that I had initially overlooked important clues regarding the history of Silver Lake that were present in current maps of this area. For example, the odd, zig-zag border between Belleville and Newark along Franklin Avenue, near Clara Maass Medical Center at the northern end of Branch Brook Park; and the existence of short streets named "Brook Street" and "Lake Street" near buildings that are called, on maps, "Silver Lake Church" and "Silver Lake Station."

Alva Street

"Alva Street!" I exclaimed to myself. "That can't be a coincidence. Edison's Plant must have been somewhere near here." I was driving south on Belmont Avenue in Belleville, looking at the flags on the light poles that said I was in the "Silver Lake District," and much to my surprise, I suddenly saw a street sign that bore the inventor's middle name. Backing up, I turned west into this short street, hoping to find something else connecting this area with Edison. In less than one hundred yards I was at the next intersection, looking at a pole that bore the signs of "Alva Street" and "Edison Street." This is a blue-collar neighborhood, with some older houses that were probably built in the nineteenth century, and some that were more recent. No large factories were visible, so I supposed that they had all been torn down. It was a cold, windy, cloudy afternoon in March, and no one was out on the streets to talk to, so I took a few pictures, and got back in my car to consult my map. Sure enough, this corner was precisely on the line between Belleville and Bloomfield, on a dotted line that cut across the large open pentagonal space on the map that I had identified as the probable location of Edison's Silver Lake Plant.

I had just come from the Bloomfield Public Library, where I had not been able to find anyone who knew anything about Edison and Silver Lake, and there was nothing in the histories of Bloomfield at that library that referred to either Silver Lake or Edison. But now I was sure that I had found the "footprints" of Edison at Silver Lake, and I decided to go to the local historical society to dig deeper into the history of this area. The people that I met the next day at The Historical Society of Bloomfield, and the documents and maps that they showed me, provided the orientation that I needed to begin to understand the disjointed bits of written and oral history, geography, photographs, and maps that I had been collecting about this area that is located northwest of Newark. During the next three weeks I spoke with librarians and local residents in Glen Ridge and Belleville, and I was shown old maps, photographs, and local histories that answered some — if not all — of my questions about the history of Silver Lake. What follows is a composite story, based on my interpolation of the information that I saw in libraries and archives, and on what I learned in conversations and personal site visits to the Silver Lake District and adjacent areas in Belleville, Bloomfield, Glen Ridge, and Newark, by car and on foot.

The Valley of Silver Lake and Branch Brook

The story of Silver Lake began with the formation of an area of low hills and wooded wetlands and meadows that is about three miles by two miles in size, roughly four thousand acres, including portions of the towns that are now known as Newark, East Orange, Bloomfield, and Belleville, New Jersey. The Silver Lake District is in the north central portion of this tract of land, just north of the place near the intersection of Bloomfield and Belmont Avenues where the borders of Bloomfield, Belleville, and Newark meet. On some maps, "Silver Lake Station" is

PHOTO FROM ROBERT B. BURNETT'S *BELLEVILLE*, 1989 (p. 25)

WHEN THERE ONCE WAS A SILVER LAKE: Silver Lake was an artificial body of water enjoyed by Essex County residents until a storm on July 30, 1889, washed out the dam that held the water in.

shown near this intersection (although the station is gone now); on other maps there is a "Silver Lake Church" here. Older maps show a "Silver Lake School" at the northwest corner of Belmont and Bloomfield Avenue, while other old maps show that a narrow lake called "Silver Lake" is the border between Newark and Belleville, from Bloomfield Avenue to Franklin Avenue.[219]

Silver Lake was thus in the lowest portion of a wide valley that was rimmed on the east by a ridgeline that is now marked on its southern extremity by the Sacred Heart Cathedral in Newark. The valley that contained Silver Lake is bordered on the west by the low ridge on which the Garden State Parkway now crosses Essex County from Exit 145 to Exit 148. The southern edge of this valley is the watershed between the Rahway and Elizabeth Rivers (which drain to the south) and the Passaic River (which drains to the north). This watershed, as we have previously seen, is now the route of Orange Street in Newark and its western extension, Main Street, in the Oranges. The northern edge of the valley of Silver Lake is marked by the gentle concave curve of Second River. This great valley is now the home of many thousands of people, and it is the site of scores of factories and parks. The valley of Silver Lake is a part of an even larger valley, which has sometimes been called the Orange Valley. The greatest of the parks in the valley of Silver Lake is Branch Brook Park in Newark, which we will return to shortly, for Branch Brook is an important part of the story of Silver Lake.

The floor of the valley of Silver Lake was sculpted by the last glaciers of the Pleistocene Age, which, as they melted and retreated, left behind a series of longitudinal moraines — running from north to south — and isolated hills known as drumlins. Some of the brooks that drained the narrow valleys between these longitudinal ridges and coursed around the hills in the Orange Valley are already familiar to us: For example, the Wigwam Brook at the base of First Mountain, and the "ill-fated" Parrow Brook, which once drained the valley to the east of the Wigwam, but is now just a sewer. The next ridgeline to the east in the Orange Valley is marked by Arlington Street in East Orange, and the Garden State Parkway, at an elevation of 180 feet. This ridge is the western border of the valley of Silver Lake. As one drives east from Arlington Street along, say, Park Avenue, the ground slopes down to a low point at Branch Brook Park, 100 feet above sea level, and then rises to 120-130 feet at the Sacred Heart Cathedral. To the north of the cathedral, along Clifton Street, elevations of 160 feet are again reached, before Park Avenue plunges down into Newark.[220]

The valley of Silver Lake tilts gently toward the north, and it is just under 100 feet above sea level where it terminates at Second River. This point is now marked by the intersection of Franklin Avenue and Mill Street, at the restaurant known as Nanina's-in-the-Park. This was a historically important area, for the Morris Canal once turned west at this location, crossing the outflow from Silver Lake on its way across Belleville into Bloomfield. This was also once the location for the dams and mills of the Hendricks family's factories, eponymic of Hendricks Field, which is across Second River at this point in Belleville. Two major watercourses once drained the valley of Silver Lake. Both are now reduced in their flow and are confined by man-made retainers of earth and concrete. One stream is known as Branch Brook, which appears above ground at various locations in Branch Brook Park. The other stream is called simply "the river" by residents of the Silver Lake District — "the river that tries to come back whenever there is a heavy rain."[221]

Water in the eastern portion of the valley of Silver Lake collects in the series of streams and ponds that are now known collectively as Branch Brook Park. We will soon read more about the creation of this park, but suffice it to say at this point that the stream that flowed into Second River here in the eighteenth century became polluted, and then obstructed,

PHOTO BY GEORGE J. HILL, M.D.

"THE RIVER THAT TRIES TO COME BACK." The river that was dammed to create Silver Lake now drains into Second River through portholes and cracks between the stones in the retaining wall shown above. The dam that retained Silver Lake washed out in 1889, two years after Edison arrived in the area.

its outflow occluded by streets and houses. It no longer drains on the surface into Second River, but its termination can be seen as a row of round portholes, one and one half feet in diameter, along the southern (right) bank of Second River, about two hundred yards east of Franklin Avenue in Newark.

The western portion of the valley of Silver Lake is now separated from the wetlands of Branch Brook Park by a low ridgeline, along Franklin Street, across the street from Clara Maass Medical Center. Water in the western portion of the valley of Silver Lake once flowed into Second River where Franklin Avenue now crosses Mill Street, a few hundred yards west of the outflow of Branch Brook Park. In the past century, the outflows from the eastern and western portions of the valley of Silver Lake were so close together at this point that there was no clear distinction between the two streams at their termination. There was, perhaps, a cloaca where the drainage from the eastern and western parts of this valley merged and entered Second River. Maps as recently as 1906 do not clearly distinguish between the mouths of Branch Book and the river that drained Silver Lake. The mouth of the Silver Lake river is now marked by a large, square open window, two feet by two feet, in the concrete wall of Second River; on an average day, it may be a dry hole, or a bit of water may be trickling out here from the Silver Lake District.

Silver Lake Had Been Created

In the eighteenth century, the flow of water in the valley of Silver Lake was so brisk that its source was called "Boiling Springs." At that time, a stream then arose near the height of land at the southern edge of this valley, beginning in what is now the city of East Orange, in the superblock bordered by Arlington, Grove, Park, and Main Streets. This stream flowed north, winding across the area where Springdale Avenue is now located, just west of the railroad station known as Ampere. It then passed through meadows and woods to the precise point that we have previously observed where Belleville, Bloomfield, and Newark meet near the intersection of Belmont and Bloomfield Avenues. About one hundred yards before it reached this point, the stream received a small branch from the west, arising between where we now find Ampere Parkway and Grove Street. About one hundred yards north of Bloomfield Avenue, the stream which I call "the river of Silver Lake," and which local residents now call simply "the river," was joined by another brook that entered from the west. This brook had taken a long, winding route from its origin west of Grove Street, passing along the course of Roosevelt and LaFrance Avenues. This brook had crossed Bloomfield Avenue at Grove Street and had then turned east.

Before it joined the river of Silver Lake, the brook had passed through the great meadows that were, in 1890, owned by John M. Dodd and Thomas A. Edison, to the west of where the Pathmark store on Belmont Avenue is now located. The brook had been joined at this point by another stream which flowed into it from the north. The stream from the north had passed under the Orange Branch Railroad (the CONRAIL tracks that still cross this great pentagonal field), draining almost the entire border between the properties of Dodd and Edison, from Franklin Avenue to Bloomfield Avenue. The free-running brook of 1890 had, by 1906, been confined within a ditch as it passed down through Edison's property along Alva Street, crossing Thomas (now Columbus) Street, then Edison Street, and finally Belmont Avenue, before joining "the river" fifty yards later at

Heckel Street. Remember Heckel, for we will later read of the unfortunate later history of this brook. Its position is now marked by a storm sewer at the corner of Heckel and Brook Streets in the Silver Lake District.[222]

The history of Belleville states that "Silver Lake had been created in the eighteenth century by the building of a dam across a stream." Maps of 1890 and 1906 show that Silver Lake extended from a dam at the corner of Franklin and Sixth Streets to the corner of Belmont and Bloomfield Avenues. It covered "an area one-half mile in length and 300 feet in width." The lake was oriented from northeast to southwest, and its eastern shore was the border between Newark and Belleville. The west bank of Silver Lake is represented by the irregular property line that now separates the back yards of the houses in Belleville that face east toward Lake Street or west toward Heckel Street. The east bank of Silver Lake can still be identified by following the irregular border between Newark and Belleville, including Lake Street (in Belleville), which is the northern extension of Newark's Tenth Street. This border veers to the west as it passes north of the location of the dam that retained Silver Lake. A tributary known as Great Meadow Brook once flowed into the east side of Silver Lake about one hundred yards north of the dam. This brook began at Park Avenue and ran along the course of what is now Ninth Street in Newark. A low ridge to the east of Ninth Street separated the drainage of this now-buried stream from the basin of Branch Brook Park.[223]

To the north of Belleville's Franklin Street, the border between Newark and Belleville follows the course of the river that once drained Silver Lake. The border initially passes north along what is now North Eighth Street, which is the northern extension of Eugene Place. It then jogs west and then north again to pass along Watchung Street. The border then again runs north along the course of what is now Franklin Avenue in Newark, and it turns east where Franklin Avenue crosses Second River. North of the dam at the foot of Silver Lake, the Silver Lake river also received water, probably seasonally, that passed north along the course of what is now North Belmont Avenue from the corner of Belmont Avenue and Franklin Street. This corner was the lowest area in the large pentagonal tract on which the Edison Plant was located, and drainage from the northern portion of the Edison property would have passed across Franklin Street at this point. The short, rather steep, downhill course of North Belmont Avenue ends in 150 yards at Newark Avenue, just south of Clara Maass Medical Center. The waters from the area of the Edison Plant would thus have passed down what is now North Belmont Avenue, then turning to the east and flowing into Silver Lake river at the corner of Newark and Franklin Avenues, and thence into Second River.[224]

It is clear from the topography of the great pentagonal meadow on which the Edison Plant was located that much of its natural drainage would have been to the north, about one hundred yards west of the Silver Lake Railroad Station. Edison's water tower at Silver Lake was located near this corner of his property, and presumably he would have retained as much as he could of the water that arose in or passed through this great meadow. We shall see that there was also drainage to the southeast from Edison's property, into the ill-fated, ditch-bound brook that passed along Alva Street.

In 1890, a small structure called the "Old Mill" was located on the north side of Franklin Street, at the northern end of Silver Lake. At that time, the Edison Manufacturing Plant was by far the largest building in this part of Belleville. The Edison Manufacturing Plant buildings were situated midway between Bloomfield Avenue and Franklin Street, on the west side of Belmont Avenue, about where the parking lot for Pathmark is now located. Silver Lake was then idyllic:

Silver Lake's dam was the site of several mills over the years. Belleville's residents used the lake for boating, fishing, and picnicking. Rowboats and canoes could be rented there. In the winter people skated while others harvested ice to be stored in icehouses standing along the eastern bank.[225]

In 1890, the Newark City Ice Company's building was located at the north-east corner of Silver Lake, on Franklin Street. A photograph of Silver Lake taken at about this time shows sailboats on the bank, rowboats on the beach, and a small island near the far shore. The hills in the background of this picture suggest that the photograph was taken from Belleville, facing Newark, for there are no hills immediately to the west of Silver Lake. To the west of Silver Lake was only the large, flat meadow that Edison was developing into his Plant. The hills in this picture thus provide additional evidence that the great valley of Silver Lake was drained by both the river of Silver Lake as well as by Branch Brook. But time was running out for Silver Lake.[226]

"Highly Offensive to Both Smell and Taste"

The body of water that was once called Silver Lake was on the south bank of the tributary of the Passaic known as Second River. The history of Silver Lake is thus a part of the history of Second River, so let us turn our attention for the time being to Second River. We had previously encountered this river, with its puzzling name, in Watsessing Park in Bloomfield, where it received the waters of Wigwam Brook and then passed to the east, crossed by the Morris Canal. To save time and trouble, let me say this: Don't even bother to look for "First River," for no river by this name appears on recent maps of Essex County, although we have previously seen that there is a stream known as "Third River" (which drains into the Passaic four miles upstream from the mouth of Second River, at the border between Essex and Passaic counties).

In only a mile and a half, Second River makes its way from Watsessing Park in Bloomfield into the Passaic River at Belleville. Second River is rarely seen these days, for there is no major road that runs along its bank. However, Belleville Avenue runs parallel to this part of Second River, along its north bank, separated from the river by Hendricks Field and Belleville Park. On its south bank, opposite Belleville Park, Second River once received the water that devolved from a series of ponds and wetlands that are now confined within Branch Brook Park in Newark. The sign that marks the northern border of the Cherry Tree Section of Branch Brook Park is actually located beside Second River, not along Branch Brook.[227]

In pre-colonial days the meadows of what is now called the Silver Lake District were surely watered by the actions of beavers, whose activities we read about previously in the western portion of the Orange Valley, along the Wigwam and Nishuane. There never was a stream that beavers didn't love to dam. The Silver Lake area once had a deep layer of sand at its base, which reduced its capacity to retain water, thus increasing its vulnerability during periods of drought. The early settlers in this area would have begun to degrade these meadows and the surrounding woods. Beavers were killed for their pelts and for food, and rich flat farmland was revealed when the beaver dams were knocked down. As the trees were felled and wells were dug, the water table would slowly fall, springs would dry up, and the meadows would become drier. The outflow of the smaller brooks and springs would become seasonal, rather than continuous. Manure from farm animals would have sullied the springs and ponds a bit, but this would still have been an attractive place to live and work. The environmental impact of English colonial farmers on this area was, however, gradually replaced by the more devastating effect of industry, which began two miles to the east, at the Passaic River, and then moved west.[228]

Second River drains into the Passaic about one mile north of Mount Pleasant Cemetery in Newark, where Mary Edison is buried. The mouth of Second River is three miles north of the center of Newark — about three miles from the Puritans' landing point on the river — and the corner of Broad and Market Streets. The geographic area for a mile or so to the north of Second River along the Passaic was originally called simply "Second River." In its early days the village known as Second River was Dutch, and its settlers worshipped in a Dutch Reform Church. To the west, along the upper reaches of Second River, English settlers spread out and established small villages that took the names of their founders. The area known by the Indians as Watsessing, which later became the town of Bloomfield, was for a time known as Wardesson (in its eastern portion) and Cranetown or Craneville (in the western portion, named for Azariah Crane, who settled there in 1694).[229]

These villages along Second River grew slowly as farming centers, but they were tied together by the Newark-Pompton Turnpike, which was developed by a wagon owner and entrepreneur named Israel "King" Crane. The Newark-Pompton Turnpike is now known as Bloomfield Avenue from the summit of First Mountain to its terminus at Broadway in Newark. To the north, the Turnpike is now known as Pompton Avenue, proceeding through Verona and Cedar Grove into Passaic County, while Bloomfield Avenue, as we have previously seen, passes west into Caldwell, where it was once known as "the Road to New-Ark." Many fine homes were built in Bloomfield before the Revolutionary War, some of which — such as Caleb Davis' house and the homesteads of Joseph and Israel Crane — still stand in the late twentieth century.[230]

In 1807, one year after Orange's secession, Bloomfield separated from Newark. Bloomfield then included the present towns of Bloomfield, Belleville, Verona, Glen Ridge, and Montclair. Belleville's industrial development continued apace, and by 1833 it was a thriving center of copper and brass factories, using locally mined copper ore. Belleville became independent of Bloomfield in 1839, and it developed into a major industrial area while the rest of Bloomfield was still largely engaged in farming. In 1830 David Oakes built his first wool factory in Belleville, and by 1850 Belleville was the location of Oakes' five-story plant for production of cassimere (a form of cashmere). Belleville was also the site of the large mills known as Bennett's Grist Mills. For several more decades Belleville continued to be a center of copper manufacturing, and it was the site of quarries which supplied sandstone for New York's brownstone houses. These industries would have used as much water as they could get access to, and they would thus have impacted on the ill-defined area to the west between Belleville and Bloomfield that was then known as the Silver Lake District.[231]

In 1857 the industrial centers of Essex County were said to be in Newark, Orange, Belleville, Montclair, and Bloomfield. By this time, Bloomfield was also participating in copper-working and woolen-goods manufacturing, although the center of Bloomfield still appeared rural as late as 1865, with dirt roads where now are seen the busy, paved streets known as Liberty Street, Broad Street, and Bloomfield Avenue. Large areas of Bloomfield were then still unsettled, but the Newark & Bloomfield Railroad ran as far out as West Bloomfield by 1856, tying this area to Newark. Montclair (formerly West Bloomfield) separated from Bloomfield in 1868; a year later, Bloomfield Seminary (now Bloomfield College) was established. As Bloomfield's industrial development picked up, stimulated by the Newark-Pompton Turnpike, the Morris Canal, and the railroad, Newark was already in the throes of intense growth.[232]

By the 1870s, the Passaic River in Newark was "highly offensive to both smell and taste." Although Newark blamed this problem on carbolic acid dumpers in Nutley, north of Belleville, it was also due to Newark's sixty miles of sewers, all of which emptied directly into the Passaic. A new reservoir for Newark city water was opened in 1873 on Clifton Avenue, about one mile south-east of Silver Lake. However, the reservoir had a leaky bottom, and by 1881 it was "dangerously polluted." Newark was repeatedly swept by episodes of typhoid fever, which the local residents believed — correctly — were related to polluted water. Eventually, the city reached farther afield for its public water supply, and in 1895 the series of streams, reservoirs, and wetlands that lay along the east bank of the Morris Canal in the northern part of Newark were transformed into Branch Brook Park — the nation's first county park. Under the guidance of the Olmsteads, who had co-designed New York's Central Park, the once polluted city reservoir in the area known as Blue Jay Swamp became the Branch Brook Park's skating rink.[233]

While Newark was cleaning up the area to the east of the Morris Canal, only a few hundred yards to the west — in the Silver Lake District of Belleville — the situation would soon be deteriorating. In 1888, Thomas Edison began to acquire land on which to build factories and homes in the Silver Lake district. Edison announced that his intentions were to beautify the area and to generate prosperity for the community. However, as we shall soon see, what happened at Silver Lake was quite different from Edison's announced intentions. The lake known as Silver Lake was destroyed in 1889, and the people of the Silver Lake District have worked for more than half a century to develop a post-Edison identity and a self-sustaining degree of prosperity.

A Pail of Fine Water

Before we direct our attention to Silver Lake in 1888, it is worth taking a closer look at the status of the Morris Canal in this vicinity, and on Thomas Edison's other manufacturing operations in Bloomfield at this point in time. We have previously seen that Edison had chosen sites near the Morris Canal for business operations in Jersey City and in Newark, and we will later see that he operated large plants near the canal and its tributaries at Lake Hopatcong and in Warren County. Shortly after he arrived in West Orange, Edison identified Bloomfield as a good place to do business, for reasons that will soon become clear.

The Morris Canal traversed Bloomfield from its southeastern corner to its northern border. Canal boats traveling west from downtown Newark turned north at First Street in Newark and then for two miles the boats skirted the western edge of the wetlands of what is now Branch Brook Park. At the northern edge of the park, just north of where Clara Maass Medical Center is now located, the Morris Canal entered Belleville and began a turn to the west that placed it immediately adjacent to the right (south) bank of Second River at the eastern border of Bloomfield. The canal followed the course of Second River for a half mile in Bloomfield, and then crossed Second River at the southern end of Walnut Street, between Newark Avenue and Montgomery Street. At this point, near the center of Bloomfield, the canal came abreast of Broad Street, and proceeded north through Bloomfield into Passaic County. The long run of the Morris Canal through Bloomfield gave residents of that town an uncommonly fine exposure to the canal. Portions of the canal still exist in Bloomfield. For example, on Berkeley Avenue just south of Jerome Place in Bloomfield, there is a bridge over the stone-lined walls of the Morris Canal, with water at its bottom.[234]

As we have previously seen, the Morris Canal passed only a few hundred yards to the east of Silver Lake, and it also traversed the area that was about one-third of a mile north of the lake. Although the canal's route through Belleville and eastern Bloomfield was generally level, a lock (Fifteen East) and a plane (Eleven East) were needed to convey boats between the higher and lower areas of Bloomfield. Photographers have the power to show what they wish to emphasize, and illustrations of the canal in this region show both pastoral and industrial scenes. For example, one contemporary photograph showed a portion of the Morris Canal in Bloomfield with earthen banks bordered by large trees. In contrast, another contemporary photograph of Bloomfield showed a group of large buildings with a caption that reads "Factories located along the canal because of easy access to coal and water." You can take your pick regarding the purity of the water in the canal: While factories adjacent to the canal in Bloomfield were emphasized in a photograph in *The Morris Canal*, it was said in *Tales the Boatmen Told* that "Industries were not located along most sections making the water pollution free."[235]

While there may have been reason to worry about the purity of water in the Morris Canal, especially as one got closer to Newark, the route of the canal provided a good slope for bringing clean water into the city from West Orange. In one of those coincidences that delight researchers, a description of the aqueduct that transported fresh water from Eagle Rock to the leaky reservoir in Newark appears in an oral history of the Morris Canal. The lake from which this fresh water was taken is probably the body of water that was called "Skating Lake" in the 1857 and 1877 maps of Llewellyn Park, and is now called Crystal Lake. As we have previously seen, Crystal Lake no longer has an outlet to the east; it now drains only into the West Branch of the Rahway River. But in 1886-1891,

> There was a stream of water that came down from Eagle Rock upon Orange Mountain. It was piped from the mountain and run under the canal just west of Newark and emptied into what is known now as Branch Brook Park. The pipe was broken on the top just after it came out from under the canal bank, and we always got a pail of this fine water at this point.[236]

On the Eve of a Boom

At about the same time that Edison was moving into his new laboratory buildings in West Orange, he was beginning his business operations in Bloomfield. In October 1887, *The Bloomfield Citizen* reported that,

A force of men are engaged at the buildings in Bloomfield Avenue known as the Bloomfield Machine Works. The building has been leased by the Edison Electric Light Company and will be used by them to supply electric light to Bloomfield and Montclair.[237]

Only nine months later, *The Bloomfield Citizen* reported that "The Edison phonograph works on Bloomfield avenue will soon be moved to West Orange."[238] Thus began what later became a see-saw pattern of establishment and disestablishment, as Edison created industries and raised expectations in Bloomfield and Silver Lake, following which he withdrew and abandoned his operations there.

Something was happening even then in Silver Lake. It is impossible for us to reconstruct the details of politics and money, and to define precisely the various alliances and opposing interests that were involved, when annexation of Silver Lake by Bloomfield was proposed in January 1889, and then rejected. Whether this was a victory or defeat for Edison was never made absolutely clear. However, the brief accounts describing this episode in the *Bloomfield Citizen* suggest that Edison wanted to have Silver Lake annexed by Bloomfield. Characteristically, he was undaunted by failure, and looked to the future rather than bemoaning the past:

14 January 1889: Residents of Silver Lake petition for the annexation of that locality. Bill to that effect presented to the Legislature by Assemblyman McGowan. Scheme defeated by opposition of Belleville and Bloomfield property owners.

19 January 1889: The Edison Electric Light Company have purchased a large tract of property near Silver Lake from the Farrand estate. It is said that they intend erecting a very large factory there in which a great many hands will be employed.

13 July 1889: Our Silver Lake friends inform us that the people of Bloomfield missed an opportunity to increase the wealth and importance of the town by their failure to help carry through the annexation scheme last winter. Silver Lake is on the eve of a boom. Thomas A. Edison has recently acquired considerable property there and is negotiating for more. It is said to be Mr. Edison's intention to begin a series of extensive improvements. The ground adjoining the lake is to be put in order and made more attractive and beautiful. A large phonograph factory is approaching completion on Belmont avenue. In view of these facts property is enhancing in value and the erection of a number of dwelling houses is being talked of.[239]

Glen Ridge

PHOTOS BY GEORGE J. HILL, M.D.

INK FACTORY IN GLEN RIDGE. Long forgotten, Edison once manufactured ink in a factory building on the bank of a brook in a residential area (above) of what was then western Bloomfield and is now Glen Ridge. Edison's ink factory is gone, and the stream is buried beneath back yards and city streets. Ironically, the site of Edison's ink factory was later contaminated with radioactive waste from an unknown source - probably the U. S. Radium Corporation - and was an EPA Superfund site when the photograph below was taken. It has since been successfully transformed into a park.

The Ink Factory: 1890-1906

WHILE Edison was purchasing and developing property in the central and eastern portions of Bloomfield and in the adjacent Silver Lake District of Belleville, he was also getting underway with a new project in the western part of Bloomfield. This area, which separated from Bloomfield in 1895, is now known as Glen Ridge. Edison's first plant there was an ink factory, which was located on the east bank of a small stream immediately northeast of the intersection of Midland and Carteret Avenues, only a few hundred yards from the border of East Orange. We know little about this ink factory, but in the history of Glen Ridge it is said that this is "where it is believed he formulated the idea for waterproof ink." The "Ink Factory" was on the map of Glen Ridge in 1890, and by 1906 it was identified as "Ruins."

The little stream on which Edison's Ink Factory was located flowed into Wigwam Brook in about three-tenths of a mile — the same Wigwam Brook on which his factory in West Orange was built in 1887. This little stream — that once crossed Midland Avenue in Glen Ridge — is, however, no longer visible. It is buried underground and its location is marked only by culverts that lead into storm sewers. A neighborhood of well-built, nicely-landscaped, carefully-maintained two to three story homes is now present for several hundred yards on each side of the location of the former ink factory. This area is, nevertheless, a troubled location. In 1997, a visitor would see that the place where the ink factory was once located, and for about half of a city block on either side of it, had recently been scraped clean, revealing reddish brown earth. No grass or trees were left. In 1997 the site of the former ink factory was surrounded by a high fence and was posted with ominous warning signs. This location had become a Superfund toxic waste project site of the U. S. Environmental Protection Agency. I will return to this subject later.[240]

The Battery Factory: 1901-1924

Edison's other project in Glen Ridge was getting underway as his ink factory was folding up. In May 1901 Thomas and Mina Edison bought a harness factory known as the Hayden Mill from the estate of Peter Hayden. This mill was located in the center of Glen Ridge. It was only a block from the principal north-south street of the community — Ridgewood Avenue — and it lay between the town's two main east-west streets — Bloomfield and Belleville Avenues. The Hayden Mill and the

PHOTOS BY GEORGE J. HILL, M.D.

BATTERY FACTORY IN GLEN RIDGE. In 1901, Edison moved into an existing factory building in the center of Glen Ridge and began to manufacture storage batteries for electric carriages. By 1906, he had expanded his factory to fill the entire property now occupied by the bleachers on the east side of Hurrell Field (background, above), from Bloomfield Avenue Arcade (below) to Belleville Avenue.

surrounding land became the location for the Edison Storage Battery Company, where the inventor "experimented on a storage battery for electric carriages." Edison preserved the two main buildings of the Hayden Mill and added several of his own, including an office building in the center of the complex. In 1906 the buildings of the Edison Battery Factory Company covered a property that was about one hundred yards long by thirty yards in width.[241]

In 1924 Edison's factory buildings were demolished and the land was converted to an athletic field for the Glen Ridge High School. The east bleachers for Hurrell Field are now located where the battery factory once stood. Perpendicular to the bleachers, along Bloomfield Avenue, is the Glen Ridge arcade, which was built in 1911. The arcade is one of the best known and most admired structures in Glen Ridge. Its graceful arches and Spanish colonial architecture are a signature piece for the community, harmonizing with the architecture of several municipal buildings across the street at the corner of Ridgewood and Bloomfield Avenues.[242]

Across Bloomfield Avenue from Hurrell Field is the deep, wooded valley of Toney's Brook, through which the railroad now known as New York to Montclair Branch of New Jersey Transit also passes. In Edison's day, this was known as the Newark and Bloomfield Branch of the Delaware, Lackawanna & Western Railroad. Toney's Brook is the largest tributary of Second River; it joins Wigwam Brook to form Second River only a mile or so below this point in Glen Ridge. The Edison Storage Battery Factory thus had close access to both an important rail line and to abundant amounts of water. The valley of Toney's Brook is arguably the deepest natural valley east of First Mountain in Essex County. It is "the glen" of Glen Ridge, a beautiful place to look down into from the concrete bridge across Bloomfield Avenue from Edison's former factory site.

* * * * *

Edison's environmental impact on Glen Ridge was relatively minimal, and his presence there has largely been forgotten. As we return to examine Edison's relationship to Silver Lake, we shall see that, in contrast to Glen Ridge, the inventor's environmental impact at Silver Lake was substantial during his lifetime. However, at Silver Lake — as elsewhere — memories of Edison have dimmed and have been sanitized with the passage of time.

Silver Lake Was No More

Edison moved out of a building on Bloomfield Avenue in April 1889 and he purchased more property in the following month near Silver Lake. Within four months, however, the idyllic valley of Silver Lake was suddenly and permanently changed.

> On 30 July 1889 a storm caused a flood that broke the dam, draining the lake's waters into the Second River. Silver Lake was no more; only the name remains. But flooding remains a problem to this day.[243]

Inexplicably, the storm of July 1889 and the destruction of Silver Lake are not mentioned in the history of Bloomfield — although the eastern portion of Bloomfield was part of the Silver Lake valley. Nor was the disappearance of the lake at Silver Lake mentioned in the accounts of Edison's business operations there, or in the oral histories of Edison's employees. Indeed, the "Silver Lake District" persisted, even though the lake was gone.[244]

In the summer of 1889, Edison rapidly continued to expand his operations in the Silver Lake District. By August 1889, within a month after the dam broke, Edison had acquired no less than fifty acres within the 120 acre pentagonal tract that is bordered by Belmont Avenue, Bloomfield Avenue, Grove Street, Watsessing Avenue, and Franklin Street — the western area of the "Silver Lake District" of Belleville, and the contiguous area in Bloomfield. This pentagonal tract was already traversed by the railroad line that until recent years ran on to Edison's Plant in West Orange. Traces of the rails still remain there, along the east side of the Battery Factory.[245]

Four months later, in December 1889, Edison suffered a major setback in Bloomfield, when the Township Committee reversed its initial acceptance of his proposal to provide public lighting for the city streets. As was the case in the question of annexation of the Silver Lake District, fierce political pressure was exerted on both sides of the issue. In contrast to its more or less neutral position regarding the annexation of Silver Lake, after taking a neutral position at the outset, the *Bloomfield Citizen* eventually published a cautious, loquacious feature article which, in effect, opposed Edison's lighting contract.[246]

The ambiguous position of the local newspaper regarding Edison's activities reflected the attitude of the people of Bloomfield, who continued to admire Edison personally for the rest of his life, yet did not regard him as one of Bloomfield's business leaders. In 1932, only one year after Edison died, the town's official history did not mention Edison or Silver Lake at any point in the text or in the index, nor were any of Edison's various businesses mentioned — although fifty-two firms were mentioned, including Edison's competitors Bakelite and Westinghouse, and his own "baby," General Electric.[247]

Bloomfield was a major center of industry in Essex County in 1892. The Oakes Wool Mill in Bloomfield "had become one of the nation's foremost makers of woolen cloth for uniforms." By the spring of 1892, Edison's operations at Silver Lake were in high gear, and the areas nearby were being developed by speculators. The *Bloomfield Citizen* reported that:

More workmen are being taken on at the Edison works in Silver Lake. . . . A great many people are looking at the lots on the old pond property which Fred L. Flohn is selling off. The Force property, formerly Mr. Farrand's, has been sold to a New York man and will be cut into building lots.[248]

Edison was not alone in his development of chemical and electrical manufacturing plants in this region. For example, Frank Sprague "built a major factory in Bloomfield in 1892 to make electric hoists," and a triangle of land between Sprague's factory and the Edison Plant in West Orange and a flag stop called Crescent (later Ampere) "became the major focus of the nation's prime regions for makers of electrical products."[249]

A Fire There Every Saturday Night

When she growing up in Bloomfield before World War I, Lucy Sant'Ambrogio was invited by friends who lived near Edison's factories in Silver Lake "to sit on their front steps on Saturday nights to watch the fires in Silver Lake. There was a fire there every Saturday night," she recalled with a chuckle in March 1998. She continued:

There were lots of fires at the Edison plant. This was about 1912 to 1914, and Edison's buildings were already deteriorating. He would build things up and then pull out. . . . They [Edison and his companies] weren't very well liked around here. They didn't pay ... They were very strict.

PHOTOS COURTESY OF NATIONAL PARK SERVICE

CHEMICALS AND FIRE: Workers in the Chemical Works Laboratory in Silver Lake on April 14, 1911, above. Fires were reportedly common at the plant. Below, the Coal Tar Products division two days after the fire of December 29, 1917.

When asked if she had ever seen Edison, Ms. Sant'Ambrogio replied:

No, but I worked for him. When I was a student, I polished records at his plant in West Orange [her hands form a circle about one foot in diameter, and her fingers indicate the thickness of the disc]. It was strict, very strict. They [the Edisons] were very remote, distant. We never saw them. He didn't get along well with the people around here.[250]

Looking at photographs of the Edison factories at Silver Lake, Ms. Sant'Ambrogio and two of her friends commented that:

It was a mess there. . . . Smoke and fires. . . . People didn't think about pollution then like they do now, but Clara Maass Hospital [about one-fourth mile northeast of Silver Lake] was built on a dump. . . The main operations of Edison were on the Belmont Avenue side, where Pathmark is now. . . . Silver Lake was pretty shallow, more like a pond than a lake, and it just dried up after Edison built his factories there.[251]

One illustration of the Silver Lake area in this period depicts the "Silver Lake Chemical Works," viewed from Alva Street, in January 1912. The picture shows a grim contrast between a fine colonial-style dwelling on the right (Belmont Avenue) side of Alva Street, and gloomy factory buildings at the left side of the picture. This picture shows in microcosm the problem of living beside the Chemical Works. The factories made a bleak backdrop for houses, in spite of newspaper reports in 1889 that "property was enhancing in value" with "the erection of a number of dwelling houses."[252]

Two photographs taken in 1913 show interiors of buildings at the Chemical Works, and we can now see why these buildings were so hazardous. One interior shows "Hydrogen-Earthen Vessels" that would hold several hundred gallons of liquids, connected to pipes, and two boxed free-standing carboys. This building probably has vertical board sides. It clearly has wooden window frames and wooden shelves, and it looks like a firetrap. The other photograph shows about a dozen men at work in the "Construction of Hydrate Building at Chemical Works." The men are laying what appear to be wooden forms for the concrete floor of what will be a massive building. It is similar to the cement buildings that were built by Edison in the first decade of the twentieth century in West Orange. Edison thought they were fireproof, although only a year later, on 9 December 1914, he learned that they weren't, and why.

PHOTO COURTESY OF NATIONAL PARK SERVICE

DANGEROUS CHEMICAL: Settling tanks for crude phenol (carbolic acid) at the Silver Lake plant on March 1, 1915 – one year before an Essex County judge ruled that phenol was hazardous and fined Thomas A. Edison Inc. for polluting a stream near Heckel Street with the chemical.

Two aerial views of the Silver Lake Plant provide a fine opportunity to see how the buildings were laid out, and how the plant developed. Although neither picture is dated, it is clear that one is somewhat earlier than the other, and both show the plant when its buildings were in good condition. In the earlier picture — which may be a drawing rather than a photograph — factory buildings fill the space that is bordered by Belmont Avenue, the railroad, and Alva Street — an area of approximately forty acres. At this time, the buildings were mainly one story high, although a two-story building can be seen that is perhaps 150 feet long. This building and the one at right angles to its southern corner provide an orientation for the second picture, which is an aerial photograph that was taken later.

The second picture was taken by Fairchild Aerial Surveys after factory buildings had been erected along the north side of the railroad, up to the corner of Belmont and Franklin, and extending west nearly half of the distance to Watsessing Avenue. (See photo, page 152). Many of the buildings north of the railroad were two stories high. By the time the second aerial view was taken, the area covered with buildings consisted of about sixty or more acres of the 120 acres in this tract. There were also several large square and rounded foundations extending along both sides of the railroad, towards the southwest corner of the tract, at Bloomfield and Watsessing. These structures appeared to be either holding tanks for liquids, or were buildings under construction, or both.

There were, in the second aerial photograph, still a few houses along Alva Street, some of which may still exist. In the later photograph, a water tower had been erected on the south side of the railroad, near the corner of Belmont and Franklin. As I previously stated, contour lines on the Orange quadrangle map suggest that this was the corner from which Edison's property once drained toward Second River. The house and brook at 45 Heckel Street, of which we will soon be reading, would have been just off of the lower right corner of the aerial photograph, but the photograph shows clearly how close this unfortunate property was to the Silver Lake Plant.

A Menace to Health

By 1915 the environment at Silver Lake had become dangerous to workers as well as to families who lived in the nearby streets, especially those downwind and downstream. As a recent graduate in chemistry from Cornell, Edward Cary should have been well prepared to work in the chemical industry, but he was unable to protect himself from injury. The new materials that were being synthesized at Silver Lake, which we now call plastics, were unexpectedly and unpredictably hazardous:

I spent nine years in charge of that plant . . . Silver Lake, yes. Then they discovered . . . . that I had lost my sense of smell, due to the carbolic acid formaldehyde fumes of what was known today as bakelite. We called it phenol resin, which was invented by the man who organized and founded the Bakelite Corporation of America.[253]

Another former employee described the "mountain of sludge" that accumulated at Silver Lake:

PHOTO BY GEORGE J. HILL, M.D.

HECKEL STREET POLLUTION: Residents of Heckel Street successfully sued Thomas A. Edison, Inc., for the discharge of carbolic acid into a stream (now covered by Brook Street) that intersected Heckel Street just to the left of the house on the left in the photo. The successful litigants in the 1916 case, Salvatore Crillo and Angelo D'Alessio, lived a few houses to the right.

[D]own at Silver lake they had a huge mountain of junk, you know, off the back of one of the active material plants . . . This was the active materials. They made the nickel and iron compounds for the storage batteries, and also I think they made certain stuff for the experiment batteries.[254]

Confirmation of the existence of fires at Silver Lake, or at least one of them, appeared in an article in 1916 in *The New York Times*, in which a 17,000-square-foot corrugated steel building burned down only thirteen months after the great fire at Edison's Plant in West Orange. Fifteen other buildings with chemicals nearby were at risk, as well as the firemen who fought this blaze in January 1916. Carbolic acid (phenol) was made in the building that burned — the same organic chemical that was involved in Edward Cary's loss of the sense of smell:

From a cause yet unsettled but supposed to have been defective light wiring, a corrugated steel building, 200 feet long by eighty-five *deep, belonging to Thomas A. Edison, and part of his chemical plant here, where he made carbolic acid, took fire late tonight. It was burned to the ground.... He estimated the loss at between $4,500 and $5,000.*[255]

In 1916 a court in Essex County, New Jersey, ruled that carbolic acid was hazardous, and that factory owners such as Edison were responsible to protect the public from exposure to it. This ruling was made in response to a suit against Edison for polluting the brook-in-a-ditch that we read about previously. The suit was decided in favor of the plaintiffs, but not without a long battle by Edison, who raised the issue of wartime needs for phenol and the importance of this chemical as a disinfectant in hospitals. Indeed, Edison received only a token financial penalty:

A long legal contest in which Thomas A. Edison and some of his companies were defendants, growing out of the discharge of acids into a stream in Belleville, ended today when Judge James P. Mylod decided in favor of the plaintiffs. The court excluded Edison as an individual, and awarded $200 damages against Thomas A. Edison, Inc., lessee of Edison's property in Belleville where carbolic acid is being made for use in war hospitals. Salvatore Crillo and Angelo D'Alessio, owners of a house at 45 Heckel Street, Belleville, were the plaintiffs. The stream polluted by the acid was found by the court to be a menace to health.[256]

Heckel Street is parallel to and one block east of Belmont Avenue, which was the eastern border of Edison's Silver Lake property. Heckel Street runs from Franklin St. to Bloomfield Avenue; it is about one-half mile in length. #45 Heckel Street is about 250 yards north of the corner of Bloomfield Avenue and Heckel Street. This address is less than 100 yards north of the intersection of Brook Street and Heckel Street, where we previously saw that a brook-in-a-ditch passed out of Edison's property and drained into Silver Lake. The Heckel Street area immediately adjacent to Edison's Silver Lake property figures prominently in the accounts of local residents who complained of environmental degradation produced by air pollution, fires, and foul water from his factories.[257]

The Death House

One of Edison's chemists tells how careless and disrespectful the Edison company — and he personally — were regarding the health and safety of the immigrant Italian families who lived near the Silver Lake

Plant. As we shall see, some of William Hand's comments do not reflect well on his own performance as an employee and as a manager, yet he is also harshly critical of Edison. In assessing his credibility, therefore, I weighed all of his comments to determine whether he was exaggerating or speculating. In this regard, I compared Hand's remarks with the statements and written reports of others about Silver Lake. Although some of the scenes and situations he described are particularly egregious, I concluded that Hand's comments are consistent with those of others that I have quoted previously:

Silver Lake was divided into the primary battery works and the Edison Chemical Works which produced potash, phenol and things like that, and the organic chemical plant which produced these so-called German chemicals, and then the fourth was the Edison plant that produced phonograph cabinets and things like that.[258]

After summarizing Edison's operations at Silver Lake in general, and his production of phenol in particular, Hand then delineated the chemical reactions that he supervised in 1926. This chemical operation was, we may say, awesome:

You start with carbolic acid, and formaldehyde in solution, in an autoclave. . . In Silver Lake today there's probably hundreds of tons of this stuff which was taken out to the dumps all because they lost control of the rate of reaction. . . . he couldn't get people to work on that job because it was explosive, and if something gave way, they'd get killed. Two investigators were killed on it. One tightened a flange and the bolt split off. He had too long a handle on the wrench — he was killed by the gas, phenol formaldehyde, coming out at great pressure. The other was sent to a sanitarium, about the same time.

Hand clearly recognized the danger and environmental hazards:

I actually had many explosions and I had found plastic over three or four blocks of houses, in Silver Lake. My laboratory was known as Hand's Death House or Hand's Mad House. Now, the first is obvious because people had been killed on it. . . . Now plastic would fill up on the inside and block the pipes and the valves, and . . . then it would break through the froth and this glasslike material would shoot up a couple

PHOTO BY NATIONAL PARK SERVICE (ABOVE)
PHOTOS BY GEORGE JAMES HILL (RIGHT)

RAILROAD AND RUBBLE: Railroad tracks run past Edison's Silver Lake factory complex in this historic photo (above). Today, the tracks are still there (left photo, opposite page), used by Conrail freight trains, just 20 feet away, off to the side, are foundation stones and other remnants of the Edison plant (right photo, opposite page). Edison's Silver Lake plant was torn down many years ago.

of hundred feet into the air, and then the wind would carry it over Silver Lake. And it caused an awful lot of trouble. The inhabitants of Silver Lake were largely Italians on filled-in land, not necessarily squatters, but when that solution with a lot of free formaldehyde and phenol was blown over their area, they couldn't stand it. They couldn't breathe.

    As a senior employee and the responsible chemist in this laboratory, Hand was an important representative of the Edison Company at Silver Lake. But he was also a brash young man, who thought it perfectly appropriate to have a derisory attitude toward the immigrants who lived near the plant. In this regard, Hand presumably reflected the attitude of Edison and other managers of factories at Silver Lake. In spite of his cavalier attitude regarding the environment and his neighbors, Hand seems not to have been surprised by their responses — fighting fire with fire, as it

were. Hand looked at the entire issue as a contest, a test of will and of cunning, rather than as a moral or ethical problem:

So they brought all kinds of damages against the Edison Chemical Plant, and every time I had trouble, they would form a queue a block long with Italians carrying dead dogs and dead cats and chickens and wash everything like that, not necessarily from the explosion . . . and they would try to collect money on them. In this case, with an Italian woman carrying a baby on her hip . . . I pinched this child and he let out a yelp and I said to the mother, "That child isn't dead, you can't collect anything on that child," and with that the whole line descended on me and I had to run for cover. I got in through a hole in the plant fence.

But that night, they . . . wrecked the laboratory. They did about $30,000 worth of damage on the laboratory. I was called and went in at about 3 o'clock in the morning — the fire apparatus had come.[259]

Hand says that Edison had given him a badge and told him to investigate what was going on in his plants there, as a sort of "intelligence officer." Hand was a determined snooper, and he didn't hesitate to prowl in the enormous, vacant, abandoned buildings at Silver Lake in the period 1924-1926.[260] Hand then describes how he discovered that mercury was being used at Silver Lake, and that workers there were unwittingly exposed to its toxicity:

There was one plant that I couldn't get into. It was always locked, so one Sunday night I returned to the plant and put up a ladder up against one of the ventilators and climbed up. . . . When I got down

PHOTOS BY GEORGE J. HILL, M.D.

FROM FACTORIES TO SUPERMARKET. Belmont Avenue marks the border between Belleville and Bloomfield. The eastern edge of what was once the location of Edison's immense Silver Lake factory complex is now a shopping center.

from the ventilator my hands were yellow. I made a quick test and I found out that yellow was mercuric oxide, and the mercuric oxide was the powder incorporated in the black iron. When the battery was charged . . . the mercuric oxide would break down and in its stead would be dropules of mercury, which increase the conductivity of the iron. There would be millions and millions of these tiny mercuric, metallic mercury droplets all through the plate. . . . When I told Edison . . . He was very, very unhappy about that because that was one of his secrets.

    I wandered around the plant. I went out to the dump. Out at the dump there was a shelter and when I went around in front of the shelter I saw a man who was a skeleton. . . . He said, "I was working in the foundry." I recognized that this man had picked up an industrial poison, and it looked very much as though we were dealing with mercury again . . . . I'm pretty sure he only lived for a few weeks after that (20). I wrote to Mr. Edison . . . His reply was "It's not as dangerous as you think it should be" (21).[261]

SILVER LAKE TODAY: A chain-link fence separates the residences in the Silver Lake district of Belleville from the supermarket on the Bloomfield side of Belmont Avenue.

Hand confirms the existence of large dumps at Silver Lake by 1926, and of abandoned buildings up to three stories high. The environment that Hand describes was deadly, even murderous, as he recounts an incident in which he was, he believes, warned to stop looking for gold that had been disappearing. Edison had directed Hand to determine what was happening to gold that was used in his chemical processes, but which was disappearing. Hand says that "I had a notion that the gold was disappearing within the company and not being stolen . . . and my judgment told me that perhaps somewhere in these ruins [at Silver Lake], gold was being secreted." He believed that he discovered a dishonest employee who "was involved with Edison in leaching this gold off."[262] One of the dumps at Silver Lake was a pile of nickel-containing batteries that was sixty feet high and covered an acre of land.[263]

It Stretches into Bloomfield

Although the oral history by William Hand suggests that by 1926 Edison's factories at Silver Lake comprised a hadean wasteland, the apparition of the demise of Edison's plant at Silver Lake was premature. In 1927, it was stated that "Oldtime firms such as Edison Storage Battery . . . remained in business" in Belleville. Four years later, in the year before Edison died, the Table of Organization of Thomas A. Edison Industries, Inc., showed that in 1930 several Divisions and other components of the Edison corporation were located at Silver Lake. These included the Edison Storage Battery Company's Chemical Works Division; the Manufacturing component of the Edison Primary Battery Division; the Wax Division of the Ediphone Division; the Radio Manufacturing component of the Edison Radio Division; and the Manufacturing component of the General Manufacturing Division. The company history of the Primary Battery Division states that in 1914-15 "All production facilities for the Primary Battery Division were consolidated in the present Silver Lake factory after fire destroyed the main Edison plant at Orange, N.J." In 1918, the "offices of the Primary Battery Division were established at Silver Lake (Bloomfield, N.J., post office). Previously they were located at Orange and in New York City."[264] In the early 1920's the E-K Medical Gas Division was established at the Silver Lake plant; nitrous oxide, oxygen, ethylene, carbon dioxide and cyclopropane for hospitals and industrial use were made there. By 1937, six years after the inventor's death, "The Edison plant has grown until it stretches into Bloomfield. It now covers about seven acres fronting on Belmont Avenue and employs 400 people."[265]

Marked Lowering of the Water Table[266]

And if this weren't enough, the land that had once been Silver Lake had suffered one more insult. Since it was invisible, this insult was not noticed immediately, but it is clear today: Not only has the lake been lost, but the water table has been lowered to such an extent that any effort to restore the lake would fail because surface water must fall as much as thirty feet below the ground before it reaches ground water. This grim assessment is based on the depth and flow rates of the six water wells that were present in or near the Silver Lake district in 1968, and a comparison of the ground water situation in this area, just west of Newark, with the history of ground water changes in the eastern part of Newark from 1879 to 1947.[267]

The Silver Lake aquifer was still an important source of groundwater as recently as 1968. There would thus be reason to hope that the aquifer could gradually be replenished if well drilling and "mining" of subsurface water were terminated, or at least restricted. The four wells clustered in the southeastern corner of Bloomfield represented nearly forty percent of all of the recorded wells in that city, and the Jack Frost well in Belleville was one of only two wells in that city that were not located immediately adjacent to the Passaic River; eight others were located on

PHOTO COURTESY OF NATIONAL PARK SERVICE

ENVIRONMENTAL DISASTER: Edison's Silver Lake Chemical Works, shown above on May 4, 1938, is undoubtedly the biggest black mark on his environmental record.

the Passaic. If these five wells could be capped, or their flow rates monitored so that the water table rose, rather than fell, from year to year, the Silver Lake aquifer would have a chance to recover. However, in 1968, Nichols estimated that by the year 1990, Essex County would need 223 gallons per person per day, which far exceeded the delivery capacity of existing wells and aquifers in the county. Water for Essex County would need to come "from surface sources," (i.e., from reservoirs outside of the county).[268] In 1951, Henry Herpers and Henry C. Barksdale pointed out that between 1879 and 1947 there had been a "marked lowering of the water table in the eastern part of the [Newark] area." The authors predicted that the trends in the Ironbound would be expected to occur in other parts of the Newark area if continued pumping exceeded the inflow from the average rainfall on the surface at Newark, which was "approximately 47 inches per year."[269]

These ground water analyses in the area near the Silver Lake District may appear to be inconsistent with reports of flooding, and of statements about "the river that tries to come back." We must, however, remember that surface water and ground water, while associated in a general way, are not directly related to each other. When the lake was present it received and retained water, at least temporarily, on an area that covered about twenty acres. This would allow for a substantial percolation of surface water into groundwater through the permeable sandy lake bottom. Furthermore, when the lake was in existence, it was surrounded by meadows and trees that also retained surface water and facilitated groundwater replacement. In contrast, the high density of paved streets and buildings at present in the Silver Lake District leads to rapid runoff of precipitation, impeding restoration of groundwater. The runoff may be on the surface, or through storm sewers such as we saw along Heckel Street. However, the low, relatively flat or concave surface of the land in the Silver Lake District, which was perfect as a lake bottom, does not readily convey rainwater down to Second River. Instead, rainwater becomes a nuisance in streets and basements.

*****

Our final view of Edison's environmental impact at Silver Lake was grim, but not hopeless. With nearly four feet of water raining down on this area every year, a determined community can address the environmental damage that was wrought long ago by the managers and workers at Edison's Silver Lake factories, and by the conversion of lake bottom and farmland to closely spaced streets and houses by Edison and other major property owners. We may wonder whether Edison and his workmen were reckless or naive, or both, but the environmental impact of their factories and shops is clear. When we read signs that say "Welcome to the Silver Lake District," and "Something's Happening" there, we can see that the Silver Lake community is, indeed, doing this.

While the Silver Lake District is slowly recovering from the environmental onslaught of the past century, we now leave Essex County, to follow Edison's "footprints" into the highest and most northerly part of New Jersey — Sussex County — where the Great Inventor once mined for iron, and where he is still remembered with admiration and affection.

Chapter 10

Iron Mining: Ogdensburg, Sparta Mountain, and Lake Hopatcong (1889-1900)

We are making a Yosemite of our own here. . . .
We will soon have one of the biggest canyons in the world.

—Thomas Alva Edison, about 1890[270]

The Edison Company brought in musicians, and they had dances in the schoolhouse at the mine on Saturday nights — the schoolhouse that is in Franklin now.

—W. C. Dolan, 1997[271]

Ogdensburg and Sparta: The Ogden/Edison Mine

IT was a cool, cloudy day in September 1997, and William C. "Doley" Dolan, the senior citizen of Ogdensburg, was relating what he had heard from his father, who had been a miner at the Edison/Ogden mine a century ago. We were standing on Edison Road at the entrance to the Sparta Mountain Wildlife Management Area. Directly in front of us was a flat, sandy area about one hundred yards wide and fifty yards deep that was surrounded by low trees. In the background, the land rose gently to the summit of the ridgeline. Behind us, across Edison Road, we had seen a glimpse, through tall trees, of what was known as the

Horseshoe Cut, which was the open pit that Edison had once mined for iron ore. Mr. Dolan continued:

> *Many of the miners lived in houses near here, on the mountain. My father and others lived in town, and walked up the road with their lunch pails every day, and back down at night. It wasn't a hard climb, and they enjoyed walking together. The spirit was good here then. The houses were taken away to Ogdensburg and Franklin after Edison left, and many are still there, in good condition. The schoolhouse was moved to Franklin, where it was used as a church building for a while.*[272]

Two weeks later, I located this old schoolhouse, weathered but sturdy, at its present location eight miles from the mine site. It is now in the woods off of Evans Street in Franklin.[273] Mr. Dolan was born in 1903, and he was ninety-three years old when he recalled his father's stories about what it was like to work for Edison's mining company, the New Jersey and Pennsylvania Concentrating Works. Before he retired, "Doley" Dolan had spent many years working as an engineer at the zinc mine on the western side of the Wallkill River valley, across the valley from the Edison mine. He was familiar with the stories that were told

PHOTO BY GEORGE J. HILL, M.D.

A SCHOOLHOUSE FOR MINERS' FAMILIES: Edison built this schoolhouse for the children of his workforce up the mountain near his mine in Ogdensburg. After Edison left, the building was moved eight miles to Franklin, where it was used as a church. Today, it stands abandoned.

PHOTO COURTESY OF NATIONAL PARK SERVICE

EDISON'S IRON MINE COMPANY BUILDINGS: The New Jersey and Pennsylvania Concentrating Works once covered the summit of Sparta Mountain in Sussex County. Today, only a large patch of sand marks the location of this factory complex (see photo on page 203).

by men who had worked for Edison, although he never saw Edison personally. Dolan had not been to the area of the Edison mine for many years, although it was only two and one-half miles from the center of Ogdensburg, because it had been privately owned and was posted with "No Trespassing" signs. The land was now owned by the state of New Jersey and the Audubon Society.

This was my second trip to Ogdensburg, searching for Thomas Edison's "footprints" in Sussex County. Four days earlier, on a glorious cool, sunny day, I had visited the president of the Ogdensburg Historical Society and looked at artifacts from the Edison era in the museum that the Society had established in Ogdensburg. I had also toured the zinc mine across the valley from Edison's iron mine, and learned something of the mining operations that had been carried out for hundreds of years in this valley and in the mountains that surrounded it — going back to the days of the Indians, the Dutch, and the early American colonists. On the day that I walked with Mr. Dolan through part of the property that Edison once owned, a gentle rain began to fall. It didn't bother him at all, but it was clear to me that the slippery rocks and leaves made it too hazardous for us to continue walking in woods that were full of old mine shafts and half-hidden, unmarked stone walls, and the remains of the foundations of buildings.

When I returned two weeks later to explore the area by myself, the hills of Sussex County had exploded with fall colors. Brilliant red maples and golden oaks stood out from the background of green trees that had not yet changed color, or were evergreen and changeless. It was hard for me to understand how Edison's biographers could have thought of this a "dreary" wilderness.[274]

Before visiting Ogdensburg, I had reviewed the latest information that was then available about the Ogden/Edison mine in the *Chronology* of the Edison Papers Project. There was but little in the *Chronology*, some seventeen items, spread over nine years from 1890 through 1898.[275] The information in the *Chronology* provided neither a starting date nor an ending date for Edison's work in Sussex County, so I was left to determine this for myself, as well as I could. I also knew from Edison's biographers that there was considerable disagreement regarding how much land Edison had owned and controlled near Ogdensburg. On my first visit to Ogdensburg, I learned that this was still an open question locally, although the prevailing belief was that:

> Edison . . . acquired title to 2,248 acres of magnetic-bearing lands in Sparta surrounding a 600-foot-wide and 11,500 foot-long body of low grade ore that had been worked sporadically since 1772 as the "Ogden group mines." . . . At least fifty workmen's houses were located in four areas — "Mudwall Row," "Summerville," "Cuckoo Flats," and "New City."[276]

If Edison had owned 2,248 acres, he would have had title to about three and one-half square miles of land. This would be an area that is, say, one mile long and three and one-half miles wide, or three and a half "sections" of land, at 640 acres per square mile "section." Whether or not this was the correct figure remains to be seen, but it provides a useful guide to visualize the amount of terrain that might have been involved in Edison's iron mining operations. I eventually decided that Edison's actual mining and milling operation was conducted on a much smaller piece of land than this. However, in the end, the larger figure — somewhere between 1,500 and 2,500 acres — also made sense, because this would have been the area required for housing at Ogden/Edison and for future development, if the mine had been commercially successful.

My goals on this site visit were to determine what this area was like when Edison arrived, and what happened to the local environment during the eleven years that Edison mined and milled iron ore near Ogdensburg. I also expected to see what had happened to the environment of Sparta Mountain and in the nearby towns, from the time that Edison left up to the present.

* * * * *

In order to place the Ogdensburg era into context, let us recall that while Edison was acquiring space for his manufacturing operations in Bloomfield and land for construction of new factories in the Silver Lake District of Bloomfield and Belleville, he also started a major endeavor in mining which continued for the last half of his life. The inventor's work in mining began in earnest with his creation of a large open-pit iron mine and an iron ore-concentrating mill in Sussex County, New Jersey in 1889. Edison's iron mining and concentrating plant was in operation at Ogdensburg and Sparta, New Jersey, until about 1900 or 1901. He then transferred his mining and milling equipment to Warren County, where he developed large open-pit limestone quarries and built a group of buildings that were used to transform limestone into Portland cement. The Edison Portland Cement Company was in operation in New Village and Stewartsville, N.J., for several years after the inventor's death.[277]

Edison's work in mining began with his interest in metallurgy, and it eventually included far-flung operations in the search for commercially useful sources of platinum, tungsten, gold, and iron. In our case study of Menlo Park, we learned of his interest in copper mining, and it is said in Ogdensburg that he offered useful suggestions to the operators of the zinc mines in Sussex County. Edison's prospectors scoured the Rocky Mountains in Canada and in the western part of the United States, and he eventually built mines and mills in areas as distant as New Mexico, Michigan, Pennsylvania, and Norway. Edison's interest in iron mining started with his studies of the use of electromagnets to concentrate low grade iron ore into high grade ore that could be sold for a profit to iron- and steel-making factories. Although he was not the first to consider this method for concentrating iron ore, he believed, rightly, that his knowledge of electricity, generators, and electromagnetism would give him the opportunity to be a leader in this field. We know from Edison's biographers that he did, indeed, develop what was then the world's largest electromagnetic separation plant for the concentration of iron ore, and that he persisted until he shut down his iron mine in New Jersey because it appeared that it was not going to be profitable. Edison finally admitted that richer natural deposits of iron near the Great Lakes could be mined and transported to steel mills at less cost than he could ever achieve.

We have seen in the previous chapter that Edison was deeply involved in his Silver Lake project in 1889. This is the same year that Edison's biographers state that his search for a source of low grade iron ore culminated in his decision to secure the rights to mine for iron near the town of Ogdensburg. The site that Edison selected in Sussex County, New Jersey, had been mined off and on for about one hundred years.[278]

From Glenmont to Ogdensburg

Much of the rougher land away from the iron industry remained in high forest at the end of the eighteenth century; the presence of wolves well beyond 1800 in Sussex County suggests that extensive areas of forest remained.

—Peter O. Wacker and Paul G. Clemens, 1995[279]

SUSSEX County was one of the last areas in the colony of New Jersey to be developed. Sussex County is in the New Jersey Highlands, which has been described as "a region of forested ridges, sparkling lakes, rivers and streams, and abundant wildlife stretching over 1,000 square miles." Sussex became a separate county only in 1753, when it separated from Morris County. Sussex County, in the Northern Highlands, was noted for its iron mining activity and the custom of running stock loose in the woods. The township of Byram, south of Ogdensburg, was said in jest to be characterized by its "rock farms."[280]

In order to understand what this part of Sussex County was like when Thomas Edison arrived, and what has happened subsequently in this vicinity, let us begin by traveling in our mind's eye from the inventor's home and laboratory in West Orange to the valley of the Wallkill River in Sussex County, where the town of Ogdensburg is located. Until the

THE IRON MINER: Edison at his mine office on Sparta Mountain. This hilltop property was long known as the Ogden Mine, but the Great Inventor changed its name to "Edison."

COURTESY OF NATIONAL PARK SERVICE

roads and highways that cross New Jersey were leveled, widened and straightened in recent years, this was a relatively remote area. It was a four hour train ride to get here in Edison's day. However, one can now easily drive on broad, limited access, divided highways all the way from West Orange, where Edison lived, to Sparta township, which was once a part of the village of Ogdensburg.

The traveler from West Orange to Ogdensburg now drives west on Interstate 280 through the great gash in First Mountain that cuts through Llewellyn Park, and then further west on Interstate 80 to Dover, a distance of about twenty-four miles on interstate highways. At this point, one proceeds to the northwest on New Jersey Route 15 for ten miles. Route 15 is not only a splendid divided highway but is rightly called a "Scenic Road," passing Lake Hopatcong and rising ever higher through the wooded foothills of the Appalachians that are called the "New Jersey Highlands." Near the western border of Morris County, at Lake Hopatcong, Route 15 passes through a large shopping center in Jefferson Township. Here, the highway is joined by County Route 615, also known as Edison Road, which connects Route 15 with the road that winds around the lake. We will return later to study this "footprint" of Edison.[281]

Route 15 then continues on to Sparta, where the traveler who seeks the site of the Edison mine exits the divided highway and turns north on Sussex County Route 517, which enters Ogdensburg in less than three miles. The thirty-seven mile trip from the Edison National Historic Site in West Orange to the intersection of Ogdensburg Road (Route 517) and Edison Street in the center of Ogdensburg now takes less than an hour.

Sources

My case study of Edison's relationship to the environment in Sussex County, New Jersey, is based on three field trips in September and October 1997 to Ogdensburg, New Jersey, and the surrounding area. While in the Ogdensburg area, I spent several hours with Mr. Wasco Hadonowetz, President of the Ogdensburg Historical Society, who oriented me to the community, and introduced me to local residents. On three occasions I visited the site of the Edison iron mine and mill, once with him and a group of others, and twice by myself.[282]

This case study also incorporates information that I gained during a private two-hour tour of the zinc mine of the Sterling Hill Mining Museum, and in a trip to the town of Franklin, about five miles north of Ogdensburg, where I visited the Franklin Mineral Museum and located the old schoolhouse that was moved from the Edison mine to Franklin.

On Main Street in Ogdensburg, I enjoyed lunch at the Lyons House, which was once a hotel where Edison is said to have stayed on many occasions when his mines were in operation. Four wooden houses that were lived in by Edison's miners are now located across Main Street from the Lyons House. Two of these so-called "Edison houses" are free-standing residential homes, and two have been brought together and converted into a store. During my visits, I was able to examine the dining areas of the Lyons House and the interior of the two "Edison houses" that have been made into a store. My informants in Ogdensburg also included Steve Misiur, tour guide and "avocational historian" of the Sterling Hill zinc mine; and Sylvia Hadonowetz, wife of Ogdensburg's historian, daughter of a miner who emigrated to America from Cornwall, England, and worked in the zinc mine at Sterling Hill.[283]

Although the site of the former Edison iron mine and mill is less than three miles east of Main Street in Ogdensburg, it would be difficult for someone to locate the Edison site without assistance, since there are no signs that point to it, or identify it. With guidance, however, the Edison mine site is readily accessible, and if the visitor has a map of the property of the New Jersey & Pennsylvania Concentrating Works to refer to, many of the roads, rocks, and pits at this place can be recognized as the remains of work performed by Edison's men.[284]

The Wallkill River Valley, from the Lenape to Edison

Archaeologists have traced human life in Northern New Jersey back to 8640 B.C.

—**Paul Horuzy, 1990**[285]

FOR perhaps 10,000 years the Lenni Lenape Indians had lived in the land that is now New Jersey, and when the first European settlers arrived this valley was occupied by a subtribe of the Lenape known as the Minisinks, the "People of the Stone Country." Some of their stone tools were made of rock that contains zinc, which becomes fluorescent under ultraviolet light. The early Dutch settlers gave the name Wallkill to the river of this valley (from Dutch, meaning "stone" + "river"), which runs parallel to, and just west of, Main Street. The rocky outcroppings above the Wallkill were obviously some type of ore, and although iron ore was plentiful on the east side of the valley, it was not known until later that the great mountains on the west side of the river were not composed of copper or iron; they were predominantly ores of zinc. This area was originally owned by the Dutch, and Dutch miners worked in the hills.[286]

In the seventeenth century, New Jersey was acquired by the English and in 1664 this area became part of the grant from King Charles II to his brother James, Duke of York. The land then passed to Sir George Carteret, and later to Anthony Rutgers. An early iron forge in this area was operated by Major Elias Ogden, where the Ogden (later Edison) Mine was located. The mine was named after Abram Ogden, who opened it in 1772. The mountain on the other side of the valley was owned by William Alexander (1726-1783), later known as Lord Stirling, who began open-cut mining there for iron in 1772, but failed because the ore was principally zincite and franklinite, and was not a good source of iron. In the nineteenth century, it became apparent that Sterling Hill (the spelling having been changed), was the world's richest source of zinc, and methods for mining, extracting, and using zinc were developed. The mine at Sterling Hill changed hands and names several times before finally becoming known as the New Jersey Zinc Company.[287]

The first English settler in the upper Wallkill valley was Robert Ogden, II, who was born at Elizabethtown in 1716, son of Robert and Hannah (Crane) Ogden; he died in 1787. Robert Ogden, II, married Phebe Hatfield and came to the upper Wallkill valley in 1765, where he founded the communities now known as Ogdensburg and Sparta, the latter town being named for his house. According to local tradition, the name "Sparta" was given to the Ogdens' house by Phebe, who saw similarities between life in the Wallkill valley in the eighteenth century and the minimalist, military environment of the ancient Greek city for which she named her house. Phebe Ogden certainly needed a sense of humor, for she and Robert had at least twenty-two children, of whom no less than seventeen survived.[288]

One of the Ogden children, Robert III (1746-1826), was the head of the Ogden family in the Wallkill valley. Like his father, Robert III was prominent in civic affairs, and he became Surrogate of New Jersey. His brothers Matthias (1754-?), Aaron (1756-1839), and Elias (1763-1805) were leaders in the Revolutionary War, and in New Jersey affairs after the war. Rebecca Ogden, a daughter of Robert Ogden, II, married Dr. Samuel Fowler, a prominent physician who became the owner of the zinc mines at Sterling Hill and Franklin. In 1830 Dr. Fowler found that zinc oxide could be substituted for white lead as a pigment for paint. Methods were eventually developed to separate zinc from the oxides of iron and manganese that were combined with it in the ore known as franklinite. After these methods were perfected, zinc mining began in earnest at Ogdensburg, and a wide range of other uses for zinc were developed, such as galvanizing of steel. Zinc mining continued at Sterling Hill for more than 150 years. It was the end of an era when the Sterling Hill mine closed in 1986, for it was the last of the underground mines in New Jersey.[289]

PHOTO BY GEORGE J. HILL, M.D.

AN EDISON HAUNT: Edison was a frequent guest at the Lyons House during his decade of mining at Ogdensburg. Now a restaurant, the Lyons House proudly features a framed newspaper clipping that describes Edison's visits.

In the meantime, the Ogdens and their successors mined the iron ore and operated iron smelters and forges at the top of the mountain on the east side of the valley. A cluster of houses around the iron mines formed a village known as Ogden Mine, or simply as Ogden. By the last decade of the nineteenth century, iron mining had greatly decreased or perhaps ceased at Ogden, although a considerable amount of low grade magnetite iron ore was still accessible at or near the surface. The Ogden mine had become no longer commercially viable as a source of iron for steel manufacturing, because of the low concentration of iron in its ore, as well as the presence of unacceptable levels of phosphorus, which produced brittle steel. However, more than one hundred iron miners and their families were still living at Ogden Mine and in Ogdensburg in 1890, when Edison began to build a large facility at Ogden to extract and purify iron ore for sale to steel manufacturers in Pennsylvania.[290]

A study of Ogdensburg and the site of the Edison mine and mill is somewhat like reading a palimpsest. That is to say, this place is like a

PHOTO BY GEORGE J. HILL, M.D.

GENERAL STORE: Two of the four Edison houses that were moved to Main Street in Ogdensburg were joined together in 1912 to form the Beierle General Store.

parchment that is used over and over again, a parchment on which there are successive layers of writing that can never be completely erased. Whether we begin at the deepest layer of the past and work forward in time, or with the present time and work backward, we are continuously impressed with the way that past and present interact. And so it is, when we look for Edison's footprints at Ogdensburg. Edison's spirit is still there, more than 110 years after he arrived and nearly a hundred years after he left, but in some respects, the signs of his previous presence are now remarkably well hidden.

This paradox becomes apparent when we look for Edison's footprints in the terrain of Ogdensburg and at the site of his mine and mill as it appears today. The reasons are twofold: the recuperative powers of Nature, when land is given a chance to recover; and the inexorable work of humans, who continue to make changes in their environment. In this case study, we shall see that Nature has reclaimed much of what had been perturbed at the site of the Ogden/Edison iron mine and mill, but urban development has continued to usurp the forests and lakes of the

PHOTO BY GEORGE J. HILL, M.D.

MINER'S HOME: This well-built house was moved to Main Street in Ogdensburg. It has been modernized and resided with new wooden clapboards.

Wallkill valley, as it has elsewhere in Sussex County and in other areas of rural northern New Jersey.

When Edison first visited Ogdensburg in October 1889, he found a town that was small but active commercially, in a part of the country that was rugged yet beautiful. Like most other rural American towns of this period, its main street was unpaved, but two railroads passed through Ogdensburg that had good connections to Newark and the industrial areas of eastern Pennsylvania. There were many men living in the valley and on the adjacent mountain who understood how to mine iron ore, and who were then unemployed. There was also abundant water and firewood for fuel, both of which Edison would need to operate his mill. Coal could be brought in and iron ore shipped out on the Ogden Mine Railroad that went directly up the north-south ridgeline to the mine site. Edison's teams of geological surveyors had combed the Appalachians with magnetometers, looking for iron ore, and here was a mine that bore the same name — Ogden — as that of his father and grandfather. We do not know if Edison was moved in any way, or even curious about, the Ogden connection, although residents in the area assume that he must have been aware of it. He was, we now know, a distant cousin of the founder of Ogdensburg, and of the original owner of the mine that he selected to be the site of this great commercial experiment.[291]

Ogdensburg offered two hotels to its visitors in the 1880s, and both are still standing on opposite sides of Main Street. The oldest, on the east side of the street, now called Lyons House, has been known by several names; David Lyon was its second owner. Edison is said to have been "a frequent guest" there when his mine was in operation. Across Main Street, on the river side of the street, was Walter Onsted's hotel, built in 1885, which became known as the Ogdensburg Hotel. Ogdensburg also had an Opera House and a General Store (which is still standing), and there was also a garage, a tavern, and a post office. The population in 1881 was about 560. One of the finest houses in town, three stories high with a mansard roof, was built sometime between 1853 and 1880 by John George, superintendent of the zinc mine. This house still stands on the west side of Main Street, opposite the end of Edison Road.[292]

PHOTO BY GEORGE J. HILL, M.D.

SPARTA MOUNTAIN: Edison's iron mine was located on the summit of what is now known as Sparta Mountain. Iron ore had been mined there many decades earlier by the Ogden family, to whom Edison was distantly related.

The Midland Railroad (now the N.Y., Susquehanna & Western) had its station on what is now known as Edison Road. The Midland ran five trains a day to Unionville and Jersey City. Several trains a day also passed through Ogdensburg en route between Jersey City and Stroudsville, Pennsylvania, on the other railroad, which was a branch of the Delaware, Lackawanna, and Western. This railroad, which is no longer in existence, had its station on Railroad Avenue, now known as Kennedy Avenue, a block north of the two hotels. Tensions existed between the townspeople and those who lived in the country, and in 1914 Ogdensburg became an independent borough, separating itself from Sparta township. The mine and mill that Edison built at Ogden Mine then became part of Sparta township, although the mine site was then and is still most directly approached from Ogdensburg.[293]

After the Edison mine closed, many of the houses that were built near the mine were moved to new locations. At least four were brought to Main Street in Ogdensburg, where they can be seen now, across from Lyons House, ranging north from Kennedy Avenue. The two that were nearest to the corner were joined in 1912 to become the Beierle General Store. These two houses were later brought together and covered by a

PHOTO BY GEORGE J. HILL, M.D.

SITE OF EDISON'S IRON SEPARATING PLANT: Today, only this patch of sand produced as a waste product of Edison's mining operation marks the location of what was once a large complex of buildings (see photo on page 191).

PHOTO BY GEORGE J. HILL, M.D.

THE HORSESHOE CUT: The huge excavation that Edison once envisioned as a new Yosemite (right) today is a modest canyon (above), reclaimed by the forest 90 years after Edison left.

single roof, while the other two are still detached, and are used as dwellings. The northern house of the detached pair has been modernized and re-sided with new wooden clapboards. The southern one of the detached pair of Edison houses in Ogdensburg is still covered with its original siding of thick wooden tongue-in-groove, shiplap boards, which are weathered but unwarped and in good condition.[294]

The "Horseshoe Cut" on Sparta Mountain: A Trip to Edison's Mine

He traveled by horse and buggy up to the plant in Sparta.

— **Paul Horuzy, 1990**[295]

COURTESY OF NATIONAL PARK SERVICE

WHEN Edison arrived in Ogdensburg, he would have approached the Ogden mine along a road that begins at Main Street about 100 yards north of the Lyons House. Now known as Edison Road, this road has been paved with asphalt in recent years, but it would have been rutted and rough in the 1890s. It is two and one-half miles from Main Street to the mine, and most of it is a steep uphill grade that would have been a hard pull then for a team of horses pulling a carriage or wagon. It would have been good exercise for workmen walking to the mine, as they did, and a slow plod for a horse and rider. My car overheated badly when I drove up this hill on one of my trips to the mine site. The road crosses the tracks of the "Susquehanna" railroad in one-half mile, and then rises steeply for another half mile. Edison Road then levels off for about one-half mile as it passes along an artificial lake known as Heater's Lake, which is Ogdensburg's municipal swimming and picnic area. Crossing the stream at the upper end of Heater's Lake, Edison Road rises steeply again for another mile, gradually turning to the south, until it reaches the crest of the ridge at an elevation of 1,200 feet.

This point (which is our goal, the entrance to the Edison mine site) is marked by a large wooden sign on the left (east) side of the road, announcing that this is "Sparta Mountain," a Wildlife Management Area under the protection of the New Jersey Department of Environmental Protection, Division of Fish, Game & Wildlife.[296]

Edison Road is posted by the New Jersey DEP on both sides with small metal signs on trees for a distance of about two miles, from Heater's Pond to an intersection about one mile beyond the sign for Sparta Mountain. It is thus only one and one-half miles along Edison Road from Main Street in Ogdensburg to the beginning of the site of the Edison mine and mill. The road is well-paved, though steep, and the site is readily accessible, if you know where it is located: look for the entrance beside the sign for Sparta Mountain Wildlife Management Area.

We are now at the site of Edison's mine and mill. But where are the ruins, and where is the devastated environment? The answer is that the buildings and equipment were all carried away, years ago, by Edison and by others, and the forest has grown back over the foundations and the mine pits. It has been written that "Only stone foundation remnants at various places off Edison Road . . . exist today." However, having read of Edison's plan to make a "Yosemite of our own here," and having seen pictures of the huge buildings that once filled frame after frame of photographs, I expected to see more here than just a sandy road that leads off into the woods. And having seen the enormous buildings of the abandoned Sterling Hill zinc mine on the other side of the valley, and the mine buildings and abandoned houses in ghost towns in the Rocky Mountains, I thought that there might be some visible trace of Edison's presence here. Indeed, I expected to find something that I could identify as Edison's work. In due time, Edison's "footprints" at this place became apparent, but I first had to get oriented in order to find them.[297]

My companions and I began by locating our position and direction on the Anderson/Bekaert map of the site of the mine and mill. This done, it was apparent that the road that led to the east into the woods was the main access road to the mill, which had been located only a few yards away from where we were then standing. We would soon proceed forward, to see what was left of the mill. But our attention was first drawn to Edison's mine, which, according to the map, was behind us, across Edison Road to the southwest.[298]

Edison referred to his mine as a new "Yosemite," and it was called "Horseshoe Cut" on the map. Barely visible through the trees and protected by a chain link fence, it now looked more like a small natural canyon than a mine pit. It was narrow, perhaps fifty yards across (the fence on the opposite side of the canyon was no more than one hundred yards away), and the two sides appeared to be no greater than forty feet high. There was a bit of water visible at the bottom of the gorge, on which autumn leaves were floating. The walls of the mine pit appeared to be of dark and weathered stone. From a distance, I would have thought that the stone was granite, although knowing that this gorge was once an iron mine, I supposed that it was iron ore, probably magnetite. The scene was a bit like The Flume in Crawford Notch, New Hampshire, or the glimpse of the base of Eagle Rock that I had finally gotten from Mountain Avenue in West Orange. The Edison mine bore no resemblance to what I expected. It was not at all like the enormous pits that exist all over America, after stone quarries have been abandoned and have filled up with water. I now finally understood what I had been told that Edison had done here: He went into an existing open pit mine with large equipment and followed the visible seam of iron ore, deepening and widening the seam. However, in spite of his grandiose words, I saw that Edison neither created a new "Yosemite," nor did he remove the top of a mountain.[299]

We turned our attention once again to the road that led to the mill site. A large evergreen tree that was adjacent to this access road may, I thought, have been spared when this road was created by Thomas Edison. The tree was a puzzle to me, and I couldn't identify it immediately. I later decided that it is probably a black spruce (*Picea mariana*). Although this location is at the southern edge of the black spruce's range, the cool climate on Sparta Mountain is apparently congenial to it. The DEP had posted signs on the evergreen tree that listed all the "Do Not's" that one could think of, except — as far as I could see in scanning the fine print — prohibition on removal of non-living and man-made objects such as foundation stones, bricks, building lumber, and metal objects. Whatever relics and remnants might exist of the eighteenth century Ogden Mine and the nineteenth century Edison mine and mill had apparently not yet been placed under DEP protection. I made a note to myself to check on this in the near future.[300]

The site of the Edison mill was now before us, less than one hundred yards from Edison Road, as we stood on a low hill, looking down at a flat sandy area about a quarter of a mile wide that was criss-crossed by all-terrain vehicle tracks and rimmed by bushes, grass, and low trees. Not a stick of wood or a piece of metal was immediately apparent, although on closer inspection there was a bit of trash on the surface here and there — beer bottles and recent household detritus. There were also a few old red bricks showing in the sand that might have been remnants of the enormous chimney that we saw in the pictures of the site.

PHOTO BY GEORGE J. HILL, M.D.

PITFALL: The woods on Sparta Mountain are laced with countless unmarked holes and dangerous clefts that were produced by two centuries of iron mining. This deep trough is one of Edison's environmental legacies.

Later, poking around in the trees and bushes at the edges of the sandy area, I found dozens of weathered boards and pieces of sawed lumber that were old enough to have been part of the Edison mill buildings, and a four-foot strip of attractive wooden molding, milled along the full length of three of its four sides, and at the ends. This site is crying out for protection, and for archaeological research, I thought.

We turned to the left, to the northeast, and tried to visualize where Edison's great reservoir was located. It had a capacity of 300,000 gallons, according to the map, and was filled from a pond, just out of sight at the east edge of the map. I later wondered if this was the pond called "Edison Pond" on modern maps. The reservoir was too far away in the woods for us to find on this rainy day. To the east, we looked at the low trees and wondered if there were any foundation stones left, or a cellar hole, at the site of Building No. 36, a dwelling which was marked as "Edison's" on the map. It would be about 500 yards away, just over the embankment where railroad tracks had once stretched across this site. If we had time, we could get there, for the trees in that direction were low and scattered. But Mr. Hadonowetz said that he had been out there once, and there was nothing remaining at that place above the ground. The search for traces of the house that might have been Edison's would, therefore, be a task for archaeology, and we thought it best not to disturb anything there.

Mr. Hadonowetz said that he understood that the sandy ground that formed the foreground of our view was all that remained of the enormous hill of sand that had been produced by the mill. The rest of the sand had been removed over the years by anyone in the vicinity who wanted it. I recalled that fine dust had been created by Edison's mill as an important step in the separation of the heavy, magnetic iron ore from the phosphorus that contaminated it, and that this dust must have had a high silica content. Photographs of the mill in operation show clouds of dust in the air, and Edison was covered with it when he came home to West Orange. The debilitating and sometimes fatal disease known as silicosis was, I thought, unknown in the 1890s, when this work was going on.

It occurred to one member of our group that we might investigate some old stone walls that we saw to our left, to the north of the Edison mill site. This suggestion proved to be fortuitous, for it led immediately to the discovery of a series of building foundations, rock-lined pits, deep crevices in the ground, and short stone walls, all of which were obviously older than the Edison mill, and for which the purposes, by and large, were mysterious to us. Mr. Dolan said that he had never been into this area, although it is within two hundred yards of Edison Road at the entrance to the mill site. In retrospect, it is remarkable that these stone foundations and rock-lined pits were preserved so well, considering the fact that hundreds of people lived and worked in this area for a century or more, and that they were located only a stone's throw from the enormous mills and buildings that Edison built in the 1890s.

Some of the areas of the old stone walls have been surrounded by chain link fences sometime within the past few decades. However, the fences have not been maintained well, and there are many gaps in the wire mesh which an unwary or foolish person could slip through to inspect the crevices and pits. One circular stone-lined pit, for example, is about seven feet in diameter, and I couldn't see the bottom of it from where I stood. It is possibly a well, although a water level is no longer apparent in it. Another pit is about five feet wide, and perhaps twenty feet long. The sides of this crevice are five to ten feet high, and it extends out of sight into the ground; it is perhaps an old surface mine. Another stone-lined pit is about forty feet long, ten feet deep, and six or seven feet wide. It is partially surrounded by a chain link fence, and it appears to be a major safety hazard, yet it would be fascinating to explore. Old pieces of wrought strap iron and iron barrel staves can be found throughout this area, as well as broken pottery, some of which may be twentieth century trash, but most of it appears to be of eighteenth or nineteenth century vintage. After we concluded our exploration of these ancient works, we discussed moving a bit to the northeast to see if we could locate the Iron Hill Cut that was shown on our map as an Edison mine. In the end, we decided not to do this, lest we tumble into the mine shaft, since no one present knew whether the Iron Hill Cut is protected by fencing, or if its edges are stable.

We then returned to Edison Road and drove about one-half mile south, to inspect the site of "Stock House 'No. 3'," which is Building No. 30 on the Anderson/Bekaert map. The southwest corner of the foundation of this building is readily visible from Edison Road, and it is only a few feet from the road. The rock foundation for this building is about six feet high and about thirty feet long, much as it appears on the map. We climbed up onto this foundation and there found three deep man-made, stone-lined, drywall troughs that extend for the entire length of the structure. Each trough is about five feet wide and six feet deep, and they are about twelve feet apart. They were deep enough and wide enough to make us look very carefully before we leaped across each one to examine the next, and before we jumped back over each one to return to the road. The function of the troughs and of the building (which is now gone) through which they passed is unclear. Perhaps, we thought, they may have been water-courses, or there may have been some sort of conveyor belts that passed along them. In any event, they were apparently upstream, so to speak, from the so-called "Briquette Loading Area" and the "Bricker Building." I marveled at how little we know about all of this, in spite of the analysis of the chemical engineering at the Edison mill that was written by Vanderbilt. It is clear that there is much work to be done to retrieve the function of each component of the mill, and to analyze the function of the complex as a whole from the perspective of the history of technology.

I was glad to have seen the location of the key components of Edison's iron mining operation — the Horseshoe Cut and the mill site — before they deteriorate any more, and to have had the opportunity to examine one of the concentrated iron ore "briquettes" that were produced by Edison's mill. My briquette was a gift of the Old Firehouse and Old Schoolhouse Museum, one of a thousand that were recovered some years ago from the mine site. It is very dark gray, almost black, and it has a powdery surface. The Edison iron ore briquette looks somewhat like the typical charcoal briquette that is used in backyard grilles, but it is about twice as large as a charcoal briquette (being two and one-half inches in diameter, and one and one-fourth inches thick). The Edison briquette is very heavy for its size, weighing fourteen ounces — nearly one pound — although it is small enough to fit into a pants pocket. A pocket compass needle is deflected twenty degrees when it is placed adjacent to the Edison briquette, which confirms that it is a concentrated mass of iron ore.

Other roads that are shown on the Anderson/Bekaert map are still visible at the mine site, although they are not passable. There were at one time 50 houses in Edison, similar to the two that can be seen at present along Main Street in Ogdensburg. None are present any longer at the mill and mine site. I could not find where the Ogden Mine Railroad and the road adjacent to it, called Ridge Road on the Franklin quadrangle map, crossed Edison Road. This area is now as quiet and free of landmarks as only a deep forest can be. When I returned alone to Sparta Mountain on 23 September, the only sound I heard was that of rain drops falling on dry leaves.[301]

This case study led me to concur with others that Edison constructed a very large mill for concentrating iron ore. However, although I concluded that the mill was large, I decided that it was not uniquely stupendous in size. In addition, although Edison's extension of the surface iron ore mine that had been started by previous owners of the Ogden Mine was also a large project, it, too, was by no means immense or monstrous. The size of Edison's mine and mill, in comparison with other facilities such as the mine and mill at Sterling Hill, were either exaggerated by Edison, or they have grown larger with storytelling as legends are wont to do.

Edison's principal objective here was to concentrate the iron in the low grade magnetite ore at Ogden, and to reduce the phosphorus in it, by a series of novel innovations that would make the mine a commercially viable source of iron for the manufacture of steel. In this regard, he was partially successful. He was, however, unable to compete with the high grade iron ore that was, by chance, discovered at about the same time at the Mesabi area in Minnesota, near Lake Superior. Edison's second objective in this project was to make money, in order to fund his research laboratory. He failed to achieve this goal. Edison also wanted to enjoy what he was doing, and in this he was successful, for he enjoyed his work at Ogdensburg. Another objective was to improve the lives of human beings, and in this he succeeded in Ogdensburg. The contemporary record, the legends, and the current assessment by local historians and the descendants of Edison's workers confirm his interest in the health and spirit of his workers and their families. While this objective may appear to be paternalistic by present standards, and his mill may have lacked the safety features that would be required in the late twentieth century, there is no reason to believe that Edison intended anything but a fair and decent life for his workers. Indeed, he provided good housing, with electricity and running water, and he was personally involved with the worklife and culture of his workers and their families. Edison stayed at the mine site, or close to it, and he regularly exposed himself to the same dangers and pleasures that his workers experienced. Another of Edison's objectives in this work, as in all of his projects, was to enhance his image, and in this he was successful in Ogdensburg, if not in the world at large. He was admired when he came to Ogdensburg, and also when he left. Edison's reputation as a man who did his best under trying circumstances persists in Ogdensburg to this day.

Finally, Edison attempted to improve the lot of miners and mine owners everywhere, and in this he succeeded. His magnetic ore separation method was said to have been useful in removing undesired iron and manganese from the zinc of franklinite ore. Edison's method may have been an important component of the continuing success of the Sterling Hill zinc mine.[302] Furthermore, Edison's production of a safe battery powered miner's lamp in 1914 was a significant advance over the previously used carbide safety lamp. The Edison safety lamp was used at Sterling Hill for the next seven decades, which is a remarkably durable record of success.

Many aspects of Edison's work at Ogdensburg are still shrouded in mystery, and will not be clarified until the archivists at the Edison National Historic Site and the Edison Papers Project's historians have had a chance to study the documents related to this period in his life. For example, we cannot say how much land Edison owned, controlled, and worked in his mining operations in Sussex County. Figures cited range from 1,000 acres, to 2,200 acres, to 16,000 acres. Having stood at the place where Edison worked, I would estimate that the effective size of the Edison mine and mill was only about 160 to 320 acres; i.e., somewhere between one quarter to one half of a square mile. The mine and mill site may have been larger, but surely not more than one square mile (640 acres), unless there are additional areas that do not appear on the Anderson/Bekaert map of his works, and are unknown to those who live in Ogdensburg and have studied his operations there. More to the point, Edison's active operations did not cover the entire area of the old Ogden

Mine, some of which remains virtually the same as it was when Edison's predecessors discontinued their operations.[303]

Recent History of the Edison Mine Site

Sparta Mountain . . . boasts mines once used by Thomas Edison. . . . a place where bobcat and coyote roam, and a place that owls, hawks, wild turkeys and blue heron call home.

— "Sparta Mountain Saved," 1997[304]

THE Sparta Mountain Wildlife Management Area (WMA) now consists of 1,394 acres, of which eighty percent is owned by the State of New Jersey, and twenty percent is owned by the New Jersey Audubon Society. Some 1,750 acres on Sparta Mountain were protected with a $5 million land acquisition that was concluded on 11 February 1997. The Fish, Game, and Wildlife Service of the Department of Environmental Protection manages the entire property, and its regulations govern all activities on the Sparta Mountain WMA. The Audubon Society owns the portion of the land that is traversed by the Highland Trail, while the Ogden/Edison mines are in the portion that is owned by the State of New Jersey. Within the WMA there is also a landlocked section to the west of Edison Road, near Hawthorne Lake, that is still privately owned. The area called "Edison" on the DEP's topographical map of the WMA is at an elevation of about 1,230 feet above sea level, and the highest point on the property is a short distance to the north of this point, at an elevation of 1,320 feet. A small body of water known as "Edison Pond" is located southeast of the point called "Edison" on the WMA topographical map.[305]

It is clear that the New Jersey Department of Environmental Protection should place a high priority on protecting the Sparta Mountain area as a historically important site. The DEP should improve its control and guidance of the public with respect to access and safety, and prohibit disturbance of historical artifacts and ruins at the Sparta Mountain Wildlife Management Area, which includes the Ogden Mine and the Edison Mine and Mill Site.

Transition from Iron to Cement

Large masses of the rock contain from 10 to 12% magnetite.

> *The existence of this large amount of iron-bearing material led to the experiments of the N.J. and Pennsylvania Concentrating Co., extending from 1889 to 1901.*
>
> — M. R. Pustay and T. K. Shea, 1982[306]

EDISON'S biographers agree that after the inventor terminated his iron mining operations in the northern New Jersey Highlands he moved much of his mining machinery and equipment to Stewartsville, near the western border of New Jersey, where he mined limestone and produced Portland cement. But when did he begin to construct a plant at Stewartsville, and when did he terminate his work at Ogden/Edison? Regarding these questions, the information provided by Edison's biographers and in the Edison Papers Project's *Chronology* is sketchy and conflicting. Pustay and Shea state that Edison worked with iron ore in New Jersey from 1889 to 1901. However, specific dates and precise locations for events related to the end of Edison's work with iron ore and the beginning of his work with limestone and cement are virtually non-existent in other publications. As I concluded my case study of Edison's mining operations near Ogdensburg, I began to wonder what the precise sequence of events was as he looked about for new ways to use his mining and milling equipment. I also wondered why Edison decided to locate his limestone mining and cement manufacturing plant at Stewartsville — or New Village, as some historians had referred to it. And, of course, I wondered what role the environment, as I have broadly defined it, played in Edison's decision to move from Sussex County to Warren County. My attention was therefore drawn to what I call Edison's "transition from iron to cement." The limestone of Warren County southwest of Ogden/Edison, in the Southern Highlands of New Jersey, and the gateway to the Southern Highlands was Lake Hopatcong.[307]

Edison and Lake Hopatcong

> *In the year 1818, a man by the name of George P. McCullough, of Morristown, New Jersey, while with a fishing party at Lake Hopatcong, conceived the plan of constructing a waterway from Phillipsburg to Jersey City, using the waters of the lake to feed the waterway.*
>
> —John Johnson, 1977[308]

I previously mentioned that, by chance, I discovered that Morris County Route 615 in Jefferson Township, just north of Lake Hopatcong and about ten miles south of Ogdensburg, is known locally as "Edison Road." I regarded this finding as a possible clue to the presence of the inventor in the vicinity of Lake Hopatcong, and I sought to determine if Edison Road/Route 615 might represent his "footprints" near the lake. My search led to conversations with several people who live or spend their holidays in this area, and to the examination of old maps, photographs, and compilations of local history. I also had the good fortune to receive copies of previously unpublished correspondence and notes made by Edison in 1900; these items came from a friend who heard that I was studying this period in the inventor's life. I eventually created a possible scenario for the chain of events that led to the inventor's transit between his mine at Ogden/Edison and his new operations in western New Jersey. The Morris Canal and Lake Hopatcong are central features in my scenario, so I begin this section of "transition from iron to cement" by describing the environment of the canal and the lake as they existed at the turn of the century.[309]

In order to recreate the environment in the area around Lake Hopatcong in the period from, say, 1890 to 1910, I will describe some of the key geographic features in this area as they exist at present, and as they existed in about 1900, when Edison was in the process of shifting his operations from Ogden/Edison to Stewartsville/New Village. As the canal continued west, it crossed the Pompton River tributary of the Passaic and passed into Morris County between Pompton Plains and Lincoln Park. The Morris Canal then followed the north bank of another tributary of the Passaic, the Rockaway River, through Montville and Boonton to Rockaway. This is now the route that is taken by U.S. Highway 202. From Rockaway, the canal proceeded west through Dover and Wharton to reach the southern tip of Lake Hopatcong, along the corridor of Interstate 80.[310]

The Morris Canal's outlet lock on Lake Hopatcong was 39.80 miles east of the Port Delaware basin on the Delaware River at Phillipsburg, N.J. For reference, we may note that, counting east from the Delaware River, Dover — which was mentioned above — was at about 48 miles, Denville was at 53 miles, Boonton was at 58, Pompton at 72, Paterson 78, Bloomfield 85, and Newark was at 90 miles from the Delaware River. Proceeding east from Newark on the Morris Canal, Jersey City was 102.30 miles from the Delaware River at Phillipsburg. There were twenty-three inclined planes and thirty-four locks on the canal, which were numbered to the east and west from the highest point on the canal: Lake Hopatcong, 914 feet above sea level.[311]

The canal turned southwest from Lake Hopatcong and passed along the southern border of Sussex County for a few miles. It then went west through Warren County to the western border of New Jersey. After Hopatcong the canal passed through Netcong, Stanhope, Byram, and Waterloo to reach Hackettstown on the route that is now followed through Allamuchy State Park by County Route 604. From Hackettstown, County Route 629 and New Jersey Route 57 are now the approximate routes that the Morris Canal took through the towns of Washington, New Village, and Stewartsville to reach Phillipsburg, where the canal terminated at the Delaware River. Along the route of the canal, we can still identify once-important locations such as Landing, near Wharton; Port Morris, at Lake Hopatcong; Netcong, which was once a reservoir for Lake Hopatcong; and Rockport, Port Murray, Port Colden, and Port Warren between Hackettstown and Phillipsburg.[312]

The Morris Canal was opened for operation from Newark to Phillipsburg in 1831, the ninety mile trip taking five days. Some 58,259 tons of commodities were transported on the canal in 1845 and commerce on the canal reached a peak of 899,220 tons in 1866. Coal was the principal product carried on the canal from 1855 on, while iron ore was another major commodity that was transported on canal boats. The route of the Morris Canal was also ideal for the construction of railroads, which provided increasing competition for the canal. The canal lost thirty-four per cent of its coal business to the Delaware, Lackawanna, and Western Railroad (D.L.&W. R.R.) in 1870. This was followed by a major loss of iron ore transportation to the Central Railroad of New Jersey (C.R.R.N.J.) in 1881. As the result of the decrease in business on the canal, by 1903 the New Jersey Legislature was considering a recommendation to abandon it. Operation of the Morris Canal was discontinued in 1924, a century after it was chartered.[313]

In spite of the bleak figures that were reported for canal business in the last decades of the nineteenth century, the Morris Canal continued to be a major source of transportation of finished goods and raw materials for communities along the western part of its course during the period from 1890 to 1910. One hundred forty-four published photographs of the canal and its environment in this period, from Wharton (Lock Three East) to Port Warren (Plane Nine West), show vibrant activity and well-loaded boats in a pleasant rural environment. This was the portion of the Morris Canal that Edison would have traveled along as he rode the D.L.&W. Railroad from his iron mine to his cement works. Photographs of the canal, the adjacent railroad line, and the bridges, farms, locks, and canal boats provide vivid illustrations of the environment in the countryside between Wharton in Morris County (where the Ogden Mine Railroad joined the D.L.& W.) and the New Village/Stewartsville area in Warren County (where Edison was securing property and building rights for his cement works).[314]

Although the canal was steadily losing business to the railroads, Edison could see that it was still an important method of transportation in the area around Stewartsville. Canal boats received large amounts of coal from railroad hopper cars at Port Delaware. And the coal used for Edison's cement plant at New Village came from canal boats that were loaded at Port Delaware (elevation 220 feet) and then docked at Henry Stone's store, eight miles east at Stewartsville (elevation 400 feet). When she was ninety-three, in 1974, Stone's daughter, Helena, recalled that:

My father sold coal — the first coal ever used at the Edison Cement Plant... And Thomas A. bought the coal from my father.... In fact he sold him, I think, all the coal they ever used there.... My father used to go out when Thomas A. came down to pick up eggs that he'd bought to bring down to Orange over the weekend. He and my father would have quite a long talk out beside the buggy that Thomas A. drove from New Village. And he would take home eggs and I suppose butter because we took in butter in exchange for food, you see.[315]

Ms. Stone recalled that her father transported the coal in a wagon drawn by two horses, and this is presumably how Edison originally got his coal. We shall see that Edison later had a railroad spur constructed to link his cement plant with the main line of the D.L.&W. Railroad in Stewartsville. The railroad spur to the Edison Portland Cement Company originated at the point where the main rail line crossed the Morris Canal — i.e., at about the same place where Henry Stone's store was located.

Concurrent Operations at Ogden/Edison and Stewartsville/New Village

How do you expect me to decide the route of a proposed road when I have no maps at Edison. Remember I have no maps here.

—Thomas Alva Edison, to Judge Elliott, 1900[316]

CORRESPONDENCE and notes that were exchanged between Edison and his employees in the spring and early summer of the year 1900 show that the inventor was still vigorously engaged in his decade-old iron mining project at Edison in Sussex County, while he was at the same time active in the development of his new cement manufacturing operation in Warren County. The fifteen pages of documents in the Pierce Papers confirm that between 10 May and 26 July 1900 Edison was simultaneously overseeing minute details of his iron and cement projects in rural New Jersey, as well as other activities that stretched across the ocean from West Orange to England. His telephone call from Sussex County to Judge Elliott in Stewartsville in Warren County on 22 June 1900 was made in response to Elliott's long telephone message on the same day which described a parcel of land that Edison wished to acquire for his cement works, but Edison could not figure out exactly what Elliott was talking about. At the age of 53, Edison was an impatient employer who rapidly became irascible when he didn't get exactly what he wanted, when he wanted it. And he did not care whether his employees understood the purpose of his request so that they could, if necessary, provide a substitute in order to meet his deadline.

Only a month earlier, Edison's anger with a hapless employee named Olmsted was ignited by Olmsted's failure to meet Edison's requirement to have fifty pounds of a certain kind of finely divided wool of a specific length delivered no later than "tonight," at the mine. The wool might have to be obtained in New York City, or from a number of "small woolen mills in the vicinity" of New York if necessary, but "It is very important we have it tonight = Don't get long staple wool but the short staple common wool that is very crinky." Edison was certain that small mills "would not refuse to sell . . . 50 lbs as a special accommodation" to him. Edison was furious with Olmsted when he was told that Olmsted could not get anything but samples, because all the mills say "they would not do carding for outside parties." In his first note to Olmsted on the 17th, Edison wrote that "I am disappointed that you fail to understand so simple a request."[317]

When Olmsted replied that he couldn't locate what Edison wanted, the inventor castigated him in a third note on the same day, by writing that "It would seem to me that any boy would understand from my telegram that I didn't want samples but wanted the stuff tonight . . . I shall not have another case like this occur again if I can help it." There is no indication in these notes why Edison had such an urgent need for wool, and what happened when it didn't arrive. It is, indeed, difficult for me to imagine what Edison needed this wool for at his iron mine, and Olmsted did not appear to know either. Could it be for use as binder in his briquettes, or for packing delicate instruments? This incident appears to be another example of the imperious, secretive behavior by Edison that the chemist, William Hand, observed at Silver Lake, and which created a difficult — even dangerous — work environment there. These notes also show that in May and June 1900 Edison intended to be very much in charge of the operations at the iron mine as well as in West Orange.[318]

One of Edison's biographers pointed out that Edison never patented the mixture and method that he used to form his briquettes of concentrated iron ore, in order to keep the method secret from his competitors. In July 1900 Edison was enthusiastic about the excellent output from his "Bricker," which had just produced a run of thirty-five tons, "not one tenth of one per cent broken." After baking, his "dead black" briquettes cooled off in six minutes and they were "perfectly water proof even when put in water hot." Edison was then responding to urgent telephone calls for briquettes, and he believed that he would be able to meet the deadline that he had received from "Stanhope" (a village on the railroad and the Morris Canal, just west of Lake Hopatcong). Others have speculated that Edison may have used molasses as a binder for his briquettes. He was also known to have used bentonite clay for this purpose, and bentonite was a key ingredient in his process for making Portland cement. The Pierce Papers provide insight into the briquetting process. In Edison's memorandum of 26 July 1900 we see that the inventor ordered fifty tons of coal tar and fifty tons of pitch, which were apparently intended to serve as a binder for his concentrated iron ore powder, and to make the briquettes waterproof.[319]

The Pierce Papers also show us that Edison was acutely aware of his geographic environment. In his three notes of 17 May 1900, Edison referred to the towns of Franklin (which is five miles north of Ogdensburg), Dover (ten miles east of Lake Hopatcong), and Stanhope (three miles west of the lake); and to the Susquehanna [railroad]. Edison's letterhead states that the "Works" [i.e., the mine] of the New Jersey and Pennsylvania Concentrating Works is "On High Bridge Branch, C.R.R. of N.J., 92 miles from Jersey City, N.J.," at "Edison, Sussex County, N.J." He also referred to his mine site as "Edison" in the hand-written note of 22 June 1900 that he addressed to the team that was buying land for him in Stewartsville. Interestingly, however, Edison did not refer to either Ogdensburg or Sparta in these papers. This is a minor point, but it reinforces my notion that Edison's connecting link with West Orange and Stewartsville was the Ogden Mine Railroad (which ran directly down the ridgeline from his mine to Lake Hopatcong). The Ogden Mine Railroad, which later became a part of the system known as the Central Railroad of New Jersey (C.R.R.N.J.), was never connected with the railroads that ran in the Wallkill River Valley two to three miles west of the mine, nor did the railroads in the Wallkill Valley connect directly to the main line of the D.L.&W. R.R.[320]

The main line of the D.L.&W. R.R., which was sometimes called just "the Lackawanna," ran west parallel to the Morris Canal from Lake Hopatcong to Stewartsville and Phillipsburg.[321] What is left of the northern route of the D.L.&W. is now known as the Montclair Branch of the Morris and Essex Rail Line of New Jersey Transit.[322] Edison referred to this branch of the D.L.&W. when he wrote on 22 June 1900:

The road that I wanted ran from the depot along the Railroad northward beyond a hill where there was bend in the railroad & then turned east across the extreme north end of our property and at juncture of the adjoining property.[323]

* * * * *

At some point in time after July 1900, Edison made his final trip down the Ogden Mine Railroad from Edison to Wharton, where he transferred to the D.L.&W. and left his iron mine behind forever. In the next three decades, Edison would travel west on many occasions from West Orange to Warren County, where he constructed a remarkable group of concrete and brick buildings and dug holes in the ground that dwarfed the new "Yosemite" that he left behind on Sparta Mountain. We now turn to Warren County.[324]

Chapter 11

Edison and Cement: Warren, Union and Essex Counties (1899-1931)

The farmers near the plant complained so much about limestone dust that the Edison lawyers bought them out, but then leased the land back to them. The limestone powder was great for the land!

—Charles Hummel, 1997[325]

IN answer to my question about the environmental impact of the Edison Portland Cement Company, Charles Hummel passed along a legend that he had heard regarding the limestone dust that was generated from Edison's quarry and cement plant at New Village, New Jersey. The farmers in the vicinity, said Hummel, had not liked the dust that Edison was producing, but in the end they were satisfied either by the improvement that limestone produced in their land, or by compensation, or both. Charles Hummel is a credible authority, for he is an acknowledged expert on Edisonia — the material objects associated with Thomas Edison or that were produced by his companies — and he is also a lecturer for the Charles Edison Foundation. Mr. Hummel's story about the farmers in New Village and Stewartsville is remarkable in that this minimally critical anecdote is the only adverse comment that I encountered in my case study of Edison's impact on the environment around his cement plant in Warren County. In contrast to the negative comments from Edison's neighbors regarding the environmental impact of his work at Menlo Park, in West Orange, and at Silver Lake, Edison's limestone quarry and cement plant were generally regarded benignly by those who lived nearby.[326]

In this case study I sought to determine the nature of Edison's personal environment in Warren County, and what impact he had on the environment there. And as in my previous case studies, I also attempted to determine what aspects of the environment led him to come to Warren County, and what objectives, if any, he had for the environment in that vicinity. The background for this case study included the comments about Edison's work with cement that appeared in the biographies of the inventor by Josephson, Conot, Melosi, Millard, Baldwin, and Vanderbilt. Several references that I used in previous case studies were also useful in this study.[327] I was guided by the advice of a number of individuals, and I developed several new sources related to Warren County and Edison's work with cement. I appreciate the suggestions and comments that I received from Charles Hummel and James ("Jim") Lee, who I have mentioned previously; and Gary Meddaugh, Marie Acceturo, Linda Kimler, Dr. Charles E. Crandall, George K. Warne, and John ("Jack") Brun. I am especially grateful for the information that Carl Brown provided to me. This study is also based on field trips that I made to Warren County on 30 September 1997 and 25 April 1998; to Union, New Jersey, on 6 August 1997; to various sites in Essex County in 1997 and 1998; and on a number of telephone conversations in 1997 and 1998.[328]

In the Beginning: Formation of the Highlands and Valleys of Western New Jersey

Limestone, which occurs mostly in the southwestern part of the region, ranges from 100 to 600 feet in thickness.
— **Alison E. Mitchell, 1992**[329]

It was this incredibly deep bed of limestone in the Southern Highlands of New Jersey that drew Thomas Edison to Warren County. By the time he came to New Village and Stewartsville, about eight miles east of the Delaware River and forty-five miles west of West Orange, Edison had learned that limestone was readily accessible in this area. And he knew that the limestone of New Village had a chemical composition that made it well suited for conversion to Portland cement. We shall later see that other aspects of the environment in this region were important for the inventor, but the physical environment — the abundant cement rock, gravel, and water — in Warren County was crucial to the success of his plan for the Edison Portland Cement Company. The physical environment of the Southern Highlands was formed over a span of time that is so great that it is difficult to grasp. As we examine the environment that Edison found here in 1900, it is important for us to recognize that:

A long series of geological events, so ancient that they probably exceed human comprehension, have shaped the physical character of the Highlands region, resulting in a varied topography characterized by ridges and valley underlain by ancient rocks — primarily Precambrian in age.... Furthermore, the region has been scoured by three glaciers that have greatly influenced the location and quality of its soils.[330]

The Precambrian (Middle Proterozoic) rocks that underlie the Highlands are the oldest in New Jersey; many are over a billion years old. The carbonate rocks of the Highlands, which include the limestone that Edison mined, are water soluble rocks that are composed of calcium carbonate and calcium-magnesium carbonate. The carbonate rocks of the Highlands also include marble, which is common in Sussex County, where Edison's iron mine on Sparta Mountain was located, and dolomite (magnesium limestone). In 1881, nine years before Edison began to acquire limestone-bearing land in the Pohatcong Creek valley above Stewartsville, it was written that:

The magnesian limestone is the common blue limestone of the Kittatinny valley and is a prevailing and important formation in Warren County. . . . [It] occupies the valley of the Pohatcong Creek from Mount Bethel to Stewartsville. . . . Between Washington and Stewartsville it averages one and a half miles [in width]. . . . The whole valley is assumed to be of limestone basis, the boundaries of which coincide with the mountains that enclose it.[331]

There is indeed a lot of limestone in this area. In the southwestern part of the Highlands, the Cambrian-Ordovician Kittatinny Formation of carbonate rock ranges from 3,000 to 4,000 in thickness, while Jacksonsonburg Limestone in this region is from 100 to 600 feet thick.[332] The ridges and valleys that characterize the New Jersey Highlands began to form with the differential erosion of the more resistant Proterozoic rocks and less resistant rocks of the Paleozoic period. The Highland ridges and valleys, which generally range from northeast to southwest, were later sculpted by the same Pleistocene glaciers that we previously encountered in our review of the geology of the Watchung Mountains in eastern New Jersey. These were the so-called Kansan and Illinoian glaciers, and the most recent icecap — the Wisconsin — which began to retreat about 20,000 years ago. The southern limit of the Wisconsin glacier left a terminal moraine which stretches from Belvidere, the shire town of Warren County, on the Delaware River, through Hackettstown and Dover to Morristown, and then southeast to Perth Amboy. Or, if you will, from the Delaware Water Gap to Lake Hopatcong and then south along the Raritan River to the Atlantic Ocean. This is the route of I-80 from Pennsylvania to Parsippany-Troy Hills, N.J., and then along I-287 to Raritan Bay and the southern tip of Staten Island, N.Y.[333]

Gravel and till deposited by the Wisconsin glacier overlie the valleys of the Highlands to a depth of up to 250 feet. Edison's environment in the Southern Highlands thus included clay, gravel, and limestone that were formed by eons of geological activity, and which were to be essential elements of his industrial environment in Warren County. These elements were necessary, but the characteristics of the physical environment were not, by themselves, sufficient for Edison to proceed with his development. As we shall soon see, the physical aspects of the geological and topographical environment of the Southern Highlands were additionally modified during the past ten to twelve millennia, especially in the past two centuries. The recent changes in the Southern Highlands were predominantly the result of human work — of the human activity that produced the environment which Edison needed for his new industrial operations in the valley of the Musconetcong River.[334]

Lenni Lenape to Daniel Beatty:
Human Impact on the Musconetcong Valley

The earliest known period of human occupation in the region is represented by the Paleo-Indian Period (10,000 - 8,000 B.C.).

— Alison E. Mitchell, 1992[335]

IT is not an easy task to recreate the environment of the earliest Native Americans who lived in the Musconetcong Valley from ten to twelve thousand years ago. This is now a valley of farms and

PHOTO BY GEORGE J. HILL, M.D.

RURAL LANDSCAPE: Pohatcong Creek still flows past broad fields and farmland in the Musconetcong Valley, where the Lenni Lenape once hunted and farmed. It was home to a major Edison industrial complex until 1942, and now the land is changing again as housing developments spring up.

factories, and of towns, roads and railroads. This area is also the home of many species of Old World plants and animals that were intentionally imported by Europeans, or that traveled with them as unintended passengers. These new species have suppressed or displaced much of the native flora and fauna. Archaeologists are, however, able to show that the Paleo-Indians of twelve millennia ago were hunter-gatherers who shared their still-cold post-glacial valley with mammoth and mastodons. These great mammals, like their hunters, are, of course, now extinct. The Plenge Site near the Musconetcong River in Warren County "represents a major encampment of the period and is one of the most important Paleo-Indian sites in the Northeast." Tools found there are similar to those in only one other Paleo-Indian location, the Debert Site in Nova Scotia.[336]

In the thousands of years between the time of the early Indians and the arrival of European colonists, the Musconetcong Valley became warmer, and its occupants grew "more efficient in their utilization of the surrounding environment." Changes in the lives of the Indians in the Musconetcong Valley have been revealed by archaeological evidence of stone toolmaking and cultivation of tobacco and other crops such as corn, beans and squash. Shards of fired clay ceramic pottery have been found and cordage manufacturing has been demonstrated in a number of campsites in the Highlands, including the Musconetcong Valley. During the Archaic Period (8,000 to 1,000 B.C.) and the Woodland Period (c.1,000 B.C. to 1,600 A.D.), "Habitation sites grew larger and became more permanent, with base camps located on large floodplains."[337]

At first glance, few signs are apparent as reminders of permanent, human-induced changes in the landscape of the valley before the arrival of European colonists. However, "Native Americans . . . had a significant and long-term impact on the landscape and land use, and on later European settlement" in this area. "Agricultural sites were generally situated near land that was easily cultivated, particularly in river bottomlands." The soil in this area was easily tilled by hoes that the Native Americans made from stone, tortoise shells, or large bones, and "New fields were cleared every few years, since soil fertility decreased with repeated use of the same land. Thus . . . the impact of Lenape farming on the landscape was extensive."[338]

During the early part of the so-called Contact Period, trade goods such as glass beads, "fragments of a clay tobacco pipe bowl, a piece of iron wire," found their way into Indian villages, although "much of this region remained unsettled by the colonists longer than most other areas of New Jersey." The Native Americans who inhabited the Musconetcong Valley called themselves the Lenni Lenape, and they were referred to by the English as the Delaware Indians. We previously encountered the Lenape in the history of European settlement of Newark and the Watchung Mountains in Essex County and of Elizabethtown in Union County. European occupation of the New Jersey Highlands began in the 1650s, when "Dutchmen from Esopus (Kingston, New York) started to dig copper out of the Kittatinny Mountain." However, the Dutch did not continue long with their mining activities: "There were no markets downriver when copper began heading for Esopus, . . . and when the English took over all of New Jersey in 1664, the Dutch just stopped digging copper and settled down to farming."[339]

The geography of Warren County offered impressive potential opportunities for industrial growth, but these possibilities were not pursued by the early English landowners. Neither William Penn (who owned five thousand acres at Foul Rift, on the Delaware) nor several other early owners of large tracts developed their properties. An exception was the iron furnace that was built at Oxford in 1743, which was "booming" by the 1750s. The Oxford Furnace was then owned by the Shippen family, and Oxford was a great social center for wealthy Philadelphians. One of the Colonial-era visitors to Oxford was the beautiful and flamboyant Miss Peggy Shippen, a niece of the owners of the Oxford Furnace, who later achieved notoriety as the wife of Benedict Arnold. We will visit Oxford again in the twentieth century, when it was the site of one of Edison's quarries.[340]

By 1809 the timber necessary to support the Oxford Furnace had been used up, and the iron forge there was shut down. However, farmland was opened up as the trees were cut, and the Southern Highlands began to show the steady, quiet progress in agricultural development which has continued up to the present time. Warren County was created by the New Jersey legislature in 1824, when it was separated from Sussex County. The new county, where Oxford, Stewartsville, and New Village were located, took the name of General Joseph Warren — a Colonial physician who was fatally wounded at the Battle of Bunker Hill. Warren County was then, as now, a region of farms and forests. As recently as 1986, the 142,000 acres of Warren County still contained the largest amount of agricultural land (59,899 acres) of any county in New Jersey. And at the same time, only Hunterdon County had as high a percentage of agricultural land (42%) and as low a percentage of urban land (21%) as Warren County. Some 37% of Warren County land (52,155 acres) was still forested in 1986.[341]

Although Warren County was predominantly a rural county when it was created, a modest level of industrial development began to take place early in the nineteenth century. Industrialization in Warren County principally developed along the routes of the Morris Canal, the Delaware River, and several of its tributaries. These streams included the Musconetcong and Pequest Rivers and Pohatcong and Lopatcong Creeks. The Morris Canal, as we have previously seen, was chartered in 1824 and began to carry freight between Phillipsburg and Newark in 1831. Phillipsburg was across the Delaware from Easton, Pennsylvania, which was built at the mouth of the Lehigh River and was the terminus of the Lehigh Canal. Not surprisingly, Phillipsburg and Easton were early rivals, with Easton, on the Lehigh, usually outstripping Phillipsburg in every way. Only in recent years has a truce been more or less agreed upon that acknowledges the mutual interdependence of both cities. Easton and Phillipsburg are now tied to each other by Interstate 78 on its way from Newark to central Pennsylvania. Photographs of Phillipsburg at the beginning of the twentieth century, when

Edison began his operations less than eight miles to the west, show an impressive array of railroad lines passing through the city. The railroads were clustered around Port Delaware — the western terminus of the Morris Canal. And in the early 1900s, Charles Ingersoll, who was later to become Edison's partner in the building of cement houses, was then building his own his industrial plant in Phillipsburg. The Ingersoll-Rand factory can be seen to this day on the south side of Interstate 78 near the Delaware River bridge in Phillipsburg.[342]

The major population centers in Warren County initially developed along the rivers and streams, as they did elsewhere in colonial America and in the early days of the Republic. Belvidere, which became the county seat, was at the mouth of the Pequest River, a few miles south of the Delaware Water Gap. Hackettstown was the principal town of the upper Musconetcong valley; it was located on the north or right bank of the Musconetcong, across the river from Morris County. Streams that arose in the broad lower valley of the Musconetcong provided water and power for other towns, such as Phillipsburg and Washington, which was originally called Mansfield. Washington was located on Pohatcong Creek, upstream from Stewartsville and New Village, while Phillipsburg was on Lopatcong Creek. Both of these streams drained directly into the Delaware River. Warren County was principally a rural area until after the Civil War, when coal arrived in sufficient amounts on the Morris Canal and railroads to fuel the development of factories and foundries. By 1880, Hackettstown had ten carriage factories and a five story brick building housing the Centenary Collegiate Institute — now Centenary College. At the same time, Washington, only a few miles away, became the organ-making center of America. Daniel Beatty's five-story factory turned out 500 organs a month until it burned down in 1881. "Beattytown" is still a charming village of nineteenth century houses on the outskirts of Washington, in Warren County, New Jersey.[343]

During the nineteenth century the Musconetcong and Pohatcong valleys were largely occupied by farmers, however, not industrial workers. The farmers in this part of Warren County were not wealthy, but they were successful in their work, and they were not poorly educated. Many sturdy and attractive buildings were built along the major roads of southwestern Warren County in the early decades of the nineteenth century. A large number of prosperous farms, with fine cut stone houses and mills and great wooden barns, were located in Stewartsville and New Village at the turn of the twentieth century, when Edison decided to go into the cement business in this area. The inventor had to learn how to function in the environment that was controlled by the farmers and owners of small businesses in this part of Warren County. As we shall see, Edison was, indeed, successful in adapting to this rural environment.[344]

From West Orange to New Village: Edison Comes to Pohatcong Creek

The road I wanted ran from the depot along the railroad northward beyond a hill where there was a bend in the railroad & then turned east across the extreme north end of our property. . . . Starting at the Lackawanna station follow along [the] rail way to the bridge on Sally Boyers place then across the valley east to the road along the mountain.

— Thomas Alva Edison, 1900[345]

In a flurry of urgent activity on the afternoon of the first day of summer in 1900, Thomas Edison personally described the right of way that he wanted to acquire for a new road that would link his cement plant near Pohatcong Creek in Warren County to a road that ran from New Village to Stewartsville, New Jersey. At the moment that the inventor was writing out this description of his proposed road to Judge Elliott, who was representing the Edison Portland Cement Company before the Township Committee in Stewartsville, he was more than thirty miles away at his iron mine in Sussex County. Several telephone messages flashed back and forth that afternoon between Stewartsville and Edison, at least three from Judge Elliott and two from the inventor. Edison twice bemoaned his lack of a map ("Remember I have no maps here"), but the inventor clarified his intentions by drawing a sketch map that indicated his recollection of the existing roads, buildings, and natural landmarks near his "Cement Co." and the "DL+W" railroad.[346]

The Edison-Elliott messages in June 1900 reveal much about the inventor's awareness of the environment, and how he thought it could be modified to suit his needs. The brief passage quoted in the epigraph for this section shows that Edison had a strong sense of space and place. He had a good memory for natural features ("hill" and "mountain") and for the built environment (e.g., railroad, depot, and road). Edison also indicates that his concept of the environment was proprietary, as he mentions "Sally Boyers place" and "our property." We shall later return to examine these communications in more detail.

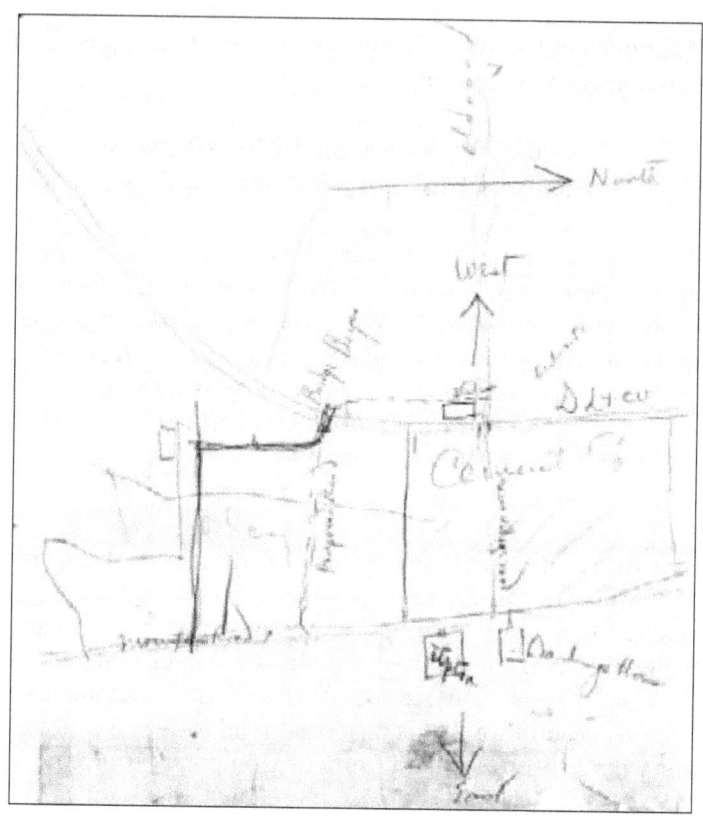

COURTESY OF PROFESSOR MARGARET PIERCE

IN EDISON'S HAND: In this map that he drew from memory, Edison visualized how his cement factory in New Village would fit into both the natural and built environment. It was adjacent to the railroad, a stream, and existing roads. He first planned the factory and then found a source of cement rock just up the road from his plant.

    The comments that Edison made, and the map that he sketched to illustrate his plan for a new road, show that his cement operations were already well underway in Warren County in June 1900. How and when, we may ask, did Edison first become acquainted with this part of New Jersey, and what was the environment like when he arrived there? It is possible now to offer a preliminary or rudimentary reply, based on a synthesis of comments made by other writers and a study of the routes that Edison would have used to reach Pohatcong Creek.[347]

PHOTO BY GEORGE J. HILL, M.D.

EDISON SLEPT HERE: The Darling house, identified by Edison on his hand-drawn map on the page at left, is where Edison stayed on overnight trips to his cement works in New Village.

Edison began his great venture with cement in Warren County at the end of 1898 and early in 1899. A few years earlier, Edison had become acquainted with the Delaware River valley and the major towns in this region in the course of developing a commercial outlet for use of his primary copper-oxide batteries. In 1893, Edison had established what was called "the first low-voltage automatic block semaphore signal in the world" near Phillipsburg, New Jersey. Five years later, in December 1898, the inventor made arrangements to visit Portland cement plants in the Lehigh valley of Pennsylvania, which was across the Delaware River to the west of Phillipsburg.

Within the next few months Edison acquired land in the Pohatcong valley a few miles east of Phillipsburg, on which he began to build his own cement manufacturing plant and where he would establish a quarry for cement rock. In June 1900, Judge Elliott referred to Edison's previous visit to this valley "last Spring" (presumably the Spring of 1899). The sketch map that Edison drew in June 1900 showed that by this time his cement company already covered more than 160 acres. The Edison Portland Cement Company would eventually acquire some 800 acres in Warren County.[348]

Regardless of his method of transportation, when Edison traveled from his iron mine in Sussex County to his operations in Warren County, he would have initially gone south to Lake Hopatcong. From there, he would have gone south-west to Hackettstown and Washington, and then west-southwest to New Village, Stewartsville, and Phillipsburg. Although roads were in existence at the turn of the century that connected these towns, and although the Morris Canal with its adjacent towpath was then still in operation between Hackettstown and Phillipsburg, the best way to make this journey at that time was by rail. The inventor would naturally view his position in Sussex County as being north of New Village, and he thus referred to the rail line through New Village as proceeding to the north, although local residents — such as Judge Elliott — thought of the rail line as proceeding east and west. After all, from their perspective, the railroad and the Morris Canal went east from Phillipsburg to Newark. In fact, the Pohatcong valley did not run either north and south, or east and west; it ran from northeast to southwest. However, although the D.L.& W. ("Lackawanna") railroad entered the valley on this orientation at Hackettstown, it gradually turned to the north and assumed a west-southwesterly course as it proceeded from Washington to Phillipsburg. Indeed, just west of Edison's property, the railroad turned even more to the north, to run on a true east-west course for about a half mile before turning southwest again to continue to Phillipsburg. This is the "bend" in the railroad that Edison referred to in his messages in June 1900 and which he showed on his sketch map, and it can be seen to this day on the Bloomsbury quadrangle map. The differences in orientation between Edison (at the iron mine) and Judge Elliott (in Stewartsville) led to confusion in their messages. What Edison referred to as south, Elliott called west. In fact, neither man was precisely correct, but no wonder that Edison complained about the lack of a map to work with in his dialogue with Elliott.[349]

When Edison traveled from West Orange to Stewartsville and New Village, the D.L.&W. railroad would surely have been his best mode of transportation. There were, of course, other possibilities, but I assume that the rail line was his usual route, and I will, in a moment, examine in some detail the environment that Edison passed through on the railroad as he went from Glenmont to his cement works. Unlike some of the great magnates of industry, Edison ordinarily traveled on the railroad as an ordinary passenger. That is to say, he did not have a private rail car, so he would usually have ridden on passenger trains. However, a major customer of the railroads, such as Edison was, has long been permitted to ride as a passenger on freight trains, usually with trainmen in the caboose or engine, or occasionally in a passenger car that was hitched into the row of freight cars. We may, therefore, assume that Edison's passage from central Essex County to western Warren County was varied and interesting, and he would have had the opportunity to look around from time to time when the train stopped to pick up or discharge passengers and freight.[350]

We know from *To Breathe the Beauty* that Edison enjoyed traveling on country roads, and we also know that he eventually had his own car and driver in Warren County. It is reasonable to assume, therefore, that he

COURTESY OF NATIONAL PARK SERVICE

PHOTO BY GEORGE J. HILL

FIRST CONCRETE ROAD: This section of Route 57 in Franklin Township is touted as the nation's first concrete road, although Edison may have first paved the road that ran through his factory complex.

explored some of the roads that then existed between West Orange and Stewartsville. Fine automobile roads that have replaced the old roads are now the easiest routes for travelers to take between these two towns. Indeed, one of these roads — Route 57 in Franklin Township — was the first concrete highway in America, and it was paved by Edison. We have previously seen that modern roads — including interstate highways, U.S. highways, state highways, and county roads — generally follow the routes of older roads that date back to colonial days. Colonial roads, in turn, were usually laid down along Indian paths and game trails that followed natural features of the landscape such as the valleys of rivers and streams, and mountain ridges and passes. Edison could have motored directly west from Llewellyn Park on Mount Pleasant Avenue to the western border of Morris County, or he could have been driven along the more northerly route of Bloomfield Avenue from his plant at Silver Lake through Caldwell and then into the center of Morris County. Both of these roads are still available for travelers. Bloomfield Avenue terminates at Route 46 in Denville. Mount Pleasant Avenue is now known as New Jersey State Route 10; it terminates at Port Morris near Lake Hopatcong, where it joins Route 46.[351]

Edison's driver would thus have been able to take the inventor to Lake Hopatcong by going west on either Mount Pleasant Avenue or Bloomfield Avenue. From Lake Hopatcong, Edison's chauffeur would then have had good roads to follow down the Musconetcong and Pohatcong valleys through Hackettstown to Phillipsburg. These routes are now called U.S. 46 and State Route 57. Scenic diversions abound on county roads along these two major highways. For example, Warren County Road 604 (Waterloo Road) runs beside the abandoned Morris Canal for about four miles on the right (west) bank of the Musconetcong River where it passes through Allamuchy State Park near Hackettstown. The railroad (now called the Boonton Branch of New Jersey Transit) hugs the opposite bank of the Musconetcong as it runs down this valley, dividing Morris and Warren Counties. Edison also had two major road systems available if he chose to take a southerly route from West Orange to Phillipsburg. From Llewellyn Park, he could have motored four miles south to South Orange, and then turned west to Morristown along the route that is now South Orange Avenue in Essex County. This road is known as the Columbia Turnpike after it enters Morris County. From Morristown, there were — and there still are — two possible routes to Phillipsburg. One route (now known as U.S. 202 and New Jersey Route 53) proceeds to the north through Morris Plains. This route passes by the historic village of Speedwell — where Morse Code was first publicly demonstrated in 1838 — and crosses Mount Pleasant Avenue at Mount Tabor, on the southern border of Parsippany-Troy Hills. In Denville, Route 53 (now known as East Main Street) ends at Bloomfield Avenue, which continues on to Lake Hopatcong as U.S. 46. This meandering way from Morristown to Lake Hopatcong is also the route that the railroad follows to Hopatcong — the D.L.&W. in Edison's day, now known as the Morristown Line of the Morris & Essex Rail Lines of New Jersey Transit. The route takes the path that it does in order to stay in the river valleys, wind around the lakes, and avoid the ridges in Morris County.[352]

The other southern route that Edison could have taken from Morristown to Phillipsburg was the Morris Turnpike, which was constructed early in the nineteenth century. This road was subsumed by the state of New Jersey in 1924, and it has been replaced by Interstate 287 and Interstate 78. It is now possible to travel at nearly a mile a minute on limited access interstate highways from Morristown to Phillipsburg. A century ago the pace was slower, and the environment along the southern route from Morristown through Clinton to Phillipsburg would have been much more tangible and accessible to the traveler than it is today.[353]

In Edison's day, the D.L.&W. Railroad had an Orange Branch that arose from the main line at Forest Hill Station, in north Newark. This branch passed west through stations at Silver Lake, East Orange, Orange, and Llewellyn Park, and it terminated at Main Street in West Orange. We have previously seen that this branch passed through Edison's property in Silver Lake, and it went within a few feet of the Edison plant in West Orange. The Llewellyn Station on this branch was the closest railroad depot to the gate of Llewellyn Park, but it would not have been Edison's best route to take to Warren County. Instead, the inventor would have been driven for one mile from either his plant or his home to the Orange Station on the Morris & Essex Line. This station was located at Lackawanna Plaza, near the corner of High Street (Scotland Road) and Main Street in Orange. At this station, a block from the First Presbyterian Church in Orange, where his Ogden ancestors are buried, Edison would have boarded the train for Morristown, Lake Hopatcong and points west — i.e., Hackettstown, New Village, Stewartsville, and Phillipsburg.

The Morris and Essex Line still exists, although it is now a branch of New Jersey Transit instead of the D.L.&W. or its successor, the Erie and Lackawanna. And although it no longer carries passengers beyond Hackettstown, the railroad tracks and right-of-way are maintained in good condition to serve as a CONRAIL freight line from Hackettstown to Phillipsburg. This rail line still passes over Edison Road as it runs between Edison's former plant and his quarry — now known as Edison Lake — in New Village. Other changes have occurred since Edison traveled this route: The trains are no longer pulled by steam engines, and I can find no trace of the rails of Edison's own Pohatcong Railroad that once ran through this valley. Furthermore, it is no longer possible to proceed directly west from Orange to Hackettstown; one must take the train east from Orange to Newark or Hoboken, and then change to a westbound train for Hackettstown. It is possible, in theory, to make the round trip from Orange to Hackettstown twice a day on weekdays, but not at all on Saturdays, Sundays, and holidays. And the Morris Canal, which in Edison's day ran along the railroad from Dover to Phillipsburg, is now almost entirely gone. Enough traces and mementos of the Morris Canal remain, however, to mark its route and to serve as a reminder of the environment that existed in Morris, Sussex, and Warren Counties when Edison arrived here a hundred years ago.[354]

During the early years of Thomas Edison's work with cement in Warren County, his total environment consisted of much more than what he encountered en route to New Village, and what he found in the valley of Pohatcong Creek. When he traveled to Warren County in 1897-1900, the inventor carried the memories of his personal and business environment in Essex County, and of the environment in the many other areas where his family, his employees, and his associates were located. Let us therefore recall a few of the other aspects of Edison's environment during this period, to show what he was thinking of, as he traveled over the mountains and rivers of New Jersey to his enterprise in Warren County.

In 1898 Edison was still intensively engaged in his iron mining operations in Sussex County — in which he had lost some two million dollars — and he was operating a very large industrial complex at Silver Lake. His Laboratory and factories in West Orange "had become overwhelmed with orders for the spring motor phonograph," and he had "a million dollar annual revenue stream" from his various businesses. Furthermore, Edison was deeply involved in the development of his new "kinetoscope," and he was deposed in West Orange in January 1900 on the "fundamental motion picture camera patent," which had been approved at the end of August 1897 but was still in litigation. Edison was also hard at work on his new iron-nickel alkaline storage battery, which he described during this period to the American Institute of Electrical Engineers. During the time that Edison was starting up his cement company he was concluding the initial phases of his work with x-rays, which he had begun in March 1896 with pioneering experimentation that led to his invention of the fluoroscope.[355]

If Edison's business environment wasn't enough to keep him occupied, he also had a family environment to be concerned about, and it was, to say the least, chaotic. Although Edison's magnificent home in Llewellyn Park was managed with grace and strength by his precociously serene second wife, his first three children were a worry and concern. Tom, Jr., had "fleeting, acute suicidal thoughts" in the spring of 1897 and by 1898 he had moved to the family's winter home in Fort Myers, Florida, for two months of rest. In the summer of 1898 Tom, Jr., moved in with a "casino girl," Mary Louise Toohey, whom he married in February 1899, only to leave her a year later. In the late 1890s, Edison's second son, William Leslie, was reported to be "slovenly and disheveled" at boarding school, while his eldest child, Marion, continued to be unhappy in her new role as a step-daughter to young Mina Edison. Edison's family environment became even more complicated in July 1898, when Mina's beloved brother, Theodore, died of wounds in the Spanish-American War. Mina was then in the late stage of her third pregnancy. The new baby, born two days later, was named Theodore, in memory of her brother. He joined Mina's first two children, Madeline (age 10) and Charles (age 8). Thomas and Mina had then been married for twelve years; he was 51 years old, and she was 33. Mina's sister, Jane, whom she adored, died four months later, and three months after this her grieving father died, leaving behind a large family that had seen its fortunes greatly diminished by a recent business recession.[356]

* * * * *

It is a sixty-five mile drive from Llewellyn Park in West Orange to Edison Road in New Village, New Jersey, along the route of the railroad that Edison would have taken in 1898. The roads are clearly marked and well-paved, and the drive can easily be made in about an hour and a half — or about the same as the scheduled time for a train ride from Orange to Hackettstown, eighteen miles up the valley from New Village.[357] Edison easily made the round trip by train from Orange to New Village in a day, and he had time enough to do almost seven hours of work at his cement plant before catching the train home. We do not know exactly when he left home, or when he got back to Glenmont, but on a typical day his train arrived at New Village at 10:40 in the morning, and his east-bound train for Orange passed through the New Village station at 5:30 in the afternoon.[358] The railroad passes near the Morristown National Historic

Site, which marks the location of Washington's Headquarters in Morristown, where the Continental Army was encamped for two winters.[359] The railroad and its accompanying highways, such as U.S 46, continues through wooded country with scattered houses and small towns that have changed little, except that they are now joined by paved roads, and trucks and cars, rather than horses and wagons.[360]

A traveler from West Orange, such as Edison, would have found the Pohatcong valley a quiet, beautiful place. Even today, one finds that entering this valley provides a sense of relief. It is a place to pause, to take photographs, to have lunch on the grass, and marvel at scenery that unfolds as the road to Phillipsburg traverses the villages of Pleasant Valley and Broadway. The traveler passes Buttermilk Bridge Road, stone houses, stone barns, and Millpond Road, to arrive at Edison Road, in New Village, sixty-five miles from Llewellyn Park in West Orange.

The CONRAIL tracks are barely visible in the valley to our left, a half-mile away, just beyond the creek. The old canal route is on the hillside to our right, marked by occasional signs and a depression in the ground here and there. We see many stone and frame houses that were here a century ago. There are also a few newer homes, some of which are built of stones (quarried from the Morris Canal's locks, we suppose) or concrete (made from Edison's cement, of course). But the spirit of this village, and of this valley, is epitomized by the slow switching of the tails of the black and white milk cows that graze along the creek below us. On the highway, we are greeted by a sign that says it all: "Welcome to Franklin Township — "A Clean Agricultural Community."

The Edison Portland Cement Company:
Plant and Quarries in New Village, Stewartsville, and Oxford

The Township committee are now here and want me to adjust the whole matter ... This puts the committee just where I have been trying to get them. ... The committee say they will make good terms with Purcell for the land this afternoon. ... The committee will make the bargain with Purcell – not me.

— Judge Elliott to Thomas Alva Edison, 1900[361]

At about noon on 22 June 1900, Judge A. Elliott telephoned from Stewartsville to Edison, who was at his iron mine in Sussex County, to get the inventor's approval for a complicated maneuver that he was undertaking in order to secure land for the cement company at a bargain price. (Only the first initial of Elliott's name appears in the record. Or is "A." his middle initial? I cannot say.) We had previously looked at portions of the messages that Edison and Elliott exchanged on this day in June 1900. We now need to review these messages in detail, to see what they tell us about Edison's impact on the environment in this part of the Pohatcong valley.[362]

Before we study the Edison-Elliott messages, however, we need to take a closer look at the Pohatcong valley itself. We have already seen that the stage was set in the spring of 1899 for the one-act play that featured Edison and Elliott, but the stage itself — the Pohatcong valley — was already in existence. The "stage" for this "play" was constructed in geological time: The Pohatcong valley was created by the action of ice, water, and wind over millions of years. We do not know if Edison passed through this valley in the winter of 1898 on his trip to study the cement plants in the Lehigh valley, but it is more than likely that he did. After all, the train from Orange to the mouth of the Lehigh River passes down this valley, through New Village and Stewartsville. The portion of the Pohatcong valley that interested Edison was about seven miles long, from the village of Pleasant Valley on the northeast to Stewartsville on the southwest.

The Pohatcong valley is about a mile wide at the upper end, just above Pleasant Valley, some 380 feet above sea level. The valley doubles in width and falls by a hundred feet or so between its origin and the point where Merrill Creek flows into it in Stewartsville. To the casual eye, the broad floor of the valley would appear to be nearly flat. However, a careful observer can see that it is tilted slightly, being lower on the southern side along the long ridge known as Pohatcong Mountain than it is along the higher and more rugged Scotts Mountain ridge that bounds the valley on the north. Scotts Mountain, cresting at 1,068 feet above Stewartsville, is also higher than the Pohatcong ridge. The highest point on the Pohatcong ridge is at 857 feet, one and one-half miles south of the site that Edison picked for his plant. The floor of the valley is relieved by the presence of several streams that flows down from gullies on the mountains, and by a row of low hills within the valley that are separated by these streams.

The most level area of the valley, well away from tributaries and hills, was the place that Edison chose to commence his operations. It was so flat at this point that Pohatcong Creek discontinued its steady downhill course and meandered for a half mile through a great bend to the south before straightening out again to proceed on down to the Delaware River. The valley was dotted with small ponds and springs. The farmland on the floor of the valley was also strewn with small sinkholes and large depressions that were caused by the limestone formations that were underneath the fields and pastures. One of the largest of the depressions, about a thousand feet in diameter, was only a half mile southwest of the property that Edison purchased. The inventor would eventually create two great quarries in this valley, one on each side of Pohatcong Creek.

The principal road through the valley was the highway from Washington, New Jersey, to Stewartsville and then on to Phillipsburg. It was called Washington Avenue then, and we now call it State Route 57. This road followed the right or north bank of Pohatcong Creek, along the base of Scotts Mountain, connecting the settlements known as Pleasant Valley, Broadway, and New Village. Along the southern rim of the valley, high up on the Pohatcong Mountain, was another road, now known as Good Springs Road, which joined the farms on this side of the valley with Stewartsville and Asbury, over Pohatcong Mountain.[363]

When Edison arrived in the Pohatcong Valley, the valley was also traversed by the Morris Canal and the D.L.&W. Railroad. The Morris Canal ran above and more less parallel to the highway along the base of Scotts Mountain, well above the right bank of Pohatcong Creek, while the railroad ran down the center of the valley, on the left bank of the creek. In the upper part of the valley the canal followed the contour line at 440 feet above sea level, and it was thus nearly one hundred feet above the valley floor. The canal was about a half mile from Edison's quarry in New Village, and a mile or so from his plant. Just below New Village, the road rose to cut across the shoulder of Scotts Mountain before descending into Stewartsville. The canal, continuing on as level a course as possible, crossed the highway and continued on down the valley below Stewartsville. The Morris Canal's former course at this point is marked by a sign on the road that connects the Stewartsville cemetery with Route 57. The course of the canal can now be identified more easily on the Bloomsbury quadrangle map than on the ground, for nearly all traces of it have been removed. The land that the canal formerly passed through has reverted to pastures, fields, and farms.

In another half mile, the Morris Canal crossed Main Street on the southern outskirts of Stewartsville and exited the valley on its last leg, passing through Port Warren to end at Phillipsburg. The railroad, in the meantime, rose from the valley floor to cross Pohatcong Creek and the Morris Canal to enter the center of the village of Stewartsville about three hundred yards south of the center of town, where Main Street crossed the highway that we call Route 57. The major commercial location at the southern end of the valley was situated at this point, in the northern part of Stewartsville, where the railroad crossed the Morris Canal, Merrill Creek, and Main Street.

When Edison arrived in the Pohatcong valley, the roads were dirt and travelers made their way locally on foot or with horses — riding or being pulled in buggies or wagons. The land was already cleared and farmed, which facilitated viewing the environment, as did the slower pace of life and the more intimate connection with nature that was present in those days, compared to the present. Edison would have walked about or ridden slowly through the valley that we now drive quickly through on well-paved roads. The roads then were muddy, snow-covered, and icy from fall to spring, and dusty and rutted in the summer. So it is not surprising that Edison would think of using his cement to pave the roads near his plant, especially when the first frail little automobiles began to appear in the valley. In his early years at New Village and Stewartsville, however, Edison traveled in the same way that the local residents did, and he met a good many of them.

Although Edison soon had his own farm, with a fine two story stone house in which to stay, when he came to Warren County he was regularly invited to eat and stay at the homes of leaders of the local communities on both sides of the Delaware River. So when Edison initiated a complex real estate transaction in New Village in June 1900, he was already well-known to the landowners in the valley, and his plans for development of a quarry and cement plant were supported by those who thought it would be good for the community. Many local people thought they, too, would profit in some way by Edison's new project. By the spring of 1900, Edison had put some of his most skillful employees to work on the cement project, and he had enlisted the assistance (at what price we do not know) of key individuals in the valley. When Edison wanted to obtain land on which to build a new road from the cement company plant to what we now call Good Springs Road, the task was apparently given to no less a person than a judge. (I am assuming that "Judge A. Elliott" refers to a magistrate or someone who held this title as an honorific, not someone whose first name is "Judge.")[364] The necessary petition was signed by thirty-five people ("I have about 35 names on my road petition"). Judge Elliott then successfully maneuvered the Township Committee into completing the acquisition of land for the road, at a price much less than it might have been. The committee members were, in fact, actually out at the desired property ("on the grounds now") at the time that Elliott called Edison on the morning of 22 June 1900 for his approval of the scheme:

> *The Township committee are now here and want me to adjust the whole matter and not go any further with my petition. . . . . This puts the committee just where I have been trying to get them. Now we can come to an agreement and think we will be able to adjust it all this afternoon. . . . I am waiting for an answer from you.*[365]

Elliott had originally proposed building a road running east ("runs East . . . as laid down in my papers") from the little railroad station at the northern edge of the cement plant, and then turning to the south. But Elliott knew that the cost of the road would be much less ("1/4 as much") if it began by running west from the station, and then turned south. So Elliott maneuvered the Township Committee into proposing a western route for the road, and the committee then went on to say that it would secure the land for the road from the owner ("The committee will make the bargain with Purcell - not me").

Elliott explained his reasoning to Edison: "I had to go to the east to get them committed in the shape I have them in now." Elliott then went on to describe the course that he proposed for the new road, referring to landmarks and property owners that Edison would remember:

> *We will start at the culvert, run west over David Purcell's, taking a little less than one acre of his land; then over our land; then over our overhead bridge; over our land; then over Fritt's to the Davis road.*

Elliott was confident that his project would work, but he had a backup plan ready in case it fell through:

> *I think they find we have them up a tree and want to adjust it all and come to an agreement now. I shall put up my notices just the same so as to hold my rights before the court on July 6th so that in case anything fails between now and then we will not have lost our rights.*[366]

Edison, however, was puzzled. At his office at the iron mine in Sussex County, he could visualize the railroad in New Village, and the station by his cement plant. He also knew where the "culvert" was, but he couldn't relate to Elliott's references to Purcell, Fritt, and Davis. Edison did, however, recall some features of the geography that Elliott had not

> Telephoned June 22, 1903
> 1:40 PM to Stewartsville
> to Stenographer R Scott
>
> How do you expect me to decide the route of a proposed road when I have no maps at Edison — I remember the road I wanted ran from the depot along the Railroad Northward beyond a hill where there was a bend in the railroad & then turned East across the extreme north end of our property and at juncture of the adjoining property owned by the man who had given an option to another party — Is this the route if not what changes do you propose making, remember I have no maps here
>
> Edison

COURTESY OF PROFESSOR MARGARET PIERCE

MAKING HIS POINT: In the days before fax machines, Edison had a hard time making Judge Elliott understand what he envisioned for his New Village factory complex. Edison had drawn a detailed map (see page 230) but Elliottt did not have the map in hand when Edison sent him this telephone message. Elliott was asking as Edison's representative in negotiations with New Village officials.

TOP PHOTO BY GEORGE J. HILL, M.D.

PHOTO AT LEFT
COURTESY OF
NATIONAL PARK SERVICE

UPTON'S HOME: Francis R. Upton, left, managed Edison's cement factory complex in New Village. Upton's home, shown above, was located next-door to the Darling house, where Edison stayed on overnight trips to his Warren County facility. Like the Darling house the Upton house is identified in the sketch map he created (see page 230).

mentioned including the road that went directly across the valley from New Village to the cement plant. He called this the "old road" and "New Village Road"; it is now known as Edison Road (County Route 633). Edison also recalled that there was a bridge on the railroad at the Boyer property. He drew a sketch map that showed what he had in mind, and replied to Elliott:

Do you mean starting at the Lackawanna station [and] follow along railway to the bridge on Sally Boyers place[,] then across the valley east to the road along the mountain? If this is the route, all right, go ahead.

[initialed] E [367]

There was no way that Edison could get his sketch map transmitted to Judge Elliott at that moment, so each man could see what the other was talking about. At 1:40 p.m., Edison continued:

I remember the road I wanted ran from the depot along the railroad northward beyond a hill where there was a bend in the railroad. . . Is this the route? If not, what changes do you propose making? Remember, I have no maps here.

Edison [368]

Edison's question showed Elliott that the inventor didn't understand the new proposal, so Elliott had to try again. He referred to the Boyer property and the bridge, because they were points that Edison could visualize. Elliott also referred again to directions (north and west), which were not helpful to Edison, whose mental orientation was ninety degrees different from Elliott's. Elliott said at 3:20 p.m.:

Mr. Edison — The route in your message is the one you and I agree upon but the committee now wish me to change. They want me to begin north of the culvert and run west over David Purcell's; then over our land and across the White Bridge over the railroad and then across our land again (Boyer field); then across Fritt's to road at Davis house, as I stated in this morning's message.[369]

Elliott was getting a bit desperate by this time, and he emphasized that Edison already knew the route that he was talking about:

> *This is the cheaper route and is the same route that you, Lehman and Darling walked over last Spring. Shall I take this last route if I can make [a] satisfactory and quick arrangement with the committee? As the committee are all here, I must know this afternoon.*[370]

Since Edison was having a problem understanding what Elliott was talking about, Elliott repeated that "the committee wish me to accept a road running west instead of east." An hour later, in the last message that we have on this subject, Elliott struggled to make clear to Edison the proposal that he had maneuvered the Township Committee into making:

> *Mr. Edison: Instead of going straight across the valley, the proposed road bears southwest from the bridge to the road at Davis house. Davis house is at the top of the little hill above the Davis crossing, which is the first crossing of our track below the plant.*
>
> Judge Elliott [371]

That Elliott was finally successful in explaining to Edison what he had in mind can be presumed from the heavy markup that appears on Edison's sketch map, in which Edison shows a new road that crosses the railroad at the bridge at Sally Boyers' place (which he and Elliott both referred to). Immediately after crossing the railroad, the new road on Edison's map turns sharply down the valley (a direction which Elliott had originally said was "west" but which in his final message he called, correctly, "southwest"). The new road on Edison's map then comes to a house, turns sharply to the left, crosses a stream, and ends at the road which we know of as Good Springs Road. The house at which the road turned was surely the one that Elliott called the Davis house. The hill which Elliott mentions, on which the Davis house stood, is easily visible on the Bloomsbury quadrangle map. The stream which Edison's sketch map shows being crossed by the new road is clearly apparent on the Bloomsbury quadrangle map. This stream flows down from Pohatcong Mountain and is a major tributary of Pohatcong Creek. The stream that Edison showed on his map runs into the valley immediately adjacent to the stone house that still stands facing the south end of Edison Road at its intersection with Good Springs Road. Edison was familiar with this house, which he called "Darling's House" on his sketch map. Upton's house, he wrote, was next to it. "Darling's" is the house where Edison stayed when he remained overnight at New Village; it was the house on the "company farm."

Parts of the "proposed road" that Elliott described and which Edison sketched in June 1900 still exist, although not all of these remnants appear on modern maps of this area. The Lackawanna station on Edison Road in New Village was removed in recent years, but a road known as Quarry Road still runs along the north side of the railroad tracks at this point, just where Edison showed it on his map. And if you continue along the north side of the railroad for three miles, you come to a short street, hardly two blocks long, called Edison Avenue, where the railroad crosses Main Street in Stewartsville. An underpass, rather than a bridge, now marks the place where the railroad crosses over Stewartsville Road, which runs past Edison's former quarry in New Village. A road known as Willow Grove Mill Road now connects Good Springs Road with New Village Road, along the route that Edison sketched for the southern part of his proposed new road. (The road that runs from the principal intersection in Stewartsville to New Village is called New Village Road, County Route 638, in Stewartsville. Its name changes to Stewartsville road when it crosses into New Village, and after it crosses Route 57 it continues on up Scotts Mountain as Montana Road.) Edison's other quarry in the Pohatcong valley, now filled with water, is located in the woods between New Village Road and Willow Grove Mill Road.

* * * * *

During the three decades from 1900 until Edison's death in 1931, the environment in the central part of the Pohatcong valley was dramatically altered by the presence of the Edison Portland Cement Company. Factory buildings were constructed and remodeled, quarries were dug and deepened, hundreds of workers and their families moved to the valley, and the by-products of this industrial development spread downwind and downstream. Edison expanded his operations to the northern border of the town of Oxford, eight miles to the northeast, where he opened another limestone quarry. New roads and railroads were built to serve Edison's quarries and his cement plant, and roads in this region were paved with concrete. These effects on the environment were consequences of the activities of Edison and his cement company.

On the other hand, some changes occurred in the environment of the valley that were unrelated to Edison's activities. For example, the Morris Canal was abandoned and its remains gradually vanished from sight, and motor vehicles began to replace the horse as the principal means of transportation within the valley. Motor vehicles continued to improve and eventually displaced trains for passenger transportation into and out of the valley. The main line of the railroad persisted, however, since motorized trucks dominated but did not completely replace trains for transportation of raw materials and finished goods. And Edison's cement company continued to operate for eleven years after the inventor's death.[372]

The definitive history of the Edison Portland Cement Company from 1900 to 1942 has not yet been written, so I have only a sketchy timeline to work with for my case study of the environmental impact of the cement company. I shall now summarize the information that I have gathered about Edison's work in Warren County. This information will then serve as a scaffold, on which I will attach the comments that I received in 1997 and 1998 from several local residents who have had a long interest in the history of this region, and who have heard or read of Thomas Edison's work in Warren County.[373]

One of the most complete analyses of Edison's work with cement that I have seen is an article written by Michael Peterson of Blairstown, N.J., in 1996. Peterson states that "Edison entered the Portland cement business" in 1902, when the "Edison Portland Cement Company was still in the design phase." The Edison Portland Cement Company, says Peterson, "remained one of the top producers of concrete and cement materials until it closed in 1942 in response to wartime energy-conservation materials."[374]

Another recent review of Edison's activities in Warren County was written in 1998 by Gladys Harry Eggler for the Warren County Cultural and Heritage Commission. Eggler states that the Edison Portland Cement Company was incorporated in June 1899 and it became the Edison Cement Corporation in December 1930. The Edison Cement Corporation was dissolved on December 22, 1942.[375]

We can get a sense of what life was like in the Pohatcong valley in 1900 by studying the photographs and stories that have been published in the histories of the Morris Canal. In his book, *The Morris Canal: A Photographic History*, Jim Lee published eight photographs of the area around Plane 8 West in Stewartsville and three pictures of the canal at Lock 7 West in New Village. Only one of these pictures was dated (ca. 1890), but Lee's photographs in general range from the 1890s to about 1910, which is roughly the period of Edison's arrival in the valley. In the

TOP PHOTO COURTESY OF THE NATIONAL PARK SERVICE
PHOTO BELOW BY GEORGE J. HILL, M.D.

FROM A CRATER TO A LAKE: Edison's quarry in New Village was so large that he built a tramway (above) to haul out cement rock. After it fell into disuse, the quarry filled with water and became Edison Lake, a 13-acre body of water (left) used for recreation by residents of Stewartsville and New Village.

PHOTO BY GEORGE J. HILL, M.D.

EDISON'S CEMENT WORKS: This 1906 factory, now used by the Victaulic Company, was once the signature building for the Edison complex in New Village.

background, we see wooded slopes on Scotts Mountain behind the canal, and scattered trees in fields of crops in the valley. The largest buildings in these pictures are Henry Stone's store in Stewartsville (two and a half stories, clapboard) and Dowling's coal loading and storage plant (three stories, clapboard). The power supply in those days was from animals: mules on the towpath, and horse-and-buggy on the roads. It was a quiet, slow-paced life in New Village then, a pace that picked up considerably when Edison's plant and quarry began to roar and smoke nearby.[376]

Many stories about New Village and Stewartsville appear in Lee's collection of *Tales the Boatmen Told*. These anecdotes give us another view of the environment in western Warren County at the turn of the century, and at least two of them mentioned Edison. For example, life on the "scows" was romantic enough for some of the boatmen, but for Charles Snyder, looking back at the age of 89, it was hard and unpleasant. When he was 21, Snyder quit and told his boss on the boat that "I'll pick bones and buy rags before I'll work for you." Snyder then settled in Stewartsville, got married, and "worked at the Edison."[377]

By the summer of 1900, Edison's cement company had expanded to cover an area between one hundred and two hundred acres in size, extending from the central line of the valley to its southwestern border on Good Springs Road. We have been told that Edison cement company's

PHOTO BY GEORGE J. HILL, M.D.

THE LABORATORY CONTROVERSY: This building, seen at the right in the photo on the opposing page, is identified by New Village residents as Edison's laboratory, although proof that Edison conducted experiments here remains elusive.

property in Warren County would later grow to include as much as 800 acres in land that was owned or controlled by the company. This was, as far as I can determine, by far the largest business operation that ever existed here, within the ten square miles of farmland bounded by Pleasant Valley on the northeast and Main Street in Stewartsville at the southwest, between Washington Avenue (Route 57) and Good Springs Road.[378]

We can be sure that at the time of its maximum size, the Edison Portland Cement Company plant consisted of dozens of buildings. One author reported that Edison had as many as ten 150-foot long kilns in operation simultaneously at New Village, each of which could produce 1,100 barrels of cement a day. We have read that his buildings were connected by a tunnel or tunnels up to one-half mile in length. Edison had his own depot on the D.L.&W. railroad, and he built a concrete pumping

PHOTO BY GEORGE J. HILL, M.D.

TOWERING SILOS: Two attached concrete silos, apparently used by Edison to store powdered cement, loom above the Victaulic site that was the headquarters for the Edison Cement Works.

station on the Pohatcong Creek where the creek crossed the road that led to his plant — the road now named for him.[379]

Edison eventually constructed a private railroad — the Pohatcong Railroad — to bring limestone from his quarry at Oxford, eight miles away as the crow flies and twelve miles by road, to his plant in New Village. Edison's cement rock quarry at New Village has long since filled with water. The water in this quarry — now called Lake Edison — is the community's swimming pond. It has a surface area that exceeds fifty acres. Its sheer walls tower sixty to eighty feet above the water line, and the walls undoubtedly extend for scores of feet below the surface. This quarry was originally dug out with an immense steam shovel, and its base was interlaced with railroad tracks. Large buildings were once located inside this quarry in New Village, far below the surface of the surrounding farmland. Edison's water-filled quarry a mile away in Stewartsville has a surface area of about thirteen acres. Man-made cliffs tower over its surface, too, and its depth can only be imagined.

A clearer view of the magnitude of these cavities on the earth's surface can be obtained by peering over the rim of the Oxford Quarry, which was known as the Edison Quarry until 1942. The Oxford Quarry, which had a surface area of about ten acres, filled with water when it was longer being mined. In recent years, this quarry has been pumped out and reopened. It now extends further than the eye can see, from the main entrance into several artificial canyons.[380]

One of the most respected authorities on the subject of Edison's work in Warren County is Carl Brown, who is the former manager of the Victaulic Company plant in New Village. Mr. Brown says admiringly of Edison, that "What he did here was tremendous." Victaulic is based in the last remaining factory building of the Edison Cement Company — a three story building that bears the date "1906" on the pediment at each end of the building. This building, adjacent to the railroad (now CONRAIL), is as large inside as a small cathedral. Yet when the Edison plant was in operation in New Village, the "1906 building" was dwarfed by the size and scope of many other buildings that extended away from it for several hundred yards on both sides of Edison Road, and behind it in the valley for two hundred yards or more toward Good Springs Road and Pohatcong Mountain. The 1906 building is clearly seen in the foreground of the illustrations in Warne's book (1991) and Eggler's paper (1998).[381]

In September 1997, I had the opportunity to see the interior of the 1906 building and to learn something of its unique nature. Initially, I was taken into the main room of the Victaulic building, which is now a galvanizing facility, by Gary Meddaugh, who is Mr. Brown's successor as the plant manager. I later saw the basement and the exterior of this building, as well as some of the other old buildings and residual structures that are near it. I will return in a moment to recall some of the features of the 1906 building in detail. After this orientation, I walked around the outside of the 1906 building to examine the abandoned buildings and ruins that are nearby. I then drove up and down the valley to get the general sense of the environment as it exists now, in order to be able to imagine it as it was during Edison's lifetime.[382]

There are several smaller buildings and ruins around the 1906 building that date back to Edison's period. The one that is in the best condition is a small one-story concrete building a few feet from the 1906 building, which is now used for storage. This building, about twenty by twelve feet in size, bears a tablet affixed to one corner bearing the date "1941." It is called "the laboratory" by Victaulic employees, because of the legend that this was Edison's laboratory at New Village. Beside and behind the 1906 building is a row of concrete arches ten to twelve

COURTESY OF
NATIONAL PARK SERVICE

MAN AND MACHINE: An Edison worker is dwarfed by the massive machinery inside the Edison Cement Works.

feet high that looks a bit like a Roman aqueduct. Two tall cement silos, attached to each other, tower over the Victaulic property at its upstream end, beyond a fence. They were apparently used by Edison for storage of powdered cement. Across Edison Road is a three-story slab-sided vacant cement building back in the trees that would pass for an unexcavated Maya temple. Beyond this abandoned concrete building is the fenced-off modern facility of the Elizabethtown Gas Company. On the other (north) side of the railroad underpass, between the railroad and Quarry Road, there are several piles of broken pieces of concrete that contain the aggregates of stones and pebbles which I associate with Edison's concrete.

The scraps of former Edison buildings are back in the trees which form the edge of the development of homes that are being constructed in the valley near the quarry, which is now known as Edison Lake. The row of decaying arches stands beside the 1906 building, which can be seen in the aerial drawing of the cement plant in Warne's *Look at Warren County* and in the photograph of the plant in 1907 in Eggler's "Edison and Warren County." Back in the weeds behind the 1906 building is a railroad tank car, sitting on railroad tracks that now connect to nothing.[383]

The "1906 building" is remarkably well preserved, given that it is ninety-two years old and has been put to hard use throughout the entire period of its existence. The basic structure appears to be very sturdy, with unusually thick walls. The 1906 building is now partially hidden behind a number of accretions that have been attached to it over the years. For example, the lower part of the long side, about two-thirds of the building's height facing the railroad, is no longer visible. Another, lower, building has been attached along this side. Above this low addition, however, the original design is clearly seen, just as it was when it was photographed in 1907. This facade consisted of a series of nine windows, separated by pillars, with additional pillars at either end. Above the windows, which are no longer visible behind the recent addition, were a series of nine matching faux windows, which are still apparent, giving the building its signature appearance. Decorative trim along the lower edge of the flat roof consists of a strip of repetitive fluting, with nineteen points on the long side and thirteen points on the narrow side of the building. If these decorative points are spaced at two and a half foot intervals, which appears reasonable, the 1906 building would be about fifty feet by thirty-two feet in size.

Victaulic has painted the exterior of the 1906 building a deep chocolate brown, giving it a well-cared for appearance. A rich, carefully groomed lawn extends to the parking lot on the northwest side of the 1906 building and stretches for about seventy-five yards to the northeast, where it terminates at a fence in front of the pair of somewhat mysterious old tall cement silos.

The 1906 building is about forty to fifty feet long and thirty or so feet wide, and it is about three stories high; i.e., thirty feet high. The principal room in the building is nearly as large as the building itself. It appears to run the length of the building, and it extends without interruption from the cement floor to the cement ceiling. The ceiling of this great hall is supported by massive cement beams, a foot or so in cross section, which run across it from side to side. Gary Meddaugh remarked that these beams are more than sufficient to bear the weight of the ceiling, and added that "Edison built things to be stronger than they needed to be!" Edison not only built on a massive scale, his cement (or more properly, his concrete) was incredibly strong.

Mr. Meddaugh showed me a hole that he had directed to be drilled through a side wall, through which a drain could be installed from the roof. This hole in Edison's ninety-year old cement was only seven by seven inches in cross section, and fifteen inches deep. Yet the task took two of his strongest workers eight hours to complete, and the men and their tools were "nearly worn out when it was done."

The basement of the 1906 building shows evidence of the evolution of use of the building from the time of its original construction up to the present. Gary Meddaugh showed me that the ground floor — the floor above the basement — is supported by three types of pillars, which were clearly constructed at different times. One type of pillar is of concrete; these were likely to have been the original supports, and are tapered slightly from base to top. Another type of pillar is of riveted steel, whereas a third type is of welded steel. Passageways out of the basement once opened into tunnels that have been mentioned by various authors. They lead to other buildings that have been destroyed or are now in ruins. Some of the tunnels have fallen down, while others are filled with water. For safety's sake, the entrances to the tunnels from the basement of the 1906 building have been closed, as if they were entrances to sewers of Paris.

The great room in the 1906 building was apparently used for different purposes between the time it was constructed and when the Edison Cement Company closed down thirty-six years later. Meddaugh related to me a legend that this large room had been a place that was used

COURTESY OF
NATIONAL
PARK SERVICE

PREFABRICATED CEMENT HOUSES: Edison constructed eleven identical houses in Union in 1912, ten of which are still standing.

by Edison to pour and test experimental mixtures of concrete. Carl Brown, on the other hand, said to me: "Did you know that there were two large generators there, so tall that they were sitting in the basement and came up through the floor?" Indeed, it seems likely that this great room was used for more than one purpose during the thirty or so years that it served the Edison company. No doubt Edison and his senior engineers needed a place where they could test various mixtures of the ingredients of cement and concrete, for such qualities as speed of setting, hardness, strength, brittleness, and resiliency (flexibility). The great hall in the 1906 building would have been an ideal place to erect wooden or iron forms for cement, or even to build a miniature house. The small adjacent building, the one that tradition calls a "laboratory," was well-situated as a place to study the qualities of the cement. This small one story building, whose walls were originally almost entirely windows (now filled in with bricks and cement) would have been cooled by breezes and very well lighted by sunlight. It would have been a perfect place to study samples of the cement as it hardened. The so-called "laboratory" building bears the inscription "1941," which is ten years after Edison died, so its original function is still a mystery.[384]

PHOTO BY GEORGE J. HILL, M.D.

WARM IN WINTER, COOL IN SUMMER: This cement house built in 1912 by Edison in Union, has been home to the Connell family for several decades.

Buildings, Pavement, and Water:
Environmental Impact of Edison's Work with Cement

No cement could have been better or more satisfactory than the Edison cement which was used exclusively in the construction of the new Yankee stadium.

— American League, 1923[385]

Cement

The trained or curious eye can see evidence of Edison's cement in count-less locations throughout New York and New Jersey. Eggler states that:

It was just a matter of time before Edison Cement Works was declared one of the biggest, producing the best. In addition to Yankee Stadium, Edison cement was used in the construction of scores of buildings and factories; the Hotel Traymore in Atlantic City, the Underwood Typewriter Building in Connecticut and Ford Motor Company buildings. It was used in the construction of New York City sewers and subways, dams and power houses. And highways. Warren County's Route 57 was a section of twenty-two miles of road paved in concrete by 1922. A State record.[386]

The earliest concrete structure built by Edison that I have found in this case study is his swimming pool at Glenmont. While the precise year of construction of the swimming pool is unknown, the gardener who was interviewed in 1965 stated that he believed that it preceded the garage and greenhouse, which are commonly said to have been built in 1908 and 1909, respectively. Although Edison was beginning to mine and crush limestone in Sussex County prior to 1898, it appears likely that the swimming pool was constructed from cement that he obtained from other sources.

In any event, it is remarkably durable. The border of the old swimming pool at Glenmont is still in good condition. It has not crumbled in the way that more recent structures made of lesser grades of cement have done — such as the cement that was used in 1974 in the remodeling of Yankee Stadium.[387]

PHOTO BY GEORGE J. HILL, M.D.

A MANSION OF CONCRETE: The Mediterranean-style home at 303 North Mountain Avenue in Upper Montclair, built of Edison concrete in 1912 in a neighborhood with "million dollar homes."

PHOTO BY GEORGE J. HILL, M.D.

DISTINCTIVE HOME: This attractive house at 740 McLaughlin Place in Orange is a three-story structure built of Edison concrete.

The largest building in New Jersey that is still standing which is made of Edison Cement is probably the Edison Storage Factory Building, across Lakeside Avenue from the Edison National Historic Site on Main Street in West Orange. The next largest building still in use in New Jersey that is made of Edison Cement, as far as I can determine, is the 1906 building of the Victaulic Corporation in New Village. There are, however, many houses and other structures that are constructed from Edison cement. For example, there are the ten remaining "Edison houses" on Ingersoll Terrace in Union, New Jersey. I have examined the exteriors of these houses, and I have talked with the owners of two of them. I was also given a tour of the ground floor of one of the Edison houses on Ingersoll Terrace. The owner described his house as being "Cool in summer and warm in winter — Wonderful house — Indestructible."

Mrs. Anne Connell is proud to have lived in the same Edison house at 983 Ingersoll Terrace in Union, N.J., for forty-five years. I took a photograph of her and her sons on the front steps in August 1997, replicating the photograph that Vanderbilt published 27 years earlier.[388]

In my neighborhood in West Orange, many of the cement sidewalks are very old and contain the black smooth basaltic pebbles that I think of as Edison concrete. The walls of my own house, built in the 1930s, are of very strong cement, and it is almost impossible to drive a nail into them. The border of my flower bed appears to be made of the same type of rough old cement as the border of Edison's swimming pool. A block away from my house, the sidewalk for more than one hundred yards along Overlook Road is made of cement that is heavily laden with black basaltic aggregate, from #3 to #33 Overlook. In front of #11 Overlook, the year 1932 is inscribed in the cement; it was laid down a year after the inventor died. I suspect that much of the cement in West Orange was made by the Edison Portland Cement Company. In Menlo Park, we saw that the magnificent art deco Edison Tower which marks the site of the inventor's laboratory building is made of Edison Portland cement, poured in 1937, six years after the inventor died.[389]

My interest in Edison has led to the identification of two more houses that are said to be made of Edison cement. Each is different from the other, and neither looks at all like the houses that were constructed on Ingersoll Terrace in Union. Both are well-maintained, handsome buildings, in neighborhoods of well-cared for houses. In Upper Montclair, the house at 303 North Mountain Avenue bears a plaque that states that it was built by Edison in 1912. This is a fine, flat-roofed

Mediterranean-style two story house in a district that is said to be of "million dollar homes," and it fits into its neighborhood very well indeed.[390] In Orange, just north of the border with South Orange, is a small, beautifully maintained three story cement house at 740 McLaughlin Place, on the corner of Valley Street, which I have been told is an "Edison House." It is unusual in that it has a rather small perimeter, yet is tall, with a roof that symmetrically tapers to the center from all four sides, and it has a chimney rising exactly from its peak. This house has small windows but it also has a wooden portico that extends toward McLaughlin Place on the south, and a room that reaches out to the west, relieving what otherwise would be a rather stark appearance.[391]

Edison also designed a number of different objects, such as furniture, phonograph cabinets, and a bathtub, that could be made from concrete. While his ideas may have been good in theory, and many of the items that he produced were both attractive and durable, Edison failed to convince the public that cement would be better for furniture than traditional materials such as wood and steel. "Regardless of its value and appearance, Edison's concrete furniture just never caught on." I have therefore not pursued a case study of this aspect of Edison's work with cement. Within only a decade or two after his death, other inventors had formulated carbon-hydrogen-based plastics that have been used to fabricate many of the objects that Edison molded from carbon-silicon-based composites in 1911-1912. It is ironic that silicon-based composites and plastics are now essential components of everyday life. They are used in products ranging from silicon "chips" to ceramic tiles. But these uses of silicon were derived from discoveries in other fields of technology, not as the result of Edison's efforts to make concrete furniture. Edison's cement piano and his other concrete household items produced no obvious environmental legacy.[392]

Water

Another environmental impact of Edison's work in Warren County was the creation of three large quarries, two of which are now filled with water. The unintended effects of these great craters have not been fully explored, but they may be far-reaching. It has been said that:

In the Highlands bedrock aquifers, pollution will spread to underlying aquifers through the system of fractures. . . . [T]he glacial valley-fill aquifers of the Highlands act as an interconnected system, lacking sufficient competent confining materials to prevent downward movement of pollution from the surface. All groundwater is vulnerable to pollution but aquifer systems dominated by fracture and open channel flow, which exist throughout the Highlands region, allow for rapid movement of contaminants with little filtration.[393]

A test in 1968 demonstrated "the rapid rate of groundwater movement possible within the Highlands region." Dye deposited in a pond in Warren County appeared at a spring a mile away in Sussex County within two hours. This pond "lies within an area underlain by cavernous limestone, which is riddled with fractures and channels."[394]

Fractures of the limestone by water wells in the Highlands have facilitated groundwater contamination from gas stations, wastewater disposal systems, sewage lines, and underground storage tanks. Although quarries are not mentioned as common causes of communications between surface water and groundwater, common sense would suggest that this is a possibility. The source of groundwater contamination is often difficult to detect, and it is "often infeasible or virtually impossible to remedy." And as groundwater is drawn down by increased use, its rapid recharge from surface water increases the threat of pollution. The large lake created by ingress of water into Edison's quarry at New Village provides a picturesque backdrop for a new housing development. However,

As the region experiences rising urban/suburban development, increased use of groundwater within the region will be in competition with the surface water diversions that supply the densely populated northeastern part of the state. Proper management of the water resources of the Highlands will require land-use planning that protects aquifer recharge areas, maintains base flows in streams and rivers, and prevents the pollution that has been detrimental to high-quality supply systems in other areas of the metropolitan region.[395]

Water quality in the Highlands affects the entire state. "At stake is roughly half of New Jersey's drinking water . . . as well as the associated wildlife habitats and recreational resources" that make this area so attractive and important.[396]

PHOTOS BY GEORGE J. HILL, M.D.

EDISON IN OXFORD: Edison Road led to Oxford Quarry, Inc., the successor company to Edison's quarrying operation in Oxford (above). Several old vehicles preserved at the site bear the legend "The Edison Quarry 1923-1942" (below).

PHOTO BY GEORGE J. HILL, M.D.

PRESERVING THE EDISON NAME: The old trucks parked at Oxford Quarry are still emblazoned with the name of the Edison Quarry on their doors.

A Mere Ghost

Today the sprawling complex which was the Edison Cement Works is a mere ghost of its former self, with just a dusting of cement still covering the nearby landscape, a reminder of what used to be.
— Gladys Eggler, 1998[397]

At this point, it is time to ask what this case study of Edison's work in Warren County has revealed about the inventor's beliefs and attitudes toward the environment, as well as his impact on the environment in Warren County and elsewhere. While it would now be difficult to find a "dusting of cement" near the former Edison plant, Gladys Eggler's lyrical metaphor is appropriate, for there is, indeed, little that remains of the structures that Edison created in New Village, and even the memory of what he did there has largely faded away. George Warne of the Warren County Cultural and Historical Commission went to the heart of the matter when he wrote: "the Edison Portland Cement Plant, now extensively demolished."[398]

The size and scope of Edison's activities in Warren County rivaled and may have even exceeded the magnitude of his previous operations in Sussex County. The largest estimates of his land acquisitions in Sussex County exceed the 800 acres that he is said to have controlled in Warren County. However, the number of buildings and the volume of work performed in Warren County appear to be greater than Edison's operations at the Ogden iron mine. The area over which his buildings and mines extended in Sussex and Warren Counties greatly surpassed anything else that Edison occupied in New Jersey. Indeed, all of the rest of Edison's property that we have examined in New Jersey (i.e., in Newark, Menlo Park, West Orange, Silver Lake, and Harrison) probably did not, in the aggregate, total as much as 800 acres. The Pohatcong valley has, however, not yet been totally transformed into mega-farms. Milk cows and sheep graze along the Pohatcong and its tributaries in the valley, and there are still a few pigs and vegetable gardens near small, well-maintained farmhouses. Suburbanization of the countryside also poses a challenge to traditional farming. Several farms in the valley have already been transformed into developments of winding streets and single family homes. One of the largest of these developments is located between Edison Lake and Edison Road.

It is now time to ask: How much of the alteration in the environment in Warren County during the past century can be attributed to the direct effect of Edison's work with Portland cement? On balance, it appears that the environmental impact of the Edison Portland Cement Company (from 1899 to 1942) and of the inventor himself (from 1899 to 1931) was initially profound, but the effect has been ameliorated during the past six to seven decades and it is virtually not apparent now. Edison's huge quarries and his great cement plant were fascinating, dramatic, noisy, dusty, smoky, and dangerous places. They were interesting from the perspectives of both science (or technology, if you wish to call it that) and management. Edison invented new methods to produce Portland cement, and through his research he set new standards of quality for the cement industry and for the use of concrete in construction. He achieved what we now call "economy of scale" with his very large mining and milling equipment, and his extra-long, automated, brick kilns were able to out-produce his competitors. Edison apparently took good care of his employees, and the environment at his quarries and his cement plant has been recalled with satisfaction by former employees and their families.

The long-term indirect impact of Edison's work in Warren County is difficult for us to assess, for although we are immersed and surrounded by the effects of Edison's work with cement and concrete, we are largely unconscious of it. The environmental impact of Edison's development of the incandescent lamp and electric power systems, of the phonograph and sound recording devices, and of motion pictures, has been well-documented and is repeatedly emphasized by historians and journalists. It is clear, however, that the environmental impact of Edison's work with cement and concrete cannot be fully assessed until the history of the Edison cement company itself is written. This task cannot be completed until the archives at the Edison National Historic Site for the period 1899-1931 have been catalogued and copied, and then studied by historians in conjunction with other sources such as deeds, diaries, account books, newspaper reports, oral histories, collections of photographs, and archaeological excavations.

*****

I now leave Warren County to study the last site in New Jersey on which a new plant, in Hudson County, was built by the Edison Corporation during the Great Inventor's lifetime.

Chapter 12

Kearny: The Battery Factory and the Model A Ford (1927-1931)

For a manufacturer it is difficult to visualize a location more ideally situated than in Kearny and it is just as difficult to find a community in which the governing body goes to greater legitimate length to encourage industry

— B. F. Morris, Thomas A. Edison, Inc., 1939[399]

CHARLES Edison, who was officially appointed as the head of the Edison corporation in 1927, soon began manufacturing lead-acid storage batteries at a new plant in Kearny, New Jersey. His father, who had been elevated to the honorary position of Chairman of the Board, disapproved of lead-acid batteries, so they were labeled with the brand name of "E-Mark" instead of mentioning Edison by name. The E-Mark Battery Corporation was organized to produce batteries for Ford motor cars, and this operation "rang up consistent profits over many years." By 1930, a year before the death of the Great Inventor, E-Mark had become one of the ten major divisions of TAE, Inc., and its plant in Kearny covered an area of several thousand square yards. In 1930 the Kearny operations were headed by E. D. Martin, Vice President of the Edison corporation and General Manager of E-Mark.[400]

In this case study, I shall review the history and geography of Kearny to explain why Charles Edison would have considered this city as a possible location for his new battery factory. I shall then describe the environment of the New Jersey Meadows at the time the Edison factory was built, and during the early years of its existence in Kearny.

This case study is based on two site visits to Kearny in May 1998, and on books and papers that I located in the Kearny Public Library and in the Kearny Museum. I was oriented to the town of Kearny by a native son and Princeton graduate, Charles E. Crandall, M.D., and by his friend, Mr. George Rogers. I also was given generous assistance and guidance by several members of the staff of the Kearny Library and Museum, including a senior volunteer at the Museum, Mr. Leo Koncher.[401]

New Barbadoes

5,308 acres of upland, extending from the point of union of the Hackensack and Passaic rivers, about seven miles northward along these rivers to a spring known as Boiling Spring.

— Grant to William Sandford, 1668[402]

THE first Englishman to settle in the area now known as Kearny, New Jersey, was a Major William Sandford, who on 4 July 1668 was granted title by Governor Carteret of New Jersey to the land between Newark and the "Barren Neck" (now Bayonne and southern Jersey City) and north to a great spring where Rutherford is now located. Sandford was then a resident of the Parish of St. Mary's on the island of Barbados, and he called his new property "New Barbadoes." The "point of union of the Hackensack and Passaic rivers" juts into Newark Bay below and to the south of the bridges of the Pulaski Skyway and Truck Routes of U.S. Highways 1 and 9. Three hundred and thirty years after Major Sandford was awarded this property for "twenty dollars sterling, yearly," it includes the towns and cities now known as Harrison, Kearny, and East Newark in Hudson County, and North Arlington, Kingsland, Lyndhurst, and Seacaucus in Bergen County. Sandford's grant also includes much of the New Jersey Meadowlands, where seventy years ago Charles Edison decided to build his new battery factory.[403]

This is confusing geography for most residents of the New York-New Jersey metropolitan region, even though it is traversed every day by millions of people and hundreds of thousands of vehicles, including cars, trucks, trains, airplanes, ferries and ships. The delta of the Hackensack and Passaic rivers and the New Jersey Meadowlands is mysterious in part because it is now crisscrossed with countless roads and railroads, and is scattered about with warehouses, factories, and abandoned property. But even before it was built up and then trashed, the Meadowlands was terra incognita: It was a low, mucky, tidal area that lacked convenient landmarks. The New Jersey Meadowlands was long regarded as a mosquito-infested swamp to be endured when passing from, say, Newark to Jersey City. By the late 1920s only two land routes went across the southern Meadowlands between Essex County and Hudson County, and the Edisons were intimately familiar with both of them.[404]

The two roads of the southern Meadowlands — one called the Belleville Turnpike and the other known as the Newark-Jersey City Turnpike — met in the eastern part of the Meadowlands and formed a single road that crossed Fish House Road on the west bank of the Hackensack River and continued on to Jersey City, where it was known as Newark Avenue. The E-Mark battery plant was built in the west-facing crotch of the "Y" that marked the intersection of the two turnpikes that came into the Meadowlands from Essex County. Thomas A. Edison, Inc. ("battery mfr"), telephone KE2-3000, was located between the south side of the asphalt road that led across the wetlands from Belleville (the Belleville Turnpike) and the north side of the cut stone turnpike that led to this intersection from Newark. The Edison plant faced the Belleville Turnpike, and for the entire period of its existence it was the easternmost property owner on this road. The Edison company's battery factory was located just east of the places where the Pennsylvania Railroad and the Erie & Lackawanna Railroad crossed the Belleville Turnpike.

The E-Mark battery factory was thus located near abundant amounts of water — to say the least — and it was adjacent to outstanding railroad connections, as well as being situated where the principal roads between Newark and Jersey City came together. These facts alone, however, would not necessarily have guided Charles Edison's eye to this spot. There was, in addition, a long history that connected the Edisons with the routes that joined at this point. These roads had been a part of the Edison family's environment for nearly sixty years.[405]

Schuyler's Purchase

One of his slaves, while plowing, turned up a peculiar green stone which ... contained 80% copper.

— Mrs. Walter C. Hipp, 1967[406]

WHEN Charles Edison selected Kearny as the site for his new battery factory, he chose a city that had a long history of industrial development. One of the earliest copper mines in New Jersey had been discovered in about 1719 immediately north of what is now the corner of Portete Avenue and the Belleville Turnpike, on the property of Captain Arent Schuyler. This copper mine was worked by power "produced by the first steam engine to America from England," which was "needed to pump out the deep shaft." Captain Schuyler had bought the Sandford property from Major Nathaniel Kingsland, who had taken it over after Sandford died. Schuyler's enterprise was the first of many businesses that thrived in Kearny. His mansion survived until 1924, when it was demolished by a land development company. Schuyler Avenue now marks the eastern base of the ridge on which most of the homes in Kearny are built, and it marks the western edge of the Meadowlands. The southern portion of the Sandford grant became known as Lodi in 1825, and then as Harrison in 1840. The New Jersey Legislature made a large portion of this township into a separate town in 1867 and called it Kearny, in honor of General Philip Kearny, who had lived there before the Civil War.[407]

Other industries developed in Kearny in the mid-nineteenth century, beginning with the Clark Thread Company in 1875, which brought "thousands" of Scottish immigrants to the region. Two additional Clark Thread mills were added in 1890. Other cotton and flax spinning mills were started in the 1870s and 1880s, and predecessors of a DuPont factory and of the Congoleum-Nairn Company were built in the 1880s. These operations began to extend industrial buildings into the western fringes of the Meadowlands. Swift & Company, Koppers Company, and the Western Electric Company had established plants in the southern part of Kearny by the beginning of the twentieth century. Indeed, by the late 1930s over one hundred companies were said to have factories in Kearny, including the battery factory of Thomas A. Edison, Inc. Charles Edison would have considered this small city as a favorable site for the establishment of his new factory, based on the history of success that other companies had demonstrated in Kearny. But there was at least one other important consideration that would have been obvious to him: Although the area in the eastern Meadowlands that Charles Edison selected was then undeveloped and uninviting swampland, it was located on the main roads that ran east from the main Edison plant in West Orange and from the Edison factory complex at Silver Lake.[408] The three roads that led to the spot where Charles Edison built the E-Mark battery factory had strong connections with shops that his father — the Great Inventor — had operated. From the east, Newark Avenue came to this intersection from Jersey City, across the Hackensack River. Newark Avenue originated at Exchange Place in Jersey City, where Thomas Edison's first shop in New Jersey was located in 1870. The Belleville Turnpike

PHOTOS BY GEORGE J. HILL, M.D.

FIRST FACTORY IN THE KEARNY MEADOWLANDS: Edison's E-Mark Battery Factory was located at the intersection of the Belleville Turnpike and Newark Avenue (now Route 508). Today, the Belleville Turnpike (shown above heading toward Jersey City) runs over the site of the former E-Mark plant. No traces remain of Edison's factory, which once looked toward Newark Bay and what is now the Pulaski Skyway (below).

came to this spot in the Meadowlands as the eastern extension of Belleville Avenue, which began at Bloomfield Avenue less than one hundred yards west of the Edison Battery Factory in Glen Ridge. Belleville Avenue passed along the north side of Edison's property in Glen Ridge, and north of the Edison plant in Silver Lake, while Bloomfield Avenue passed along the southern border of both properties. Belleville Avenue proceeded on through Belleville and crossed the Passaic River into Kearny, where it became known as the Belleville Turnpike. It rose over the ridgeline on the east bank of the Passaic and dropped down into the Meadowlands, running east to join the Newark-Jersey City Turnpike, and continuing on to Jersey City as Newark Avenue.

Only a few years after the Edison factory was built in the Meadowlands, R. Eagan built a tavern at the northeast corner of Schuyler Avenue and the Belleville Turnpike, and Eagan's Restaurant is still there. Eagan's, "Since 1933," says the sign at the corner. By 1940, this intersection at the western edge of the Meadowlands was occupied by Eagan's tavern, the Tri-County Radio and Television Laboratory, J. T. Jeffreys' gasoline station, and Schantz & VanBuren's Service Station. As the Belleville Turnpike descended from this corner into the Meadowlands, it passed by Arlington Cemetery (established in 1883) on the south and Portete Avenue (where the red sandstone cliffs marking the old Schuyler copper mine were still visible) on the north. To the east of this intersection, the vast grassy swamps of the Meadowlands then extended with few interruptions to Jersey City. The view across the Meadowlands then was broken by only a few radio towers, the railroads that crisscrossed the marshland, and the Pulaski skyway that arched along the southern horizon between Newark and Jersey City. The Meadowlands' highest point, Snake Rock, had not yet been quarried down and covered with graffiti, for the New Jersey Turnpike was not built until the 1950s.[409]

The third road that came to the new Edison factory site in the Meadowlands — the Newark-Jersey City Turnpike — began at the Passaic River in Newark and crossed the river on the short street which was called, appropriately, Bridge Street. It passed east through Harrison as Harrison Avenue, and then became the Newark-Jersey City Turnpike. To the west of the Passaic River in Newark, this road was, and is still, known as Orange Street in Newark, and as Main Street in the Oranges. Main Street reached St. Mark's Square in West Orange less than a quarter of a mile south of the Edison Plant. In earlier days, the street running north from this intersection, past Llewellyn Park and the Edison plant, was known as Valley Street, although it is now called Main Street. This ancient road continued to the west over First Mountain as Northfield Avenue and finally terminated on the west side of Second Mountain, where it joined Mount Pleasant Avenue in Livingston. The route that goes from the Livingston traffic circle to St. Mark's Church in West Orange and then on to the intersection in the Meadowlands where the E-Mark batteries were once made is now a well-paved and heavily traveled thoroughfare. It is County Road 508.[410]

A nexus of railroads was also essential for industry in the late 1930s, when trucks were less powerful and roads were not as well surfaced as they are today. The Belleville Turnpike had been a corduroy road until 1914, when it was "macadamized." Prior to this, it had been very difficult to maintain this road, and forty-five years earlier, in 1869, the Hudson County Grand Jury had actually indicted the inhabitants of Kearny for the bad condition of the turnpike. This marshy ground is still challenging terrain, and it has been written that "new roads rarely stay smooth for long in the Meadowlands. They buckle and sink and eventually begin the long journey down into the depths of the old swamp."[411]

All of the railroads that the Edison companies had used in West Orange, Silver Lake, and western New Jersey were close to the site of the E-Mark factory in the Meadowlands, either directly or through connecting lines. As recently as 1950 Kearny was still served by the Erie R.R., the Central R.R. of N.J., the Pennsylvania R.R., the D. L. & W. ("the Lackawanna"), and the Lehigh Valley R.R. In 1940 the Harrison-Kearny City Directory had finally gotten the Edison battery factory located correctly on the eastern, rather than the western, end of the Belleville Turnpike. At that time the turnpike was crossed sequentially by four railroads just west of the Edison plant: the D.L.& W., the E.R.R. (Greenwood Lake Branch), the E.R.R. (Newark & Hudson Branch) and the P.R.R. Only three other businesses were then located along the entire stretch of the Belleville Turnpike east of the railroad tracks: two radio stations (WAAT and WMCA) and the White Tar Co. of N.J. Even then, in 1950, only three other pieces of property were occupied between Schuyler Avenue and the Edison plant, a distance of three miles: a gasoline station, a real estate holding company, and the Scandia Match manufacturing plant. From the late 1920s to 1938, the Edison plant's only neighbors for three miles in the Meadowlands were radio station WAAT and a chemical manufacturer, the White Tar Company. Two years later, in 1940, a White Castle diner had opened between the tar company and the battery factory, but it disappeared during the Second World War.[412]

Edison and the Model A Ford

Organized to supply original equipment for Ford automobiles, the E-Mark operation . . .

—Venable, 1978[413]

Let us now return to Venable's comment about Ford automobiles, which I mentioned earlier in this case study. Venable, who was the biographer of Charles Edison, states unequivocally, although without elaboration, that the E-Mark battery was used in Ford cars. A bit of history of the Ford automobile and of Henry Ford's relationship with Thomas Edison is in order at this point, for it helps to explain when the E-Mark battery project started, and why.

Henry Ford was a great admirer of Thomas Edison. Ford and Edison traveled together on country roads for many summers, and Ford built a winter home near Edison's in Fort Myers. Ford credited Edison for many of his important ideas, including the concept of the assembly line, and Ford persuaded Edison to allow him to move the Menlo Park laboratory buildings to Michigan, where they became the nucleus of a museum which he established at Greenfield Village, near his plant at Dearborn. By the late 1920s, Ford and Harvey Firestone had begun to subsidize Edison's project to find a domestic source of latex for rubber production, in the event that U.S. supplies were cut off in a world war — which many leaders predicted, correctly, would begin in the 1930s. Edison was arguably the world's premier manufacturer of batteries, and he was certainly believed by Ford to be the world's most gifted battery scientist. To this background, we need to add the information that Ford was preparing to terminate manufacture of his once hugely successful, but now outdated, Model T car and begin manufacturing a new automobile, which he would call the Model A. The Model T was discontinued in 1927, and for the next four years, Ford surged forward again in sales with his new Model A automobile.[414] The Model A was the fore-runner of the automobile of today. In contrast to the Model T, the Model A had a transmission that was virtually identical in principle and in operation to the modern four speed (three forward, one reverse) transmission, with a clutch pedal to the left of the brake pedal, just as it is on modern trucks and cars. Anyone who can drive a car with a standard manual transmission will feel comfortable, even exhilarated, driving a 1928 Model A Ford. And, in contrast to the Model T, the Model A had a battery-powered "starter," rather than an arm-breaking crank. The Model A could be cranked, too, so it could be started if the battery was dead, and it broke a few arms in its day. But the battery usually worked, when it was hooked up properly.

If the sequence of my reasoning is correct, Ford and Edison (in this case Charles, who was the acting CEO of the Edison Corporation) agreed that the Edison company (or a new Edison company, as it turned out) would make a new battery (the lead-acid "E-Mark") for Ford's new-fangled automobile. Ford was going to market the Model A in 1928, so the battery would have to go into production in 1927 at the latest. This argument places Charles Edison and the E-Mark battery factory in the Meadowlands of Kearny, New Jersey, in 1927. The Table of Organization of Thomas A. Edison, Inc., shows that E-Mark was located in Kearny in in 1930. My reasoning suggests that the new company's startup year was in 1927, and Kearny was a good a place for it to be located. After all, the Old Man hated lead-acid batteries ("if God had wanted batteries to be made of lead, He would have made lead lighter"), and not even Charles would have been comfortable making them secretly in West Orange or Silver Lake. Kearny had the water, railroads, labor, and roads that were needed for the Edison factory, and undeveloped property was available in the Meadowlands. It required a spark of imagination and a pioneering spirit to build the new battery factory far out in the mosquito-infested swampland, but Charles Edison's gamble paid off.[415] In the 1930s, the E-Mark Battery Corporation was typical of the major industries

COURTESY OF THE NATIONAL PARK SERVICE

E-MARK FACTORY: No photographs have been found of the Edison plant in Kearny, but this 1930 drawing was used to illustrate the "Table of Organization of Thomas A. Edison, Inc.," that is on the wall of the Visitor's Center at the Edison National Historic Site in West Orange.

in Kearny, with respect to its size and the attitudes of its leaders regarding the rationale and objectives of its operation in the Meadowlands. A drawing of the E-Mark plant on the Organization Chart of Thomas A. Edison Industries, Inc., in 1930 shows a facility approximately one hundred yards on each side and two to three stories high, surmounted by a smokestack at least 100 feet high emblazoned with a logo and the company name, "EMARK." The principal buildings were in two parallel groups, each of which consisted of a tall central building with two shorter buildings on each side. If the cartoon drawing of E-Mark is a reasonable approximation of reality, it represents a plant with of twenty to thirty thousand net square feet, which would provide employment for several hundred workers.[416]

In 1939, B. F. Morris, who was then Vice President of TAE, Inc., and head of the E-Mark Battery Company, praised Kearny, writing that,

We have ideal transportation facilities. We have a progressive and modern school system. Taxes are reasonable and the Board of Assessors is composed of men who understand the problems of industry and cooperate whole-heartedly. The Mayor and Council will be doing a great favor to any industry which they succeed in bringing to Kearny.[417]

The fulsome praise that Morris showered on Kearny's schools and its transportation system (as well as its assessors, mayor and council) was echoed by many of the 102 companies on "Kearny's Industrial Roster" in 1939.[418] In the late 1930s, it was the stated opinion of business and government in Hudson County that Kearny was "an ideal site for an industry," and "a delightful place in which to live."[419]

The Edison battery company is not mentioned in the official histories of Kearny, and I have not found anyone who remembers that it was once out in the Meadowlands. Perhaps this is fortunate for Edison's reputation, since the Meadowlands near the Edison Battery Factory later became known as "the largest garbage dump in the world." It has been called "the nations' eyesore, the blight separating New York and America." At this point in our Case Study, the E-Mark Battery Factory appears to be the parlous nadir of Edison's worksites.[420]

* * * * *

In the last section of this case study I will examine the Great Inventor's impact on the "internal environment," or *milieu interieur*.

Chapter 13

Edison and the *milieu interieur*: Health, Hygiene, X-Rays and Radium

Oh yes, [Edison was] tremendously interested in medicine. . . but he never had much to do with physicians.

— Mina Edison, 1947[421]

MINA Edison was eighty-two years old when she was interviewed for an oral history project at Columbia University, and she was intensely protective of her husband's image. An imposing and patrician individual even when she was young, Mina was not going to yield anything except what she wanted to have made a matter of record. With that caveat, let us then continue with what Mina said about Thomas Edison and the medical profession:

Well, he would talk with them but he never had much to do with physicians. He was a pretty well man. He listened to them. I always called him my doctor. I never called in a physician, he told me what to do. . . . [He developed] Tetra-ethyl-ammonia for arthritis. It did help but Dr. Peterson who was working on it for him died and he gave it up.

I cannot directly challenge Mina Edison's statement that she was not treated by physicians, but instead let her husband tell her "what to do." However, she seems to be either exaggerating, or forgetful. We have previously read of several instances in which Thomas Edison became seriously ill during their forty-five years of married life, we know that on these occasions he was attended by physicians and surgeons. There is no reason to believe that Mina did not also receive the attention of physicians, too, at least when her three children were born. Her statement, then, tells us what she would like us to believe. Mina wished to have it recorded that Thomas Edison was a wise and creative person with respect to health and medical science. That, in fact, is a reasonable hypothesis to explore in this case study, which I call "Edison and the *milieu interieur*."

Longevity Inquiry

Chew continuously & 2 to 3 cigars daily.
— Edison, 1930[422]

IN October 1929 Edison consented to have his body measurements taken in connection with a "Longevity Inquiry" that was conducted by Professor Irving Fisher of New Haven, Connecticut. We do not know the reasons that Professor Irving marshaled to gain the inventor's concurrence. However, he must have struck a responsive chord, for Edison cooperated in what most people would think of as a thoroughly tedious and potentially embarrassing examination. The copy of the report that I have seen is not legible enough to read all of the measurements that were taken. Nevertheless, we can see that there were at least six measurements taken of various aspects of Edison's head and neck; seven of his arms, forearms, and hands; seven of his chest and abdomen; and eight measurements of his thighs, lower legs, and feet. In addition, his height was measured and he was asked such questions as "Are you tired?" (I cannot locate his answer to this question.) I presume that Edison's weight was also taken, although I cannot see a record of it on the cartoon drawings of the front and side views of a man, on which the measurements are recorded.[423]

At the age of eighty-two, Edison was a relatively short man with a large neck, chest, and abdomen. His height appears to have been 67 inches (five feet, seven inches), and his neck was 17 inches in circumference. The circumference of his head is obscured but the final digit appears to be a "4," so it was presumably 24 inches; this would give him a hat size of about 7 and five-eighths. He was 44 inches around at the shoulders, and his waist was but slightly less at 40 inches in circumference. His feet were long (12 inches from heel to longest toe) although his hands were relatively small (7 and three-fourths inches from wrist to longest fingertip). His maximum forearm diameter was 12 inches, only one inch less than his upper arm. In summary, he appeared to be a short, dumpy man with a large belly, a thick neck and large head, and small biceps muscles.

Edison was, however, undaunted by this physical evaluation, and the following year he submitted to a searching personal health history, which was called, euphemistically, a "Longevity Inquiry." Indeed, at this time, the Great Inventor was eighty-three years old; he would die just a year later. As a participant in the Longevity Inquiry, Edison personally wrote out the answers to a five page, fourteen part questionnaire. I have taken the liberty of converting the outline of the questionnaire and Edison's answers to a narrative format, which reads as follows:

LONGEVITY INQUIRY
Confidential Communication
File No. S746A

My name is Thos. A. Edison. I am a male. I was born Feby 11, 1847. My Post Office Address is Orange, N. Jersey. I am writing these answers on Oct. 12th, 1930.

My father was a lumber operator. He was in strong, robust health for most of his life. He died at 94 of old age. My mother was in medium health during most of her life, and she died of worry at the age of 70. My mother's father died at 103, and her mother died at 90. One of my brothers died at 70. One of my sisters died at 35 of tuberculosis, and another sister died of stomach trouble at the age of 77. My family has been troubled by tuberculosis.

I have been married twice, and I have six children, all of whom are in good health. Their ages are 55, 53, 50, 48, 40, and 37.

I do not recall anything special about my health as a child, but I did not have measles, whooping cough, or scarlet fever. My health from childhood to age 65 was generally robust, and it has been robust since the age of 65. I have had pneumonia, and I had a mastoid operation at the age of 35. I suffered from indigestion and gas at the age of 54, but I have not had any serious accidents, and none of these incidents had any effect on my later life.

My height is now five feet, nine and one-half inches, and I weigh 170 pounds. I have lost 28 pounds during the past five years as the result of dieting. During my middle years, I tended to be thin to moderate in weight. My body was fairly well proportioned. My posture is now slightly bent. My eyesight is good, but I have worn glasses since the age of seventy. I am very deaf and I have no teeth left. My hair is thin. My pulse rate is 74 and my blood pressure is normal for my age. I have had perfectly normal bowel movements for 78 years, and I now average a movement once a day. My only organic impairment or internal disorder is indigestion and gas.[424]

Regarding my mental attitude, I am not predisposed or inclined to nervousness, nor am I accustomed to worry. I do not have a depressing mental state. I do not derive comfort from religion, but I very much derive comfort from philosophy and literature.

I sleep well, about six hours in every twenty-four hours. In earlier life, I formerly slept less than five hours out of every twenty-four. I am a very small eater. I formerly ate three times daily, but now I take a milk diet six times daily. I am not regular in my eating habits, and I eat rapidly. I have no teeth, so I do not chew my food; my diet is now only fresh milk and orange juice. I believe that I have benefited [sic] from eating little or no flesh foods.[425]

The only liquid that I consume is milk, and I take it at mealtimes. I do not drink water. Most of my life I used plenty of spring water at meals. I took coffee very slightly, but no tea, cocoa, soda water, or mineral waters. I did not use spirituous liquors, beer, wine, or cider.[426]

Regarding bathing and physical exercise, I bathe less than once a week, in water of medium temperature. I know how to swim, but I do not swim, walk, or perform any other exercise for recreation. I do not take regular vacations. I have never participated in athletics, nor have I excelled at sports. I do not exercise to the point of perspiration; I do not exercise at all.[427]

My house has air that is as fresh as outdoors, and I sleep with the windows opened. My bedroom air has always been as fresh as outdoors, and my habits in this respect have not changed. I have practically never lived in the open air. When out of doors, I have always been in much sunlight.

Regarding my tobacco habits, I chew tobacco continuously and smoke two to three cigars daily. I consider that I am a very slight cigar smoker, but I have used chewing tobacco freely for seventy-eight [?] years. [Edison did not reply to questions about cigarettes and pipe tobacco, but he said that he did not take snuff.] *I believe that my health has been unaffected by the use of tobacco.*[428]

I do not take patent medicines or drugs habitually, or even as often as once a week. I wear woolen underclothes. With regard to my personal hygiene and environment, and my long life: I eat to keep my weight constant. I have been an extremely small eater since a boy. 2500 cc of fresh milk daily keeps my weight constant.[429]

[signed] Thos A. Edison

* * * * *

We can see from the answers to Professor Fisher's questions that Edison could be brutally realistic regarding his own health and habits, while also being forgetful or devious. Some of his answers, such as the responses about his health in childhood, conflict with well-documented statements made either by Edison himself or by others. Nevertheless, Edison's responses to the "Longevity Inquiry" provide a truly unique opportunity to see the Great Inventor's health and health habits as he wished to have them recorded at what we now know (and which he presumably believed, too) was the twilight of his life. His handwriting was clear and firm, and he wrote his name at the top of page one and the bottom of page five with no degradation in form or clarity, which shows a remarkable degree of tenacity.

Edison's comment on bathing ("less than once a week") is consistent with what others have written about his habits and on his own handwritten statement elsewhere:

Some native Races never bathe. The skin is not the proper or normal organ for the exit of dead matter. People who eat very little do not need such frequent baths, don't have scales on their backs.[430]

The inventor's handwritten statement in the Longevity Inquiry that he took "no exercise" was consistent with his derisory comment elsewhere regarding "Exercise," in which he wrote:

Riding a horse is no Exercise whatever. Every movement comes from the horse — he gets exercise if he is the motor and walks or rides a bicycle.[431]

This statement can be read as a put-down of exercise in general, not just horseback riding. The reader may recall that Edison was said to have detested horses, and at this point he provides yet another excuse to avoid getting on a horse. And although he wrote here that walking or bicycle riding would provide more exercise than horseback riding, I have never read that Edison rode a bicycle, nor did he evidence interest in walking, except out of sheer necessity.

The brief statements made by Edison in the Longevity Inquiry regarding vacations ("none") and recreation ("none") warrant a critique, inasmuch as it is a matter of record that he traveled with Henry Ford, Harvey Firestone, John Burroughs, and others for several summers

COURTESY OF NATIONAL PARK SERVICE

EDISON AND HIS FAMOUS TRAVELING COMPANIONS: Henry Ford, Harvey Firestone, John Burroughs and others on one of their famous star-studded summer vacations together.

during the period before and after World War I. Furthermore, Edison had built a home in Fort Myers, Florida, in 1886, and he spent much of his time there during the last years of his life — including 1930, when he answered the questions posed in the Longevity Inquiry. What rational explanation, therefore, can be given for his saying "none" in reply to questions about vacations and recreation? The answer is clear from Edison's responses: he regarded his trips with Ford and Firestone and the time he spent in Florida as integral parts of his working life.

Edison's mind was never at rest, and he was continuously thinking of new projects or trying out his ideas at the laboratory bench. In his simple, unguarded responses to Professor Fisher's questions — which Edison believed was a "confidential communication" — we gain better insight into the mind of the Great Inventor at the end of his life. Edison regarded Fort Myers as an essential part of his work environment, and we must bear that in mind as we examine his home, laboratory, and botanical projects in Florida. Before turning to Florida, however, we have a bit of grim business to consider, which is Edison's unfortunate experience with X-rays and his close encounter with radium.

Ionizing Radiation

Try radium if you like.
— **Thomas Alva Edison, 1903**[432]

THE discovery of X-Rays by Roentgen in 1895, and radium, which was discovered by the Curies and their assistant, Bemont, in 1898, revolutionized the field of physics and ushered in what later became known as the Atomic Age. The dangers of the ionizing radiation that is produced by X-rays and radium gradually became apparent, but not before many scientists and industrial workers had been seriously injured. Some of them would eventually die of radiation-induced diseases. Edison's flippant comment about radium in about 1903 shows that he lacked awareness of the hazard of radium. That was typical of the period. His comment also vividly demonstrates the disconnection at that time in the minds of most people, including physicists and physicians, between the effects of X-rays and radium.

We now know that these two forms of ionizing radiation produce similar biological effects, but that knowledge was lacking until the 1920s and thereafter. Edison was very familiar with X-rays, having been — early in 1896 — one of the first to experiment with these new rays in the Western Hemisphere. By 1903, when Edison joked, "try radium," one of his employees was dying of cancer induced by X-rays produced in his laboratory in West Orange, and the Great Inventor had developed a life-long personal antipathy to the use of X-rays. Yet we see that Edison did not yet recognize the dangers associated with radium, and one of the world's most notorious generators of radium-induced injuries and deaths was established within the next decade less than two hundred yards from the Edison plant.[433]

PHOTO BY GEORGE J. HILL, M.D.

GATEHOUSE TO THE EDISON PLANT: The main entrance to the Edison complex in West Orange was guarded by this gatehouse, which stands on Main Street in front of Building No. 5. The West Orange plant was the site of the experiments with x-rays that resulted in the first death from radiation exposure in the United States.

    In an astonishing coincidence that has, to my knowledge, not previously been commented upon by historians or scientists, the lethal effects of X-rays and of radium dial watch paint were first produced by two corporations that were nearly adjacent to each other in Essex County, New Jersey. Both companies were located along the Wigwam Brook, on opposite sides of Watchung Avenue, which at this point is the dividing line between the municipalities of Orange and West Orange. Thomas A. Edison, Inc., was located between Alden Street and Lakeside Avenue on the west side of Watchung Avenue in West Orange, and the U.S. Radium Corporation was located between Alden Street and the Wigwam Brook in Orange, one half block east of Watchung Avenue.[434]

COURTESY OF NATIONAL PARK SERVICE

FIRST MARTYR TO RADIATION: Clarence Dally at work on the fluoroscope, which was invented by Edison. Dally later died of cancer induced by X-rays.

What is probably the first accidental fatality from X-rays in the world (and certainly in the Western hemisphere) was the death of one of Thomas Edison's employees, Clarence Dally, in 1904, and the first death of a radium dial watch painter occurred in 1922. The unfortunate dial painter had been employed at the Radium Luminous Materials Corporation, later known as the U.S. Radium Company. My case study of "Edison and Ionizing Radiation" was performed to if any information could be found regarding Edison's work that might be connected with the U.S. Radium Corporation. I wished to see if there was a connection of some kind between these two organizations — both of which were engaged in research and development of products that utilized ionizing radiation early in the twentieth century. In the end, I was unable to establish a corporate relationship between TAE, Inc., and U.S. Radium, but the proximity of these two industrial plants had (and still has) some interesting environmental sequelae, as will soon become apparent.[435]

Beginning in March 1896, Thomas Edison — working on the west side of Watchung Avenue — inadvertently exposed his glassblower,

Clarence Dally, to a cumulative dose of X-rays that was large enough to cause cancer of the skin of his hands. In spite of treatment, which eventually included amputation of his arms, the cancer recurred and eventually spread to his chest cavity. Dally is said to have been the first person to die of X-ray induced cancer. His agony profoundly affected Thomas Edison, who had also become ill from the effects of X-rays, although Edison recovered completely. Two decades later, on the east side of Watchung Avenue, less than one hundred yards from the Edison plant, young women who were employed as dial painters of watches began to ingest lethal amounts of another form of ionizing radiation — radium.[436]

For this case study, I reviewed the files on "Radium" in the archives of the George F. Smith Library of the University of Medicine and Dentistry of New Jersey (UMDNJ), Newark, N.J., and in the West Orange Public Library. I also reviewed the archives of the Essex County Medical Society for the period 1895-1931, looking for anything related to Edison, or X-rays, or radium. These documents are now located in the UMDNJ Library. Dr. George Tselos of the Edison National Historic Site guided me to the case report of Clarence Dally in Percy Brown's article, "American Martyrs to Radiology" (1935), which was reprinted in 1995 in the *American Journal of Roentgenology*. The fortuitous publication of *Radium Girls* by Claudia Clark in 1997 was immensely helpful to me, with respect to the information that Clark assembled regarding the dial painters' problems and the status of industrial health in the period from 1914 to 1941. Christopher C. Sellers' book, *Hazards of the Job* (1997) was important in helping me to understand the history and characteristics of the workplace environment during the period that Edison was developing the fluoroscope in West Orange and radium dial paint was being prepared and used by his neighbor on the Wigwam Brook in Orange. Finally, I am indebted to Jack Stanley, whose copies of oral histories that were transcribed in the 1970s provided, by chance, one of the few specific connections that I found between the Edison corporation and U.S. Radium.[437]

* * * * *

COURTESY OF SPECIAL COLLECTIONS,
UNIVERSITY OF MEDICINE AND DENTISTRY (NOW RUTGERS UNIVERSITY),
GEORGE F. SMITH LIBRARY OF THE HEALTH SCIENCES, NEWARK

RADIUM GIRLS: Young women of the Oranges were employed by the U.S. Radium Corporation as dial painters and in the adjacent Thomas A. Edison, Inc., plant. At least one of the dial painters is known to have worked for both companies.

One of Edison's employees, A. E. Johnson, recalled in 1971 that:

We had one girl, in the early days we had one girl, I guess she was one of the first victims of radioactivity. You remember, during World War I they had a — there was a concern around here, I don't know what they were making, but anyway they were making — oh yes, they were putting lighted marks on watches that were radioactive. The girls who did these had small camel's hair brushes, and it became necessary to moisten them with their tongues, you know, and there were the first cases of radioactivity affecting individuals. And one of the girls, she came to work for me and was taken sick and died. There were quite a number. That plant was right over on the corner of the Edison property, you remember?[438]

Mr. Johnson's recollection about the "radium girl" who had worked under his supervision in the Edison plant more than fifty years earlier would be a delectation for us, if the outcome had not been so tragic. Nevertheless, Johnson's brief comment warrants a thorough exegesis, for the unfortunate, anonymous, young radium dial painter who later worked for Edison exemplifies several important aspects of the industrial environment in this "poor, residential neighborhood" of the Orange Valley in the early twentieth century.[439]

In the first place, both the radium dial painters and many of the workers in the Edison plant were young women, who were patronizingly called "girls" by their employers and supervisors. These young women were expected to be neatly dressed, punctual, and well-behaved on the job and in their personal lives. Most of them were single, and they needed work to help support their families. They were quiet, compliant, and pleasant — ideal factory workers for Edison's plant as well as for the U.S. Radium plant. Especially for tasks that required delicate manual dexterity, such as assembling "talking dolls" and polishing "Diamond Disk" phonograph records in the Edison plant, or painting the hands and numerals on watch dials at U.S. Radium. These "girls" came from blue collar families that lived in the Orange Valley near the border of Orange and West Orange, and they had little choice but to work as long and as hard as they could, in whatever environment their employer chose to provide. They were supposed to beware of exposing themselves to obvious industrial hazards such as lead, mercury, phosphorus, benzene, and asbestos. They had no reason to worry about working with radium, for until the 1920s radium was not regarded as even possibly being a hazardous substance. In the first three decades of this century, radium was actually considered by the public and many medical professionals as being a useful tonic, and this belief persisted even after radium was beginning to be suspected as the cause of disastrous jaw problems and bone cancer in dial-painters.[440]

Johnson's final sentence shows that even a half-century after the former radium dial painter worked for him, Johnson remembered that the U.S. Radium Corporation plant was very near the eastern border of the Edison property. (He said, correctly, that it was "right over on the corner.")

This fact was surely common knowledge in the 1920s and 1930s, but it has been largely forgotten in the past three decades, concurrent with the

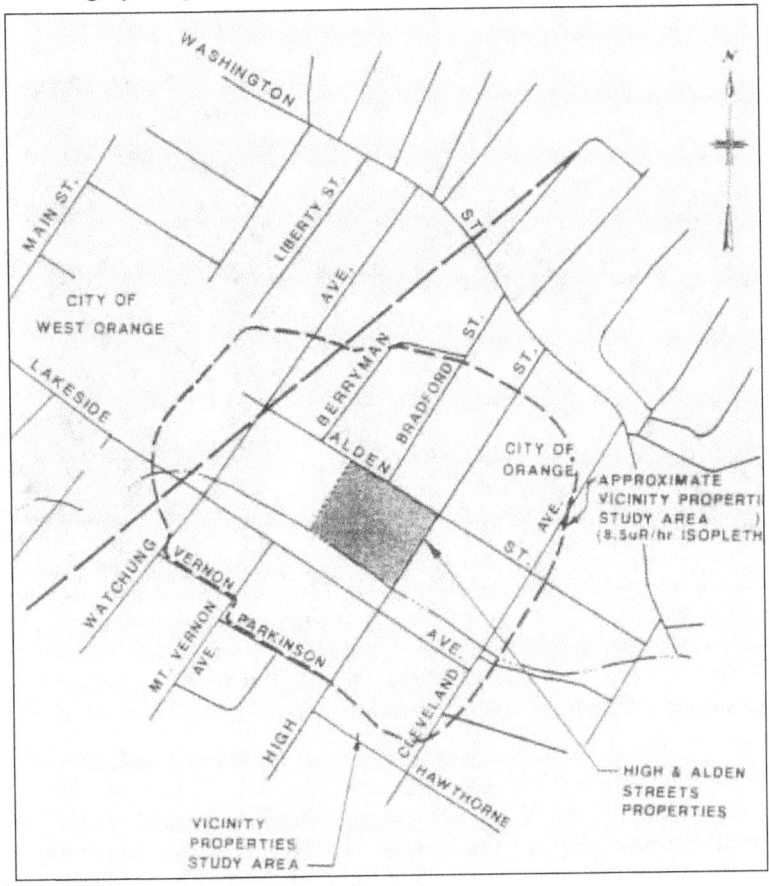

COURTESY OF SPECIAL COLLECTIONS,
UNIVERSITY OF MEDICINE AND DENTISTRY (NOW RUTGERS UNIVERSITY),
GEORGE F. SMITH LIBRARY OF THE HEALTH SCIENCES, NEWARK

SUPERFUND SITE: The black square marks the location of the U.S. Radium Corporation Superfund site. Edison's plant stretched along Lakeside Avenue from Main Street to Watchung Avenue, ending one block away from U.S. Radium. The plume of radiation in the ground extends from the Superfund site to the border of the Edison property.

destruction of most of the Edison plant buildings and the gradual demise of the former employees of both companies. Nevertheless, the purification and chemical preparation of radium near the Edison plant has had a profound, though silent, effect on the former Edison property.

PHOTO BY GEORGE J. HILL, M.D.

WIGWAM BROOK: The sparkling brook that arose near the top of First Mountain ran past Edison's home, Glenmont, then crossed under his battery factory before emerging into a concrete ditch beside the U.S. Radium Corporation.

The eastern edge of the Edison National Historic Site on Lakeside Avenue is only a few feet away from the demonstrated danger area of the U.S. Radium Corporation Superfund site. Radioactive contamination of the soil from the U.S. Radium site now extends eastward into West Orange. By 1991, radioactivity from the U.S. Radium site had spread to the base of the Edison water tower, where Crooks Pond was once located. At that time, the U.S. Environmental Protection Agency's "Vicinities Property Area Map" showed that the asphalt-paved parking lot immediately east of the Edison water tower was within the so-called "8.5 uR/hr isopleth line" of radioactivity.[441] What impact this fact will have on future plans for development of the Edison site remains to be determined. It is, however, now clear that the environment of earth and water along Alden Street, the Wigwam Brook, and the former right of way of the Orange Branch railroad on both sides of the border of Orange and West Orange has been seriously contaminated by the U.S. Radium Corporation.

I have found no evidence that suggests that the Edison Corporation was directly involved in any way with the production or use of radium. However, Thomas A. Edison, Inc., was the dominant corporation in this neighborhood, and indeed in this region of the Orange Valley. Edison thus provided the "gold standard" for environmental safety in the workplace in this part of Essex County. As the principal employer in West Orange and as an advocate for public safety, we can now see that Edison missed an opportunity to identify the hazards of a new substance (radium) that he was interested in, and to study methods to use it safely. Edison's failure to appreciate the danger of radium is understandable, for many of his contemporaries in science and business also failed to recognize the hazards of radium and other radioactive substances. Edison had been burned, literally and figuratively, by X-rays, and he had decided not to conduct further studies on that aspect of radiation.[442]

It is not surprising, therefore, that Edison instinctively avoided getting involved with this new and mysterious form of radiation, in spite of the safety — and therapeutic benefits — that its proponents claimed for radium, "radium hot springs," and "radium water." In addition, by the 1920's Edison was elderly (he was already 70 years old when radium dial paint was first used in large amounts in 1917), and he was deeply involved in research and development of other products. In the last decades of his life Edison was studying and producing batteries, cement, and — in the last years of his life — new sources of latex for rubber to be used in motor vehicle tires.

* * * * *

As I came to the end of my last case study, I realized that there are still many sites to explore and questions to ask regarding the environment of the Great Inventor. At this point, however, I decided that I had achieved what I had set out to do, which was to learn enough to be able to develop and defend my own analysis of this subject. I had studied some areas in depth that had not previously been examined or were mentioned only briefly by other historians. I had also investigated various aspects of Edison's relationship to the environment that were contested by various authorities. It is now time to proceed to the synthesis, which follows in the final Part of this book.

Part III

EDISON'S ENVIRONMENT, 1869-1931

Denouement

THE last part of this book consists of an Epilogue, Summary, Discussion, and Conclusion. In the Epilogue, I will trace the environmental legacy of Edison's life in the communities where he lived and worked in New Jersey, and in other areas where his impact was indirect, throughout the nation and the world. In my Summary, I shall recapitulate the principal environmental effects that are attributable to Edison's activities, based on the scholarship of others and on my own research (presented in Part II and in the Epilogue). In the Discussion, I examine Edison's impact on the environment in relation to the changes that have occurred in the environment, in general, throughout his lifetime, and thereafter. In my Conclusion, I shall outline the principal themes of Edison's life and work that impacted on the environment. In the end, I render my personal judgment regarding the Great Inventor's beliefs, intentions, behavior, and effects with respect to the environment.

Chapter 14

Epilogue

Man of the Millennium

Thomas Edison, the Wizard of Menlo Park, has been selected by Life *magazine as the most important figure of the millennium in a special double issue out this week.*

— *Star-Ledger*, 1997[443]

IT is a daunting task to attempt to summarize the history of Thomas Edison's environment from the moment of his death to the present time. This aspect of history has a scope that ranges from minor myths to grand pronouncements.[444] Nevertheless, let us begin.

* * * * *

As the Great Inventor's physical strength ebbed during the last years of his life, he became more sedentary, ate little, and rested in bed for longer periods of time. He was content to have a personal environment that was restricted principally to his homes and laboratories in West Orange and Fort Myers. In his eighties, Edison rarely appeared in public, and he was seen then only from a distance. He collapsed on his last major trip, in October 1929, when he was honored at the Golden Jubilee of the incandescent light in Dearborn, Michigan. However, Edison continued working on his goldenrod rubber project, and he helped Professor Fisher of New Haven with his geriatric studies. In January 1931, nine months before he died, Edison welcomed the birth of his fourth grandson, who was to be his last descendant in that generation. Near the end, Edison was virtually bedridden, and we do not know how much he participated in the plans for his services and burial. It is, however, clear that there was ample opportunity to make arrangements for Edison to lie in state at his Laboratory, for the memorial service that was held at Glenmont, and for his interment at Rosedale Cemetery in a plot overlooking the buildings of Thomas A. Edison, Inc.

The sixty-sixth anniversary of Edison's death passed in October 1997. It was not a remarkable occasion, nothing like the 150th anniversary of his birth, which was celebrated in February of that year. After all, "sixty-six years" has no special meaning, unless you are — like the writer of this book was at that time — in your sixty-sixth year of life. Those who are in this cohort have personally lived through the events that constitute the Epilogue of the Great Inventor's life. While others may consider the past sixty-six years to be "history," for children of the 1930s — for those who grew up in the Great Depression — they are, in a sense, "current events."

In spite of their relevance to me as a child of the 1930s, I shall avoid listing all of the important mileposts of the past seven decades, even those that are particularly significant with respect to the environment. Instead, I will mention a few of the highpoints, to provide a background for my comments about the changes in the environment where Edison lived and worked (i.e., in the areas of his "footprints"), and of the environmental impact elsewhere that resulted from his activities.

A world-wide war broke out only eight years after Edison died, a conflict that he and others had predicted. World War II raged from September 1939 until August 1945, when it concluded with the defeat of the Axis powers of Germany, Italy, and Japan. This war ended with the birth of the Atomic Age, which Edison had also foreseen. A "Cold War" between the U.S. and its European allies on the one hand, and the Soviet Union and its allies on the other, continued for the next four decades. It brought the world to the brink of disaster on several occasions, although thus far a nuclear holocaust has been avoided. In spite of countless smaller wars, such as those fought by many countries in Korea and Vietnam, world population more than doubled and is well on the way to doubling again. During the past seven decades, the natural environment of the world has been severely eroded by the burning of fossil fuels and tropical rainforests. The products of combustion have created a "greenhouse" effect that has raised the temperature at the Earth's surface and produced changes in weather, climate, shore-lines, and glaciers. The Earth's ground, air, and water have been sullied by long-lasting toxic chemicals and nuclear waste, the effects of which are expected to last for centuries to come. Even the oceans have become depleted and polluted.

Many animal and plant species have been extinguished, and many more are threatened.[445]

The changes in the world's environment have been devastating, but regard for "nature" and concern for the effects of industrialization on human life have begun to result in mitigating behavior by individuals, governments, and industries. Children now are taught to understand complex terms such as "habitat" and "ecology." At this point in time, it is impossible to predict whether the causes of environmental degradation in the world will be reversed by measures designed to ensure environmental protection and restoration. It is, however, possible to examine the chain of events that have occurred in the environment in local areas. In an Epilogue, we thus have an opportunity to take a longer view of the environmental legacy of the Great Inventor than was possible for Edison, personally, and for others during his lifetime.

In this sequel to Edison's life, I shall return to examine the locations that we visited in the case studies of Chapter II. We will be looking at these places for traces of Edison's "footprints." All but one of my case studies were performed in New Jersey. (The exception was a study of Edison's vacation in Winthrop, Massachusetts.) Several of the other places where Edison lived and worked are currently protected and are accessible for scholars and the general public. These include his birthplace at Milan, Ohio; the archeological excavation of his boyhood home at Port Huron, Michigan; and the reconstructed buildings at Greenfield Village, Dearborn, Michigan. The most frequently visited site related to Edison is his winter home, which is maintained as a museum in Fort Myers, Florida. In addition, at least one other site where Edison lived is preserved as a museum: Butchertown House, in Louisville, Kentucky. There may be others, of which I am unaware.[446]

There are countless other places where Edison lived, worked, or visited during his long life that would be interesting to study for local legends and evidence of his presence. To mention but a few, consider Boston and New York City, where he lived and worked; Rawlins, Wyoming, where he participated in the study of an eclipse; California, where he visited Luther Burbank; and his plants and mines in locations as disparate as Pennsylvania, New Mexico, and Michigan. The routes and locations where Edison traveled and stayed in England and France, and in the Appalachian Mountains from New Hampshire to North Carolina, would also be interesting to examine, to obtain a deeper understanding of Edison's environment.

Edison's "Footprints": The Case Studies, Revisited

Elizabeth, New Jersey

Elizabeth is now a small, ethnically diverse city that is slowly making its way back from chronic economic depression. Interest in the city's history by various groups and individuals, several of whom were mentioned in the account of my site visit, auger well for historic preservation and future research. The question of where Thomas Edison lived when his residence(s) was (were) in Elizabeth needs to be pursued lest this building or these buildings on Morris Avenue be destroyed inadvertently in the course of the urban reconstruction that is currently underway.[447]

Orange, New Jersey

Orange, New Jersey, is now a tiny municipality, compared to what it was when it included the towns that are now East Orange, West Orange, South Orange, and Maplewood. It is economically depressed, but the city government and residents of the community take pride in their city's heritage and in its future. Through no fault of its present citizens, Orange must continually confront its image as the source of unwanted radioactive pollution throughout the Orange Valley. The United States Environmental Protection Agency's U.S. Radium Corporation Superfund Site is located on Alden Street in Orange, a half block west of High Street. Workmen in their white protective "space suits" do not receive tourists at this Superfund Site along the Wigwam Brook, although visitors are of course welcome at the Edison National Historic Site, only a hundred yards to the west.

Jersey City, New Jersey

Jersey City is undergoing a major renaissance. It still is — as it was in Edison's day — a vital intersection on many routes between New Jersey and New York City. The area where Edison's shop was once located, near a Green Acres "mini-park" on the Hudson River and just north of the historic Morris Canal Basin, is safe, clean, and readily accessible by PATH or car.

Newark, New Jersey

Newark fell on hard times after Edison moved to Menlo Park. The nation's financial center shifted from Newark to New York City, in the Wall Street district that was electrified by Edison. The gradual attrition in Newark's industrial base and its economy culminated in the riots of 1967, which left the city in flames and sent shock waves into the surrounding suburbs. Since then, however, Newark has gradually recovered and it appears likely that it will resume its role as the leading city of New Jersey.[448]

The locations of the thirteen buildings where Edison lived or worked during the five years that he spent in Newark can be identified with reasonable certainty, but only one or two — both being two story brick factory buildings — are still relatively intact. A house beside the house that Edison and his bride, Mary Stilwell, moved into, and where their first child, Marion, was born, can still be seen in a run-down neighborhood near the southern end of Broad Street. Edison's house was probably similar — perhaps nearly identical — to the house that remains there, on Wright Street. The most persistent reminder that the Great Inventor once was a Newark resident is, however, seen in the signs of the ubiquitous "Edison Park Fast" parking lots (Fig. 30). Two of the "Edison Park Fast" lots are located almost exactly adjacent to three of Edison's former worksites on Edison Place in Newark. None of the thirteen sites where Edison lived or worked in Newark between 1870 and 1875 are currently registered as Newark Landmarks by the Newark Preservation and Landmarks Committee.[449]

Menlo Park, Edison Township, New Jersey

The U.S. Post Office for Menlo Park, New Jersey (zip code 08837-9998) is now located in a shopping center on a hilltop on the east side (or southeast, to be more precise) of the Amtrak railway and State Route 27. The railroad station has been moved a few hundred yards closer to Newark and it is now called Metro Park. The house that the Edison family lived in burned down about thirty years after he left Menlo Park. The location of Edison's house — on the hill just behind that boulder on the highway — is now just a depression in the ground in a patch of trees and briar bushes.[450]

Harrison, New Jersey

In Harrison, New Jersey, most of the buildings that housed the Lamp Works — which were later the General Electric Lamp Works and were subsequently used by R.C.A. — are now gone. However, the history of the past century has been kept alive for the descendants of those who worked in the great factories that were built in Harrison a hundred or so years ago. One of the buildings in this complex is still standing, at the corner of Bergen Street and Fifth Street; it may be one of the few brick factory buildings of an Edison-related company that is still extant in New Jersey.[451]

Roselle, New Jersey

Roselle was one of New Jersey's earliest planned residential communities, its gridwork of streets having been laid out nearly one hundred and thirty years ago. The terrain around the original town of Roselle eventually filled in with other streets and houses, so that Roselle is now in the center of a continuous mega-town that extends from Elizabeth (on the north) to Linden (on the south and east), and to Cranford and Roselle Park (on the west and northwest). Roselle thus outgrew the need for isolated electric power, but the memory of Roselle's unique place in the history of the urban and suburban environment is well preserved in this still-small, although no longer wealthy, residential community.[452]

Winthrop, Massachusetts

The environment of Winthrop, Massachusetts, has remained remarkably stable during the past century. Like Llewellyn Park, which later in the same year Edison and Mina Miller selected to become their residence, a visitor to Winthrop can appreciate Edison's personal environment more easily than is possible in, say, New York City, or Silver Lake, New Jersey, which have changed so dramatically since Edison was there.[453]

West Orange, New Jersey

West Orange is now the fifth largest municipality in Essex County, with a population of over thirty-nine thousand. Changes in Edison's business activities produced profound ripple effects on the local economy.

These changes continued after Edison died, with the merger of the Edison Corporation into McGraw-Edison, and with the subsequent closing of the McGraw-Edison plant. An attempt to redevelop the area around the Edison plant began by destruction of most of the plant (except for the Battery Factory, which still stands). The redevelopment plan was aborted, however, and the area where the large Edison factory buildings had been located was converted into a parking lot and a few small one-story buildings used by business and the city government. The industrialization of the Orange valley, and the industrial despoliation of the water and soil in Orange and West Orange, began long before Edison arrived, and it continued after he died. The deep wells in Orange near the Edison plant are now polluted with organic chemicals and are closed. Wigwam Brook, which flows under the old Edison plant, looks like an open sewer when it appears above ground again in Orange. The brook is now usually just a trickle of unpleasant-looking water, flowing intermittently in a concrete ditch under Watchung Avenue, through Orange — past the U.S. Radium Superfund Site — and then through East Orange, past another Superfund Site in Glen Ridge, and into Bloomfield, where it empties into Second River.[454]

Llewellyn Park is recognized by historians and ethnographers as a unique suburban enclave, the first of its kind in the United States. Llewellyn Park and its residents have always remained somewhat aloof from the affairs of West Orange. The terrible east-west gash of Interstate 280, which has divided West Orange physically and spiritually, was routed through Llewellyn Park. Llewellyn Park is still a gated community that does not welcome visitors, in general. Access to Glenmont is granted courteously, as long as the visitor has a pass from the Edison National Historic Site. The grounds of Glenmont and Llewellyn Park have changed with the passage of time, and some of the trees have added seventy summers' worth of height and breadth since the Great Inventor died. The graves of Thomas and Mina Edison, who were reinterred behind Glenmont, are an unintended metaphor for the environment at Glenmont, which is now silent and still, from a human perspective. The National Park Service's Edison National Historic Site now includes Glenmont and about fifteen acres in Llewellyn Park, and the government-owned property around the Laboratory buildings. Portions of the buildings are shown to the public on guided tours, although much of the property is off-limits to visitors. Across Lakeside Avenue from the Laboratory buildings, the Edison Storage Battery Factory stretches for a hundred yards to the south. One of Edison's biographers summarized the situation in the valley surrounding the Edison National Historic Site as follows: "The energy and activity that once permeated the site . . . are long gone, and instead a feeling of depression, both spiritual and economic, pervades the area."[455]

West Orange has gradually made its peace with Edison. After previously rejecting the notion of naming a school for the Great Inventor, the public school that is nearest the Edison National Historic Site is now known as the Thomas A. Edison Middle School. A significant recent indication that West Orange accepts — indeed is proud of — "its most famous citizen" was the tribute paid to the Great Inventor in the *West Orange Chronicle* when *Life* magazine named Thomas Alva Edison as the "Man of the Millennium. One of the principal tasks of the new city administration in West Orange is to complete the plan that has been initiated for real estate development of the Crystal Lake area near Eagle Rock at the top of First Mountain, which has been called "the last piece of undeveloped land in West Orange." The developer has agreed to build an amphitheater for public use at no cost to the township, and would "revitalize and maintain Crystal Lake, cleaning its waters and possibly stocking it with fish."[456]

Silver Lake, Bloomfield, Belleville, and Glen Ridge, New Jersey

Much of the great pentagonal field at the border of Bloomfield and Belleville where Edison built his Silver Lake plant has reverted to a status that is somewhere between "developed" and "wild." The center of this great meadow is, one might say, in limbo. The meadow is rimmed by a line of shops along Bloomfield Avenue, by two and three story warehouses and abandoned factory buildings along Grove Street, Watsessing Avenue and Franklin Street, and by homes and a small shopping center at the south corner, at Alva Street and Belmont Avenue. But there is a nature trail of sorts that crosses the meadow: A half mile hike along the CONRAIL tracks from the corner of Belmont and Franklin passes through terrain that is heavily trashed but is now quiet and remote from the noises of the city.[457]

Edison's first plant in the Silver Lake-Bloomfield-Glen Ridge area was the Edison Ink Plant, which was located in what is now a residential neighborhood at the southwest corner of Glen Ridge. In 1983 it was determined that this site was one of several locations in West Orange, Montclair, and Glen Ridge that had been made hazardous from radium-contaminated soil that was a by-product of extracting radium from ore at the U.S. Radium Corporation in Orange, New Jersey. The site was designated as a Superfund site by the U. S. Environmental Protection Agency, and it was closed in 1996. The cleanup was completed and a small community park at this site was reopened in May 1999.[458]

Essex County, New Jersey

When Edison arrived in West Orange, Essex County was largely a region of relatively isolated villages that were separated by farms, except for the city of Newark and the manufacturing plants that existed along Main Street in the Oranges, and along Bloomfield Avenue in Belleville and Bloomfield. By the time Edison died, much of the farmland in the Orange Valley had been converted to manufacturing plants and houses. On the other hand, large parts of the ridgelines of First and Second Mountains and the intermontane valley were included in reservations such as the Eagle Rock Reservation and South Mountain Reservation. Smaller parks managed by the county exist in many of the communities of Essex County, such as Irvington and Newark, and the entire system now includes 5,725 acres of land.[459]

Ogdensburg and Sparta, Sussex County, New Jersey

In no other town in New Jersey is Thomas Edison remembered with such unwavering admiration as he is in Ogdensburg, where it is said that Edison's concept of a surface mine and a magnetic separator was good, and that he was defeated only because Mesabi ore from Minnesota had a higher iron content than anything that was left at the Ogden/Edison mine. Sparta Lake and the east and south sides of Sparta Mountain, at the opposite end of Edison Road from Ogdensburg, are now staked out with new homes in upscale developments. The woods here are called "Edison Acres Park," and maps show that there is an "Edison Pond" in there someplace. The Sparta Mountain Wildlife Management Area, which includes the former Ogden/Edison mine site, was created in the nick of time. The old school building from the mine site is now abandoned and sits in the woods in Franklin, about five miles north of Ogdensburg. There are at least four of the so-called "Edison houses" remaining in Ogdensburg, and I understand that there are more in Franklin.

Warren County, New Jersey

Scotts Mountain, at the northern side of the Pohatcong Valley in Warren County, was in the news in May 1998 when the Dalai Lama visited a Buddhist retreat there. The thirty-two acre Tibetan Buddhist Learning Center in Franklin Township is only a few miles from Edison Road in New Village. However, Edison's environmental impact and legacy in Warren County is largely invisible, and most of the people with whom I spoke were unaware of the extent and duration of his limestone mining and cement-making operations there. I understand that there are still a few former Edison employees still living near New Village, Phillipsburg, and Easton, and many of their descendants are nearby. The legend that Edison stayed in the fieldstone farmhouse at the south end of Edison Road, where it meets Good Springs Road, should be investigated; and the house should be studied by an architectural historian, if the present owners concur.[460]

The *milieu interieur*

Vast changes have occurred in medicine, health, and health care during the sixty-six years since Thomas Edison died. Some of Edison's inventions played a direct or indirect role in some of these changes. Although Edison was interested in the discoveries of the great microbiologist, Louis Pasteur, who he visited in France, the work of Edison did not bear directly on the ominous new microbial environment of the late twentieth century. However, in his work with benzene, phenol, and formaldehyde, Edison was a leader in the field of organic (carbon-based) chemistry. Edison thus participated in the birth of the modern pharmaceutical industry, especially of drugs that are formulated from sterols and other chemicals derived from the hexagonal ring molecule of carbon and hydrogen known as benzene.[461] During the present century, the use and consumption of tobacco has dramatically increased throughout the world, and mortality has risen concomitantly in many countries from tobacco-related illnesses such as cancer and heart disease. The increased incidence of these diseases has been greatest in countries such as the United States where high-fat, high-calorie diets are normative, the population is relatively sedentary, and other causes of death have been reduced. Edison had strong opinions regarding tobacco and diet. Beginning when he was a boy, Edison chewed tobacco (spitting tobacco juice in whatever direction was convenient), and he began to smoke cigars as soon as he could afford them. Edison detested cigarettes, however, and he opined that cigarette paper produced hazardous products of combustion. We might be tempted to give him a mixed grade on the consistency of his views regarding tobacco, although his perspective regarding chewing tobacco, cigars, and cigarettes was not at all unusual at that time. What was unusual for the early decades of the twentieth century was Edison's attempt to find a scientific rationale for his belief that cigarettes were hazardous.

Edison's sparse diet was a puzzle to his contemporaries. He ate little or no meat, consumed few calories, and — near the end — he lived on little except whole milk and orange juice. We now know that a low calorie diet is associated with longer life than a high calorie diet, other things being equal; and that a vegetarian diet is probably safer than a diet containing meat, as long as the essential nutrients and vitamins are not neglected. Furthermore, although monotonous, a diet of whole milk and orange juice such as Edison lived on may indeed be sufficient for an adult male — notwithstanding its lack of the water-soluble vitamins and minerals normally obtained from green leafy vegetables, and its relative deficiency in essential fatty acids.

Edison was sincerely interested in medical science and technology. He correctly predicted that biologists and medical scientists would develop many new methods of treatment, and he personally tinkered in the pharmaceutical field by formulating various patent medicines. Edison's discovery of calcium tungstate as a superb fluorescent compound and his subsequent development of the fluoroscope — with its tragic accidental consequences for Clarence Dally — has not received the recognition or appreciation that it deserves. The Edison corporation's important work with medical gases, including oxygen cylinders, carbon dioxide absorbers and anesthetic gases, has largely been forgotten.[462]

On balance, however, Edison's beliefs, pronouncements, and actions related to health, hygiene, and medicine represent a simultaneous display of common sense and nonsense. He was at various times both perspicacious and obtuse. His statements about health and physiology range from honest appraisal to self-deception and dissimulation.

* * * * *

Concerns regarding the effects of industry on the health of workers and of the public are now addressed more aggressively than they were at the time of Edison's death. A new attitude toward health and safety in the workplace was coming forward even before Thomas Edison died. Thus Charles Edison, in his role as president of Thomas A. Edison, Inc., established an office within the West Orange plant for a plant nurse.[463] In the decades following Edison's death, many hazards of the workplace have been defined that were only dimly perceived or were intentionally disregarded in the 1930s. For example, employers must now provide workers with the "right-to-know" about potential hazardous substances in their environment, and employers must make material safety data sheets (MSDS) available to their workers, for all substances that have any possible toxicity.

Environmental pollution from chemicals and radiation has been increasingly recognized as a serious problem by the public and by governmental agencies during the past forty years. The seminal work in the field of chemical pollution was Rachel Carson's *Silent Spring* (1962), which dealt mainly with insecticides, principally DDT and its congeners. Even more worrisome to the public than chemical pollutants are the dangers from ionizing radiation released into the atmosphere or groundwater. That these concerns are realistic has been shown by accidents at Chernobyl, at Three Mile Island, and elsewhere.[464]

Edison was not, of course, involved in any way in the development of atomic weapons and nuclear power. However, long before World War II, Edison had identified the atom as a source of immense power, which he thought could be harnessed for the benefit of mankind. By including atomic power in his list of potential sources of energy for future exploitation, along with solar power and tidal motion, Edison showed great foresight. Edison did not, however, visualize the dark side of atomic energy that was revealed by Hiroshima and Nagasaki, the prolonged brink of the Cold War, and the contamination of many areas of the world, from Bikini to Chernobyl. In fairness to Edison, we should recall that not even Albert Einstein — who is arguably the greatest scientific genius of the Age of the Atom — foresaw all of the Pandoran consequences of atomic fission.[465]

Thomas Edison's corporate environmental legacy includes the emissions from the Edison General Electric Company, known to us as General Electric, Inc. The GE plant at Schenectady, New York, which was established by Edison personally, is now considered to be the greatest source of chemical pollution of the Hudson River. The principal pollutants emitted into the Hudson River by the GE plant are polycholorinated biphenyls (PCBs), which are used in electric transformers. In 1998, *The New York Times* stated bluntly that:

Though the company's dumping of PCB's into the Hudson ranks among the most clear-cut and destructive cases of industrial pollution, G.E. has for the last 10 years managed to stave off the costs of a cleanup.[466]

In this context, we should recall that TAE, Inc., produced a wide variety of phenolic compounds at its Silver Lake plant. The production of a "biphenyl" — a pair of phenyls — is the first step in the process of polymerization of phenyls. This is just what is needed to produce PCBs, which are biphenyls containing several chlorine atoms.

Learn and Be Inspired

As I draw the Epilogue to a close, I return to the image of Edison that has been most durable, the image that shines through into the seventh decade since his death: Edison, the Great Inventor. As the Managing Editor of his home town newspaper wrote in 1997,

West Orange's favorite son, Thomas Alva Edison, the man who electrified the modern world, has been selected by Life *magazine as the most important figure of the millennium. . . . . [P]erhaps of even greater importance than any single invention . . . [h]e built the first factory . . . models of industrial research and development.*[467]

On the occasion of her visit to West Orange in July 1998 to acknowledge the corporate gift of $5 million at the beginning of a campaign to restore Edison's laboratory and home in West Orange, Hillary Rodham Clinton expressed the importance of the Great Inventor's legacy in terms of what can be learned from studying his life in the environment where he lived and worked:

As we went through this incredible invention factory . . . I became more and more excited about the possibilities of taking this site and making it more accessible to people, enabling students who come here to learn and be inspired by what happened here so many years ago.
This, to me, is almost breathtaking because we take so much for granted about what he did here in this invention factory.[468]

Although we have seen paradoxes, uncertainties and conflicts in Edison's environmental legacy, few who have studied his life and work have failed "to learn and be inspired" by what they have observed.[469]

Summary

General Electric today doesn't make a product that in some way didn't start here.

— Chairman and C.E.O. of General Electric, at Edison National Historic Site, 14 July 1998[470]

200 miles of the Hudson river bottom were deemed a Superfund toxic site 15 years ago. . . . The General Electric Company . . . operated two factories that legally released more than a million pounds of PCB's into the river before the Government banned such discharges in 1977.

— *The New York Times*, 24 July 1998[471]

These two quotations, both of which appeared in July 1998, illustrate the paradox of Edison's environmental legacy. On the one hand, he is praised for what are believed to be positive contributions to society, while we are more inclined to forget his role in the deleterious consequences of his inventions and business operations.

If it seems excessive to link Edison with the despoliation of the mighty Hudson River, we may recall instead the fate of Wigwam Brook, which flows down The Ramble by Edison's home in Llewellyn Park. Below the Park, the brook disappears under Edison's Battery Factory, and it does not reappear until it passes beyond the land he once owned on Watchung Avenue. Although the origin of Wigwam Brook near at the top of First Mountain was dried up, paved over, and diverted by the actions of many other people, and the ditch that carries the brook beside the U.S. Radium Corporation Superfund Site was constructed by someone else, Edison and his workers were surely responsible for the disappearance of the Wigwam Brook and Cook's Pond along Lakeside Avenue. Let us therefore keep a steady eye on the entire picture of Edison and the environment, as well as we can. In this section, I will summarize briefly the main themes that have emerged in the previous chapters regarding Edison's environment, as a preamble to the next chapter, **Judging Edison**.

My review of the recent published literature led me to believe that during the early years of his life, Edison's environment was important in molding the man who, in his later years, was responsible for changing the environment of the world. Nothing that I learned in my case studies (Part II) or in studying the Epilogue to his life contradicts this hypothesis.

The home-schooled and independent boy of the rural Great Lakes basin grew into a clever, interesting young man, who struck out on his own for the cities of the East Coast. The young telegrapher and inventor of Boston and New York became the preternatural "Old Man" of Newark in the early 1870s, but even then his impact on the environment was slight, at most. The duplex telegraph and other technical modifications of the telegraph were important in that industry, but Edison' name would have been forgotten today if he had not done more than that. In the latter half of the 1870s, when he had established his first "invention factory," Edison invented the phonograph and became known as the "Wizard of Menlo Park." The environment would never be the same again. Edison's fame, however, rests on more than the phonograph; if that had been his last and greatest discovery, we would probably remember the instrument, but not the man. The phonograph was, after all, initially considered to be a curiosity, and its full impact on the environment was slow to be perceived.

Edison's development of a practical, long-burning incandescent lamp and all else that was needed to electrify and illuminate large districts was what launched him immediately and permanently into the foreground as the Great Inventor of the modern environment. But even that cluster of inventions might not have been enough to sustain his reputation as the Greatest Inventor. Nor would his development of the kinetograph and kinetoscope, the motion picture studio, and films for public viewing have kept his memory alive, even though our environment has been dramatically transformed by the movies and their sequelae. There would be little general interest in his family life, his success or failure with iron mining, cement making, rubber, and battery manufacturing, if Edison's reputation as the Great Inventor had not emerged above all of the details. His discovery of the fluoroscope would be only a minor footnote in the history of medicine, if he wasn't already the Great Inventor. There is, therefore, something more to the story of Edison and the environment which must be found in order to explain his durable reputation. This elusive quality, more than all of his inventions — both those that were patented, and those that remained trade secrets —

must be studied in order to understand Edison's impact on the environment.

Edison was immensely skillful in promoting intense interest in his inventions before they were finished, and in selling them after they were produced. It has been said by some that his greatest invention was the "invention factory," where science and technology were first joined in a modern sequence of "research and development." Others have said that his concept of an efficient multicentered but centrally coordinated business organization, "Thomas A. Edison, Inc.," was his greatest achievement, a model for the business environment of today. From scenes described by his associate M. A. Rosanoff, and others, however, we see in Edison an element of self-conscious posturing which could be called "inventing himself." We therefore have a range of additional possibilities to consider, in order to understand how Edison's reputation as the Great Inventor has survived in spite of the varied environmental effects that were produced by his personal actions, his inventions and discoveries, and his businesses. Let us keep in mind what we have learned up to this point about Edison's inventions as well as their immediate environmental consequences as we examine their sequelae from the perspective of authorities in various fields of scholarship.

Chapter 15

Judging Edison:
The Issue of Accountability

*It is the fashion to call this the age of industry. . . .
Rather, we should call it the age of Edison.
For he is the founder of modern industry in the country.*

— Henry Ford[472]

NORBERT Wiener concurred with Henry Ford, adding that "Edison's greatest invention was that of the industrial research laboratory... The GE Company, the Westinghouse interests and the Bell Telephone Labs followed in his footsteps, employing scientists by hundreds where Edison employed them by tens."[473]

A biographer sees the object of his study in a manner that inhibits viewing this individual in context. If not "larger than life," the principal character in a biography is singled out and is focused upon, like one tree in a forest. And so it has been up to now, in this book, which has concentrated squarely on Thomas Edison. In this chapter, I intend to step back from Edison to take a broader and deeper view of the Great Inventor's environment, and of his impact on the environment. I shall do this by examining some of the major components of the environment, while looking at Edison's role in these subjects, as described by his contemporaries and by observers of the environment since the time of his death. This approach is exemplified by the epigraph by Henry Ford, above, that introduced this section and the comment on Edison by Norbert Wiener that followed it; both statements appear in David Noble's work, *America by Design* (1977), which examined "science, technology, and the rise of corporate capitalism" in general, rather than focusing specifically on Thomas Edison.

In this chapter, I will examine Edison's role in the changes that have occurred in the environment of the workplace in the past century and a half; of Edison's participation in the changes that chemistry and electricity brought to the environment during the same period; of Edison's contributions to changes in health and safety (the *milieu interieur*, or "internal environment"); and Edison's place in the history of changes in the cultural and social environment. In each of these studies, I will attempt to avoid rendering a value judgment at the outset, following the principle that "one man's trash is another man's treasure." I also recognize the danger inherent in passing judgment on the ideas and work of a historical figure using information that was not available during his or her lifetime. For example, the specific hazards associated with some chemicals that Edison worked with were unknown during his lifetime (such as his new plastic polymers), although others (such as lead and mercury) had long been known to be toxic.

Human Engineering

Problems in human engineering will receive during the coming years the same genius and attention which the nineteenth century gave to the more material forms of engineering.

— **Thomas Alva Edison, 1920**[474]

In commenting on what he called "human engineering," Edison went on to say that "We have laid good foundations for industrial prosperity. Now we want to assure the happiness and growth of the workers through vocational education and guidance and wisely managed employment departments." Edison regarded this as a "great field for industrial experimentation and statesmanship."

In *America by Design*, David Noble uses Thomas Edison's statement in 1920 to introduce his chapter on "A Technology of Social Production: Modern Management and the Expansion of Engineering." Noble is a severe critic of "the rise of corporate capitalism," which he says "has to do with the nature of modern engineering" — of "corporate engineering." Noble contends that "under the name of management," engineers and "a handful of giant firms" organized "patent reform, the organization of industrial and university research, and the transformation of both public-school and higher education." Noble argues that in the guise of a new "world-view of corporate reform, . . . modern technology became a class-bound phenomenon, the racing heart of corporate capitalism." The Great Inventor's contributions to the field of corporate engineering are discussed at length by Noble, who cites Edison on no less than eleven pages in his Index. By comparison, Frederick Winslow Taylor ("the father of scientific management") was cited on fifteen pages, and Robert M. Yerkes (a pioneer "intelligence" tester and Chairman of the Psychology Committee of the National Research Council) was discussed on only six pages of Noble's book.

Noble introduces Edison's contributions to the lamentable present state of "corporate capitalism" as follows:

The development of incandescent lighting . . . dates back to the pioneering experiments of Sir Humphrey Davy, but . . . The central figure in this work, of course, was Thomas Edison. . . . Edison's investigations and experiments were inextricably informed by economic considerations; as in all engineering work, the profit motive did not lie behind the inventive activity but was bound up with it.

Edison, says Noble, "did not fit the mythical image of the humble tinkerer." Instead,

Edison was familiar with the latest scientific work and conceived his projects "systematically," consciously incorporating economic factors within technical designs . . . Edison's ultimate success depended upon the [J. P.] Morgan support . . . and Morgan was one of the first New York residents to have his home supplied with its own electric-lighting plant. In 1892 Morgan played a leading role in the formation of the General Electric Company and served on that corporation's executive board until his death in 1913.[475]

Noble considered that control of patents provided a means for large companies to dominate their segments of industry and to eliminate competition. Control was exercised by corporate acquisition of patents from penurious independent inventors, and "suppression" of work on the new inventions that were described in these patents:

The most important impetus behind the formation of the General Electric Company . . . was the patent situation. . . By the 1890s, two large companies, General Electric and Westinghouse, monopolized a substantial part of the American electrical manufacturing industry, and their success

and expansion had been in large measure the result of patent control.
Edison himself had spent more money in obtaining patents, litigating them, and preventing infringements than he had received from them.[476]

On the other hand, says Noble, Edison testified to a Congressional committee in opposition to compulsory working of patents, stating that "he knew of no instances of suppression." Noble implies that Edison was either duplicitous in his testimony, or that he did not understand what was really going on in the corporate world. Edison must have been either "a knave or a fool," as the saying goes — or both.[477]

Noble describes one of the ways that young engineers were brought into the spirit of corporate engineering:

The Edison Club was formed [in Schenectady] in 1904 and had over six hundred members by 1918. . . . The facilities included a library, bowling, pool, movies, tennis, canoeing, music, golf, and restaurants and were the setting for AIEE meetings and company-sponsored lectures. As a writer for GE described it, the club had a "university spirit," where the various social and athletic activities [offered] opportunities for the student engineers to be brought in contact with many of the officials and engineers of the company.[478]

The "spirit" of organizations like the Edison Club in Schenectady was savaged by Kurt Vonnegut in his mordantly humorous novel, *Player Piano* (1952). While Noble took a historical approach to show how young engineers were transformed by GE, Westinghouse, and other large organizations into managers who regimented workers into performing like machines, Vonnegut demonstrated the same process using the technique of science fiction. At a corporate club called "the Meadows," wrote Vonnegut, "a flat, grassy island in the St. Lawrence, . . . the most important men, and the most promising men . . . spent a week each summer in an orgy of morale building — through team athletics, group sings, bonfires and skyrockets."[479]

Vonnegut's fictive mega-corporation had its origin at "Ilium," New York, on the banks of the "Iroquois" river. At the "Ilium Works," the north end of the original building had been preserved "because of its historical interest to visitors. . . It was the original machine shop set up by Edison in 1886, the same year in which he opened another in Schenectady." As Vonnegut describes it,

> Building 58, . . . [t]he rafters still bore the marks of what Edison had done with the lonely brick barn: bolt holes showed where overhead shafts had once carried power to a forest of belts, and the wood-block floor was black with the oil and scarred by the feet of the crude machines the belts had spun.

Vonnegut's protagonist, Doctor Paul Proteus, "wished Edison could be with him to see it. The old man would have been enchanted." In his description of "Building 58," of "the Ilium Works," Vonnegut is, of course, describing the great machine shop in Building 5 of the West Orange Laboratory, which Edison first sketched out in 1886 and which was completed in 1887.[480]

In order to emphasize the Great Inventor's connection with the subsequent story of the mega-company that began at "Ilium," Vonnegut wrote that two workers in Building 58 scratched their initials "and the date, '1931,'" into the building's old bricks "in the same year that Edison had died." The homosocial nature of the Edison corporation persisted into the future:

> Doctor Katharine Finch was [Dr. Proteus'] secretary, and the only woman in the Ilium Works. Actually, she was more a symbol of rank than a real help, although she was useful as a stand-in when Paul was ill or took a notion to leave work early.[481]

Vonnegut uses the voices of his characters to describe the history of industrial revolutions. The "First Industrial Revolution devalued muscle work, then the second one devalued routine mental work." Vonnegut's secretary, Doctor Finch, wonders if there would be "a Third Industrial Revolution" and Doctor Proteus responds that, yes,

> I guess the third one's been going on for some time, if you mean thinking machines. That would be the third revolution, I guess, machines that devaluate human thinking. Some of the big computers like EPICAC do that all right.[482]

Too late, Doctor Proteus realizes that the Third Industrial Revolution is a disaster. A colleague points out to him that:

The machines are to practically everybody what the white men were to the Indians. People are finding that, because of the way the machines are changing the world, more and more of their old values don't apply any more. People have no choice but to become second-rate machines themselves, or wards of machines.[483]

In addition to Edison's direct involvement in the early history of "human engineering" in his work as an inventor and businessman, Noble also charges that the Great Inventor played a significant indirect role in the development of "intelligence" testing, which began in the United States during World War I. According to Noble, the purpose of intelligence testing at that time was "to standardize the 'human material' that comprised American society for efficient, profit-making enterprise." Noble traces Edison's involvement in intelligence testing to his position as Chairman of the Naval Consulting Board (NCB). The activities of the NCB, says Noble, were "rather fruitless," except for the "preparedness propaganda campaign" of the NCB's Industrial Preparedness Committee, which was headed by Howard E. Coffin. This committee "provided an inventory of industrial resources which would serve as the basis for the mobilization work of the Council of National Defense and the War Industries Board."[484]

Noble shows how Edison's NCB, the Council of National Defense, and the War Industries Board worked together during World War I. These three organizations utilized the National Research Council to organize the War Department's Committee on Education and Special Training (CEST), which "formally took charge of American vocational and higher education during the war," and which later developed the "famous alpha and beta intelligence tests," under the direction of Robert M. Yerkes. The poor scores achieved by recent immigrants on these tests had "an immediate and profound effect upon the great immigration debate," according to Stephen Jay Gould: "The eugenicists battled and won one of the greatest victories of scientific racism in American history. . . 'America must be kept American,' proclaimed Calvin Coolidge." In one of the central passages of his criticism of intelligence testing, Gould discusses Yerkes' work in detail in a thirty-three page section entitled "R. M. Yerkes and the Army Mental Tests: IQ Comes of Age." Gould concurs with Noble on the importance of the National Research Council in providing important academic support for Yerkes' work on intelligence testing, and thus — indirectly — for its racist consequences.[485]

Noble also shows Edison's connection with the implementation of the principles of Frederick Winslow Taylor (1856-1915), in Edison's role as the leader of a study which Noble calls the "first major social-science experiment." In 1924, when he was seventy-seven years old, Edison was the honorary chairman of a committee that conducted an evaluation of workers' activities at the Hawthorne plant of the Western Electric Company. The study showed that "a worker's productivity was a function of the attention given to him by management." This conclusion has since been called "the Hawthorne Effect." By 1924, Taylor had already been dead for nine years, but his principles of "scientific management" — which led to the initiation of the Hawthorne study — have been called "the bedrock of all work design." Taylor coined the phrase "a fair day's work," and he became famous for using a stop watch to observe workers' productivity. "His concern was with the control of labor at any given level of technology." Taylor believed that managers should assume the burden of gathering together the knowledge that had previously been possessed by workers; of removing "brain work" from the shop; and of laying out each day's work for every workman in advance.[486]

Frederick Winslow Taylor is still controversial: According to Harry Braverman (for whom Edison was *sui generis*, although not particularly admirable), "Taylorism" has "a bad odor." On the other hand, the noted conservative columnist George Will concluded, unsurprisingly, that "Taylor's legacy — a new kind of seriousness about enhancing workers' productivity — has been, on balance, benign."[487]

By associating Edison with the Hawthorne study, and thus with Taylorism, Noble again emphasizes Edison's role in what he calls "the rise of corporate capitalism." Noble does not mince words when he describes the character of modern technology, the technology that he has connected Edison with in so many ways:

Modern technology in America . . . has become merely a means to corporate ends, a vehicle of capitalist domination. . . . Corporate engineers [have] in reality served only the dominant class in society . . . which . . . must forever struggle to extract labor from, and thus to control the lives of, the class beneath it.[488]

A somewhat less passionate view of the subject of "human engineering" appears in Alfred DuPont Chandler's classic treatise, *The Visible Hand*. Those who would award to Edison a pioneering role in this field, either to praise or condemn him, will be surprised to find that Chandler barely acknowledges Edison's activities as an executive in the world of business.[489]

Electricity and Chemistry:
Edison's Contributions to the Technological Environment

The neotechnic phase was marked, to begin with, by the conquest of a new form of energy, electricity. . . . In the application of power, electricity effected revolutionary changes . . . The metallurgical industries were transformed. . . Today our industry owes a heavy debt to chemistry.

— Lewis Mumford, 1934[490]

Already the author of five books, Lewis Mumford began writing *Technics and Civilization* in 1930, the last full year of Thomas Edison's life. First published in 1934, *Technics and Civilization* has had a long-lasting impact that endures in spite of Mumford's various shortcomings in style and substance. As a contemporary of Edison in the Great Inventor's later years, and as a scholar of technology, Mumford was well-equipped to describe Edison's impact on the environment. It was, therefore, somewhat surprising to find that Mumford mentioned Edison on only three occasions in *Technics and Civilization*. This was far less attention than he paid to, say, Karl Marx, Leonardo DaVinci, Thorstein Veblen, and Roger Bacon. It was, on the other hand, more notice than Mumford granted to Benjamin Franklin or Eli Whitney, and roughly comparable to his comments on James Watt, Frederick Winslow Taylor, and Henry Ford. Let us, therefore, see what this important social critic and early environmentalist had to say about the world that Edison had helped to create with his discoveries and inventions in the fields of electricity and chemistry.

Electricity and chemistry were the central elements in the technology of what Mumford, echoing Patrick Geddes, called the "neotechnic" phase or period of civilization. The neotechnic phase — the present phase in history — was rather loosely defined by Mumford, but at one point he stated that it began with the invention of the water turbine in 1832. The neotechnic phase overlapped, but did not immediately replace the preceding phases, which he called "eotechnic" and "paleotechnic." Mumford's "eotechnic" period began in Europe in about 1000 A.D. and ended around 1750. The eotechnic was the phase of "water and wood," during which the clock, the printing press, and the blast furnace were invented, and universities, laboratories and factories were first created. Mumford's idyllic eotechnic period was replaced by the "paleotechnic," the phase of "coal and iron," beginning in about 1750 in England and about 1850 in the United States. (Mumford is a bit vague on his dates, for he also stated that the paleotechnic began in 1700 and it reached a "high point" in 1870. The paleotechnic, he says, turned "downward" in 1900.) The paleotechnic (which is an epithet for Mumford) phase was driven by the invention of the steam engine, and it was characterized by the "industrial army," railroads, and mechanized warfare. The nadir of the paleotechnic's image of blood and darkness was the Great War of 1914 to 1918.[491]

The paleotechnic period began to yield to the neotechnic in the late nineteenth century. Mumford says that the neotechnic was in "countermarch" by 1910, in spite of the Great War. The neotechnic era, in its most perfect expression, was and is a period of cleanliness, in which electricity was generated at a distance and was transported quietly by power lines to the homes and small factories where it was used. Iron was replaced by steel and hard alloys; the scientific method replaced discovery by trial and error; and quality of life became both a goal and an achievable reality. In the neotechnic period, environmental concerns were reflected in conservation of resources; in reuse of garbage, scrap, and industrial waste; and in a new "organic ideology." Mumford recognized that paleotechnic methods and mentality persisted even as the neotechnic period began to flower, and he used the term "mesotechnic" to describe the overlap between these two periods.[492]

Although Mumford mentions Edison but briefly, and only in connection with Edison's work in the fields of electricity, the phonograph, and moving pictures, he clearly situates this exemplar of "distinguished individual inventors" in the neotechnic phase. Mumford focuses on Edison's "central power station and distribution system (1882)" and his "invention of the motion picture" in 1887, "to do for the eye what he had already done for the ear." Mumford does not mention anything about Edison's work with the incandescent lamp. Indeed, in one of Mumford's frustrating lapses, he fails completely to mention the development of electric lights (except for the arc light). However, in a section entitled "Light and Life," Mumford waxes rhapsodically about the brilliant illumination that characterizes the neotechnic period:

Light shines on every part of the neotechnic world... The dark blind world of the machine, the miner's world, began to disappear... Even the unseen was, so to say, illuminated... the neotechnic was conscious of other forces equally potent under other circumstances: electricity, sound, light, invisible rays and emanations.[493]

Edison's inventions in chemistry and in the field of communications are not mentioned by Mumford. And Edison's inventions in telegraphy and telephony are not described, nor are his electrical appliances, or his discoveries of phenomena in vacuum tubes that facilitated the invention of radios and the fluoroscope. Edison's work in mining and cement making was not picked up by Mumford, nor did Mumford recognize the importance of storage batteries in the neotechnic period. Mumford, instead, was focused on transmission of high voltage alternating current generated from remotely situated dynamos and hydro-electric power. Mumford does not see that Edison, the neotechnic inventor, could also be characterized as a paleotechnic industrialist. In the 1930s, Mumford had not yet seen the failure of neotechnic industries to liberate the workforce. Mumford quotes Frederick Winslow Taylor at length, appreciatively. For example: "Taylor was able to add to the labor output per man without adding to his physical burden." Mumford also quotes Henry Ford at length, with hardly a word of criticism, since Ford appeared to Mumford to favor the small workshop:

A product that is used all over the country ought to be made all over the country... For many years we have followed the policy of making in our branches whatever parts they were able to make for the area they served.[494]

With such admiration for Taylor and Ford, it is hardly surprising that Mumford did not see anything amiss in Edison's business methods or in his factories.

* * * * *

Having seen that Lewis Mumford granted to Thomas Edison a distinct (albeit small) role in the technological environment of the neotechnic period, let us now turn to two later writers who have examined the history of technology, Arnold Pacey and George Basalla.

In 1990, Pacey examined the development of technology with a scope that was both broad and deep in his monograph, *Technology in World*

Civilization: A Thousand-Year History. Pacey provided a greatly needed integration of the history of technology in Asia with that of Europe and America, showing many ways in which inventions in Asia (especially in China) influenced the development of technology in the West. Pacey's index is poorly done, skimpy in fact, but I was unable to locate any more than two references to Edison in either the text or the Index. Both citations were in a brief section entitled "Electricity and Chemistry," which discussed developments in these related fields beginning in the 1870s.[495]

The cheap generation of electric current opened the way to a much wider use of electricity in lighting, industry and transport. In 1879 . . . Edison in America and Swan in England independently produced the first successful electric light bulbs with incandescent filaments. Within two years, Edison had small power stations supplying large numbers of his lights in both New York and London.[496]

Pacey emphasized the interrelationships between chemistry and electricity, and how the work of Edison and others in these fields was nurtured by the international environment in the late nineteenth century:

One feature of these innovations was the highly organized research work on which they depended, whether in Edison's workshop and laboratory in Menlo Park near New York, or at the Siemens and Halske works in Germany. . . Chemistry was at the centre of a great many key developments in nineteenth-century technology.

The electrical industry showed a similar development, not least because of the importance of chemistry in several of its branches. . . When Edison needed a mathematician to help design his first electricity supply systems, he employed Francis R. Upton, who had studied under H. L. F. von Helmholtz in Germany.[497]

Although Pacey's assessment of Edison is brief and oblique, his conclusions conform with others in the major studies of Edison's work that we reviewed in the Introduction. Pacey is particularly important for us, however, in that he views Edison's work in the context of a worldwide, thousand year history of technology, without focusing specifically on Edison. This is a contrast to what we and others have done in this thesis, which has been to focus on Edison's work and place it, as fairly as possible, in the context of some broader aspect of history (which, for me, is the history of the environment).

While Pacey's brief references to Edison would be sufficient to satisfy us that our subject has achieved a reasonably secure position in the history of technology, George Basalla elevates Edison to the role of a major actor on this stage. Edison not only appears far more often in Basalla's index than any other individual, his citations are widely distributed throughout Basalla's monograph. They appear in four chapters: Chapters II ("Continuity and Discontinuity"), IV ("Novelty [2]: Socioeconomic and Cultural Factors"), V ("Selection [1]: Economic and Military Factors"), and VII ("Conclusion: Evolution and Progress").[498]

Pacey's principal theory is that of "technological evolution," by which he means that technology has evolved gradually, rather than being "discontinuous." That is to say, technological change is not dependent solely on "the heroic labors of individual geniuses such as Eli Whitney, Thomas A. Edison, Henry Ford, and Wilbur and Orville Wright." Technological evolution, says Pacey, can be demonstrated through a study of artifacts. Pacey follows three themes: diversity, necessity, and technological evolution ("an organic analogy that explains both the appearance and the selection of these novel artifacts"). He agrees that "necessity is the mother of invention" in some cases, while in other situations, inventions have been made before they were needed, or their potential uses were obvious.[499]

Basalla's longest discussion of the work of Edison is his description of "Edison's Lighting System," in which he shows how the various components were designed to be compatible, similar to the design of a large machine. The entire system, said Basalla, exhibited "continuity in change," in that Edison designed it to be "an electrical analogue of the gas lighting system." The history of the development of lighting systems also shows that "Technology became a factor in international affairs and rivalries," when "the heroic inventors of one country were scarcely acknowledged in another land." The "inventor" of incandescent light bulb, says Basalla, is Edison in America, Sir Joseph W. Swan in Britain, and A. N. Lodygin in Russia. Recognition is sometimes based on "dissimulations," such as Edison's "dubious claims when he sought recognition for the invention of moving-picture apparatus."[500]

Edison's invention of the phonograph (1877) is discussed by Basalla to illustrate his contention that "the potential, as well as the immediate, uses of an invention are by no means self-evident." Basalla emphasizes that "The first uses are not always the ones for which the invention will eventually become best known." Of Edison's list of ten possible uses for the phonograph, the inventor thought the most important was "to take dictation without the aid of a stenographer," whereas recording and playing music was fourth on the list. It took twenty years for Edison to accept the fact that "the primary use of his talking machine was in the area of amusement." Basalla also reminds his readers that Edison's crude model of a phonograph, with its "tinfoil recording surface and hand crank, was just barely able to reproduce the nursery rhyme that the inventor shouted into its mouthpiece." It "was able to record less than two minutes worth of material and did so poorly." In the early 1880s, Edison believed that it "did not have 'any commercial value'." This, says Basalla, shows that "even when there is general agreement about how [an invention] is to be used, we cannot assume that it will operate as promised." Basalla emphasizes that the "selection of novelty involves risk and uncertainty," a fact forgotten when "an Edison or Ford brushed aside doubts and criticisms to bring us the electric light bulb or the Model T."[501]

Although Basalla mentioned only a few of Edison's inventions, Edison has an impressive position in the technological environment that Basalla describes. None of the personal or professional issues that we have observed in Edison are relevant to Basalla. For Basalla, Edison is not merely an "heroic genius"; he is the epitome of the inventor who facilitates the evolution of technology. Basalla uses examples from Edison's work, and from the discoveries of countless others who are either famous or unknown, to show us that:

The popular but illusory concept of technological progress should be discarded. In its place we should cultivate an appreciation for the diversity of the made world, for the fertility of the technological imagination, and for the grandeur and antiquity of the network of related artifacts.[502]

Pacey, we have seen, saw Edison as an important figure, one worth citing on at least three occasions in the history of a millennium of technological development. For Basalla, on the other hand, Edison was not only one of the "heroic" geniuses; Edison became the quintessential synthesizer in Basalla's evolutionary model of the history of technology. However, not all historians of technology and the environment see Edison in such a pivotal role. To show that Edison may be disregarded completely without diminishing the value of a scholarly discussion related to the history of technology, see the essays on "The Dilemma of Technological Determinism, edited by Merrit Roe Smith and Leo Marx, entitled *Does Technology Drive History?* (1996). I found no mention of Edison in any of the thirteen essays in this monograph, and Edison is not mentioned in the Index.

The closest Edison came to making an appearance in Smith and Marx's book, I believe, was in Thomas P. Hughes' essay, "Technological Momentum." (For the purpose of this brief discussion, it can be said that Hughes locates technological momentum "somewhere between the poles of technological determinism and social constructivism.") Hughes chose electric light and power systems to illustrate his essay, and he specifically focused on the Electric Bond and Share Company (EBASCO), which was founded in 1905 by the General Electric Company. GE, we should recall, was originally the Edison General Electric Company. Edison was still peripherally involved with GE in the first decade of the twentieth century, although he had sold his GE stock to provide funds for his iron mill and mine. Indeed, Edison's name and reputation were tied up with GE for the rest of his life; for example, GE's Lamp Works in Harrison continued to bear the Old Man's name, and he enjoyed visiting the plant in Harrison from time to time. EBASCO, we are told, reorganized its factory floor "in a manner commonly associated with Fordism." It is ironic that Henry Ford, not Thomas Edison, appears in Hughes' history of this GE-related organization. However, in his closing sentence Hughes acknowledges that something may be missing from his synthesis, or at least that the future is uncertain, when he says that "we must remind ourselves that technological momentum, like physical momentum, is not irreversible."

Water and Power: How Thomas Edison and Lewis Mumford, with Good Intentions, Helped to Ruin Two Rivers.

And It Isn't Over Yet

If atmospheric sewage was the first mark of paleotechnic industry, stream pollution was the second. The dumping of the industrial and chemical waste-products into the streams was a characteristic mark of the new order. Wherever the factories went, the streams became foul and poisonous: the fish died or were forced, like the Hudson shad, to migrate, and the water became unfit for either drinking and bathing.

— Mumford, 1934[503]

We now move forward in our examination of Edison's relationship to the environment from a general consideration of "electricity and chemistry" to a specific study of "water and power." We will see how "water and power" was viewed by Edison's contemporary, Lewis Mumford. We shall also see how the problem of water and power has been viewed by those in later generations, specifically the environmental historian, Richard White. It has already become apparent that Edison, who intended to make money from his inventions in order to make more money to keep inventing more things, inadvertently or perhaps willingly polluted the Passaic and several other rivers in New Jersey. In this section of the discussion, we shall see how Lewis Mumford, enamored by the prospect of producing "clean" hydroelectric power for his beloved neotechnic age, participated in the damming of the mighty Columbia River of the Pacific Northwest. We shall also read of the awesome consequences of that action. The Passaic and the Columbia are no longer clean, free-running rivers, nor is it clear if or when they ever will be again. Hence, "It Isn't Over Yet," or — as New Jersey's adopted son, Yogi Berra, once famously said, "It ain't over 'till it's over."

In hard-hitting prose that anticipated Rachel Carson's *Silent Spring* by some two decades, Lewis Mumford wrote of "The Destruction of Environment" in the coal-fired, paleotechnic, early Industrial Age. While Mumford acknowledged that the Industrial Revolution was ushered in with water mills, he argued convincingly that it was the coal-burning steam engine that produced the power that was needed, at any location, and at any time of year, to enable factories to reach their maximum output.[504] "During the paleotechnic phase, said Mumford, "industry depended completely upon the coal mines as a source of power." And it was not only the factories' pollution of air and water that outraged Mumford. He also saw the degradation of workers and their families in "the machine" of the paleotechnic period, and he sought to move society toward a new age — the age of chemistry and electricity that he called "neotechnic." Mumford saw lessons to be learned from the methods used in the eotechnic period that preceded the paleotechnic, and by the engineers of Rome, Greece, and Egypt. He saw special merit in the eotechnic's use of water power, which was derived from dams on rivers and artificial estuaries:

While horse power ensured the utilization of mechanical methods in regions not otherwise favored by nature, the greatest technical progress came about in regions that had abundant supplies of wind and water.[505]

Before we explore the consequences of Mumford's interest in water power, let us recall Thomas Edison's relationship to the rivers of New Jersey, as these rivers appeared in earlier chapters. Edison, as we saw in the previous section, was cited by Mumford for his work on various electrical devices. We can presume that Mumford admired Edison. (After all, Mumford quoted Henry Ford appreciatively in the early 1930s, and Edison would have been easier to appreciate than Ford.) We do not know if Mumford was aware of Edison's interest in and experience with hydroelectric power, or whether Mumford developed his fascination with hydroelectric power independent of Edison. We will shortly return to Mumford. In the meantime, consider what we have learned about Thomas Edison and the following rivers: The Elizabeth River (where his ancestor, John Ogden operated a mill in Elizabethtown); the Rahway (into which Thomas Edison's property at Menlo Park drained); the Wallkill (of which Sparta Mountain and the Edison mine at Ogdensburg formed the east bank); and the Delaware (which received Pohatcong Creek, draining the Edison Portland Cement plant in New Village). Also, the Hudson River, along which Edison's first small shop in Jersey City was located, and which the [Edison] General Electric plant in Schenectady has polluted for more than a century; and the Hackensack, which received, slowly sloshing through the tidal Meadowlands, the runoff from Edison's battery factory in Kearny.

Edison's personal impact on all of these rivers — the Elizabeth, the Rahway, the Delaware, the Hackensack, and so forth — was trivial, however, compared to his impact on the Passaic. The Passaic, as we already have seen, has been polluted by hundreds of industries and tens of thousands of people over the past three centuries, and there is no need to imply that Edison was the principal culprit in the fate of the Passaic. As Sherwin Nuland wrote in 1996, "Each drop of the Passaic River is a minute sample of the ongoing flow of human life."[506]

We have previously read of Edison's many connections with this unfortunate river. Edison's Ogden and Swaine ancestors began to cut down the forests and drain the natural wetlands in the Orange Valley and along the eastern slope of First Mountain. His distant and ancient cousins such as the Stetsons were among the first hatters in Orange, where they polluted the "ill-fated" Parrow Brook, a tributary of Second River, and thus of the Passaic. The farm of Swaine Ogden, Edison's ancestor, was at the height of land that drained into Parrow Brook and the Elizabeth and Rahway Rivers. After Parrow Brook was formally converted to a sewer that emptied into the Passaic River at Belleville, the principal tributaries of Second River were the Wigwam Brook (over which Edison built his Battery Factory in West Orange, and into which his Ink Factory at Glen Ridge drained) and Toney's Brook, along which Edison's Battery Factory in Glen Ridge was located.

What Edison did to Wigwam Brook and Toney's Brook was, however, insignificant, compared to what he did at Silver Lake. Recall, if you will, that a brook which drained into the river that once formed Silver Lake was so heavily contaminated by carbolic acid that the Edison corporation (although not the inventor, personally) was convicted of polluting the stream. And from the physical evidence (such as photographs, maps, and newspaper articles), and from oral histories by Edison's former employees and local residents, the pollution of air and water by the Edison plant in the area of Silver Lake (which drains into Second River, and thence into the Passaic) was unacceptable, even by the relatively lax environmental standards of that period.

Let us now return to Mumford, who admired Edison, and who was presumably unaware of the deleterious impact of Edison's factories on the streams that were near his factories. We cannot say if Mumford knew that Edison had built a hydroelectric plant at Appleton, Wisconsin, in the 1880s, and that Edison and Henry Ford had examined every waterwheel that they could find in Appalachia in the second decade of the twentieth century. Indeed, we should assume that Mumford did not know these details of Edison's life, since our own knowledge of these facts about Edison is derived from monographs that were published after Mumford wrote *Technics and Civilization*. However, long before Mumford became a consultant to the Columbia River Basin project, Edison had expressed his hope that alternative sources of energy, including water power, would be used in the future. Mumford would have appreciated Edison's comments in 1922, when the inventor stated:

> *Quite apart from atomic energy, the motion of the earth alone as it turns on its axis and sweeps through space would give us all the light, power, and heat that we want, and a thousand times over.* Some day, we may harness that motion. Not only that, but one day we may harness the rise and fall of the tides and imprison the rays of the sun.[507]

Although Edison was not directly involved in the Columbia River project, we shall soon see that he was indirectly involved when it began. And although Mumford did not mention the Columbia River in *Technics and Civilization*, he became intimately involved with the dams on the river. The intertwined legacy of Edison and Mumford in the damming of the Columbia River has not yet ended.

Richard White says, aptly, that the problem of the Columbia River is "Frankensteinian." White continues: "The dams on the Columbia are no longer an object of romance; they have become a necessary evil." Immediately after making this statement, White indicates that the "original passion" for damming the river began with the arrival at Portland, Oregon, in July 1880, of Henry Villard, an associate of Thomas Edison, in his steamer, *Columbia*. Villard was then "in the process of turning the Oregon Steam Navigation Company into the Oregon Railway and Navigation Company." *Columbia*, we recall from Edison's biographies, had been outfitted with incandescent lamps prepared at Menlo Park for its voyage around Cape Horn. These lights worked well, a distinct contrast to Edison's arc lights that had failed two years previously on the U.S.S. *Jeanette*. The crew ran wires from *Columbia* to the Clarendon Hotel in Portland, which was then lighted up "to the brightness of day," delighting thousands of people. A half century later, observed White, Portland, Oregon, was illuminated by electricity from the Columbia River.[508]

The process of damming the tributaries of the Columbia for hydroelectric power and water for irrigation began in 1889, soon after the arrival of Villard's steamship. But it was not until alternating current was developed — a form of power which could be transmitted for long distances — that hydroelectric power became an important prospect for the Columbia basin. Fervent environmentalists such as Gifford Pinchot supported the prospect of big government dams on the Columbia. And Lewis Mumford was already committed: "the utopia Americans saw shimmering in high-tension wires emerged most vividly in the work of Lewis Mumford." Mumford, says White, "made Great Power into social theory." Mumford himself had written in 1934 that, "Electricity . . . can be developed by energy from a large number of sources: not merely coal, but the rapidly running river, the falls, the swift tidal estuary are available."[509]

The Columbia River has now been dammed, at a cost of billions of dollars. Salmon have been blocked in their annual migrations, and the culture of the Native Americans in the region has been profoundly altered with the reduction of fish in the river. Pulp mills, side channels, pumps, cities, and ranches along the river are a part of the "second nature" that has developed in the Columbia Basin. "The Columbia, an organic machine, is at once our creation and retains a life of its own beyond our control," wrote Richard White in 1995. Mumford remained, however, both prescient as well as irritating. Mumford's final book, says White,

> *Reflected Mumford at his worst: it was dire, portentous, totalizing and omniscient. . . . Mumford's jeremiad against the megamachine recognizes that we treat nature as if it were literally a machine that can be disassembled and redesigned largely at will.*

White rejects Mumford's valedictory comments. Instead, White argues that:

> *The Columbia is not just a machine. It is an organic machine. Our tendency to break it into parts does not work. . . . It is an organic machine and has to be dealt with as such. To call for a return to nature is posturing. . . . History does not go away.*"[510]

Mumford and Edison loved dams as much as if they were beavers, and countless others who preceded and followed them in history have also seen great benefit and little if any harm from the construction of dams. In recent years, however, in addition to potential benefits, the possibility of harm from dams has gradually become apparent.

On the one hand, constraining a river with levees and dikes enables terrain that was previously wet to be exploited, and a dam creates a body of water upstream that has a wide array of uses. For example: A millpond or artificial lake provides a source of power, of potable water, and water for irrigation, aquaculture (especially of lake-living fish), commerce (i.e., navigation), industry (factories), and recreation. And such a lake is more stable, from month to month, than a freely flowing stream, which may range from flood to drought, depending on rainfall in the terrain of the river's headwaters. As, for example, the Nile River in Africa, or the Missouri River in America. Seasonal floods, such as those which devastate large areas in China, may be controlled by dams. These "benefits" have created a strong movement to dam rivers throughout the world.

On the other hand, we now know of many hazards and unfortunate consequences of dams. These range from spectacular floods due to dam failures, to more subtle evils such as schistosomiasis downstream from the Aswan dam in Egypt and perturbation of the migration of spawning salmon. As land that is normally dry is watered artificially and brought under cultivation, whatever nutrients are present are leached out, and it becomes sterile from deposits of minerals, usually alkaline, that are carried in the irrigating water. These problems are then addressed with chemical fertilizers and neutralizers, which have their own unintended consequences, including algal blooms on the surface, and pollution of groundwater aquifers. The effects of major dams on human and non-human ecology are also profound. Farms and cities supplant low-impact native cultures, and indigenous plants and animals are replaced or suppressed by domesticated species or species that, like rats and dandelions, travel where humans go. Dams may fail from earthquakes, terrorism, wars, or engineering errors which neglect to calculate the porosity of the lake bottom or the proper design and use of materials in the dam itself. It is now understood that dams must be designed to withstand the "hundred year flood," but who can say exactly what that will be? The actual cost of building and maintaining a dam may exceed its benefits, and there is no way to put a price tag on some of the consequences of dams, such as the loss of habitat and the drowning of ancient cultures.

Neither Edison nor Mumford, as far as we can tell, considered any of the negative consequences of damming rivers for hydroelectric power. Even now, there is controversy about how to prevent flooding on the Rahway River in New Jersey, and dams as far away as Laos, in Asia, are intensely contested by environmentalists. For example, serious consideration is currently being given to "channel improvements" in the Rahway River, which drains more than twenty-five miles of eastern New Jersey, from West Orange to Menlo Park. At least one consultant calls for only minimal changes in the existing storm drainage system of the Rahway, arguing that "alerting business owners and homeowners could minimize damage, even when in a major storm." In the adjacent Passaic River Basin, "buyouts have been pushed as the most effective flooding solution," instead of new channels constraining the river. In Laos, a proposed $1.4 billion, 680-megawatt project has placed the World Bank in a dilemma. The World Bank has "been badly burned by recent hydro-electric fiascoes," including its decision to cancel the "controversial $1 billion dam in Nepal." The potential benefits of the Nam Theun Two project, in the Mekong River basin, are being weighed against the environmental and cultural consequences. One Laotian engineer argued that the World Bank's action "was like a guest walking into your house and telling you to rearrange your furniture."[511]

The New York Times estimates that "America's waterways are clogged by about 70,000 dams." In August 1997, the Federal Energy

Regulatory Commission, "for the first time in its history," considered the issuance of an order to dismantle a dam — the Edwards Dam on the Kennebec River in Maine. *The New York Times* encouraged the Commission to proceed with this action, which would provide access of nine species of Atlantic fish to their traditional spawning grounds.[512]

The Electric Automobile

I told her, you young people take everything for granted, automobiles, airplanes, telephones, even electric lights. You act as if they've always been here. I remembered when they had the first electric lights at the Centennial Exhibition in Philadelphia in '76. We were little children, of course, but I remember it. It was just a toy then. Nobody thought it would ever amount to anything.

— **William Carlos Williams**[513]

Lest we leave the subject of electricity without crediting Edison for his acumen as well as his inability to anticipate the negative consequences of his ideas, let us consider the present status of the electric car. Edison was an early, fervent booster of the automobile (which he hoped would retire horses from public thoroughfares) and he hoped to develop a battery that would be efficient and effective for the motor car. His early batteries were too heavy and not efficient enough to keep pace with the internal combustion engine, and the electric car gave way to the Model T, the Oldsmobile, and the diesel engine. Edison, of course, eventually developed a commercially successful nickel-lithium-alkaline battery, and the lithium-alkaline battery continues to be immensely successful (although few today would recognize it as an Edison invention).

The idea of the electric car never died completely, because it is believed that the electric automobile will have a lighter impact on the environment than cars powered by internal combustion engines. California has recently mandated that "10 percent of the vehicles sold in the state to be emission-free starting in 2003," and "New York state law requires seven major auto makers to sell a total of 7,800 zero-emission cars in the current model year." The "Automobiles" section of *The New York Times* reviewed the performance of six electric automobiles (Chevrolet, Chrysler, Ford, Honda, Solectria, and Toyota), and concluded that "electric cars are fine, even fun, for those with a short commute, a predictable driving pattern, a willingness to be stared at — and a gasoline powered car in reserve." We can presume that Edison would have been delighted to know that the lead-acid batteries in new G.M. electric cars are now being replaced by the "more efficient nickel-metal-hydride batteries," which are already being used in the Honda and Toyota electrics. The electric light was once considered to be "just a toy," and at one time the phonograph seemed to have "no commercial value." These two inventions have since transformed the environment of the world. Who, then, can accurately predict the future of the electric automobile?[514]

A Small Amount of Harm: Incremental Pollution

A central element in this [nineteenth century] accommodation between health and commerce was a new conception of dirt. Ideas about dirt have serious political implications, as will be evident from a moment's reflection on today's struggles over toxic chemicals, radioactive waste, and other environmental pollutants.

— **Paul Starr, 1982**[515]

At this point in my discussion, I move away from Edison to examine some of the recent monographs in the field of environmental history that have a bearing on my thesis, although Edison is not personally mentioned in them. As I stated earlier in the discussion, I wish to see where Edison has been presumed by others to play a role in environmental history, either as a minor actor or as a major contributor. I have pointed out some of these associations, even when they were indirect, as in the case of the Columbia River dams and in the development of batteries for modern electric automobiles. In this section of the discussion, the reader should not expect to find any mention of Edison in the monographs that I review, but his influence will be apparent, anonymously, nonetheless.

* * * * *

While traveling in another country some years ago, I happened to pass through a beautiful forest that was considered to be a sacred place. My guide told me that when local people walked in these woods, they treated all living things with great respect. Nothing would be killed — neither plants nor animals. Why, then, I asked, are so many trees along the trail dead or dying? They seemed to me to have the marks of axes or knives around their bases. My guide answered, sadly, that wood was scarce in these mountains, and that people of this region had found a solution to the problem. Each person passing by a tree would make a small cut in its bark. Eventually the tree would die, and it could then be cut down and used for firewood or lumber. No individual killed the tree. Each small axe mark, said the guide, added only a small amount of harm to it.

In this section, I will discuss what I call the concept of "incremental pollution." I will discuss the implications for "today's struggles over toxic chemicals, radioactive waste, and other environmental pollutants" in the context of what Starr called a "new conception of dirt," and what my mountain guide referred to as "a small amount of harm." Both concepts ("dirt" and "a small amount of harm") are culturally grounded, and both can act in powerful ways to relieve individuals of anxiety for actions which degrade the environment. Many of the environmental problems that I have described around Edison's residences and factories are far more obvious today than they were when he was alive. In a few instances, such as the dangers of mercury and lead, problems were apparent contemporaneously, but workers were nevertheless exposed to toxic levels of these substances at Menlo Park and Silver Lake. The dangers of X-rays and alternating current rapidly became apparent to Edison and were addressed aggressively, while the toxicity of substances such as radium and phenol-formaldehyde compounds was appreciated far more slowly. In order to understand how employers, workers, and the public evaluate and cope with potential risks — such as those associated with Edison's plants — it is necessary to look at the subject of pollution from a cultural perspective. One of the most thoughtful analysts of this subject is Mary Douglas. While Edison or Edison's corporation do not appear specifically in Douglas' examples, she cites several subjects of interest to Edison, such as "hygiene," "X-rays," "electricity" and "the telephone," in connection with her discussion of "purity and danger," "risk and culture," and "the world of goods."

Some of the comments that Mary Douglas made about dirt more than thirty years ago provide a good starting point for this discussion:

> *As we know it, dirt is essentially disorder. There is no such thing as absolute dirt: it exists in the eye of the beholder. . . . Dirt offends against order. Eliminating it is not a negative movement, but a positive effort to organize the environment.*[516]

Douglas says that she was inspired by her husband, whose threshold of tolerance for cleanness was so much lower than hers that she found it necessary to take "a stand on the relativity of dirt." She continues:

> *Our idea of dirt is compounded of two things, care for hygiene and respect for conventions. The rules of hygiene change, of course, with changes in our state of knowledge. As for the conventional side of dirt-avoidance, these rules can be set aside for the sake of friendship.*[517]

We may recall at this point that Edison had strong beliefs regarding hygiene, but some of them were, shall we say, unconventional. He regarded regular, frequent bathing as a health hazard, and he used the floor as a spittoon. When Edison flopped on the guest room bed at Menlo Park while still dressed and with his dirty boots on, his wife was delighted to have him at home for a change — an example of what Mary Douglas would call setting aside the rules "for the sake of friendship."

To illustrate the cultural relativity of dirt (and to take a swipe at Frazer's *Golden Bough*), Douglas cites the example of a holy woman of Mysore, whose feet were ritually bathed in the most sacred of liquids: "cow-dung as a cleansing agent, . . . in a special silver vessel used only for worshipping." Frazer, says Douglas, was loath "to recognize the wisdom and philosophic depth of primitive cultures. . . All in all, Frazer's influence has been a baneful one." Douglas observes that in Hinduism, holiness and unholiness need not be absolute opposites, but can instead be relative categories. "What is clean in relation to one thing may be unclean in relation to another, and vice versa." Douglas acknowledges that "there can be a marvelous correspondence between the avoidance of contagious disease and ritual avoidance." However, she argues that "Even if some of Moses's dietary rules were hygienically beneficial it is a pity to treat him as an enlightened public health administrator, rather than as a spiritual leader."[518]

Having convinced us of the cultural relativity of dirt (or pollution, if you will) Mary Douglas turned to a study of "the world of goods," in which her trajectory again intersected with Edison's. Although Douglas did not identify Edison by name, we are well aware of his interest in inventing products that would be marketable. Indeed, his focus was repeatedly drawn to the potential market for each of his inventions. Edison would surely have agreed with Douglas, in principle, when she wrote that:

Consumption decisions become the vital source of the culture of the moment. . . . Consumption is the very arena in which culture is fought over and licked into shape. The housewife with her shopping basket arrives home: some things in it she reserves for her household, some for the father, some for the children; others are destined for the special delectation of guests.[519]

Edison would not have used the words "arena" and "delectation," but Douglas and Edison would have been congruent in respect to the importance of consumption in culture. Douglas then proceeds to develop her thesis on the technology of consumption by describing a paradox, which would have fascinated Edison. In 1979, the telephone had not yet become a commonplace household device in England. Commenting on this fact, Douglas wrote:

Surely, one would expect the telephone to have been one of [the luxuries demanded] as soon as it appeared on the market. One would have expected it to quickly become part of the technology base, as it did in the United States and as electric lighting has now done in the United Kingdom. But it did not.[520]

Douglas suggested that the lag in the use of the telephone in private homes in the U.K., compared with electric lights, related to "the way that the distribution of status interlocks with the technology of consumption." This abstruse notion is immediately followed, although not particularly well clarified, by a statement which posits that "status is related to personal availability, and the latter to the use of goods implying 'scale' of consumption." A dozen pages later, Douglas was still puzzling over the low status of the telephone in England, in comparison with other household durables. Those who owned telephones ranked them fourth on a list of "preference orderings" behind the vacuum cleaner, washing machine, and refrigerator, while non-owners ranked the phone sixth, having added television and car above it on their list of preferences. Douglas ultimately, and reasonably, concludes that the rank order of the telephone on the list of preferences depended one's thinking that,

Given the likely scale of my future consumption, given my expected permanent income, I am not likely to have friends with telephones who will telephone me, so I hardly need to install one in my home. I must

seek to synchronize my consumption activities with my friends who are subject to similar periodicity constraints.[521]

In marketing his products — such as his phonographs, toys, and lighting systems — Edison kept in mind the need to sell them to ordinary people. He would have appreciated Douglas's skepticism of governmental remedies for poverty. To some analysts, says Douglas, "the problem of poverty in the midst of industrial plenty is seen solely as an outcome of the system of production, to be solved by redistributive legislation and state control." Edison, who knew what it was like to be poor and hungry and never forgot it, would have agreed with what Douglas calls her "complementary view":

The poor are our kith and kin. Not all our relatives are likely to be among the well-to-do. If we do not know how the poor live, it can only be that we have selected against them in the constituting of our consumption rituals, and have declined invitations to join their celebrations.[522]

That this would have been Edison's position, too, can be seen from numerous anecdotes that I cited previously. Although he lived in an elegant home in West Orange, and his children had all the advantages (as well as the disadvantages) that money could bring, Edison dressed in a humble fashion, walked and worked comfortably with his "muckers" and miners, and was generous to his less-fortunate relatives and in-laws.

In 1982, Mary Douglas returned to the problem of pollution in a book-length "essay" on environmental dangers. Douglas argued that "substantial disagreement remains over what is risky, how risky it is, and what to do about it." She asked:

Can we know the risks we face, now or in the future? No, we cannot, but we must act as if we do. Some dangers are unknown; others are known, but not by us because no one person can know everything. Most people cannot be aware of most dangers at most times.... How, then, do people decide which risks to take and which to ignore?[523]

Lest it be thought that she is a relativist in all respects, unmoored and without a position or a compass, Douglas answers her own question in part by stating that "The perils of nuclear wastes and carcinogenic chemicals are not figments of the imagination." Although technology has produced specific perils and has raised many questions, Douglas also states that "Undoubtedly, also, we benefit from technology. Life expectancy continues to increase; accident rates and infant mortality are way down." Yet, nevertheless, "pollution: abuse of technology; fears for the environment" appears as one of the four items on her principal list of concerns in the area of public policy; Douglas ranks "pollution" just below "foreign affairs," and "crime"; and just above "economic failure."[524]

In order to explain why a "sudden, widespread, across-the-board concern about environmental pollution and personal contamination" has developed in the Western World, especially in the United States, Douglas describes a "cultural change" in the past generation. This "cultural change" is important for our analysis of Edison's "footprints," since it should help us to understand the reasons for our awareness (and critique) of the environmental problems that were present near his factories. In other words, we need to understand why we now point a finger at an asphalt paved parking lot and say, "There was a beautiful pond here, before Edison built his factory and drained it," whereas Edison would say, "I'll make this valley more beautiful, by dotting it with factories."

When Douglas turns to the "bundles of goods and bads" in life, which "have to be taken whole," her analysis of risk edges closer to the problem that we are wrestling with in regard to Edison and his factories. "People do not live in Los Angeles," says Douglas, "for the privilege of breathing in smog but in order to take advantage of its natural beauty, warm climate, job opportunities, and so on." Risks and rewards travel together. But not equally, through all classes of society:

The distribution of life chances through society are hardly equal. Some classes of people face greater risks than others. Poorer people, on the average, are sicker than rich, die earlier, have more accidents. We cannot say that all classes of people who incur greater risks in the course of their lives incur it voluntarily. A person might risk an industrial accident, or accept a certain degree of pollution, to being unemployed; the risk is involuntary in the special sense that people would rather things were otherwise.[525]

And then, suddenly, we come face to face with Edison — though not by name. On the subject of involuntary risk, says Douglas:

Probably the use of electricity provides the best example of the analysis of "involuntary" activity. In this case the fatalities include those arising from electrocution, electrically caused fires, the operation of power plants, and the mining of the required fossil fuel.[526]

The key word, Douglas argues, is "control." Who shall control whom, and in regard to which aspects of life? Again, Douglas' examples recall New Jersey (where asbestos was once manufactured in large amounts) and Edison (the pioneer investigator of X-rays in America):

Always there are unsuspected dangers. Always some inventions (asbestos, X-rays), introduced to make something safer, turn out to be dangerous. Always dangers that are present are ignored. Since anything and everything one does might prove risky . . . we should ask why we face some unknown risks gladly and bristle at others.[527]

Part of the problem rests with the uncertainty that is inherent in scientific investigations. Somewhat facetiously, but nevertheless on the mark, Douglas says that:

Scientists disagree on whether there are problems, what solutions to propose, and if intervention will make things better or worse. One scientist thinks of Mother Nature as merely secreting a healthy amount of dirt and another thinks of her being forced to ingest lethal pollutants. No wonder the ordinary lay person has difficulty in following the argument.[528]

To determine whether a substance is a pollutant or is a potentially useful substance may be somewhat akin to the culturally- and historically-based question of defining what is dirt, which Douglas considered in her monograph some sixteen years earlier. Furthermore, even if risk is clearly apparent,

If some degree of risk is inevitable, suppressing it in one place often merely moves it to another. Shifting risks may be more dangerous than tolerating them, because those who face new risks may be unaccustomed to them and because those who no longer face old ones may become more vulnerable when conditions change.

If this seems to be a far-fetched conjecture, we need only recall that Douglas' hypothetical situation may, indeed, have been exactly what happened when Thomas A. Edison, Inc., moved its manufacturing operations around from place to place — to Glen Ridge, Silver Lake, West Orange, and Kearny.

In her essays on dirt and pollution, consumer goods, and risk and culture, Mary Douglas clarified many of the issues that we puzzled over in our review of Edison's impact on the environment. Douglas alluded to two problems, however, which she did not deal with in depth, and we must turn to other sources for further information about these issues. One of these questions relates to the history of the environmental movement: When would it have been reasonable for Thomas Edison or the Edison corporation to have had a higher level of awareness of the hazards of the substances that were being released from the factories that it operated in New Jersey? And how can Douglas state in such a matter-of-fact manner that "The perils of nuclear wastes and carcinogenic chemicals are not figments of the imagination," while not including other chemicals such as the herbicides and pesticides described by Rachel Carson in *Silent Spring*, and various substances such as white (a.k.a. yellow) phosphorus, lead, mercury, and benzene that have long been classified as industrial toxins. Finally, although we may draw an indirect analogy in Douglas' essays to what I called "incremental pollution," in fact, I found no specific, quotable reference to this subject in her writing.[529]

Indeed, incremental and cumulative pollution is so difficult to prove that it is still not a simple matter to prove a cause-and-effect relationship between a presumed or alleged environmental pollutant that has been added in small amounts over a long period of time, and an adverse outcome. This was the allegation in the case of TCE and "perc" dumping in the Aberjona River valley in Woburn, Massachusetts, which was the subject of Jonathan Harr's *A Civil Action*. In the end, the civil cases against the alleged polluting companies were restricted, dismissed, or settled out of court for rather modest sums of money. Criminal actions were later brought because of corporate cover-ups and perjury, but this provided little satisfaction for the plaintiffs. The U. S. Environmental Protection Agency also took strong actions, declaring the area a Superfund site. The corporations involved were fined by the EPA; at last report they were preparing to close their plants in Woburn, rather than to clean up their worksites and conduct hazard-free operations in the future.[530]

* * * * *

Let us turn first to the question of the history of the environmental movement. We may recall that during World War I, soon after he became acting CEO during his father's absence as a consultant for the U. S. Navy, Charles Edison established a plant health office and an improved system for treatment of injuries. We do not know if any attention was given in the plant health office to the more subtle problems that were associated with handling toxic substances such as lead, mercury, nickel, and phenol-formaldehyde derivatives in rooms with poor ventilation. Furthermore, in the absence of evidence to the contrary, we may presume that toxic wastes were allowed to flow at will into the ground, and into adjacent streams and ponds, and that whatever blew off in fumes and smoke was considered well rid of. Llewellyn Park was upstream and upwind, and the neighborhoods downwind and downstream were poor and largely voiceless.

We may be appalled now to read about the pollution generated by factories such as Edison's, but the history of the modern environmental movement actually began long after Edison's death. Mary Douglas sets 1962, when Rachel Carson's *Silent Spring* was published, as the year in which public interest in "conservation" was strongly aroused. Douglas acknowledges that the conservation movement can be dated as far back as 1872, with the creation of Yellowstone National Park. During the next ninety years, according to Douglas, the conservation movement was largely focused on preservation of unique places, such as the Grand Canyon, and on management of wildlife and natural resources on terms that were dictated by dedicated hunters, fishermen, ranchers, and "big-interest members." Following *Silent Spring*'s publication, public interest in ecology led to the celebration of Earth Day in 1970, but the rate of growth of environmental organizations "has been considerably slower since 1972." Douglas has little to say about the history of control of industrial pollution, and Carson focused principally on the field use of herbicides and pesticides rather than on intentional or accidental pollution of the environment by industry.[531]

For the history of the awareness and regulation of industrial pollution we must turn to other sources, such as Andrew Hurley's *Environmental Inequalities*; Kai Erickson's *A New Species of Trouble*; the essays on *Risk, Environment and Modernity,* edited by Scott Lash, Bronislaw Szerszynski, and Brian Wynne; Jonathan Harr's *A Civil Action*; and Robert Gottlieb, *Forcing the Spring*. Hurley discusses "class, race, and industrial pollution" associated with the U.S. Steel plant in Gary, Indiana, from 1945 to 1980. Erickson analyzes a series of seven "modern disasters," ranging from methylmercury pollution of the river used by Ojibwa Indians in Canada in the early 1970s to the atmospheric release of radioisotopes at Three Mile Island in 1979. The essays edited by Lash, Szerszynski, and Wynne all relate to issues that are subsequent to Edison's death in 1931. Gottlieb's history of the environmental movement in the United States includes a thorough review of the history of environmentalism in America from the 1890s onward.[532]

In fairness to Thomas A. Edison, Inc., and to Edison himself, there is nothing in the monographs by Hurley, Erikson, Lash et al, Harr, and Gottlieb to suggest that the Edison Corporation's plants were operating with environmental controls that were below the contemporary standards for management of hazards in the workplace, and for the disposal of waste products from factories. Standards were low, in those days, and Edison's environmental practices were no worse — and in some areas (such as in his Laboratory, and in Sussex and Warren Counties) were probably better — than his contemporaries.

* * * * *

When I began my study of Edison and the environment, I had heard or read not a word about dangers to his workers from physical and chemical hazards, and of pollution of the neighborhoods near his plants. In the course of my reading, I found that these problems were mentioned by Edison's biographers, especially Josephson and Conot, and by other scholars. In the course of my research (presented in Part II and here), I learned of additional problems in the Edison company's workplaces and in the surrounding areas. I also had a chance to examine many of the sites personally, which gave me an additional perspective. I could usually see the nature of the terrain and adjacent dwellings better in site visits than when I tried reconstruct the inventor's "footprints" in my mind's eye from maps, photographs, and oral and written accounts. During the year in which I read about Edison and visited the sites of his residences and plants in New Jersey, I gradually developed a strong sense of unease regarding his attitude toward the environment. It seemed that he regarded nature as a commodity to be exploited, especially farmland, of which there was then seemingly an endless amount available in New Jersey. Furthermore, except for long-term, loyal employees, Edison considered his workers and the neighborhoods around his factories to be more or less expendable, if necessary. They could be exposed to air and water pollution at will, up to the limits allowed by local governments, health departments, and the courts.

It was not until I began to construct my discussion that I had the opportunity to step back from a close look at Edison, to place him in the context of his period. In this regard, I wished to see what Edison thought of "nature" and "the environment," and whether or not he acted in accordance with his beliefs. And I wished to see the extent to which Edison's notions of "nature" and "the environment" were congruent with, or at odds with, his contemporaries. In short, I began to determine whether Edison spoke with a "forked tongue" (said one thing, and did another) with respect to the environment, and whether his environmental policies were consistent with those of his contemporaries, or not.

In order to assess Edison's personal environmental philosophy, I turned again to Runes' edition of *The Diary and Sundry Observations of Thomas A. Edison*. In my previous reference to this collection of articles and essays, I mentioned some of my misgivings about it (such as, the sources are not explicitly cited; and it is clear that Runes had edited the diary that Edison wrote at Woodside Villa in 1885, with some changes in spelling, punctuation, and grammar). Nevertheless, I have no reason to doubt that the vast majority of the text is Edison's and that the year in which each statement was written is correctly stated in the endnote.

Edison mentions "the environment," and "nature" in several places in the *Diary and Sundry Observations*. And, as we have previously seen, he made a number of references in this volume to observations of flora and fauna, of human interactions with nature, and to astronomical objects. For example, at Menlo Park, on Sunday, 12 June 1885, he wrote:

> *This is by far the nicest day of the season, neither too hot nor too cold — it blooms on the apex of perfection — an Edenday. Good day for an angels' picnic. They could lunch on the smell of flowers and new mown hay, drink the moisture of the air, and dance to the hum of bees. Fancy the soul of Plato astride of a butterfly riding around Menlo Park with a lunch basket. . . . Nature is bound to smile somehow.*[533]

Elsewhere in this entry, Edison mentions his affection for Mina Miller, and he is surely writing for the record. Nevertheless, he is clever, observant, and amusing. His style is interesting; one can almost smell the flowers and the hay. He often irreverently but cheerfully refers to the Bible, as to Eden and angels in this passage. In the next passage, two days later, Edison has arrived at Woodside Villa in Winthrop, on the Massachusetts seashore, with his daughter, "Dot." They are staying at the country home of his friends, the Gillilands, with members of Mina Miller's family.

In evening went out on sea wall. Noticed a strange phosphorescent light in the west, probably caused by a baby moon just going down Chinaward. Thought at first the Aurora Borealis had moved out west.[534]

Five days later, Edison wrote that he "slept as sound as a bug in a barrel of morphine." When he awoke, he heard birds singing and commented — again with a Biblical reference:

Canary seed orchestra started up with same old tune. Ancestors of this bird sang the selfsame tune six thousand years ago to Adam down on the Euphrates, way back when Abel got a situation as the first angel.[535]

On 21 July 1885, Edison wrote that he "Saw big field of squashes throwing out their leafy tentacles to the wind . . . A spider weaves its net to catch an organized whole. How like this is to the living plant." By then, Edison had been in Massachusetts for a week, and he was evidently enamored with the Woodside Villa, Mina, and his own words.[536]

Edison's comments in *The Diary and Sundry Observations* became both more prosaic and more philosophical in his later years. Although he later abjured the humor of his entries in 1885, Edison continued to be interested in atmospheric and ecological phenomena, and in what we would now call "the environment" of "nature." Indeed, he referred specifically to nature in 1920 when he wrote that "If a bridge falls, we rebuild it . . . Nature would not take the trouble to remember such unimportant details." Edison also referred to nature in his essay on Tom Paine, who he greatly admired: "His Bible was the open face of nature, the broad skies, the green hills." Although he often referred whimsically to "Nature" (as in "Nature always knows her business"), Edison was dubious about the use of the term, "nature," as he indicated in this passage in 1920:

I believe that life, like matter, is indestructible. . . Of course, you say, it is nature. But what is nature? That seems to me to be such an evasive reply. It means nothing. It is just a subterfuge — a convenient way of shutting off further questioning by merely giving an empty word for an answer. I have never been satisfied with that word "nature."[537]

Edison's familiarity with farming led him to express his views on agriculture on several occasions. He had grown up in farming country, and his property in Menlo Park and in Warren County were in the midst of farms. In 1921, the inventor accepted what we would call the commodification of nature, and he favored pushing the land to ever greater productivity. Some critics would say that this was the philosophy that produced the Dust Bowl.

America's fertile fields always welcome willing hands. Farm labor, while it may not be immensely profitable, is always self-supporting. It converts a man from a liability to an economic asset. The automobile has made farm life more pleasant; with the telegraph, telephone, and automobile, it is possible for the farmer to keep in close touch with the city and outside world.

There are plenty of natural resources in our country to furnish the proper security to capital and to support many times the number of people that we now have.[538]

Four other comments by Edison in 1920 show his breadth of interest in "the environment," which he viewed from the perspective now referred to as "social Darwinism." In other words, Edison believed that a change in the environment forces the development of new life forms. This may occur over a space of eons ("skeletons of mammoth animals," "from fish to man," and so forth; this is pure Darwinism). It also happens within the lifetime of individuals, as when, for example, humans are given the opportunity to have artificial light available for their use (this smacks of social Darwinism):

We have seen how environment has wrought changes upon animals, and even wiped out certain species altogether — as the discovery of numerous skeletons of mammoth animals of prehistoric days has proved.

Changed conditions not only require but force new forms. When a new environment replaces an old one, old forces build in new ways, in order to adapt themselves to altered circumstances.

I think it is certain that, if our environment in future changes as materially as it has in the past, alterations as great as that from fish to man and from gills to noses will occur in the course of future ages. Then what shall we be?

Put a developed human being into an environment where there is no efficient artificial light and he must degenerate. Put an undeveloped human being into an environment where there is artificial light and he will improve.[539]

* * * * *

Although Edison can be thought of as a reactionary capitalist, because he supports the "commodification" of nature and "social Darwinism," it is clear that there is nothing in *The Diary and Sundry Observations* to indicate that Edison's behavior as an inventor and businessman conflicted with his expressed beliefs. Furthermore, his stated philosophy regarding the environment was no more rapacious than most of his contemporaries, and in many ways he showed a greater appreciation for the beauty and wonder of nature than most.

Some environmental historians do not hesitate to criticize vigorously the philosophy or decisions of individuals and groups which produced untoward outcomes, as seen from the present, looking back. This "presentist" school is exemplified by writers such as Donald Worster and Carolyn Merchant.

For example, Worster states that "The Dust Bowl was the darkest moment in the twentieth-century life of the southern plains." Worster concurs with George Borgstrom, who ranks the creation of the Dust Bowl "as one of the three worst ecological blunders in history," along with the deforestation of China's uplands in about 3000 B.C. and the destruction of Mediterranean vegetation by livestock in antiquity. Worster argues that the Dust Bowl came about because "There was nothing in the plains society to check the progress of commercial farming, nothing to prevent it from taking the risks it was willing to take for profit." In the epigraph that introduced *Dust Bowl*, Worster quotes Karl Marx's condemnation of capitalist agriculture, in which all progress is said to be "progress in the art, not only of robbing the laborer, but of robbing the soil." While Worster did not implicate Edison directly in the chain of events that created the Dust Bowl, Worster charged that American farming "has evolved further toward the Henry Ford example of using machinery and mass production to make more and more profits."[540]

Carolyn Merchant delineated the characteristics of "two types of ecological revolution — colonial and capitalist" through a study of the history of New England. The "colonial ecological revolution . . . resulted in the collapse of indigenous Indian ecologies and the incorporation of a European ecological complex of animals, plants, pathogens, and people." The "capitalist ecological revolution . . . created air pollution, water pollution, and resource depletions as externalities outside the calculation of profits." Merchant's thesis was that "ecological revolutions are major transformations in human relations with nonhuman nature." Following Worster, Merchant argues that these revolutions arise from changes, tensions, and contradictions between "a society's mode of production and its ecology." Merchant also sees these revolutions as arising from contradictions between a society's modes of production and reproduction.

Merchant also acknowledges her debt to Marx, quoting him early in her first chapter, and stating that "Both Kuhn's theory of scientific revolution and Marx's theory of social revolution are starting points for a theory of ecological revolutions." Merchant forthrightly states as a matter of fact her belief that:

Science and history are both social constructions. Science is an ongoing negotiation with nonhuman nature for what counts as reality. Scientists socially construct nature, representing it differently in different historical epochs.[541]

Merchant quoted George Perkins Marsh's observation on the "injudicious system of managing woodlands" in Vermont in 1849 and Henry David Thoreau's championship of subsistence farming in 1854. (In *Walden,* Thoreau wrote that the typical Concord farmer "knows nature but as a robber").[542]

I respect the scholarship of Worster and Merchant, and I admire their passion. Their Marxist outlook provided a useful perspective for them to organize their studies and for the preparation of their conclusions. Without a perspective, a scholar wanders and has nothing coherent to report. However, I am not persuaded that we can hold historical personages and past societies liable for all of their mistakes in judgment. Who can say whether our present beliefs and actions will withstand the test of time any better than those whom we would criticize. Should a critic such as Henry David Thoreau be regarded by his contemporaries as a fool or as a prophet, as "Chicken Little" or Cassandra? How can society decide the answer to such a question? In contrast to Merchant, I would argue that one approach to the answer is the method of science, and the other is the method of history.

As a scientist searching for truth for more than forty years, I reject the radical post-modernist view that science is "relative," and that the scientific method is severely contaminated by dogmatism, sexism, and racism. While it is true that science is "socially constructed," and that science has evolved through "different historical epochs," it is a gross error to lump science and history together, as Merchant has done. Scientists may find more than one answer to a question, but they agree on how to seek truth. The scientific method presumes that there is, somewhere out there, one best solution, and Occam's razor cuts to it. If a much better solution is proposed, it may result in the creation of a "new paradigm," as Kuhn would say. In the field of history, on the other hand, "truth" is relative; it is best found by remembering Rashomon, not Occam. In other words, I am inclined to be a relativist when I examine a historical event, for it is clear to me that there are many ways to reconstruct the past. Furthermore, if we wish to hold a historical individual or a society responsible for what we believe are errors that they committed, we should attempt to determine whether they were acting in accordance with their beliefs, or if they intentionally or inadvertently violated their own laws and codes of conduct. In this way, we may hope to learn how to distinguish between true and false prophets, which has been a problem since the earliest humans first assembled and began to communicate with each other.[543]

The *milieu interieur*: Education and Health

I like the Montessori method. It teaches through play. It makes learning a pleasure. It follows the natural instincts of the human being.

— **Thomas Alva Edison, 1914**[544]

I have been at work for some time building an apparatus to see if it is possible for personalities which have left this earth to communicate with us. . . . I am engaged in the construction of one such apparatus now, and I hope to be able to finish it before very many months pass.

— **Thomas Alva Edison, 1920**[545]

In this section of my work, I will endeavor to explain why Edison is given so little credit for his contributions to medical science, health, and education. As an inventor, Edison set the standard by which all of his successors are measured. His specific contributions are less well known to the general public, but are well described in monographs in the fields of electricity (including lighting and electrical appliances), radio and electronics, sound reproduction, moving pictures, and telegraphy. In addition, we have reviewed monographs and published articles that describe appreciatively Edison's work in inorganic and organic chemistry (including metallurgy, studies of carbon, and plastic polymers of phenol-formaldehyde), mining, battery manufacturing, cement making, and rubber production.

In addition to Edison's work in these fields of science and technology, the inventor, personally, and his corporation — Thomas A. Edison, Inc. — also made important contributions to health care through the development of the fluoroscope and the production of medical gases. And Edison was a vigorous and entertaining spokesman for innovations in education. Why, then, has so little been written about Edison's work in the health sciences and education, and why have his discoveries, his products, and his ideas in these fields largely been forgotten? The answer, I believe, lies principally in the variable quality of Edison's output in these fields. Dagobert Runes assessed Edison perceptively when he wrote that the inventor's propositions in education "show a rare combination of whimsey and deep sincerity." By the same token, Edison's seminal contributions to medical science were matched with the production of patent medicines, goofy statements about hygiene, and a belief that "scientific methods" may be used to communicate with "personalities which have left this earth."[546]

Education

In an undated essay, Edison once wrote that "The most necessary task of civilization is to teach men how to think." Edison was, however, skeptical of formal education, and on the whole, he took a dim view of America's schools. In 1925 Edison recalled that when he was a boy, "My refuge was the Detroit Public Library. I started . . . with the first book on the bottom shelf and went through the lot, one by one. I didn't read a few books. I read the library."[547]

Edison's iconoclastic opinions regarding the educational environment in America were stated bluntly, and he did not hesitate to chasten the administrators of both secondary schools and colleges. His advocacy of the Montessori method and of home schooling placed him at the leading edge of educational theory in 1914, but would have been regarded as confrontational by traditionalists. His opposition to coeducation (boys and girls "distract each other's attention"), would have raised hackles among both innovative and traditional professional educators, at least in the public schools. And his fetish for facts ("young men cannot think efficiently unless they have facts in their minds") produced "violent critics" among "the men responsible for our primary and secondary education." Edison was particularly scornful of American colleges. While he wrote that "I am all for the college men," this was faint praise which faded when he added that:

Perhaps the failure of the colleges lies principally in their lack of appreciation of the dull inferiority of the material which the lower schools deliver to them; it may be because of this that they do not go down the line to help toward the correction of a national evil.[548]

Edison was farsighted in his call for visual education ("Motion pictures can be applied to a scientific, systematic course of memory training in the schools") and the use of other new techniques ("Radio is popularizing science among the young and that is something which the schools, necessarily, have frequently failed to do"). However, Edison's sarcastic comments about deficiencies in college education and his generally critical comments about education separated him from professional educators, who would regard him as an interloper in their field, rather than as a seer. Edison's favorite intelligence test was actually a memory test, which he acknowledged was "the target of much criticism." He delighted in remembering minutiae:

Out of every thousand facts that present themselves to you, I should think that at least 990 come unobtrusively, without the slightest indication whether they are to be of any subsequent importance to you or not. If your memory is a success it will reproduce — within the proper limits of human fallibility, of course — any one of these items, when and where you want it.[549]

In spite of the mixture of whimsy and sincerity in Edison's comments on education, his name is perpetuated in this field as the eponym for the Edison Project. This for-profit educational venture was founded in 1991 by an entrepreneur, Christopher Whittle. The Edison Project, a New York company, opened twelve schools in 1995 and 1996, and in 1998 it claimed that students in these schools "had made progress on standardized reading and math tests." By 1998 the Edison Project had taken over the operation of twenty-five public schools. In May 1998, the Edison Project received a $25 million grant from the owners of The Gap clothing chain, which was intended to subsidize California school districts that wanted to hire the Edison Project to create fifteen autonomous public schools, known as charter schools. The company was founded "on the premise that a private corporation could provide a better education and make a profit while spending the same amount as most states do per pupil." About half of the Edison Project schools are charter schools, and half are run as contracts for school districts. As with Thomas Edison's own comments on education, there are many controversies associated with charter schools, for-profit schools, and the Edison Project specifically. The Edison Project has not yet posted a profit (as was also the case with some of Thomas Edison's own projects), which it attributes to continued growth. The founder of the Edison Project was quoted in May 1998 as saying that "Clearly, we have no intention of stopping our growth, so we will not post a profit."[550]

The Medical Environment

Edison's personal medical environment, his own *milieu interieur*, has been described by his biographers in considerable detail. There is no need to restate the many health problems that the inventor had in his lifetime, for these are a matter of record in his biographies (especially Conot, *Edison*), and I did not discover anything new in this regard during my case studies. It is, however, interesting to read Edison's own assessment of a particularly significant aspect of his *milieu interieur* — his deafness — which he stated "has not been a handicap but a help to me."[551]

Edison's autobiographical essay on his deafness occupies some thirteen pages of his *Diary and Sundry Observations*. In this essay, he says that "it is supposed" that the injury occurred when he was "lifted by the ears" from the ground into a baggage car when he was twelve years old. Doctors, he said, "could do nothing for me." Among the benefits of his deafness, says Edison, was that "it drove me to reading," and "deafness was an advantage to a telegrapher." He was glad to have been shut off from boring "small talk." Because of his quiet environment, Edison believed that his "nerves have not been bothered" and he was "able to write without tremor." He also believed that his work on the phonograph was enhanced by his deafness. ("I can hear anything upon the phonograph . . . The phonograph never would have been what it is now and for a long time has been if I had not been deaf.") Furthermore, "The telephone as we now know it might have been delayed if a deaf electrician had not undertaken the job of making it a practical thing." Deafness was an asset in his business activities, for he did "not rely on verbal arguments," and in his courtship, "deafness was a help." He summed it all up by saying that "The best thinking has been in solitude. The worst has been in turmoil."[552]

Edison's contributions to the *milieu interieur* of the world have not been entirely forgotten. Lawrence Altman of *The New York Times* commented in June 1997 that:

> One who suspected the dangers [of X-rays] was the inventor Thomas A. Edison. Within days after learning about Roentgen's discovery, Edison began building X-ray machines with an eye to developing a lucrative new industry. But after noting redness around his eyes and strange pitting in his assistant's skin, Edison abruptly quit. His fear of X-rays persisted throughout his life; when he collapsed at 84, four months before he died, he adamantly refused to be X-rayed.[553]

Most of Edison's work in the biological sciences has, however, been lost to memory, and much of it was, indeed, forgettable. For example, his ointment for neuralgia (a patent medicine that apparently contained morphine or cocaine, or both), and electrostimulating devices that were designed to treat a wide variety of diseases, or just to amuse the users. Edison was not a significant contributor to the toxic and microbial pollution that made Newark, New Jersey, "the nation's unhealthiest city" in the late nineteenth century, nor was he an active participant in the solution for Newark's problems. Edison was also not a significant party in what Paul Starr called "the social transformation of American medicine." He made little effort to work with physicians to develop projects that would be acceptable to the medical profession. Furthermore, his personal physicians were not connected with the main stream of the profession in Essex County, New Jersey. Edison is said by his biographers to have bullied and undercut the efforts of the local Boards of Health to have his factories reduce their output of pollutants. However, I was unable to confirm the charge that Boards of Health in Essex County were intimidated by the Edison corporation, because these Boards no longer exist and their records are unavailable.[554]

Edison was very interested in botany and both his marginal notes and his field work in Fort Myers, Florida, reveal his skill in that aspect of biology. On the other hand, he was not much of a zoologist; he was far more interested in plants than in animals, and his comments on human biology — like his comments on education — covered a spectrum that ranged from wise to ridiculous. Edison was well aware of his eccentric beliefs and behavior, and he enjoyed playing the role of a curmudgeon.

A biographer should admire his subject in order to engage fully in the task of ferreting out information and then writing it. It would be far easier to write a biography of Edison from the perspective of his other inventions, discoveries, ideas, and comments than those in the field of medicine. The best that I can do in this regard is to credit the Great Inventor for his seminal contributions to the development of the fluoroscope; to admire Edison's deep concern and remorse for accidentally exposing his employee Clarence Dally to fatal doses of X-rays; and to acknowledge Edison's leadership of the corporation that produced a wide variety of important medical gases and accessories related to medical gases. For the sake of his reputation, we can be grateful that Edison's apparatus to communicate with the world beyond the grave was never demonstrated to the public. Unless, of course, it had worked.[555]

Land and Labor

The America to which the textbooks welcomed the children of Whitney Creek was secular, progressive, rational, scientific and can-do practical — a world full of the glory of man and his achievements. . . . Much the most powerful of the godlike modern were the scientists— Franklin and his kite, Morse and the telegraph, Bell and the telephone, **Edison** *and the electric light, Marconi and the wireless.*

— **From a description of rural Montana in 1911**[556]

This drugstore sells a little bit of everything: chocolate, cigars, hammocks, fabric dyes, postcards, magazines, diaries, batteries, ice cream sodas, and more. Eye-catching posters and displays, probably nationally distributed, promote major brands and companies like Eveready, Coca-Cola, McCall's, **Edison,** *and Gillette.*

— **From a description of rural Iowa, 1922**[557]

In rural America, Thomas A. Edison and the Edison Company were icons whose names and products influenced the lives, work habits, and culture of countless men, women, and children in the first three decades of the twentieth century. From the plains of Montana to small-town Iowa, Edison's success exemplified the virtues of hard work and courage, and Edison's products — especially electric lights and the phonograph — were high on the list of desired consumer products. In this section, I continue my exploration of the impact of Edison on the environment, as he appears in the words and pictures of those who wrote about it in general, without focusing on the Great Inventor. In previous sections of the discussion, I dealt specifically with the impact of Edison's work in chemistry and electricity. I now begin to examine Edison's impact on the cultural environment. In this section I review Edison's relationship to rural culture, including land use; the labor of men, women, and children on farms and in small towns; and the acquisition of products intended to enhance comfort and pleasure in these settings.

The children of Whitney Creek, Montana, in 1911 lived in a bone-dry valley on the main line of the newly built Milwaukee Railroad. Their parents had come to this tributary of the Yellowstone River to settle on half-sections of land, hoping to prosper. Most would ultimately fail, and either perish or move on. For the first few years, however, the annual rainfall was several inches above average — enough to convince the homesteaders that "rain follows the plow" — and the thin layer of dark topsoil provided sufficient nutrients for a bountiful harvest. The children were inspired by stories in their textbooks, such as "Young Tom Edison, from a village in Ohio, makes a spectacular killing on Wall Street."

Edison and his assistants went to bed in the knowledge that they had solved the problem of electric lighting. While he slept the story of his achievement was flashed around the world. The value of the stock in his company rose from one hundred and six dollars to three thousand dollars a share.[558]

Nearly all farms and ranches were still lighted by kerosene lamps and candles in 1911, but most adults and many of the children in the Midwest and the Great Plains had seen electric lights, either in cities or on trains. And although farms and ranches depended largely on animals, manual labor, and windmills for power, rather than electricity, telephone lines were strung along fence posts from one home to the next, and tractors and trucks began to appear on the larger farms. The Morse 40-light "F"

Plant ("One Cost for Light and Power") was marketed to farmers before the First World War, and the Cletrac Tank-Type Tractor was a major advance over conventional narrow-wheeled tractors, which were often stuck in the mud. "For the modern farmhouse" in Whitney Creek, "there was mechanized music. . . The New Edison Amberola, Mr. Edison's great new phonograph with the new Diamond stylus reproducer and your choice of all brand new Diamond Amberola Records . . . Only $1.00 down!" In these selections from his "historical meditation" on rural Montana in the early twentieth century, we can see that Jonathan Raban has illustrated in several ways the powerful impact that Edison had on the lives and aspirations of those who were building hopes and creating farms in that harsh environment.[559]

Ten years after Raban's families were breaking ground in Montana, Iowa was in its eighth decade of statehood, and many of its farms were being managed by the grandchildren of those who had first settled on them. Land was more fertile in Iowa than in Montana — the black soil of Iowa appeared to be bottomless and rain was rarely scarce; flooding was more likely to be a problem than drought. Iowans, in short, were ready for consumer products in 1922, and Edison's companies were ready for them. At the rear of the drugstore that was described in the epigraph to this section, the largest poster in the store proclaims "New Edison . . . Discs." It is six feet by one foot in size, if it is an inch. The Edison poster hangs from the store's "eye-catching . . . pressed-tin ceiling," which "added elegance at a low cost." This drugstore and other businesses in small towns in Iowa were photographed in about 1922 by William H. Felton. Some of Felton's photographs were brought together in 1998 by Ginalie Swaim, who used them to illustrate an essay on small-town Iowa life in the 1920s.

A handsome phonograph cabinet with the lid open—presumably an Edison brand — stands in front of the post office at the back of the store in Felton's photograph. The floor of the store is diamond-pattern linoleum, which was "preferred over tongue-and-groove flooring because it was easier to clean and . . . more decorative." Another poster at the rear of the store advertises "Edison Records . . . $1.50." The proud owner of the store stands stiffly, smiling modestly, behind his glass-covered counter, in front of the soda fountain. He is dressed in a very modern soft collared white shirt with French cuffs and a conservatively patterned necktie. The owner and the other two men in the store must have stood quietly for some time, for the illumination in this store is largely from the front and side windows; there are only two overhead lights in view.[560]

In another small town in Iowa, an appliance store that also has a post office at the rear sells both gas stoves and electrical appliances. "An arbor of ceiling fixtures dramatically displays America's dazzling new star of the 20th century — electricity." There are also "table lamps, iron, mangles, fans, and washing machines" visible, plus what looks to me like a gleaming white horizontal butter churn. Behind a massive electric iron, and beside a table fan that is at least two feet in diameter, is a sign that beckons: "Keep Your Home Cool All Summer with a G-E Fan. The Cost is Trifling." This poster bears the familiar General Electric Company logo, with its "E" reminiscent of Thomas Edison's personal signature. The appliances in this store were largely for residents of the town; farmers and their wives came in on Saturday nights to admire but not to purchase them. The reason was that at this time, in 1923, although thirty-five percent of American homes had electricity, "only 15 percent of Iowa farm homes were equipped with electricity or gas."

Telephones, on the other hand, were immensely popular in Iowa, as they were in rural Montana in 1911. By 1917 eighty-six percent of rural Iowa homes had telephones, the highest percentage in the nation. "Operating a switchboard was traditionally women's work; it was assumed they would be more patient and courteous than male operators."

For those who purchased appliances, there were, says Ginalie Swaim, "trade-offs." Swaim cites Ruth Schwartz Cowan, who argues that:

> *Modern labor-saving devices eliminated drudgery, not labor. . . Some of the work was made easier, but its volume increased: sheets and underwear were changed more frequently, so there was more laundry to be done; diets became more varied, so cooking was more complex. . . . Finally, some of the work that had previously been allocated to commercial agencies actually returned to the domain of the housewife.*[561]

Other historians, such as Jeanne Boydston, have taken a similar position. Boydston calls Cowan's work "iconoclastic" with admiration, and she cites Cowan in several places in her own history of *Home and Work*. Cowan points out that "Happy, full-time housewives in intact families spend a lot of money to maintain their households." She also states that "at least for middle-class nonrural American families in the twentieth century . . . the functions of at least one member, the housewife, have increased rather than decreased. . . . The housewife is just about the only unspecialized worker left in America."[562]

Edison and Modernism

Few men have contributed more to the well-being and comfort of modern man than Thomas Alva Edison. The glow of the electric light, and with it the waves of immortal music come right into the homes of the world's great masses, through the inventive genius of this unassuming tinkerer; and through his efforts the theatre on the screen reaches into every hamlet on the globe.

— **Dagobert Runes, 1948**[563]

If we can turn a blind eye to Runes' hyperbole ("every hamlet on the globe" did not then, nor does every one now, have a movie theatre) and to his generic use of the word "man," we can admit the essential truth of his assessment of Edison's impact on the "modern" world. I have chosen the term "modernism" for this part of the discussion to shift the focus of Edison's impact on the cultural environment to the cities of Europe and America. I shall now move away from the rural areas of America, which were exemplified by Montana's farms in 1911 and small-town Iowa in 1922. That is not to say that farm folk and those who lived in small towns were not interested in "modern" things, or that they were not participants in "modernism." Indeed, I referred to the dress and demeanor of the pharmacist in Iowa as being "modern." And Lord and Lady Cameron, who came to Whitney Creek, Montana, from their estate in Scotland, brought "modernism" to the Yellowstone River valley (he with his polo ponies and she with her artistic photography). "Modernism" is not easy to define, but by any definition one uses, it is more visible in urban than rural society, and some aspects of modernism — such as many aspects of scholarly investigation and laboratory bench science — are difficult to sustain in a rural environment.[564]

For purposes of this discussion, I will use the term "modernism" to refer to a culture that is grounded in science-based investigation rather than on religious-based faith. That many scientists believe in a Creator or Supreme Being, and worship God (or Jehovah, or Allah, or the Great Spirit), is a paradox which shows that no definition for "modernism" can be wholly satisfactory. Edison, indeed, believed in a Creator and he did not hesitate to refer to God (often in jest). However, Edison (unlike his mother and his wife, Mina) did not believe in, or worship, the Judeo-

Christian God. I do not recall Edison ever referring to Jesus or the Holy Spirit; theological arguments were not interesting to the inventor. Thomas Edison and his father both intensely admired Thomas Paine, who was regarded by Theodore Roosevelt and many others as an atheist, although it would be more correct to say that Paine (and Edison, and Thomas Jefferson, for that matter) were Deists, not atheists or agnostics. The fine distinctions between these terms need not concern us at this point. Suffice it to say that Benjamin Franklin, Paine, Jefferson, Ethan Allen, Thoreau, Edison, Walt Whitman, and many others over the past two centuries who have had the opportunity to become intimately familiar with the Old and New Testaments saw the Bible as an important book but did not "believe" the scriptures as a matter of faith.[565]

Although Edison — scientist, inventor, Deist — was a "modern" person (and, as we shall soon see, perhaps one of the first moderns), he exhibited several characteristics which could be called "pre-modern" or "anti-modern." For example, his references to God and Biblical characters in *The Diary and Sundry Observations* were comfortable and appreciative, never hostile or scornful. (For example, "God knows we need it.") Edison's infatuation with spiritualism in his old age has generally been disregarded by his biographers and others, but it is surely anti-modern. Edison's comments on spiritualism between 1920 and 1922 were gathered together in "The Realms Beyond," a forty-one page chapter in *The Diary and Sundry Observations*, including a section on "Spiritualism." These dreams and beliefs do not represent the Great Inventor at his best. For example,

I have been at work for some time building an apparatus to see if it is possible for personalities which have left this earth to communicate with us. . . . . I am proceeding on the theory that in the very nature of things, the degree of material or physical power possessed by those in the next life must be extremely slight. . . . I am inclined to believe that our personality hereafter will be able to affect matter.[566]

The nuances of Edison's life and philosophy are not apparent to many of the writers who use him as an example of one thing or another. For example, Edison is placed solidly in the group of "the first moderns" in a recent monograph by William R. Everdell, who cites Edison's kinetograph for its "triumphant foregrounding of discontinuity." For Everdell, "discontinuity" is modernism's key theme. Edison's kinetograph movie camera, which took sixteen still photos per second, produced an image that the eye interpreted as movement — an elegant example, says Everdell, of "discontinuity." Others who Everdell said showed discontinuity and therefore were modernists included James Joyce, Walt Whitman, Albert Einstein ("the quantum of light"), and especially the impressionist artists (Georges Seurat's thousands of colored dots formed a "harmonious whole").[567]

Edison was one of the leaders of the "American Century" (1898-1998), according to David Traxel, author of *1898: The Birth of the American Century*. Traxel singled out Theodore Roosevelt, Clara Barton, Thomas Edison, Geronimo, and Adolphus Green as examples of "serious men and women pursuing what they felt to be important goals. Some of these goals now seem silly, dangerous or even wicked." Nevertheless, they were the leaders who propelled America into the modern age.[568]

There is a web of relationships that loosely ties Roosevelt, Barton, Edison, and Geronimo together. While this is of no great historical import, it shows how significant "moderns" related to each other at the turn of the century. Theodore Roosevelt, as we have previously read, had several connections with Edison. For example, his sister, Corinne, lived near the Edisons in West Orange, and Theodore's cousin, Hillbourne Roosevelt, was a sponsor of Edison's work in Menlo Park. Theodore Roosevelt was a great admirer of Leonard Wood, who — like Roosevelt — was a graduate of Harvard College. Wood was the commanding officer of the Rough Riders in Cuba until he was promoted to brigadier general and turned the command over to Roosevelt. As a young medical officer in the U. S. Army in July 1886 (the year that the Edisons moved into Glenmont), Wood played a key role in the search for the Indian leader, Geronimo, and Wood later became nationally famous when he received the Congressional Medal of Honor for his heroism in this campaign. Clara Barton, Civil War nurse and founder of the American Red Cross, was — like Edison — an adopted child of New Jersey. As one of the first female school teachers in New Jersey, Barton is regarded as an important figure in the history of New Jersey, along with Clara Maass. Maass (who is buried in Fairmount Cemetery in Newark — Mary Stilwell Edison's first resting place) was a New Jersey nurse who died of yellow fever as a volunteer in Walter Reed's experiments in Cuba at the time that Leonard Wood was the Governor General at Havana.[569]

I would mention but one final connection between Edison and modernity: The "quiet charm" of Chautauqua has become "a pattern for the Disney Institute at Disney World." As we know from Edison's biographers, the Chautauqua Institution was founded by Edison's father-in-law (Lewis Miller) and Bishop John Vincent. The Chautauqua Institution is located on Lake Chautauqua, ten miles south of Lake Erie in the southwestern corner of New York state. Thomas Edison visited Chautauqua on several occasions with Mina, and he apparently found the environment there much to his liking, in spite of the Biblical spirit that it had at the time. Disney's chief, Michael Eisner, also found the Chautauqua concept to be "winning," according to an article in *The New York Times* in August 1997. The author, Susan Spano, mentioned that "nine presidents, Amelia Earhart, Helen Keller, Rudyard Kipling, George Gershwin and Thomas A. Edison have been among those who have visited the colony."[570]

* * * * *

A reviewer of the most recent biography of John D. Rockefeller quoted E. M. Forster, who "once wrote that in his fiction he eschewed the problem of good and evil for that of good-and-evil." This notion appeals to me, for it makes it possible to admire or credit Edison for his good intentions and his achievements (as we now see them), while not needing to disregard aspects of Edison's impact on the environment which were either intentionally or unintentionally harmful. The reviewer, Jack Beatty, says that the author, Ron Chernow, "takes the incurable mixedness of life caught by Forster's hyphens as the touchstone of his involving book." Chernow is thus able to portray Rockefeller in a balanced fashion. Rockefeller, we learn was the child of a "flimflam man," who became a "rapacious billionaire." He built an immense financial empire by "malodorous means," yet he was also a "loving father" who became a "loveable old codger" in his "second career in philanthropy." Rockefeller's exhibition of "competitive cruelty unparalleled in industry," exceeded anything that Edison did, or — as far as we know — even thought of. Yet they both bewailed "ruinous competition," and attempted to suppress it. That Rockefeller was more successful than Edison in eliminating competition has left Rockefeller's name as a synonym for wealth without conscience, while Edison is now thought of by the public as the Great Inventor, whose influence on modern life is wholly benign.[571]

The subject of the "invented" image of Edison is one that needs to be revisited. Edison's environment was carefully created in some respects to show him in the way that he wanted to be seen. We have read in Rosanoff's essay how Edison carefully planned his appearance and his statements when he was interviewed by a newspaper reporter, and many of his photographs appear posed as well. Edison's invention of "Edison" may be an even more important and more durable invention than his patented and unpatented discoveries, his business organization, and the corporate research laboratory (which is now generally said to be his most important invention). By putting quotation marks around the name of Edison, I follow the current abbreviated style, called "air quotes," for such a statement, as in Pauline Maier's reference to Thomas Jefferson. ("You almost feel sorry for the real life Thomas Jefferson, except that he helped create 'Thomas Jefferson' — and at some cost to us.") In air quotes, one raises both arms and flicks the index and middle fingers to indicate that one is using slang, or quoting someone. The environment that Thomas Edison created included a permanent image of "Edison," the Old Man, sitting at his desk in Building 5, and in a chair on the lawn at Glenmont, and at his bench in the Chemistry Laboratory.[572]

* * * * *

I wish to add a few additional comments to elaborate upon my perspective on environmental history. History, it has been said, is "ultimately not a catalogue of what is true but rather of what we decide is true." It has also been said that a historian fails if he "does not analyze, does not evaluate, does not relate one piece of evidence to others, does not provide context or explain how his story fits into the larger events of which it was a part." I agree with both of those statements, and I have attempted to conform to them — although I read them long after I had done most of my research and composed most of this book. I also agree with Patricia Cohen that "location matters," and that we must try to understand "how location affects the way people live." The most important landscape, says John Cole, is the "home landscape: the place we return to in our mind's eye when we contemplate our beginnings." It is this view of landscape that I referred to when I wrote that my book would be a study of Edison's impact on "landscape and life."[573]

Finally, I have learned in the course of my research that, as with the Dead Sea scrolls, "access to related material" on Edison "is still limited." And I have grown to appreciate the fact that "The nature of scholarship in the humanities is solitary, and it has always been, by and large. . . . Scholarly work is very lonely."[574]

Chapter 16

Conclusion: The Environmental Legacy of Thomas Edison

After a while I tired of this work.
Hoeing corn in a hot sun is unattractive,
and I did not wonder that boys had left the farm for the city.

— Thomas Alva Edison, on farming, 1911[575]

I believe rural life is the basis of human happiness.
That is my ideal of civilization; I would have people live on small farms instead of surrounding themselves with artificial urban conditions.

— Thomas Alva Edison, on farming, 1911[576]

Which Edison would you have? The recollection of a man who was glad he had left the farm for good, or the man who thought that everyone should live on a farm? These two quotations, both dated 1911, illustrate the challenge and also the opportunity that Edison provides to anyone who tries to make sense of all that he said and did regarding the environment. In this Conclusion to my book, I will show that the best way to view Edison's relationship to the environment is to accept his inconsistencies. We previously read in the Denouement that "discontinuity" has been called a characteristic of the modern world. Edison's inconsistencies, which are sometimes frustrating and sometimes amusing, can thus be considered as examples of modernist discontinuities. They exempt Edison from the peril of *falso in uno* (false in one instance, therefore falsely in all). That is to say, if Edison was heedless of the environment in one place (e.g., Silver Lake), it does not mean that he was necessarily heedless of the environment everywhere his factories were located.

We have previously studied Edison's relationship to the environment by examining what had been written in recent monographs regarding his unique personal environment, and what had recently been written about his relationship to the environment in general. Under the rubric of "unique personal environment" I included a number of subjects such as chemistry and electricity, mechanical engineering and architecture, thermal problems, and auditory and visual studies. In his later years, Edison's studies of ionizing radiation, earth sciences, and biological sciences were also considered as part of his unique personal environment. Edison's "general environment" included his family environment, the "natural" environment of non-living matter and non-human life, the international environment, the "built" environment, the cultural and social environment, and health and illness (which I refer to as the "internal environment" or *milieu interieur*). The Case Study of Edison and the environment in Part II was composed of approximately twenty individual case studies. These were mainly based on site visits to locations where Edison had lived or worked. Some of the case studies included a review of documents and oral histories related to the sites and Edison's presence at them. In some of the case studies (such to locations outside of New Jersey) my observations were mainly based on review of documents and publications rather than on site visits.

    My previous comments in regard to the various aspects of Edison's environment need not be restated in detail, but it should be recalled that the hypotheses that I advanced in the Introduction and Part I were generally confirmed by my Case Study (Part II). That is to say, I suggested in the Introduction that as a boy and young man, Edison was impacted upon by various aspects of his environment, such as the components that I outlined in the previous paragraph. At an early age, he began to take the next step in his relationship to the environment, which was to take control of it. He was precocious in that regard. By the time he reached New Jersey in 1869, Edison had developed the skills that enabled him to begin to alter his surrounding environment. At Menlo Park, in the late 1870s, Edison began to change the environment of the world. I found nothing in my case studies that altered this basic hypothesis. What the case studies revealed was a substantial amount of new information that provided a more complete picture of Edison's environment, and of his impact on the environment, at many sites. Some of the charges that Edison's biographers had made regarding his noxious factories and his cavalier treatment of workers were confirmed. On the other hand, some of the environmental changes that have occurred near his plants were found to be part of larger historic trends, rather than being specifically attributable to him. The reasons for some aspects of Edison's impact on the environment became clear, although questions remained that could be answered only by future studies. Some of these studies may not be possible until the archives have been more completely indexed and copied (such as examination of the health records of his laboratory and factory employees, and correspondence with local health departments).[577]

Edison's comments on farming, which were quoted in the epigraph to this Conclusion, illustrate the ambiguity of the Great Inventor. Having seen examples of Edison's ambiguity repeatedly throughout the biographies and other monographs, and in the case studies in Part II, I suggest that ambiguity, rather than constancy, best describes his relationship to the environment. In this regard it is clear that Edison is both a traditionalist and a modernist. The "traditionalist" Edison is a descendant of English-American patriarchs who led the westward migration across the heartland of America, and who had a value system that was derived from the Colonial Protestant work ethic. This includes a sense of "place" and a sense of "family," which is epitomized by a sense of the "home place," or simply "home." On the other hand, the "modernist" Edison is an intellectually curious child of the Enlightenment, who was a rationalist, Deist, experimenter. This aspect of Edison's character includes a requirement for a laboratory, which was an intimate part of Edison's "home place" from youth to old age. Conflicts between these two viewpoints (traditionalist vs. early modernist) led to profound ambivalence in Edison's world views, and thus of his environmental perspective.[578]

I suggest that Edison's view of the environment was also influenced by five other factors: In the first place, Edison's environment was affected by his health and his concept of the internal environment, especially his deafness; and his perceptions regarding wellness, illness, disease prevention, and medicine. Next, Edison's environment was influenced by his extraordinary and exceptional imagination and inventiveness, which enabled him to visualize possible environments that were beyond the comprehension of most people (e.g., his belief in the future of atomic energy, in the 1920s). Edison's environment was also influenced by the sustained burst of invention and consumerism known as the Industrial Revolution that began in the eighteenth century, and which provided opportunities throughout the nineteenth and twentieth centuries for new inventions to be utilized in commercially successful ventures. Next, luck, or "chance," played a role in Edison's environment. Chance may provide gains or losses, depending on the circumstances, and on the responses that are made by individuals and organizations. "Chance," it has been said, "favors the prepared mind." If Edison often appeared to be unusually lucky, I would argue that this was because he was well prepared to seize the opportunity that chance provided. Finally, Edison's environment was affected by the necessity to compromise between what he believed was the right thing to do, and what circumstances forced or enabled him to do. Edison was said to have called this the problem of his "Mind One" (what should be done) versus his "Mind Two" (what had to be done).[579]

"Edison" and the "New Enlightenment"

Some authors have said that Edison's most important inventions were the phonograph, the electric lighting system, and the motion pictures, and that these three inventions transformed the environment of the world. In concurring with the importance of these inventions, I would say that they have created a new age, which I would call the New Enlightenment. Some scholars have written that Edison's most important invention was the industrial research laboratory; others say it was his creation of a model research-based business organization. Each of these positions is also defensible, yet they fail to explain the unique position that Edison holds in our imagination — in our imagined environment. Many other inventors who have altered the history of the world are unknown or are known to us only by name. Yet much has been known (or believed) about Edison by millions of people, extending over a period of more than one hundred and twenty years. This is not, I would argue, solely the result of his inventions or his systems of research and business, important as they have been. The greatest of his inventions was "Edison," the persona of the inventor's imagination, which he projected to the world.[580]

"Edison" has been an immensely successful invention. The "Old Man" of Newark became the "Wizard of Menlo Park," and the Wizard became the "Great Inventor" of the Orange Valley. The Great Curmudgeon that we glimpsed in later years was largely hidden from view; the public saw a benign character called "Edison," everyman's favorite grandfather. It was Thomas Alva Edison, more than any other person, who created a New Enlightenment.[581]

Edison imagined the New Enlightenment, he electrified and illuminated it, and he gave it vocal and visual memory. The icon of "Edison" personified and empowered the New Enlightenment, and "Edison" continues to be a powerful, positive image. The environment that Edison created can be felt in each of the places where the inventor lived and worked, and wherever else his inventions are known or used.

Appendix

Site Visits to the "Footprints" of Edison

In 1997 and 1998 I visited the following locations of Edison's homes, laboratories, business offices, manufacturing plants, and other sites of his presence in New Jersey:

Edison National Historic Site: Visits to Glenmont (26 June and 16 October 1997; 15 March 1998); Visits to Laboratory (26 June, 2 July, 9 July, 16 July, 22 July, and 29 July 1997).

Ingersoll Terrace, Union, Union Co.: The site of 10 cement houses built by Edison and Ingersoll. Went inside one; talked with residents of two; photographed several, around a U-shaped courtyard facing Ingersoll Terrace. (6 August 1997).

Newark, Essex County:

6 August 1997: 97 Wright St. (now a vacant lot with a garage attached to 99 Wright St.); 65 Bank St. (NE corner of Bank and Washington, now "Superior Court of N.J"; entrance is now 57 Bank St.); 89 South Orange Ave. (NE corner of South Orange Ave and Boston St.); 854 Broad St. (NE corner of Broad at Lafayette, now "Renaissance Center"); 24 Mechanic St. (now at or near 30-42 Edison Place, a nineteenth century brick factory building of W.V. Egbert, Inc. Plumbing and Heating, for sale by Prime Network Realtors; 10-12 Ward St. (now SE corner of McCarter Highway and Edison Place); and Gateway Hilton, where Edison's apartment was located at NW corner of Market St. and Pennsylvania Railway.

8 August 1997: 788 Broad St. (SE corner of Broad and Market Streets; now the Kinney Building, housing "Cicci" department store); 15 New Jersey Railway Avenue (now E. Raymond Plaza, directly E of Pennsylvania Station, occupied by a small park with memorial to Peter Francisco, "The Hercules of the American Independence"; "White's Building" on the Morris Canal (now the site of New Jersey Transit on N side of Raymond Boulevard, NE of Penn Station; 39 Oliver Street (an unnumbered doorway on an old, abandoned five story brick factory building of "Canrad-Hanovia, Inc." that extends E from Railway Avenue on the S side of Oliver Street); 115 New Jersey Railway Ave. (at NE corner of Green and N.J.R.R. Ave., a building now occupied by "Town Gate Manufacturing Co., which now has its entrance at 119, although the central entrance to the building, now unnumbered and closed, would have been 115); and 103-109 N.J. Railway Ave. (at SE corner of Lafayette at N.J.R.R. Ave., now the parking lot for "Lafayette Auto Parts").

16 February 1998: Fairmount Cemetery, to look for record of Mary Stilwell Edison.

26 and 28 February, and 22 May 1998: Mt. Pleasant Cemetery, to look for Mary Stilwell Edison's grave, other Edison and Stilwell graves, and Ward Mausoleum.

Eagle Rock Reservation, Essex Co.: 10 August and 25 August 1997.

Caldwell, Essex Co., home of "Tory John" Edeson, 71 Elm Road (now the home of Mr. and Mrs. Lester J. Daugherty). 12 September 1997 and 30 January 1998.

South Mountain Reservation and Washington Rock, Essex Co. 16 September 1997.

Sussex County, visiting **Ogdensburg** and **Sparta Mountain** (formerly the town of Ogden/Edison) (19 and 23 September and 6 October 1997), Sterling Hill Mining Museum (19 September), and Franklin Mineral Museum and the former Hungarian Church building [said to have been the schoolhouse at Edison/Ogden] (6 October), and Sparta (6 October 1997).

Morris County: Edison Road (County Road 615), from Route 15 in Jefferson Township to Lake Hopatcong (23 September and 6 October 1997); and along roads that follow the course of the Morristown Line and Boonton Branch of New Jersey Transit from Chatham through Morristown, Denville and Dover, to Lake Hopatcong (25 April 1998).

West Orange, Essex Co.: Examined the southwest corner of the original property of Llewellyn Park at SW corner of Prospect at Mt. Pleasant Ave., now occupied by radio station WFME, the Marvec Building, townhouses, a Japanese restaurant, the Gatehouse Restaurant, Exxon gas station, other business and homes (23 September and 7 November 1997); looked for (but did not find) an Edison cement house, said to be on Whittingham Place, near intersection of Whittingham and Northfield Ave. (26 January and 18 May 1998).

Warren County: To Stewartsville and New Village, observations of the Inclined Plane #9 on the Morris Canal, Stewartsville (now home of Jim Lee), and of the former Edison Cement Plant (now Victaulic, Inc.) on Edison Road, New Village. Also saw and photographed Lake Edison, formerly his stone quarry in New Village, now water-filled (30 September 1997), and roads that were first laid in cement by Edison (Route 57, and Edison Road, in New Village). To Oxford, the site of a quarry (29 January 1998). By automobile from West Orange to Stewartsville, along the route of the railroad, through Hackettstown, including side trips in New Village to look for historic houses and the route of the Morris Canal; and to Oxford Quarry; and then returned via I-80 (25 April 1998).

Orange, Essex Co.: U.S. Radium Corp. Superfund Site (16 October 1997); Search for an Edison "cement house," located at 740 McLaughlin Place (17 January 1998); First Presbyterian Church graveyard, gravestone of Thomas Edison's ancestor, Swaine Ogden (1 February 1998).

Rosedale Cemetery, 367 Washington St., Orange (27 and 28 March, 2 April 1998); search for Edison gravesite(s). Found the Edison mausoleum containing Charles and Carolyn's remains on 27 March. Returned to view the valley down Watchung St. from the mausoleum on 28 March. Returned to look for and find the original gravesite of Thomas and Mina Edison, 50 ft. to the N of the Edison mausoleum, between Lovejoy and Peer gravestones. Mausoleum is in lot 177 and the now-empty original site (owned by the cemetery) is lot 128, which is grass-covered and rimmed by evergreen trees and evergreen bushes. The mausoleum can be seen at the rear of 86 Watchung, and lot 128 is at the rear of the vacant lot between 76-82 Watchung (cannot be seen from Watchung St.).

Upper Montclair, Essex Co.: 303 North Mountain Ave., a cement house with a plaque over the door: "Thomas A. Edison 1912." 4 November 1997.

Edison Township, Middlesex Co.: The former site of Edison's Menlo Park Laboratory (now the Thomas A. Edison Memorial Tower and State Park), and surrounding areas. 16 November 1997, and 18 and 22 January 1998.

Elizabeth, Union, and Roselle, Union Co.: Studies of the history of Elizabeth and Union County, related to the Ogden family. Searching for where Edison lived in Elizabeth in 1870; and studying the area of Roselle where in 1883 he installed electric lights in homes, a grocery store, and in the First Presbyterian Church, powered by a generating plant located at First Ave. and Locust St. Site visits in 1998 to Roselle, N.J. on 10, 12 and 14 January; to Union and Elizabeth, N.J. on 12, 14, 16, 17, 18 and 27 January; and to Rahway, N.J., on 18 January.

Jersey City, Hudson Co.: Search for the environment that existed when Edison and Pope had their plant near the railroad yards in Jersey City in 1869-1870, which Hicks, *Roselle*, says was at 7-9 Exchange Place. From Liberty State Park, viewed buildings on Jersey City waterfront; examined New Jersey Central Railway Terminal; and photographed New York harbor, Ellis Island, Statue of Liberty, and Morris Canal basin with Jersey City to north. Toured Exchange Place and the New Jersey Green Acres Park (J. Owen Grundy Park) on the waterfront; examined and photographed present buildings there, and the old buildings that are still present in nearby streets; and studied Paulus Hook Battle Site park and monument [memorializing 19 August 1779] at Washington St. and Grand St., near Exchange Place. 31 January 1998.

Harrison, Hudson Co.: 27 and 28 February 1998, looking for site of Edison's Lamp Works; located in the area between Essex and Sussex Streets and between Fourth (now Frank E. Rodgers Boulevard) and Fifth Streets, and extending for one-half block east on the north side of Bergen Street from Fifth. Conversations with three librarians (none knew of Lamp Works) and six firemen, including a Deputy Chief, who were a great source of information and legends regarding Edison and the Lamp Works.

Bloomfield, Belleville, and Glen Ridge, Essex Co.:

10 and 11 March 1998: Searched for site of Edison's Silver Lake plant, and other locations of his operations in Bloomfield and Glen Ridge, if any. Visit to Bloomfield Public Library; nothing on Edison or Silver Lake there, although located an illustration of "Silver Lake Plant" in a book of cartoons of Edison's life (ed. by Meadowcroft, 1927). Examined and photographed ruins of Morris Canal at Berkeley Ave. Drove around the area west of the former Silver Lake station on the abandoned Orange Branch of the Erie & Lackawanna R.R., photographing corner of Alva and Edison Streets, Pathmark shopping center on Belmont Ave., and an old factory building standing at 265 Watsessing Ave. The streetlamp poles in the Belleville streets on these streets proclaim this as the "Silver Lake District." On 11 March visited the Museum of The Historical Society of Bloomfield, at 90 Broad St. Spoke with Lucy Sant'Ambroglio (curator) and Dorothy Johnson (volunteer, and Past President of the Historical Society); reviewed documents in their files.

27 and 28 March: To Glen Ridge Public Library on 27 March, where found an account of Edison's ink factory on Midland Ave., where a radium Superfund site is now located; and his battery factory on Bloomfield Ave., where the east bleachers of the Hurrell Park athletic field are now located. Also saw the Essex County Atlases of 1890 and 1906 that clarified the geography and property lines in Silver Lake. To Glen Ridge again on 28 March, to photograph the sites where the ink factory and battery factory had been located. Then to Belleville Public Library to read about Silver Lake and toured the Silver Lake District from Second River to Franklin Ave. to Franklin St. and around Clara Maass Hospital. Then walked along Heckel Street, Brook St., drove on Lake St., and walked across the pentagonal tract along railroad from Belmont Ave. to Grove St., and back; picked up shards of heavy glass (from a carboy?), an old metal toothed gear, and a flat stone that looked like an old flagstone. Talked with Belleville firemen at the former location of the Silver Lake R.R. Station (they never heard of it, but they said that "there's a river under here that keeps trying to come back").

Kearny, Hudson Co.:

21 May 1998: Drove over Clay Street bridge from Newark into East Newark (est. 1895) and then through Harrison into Kearny (founded

1867). To Kearny Public Library and Museum at 318 Kearny Ave., to look for anything I could find about Edison and the E-Mark Battery. I was oriented to the history of Kearny by Leo Koncher, Museum Volunteer; drove around the hilltop at Bergen and Devon Streets, and looked down into the Meadowlands to the east, now covered with houses and trees as far as the eye can see.

22 May 1998: Returned to Kearny for additional reading and photocopying at the Kearny Public Library. Then drove to Schuyler Ave. and N to Belleville Tpk (State Route 7). En route tried unsuccessfully to locate the gravesite of Maj. William Sandford, and Stilwell Place. Visited Arlington Cemetery and saw graves in a circle dating back to Civil War veterans. Saw site of old copper mine at Porete Ave. Drove to junction of Belleville Tpk with Newark-Jersey City Tpk (CR 508) and drove W from there into Harrison (with detours to S under Pulaski Skyway and N on Fish House Rd), and into Newark over Bridge St. bridge.

Notes

Preface – Pages xiii -xviii

[1] The importance of the A.C. Gilbert Co. in the development of young investigators was emphasized in a symposium published by New Haven University, "A. C. Gilbert, Scientific Toymaker: A Symposium," *Essays in Arts and Sciences* 25 (October 1996). This conclusion was affirmed to me by Edison's great-grandson, Dr. David Edison Sloane, who is a member of the faculty at New Haven University, during his visit to Newark, June 25-27, 1997, as a participant in the "Interpreting Edison" Conference at Rutgers-Newark. Additional details appear in Shelley Pannill, "Thomas Edison's Great-Grandson Plugs Into His Past," *Newark [N.J.] Star-Ledger* (27 June 1997). This article was based on an interview with Dr. Sloane, who is a grandson of Edison's daughter, Madeline (Edison) Sloane.

A similar recollection was described by John Kean, in recalling events in his childhood at Liberty Hall, in Union, New Jersey. Built in 1772, this house was the home of Kean's ancestor, William Livingston, who was New Jersey's first governor. "As a vibrant 10-year old, . . . young John Kean's 'successful' science experiment . . . caught fire and burned down the curtains in the children's wing." Fortunately for Kean and for posterity, the house survived in "pristine condition" (Sandy Lovell, "Historic Day in Life of Keans' Liberty Hall," *Star-Ledger* [10 July 1997]). For additional information about A. C. Gilbert and his legacy, see the websites for A. C. Gilbert's Discovery Village (<acgilbert.org>) and the A. C. Gilbert Heritage Society (<acghs.org>).

[2] The Edison family's problems during the Revolutionary War were discussed by Neil Baldwin in *Edison: Inventing the Century*, 1st paperback ed. (New York: Hyperion, 1995). Thomas Edison's relationship to the history of Essex County was briefly described in John T. Cunningham and Charles F. Cummings, *Remembering Essex: A Pictorial History of Essex County, New Jersey* (Virginia Beach, Va.: Donning Company, 1995). Specific references in Cunningham and Cummings' monograph will appear in the text of this book. I recently learned that Thomas Edison and I may be distant cousins. We are both descended from men named John Ogden (his was John Ogden of New Jersey, and mine was John Ogden of Connecticut). In contemporary documents, these two men were called "cousins," although their common grandfather in England has not been identified.

[3] Matthew Josephson, *Edison: A Biography* (New York: McGraw-Hill, 1959; reprint, with a foreword by Reese V. Jenkins, New York: John Wiley and Sons, 1992). Thomas Edison's home and laboratory are illustrated in two brochures of the National Park Service: "Glenmont" and "Edison" (West Orange, N.J.: Edison National Historic Site, [1997]). The Thomas A. Edison National Historic Site is now known as the Thomas Edison National Historical Park.

[4] Program for "Interpreting Edison" Conference held at the Robeson Campus Center, Rutgers-Newark, and Edison National Historic Site, 25-27 June 1997. ("Thomas A. Edison Sesquicentennial Conference" [Rutgers University-Newark, and U.S. Department of the Interior-National Park Service: Design Consortium, 1997]). Also, during the preparation of this book, *Life* magazine announced that it had selected Edison as "The Man of the Millennium."

Ambiguous views of Edison have been expressed by residents of the Orange Valley. For example, see Debra Galant, "Edison, the Father of Invention," *The New York Times* (1 June 1997), sec. 13, 1, 12: In the section entitled "Nationally Revered but Locally Ignored," Galant quotes John Cunningham, who approached "Gov. Brendan Byrne — who came from West Orange — to raise money for the Edison site in 1979, 'he told me point blank the state would have no interest in it. He said, 'You know, He didn't treat his people very well." In "Unloved as a Boss and a Neighbor," Galant writes: "Although Edison is venerated today, there are hints that he was not universally loved in his life. He lived in a grand home called Glenmont in West Orange in the affluent Llewellyn Park section. His neighbors may have resented the pollution, noise and riff-raff from the 10,000-worker factory nearby. Edison . . . undoubtedly demanded much of his employees [and was] . . . on the lookout for shirking." The changes to Llewellyn Park that occurred during Edison's lifetime and thereafter will be discussed later in this book.

Another skeptical view was presented by Carl Chase, "Developer Hopes to 'Light Up' West Orange: Museum Planned at Edison Factory Site," *Newark [N.J] Sunday Star-Ledger* (29 June 1997): Referring to the proposal for a $28 million conversion of the Edison Storage Battery Factory into a tourist attraction and mall, the operator of a neighboring business on Standish Avenue, Larry DiSabato, complained that, "'My brother and I were born and raised in this town.' . . . Exide Battery Co., founded by Edison, left a blighted area when it moved out in the 1960s. . . .The whole area was something Edison (Exide) had walked away from. We came in and built this up, but all of a sudden someone comes along with plans, and you gotta go?'"

In the spring of 1997 I spoke with Jim Hauk, who grew up in "the second oldest house in Bloomfield, built in 1734." Jim's father, who was 92 in 1997 (i.e., born about 1905), worked for Edison as a young man. Jim believed that his father had worked at Edison's factory at Silver Lake in Bloomfield. Jim says that his father is proud to have worked for Edison, but says, cryptically, that "It was hard." I hoped to interview his father, who apparently knew Edison, or at least saw the inventor from a distance, but he died before I could speak with him. "Silver Lake" is now a paved-over shopping center, partly in Bloomfield, and partly in Belleville. The Silver Lake train station can be seen on maps of the 1980s near the corner of Franklin Street and Belmont Avenue in Belleville. The Edison operation at Silver Lake will be discussed later.

[5] Jill Jonnes, *Empires of Light: Edison, Tesla, Westinghouse and the Race to Electrify the World* (New York: Random House, 2003); Mark Essig, *Edison and the Electric Chair: A Story of Light and Death* (New York: Walker Publishing Co., 2003); Thom Metzger, *Blood & Volts: Edison, Tesla and the Invention of the Electric Chair* (Autonomedia, 1996), and Michael Daly, *Topsy: The Startling Story of the Crooked Tail Elephant, P.T. Barnum, and the American Wizard, Thomas Edison* (New York: Grove/Atlantic, Inc., 2013).

Introduction – Pages xix-xxii

[6] David Lawrence Pierson, *History of the Oranges to 1921: Reviewing the Rise, Development and Progress of an Influential Community*, 4 vols. (New York: Lewis Historical Publishing Company, 1922), 4: 581, 584. Was it Cook's Pond, or Crook's Pond, or Crooke's Pond? Pierson twice calls it "Cook's" in *History of the Oranges*, whereas the National Park Service spells it with a "r," as "Crook's." (See David L. Uschold and George W. Curry, Cultural Landscape Report for Laboratory Unit, Edison National Historic Site: Site History, Existing Conditions, and Analysis [Boston: Olmsted Center for Landscape Preservation and National Park Service, 1997], 11, 22). A third spelling ("Crooke's Pond) appears in André Millard, *Edison and the Business of Invention* (Baltimore: Johns Hopkins University Press, 1990; Softshell Books ed., paperback, 1993), 20, Fig. 1.5.

[7] Of Edison's status in the 1920s, a current resident of West Orange recently said that "Edison was like a 500 pound gorilla. He sits wherever he wants to."

[8] Wyn Wachhorst, *Thomas Alva Edison: An American Myth* (Cambridge: MIT Press, 1981).

[9] Wachhorst, Ibid. (Gallup poll). Will Joyner, "Lessons on Life, From a Genius and a Schoolgirl," *New York Times* (8 July 1997), sec. C, p.14.

[10] Edison Papers Project (accessed 1 July 1997): "Chronology of Thomas Edison's Life, 1847-1878" (19 pp.); "Chronology of Thomas Edison's Life 1879-1931" (12 pp.). <http://www.rutgers.edison.edu>.

Part I: Edison's Environment, 1869-1931
Chapter 1: Thomas Alva Edison's Family and Footprints
Pages 1-12

[11] Matthew Josephson, foreword by Reese V. Jenkins, *Edison: A Biography* (New York: John Wiley and Sons, 1992); Robert Conot, *Thomas A. Edison: A Streak of Luck* (New York: Seaview, 1979; reprint, paperback, New York: DaCapo/Plenum, 1986); Martin V. Melosi, *Thomas A. Edison and the Modernization of America* (New York: Harper Collins, 1990); André Millard, *Edison and the Business of Invention* (Baltimore: Johns Hopkins University Press, 1990; Softshell Books ed., paperback, 1993); Neil Baldwin, *Edison: Inventing the Century*, 1st paper- back ed. (New York: Hyperion, 1995); Robert

Friedel and Paul Israel, with Bernard S. Finn, *Edison's Electric Light: Biography of an Invention* (New Brunswick, N.J.: Rutgers University Press, 1987); Charles Musser, *Thomas A. Edison and His Kinetographic Motion Pictures* (New Brunswick, N.J.: Rutgers University Press, 1995); and William S. Pretzer, ed., *Working at Invention: Thomas A. Edison and the Menlo Park Experience* (Dearborn, Mich.: Henry Ford Museum and Greenfield Village, 1993). George D. Tselos, "'Start Up at the Top and Work Down': Thomas A. Edison and the Fluoroscope," presented at "Interpreting Edison" conference, Newark, N.J., 25 June 1997. MS at library of archives, ENHS. Also, see Tselos, "New Jersey's Thomas Edison and the Fluoroscope," *New Jersey Medicine* 92 (November 1995): 731-733. Byron M. Vanderbilt, *Thomas Edison, Chemist* (Washington, D.C.: American Chemical Society, 1971; paperback ed., 1980); Wyn Wachhorst, *Thomas Alva Edison: An American Myth* (Cambridge: MIT Press, 1981); and Raymond Wile, *Edison Disc Artists and Records, 1910-1929*, ed. Ronald Dethlefson, 2nd ed. (Brooklyn, N.Y.: APM Press, 1990); Paul Israel, *Edison: A Life of Invention* (New York: John Wiley & Sons, 1998).

[12] Francis Jehl, *Menlo Park Reminiscences*, 3 vols. (Dearborn, Mich.: Edison Institute, 1937; reprint of vol. 1, with an introduction by William S. Pretzer, New York: Dover, 1990); Charles E. Frohman, *Milan and the Milan Canal: The Canal, Shipyards, Grain Port, Edison's Birthplace, The Moravians* (Sandusky, Ohio: Charles E. Frohman, 1976); Richard B. Stamps, Bruce Hawkins, and Nancy E. Wright, *Search for the House in the Grove: Archeological Excavation of the Boyhood Homesite of Thomas A. Edison in Port Huron, Michigan, 1976-1994* (Rochester, Mich.: Cultural Dynamics, 1994); John D. Venable, *Mina Miller Edison: Daughter, Wife and Mother of Inventors* (East Orange, N.J.: Charles Edison Fund, 1981; reprint, 1994); Venable, *Out of the Shadow: The Story of Charles Edison* (East Orange, N.J.: Charles Edison Fund, 1978); Norman Brauer, *There to Breathe the Beauty: The Camping Trips of Henry Ford, Thomas Edison, Harvey Firestone, John Burroughs* (Dalton, Pa.: Norman Brauer, 1995); and Virginia McAlester and Lee McAlester, with photographs by Alex McLean, *Great American Homes and Their Architectural Styles* (New York: Abbeville, 1994). For a view of Glenmont before it was modified by the Edisons, see *American Victorian Architecture: A Survey of the 70's and 80's in Contemporary Photographs* (1886; reprint, with an introduction by Arnold Lewis and notes on the plates by Keith Morgan, New York: Dover, 1975); and "Interpreting Edison" conference program, Rutgers-Newark, and Edison National Historic Site, West Orange, N.J., 25-27 June 1997.

Reese V. Jenkins, Leonard S. Reich, Paul B. Israel, Toby Appel, Andrew J. Butrica, Robert A. Rosenberg, Keith A. Nier, Melodie Andrews, and Thomas E. Jeffrey, eds., *The Papers of Thomas A. Edison*, 3 vols. (Baltimore, Md.: The Johns Hopkins University Press, 1989-1994); Ibid., *The Making of an Inventor: February 1847-June 1873*, vol. 1 (1989); Rosenberg, Israel, Nier, Andrews, eds., *From Workshop to Laboratory: June 1873-March 1876*, vol. 2 (1991);

Rosenberg, Israel, Nier, and Martha J. King, eds., *Menlo Park: The Early Years, April 1876-December 1877*, vol. 3 (1994). Thomas E. Jeffrey, ed., *A Guide to Thomas A. Edison Papers: A Selective Microfilm Edition*, 3 parts (Bethesda, Md.: University Publications of America, 1981), part 3, 1887-1898.
Edison Papers homepage: www.http://edison. rutgers.edu/&etc.

[13] Stephen Wickes, M.D., *History of the Oranges in Essex County, N.J., From 1666 to 1806* (Newark, N.J.: Ward and Techenor, 1892). David Lawrence Pierson, *History of the Oranges to 1921: Reviewing the Rise, Development and Progress of an Influential Community*, 4 vols. (New York: Lewis Historical Publishing Company, 1922). John T. Cunningham and Charles F. Cummings, *Remembering Essex: A Pictorial History of Essex County, New Jersey* (Virginia Beach, Va.: Donning Company, 1995).

Francis Dodd McHugh and Theodore McCrosky, *Master Plan of West Orange* (New York: McHugh and McCrosky, 1953); David L. Uschold and George W. Curry, *Cultural Landscape Report for Laboratory Unit, Edison National Historic Site: Site History, Existing Conditions, and Analysis* (Boston: Olmsted Center for Landscape Preservation and National Park Service, 1997); Michael H. Agar, Christopher L. Borstel, Antony B. Mason, Ingrid A. Wuebber, *Ethnographic Overview and Assessment, Edison National Historic Site, West Orange, New Jersey* (East Orange, N.J.: Louis Berger and Associates, New England Support System Office, U.S. National Park Service, and Edison National Historic Site, 1997) [a 126 page report with 1 cm. of unpaginated Appendices, in the library of the Archives, ENHS]; and Keith Spalding Robbins, "A History of the Development of the First Planned American Suburban Community: Llewellyn Park, West Orange" (master's thesis, Georgetown University, 1989) [copy in WOPL].

"New Jersey Roadmap" (New York: H. M. Gousha, 1993); "Essex County, New Jersey" (Maspeth, N.Y.: Hagstrom, 1991); "DeLorme Street Atlas USA," CD-Rom Version 3.0 for Windows (Freeport, Maine: DeLorme, 1995); "Orange, N.J." quadrangle map (Washington, D.C.: U.S. Geological Survey, 1955); and "Caldwell, N.J." quadrangle map (Ibid., 1954, photorevised 1970).

[14] Francis Jehl, *Menlo Park Reminiscences*, 3 vols. (Dearborn, Mich.: Edison Institute, 1937; reprint of vol. 1, with an introduction by William S. Pretzer, New York: Dover, 1990).

[15] Matthew Josephson, *Edison: A Biography*; Martin V. Melosi, *Thomas A. Edison and the Modernization of America*; André Millard, *Edison and the Business of Invention*; and Neil Baldwin, *Edison: Inventing the Century*. The chronology follows that of the Edison Papers Project, which is revised from time to time and is presented on the Edison Papers homepage: <http://edison.rutgers.edu/&etc.> The chronology for this summary was downloaded on 1 July 1997 and is referred to hereafter as EPP www pages.

[16] Baldwin, *Edison*, 17.

[17] "happiest time" from Melosi, *Edison*, 11 [n.d., reference not provided].

[18] Edison, introduction to *The Life and Works of Thomas Paine*, by William M. Van der Weyde, vol. 1 (New Rochelle, NY: Thomas Paine National Historical Association, 1925), vii-ix.

[19] "Chronology of Thomas Edison's Life" from Edison Papers Project (EPP): Part one: (<http://edison.rutgers.edu/chronol1.htm>) covers the period 1847-1878, while the second part (<http://edison.rutgers.edu/chronol2.htm>) covers the remaining years of his life, 1879-1931. The EPP is most complete regarding Edison's life between about 1865 and 1886.

[20] Baldwin, *Edison*, 49 (reference not given), and Josephson, *Edison*, 63, 488n (referring to [Boston] *Journal of the Telegraph* (14 June 1868 and 12 December 1868).

[21] "manufacturer" from Edison, letter to his parents, winter 1871, quoted by Josephson, Edison (85), from archives of Henry Ford Museum (489n).

[22] "minor invention" from Millard, *Edison*, 3, referring (without a specific citation) to Friedel and Israel, *Edison's Electric Light* ("invention factory"); also, Josephson, *Edison*, 131. Josephson, *Edison*, 133-134, quoting Edison to Dr. George Beard ("a minor invention..."); "first successful" from EPP www pages for 1879-1931, p.2; "I have accomplished" from Josephson, Edison, 267, 494n (from *New York Sun*, 4 Sep 1882).

[23] Edison, *Laboratory Notebooks, 1886* (ENHS), in Josephson, *Edison,* 495n.

[24] *Edison Papers Chronology, 1879-1931.*

[25] Thomas A. Edison, Inc. is often referred to in as TAE, Inc., in biographies of Edison. The movie camera and film projector of today have evolved from devices that appear in the chronology of the EPP with now-archaic names such as "kinetoscope" (the projector) (1891), which originally utilized direct viewing through a peephole; the "kinetograph" (the camera) (1894); and the "vitascope" (1896).

[26] "Tate, see that valley?" from conversation regarding the Bloomfield-Silver Lake area, quoted by Conot (*Edison*, 250, 526n) from Alfred O. Tate, *Edison's Open Door* (New York, 1938), 140.

Chapter 2: History of the Environment in the Orange Valley to 1886
Pages 13-28

[27] "spring, less constant" from Stephen Wickes, M.D., *History of the Oranges in Essex County, N.J., From 1666 to 1806* (Newark: Ward & Techenor, 1892), 13.

[28] The Orange Valley of Essex County is the area to the east of First Mountain (also known as Orange Mountain or First Watchung Mountain). The Orange Valley lies between First Mountain, on the west, and Newark Bay, on the east. (See Josephson, *Edison*, 250; Baldwin, *Edison*, 183; and Vanderbilt, *Edison, Chemist*, 113) The towns of East Orange, Orange, and South Orange are entirely

within the Orange Valley, and the eastern portion of West Orange, in which Edison lived and his Laboratory was located, is also in the Orange Valley. The Orange Valley is now usually called, simply, "the valley," by local residents.

[29] Cunningham and Cummings, *Remembering Essex*, 10-11 (showing a sketch of Eagle Rock by Harry Fenn and copies of nineteenth century paintings of the Orange Mountains by Carl August Sommer and Martin J. Heade).

[30] On September 9, 1997, Mr. William Bolan, who grew up in the Oranges, said that the rock outcropping with the flagpole, adjacent to Highlawn Pavilion, is indeed the place that has long been known as Eagle Rock. It is said to be 627 feet above sea level" (personal communication). Also, see: Rebecca Goldsmith, "Status Seekers Claim the High Ground," *Newark (N.J.) Star-Ledger* (23 August 1998), 45.

[31] Henry Herpers and Henry C. Barksdale, *Preliminary Report on the Geology and Ground-Water Supply of the Newark, New Jersey, Area* (New Jersey Department of Conservation and Economic Development, Division of Water Policy and Supply, 1951); William D. Nichols, *Ground-Water Resources of Essex County, New Jersey* (U.S. Geological Survey, 1968); William B. Gallagher, *When Dinosaurs Roamed New Jersey* (New Brunswick: Rutgers University Press, 1997); Tom Johnson, "The Watchungs: Jersey's Jurassic Backbone," *Newark (N.J.) Star Ledger* (31 August 1997), sec. 1, pp. 1, 8-9; Avery Ala Drake, Jr., et al., *Bedrock Geologic Map of Northern New Jersey* (U.S. Geological Survey, 1996); *Encyclopaedia Britannica, Macropaedia*, 15th ed., "Geochronology: The Interpretation and Dating of the Geological Record"; and telephone conversations with Bill Graff (1 August and 8 September 1997) and Richard A. Volkert (9 September 1997) of the New Jersey Geological Survey.

[32] Cunningham and Cummings, *Remembering Essex*; Wickes, *History of the Oranges*; David Lawrence Pierson, *History of the Oranges to 1921: Reviewing the Rise, Development and Progress of an Influential Community*, 4 vols. (New York: Lewis Historical Publishing Company, 1922); Rick Gore, "The Most Ancient Americans," *National Geographic* 192, no. 4 (October 1997): 92-99; *Britannica, Micropaedia*, 15th ed., "Delaware" [Lenni Lenape] and "Newark". The following maps were used in describing the Watchung Mountains and the Orange Valley: Map of Essex County (Maspeth, N.Y.: Hagstrom, 1991); New Jersey Road Map (New York: Simon & Schuster/H.M. Gousha, 1993); and the U.S. Geological Survey quadrangle maps of Orange, N.J. (1955), Caldwell, N.J. (1954), Roselle, N.J. (1955), and Elizabeth, N.J-N.Y. (1967).

[33] The truth of the matter, as can be seen on the maps, is much more complex. As we saw earlier, First Mountain runs in a course that is oblique on the map, as is the course of the Hudson River, and the orientation of Manhattan; they all run from north-northeast ($25°$) to south-southwest ($205°$). Newark is thus actually southeast, not east, of Eagle Rock. To be precise about it, 125th Street in New York City is directly east of Eagle Rock.

[34] If we turn slightly to the right at this point, we could have seen — before the terrorist attacks on September 11, 2001 — the Twin Towers of the World Trade Center. This is the line of sight that identifies, in the middle distance, the location of the northern part of Newark. By turning a bit more to the right, the center of Newark, where Edison lived and worked in the 1870s, is seen, four miles away, just beyond the treetops. Just east of Newark, across the Passaic River in Hudson County, New Jersey, are the towns of Harrison, where Edison's lamp works factory was located, and Kearny, where he had a battery factory.

We can thus begin to visualize another unusual aspect of this valley. It is drained by three rivers, which do not join each other. This is a contrast to the usual notion of "a valley," such as the great central valley of the United States, which is drained by the Mississippi River and its tributaries, the Missouri River and the Ohio River. Although all the water of the eastern valley of Essex County eventually flows into the Atlantic Ocean, the rivers that drain the eastern valley do not represent a single river system. The Passaic River drains into the Atlantic via Newark Bay, while the Elizabeth and Rahway Rivers each drain separately into the Arthur Kill, between New Jersey and Staten Island, and thence into the ocean. The Elizabeth River is formed in the southeastern part of the valley, in the area between Maplewood and Irvington. The Elizabeth then passes under the Garden State Parkway and flows into the Arthur Kill in Elizabeth, New Jersey, near the Newark Airport and Exit 13 on the New Jersey Turnpike. The Elizabeth River will be seen again in this book, as part of the historical environment of the Edison family. The Rahway River valley also reappears in Edison's environment, and we will later examine it more closely. The western ends of Main Street and of Park Avenue from Newark to West Orange are near the base of First Mountain, a few hundred yards from the Edison water tower. However, the watershed or divide between the Passaic and Rahway Rivers does not end at this point; instead, the watershed continues across First Mountain, following the route of Mt. Pleasant Avenue.

Neil Baldwin says that Thomas Edison's great-grandfather, John ("Tory John") Edeson and his wife, Sarah (Ogden), owned two tracts of land in Caldwell (*Edison*, 4, 193). The Edeson house is still standing in Caldwell (its present address is 71 Elm Road). The house faces south, and the eight-inch wide pine floorboards that testify to its antiquity are visible in a room at the rear on the first floor. A 1774 map showing the Edison/Edeson property appears in Lynn G. Lockward, *A Puritan Heritage: The First Presbyterian Church in Horse-Neck* (Caldwell, N.J., 1955), 65, Fig. 48D. A photograph of the Edison house appears in Sister Loretta Claire, O.P., and Norman J. Brydon, *Caldwell, Yesterday and Today: 1776-1976* (Caldwell, N.J.: Caldwell Bicentennial Committee, 1976), 44-A. As of September 1997, the house had been owned and occupied for 45 years by Mr. and Mrs. Lester J. Daugherty.

[35] A sign on South Orange Avenue states that South Mountain Reservation includes 2,048 acres. A square mile is 640 acres, so three square miles totals 1,920 acres.

[36] The site called "Washington Rock" is marked by a large granite boulder, about three and one-half feet high, three feet wide, and three feet deep. The north side of the boulder has a flat sculpted surface, receding at about a 30-degree angle, and two bronze plaques are affixed to it. Their inscriptions read as follows:

TRADITION PLACES GEORGE WASHINGTON HERE, IN THE SUMMER OF 1780, OBSERVING AMERICAN TROOPS THWART BRITISH EFFORTS TO REACH MORRISTOWN AND DESTROY HIS BASE OF SUPPLIES...

* * * * *

WASHINGTON ROCK HISTORIC SITE REDEDICATED JUNE 1992 "LEST WE FORGET" / 1st MOUNTAIN CHAPTER N.J. SOCIETY SONS OF THE AMERICAN REVOLUTION

The site of the battle of 23 June 1780 at the bridge on Vauxhall Road at its intersection with Millburn Ave., on the border of Union and Essex Counties, is marked by a plaque which reads:

AT THIS SITE DURING THE BATTLE OF SPRINGFIELD ON JUNE 23, 1780, THE AMERICANS, CONSISTING OF CONTINENTAL DRAGOONS AND THE MILITIA OF THIS AND SURROUNDING NEIGHBORHOODS, UNDER COLONEL "LIGHTHORSE HARRY" LEE, COLONEL MATTHIAS OGDEN...

[37] Other water also flows into the Rahway from the north. For example, the West Branch of the Rahway drains the southern portion of the valley between First Mountain and Second Mountain; the East Branch and the West Branch merge south of Millburn, in Union County.

Chapter 3: In the Valley – Pages 29-42

[38] "At the union," from Wickes, *History of the Oranges*, 21.

[39] St. Mark's Church is perched on the low hill that dominates the intersection of Main Street, Valley Road, and Northfield Avenue, thrusting its spire high above the roads and sidewalks.

[40] Wickes, Ibid., 46. Newark was originally known as "Town on Passaic River" (Cunningham and Cummings, *Remembering Essex*, 20-21), or "Pesayak Towne" and later as New Milford (Britannica, *Micropaedia*, 15th ed., "Newark, N.J."). The U.S. Geological Survey benchmark of 182 feet at the entrance to Llewellyn Park, two blocks north of St. Mark's Church, is almost exactly 400 feet lower than Eagle Rock (Orange, N.J., quadrangle map).

[41] Herpers and Barksdale, *Ground-Water of Newark*, 17 ("relatively simple"); Britannica, *Macropaedia*, 15th ed., vol. 19, 877.

[42] Herpers and Barksdale, Ibid. Also, Britannica, *Macropaedia*, 15th ed., vol. 19, 877-879.

[43] The Tertiary Period was followed by the Quaternary Period, which is the last (and current) period in geological history. See Gallagher, *Dinosaurs*, 5; and *Britannica*, 780, 888; and *National Geographic* (192 [4] Oct 1997: 95).

[44] Nichols, *Ground Water of Essex County*, Figs. 2 and 3 (maps), 4-6, 20, and 29. Also, Drake, *Bedrock Geological Map of Northern New Jersey*; and "Revised Work Plan for Remedial Investigation and Feasibility Study, U.S. Radium

Corporation Site, City of Orange, Essex County, New Jersey" (Paramus, N.J.: Malcolm Pirnie, Inc., for U.S. Dept. of Environmental Protection, 1990), 24.

[45] Herpers and Barksdale, *Ground-Water of Newark*, 17. *National Geographic* 192, no. 4 (October 1997): 95.

[46] Cunningham and Cummings, *Remembering Essex*, 15. Britannica, *Micropaedia*, 15th ed., vol. 3, 970. Wickes, *History of the Oranges*, 1-2.

[47] Cunningham and Cummings, *Remembering Essex*, 16-17.

[48] Britannica, *Micropaedia*, 15th ed., 3:970; and *Newark (N.J.) Star-Ledger*, 31 August 31, sec. 1, p. 8.

[49] Wickes, *History of the Oranges*, 16. Pierson, *History of the Oranges to 1921*, vol. 2, 414.

[50] Quotations from Wickes, Ibid., 49. Pierson, Ibid., 581.

[51] Wickes, Ibid., 13, 15, 49.

[52] Wickes, Ibid., 58-65. Pierson, Ibid., 425. John R. Stilgoe, *Borderland: Origins of the American Suburb, 1820-1939* (New Haven: Yale University Press, 1988), 47: "Map of Thirty Miles Around New York City," from James Monteith, *Youth Manual of Geography*, 1854.

[53] Wickes, Ibid., 16. Pierson, Ibid., 419. "Parrow" is now pronounced "pear-oh," as in "Ross Perot."

[54] Pierson, Ibid., 422-423.

[55] Pierson, *History of the Oranges*, vol. 4, 579-586.

[56] Cunningham and Cummings, *Remembering Essex*, 18-19. The story of Williamstown is told on a plaque erected by the Charles Edison Foundation at Tory Corner, about one-half mile north of the Edison Laboratory at Lakeside Avenue.

[57] Pierson, *History of the Oranges*, vol. 3, 452. Statements regarding the size of Orange (2.2 square miles), West Orange (12.1 square miles), and Newark (24.14 square miles) from Engineering Departments of these three cities, by telephone, on 15-16 September 1997. The conventional date for the establishment of Llewellyn Park is 1857. However, the American Society of Landscape Architects gives the date as 1853 (Arnold R. Alanen, "New Towns and Planned Communities," in *American Landscape Architecture: Designers and Places*, ed. William H. Tishler [Washington, D.C.: Preservation Press, 1989], 176). Also, see Keith Spalding Robbins, "A History of the Development of the First Planned American Suburban Community: Llewellyn Park, West Orange" (master's thesis, George Washington University, 1989), 1, 21, 23; Leah Brodbeck Burt, *Historic Furnishings Report* (Glenmont: Edison National Historic Site, n.d.), 13; Stilgoe, *Borderlands*, 53; Michael H. Agar et al., *Ethnographic Overview and Assessment, Edison National Historic Site, West Orange, New Jersey* (East Orange, N.J.: Louis Berger and Associates; and Boston: New England System

Support Office, National Park Service, 1997), 16; Francis Dodd McHugh and Theodore McCrosky, *Master Plan of West Orange* (New York: McHugh and McCrosky, 1953), 32, and Table P-VI, preceding p.16.

[58] Pierson, *History of the Oranges*, vol. 1, 397-413, 474; and vol. 4, 579-86.

[59] Conversations with residents of the Orange Valley (Sept. and Nov. 1997): Charles Crandall, M.D., Mrs. Diane Ventuno, Mrs. Alice Meyers, and Mr. Thomas Duffy. Also, see William Hemmingway, "Coasting All Year Round" *Harper's* (10 April 1894), a portion of which is reprinted and illustrated at the website for "Gravity Railroad — The Oranges, NJ."

[60] Pierson, *History of the Oranges*, 463 (strikes); 425 (trolleys).

[61] Stilgoe, *Borderland*, 52-55. Also, see Robbins, "Llewellyn Park," x (Fig. 1-2 ["Llewellyn Park: Prospectus Map of Llewellyn Park 1858"]).

[62] Stilgoe does not say whether Matthias Ogden Halsted was a member of the Ogden family of New Jersey, and thus a relative of Thomas Edison. However, it would be a good guess to say that he was. Also, see Agar, *Ethnographic Overview*, 16; and *Concise Dictionary of American Biography* (New York: Charles Scribner's Sons, 1964), 748-749 (Olmsted).

[63] Robbins, "Llewellyn Park," Fig. 3-1 ("Northwest Part of Llewellyn Park or 'The Ramble,'" Drawn by Eugene Baumann, 1859), 57; and Figure 1-2, page x; also, Wickes, Ibid.,

[64] Wigwam Brook had more than one source. See Wickes, Ibid., 14-15.

[65] Stilgoe, *Borderland*, 55 ("long-haired men" and "privacy").

[66] McAlester and McAlester, *Great American Homes*, 152-65.

Part II – Edison's Environment, 1869-1931 – Pages 42-46

[67] Thomas A. Edison, *The Diary and Sundry Observations of Thomas Alva Edison*, ed. Dagobert D. Runes (New York: Philosophical Library, 1948), 19; and Edison, *The Diary of Thomas A. Edison* (Old Greenwich, Conn.: Chatham Press, n.d. [1971]), 46.

[68] "The Great Inventor" appears in M. A. Rosanoff's memoir, "Edison in His Laboratory," *Harper's* 39 (1932): 402-417 (409), copy in Jack Stanley Papers.

[69] The Edison Papers Project states that on 12 September 1869 Edison moved to Elizabeth, N.J., to board with James Pope's mother (*Edison Chronology, 1847-1878*, p.3 of 19).

Chapter 4: The Early Days: Elizabeth, Jersey City, and Newark (1869-1875) – Pages 47-74

[70] Aquilina, Koles, and Turner, *Elizabethtown*, 69.

[71] Edison Papers Project, www Edison Chronology, 1847-1878 (<http://edison.rutgers.edu/ chron1.htm> [7/1/97]), page 4 of 19; and Edison Papers, v.1, 148 (map).

[72] Site visits to Elizabeth, N.J., 10 and 14 January 1998.

[73] Site visits to Elizabeth, N.J., 14, 16, and 17 January 1998. Also: conversations with William Frolich, President of Roselle, N.J., Historical Society, 14 January; with his sister, Mrs. Betty (Frolich) Edwards, who resides at 573 Morris Ave., which was formerly numbered as 567, four house lots west of 559 Morris Ave., 16 January; and with Charles Shallcross, Past President, Union County Historical Society, 21 January. Consultations in January 1998 with Charles Boll, Elizabethtown Room, Elizabeth Public Library, and Katherine Craig, Boxwood Hall State Historic Site.

And the following maps of Elizabeth, N.J. at Elizabeth Public Library: Ernst L. Meyer, *Map of Elizabethtown, N.J., at the Time of the Revolutionary War, 1775-1783* (New York: J. Schekler, 1879); Jacob L. Bauer (compiler), *Map of the City of Elizabeth, New Jersey* (n.p., 1902); *Insurance Maps of Elizabeth, New Jersey*, 2 vols. (New York: Sanborn Map Co., 1922). Also: *Union /Hudson/Essex Counties Atlas* (Maspeth, N.Y.: Hagstrom, 1987); and *Elizabeth, N.J.-N.Y.* quadrangle map (U.S. Geological Survey, 1967).

[74] *Elizabeth Directory for 1870*, 166-7.

[75] *Elizabeth Directory for 1870*, 23.

[76] *Maps of Elizabeth* (1922), vol. 1, map 3 (245 Morris Ave.), and vol. 2, map 217 (559 Morris Ave.); *Map of Elizabeth* (1902), plate 2 (245 and 559 Morris Ave., and west end of Cherry St.).

[77] Personal communication, Charles Shallcross, Elizabeth, N.J., 21 January 1998.

[78] *DeLorme Street Atlas USA*. CD-Rom Version 3.0 for Windows (Freeport, Me.: DeLorme, 1995).

[79] Personal communication, Joseph Knapp, Union Co., N.J., 2 February 1998.

[80] The western limits of Elizabeth were west of this point in 1780, but by 1870 the city limits were east of what is now called North Avenue. The city line between Elizabeth and Union was, in 1870, close to the western end of Cherry Street and the house that is now numbered 559 Morris Avenue. The city limits were pushed back to North Avenue in the twentieth century.

[81] Ian Donnachie and George Hewitt, *Historic New Lanark: The Dale and Owen Industrial Community Since 1785* (Edinburgh: Edinburgh University Press, 1993); and Anthony F. C. Wallace, *Rockdale: The Growth of an American Village in the Early Industrial Revolution* (New York: W. W. Norton, [1972] 1980).

[82] The first railroad to reach Elizabeth was the New Jersey Railroad, chartered in 1832, according to Thayer, *Old Elizabethtown*, 248-249.

[83] Aquilina, Koles, and Turner, *Elizabethtown*, 61 (photograph of 233 Broad Street in 1869). In 1869, 233 Broad Street -- the First National Bank Building -- was at the corner of a major intersection, and railroad tracks were nowhere in the vicinity; the bank building was destroyed by fire in 1890. In 1998, 233 Broad

Street is immediately adjacent to the railroad tracks, across Broad Street from New Jersey Transit's Elizabeth Station.

[84] Aquilina, Koles, and Turner, *Elizabethtown*, 70 (Singer's factory); 68 (92 Broad Street).

[85] Aquilina, Koles, and Turner, *Elizabethtown*, 9 (history); personal communication from City Engineer, January 1998 (11.7 square miles). Newark's area at present is about 24 square miles in size.

[86] Aquilina, Koles, and Turner, *Elizabethtown*, 74 (1891).

[87] The outline of the house at 559 Morris Avenue appears on the 1902 map of Elizabeth, and a small but detailed floor plan of the first floor of this house appears on the 1922 map. The barn is shown at the rear of the property on the 1922 map.

[88] No newspaper articles associating Edison with 559 Morris Ave. could be located by the Elizabeth Public Library or the Union County Historical Society.

[89] J. Maurice Hicks, *Roselle, New Jersey: Site of Thomas Alva Edison's First Village Plant* (Roselle: Roselle Historical Society, 1979), 9.

[90] "Liberty State Park" (New Jersey Department of Environmental Protection, 1996); "The Historic Trilogy: The Statue of Liberty, Ellis Island, The CRRNJ Terminal" (N.J.D.E.P., n.d. [1997]); "Interpretive Programs . . . Offered at Liberty State Park" (Ibid.); and "Liberty State Park Conservancy" vol. 1 (no. 2, Fall 1997).

For information regarding the Morris Canal, see: James Lee, *The Morris Canal: A Photographic History* (Easton, Md.: Delaware Press, 1994), "Morris Canal Distances," 6-7; James Lee (ed.), *Tales the Boatmen Told: Recollections of the Morris Canal* (Easton, Md.: Delaware Press, 1977); and Julian R. Tinkham, *Map and Illustrations of the Morris Canal Water Parkway* (Montclair, N.J.: Morris Canal Parkway Association, 1914; reprinted by Russell H. Harding, 1975).

[91] http://edison.rutgers.edu/chron1.htm (7/1/97): *Edison Chronology, 1847-1878*, p. 3 of 19.

[92] Inscriptions transcribed on site visit to Jersey City, N.J., 31 January 1998; William Faden, *The Province of New Jersey, Divided into East and West, Commonly Called the Jerseys*, 2nd ed. (Charing Cross, London: Faden, 1778; reprint from U.S. National Park Service, Morristown, N.J., 1995); and *Union /Hudson/Essex Counties Atlas* (Maspeth, N.Y.: Hagstrom, 1987). More of the history of Paulus Hook in the Revolutionary War appears in Thayer's *Old Elizabethtown*, 119-121, 147; and Lynn G. Lockward, *A Puritan Heritage: The First Presbyterian Church in Horse-Neck (Caldwell, N.J.)* (N.p., 1955), 56.

[93] Cunningham and Cummings, *Remembering Essex*, 59, 83.

[94] Ibid., 44, 174.

[95] Cunningham, *Newark*. 181-182 (leather); 176-180 (Ballantine, Clark, New Jersey Zinc Co., and Weston).

[96] Cunningham and Cummings, *Remembering Essex*, 67 (flour mill). The total length of the Morris Canal was 102.30 miles. See Lee, *Morris Canal*, 3 (map) and 4-7 (history and mileposts).

[97] *City of Newark, N.J.* (New York: C. R. Parsons, 1874). [map, framed under glass on the wall of the Newark Room, Newark Public Library]; and *Newark -- New Jersey* (Newark: T. J. S. Landis, 1916) [map, "Prepared under the direction of the Committee of One Hundred, for the 250th Anniversary of the founding of Newark"; framed under glass on the wall of the Newark Room, Newark Public Library].

[98] Reese V. Jenkins, Leonard S. Reich, Paul B. Israel, Toby Appel, Andrew J. Butrica, Robert A. Rosenberg, Keith A. Nier, Melodie Andrews, and Thomas E. Jeffrey, eds., *The Papers of Thomas A. Edison*, 3 vols. (Baltimore, Md.: The Johns Hopkins University Press, 1989-1994); Ibid., *The Making of an Inventor: February 1847-June 1873*, vol. 1 (1989), 148.

[99] Rosenberg, Israel, Nier, Andrews, eds., *Edison Papers*, vol. 2, *From Workshop to Laboratory: June 1873-March 1876* (1991), map p.2.

[100] Francis Jehl, *Menlo Park Reminiscences*, 3 vols. (Dearborn, Mich.: Edison Institute, 1937; reprint of vol. 1, with an introduction by William S. Pretzer, New York: Dover, 1990), 48 (photograph of Edison's shop at 10-12 Ward St.).

[101] Conversation with a Newark police officer, 6 August 1997; conversation with Bernie Williams and Robert McLean, 7 August 1997.

[102] Baldwin, *Edison*, 53. Cunningham and Cummings, *Remembering Essex*, 16 (Robert Treat's house). Also, Cunningham, *Newark*, 189 (history of *Daily Advertiser* and photo of building with "Newark Advertiser" sign); and 232-233 (history and photo of Kinney Building, looking north on Broad Street across the intersection with Market Street).

[103] *Edison Papers*, vol. 2, unnumbered p.2.

[104] *Edison Chronology, 1847-1878*, Pages 8-10 of 19. This corner is about 200 yards east of the UMDNJ campus in the Central Ward of Newark, within the recently constructed Society Hill section of townhouses. The environment on the gentle hillside at this location would have been pleasant. South Orange Avenue slopes upward as it passes west to South Orange and on to Morristown from its origin near the courthouse. The view of downtown Newark and of points to the east is very attractive from the place where the Edison house was once located.

[105] Building #6 in *Edison Papers*, vol. 1, 148.

[106] It is probably similar, if not identical, to the house that Edison, his wife Mary, and his daughter Marion lived in at 97 (then number 53) Wright Street from December 1871 until the fall of 1875, when they moved to an apartment on Bank Street (See Fig. 12 for 97-99 Wright St.).

[107] Cunningham, *Newark*, 184.

108 I refer to the death of Mary Stilwell Edison, and Edison's subsequent abandonment of Menlo Park, which was followed by his decision in the late 1920s to allow Henry Ford to move all the buildings that were there to Dearborn, Mich.

Chapter 5: The Wizard in Menlo Park
(1876-1931) – Pages 75-104

109 A Rutgers University historian involved in the Edison Papers Project made this comment in the summer of 1997.

110 An 1876 map of Menlo Park shows a development planned that extended from Thornall Road to Pacific Avenue, and from Frederick Street to Cedar Street.

111 The Edison property is located on Christie Street, just 300 yards south of Wood Avenue and the Amtrak Metropark station.

112 Marion Edison Oser, "Early Recollections," Voicewritten March 1956, 1. Jack Stanley Papers.

113 David Trumbull Marshall, *Boyhood Days in Old Metuchen* (Metuchen, N.J.: Metuchen Regional Historical Society by Quinn & Boden Co., 1977; reprint of 2nd ed. [Flushing, N.Y.: Case Publishing Co., 1930]), 115.

114 Marshall, Ibid., 58 (schoolteacher); 139 ("My Father and Mother, with their seven children, lived at the Parsonage of the Presbyterian Church, the Minister . . . boarding with us"); 10 (born 27 November 1865); 139 ("In 1876 Thomas A. Edison moved from Newark to his new Laboratory at Menlo Park"); 56 (batteries . . . sulfuric acid); 29 ("country . . . children"); 197-198 ("Sunday school"); and 139 ("wild over it").

115 Marshall, Ibid., 141, 145 ("The room where I worked at the Orange Laboratory was next to the one where Mr. Edison tried out the various phonograph cylinder mixtures. Day after day, for months on end, I have heard Mr. Edison repeat his favorite test verse . . . 'The boast of heraldry, the pomp of pow'r / And all that beauty, all that wealth e'er gave / Await alike the inevitable hour; / The paths of glory lead but to the grave."); 161-162 (Lamp Factory, 1881-1910); 141 ("for use at our church"); 152 (lake at Menlo Park, emphasis in original); and 164-165 (fish . . . little boy).

116 Marion Oser, "Recollections," 1-5. Marshall confirms the accounts of others, including Marion, of Edison's long hours at the laboratory (*Boyhood Days in Old Metuchen*, 167, quoting H. Alexander Campbell).

117 Marion Oser, "Recollections," 3.

118 Ibid.

119 Marshall knew the three children of Thomas and Mina Edison. He recalled that "Mine Gully is located about a mile north of the old Edison Laboratory at Menlo park (177). Mine Gully was used as a picnic grounds by the "Edison Outing Club" for many years after Edison left Menlo Park (photo, 182).

120 Marion Edison Oser, Ibid.

[121] The maps that I used to construct my composite historical map of Menlo Park were: "Menlo Park," on *Raritan Township*, 1876 (scale 400 feet to the inch) [photocopy kindly provided by George Campbell, Edison Tower museum, Edison Township, N.J.]; "Map Showing Location of Edison Buildings at Menlo Park, N.J. 1876-1882," 16 May 1925 (scale 200 feet to the inch) [from George Campbell]; map of Menlo Park, N.J. (5 March 1936), reproduced in William S. Pretzer, ed., *Working at Invention: Thomas A. Edison and the Menlo Park Experience*. (Dearborn, Mich.: Henry Ford Museum and Greenfield Village, 1993), 13; and in Jehl, *Reminiscences*, 220; *Perth Amboy, N.J.* quadrangle map; *Middlesex County* (Chicago: Rand McNally, 1989); and *New Jersey* (New York: Gousha/Simon & Schuster, 1993). A reproduction of the 1876 map of Menlo Park by the Edison Papers Project is available on their www site (http://edison.rutgers.edu/mpmap.htm [1 July 1997]); it is enlarged, and not to scale. The state of New Jersey does not have available a map of the property which it owns at and near the Edison Tower in Edison Township (conversation with Susan Herron, Superintendent of Cheesequake State Park, 23 January 1998).

[122] In designing this imaginary tour around Menlo Park, New Jersey, I have been influenced by the work of Robert Venturi and his associates, exemplified by their design of Franklin Court for the American bicentennial in Philadelphia (1976). (Roger K. Lewis, "Introduction," and John Andrew Gallery, "Venturi, Rauch and Scott Brown," in Diane Maddex, ed., *Master Builders: A Guide to Famous American Architects* [Washington, D. C.: Preservation Press, 1985], 10, 178-180).

[123] Pretzer, *Menlo Park*, 13 (Fig. 2).

[124] Marshall, *Boyhood Days in Old Metuchen*, 153.

[125] Outcault's painting is reproduced in Robert Friedel and Paul Israel, with Bermard S. Finn, *Edison's Electric Light: Biography of an Invention* (New Brunswick, N.J.: Rutgers University Press, 1987), 31. Henry Ford Museum & Greenfield Village brochure, "Come See 200 Years of American History" (Dearborn, Mich., 1998). .

[126] Pretzer, *Menlo Park*, 59 (Fig. 50); and "Edison's 'First 100 Years'" *Pathfinder* (vol. 54, No. 4.), 12 February 1947, 25.

[127] Marshall, *Boyhood Days*, 144-150; and William H. Meadowcroft., *The Boys' Life of Edison, with Autobiographical Notes by Mr. Edison* (New York: Harper & Row, 1911; 1949 edition), ix, 171-173, and 4th unnumbered page following p. 148.

[128] Pretzer, *Menlo Park*, 24 (Fig. 13).

[129] Pretzer, *Menlo Park*, 49 (Fig. 40).

[130] Jehl, *Reminiscences*, 30.

[131] Pretzer, *Menlo Park*, 77 (laboratory, Fig. 62); Jehl, *Reminiscences*, 353 (steel tower).

[132] Pretzer, *Menlo Park*, 123 (Fig. 102).

[133] Jehl, 14, *Reminiscences*; and Pretzer, *Menlo Park*, 20 (Fig. 9).

[134] Jehl, *Reminiscences*, 270.

[135] *Frank Leslie's Illustrated Newspaper* (10 January 1880); and John T. Cunningham, *Thomas Edison: They Called Him Wizard* (Newark: Public Service Electric & Gas Co., 1979), 17. Also, Francis Trevelyan Miller, *Thomas A. Edison: Benefactor of Mankind. The Romantic Life Story of the World's Greatest Inventor* (Philadelphia: John C. Winston Co., 1931), facing 144.

[136] Pretzer, *Menlo Park*, 20 (Fig. 10).

[137] Theodore Davis, "Edison's Home, Menlo Park, New Jersey." Engraving, 1880 (Reproduction, Alexandria, Va.: American Heritage Engravings, n.d. [ca. 1996]).

[138] Jehl, *Reminiscences*, 218 and 353.

[139] Friedel and Israel, *Electric Light*, 63; also in Vanderbilt, *Edison*, 62.

[140] Mr. George Campbell, curator, told me the story of the lamp and the two towers, and I saw the little blue-green incandescent lamp glowing within a protective sealed glass case in a room in the base of the cement tower at the time of my site visit, 16 November 1997. The history of the construction of the cement tower is from the brochure, "Edison Tower at a Glance" (n.d.), provided at the Edison Tower, Menlo Park, N.J. The tower was built in the eight months from June to December 1937.

[141] Site visits, 16 November 1997 and 22 January 1998.

[142] It was exactly 10.2 miles on the Morris Canal from its beginning at Jersey City to Lock Nineteen East in Newark (Lee, *Morris Canal*, 7), and it is thirteen miles from Penn Station in Newark to Metro Park Station at Iselin, a few hundred yards north of the old Menlo Park station (see Amtrak schedules).

[143] Roger Rosenblatt, "Winter Lights," *Time* (16 February 1998): 106.

[144] *Edison Chronology, 1879-1931*, http://edison.rutgers.edu/chron2.htm, pp. 2-4 (1 July 1997). A map of the Pearl Street district that was electrified by Edison appears in Friedel and Israel, *Electric Light*, 206; the precise address of the station was given in James G. Cook, *Thomas Alva Edison: His Fertile Mind Forged Much of Our Country's Growth* (Southfield, Mich.: Thomas Alva Edison Foundation, 1976), n.p. (chronology, 4 September 1882).

[145] Marion Edison Oser mentions four residences that her family had in New York City: the Lenox, opposite her father's business at 65 Fifth Avenue; the hotel Clarendon, on Union Square; a house in Gramercy Park; and (following his engagement to Mina Miller but prior to moving to West Orange) a residence at the Hotel Normandy across from the Metropolitan Opera House ("Early Recollections," 5-6).

I will not seek for additional examples of this type, however, because my principal interest is on the impact of Edison on other aspects of the environment, such as the earth, air, water, and biota of rural areas — of regions that were only minimally transformed prior to his arrival — and of the *milieu interieur* — the internal environment of the body.

Edison's business addresses in New York City included: 65 Fifth Avenue (his main office, and the address of the Edison Electric Illuminating Company); 255 and 257 Pearl Street (Friedel and Israel, Ibid., 211); 65 Washington Street (Edison Electric Tube Co. [Friedel and Israel, Ibid., 195]; and 17th and Avenue B (Bergman & Co. [Friedel and Israel, Ibid., 201). Photographs of the front exteriors of the Edison Machine Works at 104 Goerck Street and of the Edison Electric Light Company, taken in 1881, appear in Ronald W. Clark, *Edison: The Man Who Made the Future* (New York: G. P. Putnam's Sons, 1977), 116-117. The address on Goerck Street is from Friedel and Israel, Ibid., 195. One of Edison's first projects in New York was the installation of lighting in the lithography shop of Hinds, Ketcham & Co., at 213 Water Street, in 1881; a drawing of this building appears in Friedel and Israel, Ibid., 200.

Chapter 6: Harrison, Roselle and Winthrop: Lampworks, Light and Nature (1882-1892) – Pages 105-116

[146] Cook, *Edison: His Fertile Mind*, s.v., 1882.

[147] Robert Conot, *Thomas A. Edison: A Streak of Luck.* (New York: Seaview, 1979; reprint, paperback, New York: DaCapo/Plenum, 1986), 200.

[148] Matthew Josephson, *Edison: A Biography* (New York: McGraw-Hill, 1959; reprint, with a foreword by Reese V. Jenkins, New York: John Wiley and Sons, 1992); Martin V. Melosi, *Thomas A. Edison and the Modernization of America* (New York: Harper Collins, 1990); André Millard, *Edison and the Business of Invention* (Baltimore: Johns Hopkins University Press, 1990; Softshell Books ed., paperback, 1993); and Baldwin, *Edison.* Conversation with Douglas Tarr, June 1997; and with Robert A. Rosenberg, Paul Israel, and others at "Interpreting Edison" Conference, Rutgers University, Newark, N.J., June 1997.

[149] Conot stated that the Lamp Works was in East Newark.

[150] Henry A. Mutz, *Harrison: The History of a New Jersey Town* (Harrison: Harrison Bicentennial Committee, 1976), 29, 37-38 [illustration of "Edison Lamp Works, General Electric Company" from a vantage point about 60 feet in the air, looking north up Fifth Street from Essex Street]; Edward Doyle, Jr., *Harrison: A Brief History of an American Town* (n.p., n.d. [after 1976]), [photo: "1890 -- Edison Lamp Works. This plant was . . . located on Bergen Street"]; and Edison Papers Project, *Edison Chronology, 1879-1931*, p.7. Also, *Pictorial History of the Edison Lamp* (Harrison, N.J.: Edison Lamp Works, n.d.; Courtesy of the Charles Hummel Collection; purchased at ENHS, 1998); and *The Edison Era 1876-1892: The General Electric Story* (Schenectady, N.Y.: Algonquin Chapter,

Elfun Society, 1976), 23 [purchased at ENHS, 1998].

[151] Edison, quoted in Meadowcroft, *Boys' Life of Edison,* 157-158.

[152] Alfred O. Tate, *Edison's Open Door: The Life Story of Thomas A. Edison, A Great Individualist* (New York: E. P. Dutton & Co., 1938), 133-135. The Duke of Marlborough who visited A. O. Tate and Edison in 1887 was a descendant of John Churchill, the first Earl of Marlborough and one of England's most famous generals, and his wife Sarah. See: "Marlborough, Duke of," in *Enclyclopaedia Britannica*; and Norman A. Bergman, "Georgiana, Duchess of Devonshire, and Princess Diana: A Parallel" *Journal of the Royal Society of Medicine* 91 (April 1998): 217-219. Also, Londa Schiebinger, *The Mind Has No Sex? Women in the Origins of Modern Science* (Cambridge, Mass.: Harvard University Press, 1989), 47-59. Edison's letter to the Duke of Marlborough of 27 June 1891 was quoted in Conot, *Edison,* 300, 533n. Also, see Edison, *Diary and Sundry Observations*, 147 ("now located at Harrison"); and *The Edison Era 1876-1892.*

[153] This building is the pride and joy of those who were sad to see the destruction of the other Lamp Works buildings, and it is not currently scheduled to be removed. I cannot say whether this building on the north side of Bergen Street, extending east from Fifth for one-half block towards Sixth, was incorporated in the Lamp Works during the period of Edison's ownership, 1882-1892, but the Harrison Fire Department watches carefully over it because of its connection with the legacy of Edison. Conversation with Harrison Fire Department firemen and Deputy Chief, 28 February 1998. The Deputy Chief stated sadly that in 1975 he was one of those who worked for the company that cleaned out the R.C.A. buildings ("we saved everything") and then leveled them to clear the land for the shopping centers that face Bergen Street between Frank E. Rodgers Boulevard and Fifth Street. The cream-colored brick three story building that was originally part of the Lamp Works, and that still stands at the corner of Fifth and Bergen Streets, is easily visible from the westbound lanes of Interstate 280, two-tenths of a mile west of Exit 16 into Harrison, and about 100 yards north of I-280.

[154] Conversation in Harrison Fire Department, 28 February 1998; the officers asked not to be credited by name.

[155] *Edison Chronology, 1879-1931*, p.3.

[156] Site visits to Roselle, N.J., on 10, 14 and 17 January 1998. Conversations with the Rev. Dr. J. Max Creswell (died 17 July 2016), sixth Pastor of the First Presbyterian Church in Roselle; Mrs. Betty Olson, Librarian of the Roselle Public Library; and Mr. and Mrs. William Frolich. Mr. Frolich is President of the Roselle Historical Society, and Mrs. (Ruth) Frolich grew up in Bloomfield; she is the only person that I have spoken with who saw Edison while he was alive -- when the inventor was in a large open touring car in a parade on Bloomfield Avenue in [probably] 1929.

Sources for the history of Edison's relationship to Roselle include: Signs and plaques at the northeast corner of First Ave. and Locust St. (now occupied by

Twin Boro Lumber and Supply Co.), and at the First Presbyterian Church, at the southwest corner of Fifth Ave. and Chestnut St. Also: Creswell, *Newspaper Transcriptions: First Presbyterian Church, Roselle, New Jersey* (privately printed, 1990-1994) [copy at church and library], s.v. 1883, 1949, 1983; Aquilina, Koles, and Turner, *Elizabethtown*, 69; Evelyn Naomi Olson, "Thomas Alva Edison and His Influence in Roselle, New Jersey" (MS in Roselle Public Library, 1977), 5-15; William Frolich and Helen Heumann, *The Centennial History of the Borough of Roselle* ([Roselle Historical Society, 1994], 1-10); "Typical Lighting Systems in 1884" in *A General Electric Scrapbook History* (1953), 7; and Hicks, *Roselle*, 1-74.

The original wood frame church building was built in 1868, and the Electrolier (pronounced "Elec-tro-LEER") was turned on in April 1883. In 1892 a larger wood frame building was built beside the original building to serve as a new sanctuary. The original building was destroyed by fire on 16 December 1949, and was replaced by a brick parish house. The larger building was saved from destruction, and is attached to the brick building by a short passageway. The Electrolier was badly damaged in the fire, and although it now looks as it did originally, that is because the restoration by a firm in Newark was done so well. The three-story manse, two houses west, was one of the houses that was originally electrified by Edison in Roselle.

[157] Frolich and Heumann, *Roselle*, 9 (photo of thirty-bulb "electrolier'); 10 (photo of Edison generating station and plaque at corner of First Ave. and Locust St.).

[158] Fairmount Cemetery was established in 1855. It is in the western portion of Newark between Central and South Orange Avenues, and between 12th and 18th Streets, its northwest corner being a few feet into the town of East Orange. Several prominent residents of the area are buried there, including Clara Maass, R.N., the heroine of yellow fever experiments who died in Cuba. Mt. Pleasant Cemetery was established in 1844. It is located just north of Park Avenue in the northern part of Newark, between Broadway and McCarter Highway. Mt. Pleasant Cemetery was one of the earliest planned, secular cemeteries in America. It was for many years the burial place for the wealthy, famous descendants of the founders of Newark, as is apparent on a drive through its winding roads. Both Fairmount and Mt. Pleasant Cemeteries are well-maintained, although Mt. Pleasant conveys an older look and feeling, with its entry bell, its brownstone office buildings and gate, and its larger trees and more variegated landscape. Mt. Pleasant Cemetery was added to the National Register of Historic Places in 1988.

Thomas A. Edison purchased two lots in the most easterly part of the cemetery, on a road known as Passaic, on a bluff overlooking the Passaic River. His lots (10-11, in Section 2) are only 50 feet south of the great mausoleum of the Ward family. We recall at this point that Mary Stilwell Edison's physician in her last illness was one Leslie Dodd Ward, M.D. (1845-1910), whose autobiography states that he was a descendant of the "prominent" Dodd and Ward families of Newark.

[159] Thomas A. Edison, facsimile of diary from 12 July 1885 to 20 July 1885, pp. 27-70 in Kathleen L. McGuirk (ed.), *The Diary of Thomas A. Edison* (Old Greenwich, Conn.: Chatham Press, 1971), 63.

[160] McGuirk, *Diary of Edison*, 12-13.

[161] McGuirk, Ibid., 27 (sunbeams); 65 (ant nests); 65 (No. 1 and No. 2 minds).

[162] McGuirk, Ibid., 27 (smoking); 64 (Satan).

Chapter 7: Edison's Glenmont: At Home in Lewellyn Park
Pages 117-136

[163] Michael H. Agar and Louis Berger & Associates, *Ethnographic Overview and Assessment: Edison National Historic Site, West Orange, New Jersey* (West Orange, N.J.: U.S. National Park Service, 1997).

[164] Of the many other logistical problems that I have encountered, I will mention only one at this point: The National Park Service brochure that is its only official description of Glenmont has been out of stock for several months, and – according to Park rangers at the ENHS on 14 March 1998 – is unlikely to be in stock again for several more months. The ENHS did not save a copy of this brochure from which secondary photocopies can be made.

[165] Kenneth Goldstein, Interview with Madeline Edison Sloane, 1 December 1972, page 12 (Jack Stanley Papers).

[166] Madeline Edison appears to have been a remarkably warm and interesting person, judging by the comments made to me by many people who knew her, including her grandson, her contemporaries (some of whom are still alive in 1998), and friends of her sons. For example, her half-sister, Marion Edison Oser commented in 1956 that "My sister, Madeline, was a fascinating child and she has brought me all the happiness I had hoped for having a sister" (Oser, "Early Recollections," 8).

[167] Agar, Berger & Associates, *Ethnographic Overview*, 15

[168] Llewellyn Park was more precisely defined by 1877 and was smaller than it was shown to be on maps drawn in 1857 and 1858. An old map of "Llewellyn Park, West Orange, New Jersey," was found on 25 September 1997, at the Church of the Holy Innocents in West Orange. The map is framed under glass and hangs on the wall of the Undercroft of the church. It is not dated, but on it is written in ink, "Sep 23 77 [s] J. A. McDonald."

[169] The remnants of the Morris Canal in Bloomfield and Belleville can be seen on the Hagstrom *Atlas* map of Essex County (Map 8)

[170] Milton Marmor, Interview with Mrs. Thomas A. Edison, 10 January 1947, page 6 (Jack Stanley Papers). On the other hand, Mina's stepdaughter, Marion Edison Oser, was not at all reluctant to describe the scene (Oser, "Early Recollections," Voicewritten March 1956, page 6; Jack Stanley Papers).

[171] Goldstein, Interview with Madeline Edison Sloane, 1 December 1972, 25-26 (reason for purchasing Glenmont); 1972, 12 and 13 March 1973, 46 (busy, happy).

[172] On 15 March 1998, I viewed a few of the titles of the books in the original collection at Glenmont from the visitor's stance in the doorway to the library on the first floor. All of them were works on history.

[173] Uschold and Curry, *Cultural Landscape Report*, Appendix B (National Register of Historic Places Inventory -- Nomination Form, 1978), Description, p.2. Also, Virginia McAlester and Lee McAlester, with photographs by Alex McLean, *Great American Homes and Their Architectural Styles* (New York: Abbeville, 1994), 156; and Madeline Edison Sloane, in Goldstein, Interview, 1973, 34, in Jack Stanley Papers).

[174] Uschold and Curry, Ibid., Appendix B, Continuation pages, 7-9.

[175] Ibid., 6-7

[176] Ibid., 8-11.

[177] Interview with Glenmont's gardener, W. I. Halstrom, by Park Historian Arthur Spiegler, 9 October and 22 November 1965; in Jack Stanley Papers.

[178] Uschold and Curry, op. cit., 8. Interviews with Halstrom, 1965 (in Jack Stanley Papers).

[179] Halstrom, Interview, 2-4.

[180] Halstrom, Interview, 5 (swimming pool); 6-7 (1907); 7 (barn wasn't moved); 11 (in the stables); 12 (hold no water).

[181] Halstrom, Interview, 12 (chestnut trees); 13 (red oak); 16 (raspberries); 17 (dug them out); 18-19 (peach tree); 20 (dahlias); 22-23 (palms); 23 (rose garden); 24-25 (Taxus); 25 (crabapple); 27 (grounds first); 28 (cows died); 29 (weeds).

[182] The 1857 map of Llewellyn Park that is reproduced on a sign near the Greenhouse and Potting Shed gives an excellent overview of the Park and the surrounding areas as they existed thirty years before the Edisons arrived.

[183] Goldstein, Interviews with Madeline Edison Sloane (1972, 19; and 1973, 64-65). Madeline's portrait on the first floor of Glenmont portrays her as a sultry, mischievous, young woman.

[184] *Newark (N.J.) Star Ledger*, "Essex," (13 March 1998), 33 (90,000 cars).

[185] A set of notecards illustrated with photographs from the Collections of the New Jersey Historical Society demonstrates the importance of horses in Essex County at the end of the nineteenth century.

[186] The first hats in Orange were made by one James Condit in 1785, according to Cunningham and Cummings, *Remembering Essex*, 35-36. I cannot show a relationship between this James Condit and Edison, although Edison's great-great-great aunt Elizabeth Ogden married Nathaniel Condit of Orange. There are no

less than forty-five Condits listed in the Ogden genealogy (Wheeler, *Ogden Family*, 481-482), all of whom would be kinsmen or in-laws of the Edisons. Cunningham and Cummings state that "The most prominent hat name in Orange was Stetson. The first of the famous family, Stephen began in 1790" (36). According to Wheeler, Isabella Leonard (1822-1891) married Marcus Mitchell, brother-in-law of Col. Napoleon Stetson, "hat manufacturer of Orange," and Isabella's older brother, William (b. 1814) married Martha Stetson (230). Isabella and William Leonard were third cousins of Thomas Edison's father, Samuel Ogden Edison, Jr. (343)

[187] Although Crystal Lake at the summit of the ridgeline of First Mountain, near Eagle Rock Avenue, is shown to be one of the origins of Wigwam Brook in the 1857 and 1858 maps of Llewellyn Park, this Crystal Lake no longer drains to the east. Crystal Lake's present drainage is to the west, into the valley of the West Branch of the Rahway River.

[188] David Lawrence Pierson, *History of the Oranges to 1921: Reviewing the Rise, Development and Progress of an Influential Community*, 4 vols. (New York: Lewis Historical Publishing Company, 1922), 4: 581, 584.

Chapter 8: Edison in West Orange: Laboratory and Factories
Pages 137-150

[189] Uschold and Curry, *Cultural Landscape Report*, Appendix A, 1.

[190] Ernest Stevens, interviewed by Ken Goldstein, 20 June 1973. Stevens was born 15 December 1893 and he worked for Edison in West Orange when the Great Inventor was "around 78, 79" (i.e., about 1925-26). Stevens was Edison's driver and he helped him to do experiments and make recordings of music. Stevens said that he "always looked up to him and thought he was the world's greatest man." Stevens described Edison as "a very pleasant old gent, really" (Interview #1of Stevens by Goldstein, p. 23, in Jack Stanley Papers).

[191] The number of documents in the archives at the Edison National Historic Site has been estimated by various authors to be anywhere from 1.5 to 5.5 million. *Cultural Landscape Report*, 5.

[192] Uschold and Curry, op. cit., Appendix D: "the Environment" is defined as "the general external influences effecting [sic] the historic landscape, the off-site larger physical and visual context which contains or encompasses the historic landscape." This consists of two elements, the "natural," and the "social/cultural" components. "Natural" is defined as "the natural physical form and features of the surrounding environment that has or does directly effect [sic] the historic landscape (major landforms, ridges/valley, vegetation, water bodies, wetlands, etc.)." "Social/Cultural" is defined as "the general human overlay on the physical form of the surrounding environment that has or does directly effect [sic] the historic landscape (general land use, zoning, legal restrictions, transportation, utilities, population, political jurisdiction - state, county, city, village, town, etc.)."

Within or directly adjacent to a historic setting (i.e., within the Environment, as defined above), Uschold and Curry consider the following aspects: landscape setting; natural systems and features (including physiography, geology, hydrology, ecology, and climate); topography; buildings and structures (including mechanical systems and site engineering systems); vegetation; spatial organization (including views [natural, uncontrolled] and vistas [controlled or designed]); circulation; water features; and furnishings and objects, which provide detail and diversity (11-12).

[193] Ibid., 107-108.

[194] Ibid., 1, 9, 20, 24: "Shortly after Edison had purchased Glenmont, his West Orange home in Llewellyn Park, he decided to build the Edison Laboratories on a nearby site, less than 1,000 feet away. The site he chose for the Edison Laboratories was a meadow located on the town's main street, Valley Road" (20)

[195] Ibid., 1 (physical changes); 2 ("West Orange Plant"); 12 (7.5 acres); 2 (at his home).

[196] Ibid., 2-3.

[197] Ibid., 8, showing sketch in Millard, 1990.

[198] Ibid., 91-92.

[199] Ibid., 12 (mostly meadow); 13 (planted on the site); 14 (other sides); 17 (Gate House); 18 (Black Maria); 20 (Alden Street).

[200] Ibid., 26 (7.5 to 26.26 acres, citing deeds researched); and Appendix A, 1-2; 26 (seventy-three percent); 36 (fire protection).

[201] Ibid., 27 (railroad tracks); 35-36 (Cement Company); 28-29 (chaotic).

[202] M. A. Rosanoff, "Edison in His Laboratory" *Harper's* (September 1932), 402-417 [copy in Jack Stanley Papers]; 408 (sleep . . . spittoon); 409 ("The Great Inventor"); 411 ("receptive mind". . .junk); 413.

[203] Uschold and Curry, op. cit., 28 (densely developed); 29 (West Orange Plant); 31 (Phonograph Works); 35 ("cluttered" appearance); 28; photo (41), "West Orange Plant after fire, 1914, Fig. 3.1, from Album 10, Cat. 5209, EDIS archives."

[204] The Essex County Medical Society was established in May 1816 and its archives are now held at the George F. Smith Library of the University of Medicine and Dentistry of New Jersey, Newark. I reviewed five volumes of Minutes and other business: 26 April 1865 - 3 May 1892; 5 April 1892 - 4 April 1905; 3 April 1906 - 6 April 1909; 5 April 1910 - 9 May 1916; and 13 October 1916 - 23 September 1929

[205] National Fire Protection Association and National Board of Fire Underwriters, *Report on Fire: The Edison Phonograph Works, Thomas A. Edison, Inc., West Orange, N.J., December 9, 1914*, 34. [copy at ENHS archives]

[206] Interview with Edward J. Daly at Edison National Historic Site, 28 February 1973 (in Jack Stanley Papers), 3-4 (didn't get paid); 24 (the whole town); 24-25 (might get it); 30 (no transportation).

[207] Uschold and Curry, op. cit., 42-44, with photograph "West Orange Plant after reconstruction," ca. 1917 (10.380/25, EDIS archives).

[208] Ibid., 44 (citing Mary Anne Hellrigel, "Thomas A. Edison and the Mountain Society: West Orange During the Edison Era" [Paper delivered at a Centennial Symposium, West Orange, N.J., April 25, 1987, 9-10]).

[209] Interview with Ernest Stevens of Montclair, N.J. (born 15 December 1893) by Ken Goldstein, 20 June 1973 (in Jack Stanley Papers), 22 ("world's greatest man"); 23 ("He didn't care"); 28 (West Orange).

[210] Interview with Edward Cary (born 6 August 1894), by Ken Goldstein at Lakewood, N.J., 6 June 1973 (in Jack Stanley Papers), 4 (assistant treasurer); 9 (do all right); 16 (self-educated); 17 (very generous).

[211] Uschold and Curry, op. cit., 91.

[212] During the last years of Edison's life, "research and experimentation declined at the West Orange Plant and the manufacturing of low-risk products became the plant's primary focus. The Edison Laboratories were transformed from an active research facility into a simple, routine production facility." A number of changes occurred in the environment of the Plant, which can still be recognized. For example, "The Edison Laboratories' water system was further modified with the addition of a 75,000 gallon water tower in 1926. . . The 132-foot high tower was constructed to supply water for emergencies." Uschold and Curry, op. cit., 55 (production facility); 53 (4 feet wide); 51 (emergencies); 47 (when damaged).

Chapter 9: Destruction of Silver Lake: Bloomfield, Belleville, Glen Ridge – Pages 151-188

[213] Interview with former Edison employee, William H. Hand, at Columbia University by Kenneth Goldstein, 15 March 1973.

[214] The earliest reference that I have located to Edison in Bloomfield/Silver Lake is 1887, and the last date is 1937 --six years after he died -- so this case study is said to be for the period 1887-1931. What I mean by "Bloomfield/Silver Lake" will be revealed in the text. A copy of the Organization Chart of Thomas A. Edison Industries (1930) was made for me by Doug Tarr, Edison National Historic Site. This chart shows ten major divisions, which are illustrated with small cartoon drawings, plus four "Other Divisions" and three "Associated Industries." Four of the major Divisions had manufacturing plants in Silver Lake in 1930: Edison Storage Battery Company (Chemical Works Division); Edison Primary Battery Division; Ediphone Radio Division (Radio Manufacturing); and the General Manufacturing Division, which was depicted by a drawing that showed two large buildings with seven or eight smokestacks and a water tower.

[215] There is nothing in the *Edison Chronology* of the Edison Papers Project regarding Bloomfield, Belleville, Glen Ridge, or Belleville, except "1890 Aug

Purchases property in Silver Lake, New Jersey (now the Bloomfield-Belleville area); locates the plant of the Edison Manufacturing Company on the site" (http://edison.rutgers.edu/chron2.htm [accessed 7/1/97], page 7 of 12). Uschold and Curry, *Cultural Landscape Report*, 467-469.

[216] Maps used in this case study of Silver Lake include: *Orange, N.J.* (1981) and *Elizabeth, N.J and N.Y.* (1981) quadrangle maps; Hagstrom maps of *Union/Hudson/Essex Counties* (1987) and *Essex County* (1991); Avery Ala Drake, Jr., et al, *Bedrock Geologic Map of Northern New Jersey* (1996); maps in William D. Nichols, *Ground-Water Resources of Essex County, New Jersey* (1968); map of *Bloomfield, N.J.* (1857), framed, at The Historical Society of Bloomfield, N.J.; *Robinson's Atlas of Essex County, New Jersey* (New York: B. Robinson, 1890); Ellis Kiser, *Atlas of Essex County, New Jersey*, vol. 3 (Philadelphia: A. H. Muller & Co., 1906); and copies of five archaic maps in the Glen Ridge Public Library in "Barrows Collection Inventory" [photographic negatives and positives], *Glen Ridge Historical Collection Indexes*: (1) "Map, Newark, Elizabeth, Paterson, [n.d.], very early"; (2) "Map, early Bloomfield, including Belleville and Montclair" [n.d.]; (3) "Map Montclair, Glen Ridge, Bloomfield, Belleville, ca. 1776"; (4) "Map, Bloomfield about 1830"; and (5) "Map, Glen Ridge, 1895, from the Hughes map of 1865."

[217] "Time is of the essence" is an important term in contract law, and I have learned that it is also important in oral history. For example, in June 1997 I learned from Jim Hauk, of Bornstein & Sons Plumbing and Heating, that his father, Fred Hauk, then 93, had worked for Edison and had attended his funeral in 1931. The elder Mr. Hauk lived on Montgomery Street in "the second oldest house in Bloomfield," built in 1734. I missed the opportunity to meet the elder Mr. Hauk.

[218] The Silver Lake District of Belleville is the portion of Belleville that is south of Second River. It is a triangular piece of land that is about one and one-fourth miles long on its east side (Bloomfield) and its west side (Newark), and about one-half mile wide at its base, on its north side, which is Second River. The Silver Lake District thus covers about 240 acres of land. Blue banners bearing the legend "Something's Happening . . . " are hung on poles on major streets throughout the district, and cheerful heart-shaped signs on major streets at entry points state: "Welcome to Silver Lake, Belleville, N.J. / Silver Lake Civic Association / Founded May 1993 / UPP Program." The Silver Lake Civic Association phone number is that of the Silver Lake Baptist Church: (973) 751-2247. Kiser, *Atlas of Essex County*, Plate 15.

[219] The Silver Lake Railroad Station is shown on the 1987 and 1991 Hagstrom maps of Essex County, just east of the corner of Belmont Avenue and Franklin Street in Belleville. *Robinson's Atlas of Essex County* (1890), Plate 29; and Kiser, *Atlas of Essex County*, Plates 11 and 15. The "Silver Lake Church" appears on the *Orange* quadrangle map on the north side of Franklin St. in Belleville, between

Florence Ave. and Frederick St. *Robinson's Atlas*, Plate 29).

[220] For elevations, see *Orange, N.J.* (1981) quadrangle map.

[221] Comment of a Belleville fireman to the author, 31 March 1998.

[222] *Robinson's Atlas* (1890) and Kiser, *Atlas* (1906).

[223] Robert B. Burnett, *Belleville: 150th-Anniversary Historical Highlights, 1839-1989* (Belleville, N.J.: 150th-Anniversary Committee, 1991), 24-25; Kiser, *Atlas*.

[224] *Orange, N.J.* quadrangle map (1981); Hagstrom maps of *Union/Hudson/Essex Counties* (1987) and *Essex County* (1991); *Robinson's Atlas of Essex County* (1890); Kiser, *Atlas of Essex County* (1906).

[225] Burnett, *Belleville*, 24-25.

[226] *Robinson's Atlas* (1890), Plate 29.

[227] Cunningham and Cummings, *Remembering Essex*, 36 (Second River was founded by the Dutch); 47 (The Dutch Reformed Church and a small cluster of adjacent houses along the Passaic in Belleville are shown in a painting [ca. 1840]). Also, Burnett, *Belleville*, 1-3 (From the seventeenth century "until 1797 people referred to Belleville as Second River"). See Fleming, *A History of New Jersey*; Morison, *Oxford History of the American People*, 56-57, 75-77; and Langer, *Encyclopedia of World History*, 438-439.

[228] A. E. Johnson at Edison National Historic Site, 29 March 1971 (sandy soil), in Jack Stanley Papers (23).

[229] The original Indian name for Bloomfield (Watsessing) was given in *History of Bloomfield, New Jersey* (1932). For early English settlers in Bloomfield see Cunningham and Cummings, *Remembering Essex*, 18 (Wardesson), 19 (Cranetown and Azariah Crane).

[230] Cunningham and Cummings, *Remembering Essex*, 22 (Caleb Davis' home); 24 (Joseph Crane homestead); 38-39 (Israel Crane and the Turnpike). Cunningham and Cummings state that Israel "King" Crane was a descendant of two founders of Newark, Jasper Crane and Robert Treat. Jasper Crane, was also, by the way, a kinsman of Thomas Edison. In Wheeler, *Ogden Family*, 344, Thomas Alva Edison appears as person #3214. A first cousin of Edison's ancestor, Swaine Ogden, #16 Robert Ogden, was married to Hannah Crane, daughter of Jasper Crane and Joanna Swaine (58). Hannah Crane came from Branford, Conn., to Newark in 1667; her mother was surely a relative of Captain Samuel Swaine, who was also Edison's ancestor. Edison would have been unaware of all these connections with the early settlers of Bloomfield when he began to purchase land at Silver Lake in 1888, but after Wheeler's book appeared in 1907 he and Mina had access to this information. Although I cannot prove that Edison was aware of his connections with the Ogden family, the National Park Service guide at Glenmont on 11 March 1998 stated that Madeline Edison Sloane "was a member of the D.A.R. on both sides of her family," which strongly suggests that the women in Edison's family were attentive to their genealogies.

[231] Cunningham and Cummings, *Remembering Essex*, 40 (1807); 40 (Bloomfield included Belleville, etc.); 40 (1833); 58 (1839); 26 (Bennett's Grist Mill); 50 (1850). Bloomfield was named for General Joseph Bloomfield (1755-1825), who was the fourth Governor of New Jersey. He also happened to be a kinsman of Thomas Edison. As a great-great grandson of John "The Pilgrim" Ogden, founder of Elizabeth, Joseph Bloomfield was a third cousin of Thomas Edison's great-grandmother, Sarah Ogden Edison. Bloomfield is person #349 in Wheeler, *Ogden Family* (p.88), a descendant of the same Robert Ogden who was married to Jasper Crane's daughter, Hannah.

[232] Cunningham and Cummings, *Remembering Essex*, 55 (1857); 56 (copper-working and woolen); 64 (1865); 56 (1856); 58 (1868); and 60 (Bloomfield College).

[233] John T. Cunningham, *Newark* (Newark, N.J.: New Jersey Historical Society, 1988), 224 (1870s); 224-225 (1873, 1881, 1895). "Highly offensive to both smell and taste" is a quotation from "Official reports in 1872 and 1873" (224). The Skating Rink in Branch Brook Park is in the center of the stone-lined structure that once was the reservoir; it is seen on current maps of Newark, immediately west of Sacred Heart Cathedral, in the southern portion of the park. At its eighty-third Annual Meeting on 5 April 1899, Charles F. Underwood, M.D., President of the Essex County Medical Society, "referred in most scathing terms to the action of the Board of Works in ordering the water of the Passaic River turned into the reservoir of the city in the month of February last." (Archives of the ECMS, UMDNJ-George F. Smith Library).

[234] James Lee, *The Morris Canal: A Photographic History* (Easton, Pa.: Delaware Press, 1979); Hagstrom maps of *Union/Hudson/Essex Counties* (1987); author's site visit to Berkeley Ave., Bloomfield, 10 March 1998.

[235] The pastoral scene is in Russell H. Harding, *Illustrations of the Morris Canal Water Parkway: A Recreation Project 100 Miles Long*, (Montclair, N.J.: Morris Canal Parkway Assoc., 1914, reprinted 1975), Fig. 1. The factory complex is shown in Lee, *Morris Canal*, 112; 110 (swimmers at Bloomfield). Lee (ed.), *Tales the Boatmen Told: Recollections of the Morris Canal* (Easton, Pa.: Delaware Press, 1991), 83 (winter sledding); 48 (swimming hole); 48 (industries . . . pollution free, in the legend of a picture showing swimmers in Bloomfield).

[236] George Mowder [1875-1968], in Lee (ed.), *Tales the Boatmen Told*, 180: In 1953 Mowder, a former "boat boy" who later became a canal boat captain, recalled his experiences on the Morris Canal between 1886 and 1891.

[237] Transcriptions from *Excerpts from Early Bloomfield, N.J., Newspapers 1872-1895*, compiled by Sallie Black and Margaret A. Riggin (Bloomfield: Historical Society of Bloomfield, 1982) [this volume was the only one completed by Black and Riggin]. This volume contains thirteen references to "Edison" (four to Edison Co., six to Edison Electric Light Co., and three to Edison Phonograph Works), and three to "Annexation of Silver Lake." All the articles quoted are from *The*

Bloomfield Citizen, and the pages cited are from Black and Riggin: 184 (8 October 1887).

[238] *The Bloomfield Citizen*, in Black and Riggin, *Excerpts*, 198 (14 July 1888). There is no indication that Edison's decision to move his Phonograph Works from Bloomfield to West Orange was related to the terrible weather that this region had survived between October 1887 and July 1888 -- the winter of the so-called "Blizzard of '88," which dumped more than 40 inches of snow onto New England and New York. The Arctic explorer, General Augustus W. Greeley, wrote that "This storm is by no means as violent as others which have occurred in the eastern part of the United States. . . . It is noted, however, as being one in which an unusual amount of snow fell" (*National Geographic* 193 [No. 5, May 1998], n.p. [Millennium Moments]). The environmental influences of weather and climate appear to have had little effect upon Edison's activities as an inventor and businessman.

[239] *The Bloomfield Citizen*, in Black and Riggin, *Excerpts*, 249 (14 January 1889); 204 (19 January); 227 (13 July).

[240] When we saw that the ink factory was located at Midland and Carteret, the librarians at the Glen Ridge Public Library said that they believed this area was now a toxic waste site. Radiation in tailings from the now-defunct U.S. Radium Corp. in Orange, N.J., is believed to be the source of the problem in several sites such as this in Essex County, although records (in the Special Collections of the Smith Library of the UMDNJ in Newark) from the U.S. Radium Corp. do not show where the pitchblende from Colorado that they processed was later dumped.

[241] Ronald Traviano (editor), *Glen Ridge Heritage* (Glen Ridge, N.J.: Bicentennial Committee, 1976), 15-16 (photo of Hayden Mill, and quotations regarding ink factory and battery factory). In 1976 an older resident of Glen Ridge recalled seeing Edison's car being towed after the battery failed. Also, *Robinson's Atlas of Essex County* (1890), Plate 5 (Ink Factory) and Plate 20 (P. Hayden Estate Essex Brass & Silver Rolling Mill); and Kiser, *Atlas of Essex County* (1906), Plate 19 (ink factory ruins) and Plate 20 (Edison Storage Battery Co.).

[242] Cunningham and Cummings, *Remembering Essex*, 132 (The Glen Ridge Stores, an early upscale shopping center, were built in 1911); 126: (The DL & W railroad was electrified in 1920 through the Oranges to Short Hills, and to Bloomfield, Glen Ridge, and Montclair).

[243] Burnett, *Belleville*, 24-25.

[244] The Free Public Library of Bloomfield (editors), *Bloomfield, New Jersey* (Bloomfield: The Independent Press, 1932).

[245] For the land acquisitions, see Black and Riggin, *Excerpts*: 20 April 1889: "The large brick building on Bloomfield avenue, lately occupied by Mr. T. A. Edison, is now being fitted up as a manufactory of patent cream separators, used in the production of butter" (210); 25 May 1889: "Mr. Thomas A. Edison has added to his extensive tract of property near Silver Lake the firm of Mr. Aaron

Kent, on Franklin Street" (214); 24 August 1889: "The Edison Company have purchased an additional six acres of property from the Farrand estate. They now have a frontage on Bloomfield avenue, Franklin street and Watsessing avenues. Their recent purchases aggregate 50 acres. It is said that the construction of a large brick building will shortly be commenced near the Orange Branch, Erie Railroad, which runs through the property" (238).

[246] For the street lighting contract, see: 9 November 1889: "The Edison Electric Light Company [for street lighting] . . . It is understood will be located at the junction of Glenwood avenue and the D.L.&W. R.R. west of the track and south of the avenue" (242); 23 November 1889: "The Electric Light Contract" [Editorial] "Several weeks ago the Township Committee passed a resolution accepting the bid of the Edison Company for lighting the streets. . . . We believe there is little of opinion relative to the expediency of having the streets lighted by electricity in the Edison Company's bid" (243-245); 28 December 1889: "Electric Lighting Postponed" [feature article] "The adoption of electric light in place of gas in this town has been indefinitely postponed. . . . [public sentiment was strongly opposed] against the United Edison Electric Light Company . . . experimental . . . dangerous . . . introduction of wires into the public streets." A citizen from Glen Ridge, which was then part of Bloomfield, opposed overhead wires, others opposed the amount of the contract, and *The Bloomfield Citizen* observed that there was eager competition "among the several electric light companies" (246-248).

[247] *Bloomfield, New Jersey* (1932); see especially Charles C. Ferguson, "Industrial Development" (41-48). Also, 149 articles on the history of Bloomfield by Herbert Fisher, published in the *Bloomfield Independent Press* from 16 June 1960 to 18 April 1963, bound by The Historical Society of Bloomfield, 31 January 1977 [in Bloomfield Public Library]; none of these articles mention Edison or Silver Lake. In contrast to the neglect of Edison and Silver Lake in these histories of Bloomfield, an undated photograph of Thomas Edison chatting with the Rev. Frederick Willey in Bloomfield exists in the archives of the Edison National Historic Site. The photograph is reproduced in "Thomas Edison and the Bloomfield Connection," *Newsletter* of The Historical Society of Bloomfield (September 1996), 3. The legend for the photo states that "Edison had factories and warehouses in Bloomfield."

[248] Black and Riggin, *Excerpts*, 362 (16 April 1892).

[249] Cunningham and Cummings, *Remembering Essex*, 86-88. Ampere is still seen on the map of Essex County at North 16th and 4th Avenue in East Orange, one block north of Park Avenue and a block west of the border with Newark. The center of this "triangle" would be at about where Glenwood Street, Boyden Street and Dodd Street meet near Wigwam Brook at Watsessing Park in Bloomfield. A cluster of old brick buildings is still located at this point, on Glenwood Street near Franklin Street in East Orange, on which is a sign that states "Manufacturer's Village (About 1880) . . . Space for Rent."

[250] Conversations and Documents Related to Edison, 11 March 1998, at the Museum of the Historical Society of Bloomfield, New Jersey, 90 Broad Street, Bloomfield, N.J. I met and spoke with Ms. Lucy Sant'Ambrogio, curator; Ms. Dorothy Johnson, Past President, The Historical Society of Bloomfield, and retired Librarian of the Bloomfield Public Library; and a former Postmaster of Bloomfield. I also reviewed all the Museum's information about Edison, which consisted of two vertical files about two inches thick, and the file regarding a lecture on Edison and Bloomfield given in Bloomfield on 12 September 1996 by Dr. George Tselos of the Edison National Historic Site. I reviewed a bound volume of typed excerpts from Bloomfield newspapers (see below), and studied the map of Bloomfield (1857) on the wall of the library. Ms. Sant'Ambrogio grew up in Bloomfield. When I asked about Edison and Silver Lake, she volunteered: "I had friends [?the Gianottis] who lived northeast of Edison's plant at Silver Lake, at about Franklin and Florence Streets in what is now Belleville."

[251] Conversations at the Museum of the Historical Society of Bloomfield, 11 March 1998, continued. Ms. Dorothy Johnson is a volunteer at the Museum. Her memories go back to the 1940s, perhaps the 1930s, and she was surprised when I told her that I had not been able to determine when Silver Lake became a part of Bloomfield and Belleville. She thought that Silver Lake had "always" been in Bloomfield and Belleville. The retired Postmaster said that from my remarks, he now understood why he used to see letters addressed to people in "Silver Lake, N.J.," rather than Bloomfield.

I showed Ms. Sant'Ambrogio, Ms. Johnson, and the retired Postmaster the information that I had located which indicated that Silver Lake was not a part of Bloomfield in 1857 (the map) or in 1889 (newspaper article), or probably in 1932 (since Edison or Silver Lake do not appear in the town's history, *Bloomfield, New Jersey*, published in that year by The Free Public Library of Bloomfield). All agreed that the lack of recognition by people in Bloomfield (in the 1930s and thereafter) of the work that Edison had done in Silver Lake was related to the bad feeling that was engendered by Edison's operations at Silver Lake. It was not because Silver Lake wasn't technically a part of Bloomfield at the time that Edison was there.

[252] Four photographs of Silver Lake, N.J., from the ENHS archives were provided to The Historical Society of Bloomfield by Dr. George Tselos for his lecture on 19 September 1996:

"Silver Lake Chemical Works Viewed from Alva St." (01/03/1912). 10.350/ 7 Neg. No. 619A.

"Hydrogen-Earthen Vessels at Chemical Works" (06/18/1913). 10.350/ 113 Neg. No. 1823.

"Construction of Hydrate Building at Chemical Works, Silver Lake, N.J." (11/18/1913). 10.350/118 Neg. No. 2187.

"Aerial View of Silver Lake Chemical Works" 10.350/4 Photographer: Fairchild Aerial Surveys, Inc. [date and negative number were cut off the bottom of the copy].

An earlier aerial view (perhaps a drawing) of the Silver Lake Plant appears in the unnumbered centerfold of William H. Meadowcroft (ed.), *The Life of Thomas A. Edison,* by Arthur Palmer (N.p. [?New York]: King Features, 1927).

[253] Interview with former Edison employee, Edward Cary (born 6 August 1894), by Ken Goldstein at Lakewood, N.J., 6 June 1973 (in Jack Stanley Papers), 3-4. Cary came to work for Edison in 1915.

[254] Interview with former Edison employee, A. E. Johnson, at Edison National Historic Site, 29 March 1971 (in Jack Stanley Papers), 22. Johnson continues, explaining that an effort was made to see if the "mountain of sludge" contained enough of value to warrant development of a recycling process: "Doherty ran a qualitative test and found out that there was quite a lot of nickel in it, enough nickel to warrant a, working out a recovery program. . . . he gave a report to the Old Man, that there was a large pile of muck down at the lake that he believed might contain enough metal to make it worthwhile saving."

[255] "An Edison Building Burns: Inventor Says He Will Rebuild Silver Lake Plant in 48 Hours - Silver Lake, N.J., Jan. 9" *New York Times* (10 January 1916). [copy in Jack Stanley Papers].

[256] "Edison Loses Acid Suit: Court Holds that Drainage from Plant is a Menace to Health" "Montclair, N.J., April 19" *New York Times* (20 April 1916). [copy in Jack Stanley Papers].

[257] 25 Heckel Street is immediately opposite the end of Brook Street at its intersection with Heckel Street; 45 Heckel Street is less than a block north of this point. The presence of the ill-fated brook under the ground here is apparent from the presence of storm sewers between 25 and 45 Heckel Street.

[258] Interview with William H. Hand at Columbia University by Kenneth Goldstein, 15 March 1973, 9. Hand was twenty-four years old, a recent graduate in science from Haverford College, when Edison offered him employment in June 1924.

[259] Hand, Interview by Goldstein, 17 (rate of reaction); 18 (sanitarium); 24 (Death House . . . fire apparatus had come). The phenol-formaldehyde substance described by Hand was Edison's competition to Leo H. Bakeland's "Bakelite," the phenol-formaldehyde compound that Bakeland devised in 1909, and manufactured in Bloomfield, N.J. According to *Britannica* (15th edition, 1980), Bakelite is a registered trademark of the Union Carbide Corporation. "It displaced celluloid for nearly all applications early in the 20th century" (*Micropaedia*, vol. 7, 933).

[260] Hand: "Thomas Edison built a chemical plant at Silver Lake, N.J. . . . In that chemical plant Edison had German chemists. These chemists produced many of the critical chemicals which ordinarily had come from Germany. Now . . . history shows that Edison's work in this chemical plant aided the United States greatly in World War I. But in my intelligence work I came across a secret Army report . . . which stated that the work of Thomas A. Edison Chemical Plant at Silver Lake

had produced nothing that got into the economy, because, after the war, Army intelligence agents found most of the material that they produced in the Edison Chemical Plant in cellars in Paterson and Passaic. In other words, the undercover German agents had bought all of this manufactured material and just took it off the market by hiding it in these diverse cellars (Interview by Goldstein, 6).

"I would think that I found that document about 1926 . . . They were in a file, yes. But the file, don't forget this, at that time the plant had been shut down and the plant had been abandoned and that's why it wasn't found before" (9).

[261] Hand, Interview by Goldstein, 10-11 (his secrets); 14 (discovered that). Hand emphasizes what he considers as Edison's deliberate disregarding of safety, and his obsession with secrecy by telling another story about mercury: "[T]here was a Negro working at the machine where the plates were broken apart. . . . I noticed that he gold teeth had turned silver, and I suspected right then that there was mercury in the atmosphere. . . I took a sample from the dust bin . . . took it to the laboratory, put it under a microscope . . . with a very powerful beam of light, and I found that the black iron . . . was filled with starlike globules of metallic mercury. . . When I wrote to Mr. Edison I said, 'It is a dangerous situation . . .' and in typical Edison disregard for what I had said, he sent me a note, which I have on file, 'You don't get mercury poisoning unless the mercury gets into the mouth.' . . . So he was very unhappy that I had discovered that" (14).

[262] Hand, Interview by Goldstein, 29 (I had a notion . . . gold off). Hand worked for Edison from 1924 until he quit in 1930 (32-39).

[263] Regarding a massive dump of old batteries at Silver Lake, Hand says that "The Edisons bought great quantities of the iron nickel batteries, Edison batteries which had failed, and stored them at Silver Lake . . . the idea being that they would recover the metallic nickel (11). . .The International Nickel Company came to Edison and said . . . 'Stop the practice or we'll raise the price of nickel. . . .' So he abandoned this great inventory of old batteries which must have been 60 feet high in a truncated shape covering an acre" (13).

[264] A reduced scale copy of the Organization Chart of Thomas A. Edison Industries (2 January 1930) was provided by Doug Tarr of the Edison National Historic Site; a large copy was framed on the wall of the visitors' center at the ENHS. A copy of R. E. Trout and R. St. Weston [?] "Edison Signal Batteries 50 Years of Progress" (Bloomfield, N.J.: Thomas A. Edison, Inc., 1939) [unpaginated, 9 pp.] was provided to the author on 15 April 1998 by Lucy Sant'Ambrogio of the Historical Society of Bloomfield; quotations from pp. 7, 8.

[265] Federal Writers' Project, *A History of Belleville, New Jersey* [n.d., ca. 1937], 94-95 (copy from Frederick Lewis, Librarian, Silver Lake Branch, Belleville Public Library).

[266] We have now seen that between 1887 and 1931, the environment at Silver Lake had been changed dramatically. About 120 acres of farmland that were part of the bed of a prehistoric shallow lake with a sandy bottom had become a complex

of chemical and woodworking factories that produced prodigious amounts of noxious and toxic smoke, fumes, and particulate debris. There were intermittent fires and explosions, which were frequent enough to cause youngsters in the area to joke about "fires every Saturday night." Carbolic acid and other chemicals were discharged into local streams. The underground aquifer was being drained into a water tower. Train traffic through the area had increased, with attendant noise, smoke, and hazards to pedestrians, horse-drawn wagons and carriages, and motorized vehicles. The population density increased, as workers, their families, and others moved into the adjoining areas. Then the factories were gradually abandoned and employment wound down. The Silver Lake District became a nightmarish wasteland of huge, empty, falling-down factories. The quiet farmland of the Silver Lake District of Belleville and the adjacent area in Bloomfield had been transformed into a new and deadly environment; it was covered with trash and embedded with poisons.

[267] Nichols, *Ground-Water Resources of Essex County, New Jersey*, 27, Fig. 2 [map], and Table 2.

[268] Nichols, *Ground-Water Resources*, 27.

[269] Henry Herpers and Henry C. Barksdale, *Preliminary Report on the Geology and Ground-Water Supply of the Newark, New Jersey, Area*, ([Trenton, N.J.]: State of New Jersey Department of Conservation and Economic Development, 1951), 11-13; Fig. 1. The map of the Newark area in Herpers and Barksdale includes the Silver Lake District at its upper left corner.

[270] Josephson, *Edison*, 368, 496n. The original source of the quotation is unclear.

Chapter 10: Iron Mining: Ogdensburg, Sparta Mountain, Lake Hopatcong (1889-1900) – Pages 189-220

[271] William C. "Doley" Dolan to the author, 23 September 1997. Mr. Dolan is a descendant or kinsman of William and Mary Dolan, whose son, Patrick J. Dolan (b. 1869), was the first mayor of Ogdensburg. Paul Horuzy (ed.), *The Odyssey of Ogdensburg and the Sterling Hill Zinc Mine: The Story of the Growth of a Mining Town and Its Unique Place in Science and History* (Ogdensburg, N.J.: Sterling Hill Mining Co., 1990), 14-15.

[272] Wasco Hadonowetz of Ogdensburg introduced the author to William C. Dolan on 19 September 1997, saying that Mr. Dolan's father had worked for Edison at the iron mine and mill on Sparta Mountain. The quotation referenced in this note is a composite of comments made to the author by Mr. Dolan on 19 and 23 September.

[273] The schoolhouse at Edison/Ogden was moved to Franklin, where it was first used as a church by the Hungarian community, and was later transferred to the Presbyterian church. It has been modified by an addition and by interior remodeling, and it was abandoned sometime in the past decade. Although the

church school addition has deteriorated very badly, the original historic schoolhouse is still in excellent condition. The shiplap or clapboard siding and decorative trim have withstood well the severe weather in Sussex County, and the building could easily be restored to its original condition. This building is mentioned in Vanderbilt, *Edison, Chemist*, 176. Its address would be 13 Evans Street (Conversations with Mr. and Mrs. John L. Baum of the Franklin Mineral Museum, and a Mrs. Strok of 17 Evans St., Franklin; also "Franklin Mineral Museum, Inc." [brochure, n.d. (c. 1997)]).

[274] Pejorative comments of Edison's biographers regarding Ogdensburg appear in Melosi, *Edison*, 118-120 ("dreary" highlands); Conot, *Edison*, 347-348 ("harsh," "wilderness"); and Baldwin, *Edison*, 217-245 ("dirty ruined hills," "grimy").

[275] *Edison Chronology, 1879-1931* (http://edison.rutgers.edu/chron2.htm.7/1/97), pages 6 to 10 of 12.

[276] Duane Pierson, *Images of Sparta: An Historical Narrative* (Newton, N.J.: Minisink Press, 1981), 46.

[277] The year that Edison's iron mining and iron ore concentrating plant shut down has not been determined. Although several sources give the year as 1900, the termination year was not specified in the Edison Papers Project *Chronology*. The latest year that I have located is 1901, which was given in M. R. Pustay and T. K. Shea, *Abandoned Iron Mines of Sussex County, New Jersey* (Trenton: New Jersey Department of Labor, Mine Safety Section, 1982) [obtainable from this department at CN 386, Trenton 08625], 32. For Edison's cement works, the most complete analysis that I have located is in Vanderbilt, *Edison, Chemist*.

[278] For the history of the Ogden family in Ogdensburg and Sparta, see Horuzy (ed.), *Odyssey of Ogdensburg*, 6-8, 14. "The original Ogden property was eventually divided by the Lantermanns and the McKernans. The Lantermann property was purchased by Patrick Madden," who built a General Store on the farm and added an Opera House on the second floor (14). The building with the Opera House and General Store is still standing on Main Street in Ogdensburg.

[279] Wacker and Clemens, *Land Use in Early New Jersey*, 79.

[280] Alison E. Mitchell, *The New Jersey Highlands: Treasures at Risk* (Morristown, N.J.: New Jersey Conservation Foundation, 1992), 1 ("1,000 square miles"). Also, see Wacker and Clemens, *Land Use in Early New Jersey*, 223-5.

[281] The route from West Orange to Ogdensburg is shown on H. M. Gousha, *New Jersey Roadmap* (New York: Simon & Schuster, 1993). Other maps used in this case study include the U.S. Geological Survey *State of New Jersey Base Map with Highways* (1978) and *State of New Jersey Base Map with Highways and Contours* (1978); and *DeLorme Street Atlas U.S.A. 5.0* CD-Rom (Yarmouth, Me., 1997), focused on the vicinity of Ogdensburg, NJ (which shows "Edison" as if it were still a town, located exactly where it was in 1900).

Also, the following U.S. Geological Survey quadrangle maps: *Dover, N.J.* (1981), showing the route of Interstate 80 in Morris County and New Jersey 15 in

Sussex County, including the northern part of Lake Hopatcong and the villages of Woodport, Hurdtown, and Espanong, Tierney's Corner (where Route 15 is intersected by County Road 615, which is now called Edison Road, although it was known as Cooper Road when this map was made), and the southeastern part of Sparta Township; *Franklin, N.J.* (1954, photorevised 1971), showing the town of Ogdensburg, a little village named Edison with a mine pit beside it and Edison Pond to the east, the route of an "Old Railroad Grade" that proceeds south from the Edison mine into Morris County [this railroad should, but does not, appear on the adjacent *Dover* quadrangle map], and most of the village of Franklin; *Stanhope, N.J.* (1981), showing the southern portion of Lake Hopatcong and the southern part of Sparta Mountain; *Newton East, N.J. (1954*, photorevised 1971), showing the western portion of Sterling Hill adjacent to Ogdensburg on the western rim of the Wallkill River valley; and *Hamburg, N.J.* (1954, photorevised 1971), showing the northern portion of the village of Franklin in Sussex County.

[282] I made field trips to Ogdensburg on 19 and 23 September and 6 October 1997, and had telephone conversations with Mr. Wasco Hadonowetz on 18, 23, and 24 September. On my third trip, I also visited Franklin, N.J., and studied the old schoolhouse from the Edison mine, which now is an abandoned church building. See: *The Story of Ogdensburg* (Ogdensburg [N.J.]: Ogdensburg Bicentennial Committee, n.d. [about 1976]), from the Sussex County Library, Newton, N. J.; and Pierson, *Images of Sparta*. Also, Pete J. Dunn, *The Story of Franklin and Sterling Hill* (Washington, D. C.: Department of Mineral Sciences, Smithsonian Institution, 1997); Horuzy (ed.), *Odyssey of Ogdensburg*; *Sterling Hill Mining Museum Map and Guide* (Ogdensburg: Sterling Hill Mining Museum, n.d. [1997]); and Pustay and Shea, *Abandoned Iron Mines of Sussex County*. Additionally, Karl Anderson, *Location of Buildings: Works of New Jersey & Pennsylvania Concentrating Works, Edison, Sussex Co., N.J.* ([1893, corrected to Nov. 1899], copied by Anderson on 8-30-1973, to which he added roads, mine cuts and a power line from a 1973 real estate atlas of Sussex County); this map was "Redrawn 9-12-1980 by J. J. Bekaert." Illustrations of the mine are in Conot, *Edison*; Baldwin, *Edison*; and Byron M. Vanderbilt, *Thomas Edison, Chemist* (Washington, D.C.: American Chemical Society, 1971; paperback ed., 1980). The question of the nature of Edison's personal living environment at the mine site is still obscure. Three newspaper clippings, framed and hanging on the wall of Lyons House (source and date not specified), state that: "Thomas Edison was a frequent guest of the Lyons House while working at the Edison Mines."

[283] An interview with Mr. Dolan on 22 May 1990, and his photograph, appear in *Odyssey of Ogdensburg*, 35. During my trip to the Edison mine/mill site with Mr. Dolan on 23 September 1997, he told me that he had never previously gone as far back into the area of the old mines (that pre-dated Edison's work) than we went on that date. The amenities, according to Mr. Dolan's father, included dances on Saturday night with musicians who were brought in by Edison, and good housing on the mountain, with electricity and running water.

284 The map of Ogdensburg and Franklin in *Odyssey of Ogdensburg* (8) states that Edison Road in Ogdensburg is the route "to Edison's mine." The location of the Edison mine and the pit known as the Horseshoe Cut can be seen on the *Franklin* quadrangle map at about N41^{0}3', W74^{0}34'. Details of the sites of buildings at the mine appear on Karl Anderson's map, *Location of Buildings* (1973), previously referred to.

285 Horuzy (ed.), *Odyssey of Ogdensburg*, 5.

286 Pierson, *Images of Sparta*. Horuzy (ed.), *Odyssey of Ogdensburg*, 3.

287 Pierson, *Images of Sparta*; Horuzy (ed.), *Odyssey of Ogdensburg;* and *Sterling Hill Mining Museum Map and Guide*.

288 Robert Ogden II was a distant cousin of Thomas Edison's Ogden ancestors. (Recall that Edison's father was Samuel Ogden Edison, Jr.) The relationship between Robert Ogden and Thomas Edison can be parsed from a study of the charts in Wheeler, *Ogden Family*. Sparta separated from Ogdensburg in 1845, according to a sign at the border of Sparta on State Route 15. The Ogden/Edison mine is located within the township limits of Sparta, although it is closer to the center of Ogdensburg. The mine site is now marked by a sign that calls it "Sparta Mountain," protected by the New Jersey Department of Environmental Protection, Division of Fish, Game & Wildlife, and there is no sign at this site now that identifies it with Thomas Edison's previous presence there.

289 According to Dunn, *Franklin and Sterling Hill*, the three main zinc-containing ores at Sterling Hill are franklinite, willemite, and zincite (85). Franklinite is non-fluorescent. Willemite is zinc silicate; it produces a green color in fluorescence (under ultraviolet light) and in phosphorescence (visible color that persists in darkness after activation by ultraviolet or intense visible light). Zincite, which is zinc oxide, is the most valuable of the three zinc ores, since there are many commercial uses for zinc oxide, including the manufacture of paint and pharmaceutical products.

290 A copy of the 1880 U.S. census of "Ogden Mine" [village], Sparta Township, is on file at the Old Firehouse and Old Schoolhouse Museum in Ogdensburg. It shows, by my count, 300 people in 47 families who were then living in the village of Ogden Mine. In addition, by Mr. Hadonowetz's count, this census shows 104 with the occupation of iron miner in Ogden Mine and 23 with the same occupation in the town of Ogdensburg.

291 Wasco Hadonowetz calculates that Edison's first visit to Ogensburg occurred on 8 October 1889, based on the information in Conot, *Edison*, 287.

292 Horuzy (ed.), *Odyssey of Ogdensburg*: "Edison spent much time in Ogdensburg and the villagers were fascinated and enthralled with the famous inventor's presence. . . . He stayed at the Lyon House (later Sweney's)." (11-12).

293 The railroads in the vicinity of Ogdensburg at the turn of the century are shown on a map in Lee, *Morris Canal*, 3. Also see Mitchell, *New Jersey Highlands*, "Historic Railroads," 35-38.

[294] The four "Edison houses" appear in an old photograph in Horuzy (ed.), *Odyssey of Ogdensburg*, 16. Two of the houses are used as dwellings in Franklin, according to John L. "Jack" Baum, on 4 May 1998 Mr. Baum (b. 1916) was formerly Resident Geologist at the Franklin Mine; his biography and photograph appear in Dunn, *Franklin and Sterling Hill*, 64.

[295] Horuzy (ed.), *Odyssey of Ogdensburg*, 12.

[296] The Edison mine site appears on the *Franklin* quadrangle as a small cluster of buildings at a place identified on the map as "Edison," across Edison Road from a horseshoe-shaped mine, marked with the symbol of a pick and shovel. The "Horseshoe Cut" is correctly marked, but the buildings are now gone. This spot is shown as a place called "Edison" on the *DeLorme Street Atlas USA 5.0* CD-rom (Yarmouth, ME, 1997), at coordinates $N41^{0}03.836'$, $W74^{0}34.064'$.

[297] Quotation from Horuzy (ed.), *Ogdensburg*, 11 ("stone foundation remnants").

[298] Anderson, *Location of Buildings: Edison, Sussex Co.*

[299] The relatively small area that was occupied by Edison's Horseshoe Cut and ore-milling plant is a distinct contrast to the very large open pit mines at Franklin and Sterling Hill, as shown in Dunn, *Franklin and Sterling Hill*. See, for example, what Dunn properly calls the "massive" open cut at Franklin (pp. 26-27); the "great Taylor Mill" on the rim of the very large Buckwheat Cut (pp. 41-42); and the "great Palmer Mill" (pp. 46-47).

[300] My identification of this tree as a black spruce (*Picea mariana* [Mill.]) is based on the description, photographs and map in *National Audubon Society Field Guide to North American Trees: Eastern Region* (New York: Chanticler Press, Inc., [1980] 1996), 284, Plates 24 and 481; and C. Frank Brockman, *Trees of North America* (New York: Golden Press, 1968), 38-39.

[301] On October 1, 1997, Doug Tarr of the ENHS said that the "White House" where Edison lived when he stayed at the mine was located in Cuckoo Flats, not at the site shown on the Anderson map as "Edison?"

[302] I am indebted to the comments of Steve Misiur at the Sterling Hill Mining Museum for informing me of Edison's contributions to the magnetic separation of iron from franklinite at Sterling Hill.

[303] Pustay and Shea, *Abandoned Iron Mines of Sussex County*, Introduction (1-12); Ogden Mine (32-34); Plates I (Overview) and 28-30 (Ogden Mines).

[304] Lisa Martins, "'Cabinet on Road' Makes a Stop: Sparta Mountain Saved," in *New Jersey Herald* (12 February 1997).

[305] The size and ownership of the Sparta Mountain WMA were described in a telephone conversation between the author and Tony Petrangelo, Chief of the Fish, Game, and Wildlife Service, New Jersey Department of Environmental Protection, on 1 October 1997. A map of the "Sparta Mt. WMA" was provided by the secretary to Mr. Petrangelo (undated).

The Sparta Mountain purchase is described in the following publications that I received from Mr. Petrangelo: Jeff Woosman, "State, Private Groups Help Preserve Sussex Space: Real Mountain News," *Morris Co. (N.J.) Daily Record* 1, no. 5 (Spring 1997); Martins, "Sparta Mountain Saved"; James F. Hall, "Justification for Acquisition of Sparta Mountain [with $700,000 of Green Acres funds]," Project No. 5SH2004A, 25 July 1996 (Assistant Commissioner, N.J. DEP); *Regulations of Division of Fish, Game, and Wildlife*, Chapter 7, Subchapter 2, "Use of All Land and Water Areas Under the Control of the Division of Fish, Game and Wildlife" (17 June-19 August 1996) [in contrast to the opinion of the DEP, there are NO signs here regarding prohibition of removal of rock, sand or water; or artifacts such as building materials or manufactured objects].

[306] Pustay and Shea, *Abandoned Iron Mines of Sussex County*, 32. The date given here, 1901, is not referenced. If correct, it would extend Edison's operations in Sussex County for one year longer than any other author that I have read, and thus overlapping for an additional year with the work that he was beginning with limestone and cement in Warren County.

[307] Mitchell, *New Jersey Highlands*, "Carbonate Rocks," 5-7; and "The Morris Canal and Historic Railroads," 34-38.

[308] John Johnson, in Lee (ed.), *Tales the Boatmen Told* (original ed., 1977), 145.

[309] My investigation of Edison Road/Route 615 in Morris County began in conversations in September 1997 with several people near the large Pathmark store on Route 15 in Jefferson Township. No one that I spoke with could imagine any reason for this street being named for Edison, other than that he was a famous person. None were aware of any connection between this point and Sparta or Ogdensburg. However, after I saw the route of an old railroad marked on the *Franklin* quadrangle map, extending almost due south to this location from the old Edison/Ogden mine, I realized that this was the Ogden Mine Railroad, which ran between Lake Hopatcong and the mine village known as Edison.

[310] H. M. Gousha, *New Jersey Roadmap*; and Lee, *Morris Canal*, 3 (map of Morris Canal). According to Mitchell, *New Jersey Highlands*, in western New Jersey the corridor of Interstate 80 is the lower limit of the last ice to cover New Jersey -- the Wisconsin glacier. The terminal moraine of this glacier is "the most prominent glacial feature in the Highlands, . . . stretching across the region from Belvidere on the Delaware River, through Hackettstown and Dover, to Morristown" and then southeast to Perth Amboy (4). We had previously observed that the Morris Canal passed north from Bloomfield into Passaic County, as it crossed the Passaic River into Paterson. To the west of Paterson, the canal remained north and then west of the Passaic River. After leaving Paterson, the canal crossed the Ramapo River tributary of the Passaic at Mountain View on the Pompton Turnpike (now Route 23).

[311] Lee, *Morris Canal*, 3-4 (locks and planes); 6-7 (distances); 59 (elevation).

[312] H. M. Gousha, *New Jersey Roadmap*; and Lee, *Morris Canal*, 3 (map of Morris Canal).

[313] Lee, *Morris Canal*, 4-5.

[314] Lee, *Morris Canal*, 27-79 (127 photographs of canal from Wharton [formerly called Port Oram, where the "Port Oram Iron Company," shown on p.79, was located] to Port Warren); and Tinkham, *Morris Canal Water Parkway* (Nos. 41-57). Tinkham gives the altitude of the canal at Lake Hopatcong as 928 feet, in contrast to Lee's 914 feet. Tinkham: "The D.L.&W. parallels the canal from Paterson to the Delaware River. . . the Morris County Electric Railway is reached [by the canal] at Boonton, Rockaway, Dover, Wharton, Ledgwood and Hopatcong." Tinkham asserted in 1914 that the beginning of the Morris Canal Parkway "should be at Roseville in Newark, where the canal is crossed by the D.L.&W. R.R. tracks."

[315] Lee (ed.), *Tales the Boatmen Told*, photo, 4; *Bloomsbury, N.J.* and *Eaton, Pa.-N.J.* quadrangle maps; and Helena W. Stone, in Lee (ed.), Ibid., 234-235.

[316] Edison: Handwritten note, telephoned 1:40 p.m., 22 June 1900, to Judge Elliott at Stewartsville, N.J. from mine site at Edison, N.J. (Pierce Papers, p.13).

[317] Pierce Papers, p.2 (Edison to Olmsted, 17 May 1900) [It is not clear whether Olmstead or Olmsted is the correct spelling, since both spellings appear in these papers].

[318] Ibid., pp. 3-6 (Edison to Olmsted, and Olmsted's reply, 17 May 1900).

[319] Ibid., pp. 14-15 (Edison to Mallory, 26 July 1900).

[320] Lee, *Morris Canal*, 5.

[321] Mitchell, *New Jersey Highlands*, "Historic Railroads" and "Highlands Railroads Today," 35-38. About fifteen miles east of Lake Hopatcong, between Rockaway and Montville, the D.L.&W. divided into two branches, each of which reached Newark. The northern branch of the D.L.&W. ran from this point along the side of the Morris Canal to Paterson and then south into Newark along the route that we previously observed that the canal followed through Bloomfield and Belleville. The southern branch, which was a more direct route home for Edison, was known as the Morris and Essex Branch; it passed south into Morristown and then east through the Oranges. The D.L.&W. R.R. (which later became the Erie and Lackawanna R.R. and is now one of the lines of New Jersey Transit) ran east from Lake Hopatcong to Newark. The northern and southern routes joined at the Roseville Station in Newark, just west of Branch Brook Park.

[322] New Jersey Transit, "Morris & Essex Lines" (1997). New Jersey Transit passenger trains no longer stop at the West Orange station on their way in from Hackettstown, but the railroad that Edison used is still in operation and the express run from Hackettstown to Newark now takes only one hour and twenty-five minutes. It no longer extends west of Montclair, although a connector has been proposed that may once again enable train travelers to proceed west out of Montclair. The southern branch of the Morris and Essex Rail Line, now

known as the Morristown Line, still goes as far as west as Hackettstown, thirteen miles west of Lake Hopatcong. Hackettstown is half way from Lake Hopatcong to New Village. This would have been the rail line that Edison took when he traveled between his iron mine and the property that he was acquiring in New Village for his cement plant.

[323] Pierce Papers, p.13 (Edison to Judge Elliott, 1:40 p.m., 22 June 1900).

[324] Some of Edison's factory buildings remain in New Village, as do three of his great stone quarries in this vicinity. Edison indelibly transformed the environment of New Village, Stewartsville, and Oxford, New Jersey, in ways that are still very visible, yet which are not unpleasant or unappreciated. Edison Portland Cement was used to construct buildings and other structures which have been very durable but which have had a mixed report card from the environmental perspective. The Ogden Mine Railroad was removed for scrap during World War II, according to John T. Cunningham, *Railroading in New Jersey* [Newark, N.J.?]: Associated Railroads of New Jersey, [1951?], in which a photograph of the abandoned railway is shown, prior to its removal.

Chapter 11: Edison and Cement: Warren, Union and Essex Counties (1899-1931) – Pages 221-266

[325] Charles Hummel, personal communication to the author, 13 October 1997.

[326] New Village and Stewartsville are adjacent communities in Franklin Township, Warren County, New Jersey. Edison's cement plant and quarry were in New Village, but his post office address was Stewartsville, and the same is true for Victaulic, which now occupies Edison's old 1906 factory building on Edison Road in New Village. New Village and Stewartsville are adjacent communities in Franklin Township, Warren County, New Jersey. Edison's cement plant and quarry were in New Village, but his post office address was Stewartsville, and the same is true for Victaulic, which now occupies Edison's old 1906 factory building on Edison Road in New Village.

[327] Sources and references cited in previous sections include Josephson, *Edison*; Conot, *Edison*; Melosi, *Edison*; Millard, *Edison*; and Baldwin, *Edison*. Also, Vanderbilt, *Edison, Chemist*; Lee, *Morris Canal*; Lee (ed.), *Tales the Boatmen Told*; Tinkham, *Morris Canal Water Parkway*; Wacker and Clemens, *Land Use in Early New Jersey*; and Mitchell, *New Jersey Highlands*. Relevant illustrations appear in Clark, *Edison*, 198 (photograph of a cement phonograph cabinet); and in Meadowcroft (ed.), *Life of Thomas A. Edison*, unnumbered centerfold. Information regarding this period in Edison's life was in the *Edison Chronology* of the Edison Papers Project (http://edison.rutgers.edu/chron2.htm, 7/1/97); and Ibid., 5/10/98 (items were found in the years 1898 and 1907).

[328] I reviewed the following monographs and articles for this section: Michael Peterson, "Thomas Edison's Concrete Houses," *Invention and Technology*

(Winter 1996): 50-56; "Edison's Concrete Houses," *Fine Homebuilding* (March 1998), back cover; George K. Warne, *A Look at Warren County* (Belvidere, N.J.: Warren County Cultural and Heritage Commission, 1991), 32 (photograph of Edison's quarry in operation in New Village, and "bird's eye" drawing of the Edison Portland Cement Plant); Newark, N.J., *Star Ledger* (19 March 1992), "In the Towns," page NW-1; Dennis N. Bertland, *Early Architecture of Warren County* ([Belvidere, N.J.] Warren County Board of Chosen Freeholders, n.d. [1976]), 6: Elisha Thatcher House, 50 Good Springs Road, Franklin Township, between New Village and Broadway; James P. Snell, *History of Sussex and Warren Counties, New Jersey, with Illustrations and Biographical Sketches of its Prominent Men and Pioneers* (Philadelphia: Everts & Peck, 1881); and John T. Cunningham, *This is New Jersey*, 4th edition (New Brunswick, N.J.: Rutgers University Press, 1994), 20-31 ("Warren: Rural Destiny"), and 28 (on Edison's plant, and the Vulcanite Portland Cement Company in Alpha, N.J.).

Some aspects of the history of the Morris Canal and Warren County were clarified for me by James Lee, Port Warren, N.J. On 30 September 1997 Mr. Lee told me how to find Edison's quarry in Stewartsville -- a place where Mr. Lee swam when he was a boy. Various aspects of the history of Edison's plant, quarry, and cement road in New Village were described and shown to me on the same day by Gary Meddaugh and Bill Mogilski of Victaulic, Stewartsville and New Village, N.J. With their help, I found the large body of water known as "Edison Lake," which was formerly Edison's quarry in New Village. Marie Acceturo, Oxford, N.J., helped me find Edison's quarry in Oxford on 25 April 1998; and George Campbell, Curator, Edison Memorial Tower, Edison Township, Middlesex County, N.J., showed me two bricks that were salvaged from a wall of Edison's cement kiln at New Village. I conducted interviews by telephone with Carl Brown of Easton, Pa., on 28 April 1998, and with Linda Kimler, Oxford, N.J., on 13 May 1998 (See Appendix for details of these conversations). I spoke by telephone with George K. Warne of the Warren County Historical and Cultural Commission, Oxford, N.J., on 13 May 1998.

A copy of the Organization Chart of Thomas A. Edison Industries (1930) was made for me by Douglas Tarr, Edison National Historic Site. This chart shows that one division of TAE, Inc. was "Edison Portland Cement Company / W. D. Cloos, Vice Pres. & Genl. Mgr / Manufacturing, New Village, N.J. – Pohatcong Railroad Co. / Selling, Orange, N.J., New York, Boston, Philadelphia."

Houses built from Edison Portland Cement were described to me by Helen McGuirk, of 96 Whittingham Place, West Orange (at the corner of McLaughlin Place and Valley St., Orange); and by Clifford F. Lindholm, III, of Montclair, N.J. (303 No. Mountain Ave., Upper Montclair). On 6 August 1997 I was oriented to the houses built by Edison on Ingersoll Terrace in Union, N.J., by Mrs. Anne Connell and her sons, Roger and Dennis, and by their adjacent neighbors, who showed me through the ground floor of their cement house.

The librarians of the Franklin Township Branch of the Warren County Library in Washington, N.J., kindly made their books and vertical files on the history of Warren County available for my review. Although there was nothing on Edison's work in Warren County in the files of this library, several issues of *The Furnace* (Newsletter of the Warren County Cultural and Heritage Commission) for 1995-1996 provided useful background information regarding Warren County history.

Professor Margaret Pierce of Knoxville, Tenn., generously provided me with copies of several pages of Edison's correspondence and notes, and a sketch map of the area of the plant in New Village that was drawn by Edison in 1900. Other maps used for this case study include the 7.5 minute quadrangle maps of *Bloomsbury, N.J.* (showing Stewartsville and New Village); and *Easton, Pa. and N.J.* (showing Phillipsburg, N.J.). Also: *New Jersey Roadmap* (Maspeth, N.Y.: American Map Co., n.d. [ca. 1997]); *New Jersey Roadmap* (New York: H. M. Gousha, 1993), and Ibid. (1996); *Morris/Sussex/Warren Counties Atlas* (Maspeth, N.Y.: Hagstrom Map Co., 1997); New Jersey Transit, "Morris & Essex Lines" (1997), and "Boonton Branch" (1998); and maps of the area from Easton, Pa.. to Hackettstown, N.J. printed from *DeLorme Street Atlas USA* 5.0 CD-Rom (1997) at scales of 1:250,000 to 1:7,812, showing the route of the Morris Canal, adjacent railroads, and Edison's quarries at Stewartsville, New Village, and Oxford, N.J.

[329] Mitchell, *New Jersey Highlands*, 5 (citing R. Dalton and F. J. Markewicz, "Stratigraphy and Characteristics of Cavern Development in the Carbonate Rocks of New Jersey" [*Bulletin of the National Speleological Society* 34 (number 4, 1972): 115-128]).

[330] Mitchell, *New Jersey Highlands*, 3.

[331] Snell, *History of Sussex and Warren Counties*, 477.

[332] Mitchell, *New Jersey Highlands*, 3-5. John L. "Jack" Baum, Curator of the Franklin Mineral Museum, said to me on 4 May 1998 that "There are 22 miles of marble up here.

[333] Mitchell, *New Jersey Highlands*, 4 (lower border of Wisconsin glacier's terminal moraine "terminating at what is now Perth Amboy"); 18 ("southernmost advance of the Wisconsin Glaciation . . . south of Interstate Route 80").

[334] Vanderbilt describes the use of clay, sand and gravel, and various types of limestone in the manufacture of Portland cement and concrete (*Edison, Chemist*, 179-183).

[335] Mitchell, *New Jersey Highlands*, 14.

[336] Mitchell, Ibid., 15.

[337] Mitchell, Ibid., 16.

[338] Mitchell, Ibid., 15-16.

[339] Mitchell, Ibid., 17 ("iron mine . . . other areas in New Jersey); Cunningham, *This is New Jersey*, 21 ("Kittatinny Mountain . . . down to farming").

[340] Cunningham, op. cit., 21-23.

[341] Cunningham, Ibid., 24 (Oxford furnace; formation of Warren Co.); Mitchell, *New Jersey Highlands*, 108 (land use).

[342] Mitchell, Ibid., 34-35 (Morris Canal); Lee, *Morris Canal*, 8-9 (Port Delaware and the railroads at Easton and Phillipsburg); telephone interview with Carl Brown, Easton, Penn., 28 April 1998 (Ingersoll-Rand).

[343] Cunningham, op. cit., 25-27.

[344] Mitchell, op. cit., 41. Also see Bertland, *Early Architecture of Warren County*, 47-75: There are 22 historic buildings in the "Middle Musconetcong and Pohatcong Valleys," of which the closest to Edison Road in New Village are seven old stone houses along about a two mile stretch of Abbott Road (which parallels Edison Road to the northwest). One is the Warne-Castner House (1815) on Asbury's Main Street; another is Benjamin Warne's House and Mill (1810) on Route 57 in Broadway. The nearest historic building to the Edison plant in New Village that is illustrated in Bertland is the Elisha Thatcher House (1817) on Good Springs Road, "overlooking Pohatcong Creek" (p.54). It is less than a mile from Edison Road.

[345] Edison to Judge Elliott, 22 June 1900 (Pierce Papers, pp. 12, 13; map, p.9).

[346] What Edison labeled as "Mountain Road" on his sketch map is now called Good Springs Road, and the labels "DL+W" and "Cement Co." appear in his handwriting on the map (Pierce Papers, p.9). He twice said "I have no maps" in his telephone message at 1:40 p.m. on 22 June 1900 to Judge Elliott (Pierce Papers, p.13).

[347] Edison's communications of 22 June 1900 provide an unusually detailed glimpse into the way that he conducted operations in Warren County. It has been difficult to relate what Edison did in Warren County to what he was doing elsewhere at the same time, because exact dates for Edison's operations in Warren County have not been presented by any of the authorities that I have studied as background for this case study. As will become apparent -- even the years of Edison's business operations in Warren County are difficult to determine from existing summaries of his work. For example, as of 1 July 1997, the Edison Papers Project *Chronology* provided only two statements regarding Edison and cement: "December 1898: Prepares to visit Pennsylvania's Lehigh Valley region to observe Portland Cement plants" and "Fall 1907: Receives national attention for his proposed poured concrete house." Baldwin is typical of Edison's biographers. He refers to a few years (e.g., the inventor's proposal for a poured cement house in 1901 [*Edison, 298*]; and his royalties of "one cent on every barrel of cement produced by other companies" in the 1920s [279]), but Baldwin does not state when Edison started work in New Village.

In *Edison, Chemist*, Vanderbilt presents the most thorough analysis that I have seen of the chemical and engineering practices that Edison employed to manufacture cement, but Vanderbilt provides few dates and details of the business history of the cement company. A much more complete summary of the company's history appears in Conot, *Edison*, 346-348.

[348] Trout and Weston, *Primary Battery Division: 50 Years of Progress*, 2: "1893: Edison-Leland cells were used for operating the first low-voltage automatic block semaphore signal in the world near Phillipsburg, N.J. This was the earliest application of copper-oxide cells at way-side block signals." Edison Papers Project *Chronology, 1879-1931*, 10 (for Lehigh valley, 1898). Pierce Papers, 10: "This . . . is the same route that you, Lehman and Darling walked over last Spring" (Judge Elliott to Edison: 22 June 1900, 3:20 p.m.). My estimate of the size of Edison's plant in 1900 (somewhat over 160 acres) is based on the size and shape of the area which Edison indicated was the "Cement Co." on his sketch map, and transferring the boundaries of this property to the *Bloomsbury* quadrangle map. Edison showed that his "Cement Co." extended from the railroad to what is now Good Springs Road, a distance of about one-half mile. It was rectangular, with the frontage along both the railroad and Good Springs Road (which he called "Mountain Road") being slightly longer than the frontage along Edison Road (which he called "New Village Road"). A square piece of land that is one-half mile on each side is 160 acres in size. Several authors state that Edison acquired 800 acres of land for his cement operations (e.g., Baldwin, and Vanderbilt, *Edison*, 183), but I have not been able to confirm the validity of this statement; for example, I do not know if it includes his quarry in Oxford, N.J. Carl Brown believes that Edison's operations in New Village and Stewartsville utilized about 100-200 acres of land, although he believes that Edison may well have had leases and deeds to larger tracts than that.

[349] The proposed road would run along the railroad for a short distance and then take a right angle turn to join the Mountain Road. Judge Elliott said that "The road as laid down in my papers is north of the Lackawanna and runs East." Edison was puzzled and irritated, for he thought that the proposed road would have to *turn* on the north side of his property to run east. The situation was confounded because the judge was trying to get permission for an access road at the best possible price. He was feinting by proposing a road that ran east along the railroad but he wanted to build a road that ran west along the railroad. If it is difficult for the reader to comprehend all of this, rest assured that it was no less difficult for Edison and Elliott to communicate with each other about it. If Edison could have FAXed his sketch map to Elliott, it would have been helpful, but the two men were able to communicate only by telephone, and through intermediaries at that; Edison's stenographer was one R. S. Cobb.

[350] Edison's love for riding on freight trains was documented by photographs, including one of the inventor standing on the cowcatcher, as he was said to have done many years earlier near Rawlins, Wyoming. See Norman Brauer, *There to Breathe the Beauty: The Camping Trips of Henry Ford, Thomas Edison, Harvey Firestone, John Burroughs* (Dalton, PA: Norman Brauer, 1995).

[351] For roads mentioned in this paragraph, see Hagstrom's *Morris/Sussex/Warren Counties Atlas*; and *DeLorme Street Atlas USA* CD-Rom 5.0 (1997), focused on Hackettstown, N.J., and magnified to a scale of 1:31,250 (one-half mile to the inch), which shows the Morris Canal from Hackettstown to Waterloo Lakes. A sign on Route 57 about one mile southwest of the intersection with Edison Road states: "Entering Franklin Township / The Concrete Mile / Built in 1912 by Thomas Edison / First Concrete Highway in America." Although Edison drove his own horse and buggy when he was in New Village, he also had an automobile there. Helena Stone said on 15 December 1974 that Edison used to drive a buggy from New Village to her father's store in Stewartsville "to pick up eggs that he'd bought to bring down to Orange over the weekend" (in Lee, *Tales the Boatmen Told*, 234-235). On 28 April 1998 Carl Brown told me about Edison's car and driver in New Village.

[352] "Historic Speedwell, 333 Speedwell Ave., Morristown . . . This is the site of the 1838 first public demonstration of Morse Code" (Newark *Star Ledger*, "New Jersey Fun Guide" [3 May 1998], 22).

[353] The Morris Turnpike became a state road in 1924 (Warren County Cultural and Heritage Commission: *The Furnace*, vol. 6, no. 3, July 1996: 1, 4).

[354] The scheduled train ride from Orange Station to Hackettstown would now take about one and one-half hours, although the total elapsed time to make the trip would be longer, because of the zig-zag route that must be taken to make the necessary connections (see New Jersey Transit, *Morris & Essex Lines* schedule, 1997). I have been unable to verify that it is now possible to make the round trip from Orange to Hackettstown in three hours, because of the lack of weekend and holiday trains, and a change in the weekday train schedule that left me stranded at the station on my attempt to recreate Edison's trip.

[355] Baldwin, *Edison*, 273 (motion picture patent); 274 (kinetoscope); 279 (West Orange factory and million dollar revenue); 283 (storage battery). Francis Upton, the "brilliant graduate of Bowdoin and Princeton" who had joined Edison at Menlo Park (Conot, *Edison*, 490), left the Lamp Works in 1894 and became a senior engineer at the iron mine. I believe that he moved with Mallory from the iron mine to the cement project, for his name appears on Edison's sketch map of 22 June 1900, as follows: A house labeled "Upton" in New Village/Stewartsville appears on Edison's map of June 1900. It is located near the corner of what Edison called "New Village Road" (now Edison Road) and "Mountain Road" (now Good Springs Road), immediately adjacent to, and southwest of, what Edison labeled as "Darling's House." The latter house, which stood on Mountain Road opposite the end of New Village Road, is where Edison usually lived when he stayed in New Village, according to Carl Brown (interview with author, 28 April 1998); it was the house on the "company farm." I have found no other record that confirms Upton's presence at the cement plant, but at Menlo Park, Upton's house was very close to Edison's. And if what Mr. Brown recalls

from conversations with former employees of Edison is correct, the house labeled "Upton" was only a few away from Edison's house in New Village. Francis Upton and Thomas Edison remained close for the rest of Upton's life, and Upton's sons, Francis (Jr.) and Curtis, were friends of Thomas Edison's son, Charles. The three young men had some hilarious experiences together in Colorado and California in about 1913 (Venable, *Out of the Shadow*, 41-44). Francis Upton, Sr., died of abdominal cancer in 1921 (Conot, *Edison*, 438).

[356] Baldwin, *Edison*, 260 (Tom, Jr., 1897-1898); 261 (William Leslie at boarding school); and 267-270 (deaths of Theodore [July 1898], Jane [November 1898], and Lewis [February 1899] Miller; birth of Theodore Edison [July 1898]).

[357] Individual Line and Branch schedules do not show the entire picture of New Jersey Transit's routes in this part of New Jersey. The best view is obtained by examination of the map of New Jersey Transit's rail lines, framed on the wall of Penn Station in Newark. Pennsylvania Station was completed in 1935, four years after Edison died. Penn Station replaced the Market Street Station that had served the Pennsylvania Railroad in Newark since the 1830s. (See plaque designating Penn Station as a National Historic Site.) The Pennsylvania Railroad's Market Street Station was about one hundred yards south of the present location of Penn Station, which would have placed it almost immediately across the street from Edison's factory on Ward Street.

[358] William H. Meadowcroft, *The Boy's Life of Edison, with Autobiographical Notes by Mr. Edison* (New York: Harper & Row, 1911; 1949), 192-193: "[W]hen the cement plant was nearly finished . . . he went up to look it over and see what needed to be done. On the arrival of the train at ten-forty in the morning he went to the mill, and, starting at one end, went through the plant to the other end, examining every detail. . . . In the afternoon, at five-thirty, he took a train for home, and on arriving there a few hours later got out some note-books and began to write from memory the things needing change or attention." Meadowcroft was Edison's Private Secretary from 1909 to 1931. He succeeded Alfred O. Tate, whose recollections of Edison and the Duke of Marlborough were mentioned in the case study of Harrison, N.J. (Conot, *Edison*, 487).

[359] Washington's army camped in Morristown in the winters of 1777-1778 and 1779-1780 (Cunningham, *This is New Jersey*). The Morristown National Historic Park marks the winter encampment of the Continental Army in 1779-1780 (*Newark [N.J.] Star Ledger* "New Jersey Fun Guide" [3 May 1998], 22).

[360] See New Jersey Transit, "Boonton Line" (Effective April 5, 1998, through Fall 1998); Jeff Woosnam, "Musconetcong Neighbors Help Bring a Lake Back to Health: Stanhope Planning Board to Mark Success in Clearing the Waters," *Newark [N.J.] Star Ledger* (17 May 1998), Section 1, 44; Lee, *Morris Canal*, 54-57 (views of Stanhope ca. 1892 and "a reservoir, later named Lake

Musconetcong"); Lake Hopatcong "State's Largest Lake," in AAA Clubs of New Jersey, "New Jersey Road Scholar (n.d., ?1997), 16; and green-lined scenic routes on H. M. Gousha's *New Jersey Roadmap* (1996).

[361] Telephone message from Judge A. Elliott, at Stewartsville, N.J., to Edison, at Edison/Ogden, N.J., 22 June 1900 (Pierce Papers, 3-4).

[362] Messages exchanged between Judge A. Elliott and Edison, 22 June 1900, and Edison's sketch map of the property surrounding his "Cement Co." (Pierce Papers, pages 8-13).

[363] New Jersey Route 57 was called Washington Avenue in one of the oral histories in Lee (ed.), *Tales the Boatmen Told*, and in Gladys Harry Eggler, "Thomas Alva Edison and the Warren County Connection" *The Furnace* [News Quarterly of the Warren County Cultural and Heritage Commission, Oxford, N.J.] vol. 8, no. 2 (April 1998): 1-3. The distances, roads, depressions, elevations, and other geographic features are taken from the *Bloomsbury* quadrangle map.

[364] The Edison "company farm" was described to me by telephone on 28 April 1998 by Carl Brown (See Appendix for details of this conversation). This paragraph draws on the statement by Judge A. Elliott to Edison by telephone on the morning of 22 June 1900 (Pierce Papers, 8).

[365] Elliott to Edison, morning, 22 June 1900 (Pierce Papers, 8).

[366] Elliott to Edison, Ibid.

[367] Warren County Board of Chosen Freeholders, *Warren County* [map] (Convent Station, N.J.: General Drafting Co., Inc., 1988); Edison to Elliott [22 June 1900] (Pierce Papers, 12).

[368] Edison to Elliott via R. S. Cobb, 1:40 p.m., 22 June 1900 (Pierce Papers, 12).

[369] Elliott to Edison, 3:20 p.m., 22 June 1900 (Pierce Papers, 10).

[370] Ibid.

[371] Elliott to Edison, 4:15 p.m., 22 June 1900 (Pierce Papers, 11).

[372] The Edison Cement Company and Edison Quarry went out of business in 1942.

[373] Comments made by Edison's biographers, regional historians, and historians of the building trades are largely undocumented and often appear to be unreferenced restatements of statements made by other writers. Oral history may provide depth and detail, but many comments from those who have lived in Warren County during the past century must be regarded as interesting but unconfirmed legends and stories.

[374] Michael Peterson, "Thomas Edison's Concrete Houses" *Invention & Technology* (Winter 1996): 50-56. Also, *Fine Homebuilding* (March 1998), back cover. *Scientific American* (1911), quoted in Peterson, "Edison's Concrete Houses."

[375] Eggler, "Edison and Warren County." *Washington [N.J.] Star* (1902), quoted in Eggler, "Edison and Warren County."

[376] Lee, *Morris Canal*, 6. Photographs of the canal and its surrounding environment from Stewartsville to Broadway, N.J., appear on pp. 33-36.

[377] Lee (ed.), *Tales the Boatmen Told*, 234-235 (Stone's store in Stewartsville); 97-98 ("New Village was a small settlement" . . . "of Italian extraction" . . . "social event"; 6 (sawmills); 111 (seven miles); 128 (fresh bread); 117 ("a girl"); 203 ("worked at the Edison").

[378] My statement that 800 acres represents one-eighth of the land in the valley refers to the middle portion of the Pohatcong valley, between the village of Pleasant Valley and Stewartsville. This part of the Pohatcong valley is about seven miles long and one to two miles in width.

[379] Vanderbilt, *Edison, Chemist*, 126 (ten kilns; 1,100 barrels per day per kiln). The kilns are now gone, but the bricks were salvaged and sold as mementos. Two are in the museum at the Edison Memorial Tower in Menlo Park, Edison Township, New Jersey.

[380] The immense steam shovel is shown in the interior of the New Village quarry in Warne, *A Look at Warren County*, 32. In recent years the Edison Quarry, now known as Oxford Quarry, has been pumped out and enlarged, and because the land is private, I cannot estimate its present size.

[381] Warne, *A Look at Warren County*, 32. Also: Eggler, "Edison and Warren County," 2 (photograph dated 1907); and "Edison Portland Cement Works, New Village, New Jersey" in the centerfold (unnumbered) of Meadowcroft (ed.), *Life of Thomas A. Edison.*

[382] Site visit and conversation with Gary Meddaugh at the Victaulic plant, New Village, N.J., 30 September 1997, and with a long-term Victaulic employee, Bill Mogilski.

[383] The two cement silos on the northeast side of the Victaulic building (Edison's 1906 building) are the tallest remnants of cement works (*Newark [N.J.] Star Ledger*, "In the Towns," 19 March 1992, p. NW-1).

[384] Although the staff at the Edison National Historic Site does not accept the notion that Edison had a "laboratory" at his cement plant, Vanderbilt and Peterson state that the inventor conducted studies of his cement and concrete mixtures at this plant, and common sense would yield the same conclusion. Vanderbilt, *Edison, Chemist*; and Peterson, Ibid.

[385] The American League and the White Construction Company, "singing Edison's praises," as quoted in Eggler, "Edison and Warren County," 2.

[386] Eggler, Ibid.

[387] A 500-pound concrete and steel beam fell from the roof of Yankee Stadium onto seats below it at 3 p.m. on 13 April 1998. *The New York Times* states that

the stadium was built by the White Construction Company of New York City, using "2,300 tons of steel, a million brass screws, 20,000 cubic yards, and a million feet of Pacific fir" (19 April 1998, "Metro" Section, 1, 39). The stadium "underwent a $100 million renovation during the 1974 and 1975 seasons that essentially added a new skin over the stadium's 1923 foundation. But by 1979, city officials found that design errors and poor workmanship were causing leaks and cracks in the concrete around two main expansion joints" (Ibid., 14 April 1998, 1, C3). The prevailing view in New Village, expressed by Carl Brown, is that the beam fell because the structure had been weakened during the remodeling, and that it was not a failure of Edison's cement. For the history of cement structures at Glenmont, see interviews with W. I. Halstrom, 1965 (Jack Stanley Papers).

[388] Vanderbilt, *Edison, Chemist*, 195. On 6 August 1997, I visited with Mrs. Sylvester (Anne) Connell and her twin sons Roger and Dennis at their house on Ingersoll Terrace, and had a tour of the ground floor of the "Edison house" adjacent to theirs.

[389] Edison cement is very durable, but not even Edison cement lasts forever. When Edison's factory buildings were being torn down in West Orange in the 1950s, his youngest son, Theodore, came to the Village Camera store in South Orange to buy a Polaroid camera to record the sad event. Carl Kantrowitz, who sold him the camera, told me that Theodore Edison had tears in his eyes, as he remarked that "They couldn't knock those buildings down. They'll have to blow them up." And they did.

[390] "Upper Mountain Avenue . . . the exclusive neighborhood . . . of million-dollar houses" (*Star Ledger* 19 March 1997).

[391] My attention was called to the house at 303 North Mountain Ave., Upper Montclair, by Clifford F. Lindholm, III, who said that he had seen an article about it in the local paper. I saw the house on 4 November 1997. On 17 January 1998, Mrs. Ronald (Helen) McGuirk of West Orange told me about 740 McLaughlin Place in Orange, which is now owned by her in-laws.

[392] Peterson, "Edison's Concrete Houses."

[393] Mitchell, *New Jersey Highlands*, 62-63.

[394] Mitchell, Ibid., 63.

[395] Mitchell, Ibid., 64-65.

[396] Mitchell, Ibid., 64-65.

[397] Eggler, "Edison and Warren County," 3.

[398] Warne, *Warren County*, 32. The Pohatcong Creek now flows quietly through the farms of the valley, much as it did before Edison arrived. Pohatcong Creek and its tributaries are no longer used for water power, nor is the Morris Canal inundated any longer by streams that course down the sides of Scotts Mountain into the creek. These streams are channeled under Route 57 by culverts, and the

highway itself is now wide and smooth. Edison's cement is still visible in the pavement of Route 57 but it is easier to see it on Edison Road, also known as County Route 633, where the traffic is slower and less frequent. Edison Road was repaired between the fall of 1997 and the spring of 1998, and it is now a very pleasant, scenic route. I suspect, although I cannot prove it, that Edison probably paved this road — the road to his plant — as a test, before he offered to pave the main road between Washington, New Jersey, and Phillipsburg.

Agricultural methods have changed in many ways since Edison's day, and "agribusiness" has begun to arrive in the Pohatcong valley. There are fewer trees in the valley than there were in 1900, and the fields are larger and more uniform in appearance. The fields now are mostly grass and grain, rather than a diverse mix of crops. A large chicken farm is located on the south / southwest bank of the Pohatcong, along Good Springs Road, between the Elisha Thatcher House and Edison's 1906 building that is used by Victaulic. The one story high shed or barn on the ISE chicken farm covers several acres of land and produces eggs and manure on a scale that could hardly be imagined by farmers at the turn of the century. Edison would have understood this type of mass production, for he used the same method in his factories.

There are now very few visible reminders of Edison's long years of activity in the Pohatcong valley and in Oxford, New Jersey. Maps of Warren County show three streets that bear his name (Edison Avenue in Stewartsville, Edison Road in New Village, and Edison Road in Oxford); there is a sign on Route 57 just west of Edison Road in New Village that says it was paved by Edison in 1912; and a sign has been erected in the new housing development on Cliffside Drive near Pohatcong Creek that calls his large quarry "Edison Lake." That's all that I could locate that mentions Edison on signs or plaques in Warren County, after many hours of research, many conversations with local residents and former residents, and more than eight hours spent on site visits in Warren County.

The most senior people that I spoke with in the municipal building in Stewartsville did not know that Edison had ever been in their town, nor were they aware of the significance of a short street called Edison Avenue a few blocks from the municipal building. Furthermore, on the day of my visit to the Franklin Township Branch library I could not find anyone who knew that Edison had once worked in New Village and Stewartsville, and there is no "vertical file" on Edison or his cement company in that library. Edison has only recently been profiled in the Warren County Cultural and Heritage Commission's News Quarterly, and his work is shown in only two pictures (without a narrative) in the Commission's 1991 history of Warren County. The histories of the Morris Canal have little to say about Edison and no illustrations of his work in Warren County, although his plant was less than a mile from the canal.

A study of the important early buildings in Warren County in 1976 described in detail an old house on Good Springs Road near the Edison plant (the Elisha Thatcher House, built about 1817).

However, this book does not mention Edison or a similar old stone farmhouse that stands at the corner of Good Springs and Edison Roads, where Edison is said to have stayed when he remained overnight at his plant. Several residents of Oxford were not aware that the road leading to the Oxford Quarry is called Edison Road on the current official map of Warren County, and I have not been able to locate anyone — including the official spokesperson of the Oxford Quarry — who knows when Edison first came to Oxford. The doors on two old vehicles that are located just inside the entrance to the quarry are painted with the inscription "Edison Quarry 1923-1942," but the vehicles are inside the quarry gate, and the words "Edison Quarry" are not visible to passersby unless they enter the quarry.

It has been assumed that Edison opened his quarry at Oxford in 1923, although historians of Edison's work with cement suggest that the limestone at Oxford was an important component of his cement as early as the first decade of the twentieth century. Efforts are being made by Victaulic to preserve the remaining traces of Edison's work in New Village, but CONRAIL recently demolished the little railroad station that once serviced the Edison Cement Company's plant. Carl Brown is a visiting teacher in the Franklin Township grade school. Mr. Brown tells the children about Edison and cement, but school children are likely to see more signs that point out the former route of the Morris Canal than they are to see signs that mention Edison.

Chapter 12: Kearny: The Battery Factory and the Model A Ford (1927-1931) – Pages 267-276

[399] B. F. Morris, in "Kearny's Industrial Leaders Say," *Why Kearny, New Jersey* (Kearny, N.J.: Mayor and Council of Kearny, 1939), n.p. [copy provided by George Rogers, Kearny, N.J., 28 April 1998]

[400] Venable, *Out of the Shadow*, 83 ("Over his father's objections -- Thomas looked down on lead-acid storage batteries -- Charles launched a line of such batteries at a new plant constructed in Kearny, in the New Jersey Meadows. . . to supply original equipment for Ford automobiles"). I first read about E-Mark on 17 July 1997 in Venable's book, and I have not been able to determine the dates for startup and termination of the E-Mark Corporation. The E-Mark Battery does not appear in the *Edison Chronology* of the Edison Papers Project.

Thomas Edison had long pursued a different approach to storage batteries, which had culminated in success with his invention of an iron-nickel-lithium-alkaline battery. Edison's alkaline battery was manufactured by TAE, Inc., at the Edison Storage Battery Company plant in West Orange and by the Edison Primary Battery Division in Silver Lake, New Jersey.

[401] Other primary and secondary sources include: Emma May Vilardi, *Heritage and Legacy: Town of Kearny* (Kearny, N.J.: Kearny Centennial Commission, 1967); Vilardi, "Heritage & Legacy: A History of Kearny from 1606-1955" [typed

MS, 424 pp. in 2 vols., in Kearny Public Library, n.d. (ca. 1967)]; Mrs. Walter C. Hipp, "A Profile of the Town of Kearny's History" (1967); Hipp, *This Is Your Town, Kearny: A Bicentennial Tour of Its Historic and Notable Places* (Kearny, N.J.: American Revolution Bicentennial Commission of Kearny, 1980); Anon., "History of Kearny" (n.d.); Robert MacFadyen and John P. Deley, *75th Anniversary Journal* (North Arlington, Bergen Co., N.J.: Journal Committee, [ca. 1971]); Robert Sullivan, *The Meadowlands* (New York: Scribners, 1998); *Risk Assessment for Chromium Sites in Hudson County, New Jersey* (Trenton, N.J.: Department of Environmental Protection, State of New Jersey, 1989); *Draft Environmental Impact Statement on the Special Area Management Plan for the Hackensack Meadowlands District, NJ* (U.S. Environmental Protection Agency, 1995), Appendices A-I. Also, *Harrison-Kearny Directory* (Newark, N.J.: Price & Lee Company) for all years available from 1929 through 1956 (1929, 1938, 1940, 1950, 1952, 1954, and 1956); and *Union/Hudson/Essex Counties Atlas* (Maspeth, N.Y: Hagstrom, 1987). Mr. Koncher was thanked by Robert Sullivan in his notes (*The Meadowlands*, 216).

[402] Vilardi, *Heritage and Legacy*, 2.

[403] Vilardi, *Heritage and Legacy*, 2.

[404] For additional details about the geological history of this region of New Jersey and the history of the early contacts between the Native Americans and the European settlers who displaced them, see: Vilardi, *Heritage and Legacy*; Hipp, "Kearny's History"; and Sullivan, *The Meadowlands*. Vilardi says that Sandford settled with local Indian leaders, who were known collectively as the Meghectecock (pp. 2-3), while Hipp refers to a transaction between Sandford and Chief Tantaqua of the Hackensack Indians (p.1). Anon., "History of Kearny," states that the area of Kearny was once known as Michgecticok. Sullivan says that this region was the bed of a great glacial lake known as Lake Hackensack that began to recede in 8000 B.C. (p.16).

[405] *Harrison-Kearny Directory*, 1938; and *Union/Hudson/Essex Counties Atlas*. It is now impossible for an ordinary visitor to examine the area where the Edison battery factory was located, for the eastern portion of the Newark-Jersey City Turnpike just before it meets the Belleville Turnpike is now the fenced and guarded property of New Jersey Transit. County Road 508 (which is the modern designation for this ancient route) detours around the New Jersey Transit property on the bridge that conveys State Route 7 and County Road 506 (the Belleville Turnpike), and it joins the ancient highway of cut stones a half mile west of the intersection of County Roads 506 and 508. The old road has been resurfaced with asphalt, but heavy traffic has worn away the upper layers in some areas, revealing the stone turnpike underneath it.

[406] Hipp, "Kearny's History," 1.

[407] Anon., "History of Kearny, 1; and Hipp, "Kearny's History," 1. Kingsland, New Jersey, is named for Major Kingsland. General Kearny had been killed at

the Battle of Chantilly, Virginia, on 1 September 1862, and he was initially buried near his home overlooking the Passaic River. (His remains have been removed to the National Cemetery at Arlington, Virginia, where they lie under an imposing statue of Kearny on horseback, uphill from the Tombs of the Unknowns.) Dates and locations in the history of Kearny vary in different sources. For example, Hipp states that the "nine and a third square miles" that is now Kearny, N.J. was part of "the original Crown Grant of 30,000 acres" which Sandford obtained. Vilardi, on the other hand, quotes the original deed as having stated that Sandford obtained 5,308 acres. Sandford's death is given as 1692 in the Kearny Museum, while Hipp states that it was in 1708. Hipp writes that Sandford's heir, Nathaniel Kingsland, sold the tract to Arent Schuyler in 1710 for 300 English Pounds, while the recent anonymous "History of Kearny" states that it was purchased by Schuyler in 1719 for 350 pounds.

Schuyler is memorialized in a major north-south road, Schuyler Avenue, which runs for more than three miles along the base of the hill that is the western buttress of the Meadowlands. Sandford Avenue, on the other hand, is only two hundred yards long, a minor street just east of the intersection of Schuyler and Harrison Avenues. Sandford fares better than Ogden, however; Ogden Avenue, at the same intersection, is less than one hundred yards long. This intersection was once the principal crossroads of the region, and it is now on the city line between Kearny and Harrison.

[408] Anon., "History of Kearny, 1; Hipp, "Kearny's History," 1; and "Kearny's Industrial Roster," in *Why Kearny, New Jersey* (n.p.).

[409] See Sullivan, *The Meadowlands*; and *Harrison-Kearny Directory*, 1940 (1043-4); 1950 (1018); 1952 (840); 1954 (pink p.10). The New Jersey Turnpike appears for the first time crossing Belleville Turnpike in 1954. The Edison plant is no longer listed in the *Directory* in 1956.

[410] In Hudson County, the eastern end of C.R. 508 now appears to be located at the intersection of the Belleville Turnpike and the Newark-Jersey City Turnpike, rather than at the Hudson River, at the eastern end of Newark Avenue in Jersey City. From its origin in the Meadowlands of Kearny, C.R. 508 passes through Harrison and crosses the Passaic River into Newark, in Essex County. It then jogs south for a few blocks along McCarter Highway before passing west through Newark and the Oranges on Central Avenue, just south of I-280. Central Avenue is now a wider and less crowded thoroughfare than Orange Street in Newark and its western extension, Main Street, in the Oranges. At the western end of Central Avenue, at Valley Road in West Orange, C.R. 508 jogs north again to meet Northfield Avenue at St. Mark's Square. C.R. 508 then proceeds west to Livingston Circle where it ends at the intersection of West Northfield Road and Mt. Pleasant Avenue.

[411] Hipp, "Kearny's History," 2 ("macadamized" and "indicted"); and Sullivan, *The Meadowlands*, 17 ("long journey").

[412] *Harrison-Kearny Directory* for all years available from 1929 through 1950 (1929, 1938, 1940, 1950)

[413] Venable, *Out of the Shadow*, 83.

[414] *Encyclopaedia Britannica*, (s.v.) Henry Ford. The Model T was discontinued in 1927, and the V-8 engine was introduced in 1932. The Model A (with a four-cylinder engine) was dated 1928, 1929, 1930, and 1931. I owned and drove two of the 1931 models. My brother, Thomas D. Hill, Ph.D., who was an aeronautical engineer, recalls the E-Mark battery.

Another connection between Henry Ford and the city of Kearny was mentioned by Sullivan, in *The Meadowlands*. A retired Kearny policeman pointed out to Sullivan the location of what he said was Henry Ford's first factory; he also pointed out the location of what he said was the first cement road built by a machine. These legends may have conflated Edison and Ford, since Thomas A. Edison, Inc., built batteries for Ford, and Edison also was a pioneer in cement roadbuilding. We have previously read that the first cement road in America was built by Edison in Warren County in 1912.

[415] Edison's comment about God and lead is paraphrased from one of Edison's biographies; I regret that I do not recall which one it appeared in.

[416] Thomas A. Edison Industries "Organization Chart" (1930) [from Edison National Historic Site].

[417] Morris, "Kearny's Industrial Leaders."

[418] "Kearny's Industrial Roster," with Morris, "Kearny's Industrial Leaders."

[419] Morris, "Kearny's Industrial Leaders": By 1939, Kearny, New Jersey, had become the base of such companies as New Jersey Bell, Public Service Electric and Gas, Koppers Coke and Gas, Swift & Co., and Coca-Cola. The Kearny Works of the Western Electric Company was built in 1922, and in 1931 this plant was enlarged to cover 139 acres "on the Kearny peninsula." E. I. DuPont de Nemours & Co. had a manufacturing plant in Kearny since before 1920, and by 1939 Congoleum-Nairn, Inc., had operated its plant in Kearny for over 50 years. These and other businesses praised Kearny for its labor supply and for its "good housing accommodations for workers at all compensation levels." Kearny was blessed with excellent water and "proximity to major railroads" and highways, and above all by its "low tax rate" and the "cooperative attitude of town officials." The toxic waste that has accumulated in the Meadowlands over the past few decades makes us wonder if "compliant" rather than "cooperative" would have been a more appropriate adjective to describe the attitude of the city's elected leaders.

[420] At the time of Thomas Edison's death, the E-Mark plant in Kearny would have been similar in size and in its environmental impact to the plant that the inventor had established forty-five years earlier in Silver Lake, only a few miles from Kearny. At the time of Edison's death, the Lamp Works in Harrison continued to be in operation on a large scale. It was by then officially known as

the General Electric Lamp Works, but it was still regarded as "Edison's Lamp Works" by the older residents of Hudson County. However, although the Lamp Works is still remembered locally in Kearny and Harrison as having been Edison's, the Edison Battery Factory in Kearny faded from memory after it was closed in the early 1950s. Thomas A. Edison, Inc., Battery Manufacturers, disappeared from the Kearny City Directory between 1954 and 1956.

One of the volunteers at the Kearny Museum said that her mother had worked for "the Edison Company" in Harrison, and later for RCA. She did not realize that Thomas Edison had withdrawn from General Electric before the beginning of the twentieth century, nor did she know anything about an Edison battery factory in Kearny, although she had always lived in Harrison and Kearny.

Sullivan, *The Meadowlands*, 16-17 ("garbage dump . . . "blight"). For toxic waste levels and comments, see: *Chromium Sites in Hudson County* (1989); and *Management Plan for the Hackensack Meadowlands District* (1995). The Essex County Executive -- the top elected official in the county -- in the early 1980s once said in jest that one of the garbage piles could be named for him: "Mount Shapiro" (Peter Shapiro, speaking to the New York Head and Neck Society, at the Harvard Club of New York, ca. 1985). He was referring to a long narrow hill, covered with grass and small trees, on the south side of I-280, between I-280 and the Passaic River, south of the intersection of I-280 and C.R. 508.

Chapter 13: Edison and the *milieu interieur* – Pages 277-291

[421] Goldstein, Interview with Madeline Edison Sloane, 1972, 10.

[422] Edison's handwritten answer to the question of his own "Tobacco Habits," 12 October 1930 ("Longevity Inquiry," Jack Stanley Papers).

[423] "Measurements," 2 October 1929. Record S608-G, bound with "Longevity Inquiry," Record 746A, 12 October 1930, of Thomas A. Edison (Jack Stanley Papers).

[424] Longevity Inquiry, V - Present Physical Condition. Q: State the facts in regard to your bowels. A: (handwritten) perfect for 78 years. Q: Average number of movements per day. A: (underlined) Once a day (handwritten) now. Q: As far as you are aware have you any organic impairment . . . ? A: (handwritten) only indigestion or gas.

[425] Longevity Inquiry, VIII - Food. Q: How many times do you usually eat each day? A: (circled) 3. (handwritten) milk died now no teeth. Q: What foods do you eat? Underscore all foods used ordinarily . . . (handwritten) only milk orange juice now. [The answer, "benefited" to the question regarding abstaining from flesh foods was handwritten with a flourish]

[426] Longevity Inquiry, IX - Drinking. Q: How much water do you drink? A: (handwritten) only kind from milk. Q: State the character of the water you drink? A: Most of life used spring water at meals plenty.

[427] Longevity Inquiry, X - Bathing and Physical Exercise. Q: What has been your custom as to vacation? A: (handwritten) none. Q: What has been your custom as to recreation? A: (handwritten) none.

[428] Longevity Inquiry, XIV - General. Q: Tobacco Habits. A: (handwritten) Chew continuously & 2 to 3 cigars daily.

[429] Ibid., continued. Q: Do you have any well-defined method of living, particularly with regard to personal hygiene and environment, for the purpose of prolonging your life and of making your existence a healthy, useful and happy one? . . . What factor or factors in your opinion have contributed most to your own long life? A: (handwritten) Eat to keep weight constant. Extremely small eater since a boy. 2500 cc fresh milk daily keeps weight constant.

[430] From marginalia entitled "on Bathing," transcribed by Jack Stanley in Edison's library at Glenmont, handwritten by Edison in one of his books (shown to me by Mr. Stanley 28 January 1998).

[431] From marginalia entitled "Exercise," transcribed by Jack Stanley in Edison's library at Glenmont.

[432] Attributed to Edison by Rosanoff, "Edison in His Laboratory" (emphasis on radium in original, not shown here).

[433] See *Britannica* for further details regarding the history of the discovery of X-rays and radium. The comments on Edison's work with X-rays are drawn from George Tselos' paper on Edison and the fluoroscope ("Start Up at the Top and Work Down"), which he presented at the Edison Conference in Newark, N.J, in June 1997. See also Percy Brown, "American Martyrs to Radiology," reprinted in *American Journal of Roentgenology* (January 1995): 237-239; Tselos, "New Jersey's Thomas Edison and the Fluoroscope" *New Jersey Medicine* 92, no. 11 (November 1995): 731-733; and Claudia Clark, *Radium Girls* (Chapel Hill: University of North Carolina Press, 1997), 41-43 ("Gamma radiation is indistinguishable from X rays, albeit very high-energy X rays, except for its source in radioactive transformations").

[434] A friend of mine says that he spoke of my interest in Edison and the subject of radiation and radium to Claudia Clark, author of *Radium Girls*. Ms. Clark, he said, replied that she had not realized that the Edison plant was so close to the U.S. Radium Corporation plant. In the summer of 1997 I could not find anyone at the ENHS who was aware of the proximity of the U.S. Radium Superfund site to the former Edison plant property line.

[435] Clark, *Radium Girls*: The Radium Luminous Materials Corporation was founded by Dr. Sabin von Sochocky, who invented luminous radium paint (vii). His corporation was taken over and renamed as U.S. Radium in 1921 (33). Soon thereafter, von Sochocky began to suspect that the dial painters' illnesses were due to radium. He worked closely with Harrison S. Martland, M.D., the Essex County Medical Examiner (178), to study the dial painters' illnesses and to measure the

levels of radium in their bodies. In 1925 Martland found that von Sochocky was radioactive, and the latter died in 1928 of radium-induced chronic anemia (127).

[436] Clark, *Radium Girls*, 40: "The first death from X-ray-induced cancer was in 1904." Percy Brown states that Clarence Dally, in 1904, was the first to die of X-ray induced cancer ("American Martyrs to Radiology"). Radium dial painting began in 1913, but the major exposure of dial painters at the facility in Orange, N.J. began in 1917, coincident with the need for luminous watches for the U.S. war effort. About 2,000 dial painters were exposed to radium paint between 1917 and 1927, and another 2,000 were exposed between 1927 and the end of World War II in 1945. Clark says that the tenth dial painter died of radium injury in 1927 (19), although none who began painting after 1927 have died of radium-induced cancers (199).

[437] I reviewed the file folders on "Radium" in the archives of the UMDNJ Library on 21 July 1997; at that time the files totaled approximately 10 inches of linear space. They were mainly related to the radium dial watch painters at the U.S. Radium plant in Orange, N.J., and to the subsequent history of this site up to the present. It is now a U.S. EPA Superfund toxic waste site. Also, see William D. Sharpe, "Chronic Radium Intoxication: Clinical and Autopsy Findings in Long-Term New Jersey Survivors," in *Environmental Research* 8, no. 3 (December 1974): 243-383.

The Essex County Medical Society archives at the UMDNJ Library comprise the bound records of Minutes of the Council of the ECMS and of various Committees of the ECMS. I reviewed these records at the offices of the ECMS in Verona, N.J. in July 1997; they were later transferred to the George F. Smith Library of the Health Sciences of the UMDNJ (now Rutgers) in Newark. I found nothing that was related to radium or X-rays in the ECMS archives. The only comment about Edison (which had nothing to do with either form of ionizing radiation) appeared in the Minutes of the ECMS Council meeting on 26 October 1931, two weeks after the inventor died: "Report of the unethical action of Dr. Howe of New York, as consultant in case of Mr. Edison, taking the case out of the hands of one of our members, resulted in 'no action' because having no complaint from the member."

See A. E. Johnson, Interview [below] ("radium girl" employed by Edison); and Christopher C. Sellers, *Hazards of the Job: From Industrial Disease to Environmental Health Science* (Chapel Hill, N.C.: University of North Carolina Press, 1997).

[438] A. E. Johnson, Interview, 29 March 1971, page 11; Interviewer unknown (probably Kenneth Goldstein), in Jack Stanley Papers. *Newark Evening News* (29 June 1925), 1, 4.

[439] "poor, residential neighborhood," quoted in Clark, *Radium Girls*, 33.

[440] The working conditions and the young women who were employed in the Edison plant in West Orange were described by Edison's biographers. I also heard

of them in the course of my site visits in Bloomfield, Harrison, and Kearny. At The Historical Society of Bloomfield, I met one of Edison's "girls" (Lucy Sant'Ambrogio); my conversation with her appears above in the case study of Silver Lake. At the Kearny Museum, I met the daughter of a woman who had, when she was "a girl," worked for the Edison Lamp Works in Harrison. In 1926, the list of "compensable workplace diseases" in New Jersey included, in addition to those listed in the text, arsenic, methanol, and chromium. Radium was not added to the official list until after the dial painters' illnesses were studied and compensated by their employers (Clark, *Radium Girls*, 115). "Radiothor," made by Bailey Radium Laboratories in Orange, N.J., in the 1920s, used the slogan "Gimme a Gamma." The UMDNJ Library archive's "Radium" file includes a notice that the UMDNJ Radiation Safety Office received an empty "Radiothor" water bottle on 24 January 1989. The accompanying description states that "Radiothor" was made by Bailey Radium Laboratories, Inc., 336 Main St., East Orange, N.J.

[441] "Vicinity Properties Area Map, U.S. Radium Site" in *Revised Work Plan for Remedial Investigation and Feasibility Study* (U.S. EPA Work Assignment No. 004-2L67) (vol. 1) (Paramus, N.J.: Malcolm Pirnie, Inc., 1990), Fig. 2-3; and "U.S. Radium Corporation Site," in *EPA Region 2 Superfund Update,* February 1991, in UMDNJ George F. Smith Library archives, "Radium" file, 21 July 1997. At its peak level of operation in the 1920s, one-half ton of carnotite ore from Colorado was processed daily at the U.S. Radium plant in Orange, N.J. (Malcolm Pirnie report, p. 2-5). The "Vicinity Properties Area Map" shows that radioactive contamination of the soil extends well into the area that was once occupied by TAE, Inc. An 8.5 uR/hr isopleth line surrounding the High & Alden Streets Properties of the U.S. Radium Superfund site extends for about one-half block into West Orange along Watchung Avenue between Lakeside Ave. and Alden Street. This portion of the TAE, Inc., property was previously the site of the body of water once known as Cook's Pond.

[442] Brown, "American Martyrs to Radiology": Clarence Madison Dally (1865-1904) began to work for Edison at the Lamp Works in Harrison, N.J., in 1889. His father and three of his brothers also worked for Edison as glass-blowers. According to Brown, Edison stated that "I started in to make a number of these [fluorescent] lamps, but I soon found that the x-ray had *affected poisonously my assistant, Mr. Dally*, so that his hair come out and his flesh commenced to ulcerate. I then concluded it would not do, and that it would not be a very popular kind of light" (emphasis in original). Brown does not mention Edison's own visual symptoms, skin lesions, and abdominal complaints, which were described in Chapter III of this book, and in Tselos' MS, citing *Journal of the American Medical Association* 41:499, 1903. The danger of X-rays became personally apparent to Dr. Percy Brown, who was a radiologist at Children's Hospital in Boston. Dr. Brown developed an X-ray induced cancer, from which he died in 1950 at the age of 75 (Editor's footnote on "American Martyrs to Radiology").

Part III
Edison's Environment, 1869-1931 – Page 293
Chapter 14: Epilogue – Pages 295-309

[443] Lisa Peterson, "Edison's Genius Makes Him the Man of the Millennium," Newark (N.J.) *Star-Ledger*, 30 September 1997, 19.

[444] Conot, *Edison*, 451-458. On 22 November 22 1997, Claire Griese and her sister, Lee B. Williams (daughters of John Lloyd Burgess, late Warden of the Essex County House of Detention), provided additional information about Edison's last years and his funeral. Claire Griese's husband had worked at "the new Edison laboratory," and he knew Charles and Theodore Edison. He confirmed what I had also heard from George Campbell (at the Edison Tower) and Charles Hummel (of the Charles Edison Fund), that the last breaths of Thomas Edison were captured by Charles Edison in a test tube (Mr. Williams says, "three tubes," he believes), which after being sealed up, were — and presumably are still — at the Edison-Ford Museum in Fort Myers, Florida.

The actual statement in *Life* magazine is rather cryptic but the intent is surely to cast him as the Man of the Millennium: "The 100 People Who Made the Millennium: 1. Thomas Edison... Because of him, the millennium will end in a wash of brilliant light rather than in torchlit darkness as it began" (*Life*, Fall (October) 1997, 135, 147). Edison's discoveries as "The Wizard of Menlo Park" were also listed as #11 (the eleventh most important) among the 100 most significant events of the millennium (p.120). Edison immediately became known as "The Man of the Millennium," although this term does not actually appear in the brief paragraphs about him in *Life* magazine.

[445] I will elaborate below on the world's problems from chemical pollution, in discussing Edison's contributions to these problems. See William J. Broad, "Two Views from the Greenhouse," review of *Is the Temperature Rising? The Uncertain Science of Global Warming*, by S. George Philander; and *Climate of Fear: Why We Shouldn't Worry About Global Warming*, by Thomas Gale Moore (*New York Times Book Review* [n.d., 1998], 21).

[446] A map of "Louisville/Jefferson County Attractions" shows "Thomas Edison's Butchertown House/Museum" at 729 East Washington Street, near the intersection with Clay Street (*Louisville: Your Kind of Place, Any Way You Say It* [Rand-McNally, 1996]). A picture postcard shows that the Butchertown House is a one-story brick building, painted light gray, with a new metal roof, painted red (Louisville, Ky: Postal Color Corp., n.d.); *Early American Inventions 1794 to 1906* (Historical Documents Co., 1969).

[447] For a curious bit of history of the Royal Colony of New Jersey in 1702, see Paul Lewis, "Did the Envoy of a Queen Really Dress in Drag?" *New York Times*, Arts and Ideas sec. (21 March 1998), B9, Review of Patricia U. Bonomi, *The Lord Cornbury Scandal: The Politics of Reputation in British America*.

[448] Newark's population of 275,221 exceeds by nearly 50,000 that of the next largest city in the state (Jersey City, with 228,537). Census figures from *Physician Membership Directory: 1997-1998* (Lawrenceville, N.J.: Medical Society of New Jersey, 1997).

Newspaper stories about the events of 12-17 July 1967, and the subsequent changes in Newark appeared on the thirtieth anniversary of these riots in the *Newark (N.J.) Star-Ledger,* 13 July 1997, 1, 28-30; *Star-Ledger,* 14 July 1997, 1, 10-13; and the *New York Times,* 14 July 1997, A1, B4. See: Ted Sherman, "Newark: The Next Chapter," in *Newark (N.J.) Star-Ledger,* 13 July 1997, and Mary Jo Patterson, Ibid., 14 July 1997. [The map of the affected area that accompanied his article ended, erroneously, at the city limits of Newark]. Also: Ronald Smothers, "In Riots' Shadow, a City Stumbles On," in *New York Times* (14 July 1997), A1, B4.

For recent successes and plans for development in Newark, see: Peggy McGlone, "NJPAC's Debut Season Soars to Success," in *Newark (N.J.) Star-Ledger,* 19 June 1998, 27; and *Star-Ledger,* 5 May 1998, "New Jersey Section," photo with overlay, 25. Another possible site under consideration for the Sportsplex is a few blocks south, at the corner of McCarter Highway and Edison Place. This was once the site of Edison's Ward Street shop.

[449] The Newark Preservation and Landmarks Committee was established in 1973. As of May 1997, more than 60 buildings, districts, parks and sites in Newark were listed on the National and State Registers of Historic Places. "Buildings once registered but later demolished are not listed" (Brochure, n.d. [1998], Newark Preservation and Landmarks Committee, P.O. Box 1066, Newark, NJ 07101).

[450] For recent scholarship on the Menlo Park, see Vito Massa, Jr., "A Geophysical and Geological Investigation of the Edison Copper Mine," M.Sc. Thesis, Department of Geology, Rutgers University, 1979/1980.

[451] *Price Schedules of Standard Large Edison Mazda Lamps: April First Nineteen Twenty-Two* (Harrison, N.J.: Edison Lamp Works of General Electric Co., 1922).

[452] It has also been said that one year earlier (1882) "Edison designs first hydroelectric plant, Appleton, Wis." See: Bernard Grun, *The Timetables of History*, 3rd. ed. (New York: Simon & Schuster, 1991), 1882.

[453] Edison, *The Diary of Thomas A. Edison*, ed. Kathleen L. McGuirk (Old Greenwich, Conn.: Chatham/Viking, n.d. [1971]).

[454] Christopher M. Loder, "Town Doesn't Like Soil that Glows in the Dark," in *Newark (N.J.) Star-Ledger,* 3 July 1997, 31.

[455] James F. O'Gorman, "The Hidden Half of Central Park," review of *Country, Park & City: The Architecture and Life of Calvert Vaux*, by Francis R. Kowsky, *New York Times Book Review*, 22 March 1998, 10. Venable states that Charles Edison obtained the stone for his house, "Landmore," in Llewellyn Park from a limestone quarry operated by Edison in Sussex County (*Out of the Shadow*, 68).

"Edison Site to be Closed for Repairs," *West Orange (N.J.) Chronicle*, 14 August 1997, 2. Uschold and Curry state that the laboratory buildings and 1.51 acres were given to the government in 1955 (*Cultural Landscape Report*, 60), whereas Venable states that this gift was made on 14 July 1956 by TAE, Inc., and Glenmont was given to the government three years later by McGraw-Edison (*Out of the Shadow*, 237). The events of 1963-1964 and the acreages of NPS properties are from *Cultural Landscape Report*, 70-80. The name of Valley Road was changed to Main Street during the period 1955-1995 (p.85). Uschold and Curry, *Cultural Landscape Report*, 66-67 (Japanese lanterns), 98-100 (park-like character; spruce trees). Carl Chase, "Developer Hopes to 'Light Up' West Orange," *Newark (N.J.) Star-Ledger*, 29 June 1997, sec. 1, 27. Michael H. Agar and Louis Berger & Associates, *Ethnographic Overview and Assessment: Edison National Historic Site, West Orange, New Jersey* (West Orange, N.J.: U.S. National Park Service), 100. Frank Fleischman, III, "AP Results Place School District with Nation's Elite, in *West Orange (N.J.) Chronicle*, 19 March 1998, 1. Also, *New York Times*, 9 October 1997 (wealthy suburb); and *West Orange (N.J.) Chronicle*, 10 July 1997 (tax abatement zone). Fleischman, "Properties Declared Landmarks," in *West Orange (N.J.) Chronicle*, 5 March 1998, 1, 8.

[456] Kevin C. Dilworth, "20-Year West Orange Mayor Leaves Office," in *Newark (N.J.) Star-Ledger*, 30 June 1998, 17, 19; and *Star-Ledger*, 19 July 1998. For the history of the proposed "Crystal Woods" development near Crystal Lake, see *West Orange (N.J.) Chronicle*, 31 July 1997, 1; 7 August 1997, 1; 4 September 1997; and 9 October 1997, 3; and Robbins, "A History of the Development of the First Planned American Suburban Community: Llewellyn Park, West Orange" (Master's thesis, Georgetown University, 1989): "Llewellyn Park: Prospectus Map of Llewellyn Park, 1858," p.x, Fig. 1-2; and "Llewellyn Park: Northwest Part of Llewellyn Park or 'The Ramble,'" p.57, Fig. 3-1. The Thomas A. Edison Junior High School (elsewhere called a Middle School) is shown in the *Suburban Essex Magazine* (September 1997), reverse of p.37. Edison was called "the most famous citizen" of West Orange in the West Orange (N.J.) Laboratory Notebook (Spring 1998), 1. The "Man of the Millennium" article appeared in the *West Orange Chronicle*, 9 October 1997, as a full front page, three-part story with three photographs. Former New Jersey Governor Brendan Byrne — who verbalized in a previous chapter the ill-will towards Edison that remains in the valley — put a brighter spin on the subject when he was interviewed following the visit of First Lady Hillary Rodham Clinton to the ENHS on 14 July 1998. In 1979, Byrne had said to John Cunningham that the state of New Jersey "would have no interest" in raising money to preserve the Edison site, and he added that "You know, he didn't treat his people very well" (*New York Times*, 1 June 1997, 12). On 14 July 1998, however, Byrne said that "As a person who was born and grew up in West Orange, I'm glad to see preservation efforts continue for this site" (*West Orange Chronicle*, 16 July 1998, 1, 5).

[457] Kelly Heyboer, "Belleville Files Suit to Block Subway," in *Newark (N.J.) Star-Ledger*, 21 June 1998, 29; and Heyboer, "Short Rail Link to Rumble over Long Memories in Montclair," *Newark (N.J.) Star-Ledger*, 12 April 1998, 27, 29. Russell Banks wrote that Glen Ridge "does indeed resemble Ozzie and Harriet Nelson's neighborhood." See: Banks, review of *Our Guys: The Glen Ridge Rape and the Secret Life of the Perfect Suburb*, by Bernard Lefkowitz, *New York Times Book Review*, 3 August 1997, 7; and 5 July 1998, 20.

[458] Kelly Heyboer, "EPA Says End Is Near for Cleanup," *Newark (N.J.) Star-Ledger*, 19 July 1998, sec. 1, 43.

[459] Since about 1987 the Essex County Park System has included some 5,725 acres of parks and other properties, including South Mountain Reservation (over 2,000 acres) at the southern end of the portion of First Watchung Mountain in Essex County, and Eagle Rock Reservation (more than 400 acres) at the northwest corner of Llewellyn Park. In the summer of 1997 a proposal was under consideration to add a 226-acre property known as "Hilltop" in the northern part of Essex County, between Cedar Grove and Caldwell. A final decision on this proposal has not yet been reached. See: Diane C. Walsh, "Idea Grows to Keep Hilltop Crest Green," in *Newark (N.J) Star-Ledger*, 26 August 1997, 13.

[460] David VanHorn and Art Charlton, "Dalai Lama Uplifts His Legions: 'The Essence of Sweetness'," in *Newark (N.J.) Star-Ledger*, 8 May 1998, 1. David Quammen pointed out that John McPhee "would travel back and forth across the United States on Interstate 80," which McPhee used as "'a sort of cross section of North America at about the 40th parallel'" (Quammen, review of *Annals of the Former World*, by McPhee, *New York Times Book Review*, 5 July 1998, 9). For example, Interstate 80 appears as a reference point in McPhee's *Assembling California* (New York: Farrar, Straus & Giroux, 1993), 69. John Noble Wilford, "Earliest Known Fake Stone Is Discovered in Southern Iraq," *New York Times*, 30 June 1998; and "It should be noted that the materials fell from a section [of Yankee Stadium] installed in a renovation that took place in the early 1970's" (*New York Times*, 16 April 1998, A22). A source for additional information regarding the Edison Portland Cement Co. was mentioned to me on 30 September 1997 by Jim Lee of Stewartsville, N.J.: Martin (Marty) Kane, a historian of cement manufacturing in New Jersey and Pennsylvania (923) 266-2103.

[461] The "multilayered meanings of tuberculosis as they have evolved over more than a century" were explored by Katherine Ott in 1997. See: Barbara Bates, "Tuberculosis," review of *Fevered Lives: Tuberculosis in American Culture*, by Ott, *Journal of the American Medical Association* 277, no. 21 (4 June 1997): 1732-1733. For additional information regarding tuberculosis, "the greatest killer in history," which caused the deaths of "approximately a thousand million human beings" in the nineteenth and twentieth centuries, including members of Edison's family, see Frank Ryan, M.D., *The Forgotten Plague: How the Battle Against Tuberculosis Was Won — And Lost* (Boston: Little, Brown, [1992] 1993).

[462] It was reported in September 1997 that Edison "arranged the first public display of the x-ray tube at an 1896 exposition." See: David Rhees, "Marvels on Display," review of *Exhibiting Electricity*, by K. G. Beauchamp, *Science* 277 (5 September 1997): 1444-1445.

[463] During World War I, when Thomas Edison was away from West Orange, Venable reports that "Charles proceeded to implement some of his ideas for improvement such as improved medical service" (*Out of the Shadow*, 76-77).

[464] Rachel Carson, *Silent Spring* (1962. New York: Houghton Mifflin, 1994); Jonathan Harr, *A Civil Action* (1995. New York: Vintage Books/Random House, 1996); Vincent Kiernan, "Getting an Inside Look at the Chernobyl Reactor," *Chronicle of Higher Education* (17 July 1998): A20.

[465] Edison was quoted in 1947 as having said, when asked if he could invent a weapon deadlier than any in existence: "Yes, I could . . . but I have no intention of doing so. I want to save and advance human life, not destroy it. The dove is my emblem" (from Anon., "Edison's First 100 Years," *Pathfinder* 54 (no. 4, February 1947): 22-29 [copy in vertical file on "Edison," Bloomfield, N.J., Public Library].

[466] Elizabeth Kolbert, "In PCB Fight, It's the Nun vs. the C.E.O," in *New York Times*, 25 May 1998, Metro sec., B1.

[467] John P. Nole, Jr., "Edison 'Man of the Millennium'," *West Orange (N.J.) Chronicle*, 9 October 1997, 1.

[468] Dilworth and Kunkle, "Hillary Lights Up Edison Site's Future."

[469] Hillary Rodham Clinton's comment recalls the phrase from Geoffrey Chaucer that describes the Clerk of Oxenford: "And gladly wolde he lerne, and gladly teche" (*The Canterbury Tales* [circa 1387], Prologue, Line 308). The phrases in Chaucer and Clinton both begin with variations on the verb "to learn" (Chaucer "lerne," and Clinton "to learn"). This is followed by another worthy action that is derived from the first and is joined to it by the conjunction "and." In Chaucer, it is "teche," while Clinton says "be inspired." Both verbs are variations on the same theme: The goal of modern pedagogy is not just "to teach" passive learners, but instead to have students "be inspired" to learn. Edison favored the active approach that Clinton articulated.

[470] John F. Welch, Jr., Chairman and C.E.O. of General Electric, quoted in Dilworth and Kunkle, "Hillary Lights Up Edison Site's Future." Also: "Hillary Rodham Clinton . . . announced a $5 million corporate gift to launch a massive restoration. . . Although GE has become a conglomerate whose businesses spread far beyond electric home appliances to plastics, broadcasting mutual funds and other financial services, Edison's legacy endures, . . . Welch joked of Clinton, 'She had the idea we ought to cough up the money'."

[471] Andrew C. Revkin, "Toxic Chemicals from 70's Still Pollute Hudson, Study Says," *New York Times*, 24 July 1998, Metro sec., B1, B9.

Chapter 15: Judging Edison: The Issue of Accountability – Pages 311-358

472 Henry Ford, *Edison as I Knew Him*, quoted in Gilman M. Ostrander, *American Civilization in the First Machine Age* (New York: Harper & Row, 1970), 217 (cited by David F. Noble, *America by Design: Science, Technology, and the Rise of Corporate Capitalism* (New York: Alfred A. Knopf, 1977; New York: Oxford University Press, paperback ed., 1979), 113.

473 Norbert Wiener, quoted in Ostrander, *American Civilization*, 218 (cited by Noble, *America by Design*, 113).

474 Edison, from an editorial in *Industrial Management and Engineering Magazine* (October 1920), 4 (cited by Noble, *America by Design*, 257).

475 Noble, *America by Design*, 8-9.

476 Noble, Ibid., 9-10 (patent control); 98 (received from them).

477 Noble, Ibid., 106.

478 Noble, Ibid., 173.

479 Kurt Vonnegut, *Player Piano* (1952; New York: Bantam Doubleday Dell, paperback ed., 1980), 34.

480 Vonnegut, Ibid., 6-7.

481 Vonnegut, Ibid., 11 (Edison died); 2 (leave work early). The "homosocial" nature of Edison's laboratory was mentioned in one of the biographies of Edison (I believe it was by Musser). Neither Noble nor Vonnegut, I think, mention the racial makeup of Edison's laboratory and managerial workforce, which was nearly all white. This phenomenon was so common in those days that Edison was not mentioned in David R. Roediger, *The Wages of Whiteness: Race and the Making of the American Working Class* (New York: New Left Books/Verso, [1991]; paperback ed., 1993). Nor is Edison mentioned in the review of the history of "society, environment, and place" in Laura Pulido, *Environmentalism and Economic Justice: Two Chicano Struggles in the Southwest* (Tuscon: The University of Arizona Press, 1996). Pulido is concerned, as I am, with "subaltern environmentalism," defined as the "environmentalism of everyday life" (190).

482 Vonnegut, Ibid., 13.

483 Vonnegut, Ibid., 251.

484 Noble, Ibid., 231 (human material); 149 (Naval Consulting Board). Noble's scorn for the Naval Consulting Board sets something of a record. He disposes of its work in two sentences: "The major activity of the NCB throughout the war was a rather fruitless one: the screening of public suggestions and inventions for possible military value. (Of 110,000 suggestions, only 110 merited detailed examination, and only one actually went into production.)." Noble was determined to avoid any imputation of benefit from the work done by Edison and the NCB. I believe that Noble overreached and thus disregarded serious, useful work by Edison and the NCB on behalf of the Navy and of the American government during World War I.

At the time, the Navy's uniformed leaders were uneasy about Edison, who was not only a civilian, but a thorny curmudgeon who was so famous that he was virtually untouchable. The Navy eventually came to recognize Edison's contributions, and it named two warships for him (the destroyer U.S.S. *Edison* and the nuclear submarine U.S.S. *Thomas A. Edison*). The Navy awarded him the Distinguished Service Medal and his bust reposes in a prominent location at the Navy's principal research facility. Edison's work with the Navy began long before World War I, with his development of the Edison-Sims torpedo and batteries for submarines (such as the ill-fated S-2, *Skipjack*). His batteries were important power sources for warships for several decades and his son Charles, following in his father's footsteps, served as Secretary of the Navy under Franklin D. Roosevelt.

For details regarding the attempt by Edison in 1879 to provide a lighting system for a U.S. Navy ship, see Francis Jehl, *Menlo Park Reminiscences* (1937; New York: Dover, 1990) vol. 1, 290-297, 302-303; George Washington De Long (ed. Emma De Long), *The Voyage of the Jeanette: The Ship and Ice Journals of George W. De Long* . . . (Boston: Houghton, Mifflin Co., 1884), vol. 1, 155-163; and Leonard F. Guttridge, *Icebound: The Jeanette Expedition's Quest for the North Pole* (Annapolis, Md.: Naval Institute Press, 1986), 59-61, 106-107.

For information regarding the U.S.S. *Edison*, see Theodore Roscoe, *United States Destroyer Operations in World War II* (Annapolis, Md.: Naval Institute Press, 1953), 11, 20,70; and Samuel Eliot Morison, *The Two Ocean War: A Short History of the United States Navy in the Second World War* (Boston: Little, Brown, 1963), 107, 340, 355. Regarding the U.S.S. *Thomas A. Edison* and nuclear submarines in general, see General Dynamics Co. Program, *U.S.S. Thomas A. Edison Launching* (15 March 1960); Norman Polmar, *The Ships and Aircraft of the U.S. Fleet*, 14th ed. (Annapolis, Md.: Naval Institute Press, 1987), 65; and Tom Clancy, *The Hunt for Red October* (Annapolis, Md.: Naval Institute Press, 1984).

[485] Noble, Ibid., 150 (National Research Council); 214 (CEST); 222 (alpha and beta tests); 229 (Yerkes). Stephen Jay Gould, *The Mismeasure of Man* (New York: W. W. Norton, 1966; paperback, 1981), 261 (great immigration debate); 262 (Calvin Coolidge); 222-255 ("R. M. Yerkes . . . ").

[486] Noble, Ibid., 318-319 (Hawthorne Effect). Harry Braverman, *Labor and Monopoly Capital: The Degradation of Work in the Twentieth Century* (New York: Monthly Review Press, 1974), 87 (bedrock); 110 (His concern); 112-118 (the three principles of management); 87 (Taylorism).

[487] Braverman has little to say about Edison (his remarks are confined to pp. 163-165 of *Labor and Monopoly Capital*), and he dismisses what he calls "Edison's laborious trial and error" methodology in a neologism: "Edisonian" (165). The "human relations" school of management emerged from the Hawthorne study, which found that the "lowest producer in the room ranked first in intelligence and third in dexterity; the highest producer in the room was seventh in dexterity and

lowest in intelligence" (100). George F. Will, "A Faster Mousetrap," review of *The One Best Way: Frederick Winslow Taylor and the Enigma of Efficiency*, by Robert Kanigel. *New York Times Book Review* (15 June 1997): 8, 10.

[488] Noble, Ibid., 321 (capitalist domination); 323-4 (class beneath it).

[489] Alfred DuPont Chandler, *The Visible Hand: The Managerial Revolution in American Business* (Cambridge, Mass.: Belknap Press, 1977). Chandler devotes much attention to the DuPont family (well, his middle name is DuPont), John D. Rockefeller, Sr., Andrew Carnegie, and Jay Gould. Nevertheless, the table of organization for Thomas A. Edison, Inc., in 1930, 20 months before Edison died, looks remarkably like Chandler's "basic hierarchical structure of modern business enterprise" (p.2). A copy of the table of organization of TAE, Inc., is on the wall of the Edison National Historic Site, and was reproduced for me by the archivists of the ENHS.

[490] Lewis Mumford, *Technics and Civilization* (New York: Harcourt, Brace & World, 1934; paperback ed., 1963): 221-222 (electricity . . . metallurgical), 234 (debt to chemistry).

[491] Mumford, *Technics and Civilization*: 110 (three phases, defined), 134ff (eotechnic characteristics), 155 (paleotechnic), 174 (industrial army), 195 (war), 199 (railroads).

[492] Mumford, *Technics and Civilization*: 213 (water turbine), 214 (countermarch), 248-254 (cleanliness), 255 (conservation), 368 (organic ideology), 170 (usable garbage), 233 and 255 (conservation and reuse of scrap and industrial waste), 265 (mesotechnic).

[493] Mumford, Ibid.: 218 (distinguished inventor), 221 (1882), 251 (1887), 245-250 (Light and Life), 245-246 (quotation).

[494] Mumford, Ibid.: 385 (Taylor), 226 (Ford).

[495] Arnold Pacey, *Technology in World Civilization: A Thousand-Year History* (Cambridge, Mass., 1990; paperback ed. 1991). Not in Pacey's Index, but appearing in the text, was Edison's competitor, Leo Bakeland, who made "bakelite" in 1907; it was said to be the "first plastic material for which the necessary large molecules were synthesized" (176).

[496] Pacey, *Technology in World Civilization*, 168-170 ("Electricity and Chemistry"), 168 (Edison and Swan).

[497] Pacey, Ibid., 170 (Edison and Upton).

[498] George Basalla, *The Evolution of Technology* (Cambridge: Cambridge University Press, 1988). In Basalla's Index, there are eight separate citations to Edison, and these are spread over a total of 13 pages of the text. By comparison, Heinrich Hertz has six citations, on a total of seven pages; Galileo has only two; Augustus H. Pitt-Rivers has four citations (on eight pages); and James Watt has seven, on seven pages. As often, errors and omissions may occur. For example, another citation for Edison is not in the Index, but he also appears on p.26, in a

list of "individual geniuses," along with Eli Whitney, Henry Ford, and the Wright Brothers.

[499] Basalla, *The Evolution of Technology*, 6-7.

[500] Basalla, Ibid., 45-49 (gas lighting system), 60 (in Russia), 61 (moving-picture apparatus).

[501] Basalla, Ibid., 139 (self-evident), 141 (best known), 140-141 (amusement), 143 (Model T).

[502] Basalla, Ibid., 218.

[503] Mumford, *Technics and Civilization,* 169-170.

[504] The truth of Mumford's statements regarding the transition from water power to steam in the Industrial Revolution in Scotland can be seen in the use of water power for cotton mills and its replacement by steam engines in Ian Donnachie and George Hewitt, *Historic New Lanark: The Dale and Owen Industrial Community Since 1785* (Edinburgh: Edinburgh University Press, 1983). For a similar pattern in the nineteenth century in Pennsylvania, see Anthony F. C. Wallace, *Rockdale: The Growth of an American Village in the Early Industrial Revolution* (New York: Alfred A. Knopf, 1972; paperback ed., New York: W. W. Norton, 1980).

[505] Mumford, *Technics and Civilization*, 222 (coal mines), 113 (wind and water).

[506] Sherwin B. Nuland, "Introduction" in *The Collected Stories of William Carlos Williams* (New York: New Directions Publishing Corp., 1961; paperback ed., 1996), xii.

[507] Edison (1922), quoted by Dagobert Runes (ed.), *The Diary and Sundry Observations of Thomas A. Edison* (New York: Philosophical Library, 1948), 93.

[508] Richard White, *The Organic Machine* (New York: Hill and Wang, 1995), 47 ("Frankensteinian"), 48-49 (Villard), 49-50 (illumination of Portland by Columbia River power).

[509] White, *The Organic Machine*, 55 (Pinchot . . . Mumford). Mumford, *Technics and Civilization*, 222 (electricity can be developed). When in 1922 Edison hoped to "harness the rise and fall of the tides," he antedated by about twelve years Mumford's reference to "tidal estuary" as a potential source of electrical power.

[510] White, *The Organic Machine*, 109-112.

[511] Tom Johnson, "Flooding Compels New Look at River," *Newark [N.J.] Star-Ledger*, 29 September 1997, 1,15; and Peter Waldman, "Electrical Storm: Dam Proposed for Laos is of Immense Meaning to an Array of Interests," *Wall Street Journal*, 12 August 1997, A1, A6.

[512] "Freeing the Kennebec River," *New York Times*, 9 August 1997, 22.

[513] William Carlos Williams, M.D., who lived from 1883 to 1963, did not personally see the arc lights in Philadelphia in 1876; the quotation is from "The Pace that Kills" in his *Collected Stories,* which were originally published between 1932 and 1950.

[514] Andrew Pollack, "Charge! Doing an Electric Commute," *New York Times*, 26 July 1998, Automobiles, sec. 12, 1; also, Ibid., "Keeping Current: Electrics in New York."

[515] Paul Starr, *The Social Transformation of American Medicine: The Rise of a Sovereign Profession and the Making of a Vast Industry* (New York: Basic Books, 1982), 189.

[516] Mary Douglas, *Purity and Danger: An Analysis of Concepts of Pollution and Taboo* (New York: Praeger Publishers, 1966), 2 (dirt is disorder).

[517] Douglas, Ibid., viii (relativity of dirt), 7 (sake of friendship).

[518] Douglas, Ibid., 9 (holy woman), 24 and 28 (Frazer), 29 (Moses).

[519] Mary Douglas and Baron Isherwood, *The World of Goods* (New York: Basic Books, Inc., 1979), 57.

[520] Douglas and Isherwood, *The World of Goods*, 112.

[521] Douglas and Isherwood, Ibid., 126-127.

[522] Ibid., 204-205

[523] Mary Douglas and Aaron Wildavsky, *Risk and Culture: An Essay on the Selection of Technical and Environmental Dangers* (Berkeley: University of California Press, 1982), 1.

[524] Douglas and Wildavsky, Ibid., 1-2.

[525] Douglas and Wildavsky, Ibid., 18.

[526] Ibid., 19.

[527] Ibid.

[528] Douglas and Wildavsky, *Risk and Culture*, 63.

[529] For the history of knowledge of the toxicity of these and other chemicals with which Edison worked, see Carl Zenz, M.D., Sc.D., *Occupational Medicine: Principles and Practical Applications* (Chicago: Year Book Medical Publishers, 1975), 2nd ed. (e.g. 547-582 [lead], 590-596 [mercury]); and *The International Technical Information Institute, Toxic and Hazardous Industrial Chemicals Safety Manual for Handling and Disposal with Toxicity and Hazard Data* (Tokyo: International Technical Information Institute, 1985) (e.g., 297-298 [lead], 313-315 [mercury]). The serious and potentially fatal hazards of working with these substances, and the symptoms and signs of pre-fatal toxicity, have been known for centuries. The dangers of ionizing radiation (e.g., radium and x-rays) and of organic chemicals were less well understood until the twentieth century.

[530] Jonathan Harr, *A Civil Action* (New York: Random House; Vintage Books ed., 1995).

[531] Rachel Carson, *Silent Spring* (1962; New York: Houghton Mifflin Co., 1994).

[532] Andrew Hurley, *Environmental Inequalities: Class, Race, and Industrial Pollution in Gary, Indiana, 1945-1980* (Chapel Hill, N.C.: University of North

Carolina Press, 1995); Kai Erickson, *A New Species of Trouble: The Human Experience of Modern Disasters* (New York: W. W. Norton, [1994]; 1995); Scott Lash, Bronislaw Szerszynski, and Brian Wynne (eds.), *Risk, Environment, and Modernity* (London: Sage Publications, 1996); Harr, *A Civil Action*; and Robert Gottlieb, *Forcing the Spring: The Transformation of the American Environmental Movement* (Washington, D.C.: Island Press, 1993).

[533] Runes (ed.), *Diary and Sundry Observations*, 5.

[534] Ibid., 15.

[535] Ibid., 29.

[536] Ibid., 35.

[537] Ibid., 51 ("Nature . . . business"), 220 (bridge falls), 157 (green hills), 241-242 (life . . . "nature").

[538] Ibid., 188 (outside world) ,192 (now have).

[539] Ibid., 237 (mammoth animals); 226-232 (three other quotations).

[540] Donald Worster, *Dust Bowl: The Southern Plains in the 1930s* (New York: Oxford University Press, 1979; paperback ed., 1982), 1-8.

[541] Carolyn Merchant, *Ecological Revolutions: Nature, Gender, and Science in New England* (Chapel Hill, N.C.: University of North Carolina Press, 1989), 2-4.

[542] Merchant, *Ecological Revolutions*, 1 (Marsh), 258 (Thoreau). Merchant cites Henry David Thoreau, *Walden, or Life in the Woods and On the Duty of Civil Disobedience* (1854; Reprint ed., New York: Harper and Row, 1965), 123.

[543] Thomas Kuhn, *The Structure of Scientific Revolutions* (Chicago: University of Chicago Press, 1962; paperback ed., 1996). *Rashomon* (Akiro Kurosawa, director, Japan, 1950) was a landmark movie which depicted an encounter in the woods in Japan between a man and a woman, told from the point of view of each person. Was it a rape, or not? The answer was never made clear in this quintessential "he said, she said" tale. "Occam's razor" refers to the principle that the simplest solution to a question is the correct answer.

[544] Runes (ed.), *Diary and Sundry Observations*, 112.

[545] Runes, Ibid., 233-234.

[546] For the Edison corporation's work with medical gases, see "EK Medical Gas laboratories, Inc." (date stamped: 21 Sep '37, page 10 and handwritten addition on 15 December 1938 referring to "vol. 14, Pg 59," and typed addition on 21 December 1938), from Archivist, ENHS, attached to Thomas A. Edison, Inc., "Annual Report" (1950), Title page and p.14. Also, Interview with Edward J. Daly, 28 February 1973, p.34 (Jack Stanley Papers); and John D. Venable, *Out of the Shadow: The Story of Charles Edison* (East Orange, N.J.: Charles Edison Fund, 1978), 60. Runes, Ibid., xii (whimsey), 233 ("scientific method" in spiritualism). For Edison's role as the pre-eminent inventor in American history, see Henry Pitroski, "An Independent Investigator," *American Scientist* 86 (May-

June 1998): 222-225. Pitroski wrote primarily about the work of Jerome H. Lemelson, who died at the age of 74 on 1 October 1997. *New York Times*, (4 October 1997), B6 ("When all of the patents are granted, only Edison will lay claim to more.").

[547] Runes, Ibid., 107 (necessary task), 45 (Detroit Public Library).

[548] Runes, Ibis., 124 (coeducation), 135 (college men), 131 (failure of colleges).

[549] Runes (ed.), *Diary and Sundry Observations*, 144-145 (motion pictures . . . radio . . . general intelligence test), 116-118 (990 out of a thousand facts).

[550] Jacques Steinberg, "Teachers Union Calls Edison Schools Project Unimpressive," *New York Times* (8 May 1998); and Somini Sengupta, "Edison Project Gets Aid to Open New Schools," *New York Times* (27 May 1998), A12.

[551] Runes (ed.), Ibid., 44.

[552] Runes (ed.), Ibid., 44-56.

[553] Lawrence K. Altman, "The Inside Story," review of *Naked to the Bone* by Bettyann Holtzmann Kevles, *New York Times* (29 June 1997), 31.

[554] Starr, *Social Transformation of American Medicine*; Stuart Galishoff, *Newark: The Nation's Unhealthiest City, 1832-1895* (New Brunswick, N.J.: Rutgers University Press, 1988).

[555] Edison was hardly alone in being enamored by spiritualism. See: Richard Brookhiser, "The Happy Medium," review of *Other Powers: The Age of Suffrage, Spiritualism, and the Scandalous Victoria Woodhull* by Barbara Goldsmith; and *Notorious Victoria: The Life of Victoria Woodhull, Uncensored* by Mary Gabriel, *New York Times Book Review* (29 March 1998), 11. A photograph of "radium girls" at work in the U.S. Radium Corp. plant in 1922 appears in *Newark [N.J.] Star-Ledger* (21 June 1998), 21.

[556] Jonathan Raban, *Bad Land: An American Romance* (New York: Random House; Vintage Books ed., 1996), 169 (emphasis added).

[557] Ginalie Swaim, "'Show Them the Goods': Small-Town Iowa Businesses in the 1920s, As Photographed by William H. Felton," *Iowa Heritage Illustrated* (Spring 1998), 38 (emphasis added).

[558] Raban, *Bad Land*, 30 (rainfall figures), 31 ("rain follows the plow," quoting Professor Agassiz, in 1867), 170 (apparently quoting an unnamed schoolbook which he found in an abandoned farmhouse near Mildred or Ismay [aka Joe], Mont., in the early 1990s) (emphasis added).

[559] Raban, *Bad Land*, 192-194 (Cletrac [one of these tractors, a relic, is now exhibited at Metzger's Farm, on the north side of Northfield Road in West Orange], Morse 40-light "F" Plant, New Edison Amberola).

[560] Swaim, "Small Town Iowa Businesses," 38-39.

[561] Ruth Schwartz Cowan, *More Work for Mother* (New York: Oxford, 1983), cited by Swaim, "Small Town Iowa Businesses," 43.

[562] Jeanne Boydston, *Home and Work: Housework, Wages, and the Ideology of Labor in the Early Republic* (New York: Oxford University Press, 1990), xvi (also see review of Cowan on pp xvi-xvii, and citation on 128). Cowan, "The 'Industrial Revolution' in the Home: Household Technology and Social Change in the Twentieth Century,'" *Technology and Culture* 17 (1976): 1-23 (quotations from 21-22). Also, see Liz McMillen, "Two Scholars Find that Americans Have More, Not Less, Free Time," review of *Time for Life: The Surprising Ways Americans Use Their Time*, by John P. Robinson and Geoffrey Godbey, *Chronicle of Higher Education* 44 (26 September 1997), A16.

[563] Runes (ed.), *Diary and Sundry Observations*, xi.

[564] *Webster's New World Dictionary*, 3rd College ed., 1988: Among the definitions of "modern" are "of the present or recent times; of or relating to the period of history after the Middle Ages, from c. A.D. 1450 to the present day," etc. Among the definitions of "modernism" are "modern practices, trends, ideas, etc., or sympathy with any of these"; "any of several movements variously attempting to redefine Biblical and Christian dogma and traditional teachings in the light of modern science, historical research, etc."; and "the general trend in the methods, styles, and philosophy of modern artists involving a break with the traditions of the past and a search for new modes of expression." *The Random House Dictionary of the English Language*, unabridged ed., 1967: Definitions of "modern" include "of or pertaining to present and recent time, not ancient or remote"; "of or pertaining to the historical period following the Middle Ages"; "of, pertaining to, or characteristic of contemporary styles of art, literature, music, etc., that reject traditionally accepted or sanctioned forms and emphasize individual experimentation and sensibility"; characteristic of present and recent time." Definitions of "modernism" include "modern character, tendencies, or sympathy with is modern."; "a modern usage or characteristic"; and "the liberal theological tendency in Protestantism in the 20th century."

[565] Many other writers have compared Edison to one or another of the men listed in this paragraph, although not always with respect to their perspectives on organized religion. Dagobert Runes, for example, wrote that "Edison was almost Franklinian in his defiance of the doctrines of pure science," in *Diary and Sundry Observations*, xi.

[566] Runes (ed.), *Diary and Sundry Observations*, 78 (God knows), 233-237 (quotation). Regarding Paine, Edison wrote that "I have always been interested in this man. . . My father had a set of Tom Paine's books on the shelf at home. . . I consider Paine our greatest political thinker. . . When Theodore Roosevelt termed Tom Paine a dirty little atheist he surely spoke from lack of understanding. . . I was always interested in Paine the inventor. He conceived and designed the iron bridge and the hollow candle; the principle of the modern central draught burner. The man had a sort of universal genius" (Ibid., "The Philosophy of Paine," 151-158).

[567] Hugh Kenner, "A Change of Mind," review of *The First Moderns* by William R. Everdell, *New York Times Book Review* (29 June 1997), 24.

[568] David Traxel, *1898: The Birth of the American Century* (New York: Alfred A. Knopf, 1998). Traxel's comments were made in response to the review of his book on 24 May 1998 in *The New York Times Book Review*.

[569] Joseph Hamblen Sears, *The Career of Leonard Wood* (New York: D. Appleton and Co., 1919), 39-41. "To General Leonard Wood," a poem by Corinne Roosevelt Robinson, Theodore's sister, appears on unnumbered p. 5.

[570] Susan Spano, "Chautauqua's Quiet Charm," *New York Times* (3 August 1997), Travel sec. (sec. 5), 6, 16.

[571] Jack Beatty, "A Capital Life," review of *Titan: The Life of John D. Rockefeller, Sr.* by Ron Chernow, *New York Times Book Review* (17 May 1998), 10, 11.

[572] Pauline Maier, "Jefferson, Real and Imagined," *New York Times* (4 July 1997), A19.

[573] Mark Dodson, *New York Times* (13 April 1998), Letters, A26 (history). Arnold R. Isaacs, review of *Code-Name Bright Light* by George J. Vieth, *New York Times Book Review* (n.d., 1998), 22 (what a historian is supposed to do). Patricia Cohen, "Geography Redux: Where You Live Is What You Are," *New York Times* (21 March 1998), Arts & Ideas sec., B7, B9 (Location matters). John N. Cole, "On the Ocean, Looking Back," *New York Times*, 11 June 1998, A11.

[574] Haim Watzman, "Study of the Dead Sea Scrolls Enters a New Era," *Chronicle of Higher Education* (1 August 1997), A14, A15. The quotation on the loneliness of the scholar is from a lecture given by Alison F. Richard, Provost of Yale University, New Haven, Conn., 24 April 1998.

Chapter 16: Conclusion: The Environmental Legacy of Thomas Edison
Pages 359-362

[575] Edison, quoted in William H. Meadowcroft, *Boys's Life of Edison with Autobiographical Notes by Mr. Edison* (New York: Harper & Row, 1911; 1949 edition), 18. Edison intended for Meadowcroft's readers to understand his distaste for life on the farm (ix).

[576] "Edison's Latest Discovery," *New Haven [Conn.] Leader*, 21 October 1911. The *New Haven Leader*, with tongue somewhat in cheek, asked Mr. Edison rhetorically if he would invent "a land system," "an educational system," "an economic system," to make this ideal possible, and also invent "a means of getting them adopted and placed in operation?" The *Leader* continued: "If you do these things, Mr. Edison, all your other useful and famous inventions will be submerged in the glory of this final triumph and you will be remembered forever as the inventor of human happiness."

[577] As an example of historic trends that degraded the environment and of environmental changes that tend to restore or improve it (only some of which were related to Edison's presence), consider what we have seen in West Orange:

The following sequence of events led to environmental degradation in the Orange Valley:

1. Forests, wetlands, and habitat for large animals were converted to farmland.
2. Industrialization of farmland occurred with construction of small mills and family factories, then large factories and pollution (e.g., Parrow Brook in Orange).
3. Major industrial development, beginning with the Edison factories. Wigwam Brook was covered over.
4. Radium contamination, especially by U.S. Radium Corporation.
5. Deep wells were contaminated with "volatile organics" from unknown sources, some of which were probably from Edison's plants.
6. Urban housing "blight" occurred along Main Street in West Orange. This followed the destruction of the Edison plant by urban redevelopment, and was not directly due to Edison's work.
7. Construction of Interstate 280, with loss of about 200 acres of Llewellyn Park, noise pollution, neighborhood disruption in West Orange, alterations in natural watercourses. Edison had nothing to do with this.
8. "Urban renewal" that tore down the Edison factories and other buildings, including the oldest house in West Orange, but did not "renew" the community; an "enterprise zone" is still declared for the Valley, east of Main Street.

Environmental conservation and restoration efforts have occurred, including:

1. Llewellyn Park persists; it is a Registered National Historic Landmark.
2. Sewer systems were created.
3. Town and county parks were established.
4. West Orange Historical Commission is designating historic districts.
5. National Park Service is a partner in preserving the Edison properties and the neighborhood; the Friends of Edison National Historic Site has been founded.

[578] Others have observed the ambivalent or ambiguous nature of Edison's character. For example, John M. Staudenmaier, "Edison: The Ambivalent Oracle," oral presentation at "Interpreting Edison" conference, 25 June 1997.

Wyn Wachhorst attempts to explain what he regards as Edison's ambiguous nature on the basis of a conflict between "Edison . . . the prophet of the liberal, secularized Protestant gospel of progress with its linear assumption of man's limitless perfectibility," in contrast to Edison as " 'the Old Man' — an indomitable eccentric in the pursuit of excellence, dreaming the impossible dream, sticking like hell, tending the machines — he is a more transcendent figure. He is the archetypal modern individual, an existential hero choosing the task of Sisyphus over the loss of identity which accompanies flight from conflict. (Wachhorst, *Edison*, 222).

While Wachhorst's two views of Edison are sufficiently disparate to account for ambiguity, they are both variants on a theme of modernity. I find in Edison a greater degree of ambiguity than Wachhorst does. My explanation is based on the fact that not all nineteenth century American Protestants were secularized. To the contrary, many people, including those in frontier towns such as Milan, Ohio, and Port Huron, Michigan, where Edison grew up, had a cyclical view of life with its seasons and generations — they had a pre-modern epistemology.

I therefore propose a sharper contrast than that espoused by Wachhorst; in my view, Edison can be characterized on the one hand as a "traditionalist," while also being a "modernist."

[579] "*Dans les champs de l'obseration le hasard ne vavorise que les espirits prepares*" (In the field of observation, chance favors the prepared mind). Josephson writes, without a citation, that it was Pasteur who said: "Chance favors the mind that is prepared." (Josephson, *Edison*, 158). Rene Vallery-Radot, *The Life of Pasteur* (trans. Mrs. R. L. Devonshire, 1919) attributes it to the Inaugural Address made by Pasteur as the newly appointed Professor and Dean (Sep 1854) at the opening of the new Faculté des Sciences at Lille (7 Dec 1854) (https://todayinsci.com/P/Pasteur_Louis/PasteurLouis-Quotations.htm, 14 March 2017).

Regarding "Mind One" and "Mind Two," see Edison's diary entry for 20 July 1885: "My No. 2 mind (acquired mind) has succeeded in convincing my No. 1 mind (primal mind or heart) . . ." (Runes [ed.], *Diary and Sundry Observations*, 34). Conot writes of Edison's conscience (or lack of it) at various places; e.g., he quotes Edison as saying: "My conscience must be incrusted with a sort of irreligious tartr" (*Edison*, 238; citation in 525n to Edison's diary entry, 12 July 1885). The entry in Runes is actually "My conscience seems to be oblivious of Sunday. It must be incrusted with a sort of irreligious tartr" (8).

[580] If the term, "New Enlightenment," was coined by someone else, I have inadvertently used it here without attribution. I trust the reader will see that I intend to use this term to refer to the period in which we now live. This term indirectly refers to the Age of Enlightenment, and I use it to refer to Edison with pun intended. The New Enlightenment begins with Edison's invention of the phonograph in 1877. It includes his inventions in the fields of electricity and lighting, and in motion pictures.

[581] My view of Edison as a Great Curmudgeon in his dotage is reinforced by the reminiscences of William Hand, who worked with Edison at West Orange, Silver Lake, and Fort Myers, Fla., when he (Edison) was in his late 70s and early 80s. We have read excerpts from Hand's narrative about Silver Lake and West Orange; the Fort Myers section can be found in the transcript in the Jack Stanley Papers and [presumably] at the Columbia University Library, New York City.

Bibliography

Books and Articles

Agar, Michael H., Christopher L. Borstel, Antony B. Mason, Ingrid A. Wuebber. *Ethnographic Overview and Assessment, Edison National Historic Site, West Orange, New Jersey*. East Orange, N.J.: Louis Berger and Associates, New England Support System Office, U.S. National Park Service, and Edison National Historic Site, 1997. [a 126-page report with 1 cm. of unpaginated Appendices, in the library of the Archives, ENHS]

Alanen, Arnold R. "New Towns and Planned Communities," in *American Landscape Architecture: Designers and Places*. Edited by William H. Tishler. Washington, D.C.: Preservation Press, 1989.

Ambrose, Stephen E. *Undaunted Courage: Meriwether Lewis, Thomas Jefferson, and the Opening of the American West*. New York: Simon & Schuster, 1996; Touchstone edition, 1997.

American Victorian Architecture: A Survey of the 70's and 80's in Contemporary Photographs. 1886; reprint, with an introduction by Arnold Lewis and notes on the plates by Keith Morgan, New York: Dover, 1975.

Anderson, Alice Hardiman, and Daniel M. Ogden, Jr. *A History of the Robert S. Ogden Family*. Washington, D.C.: n.p., 1986.

Aquilina, Charles L., Richard T. Koles, and Jean-Rae Turner. *Elizabethtown and Union County: A Pictorial History*. Norfolk, Va.: Donning, 1982.

Aries, Philippe. *The Hour of Our Death*. New York: Knopf, 1981; paperback, 1991.

Baldwin, Neil. *Edison: Inventing the Century*. 1st paperback ed. New York: Hyperion, 1995.

Bergman, Norman A. "Georgiana, Duchess of Devonshire, and Princess Diana: A Parallel." *Journal of the Royal Society of Medicine* 91 (April 1998): 217-219.

Bertland, Dennis N. *Early Architecture of Warren County*. Belvidere, N.J.: Warren County Board of Chosen Freeholders, n.d. [1976].

Black, Sallie, and Margaret A. Riggin. *Excerpts from Early Bloomfield, N.J., Newspapers 1872-1895*. Bloomfield: Historical Society of Bloomfield, 1982. [copy at The Bloomfield Historical Society]

[Bloomfield Public Library] Free Public Library of Bloomfield (eds.) *Bloomfield, New Jersey*. Bloomfield: The Independent Press, 1932.

[Belleville, N.J.] Federal Writers' Project. *A History of Belleville, New Jersey*. Np., n.d. [ca. 1937] [copy from Frederick Lewis, Librarian, Silver Lake Branch, Belleville Public Library]

Brauer, Norman. *There to Breathe the Beauty: The Camping Trips of Henry Ford, Thomas Edison, Harvey Firestone, John Burroughs*. Dalton, Pa., 1995.

Braverman, Harry. *Labor and Monopoly Capital: The Degradation of Work in the Twentieth Century*. New York: Monthly Review Press, 1974.

Brockman, C. Frank. *Trees of North America*. New York: Golden Press, 1968.

Bunnell, Paul J. *The New Loyalist Index*. Bowie, Md.: Heritage Books, 1989.

Burnett, Robert B. *Belleville: 150th-Anniversary Historical Highlights, 1839-1989*. Belleville, N.J.: 150th-Anniversary Committee, 1991.

Bush-Brown, James and Louise. *America's Garden Book*. New York: Scribner's, 1939. New Revised edition, 1958.

Cannon, Bradford. *The Way of an Investigator*. 1945. Reprint, New York: Harper, 1961.

Carson, Rachel. *Silent Spring*. 1962. New York: Houghton Mifflin, 1994.

Castiglioni, Arturo. *A History of Medicine*. Translated and edited by E. B. Krumbhaar. New York: Alfred A. Knopf, 1941.

Chandler, Alfred DuPont. *The Visible Hand: The Managerial Revolution in American Business*. Cambridge, Mass.: Belknap Press, 1977.

Claire, Sister Loretta, O.P., and Norman J. Brydon. *Caldwell, Yesterday and Today:1776-1976*. Caldwell, N.J.: Caldwell Bicentennial Committee, 1976.

Clancy, Tom. *The Hunt for Red October*. Annapolis, Md.: Naval Institute Press, 1984.

Clark, Ronald W. *Edison: The Man Who Made the Future*. New York: G. P. Putnam's Sons, 1977.

Conot, Robert. *Thomas A. Edison: A Streak of Luck*. New York: Seaview, 1979. Reprint, paperback, New York: DaCapo/Plenum, 1986.

Cook, James G. *Thomas Alva Edison: His Fertile Mind Forged Much of Our Country's Growth*. Southfield, Mich.: Thomas Alva Edison Foundation, 1976.

Cowan, Ruth Schwartz. "The 'Industrial Revolution' in the Home: Household Technology and Social Change in the Twentieth Century." *Technology and Culture* 17 (1976): 1-23.

Creswell, J. Max. *Newspaper Transcriptions: First Presbyterian Church, Roselle, New Jersey*. Privately printed, 1990-1994. [copy at church and Roselle Public Library]

Cronon, William. *Changes in the Land: Indians, Colonists, and the Ecology of New England*. New York: Farrar, Straus & Giroux, 1983. Paperback edition, Hill and Wang, 1992.

Cronon, William. *Nature's Metropolis: Chicago and the Great West*. New York: Norton, 1991. Paperback edition, 1992.

Crosby, Alfred W. *Ecological Imperialism: The Biological Expansion of Europe, 900-1900*. Cambridge: Cambridge University Press, [1986] 1993.

Cunningham, John T. *Thomas Edison: They Called Him Wizard*. Newark, N.J.: Public Service Electric & Gas Co., 1979.

Cunningham. *Newark*. Revised and Expanded Edition. Newark, N.J.: New Jersey Historical Society, 1988.

Cunningham. *Railroading in New Jersey* [Newark, N.J.?]: Associated Railroads of New Jersey, [1951?].

Cunningham. *This Is New Jersey*. 4th ed. New Brunswick, N.J.: Rutgers University Press, 1994.

Cunningham, and Charles F. Cummings. *Remembering Essex: A Pictorial History of Essex County, New Jersey*. Virginia Beach, Va.: Donning Company, 1995.

Dalton, R., and F. J. Markewicz. "Stratigraphy and Characteristics of Cavern Development in the Carbonate Rocks of New Jersey." *Bulletin of the National Speleological Society* 34, no. 4 (1972): 115-128.

Daly, Michael. *Topsy: The Startling Story of the Crooked Tail Elephant, P.T. Barnum, and the American Wizard, Thomas Edison*. New York: Grove/Atlantic, Inc., 2013.

De Long, George Washington. *The Voyage of the Jeanette: The Ship and Ice Journals of George W De Long ...* 2 vols. Edited by Emma De Long. Boston: Houghton, Mifflin & Co., 1884.

Demos, John. *A Little Commonwealth: Family Life in Plymouth Colony*. New York: Oxford University Press, 1970. Paperback edition, 1971.

Donnachie, Ian, and George Hewitt. *Historic New Lanark: The Dale and Owen Industrial Community Since 1785*. Edinburgh: Edinburgh University Press, 1993.

Douglas, Mary. *Purity and Danger: An Analysis of Concepts of Pollution and Taboo*. New York: Praeger Publishers, 1966.

Douglas, and Baron Isherwood. *The World of Goods*. New York: Basic Books, Inc., 1979.

Douglas, and Aaron Wildavsky. *Risk and Culture: An Essay on the Selection of Technical and Environmental Dangers*. Berkeley, Calif.: University of California Press, 1982.

Doyle, Edward, Jr. *Harrison: A Brief History of an American Town*. n.p., n.d. [after 1976].

Drake, Avery Ala, Jr., Richard A. Volkert, Donald H. Monteverde, Gregory C. Herman, Hugh F. Houghton, Ronald A. Parker, and Richard F. Dalton. *Bedrock Geologic Map of Northern New Jersey*. U.S. Geological Survey, 1996.

Dunn, Pete J. *The Story of Franklin and Sterling Hill*. Washington, D.C.: Department of Mineral Sciences, Smithsonian Institution, 1997.

Edison, Thomas A. Introduction to *The Life and Works of Thomas Paine*, by William M. Van der Weyde. Vol. 1. New Rochelle, NY: Thomas Paine National Historical Association, 1925.

Edison. *The Diary and Sundry Observations of Thomas Alva Edison*. Edited by Dagobert D. Runes. New York: Philosophical Library, 1948.

Edison. *The Diary of Thomas A. Edison.* Edited and with an Introduction by Kathleen L. McGuirk. Old Greenwich, Conn.: Chatham/Viking, n.d. [1971]. Contains facsimile reproduction of Edison's holographic diary from July 12 to July 20, 1885 (pp. 27-70).

[Edison]. *The Papers of Thomas A. Edison,* 3 vols. Edited by Reese V. Jenkins, Leonard S. Reich, Paul B. Israel, Toby Appel, Andrew J. Butrica, Robert A. Rosenberg, Keith A. Nier, Melodie Andrews, and Thomas E. Jeffrey. Baltimore, Md.: Johns Hopkins University Press, 1989-1994. Jenkins, Reich, Israel, Appel, et al. *The Making of an Inventor: February 1847-June 1873.* Vol. 1, 1989. Rosenberg, Israel, Nier, and Andrews, eds., *From Workshop to Laboratory: June 1873-March 1876.* Vol. 2, 1991. Rosenberg, Israel, Nier, and Martha J. King, eds., *Menlo Park: The Early Years, April 1876-December 1877.* Vol. 3, 1994.

[Edison] Thomas Edison, *Henry Ford Winter Estates, Fort Myers, Florida* (Kansas City, Mo.: Terrell Publishing Co., n.d., [ca. 1997]).

[Edison] "Edison's Concrete Houses." *Fine Homebuilding,* March 1998, back cover.

Elizabethtown Directory for 1870: A Business Directory of Rahway and Plainfield and an Appendix of Much Useful Information. Elizabeth, N.J.: Fitzgerald and Dillon, 1870.

Erickson, Kai. *A New Species of Trouble: The Human Experience of Modern Disasters.* New York: W. W. Norton, 1994. Paperback edition, 1995.

Essig, Mark. *Edison and the Electric Chair: A Story of Light and Death.* New York: Walker Publishing Co., 2003.

Faragher, John Mack. *Sugar Creek: Life on the Illinois Prairie.* New Haven: Yale University Press, 1986.

Fleming, Thomas. *New Jersey: A History.* New York: Norton, 1984.

Folsom, John Fulford, Benedict Fitzpatrick, and Edward Conklin. *The Municipalities of Essex County, New Jersey 1666-1924.* New York: Lewis Historical Publishing Co., 1925.

Franklin, Benjamin. *The Autobiography of Benjamin Franklin.* 1771. Reprint, New York: Washington Square Press, 1961.

Friedel, Robert, and Paul Israel, with Bernard S. Finn. *Edison's Electric Light: Biography of an Invention.* New Brunswick, N.J.: Rutgers University Press, 1987.

Frohman, Charles E. *Milan and the Milan Canal: The Canal, Shipyards, Grain Port, Edison's Birthplace, The Moravians.* Sandusky, Ohio: Charles E. Frohman, 1976.

Frolich, William, and Helen Heumann. *The Centennial History of the Borough of Roselle.* N.p., n.d. [Roselle, N.J.: Roselle Historical Society, 1994].

Galishoff, Stuart. *Newark: The Nation's Unhealthiest City, 1832-1895.* New Brunswick, N.J.: Rutgers University Press, 1988.

Gallagher, William B. *When Dinosaurs Roamed New Jersey.* New Brunswick: Rutgers University Press, 1997.

Garrison, Fielding H. *An Introduction to the History of Medicine*. 4th ed. 1913; revised, 1929. Reprint, Philadelphia: W. B. Saunders, 1960).

Gilbert, A.C. "A. C. Gilbert, Scientific Toymaker: A Symposium." *Essays in Arts and Sciences* 25 (October 1996).

Glen Ridge Public Library. "Barrows Collection Inventory," Glen Ridge Historical Collection Indexes. Nd. [a notebook describing the files of photographic negatives and positives in the collection.

Gore, Rick. "The Most Ancient Americans." *National Geographic* 192, no. 4 (October 1997): 92-99.

Gottlieb, Robert. *Forcing the Spring: The Transformation of the American Environmental Movement*. Washington, D.C.: Island Press, 1993.

Gould, Stephen Jay. *The Mismeasure* of Man. New York: W. W. Norton, 1966. Paperback edition, 1981.

Grove, Richard H. *Green Imperialism: Colonial Expansion, Tropical Island Edens and the Origins of Environmentalism, 1600-1860*. Cambridge: Cambridge University Press, 1995. Paperback edition, 1996.

Grun, Bernard. *The Timetables of History*. 3rd ed. New York: Simon & Schuster, 1991.

Guttridge, Leonard F. *Icebound: The Jeanette Expedition's Quest for the North Pole*. Annapolis, Md.: Naval Institute Press, 1986.

Hafner, Arthur W. (ed.). *Directory of Deceased American Physicians 1804-1929*. Chicago: American Medical Association, 1993.

Halgrim, Robert P. *Winter Estates, Fort Myers, Florida: Thomas Edison and Henry Ford*. Kansas City, Mo.: Terrell Publishing Co., n.d. [ca. 1997].

Halsey, Edmund Drake. *Descendants of Robert Ogden*, 2d, 1716-1787. Amenia, N.Y.: Walsh and Griffin, 1896.

Harr, Johnathan. *A Civil Action*. 1995. New York: Vintage/Random House, 1996.

Harrison-Kearny Directory. Newark, N.J.: Price & Lee Co., 1929, 1938, 1940, 1950, 1952, 1954, 1956.

Harte, Bret. *The Writings of Bret Harte*. 1882. Boston: Houghton Muffin & Co., 1910, vol. 12 ("Copperhead," 1864; "Caldwell of Springfield," 1873).

Herpers, Harry, and Henry C. Barksdale. *Preliminary Report on the Geology and Ground-Water Supply of the Newark, New Jersey, Area*. New Jersey Department of Conservation and Economic Development, Division of Water Policy and Supply, 1951.

Hicks, J. Maurice. *Roselle, New Jersey: Site of Thomas Alva Edison's First Village Plant*. Roselle: Roselle Historical Society, 1979.

Hipp, Mrs. Walter C. "A Profile of the Town of Kearny's History." Kearny, N.J.: Kearny Public Library, 1967.

Hipp, Mrs. Walter C. *This Is Your Town, Kearny: A Bicentennial Tour of Its Historic and Notable Places*. Kearny, N.J.: American Revolution Bicentennial Commission of Kearny, 1980.

Horuzy, Paul, ed. *The Odyssey of Ogdensburg and the Sterling Hill Zinc Mine: The Story of the Growth of a Mining Town and Its Unique Place in Science and History*. Ogdensburg, N.J.: Sterling Hill Mining Co., 1990.

Howell, George Rogers. *The Early History of Southampton, LI., New York, with Genealogies*. 2nd ed. Albany [N.Y.]: Weed, Parsons and Co., 1887. Facsimile reprint, Bowie, Md.: Heritage Books, 1989.

Hoyt, James. *"The Mountain Society": A History of the First Presbyterian Church, Orange, N.J.* New York: Saxton, Barker & Co, 1860.

Hurley, Andrew. *Environmental Inequalities: Class, Race, and Industrial Pollution in Gary, Indiana, 1945-1980*. Chapel Hill, NC.: University of North Carolina Press, 1995.

International Technical Information Institute. *Toxic and Hazardous Industrial Chemicals Safety Manual for Handling and Disposal with Toxicity and Hazard Data*. Tokyo: International Technical Information Institute, 1985.

Israel, Paul. *Edison: A Life of Invention*. New York: John Wiley & Sons. 1998.

Jackson, Donald Dale. "A Stout Ship's Heartbreaking Ordeal by Ice." *Smithsonian* (March 1997), 86-98.

Jehl, Francis. *Menlo Park Reminiscences*, 3 vols. Dearborn, Mich.: Edison Institute, 1937. Reprint of Vol. 1, with an introduction by William S. Pretzer, New York: Dover, 1990.

Jonnes, Jill. *Empires of Light: Edison, Tesla, Westinghouse and the Race to Electrify the World*. New York: Random House, 2003.

Josephson, Matthew. *Edison: A Biography*. New York: McGraw-Hill, 1959. Reprint, with a foreword by Reese V. Jenkins, New York: John Wiley and Sons, 1992.

[Kane, Elisha Kent] Villarejo, Oscar M, ed. *Dr. Kane's Voyage to the Polar Lands*, by Johan Carl Christian Peterson. Philadelphia: University of Pennsylvania Press, 1965.

Kiser, Ellis. *Atlas of Essex County, New Jersey*. Philadelphia: A. H. Muller & Co., 1906.

Kubler-Ross, Elizabeth. *On Death and Dying*. New York: Macmillan, 1969.

Kuhn, Thomas. *The Structure of Scientific Revolutions*. Chicago: University of Chicago Press, 1962. Paperback edition, 1996.

Lash, Joseph P. *Eleanor and Franklin*. New York, 1972.

Lash, Scott, Bronislaw Szerszynski, and Brian Wynne, eds. *Risk, Environment, and Modernity*. London: Sage Publications, 1996.

Lee, James. *The Morris Canal: A Photographic History*. Easton, Md.: Delaware Press, 1994.

Lee, ed. *Tales the Boatmen Told: Recollections of the Morris Canal*. Easton, Md.: Delaware Press, 1977.

Lockward, Lynn G. *A Puritan Heritage: The First Presbyterian Church in Horse-Neck*. Caldwell, N.J., 1955.

MacFadyen, Robert, and John P. Deley. "75th Anniversary Journal." North Arlington, N.J.: Journal Committee, n.d. [ca. 1971].

MacInnes, Margo. *Thomas A. Edison's Menlo Park Laboratory Including the Sarah Jordan Boardinghouse*. Dearborn, Mich.: Henry Ford Museum & Greenfield Village, 1990.

Maddex, Diane, ed. *Master Builders: A Guide to Famous American Architects*. Washington, D.C.: Preservation Press, 1985.

Maddex, and Janet Walker, eds. *American Landscape Architecture: Designers and Places*. Washington, D.C.: Preservation Press, 1989.

Marshall, David Trumbull. *Boyhood Days in Early Metuchen*. 1929. Metuchen, N.J.: Metuchen Regional Historical Society by Quinn & Boden Co., 1977. Reprint of 2nd ed., Flushing, N.Y.: Case Publishing Co., 1930.

McAlester, Virginia, and Lee McAlester, with photographs by Alex McLean. *Great American Homes and Their Architectural Styles*. New York: Abbeville, 1994.

McGoldrick, Monica. *You Can Go Home Again: Reconnecting with Your Family*. New York: Norton, 1995.

McGuffey, W[illia]m H. *McGuffey's New Fourth Eclectic Reader: Instructive Lessons for the Young*. Cincinnati: Wilson, Hinkle & Co., 1857.

McGuffey, W[illia]m H. *McGuffey s New Eclectic Spelling-Book: Embracing a Progressive Course of Instruction in English Orthography and Orthoepy; Including Dictation Exercises*. Cincinnati: Wilson, Hinkle & Co., 1865.

McGuirk, Kathleen L. Introduction to *The Diary of Thomas A. Edison*, by Thomas A. Edison. Old Greenwich, Conn.: Chatham/Viking, n.d. [1971].

McHugh, Francis Dodd, and Theodore McCrosky. *Master Plan of West Orange*. New York: McHugh and McCrosky, 1953. [copy in the West Orange Room, West Orange Public Library]

McMillen, Liz. "Two Scholars Find that Americans Have More, Not Less, Free Time." Review of *Time for Life: The Surprising Ways Americans Use Their Time*, by John P. Robinson and Geoffrey Godbey. *Chronicle of Higher Education* 44 (September 26, 1997), A16.

McNeill, William H. *Plagues and Peoples*. New York: Doubleday, 1977. Anchor Book, 1989.

McPhee, John. *Assembling California*. New York: Farrar, Straus & Giroux, 1993.

Meadowcroft, William H. *The Boys' Life of Edison, with Autobiographical Notes by Mr. Edison*. New York: Harper & Row, 1911; 1949 edition.

Meadowcroft, ed. *The Life of Thomas A. Edison ...* , by Arthur Palmer. n.p. [?New York]: King Features, 1927.

Medical Society of New Jersey. *Physician Membership Directory: 1997-1998.* Lawrenceville, N.J.: Medical Society of New Jersey, 1997.

Metzger, Thom. *Blood & Volts: Edison, Tesla and the Invention of the Electric Chair.* N.p.: Autonomedia, 1996.

Melosi, Martin V. *Thomas A. Edison and the Modernization of America.* New York: Harper Collins, 1990.

Merchant, Carolyn. *Ecological Revolutions: Nature, Gender; and Science in New England.* Chapel Hill, N.C.: University of North Carolina Press, 1989.

Millard, Andre. *Edison and the Business of Invention.* Baltimore: Johns Hopkins University Press, 1990. Softshell Books, 1993.

Miller, Francis Trevelyan. *Thomas A. Edison: Benefactor of Mankind. The Romantic Life Story of the World's Greatest Inventor.* Philadelphia: John C. Winston Co., 1931.

Mitchell, S. Augustus. *First Lessons in Geography for Young Children.* Philadelphia: J. H. Butler & Co., 1874.

Mitchell, Alison E. *The New Jersey Highlands: Treasures at Risk.* Morristown, N.J.: New Jersey Conservation Foundation, 1992.

Mitford, Jessica. *The American Way of Death.* New York: Simon & Schuster, 1963.

Morison, Samuel Eliot. *The Second Voyage of Christopher Columbus from Cadiz to Hispaniola and the Discovery of the Lesser Antilles.* Oxford: Clarendon Press, 1939.

Morison. *Admiral of the Ocean Sea: A Life of Christopher Columbus.* Boston: Little, Brown, 1942.

Morison. *The Two Ocean War: A Short History of the United States Navy in the Second World War.* Boston: Little, Brown, 1963.

Morison. *The Oxford History of the American People.* New York: Oxford University Press, 1965.

Morris, B. F. "Kearny's Industrial Leaders Say." In *Why Kearny, New Jersey.* Kearny: Mayor and Council of Kearny, 1939.

Mumford, Lewis. *Technics and Civilization.* New York: Harcourt, Brace and World, 1934. Reprint, with a new introduction by the author, New York: Harcourt, Brace and World, Harbinger Books, 1963.

Musser, Charles. *Thomas A. Edison and His Kinetographic Motion Pictures.* New Brunswick, N.J.: Rutgers University Press, 1995.

Mutz, Henry A. *Harrison: The History of a New Jersey Town.* Harrison, N.J.: Harrison Bicentennial Committee, 1976.

National Audubon Society Field Guide to North American Trees: Eastern Region. New York: Chanticler Press, 1980; 1996 edition.

National Fire Protection Association and National Board of Fire Underwriters. *Report on Fire: The Edison Phonograph Works, Thomas A. Edison, Inc., West Orange, N.J.*, December 9, 1914. N.d. [?1915]. [copy at ENHS archives]

New Jersey Department of Environmental Protection. *Risk Assessment for Chromium Sites in Hudson County, New Jersey.* Trenton, N.J.: Department of Environmental Protection, 1989.

Nichols, William D. *Ground-Water Resources of Essex County, New Jersey.* U.S. Geological Survey, 1968.

Noble, David F. *America by Design: Science, Technology, and the Rise of Corporate Capitalism.* New York: Alfred A. Knopf, 1977. Paperback edition, New York: Oxford University Press, 1979.

Northedge, F. S. *The League of Nations: Its Life and Times 1920-1946.* New York: Holmes & Meier, 1986.

Nuland, Sherwin B. *How We Die: Reflections on Life's Final Chapter.* New York: Knopf, 1994.

Nuland. "Introduction." *The Collected Stories of William Carlos Williams.* New York: New Directions Publishing Corp., 1961. Paperback edition, 1996.

[Orange, N.J.] "Inscriptions from Monumental Stones in the Public Cemetery at Orange Formerly Orangedale 1847." vol 2 (N.p., n.d.[?1847]). [An unpaginated notebook in the archives of the First Presbyterian Church, Orange, N.J., courtesy of Robert M. Reed, Historian of the church]

Pacey, Arnold. *Technology in World Civilization: A Thousand-Year History.* Cambridge, Mass.: MIT Press, 1990. Paperback edition, 1991.

Paterson, Thomas J., J. Garry Clifford, and Kenneth J. Hagan. *American Foreign Relations: A History to 1920.* 4th ed., vol. 1. Lexington, Mass.: Heath, 1995.

Peterson, Michael. "Thomas Edison's Concrete Houses." *Invention and Technology.* Winter 1996, 50-56.

Pierson, David Lawrence. *History of the Oranges to 1921: Reviewing the Rise, Development and Progress of an Influential Community.* 4 vols. New York: Lewis Historical Publishing Company. 1922.

Pierson, Duane. *Images of Sparta: An Historical Narrative.* Newton, N.J.: Minisink Press, 1981.

Pretzer, William S., ed. *Working at Inventing: Thomas A. Edison and the Menlo Park Experience.* Dearborn, Mich.: Henry Ford Museum and Greenfield Village, 1993.

Pinneo, T. S., M.D. *Pinneo's Primary Grammar of the English Language, for Beginners.* Cincinnati: Winthrop B. Smith & Co., 1854.

Pitrosky, Henry. "An Independent Investigator." *American Scientist* 86 (May-June 1998): 222-225.

Polmar, Norman. *The Ships and Aircraft of the U.S. Fleet.* 14th ed. Annapolis, Md.: Naval Institute Press, 1987.

Pulido, Laura. *Environmentalism and Economic Justice: Two Chicano Struggles in the Southwest*. Tuscon, Ariz.: University of Arizona Press, 1996.

Pustay, M. R., and T. K. Shea. *Abandoned Iron Mines of Sussex County*, New Jersey. Trenton, N.J.: New Jersey Department of Labor, Mine Safety Section, 1982.

Pyne, Stephen J. "Firestick History." *Journal of American History* 76 (March 1990):1132-1141.

Raban, Jonathan. *Bad Land: An American Romance*. New York: Random House, Vintage Books, 1996.

Ray, Joseph, M.D. *Ray's Arithmetic, Third Book: Practical Arithmetic by Induction and Analysis*. 1,000th [sic] ed. Cincinnati: Winthrop B. Smith & Co., 1857.

Robbins, Keith Spalding. "A History of the Development of the First Planned American Suburban Community: Llewellyn Park, West Orange." Master's thesis, Georgetown University, 1989. [copy in West Orange Public Library]

Robinson, B. *Robinson's Atlas of Essex County, New Jersey*. New York: B. Robinson, 1890.

Robinson, Corinne Roosevelt. "To General Leonard Wood." In Joseph Hamblen Sears, *The Career of Leonard Wood*, 5. New York: D. Appleton and Co., 1919.

Robinson, Enders A. *Salem Witchcraft and Hawthorne's House of the Seven Gables*. Bowie, Md.: Heritage Books, 1992.

Roediger, David R. *The Wages of Whiteness: Race and the Making of the American Working Class*. New York: New Left Books/Verso, 1991. Paperback edition, 1993.

Rosanoff M. A. "Edison in His Laboratory." *Harper's* (Sept 1932), 402-417.

Roscoe, Theodore. *United States Destroyer Operations in World War II*. Annapolis, Md.: Naval Institute Press, 1953.

Runes, Dagobert D. "Preface." *The Diary and Sundry Observations of Thomas Alva Edison*. New York: Philosophical Library, 1948.

Savary, W. A. "Connection of the Family of Edison the Inventor with Digby, Nova Scotia." *New England History Genealogical Record* 48 (April 1894): 199.

Schiebinger, Londa. *The Mind Has No Sex? Women in the Origins of Modern Science*. Cambridge, Mass.: Harvard University Press, 1989.

Schivelbusch, Wolfgang. *The Railway Journey: The Industrialization of Time and Space in the 19th Century*. Berkeley: University of California Press, 1986. Originally published as *Geschichte der Eisenbahnreise*. Munich: Carl Hanser Verlag, 1977.

Scott, George. *The Rise and Fall of the League of Nations*. New York: Macmillan, 1973.

Sennet, Richard. *Flesh and Stone: The Body and the City in Western Civilization*. New York: Random House, 1994; Norton paperback, 1996.

Sears, Joseph Hamblen. *The Career of Leonard Wood*. New York: D. Appleton and Co., 1919.

Shakespeare, William. *The Tempest*. Edited by David Home. New Haven: Yale University Press, 1955.

Shaw, William H. *History of Essex and Hudson Counties, New Jersey*. Philadelphia: Everts & Peck, 1884.

Sharpe, William D. "Chronic Radium Intoxication: Clinical and Autopsy Findings in Long-Term New Jersey Survivors." *Environmental Research* 8, no. 3 (December 1974): 243-383.

Sinclair, Donald Arleigh. *A New Jersey Biographical Index*. Baltimore: Genealogical Publishing Co., 1993.

Slocum, Joshua. *Sailing Alone Around the World*. 1900. Annapolis, Md.: U.S. Naval Institute Press, 1985.

Smith, Roswell C. *Practical and Mental Arithmetic, on a New Plan ...* New York: Daniel Burgess & Co., 1835.

Snell, James P. *History of Sussex and Warren Counties, New Jersey with Illustrations and Biographical Sketches of its Prominent Men and Pioneers*. Philadelphia: Everts & Peck, 1881.

Sobel, Dava. *Longitude: The True Story of a Lone Genius Who Solved the Greatest Scientific Problem of His Time*. New York: Walker, 1995.

Stamps, Richard B., Bruce Hawkins, and Nancy E. Wright. *Search for the House in the Grove: Archeological Excavation of the Boyhood Homesite of Thomas A. Edison in Port Huron, Michigan, 1976-1994*. Rochester, Mich.: Cultural Dynamics, 1994.

Stark, James H. *The Loyalists of Massachusetts and the Other Side of the American Revolution*. Boston: W. B. Clark Co., 1910. Reprint edition, Bowie, Md.: Heritage Books, 1988.

Starr, Paul. *The Social Transformation of American Medicine: The Rise of a Sovereign Profession and the Making of a Vast Industry*. New York: Basic Books, 1982.

Stilgoe, John R. *Borderland: Origins of the American Suburb, 1820-1939*. New Haven: Yale University Press, 1988.

Sullivan, Robert. *The Meadowlands*. New York: Scribners, 1998.

Swaim Ginalie. " 'Show Them the Goods': Small-Town Iowa Business in the 1920s, as Photographed by William H. Felton." *Iowa Heritage Illustrated* (Spring 1998): 38-39, 43-45.

Tate, Alfred O. *Edison's Open Door: The Life Story of Thomas A. Edison, A Great Individualist*. New York: E. P. Dutton & Co., 1938.

Taylor, Frederick Winslow. *Scientific Management*. New York: Harper and Brothers, 1947.

Thoreau, Henry David. *Walden, or Life in the Woods and On the Duty of Civil Disobedience*. 1854. Reprint edition, New York: Barnes and Noble, 1993.

Thorpe, Patricia. *The American Weekend Garden*. New York: Random House, 1988.

Tinkham, Julian R. *Map and Illustrations of the Morris Canal Water Parkway*. Montclair, N.J.: Morris Canal Parkway Association, 1914. Reprint, by Russell H. Harding, 1975.

Traviano, Ronald (ed). *Glen Ridge Heritage*. Glen Ridge, N.J.: Bicentennial Committee, 1976. [at Glen Ridge Public Library]

Trout, R. E., and R. S. Weston. "Edison Signal Batteries 50 Years of Progress." Bloomfield, N.J.: Thomas A. Edison, Inc., 1939. [copy from Lucy Sant'Ambroglio, The Historical Society of Bloomfield]

Ulrich, Laurel Thatcher. *A Midwife's Tale: The Life of Martha Ballard, Based on Her Diary, 1785-1812*. New York: Vintage Books, 1990.

Uschold, David L., and George W Curry. *Cultural Landscape Report for Laboratory Unit, Edison National Historic Site: Site History, Existing Conditions, and Analysis*. Boston: Olmsted Center for Landscape Preservation and National Park Service, 1997. [a 112-page report with about 27 pages of unpaginated Appendices, in the library of the archives, ENHS]

United States Environmental Protection Agency [U.S.E.P.A.]. "Vicinity Properties Area Map, U.S. Radium Site." In *Revised Work Plan for Remedial Investigation and Feasibility Study*. Vol. 1. Paramus, N.J.: Malcolm Pirnie, Inc., 1991.

U.S.E.P.A. "U. S. Radium Corporation Site." In *EPA Region 2 Superfund Update*. U.S.E.P.A., 1991.

U.S.E.P.A. *Draft Environmental Impact Statement on the Special Area Management Plan for the Hackensack Meadowlands District*. U.S.E.P.A., 1995.

United States Department of State. *Papers Relating to Foreign Relations of the United States: Diplomatic Papers 1931-1933*. 13 vols. Washington: U.S. Government Printing Office, 1949-1952.

Vallery-Radot, Rene. *La Vie de Pasteur*. 21st ed. Paris: Hachette, 1922.

Vallery-Radot. *The Life of Pasteur*. Translated by Mrs. R. L. Devonshire. Introduction by Sir William Osler. Garden City, N.Y.: Garden City Publishing, n.d. Originally published as *La Vie de Pasteur*.

Vanderbilt, Byron M. *Thomas Edison, Chemist*. Washington, D.C.: American Chemical Society, 1971. 2nd printing, paperback, 1980.

Venable, John D. *Out of the Shadow: The Story of Charles Edison*. East Orange, N.J.: Charles Edison Fund, 1978.

Venable. *Mina Miller Edison: Daughter, Wife, and Mother of Inventors*. East Orange, N.J.: Charles Edison Fund, 1981. Reprint, 1994.

Venable. *A Brief Biography of Thomas Alva Edison*. N.p. (prob. Charles Edison Fund), n.d. (prob. 1980s).

[Vermilye, Anna S.], *Ogden Family History: In the Line of Lieutenant Benjamin Ogden...* Orange, N.J.: Orange Chronicle Co., 1906. [copy at Alexander Library, Rutgers University]

Vilardi, Emma May. *Heritage and Legacy: Town of Kearny.* Kearny, N.J.: Kearny Centennial Commission, 1967.

Vilardi. *Heritage and Legacy: A History of Kearny from 1606-1955.* Kearny, N.J.: Kearny Public Library, ca. 1967.

Vonnegut, Kurt. *Player Piano.* 1952. Paperback edition, New York: Bantam Doubleday, 1980.

Wachhorst, Wyn. *Thomas Alva Edison: An American Myth.* Cambridge, Mass.: MIT Press, 1981.

Wacker, Peter O., and Paul G. Clemens. *Land Use in Early New Jersey: A Historical Geography.* Newark, N.J.: New Jersey Historical Society, 1995.

Wallace, Anthony F. C. *Rockdale: The Growth of an American Village in the Early Industrial Revolution.* New York: W. W. Norton, 1972.

Warne, George K. *A Look at Warren County.* Belvidere, N.J.: Warren County Cultural and Heritage Commission, 1991.

Wheeler, William Ogden. *Inscriptions on Tombstones and Monuments in the Burying Grounds of the First Presbyterian Church and St. John Church, Elizabeth, New Jersey, 1664-1892.* New Haven, Conn.: Tuttle, Morehouse & Taylor, 1892.

Wheeler William Ogden. (comp.). Edited by Lawrence Van Alstyne and Charles Burr Ogden. *The Ogden Family in America Elizabethtown Branch and their English Ancestry. John Ogden, the Pilgrim and His Descendants 1640-1906: Their History, Biography and Genealogy.* Philadelphia: Lippincott, 1907. With Thirty-Seven Charts [bound separately, untitled, at Alexander Library, Rutgers University; charts are present; text is missing, January 1998]. Facsimile reprint of text, not including charts [Salem, Mass.: Higginson, 1998].

White, Richard. *The Organic Machine.* New York: Hill and Wang, 1995.

Whittemore, Henry. *Founders and Builders of the Oranges.* Newark, N. J.: Hardham, 1896.

Wickes, Stephen, M.D. *History of the Oranges in Essex County, N.J., From 1666 to 1806.* Newark, N.J.: Ward and Techenor, 1892.

Wile, Raymond. *Edison Disc Artists and Records, 1910-1929*, 2nd ed. Edited by Ronald Dethlefson. Brooklyn, N.Y.: APM Press, 1990.

Williams, William Carlos. *The Collected Stories of William Carlos Williams.* New York: New Directions Publishing Corp., 1961. Paperback edition, 1996.

Worster, Donald. *Dust Bowl: The Southern Plains in the 1930s.* New York: Oxford University.

Zenz, Carl, M.D., Sc.D. *Occupational Medicine: Principles and Practical Applications.* 2nd ed. Chicago: Year Book Medical Publishers, 1975.

Standard References

The Bantam New College French and English Dictionary. New York: Bantam Books, 1972.
Bartlett's Familiar Quotations, 13th ed. Boston: Little, Brown, 1955.
Burt's French-English Dictionary. New York: A. L. Burt, n.d. [1952?].
Chaucer, Goeffrey. *The Canterbury Tales.* [circa 1387].
The Chicago Manual of Style, 14th ed. Chicago: University of Chicago Press, 1993.
Concise Dictionary of American Biography. New York: Scribners, 1964.
Encyclopaedia Britannica, 15th ed. Chicago: Encyclopaedia Britannica, 1989.
An Encyclopedia of World History. Revised 3rd ed. Cambridge, Mass.: Houghton Muffin, 1952.
Heath's New French and English Dictionary. Boston: D. C. Heath, 1932.
The Layman's Parallel Bible, 6th printing. Grand Rapids, Mich.: Zondervan Corp. 1973 (For King James Version [KJV], Modern Language Bible [MLB], Living Bible [LB], and Revised Standard Version [RSV]).
The Random House Dictionary of the English Language. Unabridged edition, New York: Random House, 1967.
Webster's New World Dictionary. 3rd collegiate ed. New York: Simon & Schuster, 1988.

Newspapers, Brochures, Maps, Unpublished Material, and Ephemera

AAA Clubs of New Jersey. "New Jersey Road Scholar." [?1997]. [brochure]
Acceturo, Marie. Telephone conversation with the author, April 25, 1998. Mrs. Acceturo lives near the oxford Quarry, which was originally the Edison Quarry, in Oxford, N.J.
Albion, Michele Wehrwein. Panel discussion on "Interpreting Edison at Historic Sites and Museums." "Interpreting Edison" conference, Rutgers University, Newark, N.J., June 26, 1997.
Altman, Lawrence K. "The Inside Story." Review of *Naked to the Bone*, by Bettyann Holtzmann Kevles. *New York Times*, June 29, 1997, 31.
Amtrak. "Northeast Corridor Services: Amtrak Train Timetables" (April 1988): 2.
Anderson, Karl. *Location of Buildings: Works of New Jersey & Pennsylvania Concentrating works, Edison, Sussex Co., N.J. 1893, corrected to 1899 and 1973.* Redrawn by J. J. Bekaert, 1980. [copy given to the author by Wasco Hadonwetz, who obtained his copy from the ENHS Archives]

Banks, Russell. Review of *Our Guys: The Glen Ridge Rape and the Secret Life of the Perfect Suburb*, by Bernard Lefkowitz. *New York Times Book Review*, August 3, 1997 and July 5, 1998.

Bates, Barbara. "Tuberculosis." Review of *Fevered Lives: Tuberculosis in American Culture*, by Katherine Ott. *Journal of the American Medical Association 277* (June 4, 1997): 1732-1733.

Baum, John L. ("Jack"), and Mrs. Frank (Augusta) Baum. Conversations with the author, October 6, 1997 and May 4, 1998. Mr. Baum was Resident Geologist at the Franklin Mine in Sussex County until he retired. He is now Curator of the Franklin Mineral Museum, Franklin Township, Sussex County, N.J.

Beatty, Jack. "A Capital Life." Review of *Titan: The Life of John D. Rockefeller, Sr.*, by Ron Chernow. *New York Times Book Review*, May 17, 1998, 10, 11.

"Bloomfield, New Jersey." 1857. [map framed under glass at The Historical Society of Bloomfield]

Bloomfield (N.J.) Citizen, 1887-1889 [Excerpts in Black and Riggin, *Excerpts*]

Bloomfield (N.J.) Independent Press, June 16, 1960-April 18, 1963. [Articles by Herbert Fisher on the history of Bloomfield, bound by The Historical Society of Bloomfield, in Bloomfield Public Library]

Bloomsbury, N.J. quadrangle map. U.S. Geological Survey, 1954, photorevised 1971.

"Boxwood Hall." New Jersey Department of Environmental Protection, 1998.

Broad, William J. "Two View from the Greenhouse." Review of *Is the Temperature Rising? The Uncertain Science of Global Warming*, by S. George Philander; and *Climate of Fear: Why We Shouldn't Worry About Global Warming*, by Thomas Gale Moore. *New York Times Book Review*, n.d. 1998, 21.

Brookhiser, Richard. "The Happy Medium." Review of *Other Powers: The Age of Suffrage, Spiritualism, and the Scandalous Victoria Woodhull*, by Barbara Goldsmith, and *Notorious Victoria: The Life of Victoria Woodhull, Uncensored*, by Marie Gabriel. *New York Times Book Review*, March 29, 1999, 11.

Brown, Carl. Telephone conversation with the author on April 28, 1998. Mr. Brown is the retired General Manager of Victaulic Co., New Village, N.J. He has maintained an interest in the former employees of the Edison Portland Cement Co., which formerly occupied the building that Victaulic now uses.

Caldwell, N.J. quadrangle map. Washington, D.C.: U.S. Geological Survey, 1954, photorevised 1970.

Campbell, George. Conversations with the author on November 16, 1997, and January 18, 1998. Mr. Campbell is the Curator of the Edison Memorial Tower, Menlo Park, Edison Township, Middlesex Co., N.J.

Cary, Edward. Interview by Kenneth K. Goldstein, June 6, 1973. Jack Stanley Papers.

Chudio, Bohdan, M.D. Conversation with the author, December 20, 1997.

Connell, Mrs. Sylvester (Anne); and her sons, Roger and Dennis. Conversation with the author, August 6, 1997. Mrs. Connell and her sons have lived in a cement "Edison House" on Ingersoll Terrace in Union, N.J., for many years.

Craig, Katherine. Interview with the author, January 21, 1998. Ms. Craig is the caretaker of Boxwood Hall, a New Jersey Historic Site at 1073 East Jersey Street, Elizabeth, N.J.

Crandall, Charles, M.D. Conversations with the author, 1997, 1998.

Creswell, J. Max. *Newspaper Transcriptions: First Presbyterian Church, Roselle, New Jersey.* N.p., 1990-1994. [copies at the church and Roselle Public Library]; and conversations with the author, January 12 and 14, 1998.

Daly, Edward J. Interview at Edison National Historic Site, February 28, 1973. Jack Stanley Papers.

Davis, Theodore. "Edison's Home, Menlo Park, New Jersey." 1880. Reproduction, Alexandria, Va.: American Heritage Engravings, n.d. [ca. 1996]

DeLorme Street Atlas USA. CD-Rom Version 3.0 for Windows. Freeport, Maine: DeLorme, 1995; also Version 5.0, 1997.

Dolan, William C. Conversation with the author, September 23, 1997. Mr. Dolan is one of the oldest residents of the Ogdensburg, N.J., area; his father was a miner at the Edison mine there.

Dover, N.J. quadrangle map. U.S. Geological Survey, 1981.

Early American Inventions 1794 to 1906. Historical Documents Co., 1969.

Easton, Pa. and N.J. quadrangle map. U.S. Geological Survey, 1954, photorevised 1971.

Edison National Historic Site [E.N.H.S.]. "Glenmont" and "Edison." Brochures. [1997]

E.N.H.S. 'Glenmont: A Walking Tour of the Grounds." Brochure [1998].

E.N.H.S. "Edison's Home, Glenmont, "Llewellyn Park," "Greenhouse and Barn," "Garage," and "National Historic Site Glenmont." Illustrated signs on the grounds and plaque at the front door of Glenmont, 1998.

Edison Papers Project's homepage, cited July 1, 1997. "Chronology of Thomas Edison's Life, 1847-1878" (19 pp.); "Chronology of Thomas Edison's Life, 1879-1931" (12 pp.). http://www.rutgers.edison.edu

Edison, Thomas A. *A Guide to Thomas A. Edison Papers: A Selective Microfilm Edition,* 3 parts. Edited by Thomas E. Jeffrey. Bethesda: University Publications of America, part 3. 1887-1898, 1981.

Edison. Letters and notes, 15 pp., 1900. Pierce Collection of Edison papers. Knoxville, Tenn.

[Edison] "Measurements." 1929. Jack Stanley Papers.

[Edison] "Longevity Inquiry." 1930. Jack Stanley Papers.

[Edison] "On Bathing," and "Exercise." Marginalia, n.d. Jack Stanley Papers.

[Edison] "Organization Chart of Thomas A. Edison, Inc. Industries." 1930. [full size reproduction on the wall of Visitors Center, ENHS; reduced copy made for me ENHS archivists, 1997]

[Edison] "Interpreting Edison" conference. "Thomas A. Edison Sesquicentennial Conference" Program. Rutgers University-Newark, and U.S. Department of the Interior-National Park Service: Design Consortium, 1997.

[Edison] *Life*, Fall (October) 1997, 135, 147. ["The 100 People Who Made the Millennium"]

Edison, Mrs. Thomas A. Interview with Milton Marmor, January 10, 1947. Jack Stanley Papers.

[Edison National Historic Site Archives] Photographs of Silver Lake, N.J. [provided by George Tselos, Ph.D., Archivist, to The Bloomfield Historical Society]

E.N.H.S. Archives. Photographs of Edison mining operations, Sussex County, N.J. [provided by ENHS archives to Old Schoolhouse and Firehouse Museum, Ogdensburg, N.J.]

"Edison Tower at a Glance" N.d. [?1997]. [brochure at Edison Memorial Tower, Menlo Park, Edison Township, Middlesex Co., N.J.]

Edwards, Mrs. Bertha Elizabeth "Betty" (Frolich). Interview with author, Elizabeth, N.J., January 16, 1998.

[Edison] "E-K Medical Gas Co., Inc." 1937 [from Archives, ENHS, attached to "Annual Report," Thomas A. Edison, Inc., 1950]

[Edison] Thomas A. Edison, Inc. "Annual Report" 1950.

[Edison-Ford Winter Estates] "Edison-Ford Winter Estates." Florida Attractions Association, n.d. [ca. 1997]. [brochure]

[Edison-Ford Winter Estates] "Thomas A. Edison's Winter Home and Museum." Dynamic Impressions, n.d. [ca. 1997]. [brochure]

[Edison-Ford Winter Estates] Photocopied pages, incompletely tiled, 1969-1994. [from Edison-Ford Winter Estates, Fort Myers, Fla.]

[Elizabeth, N.J.] "Map of the City of Elizabeth, New Jersey." Compiled by Jacob L. Bauer. N.p., 1902.

[Elizabeth, N.J.] *Insurance Maps of Elizabeth, New Jersey*. 2 vols. N.Y.: Sanborn Map co., 1922.

Elizabeth, N.J-N.Y. quadrangle map. U.S. Geological Survey, 1967; and 1981.

[Elizabethtown, N.J.] Meyer, Ernst L. "Map of Elizabethtown, N.J., at the Time of the Revolutionary War, 1775-1783." N.Y.: J. Scheckler, 1989.

Ellenberger, Arthur. Conversation with the author, Verona, N.J., 1998.

"Essex County, New Jersey [Map of]." Maspeth, N.Y.: Hagstrom, 1991.

Essex County (N.J.) Medical Society archives, at UMDNJ-George F. Smith Library, Newark, N.J. [volumes of Minutes and other business for 26 April 1865-23 September 1929]

Faden, William. *The Province of New Jersey, Divided into East and West, Commonly Called the Jerseys*, 2nd ed. Charing Cross, London: Faden, 1778; reprint from U.S. National Park Service, Morristown, N.J., 1995. [map]

Fagg, John E. *A History of the Church of the Holy Innocents 1872-1972* [West Orange, N.J., 1972].

Fouché, Rayvon. "An African-American in the Edison System: The Assimilation of Lewis Howard Latimer." Presented to "Interpreting Edison" Conference, Rutgers University, Newark, N.J., June 25, 1997.

Frank Leslie's Illustrated Newspaper (January 10, 1880) [view of Menlo Park reproduced in part in Cunningham, *Edison ... Wizard*, 17; and reproduced completely but reduced in size in Miller, *Edison: Benefactor*, facing 144]

"Franklin Mineral Museum, Inc." [Franklin, N.J.], n.d.[ca. 1997]. [brochure]

Franklin, N.J. quadrangle map. U.S. Geological Survey, 1954, photorevised 1971.

The Furnace. [Newsletter of the Warren County Cultural and Historical Commission]

Frolich, William and Ruth. Interview with the author, Roselle, New Jersey, January 14, 1998. Mr. Frolich was President of the Roselle Historical Society.

General Dynamics Company. Program for the *U.S.S. Thomas A. Edison* Launching. March 15, 1960.

[General Electric Co.] "*Price Schedules of Standard Large Edison Mazda Lamps: April First Nineteen Twenty-Two.*" Harrison, N.J.: Edison Lamp Works of general Electric Co., 1922.

[General Electric Co.] 'Typical Lighting Systems in 1884." In *A General Electric Scrapbook History*. N.p. [General Electric Co.], 1953.

[General Electric Co.] *The Edison Era 1876-1892: The General Electric Story*. Schenectady, N.Y.: Algonquin Chapter, Elfun Society, 1976. [purchased at ENHS Information Desk, 1998]

Graff, Bill (August 1 and September 8) and Richard A. Volkert (September 9), New Jersey Geological Survey, telephone conversations with author, August 1-September 9, 1997.

Gustafson, Elmer. Conversation with the author, November 1997. Mr. Gustafson had worked for the Rosedale Cemetery at the time that Mina Edison was buried there.

Haberman, Clyde, with Stephen Wilkes. "The Other Ellis Island." *New York Times Magazine*, March 22, 1998, 43-46.

Hadonowetz, Wasco. Conversation with the author, September 18, 19, 23, and 24, 1997. Mr. Hadonowetz is President of the Ogdensburg, N.J., Historical Society, and Curator of the Old Firehouse and Old Schoolhouse Museum in Ogdensburg.

Hall, James F. "Justification for Acquisition of Sparta Mountain," Project No. 5SH2004A. N.J. Department of Environmental Protection, 1996.

Halstron, W.I. Interviews by Arthur Spiegler, October 9 and November 22, 1965. In Jack Stanley Papers.

Hamburg, N.J. quadrangle map. U.S. Geological Survey, 1954, photorevised 1971.

Hand, William H. Interview by Kenneth K. Goldstein, March 15, 1973. In Jack Stanley Papers.

[Harrison, N.J.] *Pictorial History of the Edison Lamp.* Harrison, N.J.: Edison Lamp Works, n.d. [reproduction available at Information Desk, ENHS]

Hauk, James. Conversation with the author, June 1997. Mr. Hauk's father, Fred Hauk, of Bloomfield, N.J., had worked for Edison.

[Henry Ford Museum & Greenfield Village, Dearborn, Mich.] "Come See 200 Years of American History," 1990.

Hill, George J. "'These Troublous Days': The United States and the League of Nations, 1931-1933." Paper presented to Graduate Student Symposium, Rutgers University, January 1997.

Holzer, Harold. "Lincoln's Early Years: A Pilgrimage to the Family's Kentucky and Indiana Cabins Reveals a Harsh Frontier Life." *New York Times* (February 8, 1998).

Hummel, Charles. Conversations with the author, 1997-1998: September 4, 1997, et seq.

Isaacs, Arnold R. Review of *Code-Name Bright Light*, by George J. Vieth. *New York Times Book Review*, n.d. 1998, 22.

Johnson, A. E. Interview at Edison National Historic Site, March 29, 1971. In Jack Stanley Papers.

Johnson, Dorothy. Conversation with the author, March 11, 1998. Mrs. Johnson is a Past President of The Historical Society of Bloomfield (N.J.).

Journal of the Medical Society of the New Jersey 7 (September 1910).

Kantrowitz, Carl. Conversation with the author, 1997.

[Kearny, N.J.] "History of Kearny." Kearny, N.J. Public Library, n.d.

Kenner, Hugh. "A Change of Mind." Review of *The First Moderns*, by William R. Everdell. *New York Times Book Review*, June 29, 1997, 24.

Kiernan, Vincent. "Getting an Inside Look at the Chernobyl Reactor." *Chronicle of Higher Education* (July 17, 1998): A20.

Kimler, Linda. Telephone conversation with author on April 28, 1998. Ms. Kimler handles public relations for the Oxford Quarry, Inc., which was the Edison Quarry in Oxford, N.J., from 1923 to 1942.

Knapp, Joseph. Telephone conversation with author regarding history of Union County, N.J., February 2, 1998. Mr. Knapp is President of Sailer & Sailer, Elizabeth, N.J.

Kurosawa, Akira. *Rashomon* (film). Japan, 1950.

Lee, James. Conversation with the author, September 30, 1997. Mr. Lee is an author and historian of the Morris Canal. He lives in a former canal plane-tender's home in Warren County that he has restored.

"Liberty State Park." New Jersey Department of Environmental Protection, 1996.

"Liberty State Park Conservancy," vol. 1, issue 2 (Fall 1997). [copy at Liberty State Park, Jersey City, N.J.]

[Llewellyn Park] 1857 map, reproduced on sign near Greenhouse and Potting Shed at Glenmont, 1998.

"Llewellyn Park, West Orange, New Jersey." N.p., n.d. [J.A. McDonald, 1877] [map, framed under glass on the wall of the undercroft, Church of the Holy Innocents, West Orange, 1998]

Louisville: Your Kind of the Place, Any Way You Say It. Rand-McNally, 1996.

Martins, Lisa. "'Cabinet on Road' Makes a Stop: Sparta Mountain Saved." *New Jersey Herald*, February 12, 1997.

McGuirk, Helen. Conversation with the author, 1998. Ms. McGuirk is a retired bank executive who lives near the corner of Northfield Ave. and Whittingham Pace in West Orange. Her in-laws own a house built of Edison Portland Cement in Orange, N.J.

Meddaugh, Gary. Conversation with the author, September 30, 1997. Mr. Meddaugh is General Manager of the Victaulic plant at the new Village, N.J. The principal building of this plant was built by the Edison Portland Cement co. in 1906.

"Menlo Park," on Raritan Township, 1876. [map, at Edison Memorial Tower, Menlo park, Edison Township, Middlesex Co., N.J.]

[Menlo Park] "Map Showing Location of Edison Buildings at Menlo Park, N.J., 1876-1882," 1925 [at Edison Memorial Tower, Menlo Park, Edison Township, Middlesex Co., N.J.]

Meyers, Alice. Conversation with the author, West Orange, N.J., November 5, 1997.

"Middlesex County, New Jersey." New York: Rand McNally, 1989.

Millidge, Thomas. "Map of Part of Horse-Neck Tract," 1774. Reproduced in Lockward, *Horse-neck*, 48-D-E.

Misiur, Steve. Conversation with the author, September 19, 1997. Mr. Misiur is a former zinc miner who now works as a tour guide at the Sterling Hill Mining Museum. He and an associate are constructing a new tunnel as a demonstration project funded in part by the Charles Edison Foundation, in recognition of the contributions of Thomas A. Edison to the technology and safety of mining.

Mogilski, Bill. Conversation with the author, September 30, 1997. Mr. Mogilski has worked at Victaulic, Inc., New Village, N.J., for about 25 years, in the cement building built by Edison in 1906.

Morris/Sussex/Warren Counties Atlas. Maspeth, N.Y.: Hagstrom Map Co., 1997.

Mount Pleasant Cemetery, Newark, N.J. "Cemetery Register."

National Geographic 193, no. 5 (May 1998): "Millennium Moments."

New Haven (Conn.) Leader, October 21, 1911.

New Jersey Department of Environmental Protection [N.J.D.E.P]. "The Historic Trilogy: The Statue of Liberty, Ellis Island, The CRRNJ Terminal," N.d. [1977].

N.J.D.E.P. "Interpretive Programs ... Offered at Liberty State Park," N.d. [1997].

N.J.D.E.P. Regulations of Divisions Fish, Game, and Wildlife, Chapter 7, Subchapter2: "Use of All Land and Water Areas Under the Control of the Division of Fish, Game, and Wildlife," 1996.

New Jersey Historical Society. "Illustrated Notecards, 1895-1913."

"New Jersey Road Map." New York: Simon & Schuster/H.M. Gousha, 1993 and 1996 editions.

"New Jersey Transit [N.J. Transit]. "Morris & Essex Lines," 1997. [timetable]

N.J. Transit. "Boonton Branch," 1998. [timetable]

[New Jersey] "State of New Jersey Base Map with Highways." U.S. Geological Survey, 1978.

[New Jersey] "State of New Jersey Base Map with Highways and Contours." U.S. Geological Survey, 1978.

New York Times, January 10, 1916 [copy in Jack Stanley Papers]; April 20, 1916 [in JSP]; May 30, 1925 [UMDNJ-GFS Library, "Radium" file]; June 1-July 14, 1997; August 9, 1997; October 9, 1997; and March 21-July 26, 1998.

"Newark — New Jersey." Newark: T. J. S. Landis, 1916. [map, framed, on wall in Newark Room, Newark Public Library]

Newark (N.J.) Star Ledger and *Sunday Star Ledger*, March 19, 1992; March 19, 1997; June 27-August 31, 1997; September 29-30, 1997; March 13-29, 1998; April 12, 1998; May 3-17, 1998; June 19-August 23, 1998.

[Newark, N.J.] "City of Newark, N.J." New York: C. R. Parsons, 1874. [map, framed, on wall in Newark Room, Newark Public Library]

Newark [N.J.] Preservation and Landmarks Committee, Brochure, [1998].

Newton East, N.J. quadrangle map. U.S. Geological Survey, 1954, photorevised 1971.

O'Driscoll, Robert, M.D. Conservations with the author 1998.

O'Gorman, James. "The Hidden Half of Central Park." Review of *Country, Park, & City: The Architecture and Life of Calvert Vaux*, by Francis R. Kowsky. *New York Times Book Review*, March 22, 1998, 10.

Olson, Evelyn Naomi. "Thomas Alva Edison and His Influence in Roselle, New Jersey." MS in Roselle Public Library, 1977.

Orange, N.J. quadrangle map. U.S. Geological Survey, 1955; and 1981.

Oser, Marion Edison. "Early Recollections," Voicewritten Interview, March 1956. Jack Stanley Papers.

Pathfinder 54 (No. 4, 12 February 1947): 25. "Edison's First 100 Years'" [copy in Bloomfield, N.J., Public Library, vertical file on "Edison"]

Perth Amboy, N.J. quadrangle map. U.S. Geological Survey, 1956, photorevised 1981.

Penkara, Joe. Telephone conversation with the author, September 29, 1997. Mr. Penkara is Regional Superintendent in Franklin Township, Sussex County, for the Fish, Game, and Wildlife Service, New Jersey Department of Environmental Protection. He is responsible for the Sparta Mountain Wildlife Management Area (formerly the Edison mine).

Petrangelo, Tony. Telephone conversation with the author, October 1, 1997. Mr. Petranglo is Chief of the Fish, Game, and Wildlife Service, New Jersey Department of Environmental Protection.

Pinsky, Robert. Review of *The Meadowlands*, by Robert Sullivan. *New York Times Book Review*, May 1998, 7.

Pyne, Stephen J. Quoted by Peter Monaghan, "The Flames of World History: A 'Scholar on Fire' Creates a Field of Study." *Chronicle of Higher Education* (October 31, 1997), A15.

Quammen, David. Review of *Annals of the Former World*, by John McPhee. *New York Times Book Review*, July 5, 1998, 9.

"Radium." Archives, UMDNJ-George F. Smith Library. [vertical file]

Redpath, Mrs. Robert U. (Nancy). Telephone conversation with the author, February 8, 1998.

Rhees, David. "Marvels on Display." Review of *Exhibiting Electricity*, by K.G. Beauchamp. *Science* 277 (September 5, 1977): 1444-1445.

Richard, Alison F. Remarks at Panel Discussion on "Yale as an Intellectual Community." New Haven, Conn., April 24, 1993.

Robbins, Mrs. Charles F. (Margaret). Conversation with the author, 1997. *Roselle, N.J.* quadrangle map. U.S. Geological Survey, 1955.

Rosedale Cemetery, Orange, N.J. Filecards for Edisons: Thomas A., Mina Miller, Charles, and Carolyn Hawkins.

"Rosedale Cemetery." Orange, N.J., 1997 [map]

Rosenblatt, Roger. "Winter Lights." *Time*, February 16, 1998, 106.

Sant' Ambrogio, Lucy. Conversation with the author, March 11, 1998. Ms. Sant' Ambrogio is Curator of the museum of The Historical Society of Bloomfield. As a young woman, she worked as a record polisher in the Edison Phonograph Co. works in West Orange.

Scientific American (February 23, 1884), cover.

Shallcross, Charles. Interview with author by telephone, January 21, 1998. Mr. Shallcross was President of the Union County Historical Society.

Shapiro, Peter. Remarks to New York Head and Neck Society, ca. 1985. Mr. Shapiro was the County Executive of Essex County, N.J., in the early 1980s.

Sloane, Madeline Edison. Interview by Kenneth K. Goldstein, March 13, 1973. Jack Stanley Papers.

Stanhope, N.J. quadrangle map. U.S. Geological Survey, 1981.

Stevens, Ernest. Interview by Kenneth K. Goldstein, June 20, 1973. In Jack Stanley Papers.

Suburban Essex Magazine, September 1997.

Tarr, Douglas. Conversations with the author, 1997-1998: July 8, 1997 *passim*. Mr. Tar is Archives Technician, Edison National Historic Site.

Tselos, George D. "'Start Up at the Top and Work Down': Thomas A. Edison and the Fluoroscope." Paper presented at "Interpreting Edison" conference, Newark, N.J., June 25, 1997. MS at library of Archives, ENHS. Also see: Tselos. "New Jersey's Thomas Edison and the Fluoroscope." *New Jersey Medicine* 92 (November 1995): 731-733.

Tselos, George D. Conversations with the author, 1997-1998: July 2, 1997 *et seq*. Dr. Tselos was Archivist, Edison National Historic Site.

"Union/Hudson/Essex Counties Atlas." Maspeth, N.Y.: Hagstrom, 1987.

United States Census, 1880. "Ogden Mine" [village] and "Ogdensburg," Sparta Township, State of New Jersey. [copy at Old Firehouse and Old Schoolhouse Museum, Ogdensburg, N.J.]

[U.S. Radium Corporation] *Revised Work Plan for Remedial Investigation and Feasibility Study, U.S. Radium Corporation Site, City of Orange, Essex County, New Jersey*. Paramus, N.J.: Malcolm Pirnie, Inc., for U.S. Department of Environmental Protection, 1990. [copy in U.S. Radium Corp. file, Archives, George F. Smith Library, UMDNJ-Newark].

Wall Street Journal, August 12, 1997.

Warne, George K. Telephone conversation with the author on May 13, 1998. Mr. Warne is the author of a history of Warren County, N.J. He is at the Warren County Historical and Cultural Commission, Oxford, N.J.

Watzman, Haim. "Study of the Dead Sea Scrolls Enters a New Era." *Chronicle of Higher Education*, August 1, 1997, A14.

West Orange (N.J.) Chronicle, July 10-Ocotober 9, 1997; March 5-19, 1998; and July 16, 1998.

West Orange (N.J.) Laboratory Notebook," Spring 1998.

Will, George F. "A Faster Mousetrap." Review of *The One Best Way*, by Robert Kanigel, *New York Times Book Review*, June 15, 1997, 8, 10.

Williams, Mrs. Lee (Burgess). Conversation with the author, November 1997. In October 1931, Mrs. Williams was taken by her father to see Edison, when he lay in the Laboratory for people to pay their respects, following his death.

Williams, Steve. "Port Huron Museum." Paper presented at the "Interpreting Edison" conference, Newark, N.J., June 26, 1997.

Willman, Alex and Scott. Interviews by author, February 26 and 28, and March 2 and 3, 1998. The Willmans, father and son, are administrators of Mount Pleasant Cemetery, Newark, N.J.

Woods, Marianne Berger. "Reinventing the Inventor: Images of Edison over the Years." Ibid., June 27, 1997.

Woosman, Jeff. "State, Private Groups Help Preserve Sussex Space: Real Mountain News." *Morris County (N.J.) Daily Record* 1, no. 5 (Spring 1997).

Citations Taken from Secondary Sources

Bernard, Claude. *Lecons sur les phenomenes de la vie*. 2 vols. Paris: Balliere, 1878. Quoted in Castiglioni, *History of Medicine*, 683.

Brown, Percy. "American Martyrs to Radiology." 1936. Reprinted in *American Journal of Roentgenology* (January 1995): 237-239. Quoted in Tselos, "Start Up at the Top," MS, 9.

Burt, Leah Brodbeck. "Historic Furnishings Report." Glenmount: Edison National Historic Site, n.d. (prob. 1980s), 13. Quoted in Robbins, "Llewellyn Park," 23.

Burroughs, John. *Journal*. Quoted in Brauer, *There to Breathe the Beauty*, xii.

Edison, Thomas A. *The Weekly Herald*. 1862. Newspaper. Copy reprinted in Stamps, Hawkins, and Wright, *House in the Grove*, 39, Fig. 2.10

Edison. Editorial in *Industrial Management and Engineering Magazine* (October 1920), 4. Quoted in Noble, *America by Design*, 257.

Edison. *Journal of the American Medical Association* 41 (1903):499. Quoted in Tselos, "Start Up at the Top," MS, 11.

Ford, Henry. *Edison as I Knew Him*. Quoted in Gilman M. Ostrander, *American Civilization in the First Machine Age* (New York: Harper & Row, 1970), 217. Quoted in Noble, *America by Design*, 113.

Holly, Henry Hudson. *Modern Dwellings in Town and Country*. 1878. Quoted in McAlester and McAlester, *Great American Homes*, 152-165.

Liedsman. Letter to Edison, and marginal notation, May 3, 1921, ENHS. Quoted in Tselos, "Start Up at the Top," MS, 1

Sloane, Madeline Edison. Interview, *Baltimore Sun*, October 19, 1969. Quoted in Conot, *Edison*, 377, 543n.

Spilsburg E. G. *Trans. American Institute of Mining Engineers* 27 (1897): 452. Quoted in Vanderbilt, *Edison, Chemist*, 167-168, 352n.

Vallery-Radot, Rene. *Vie de Pasteur*. Paris, 1900. Quoted in Josephson, *Edison*, 336, 495n.

Walter, Dave, ed. *Today Then: America's Best Minds Look 100 Years Into the Future on the Occasion of the 1893 World's Columbian Exposition*. Helena, Mont., 1992. Quoted in Baldwin, *Edison*, 237, 475n.

Index

This index was prepared for the first edition of Edison's Environment, and the page numbers may be off by one or two pages in either direction in this edition.

A Civil Action, 337, 339
Abel, 341
Aberjona River, 337
Acceturo, Marie, 222
Adam, 341
Africa, 328
Agriculture, 31, 265, 341, 343
Akron, Ohio, 10.
Alexander, William, Lord Stirling, 197
Alfieri Building, 81, 90-91
Allah, 354
Allamuchy State Park, 214, 234
Allegheny River, 32
Allen, Ethan, 116, 125, 354
Alpha, N.J., 316
Altman, Lawrence, 348
American Institute of Electrical Engineers [AIAA], 236, 314
American Journal of Roentgenology, 286
American League, 255
American Red Cross, 355
Ampere Parkway (Belleville, Bloomfield), 160
Ampere railway stop, 173
Amtrak, 27, 51, 64, 70, 76, 78, 299
Anderson/Bekaert map, 205, 210, 211
Andrus house (Menlo Park), 85
Appalachian Mountains, 18-19, 194, 200, 297, 326
Appleton, Wis., 326

Archaeologists, 98, 197, 225
Archaic Period, 226
Arlington Cemetery, 272, 367
Arlington Street (East Orange), 122, 157
Armitage, Walter, 48
Arnold, Benedict, 227
Arthur Kill, 23, 57
Asbury, N.J., 239
Ashland Avenue (West Orange), 118, 122, 142
Asia, 31, 320, 329
Aswan, Egypt, 328
Atkinson, Mr., 129
Atlantic City, N.J., 257
Atlantic Ocean, 18-19, 23, 224
Atomic Age 283, 296, 306
Audubon Society, 191, 211-212
Aurora Borealis, 341
Automobiles, 127, 184, 240, 273, 330-331

Bacon, Roger, 318
Bakelite Corporation of America, 177
Baldwin, Neil, 3, 100, 369
Ballantine, Peter, 60
Bank Street (Newark), 64, 70, 72, 363
Barbados, 268
Barksdale, Henry C., 187
Barren Neck, 268
Barstow, William Slocum, 95
Barton, Clara, 355

Barzilla, Ayars, 48
Basalla, George, 320-321
Batchelor, Charles, 85, 92, 94
Bathing, 98, 110, 280-1, 324, 332
Bayonne, N.J., 268
Beatty, Daniel, 224, 228
Beatty, Jack, 356
Beattytown, N.J., 228
Beavers, 33, 163, 328
Belknap, Edwin S., 48
Bell Telephone Labs, 311
Bell, Alexander Graham, 108, 349
Bell, Chichester, 108
Belleville Avenue (Glen Ridge and Belleville), 162, 170-171, 270-2
Belleville Park, 162
Belleville Public Library, 367
Belleville Turnpike, 269-273, 367
Belleville, N.J., 165, 168, 172, 185-6
Belmont Avenue (Belleville and Bloomfield), 156, 366-367
Belvidere, N.J., 224, 227
Bergen County, 20, 32, 268
Bergen Street (Harrison), 107-110, 300, 366-367
Bergman Company, 102
Berkeley Avenue (Bloomfield), 166, 366
Berra, Yogi, 324
Bible, 340-341, 354-355.
Black Maria, 141
Bloomfield Avenue (Essex County), 21, 23, 34, 39, 122, 156, 160-161, 163-164, 167, 170-172, 178, 233-234, 270, 302-303, 367
Bloomfield Citizen, 167, 172-173
Bloomfield College, 164
Bloomfield Historical Society, 118, 156, 367
Bloomfield Machine Works, 167
Bloomfield Public Library, 155, 366

Bloomfield Seminary, 164
Bloomfield, N.J., 39, 163-4, 172, 193
Bloomsbury, N.J., 232, 240, 245
Blue Jay Swamp (Newark), 165
Bogen, William, 84
Boiling Springs (Silver Lake), 159, 268
Boonton Branch (New Jersey Transit), 234, 364
Boonton, N.J., 214, 234, 364
Borgstrom, George, 343
Boston Street (Newark), 70, 72, 363
Bound Brook, N.J., 31
Bouton, Edward L., 48
Boy Scouts, 32
Boyden, Jeanne, 352
Boyden, Seth, 59
Boyers, Sally, 228-229, 242, 245
Boynton Beach, Fla., 86, 100
Bradley, Alva, 5
Bradley, Leverett, 57-58
Branch Brook Park (Newark), 123, 155-158, 161-162, 165-166, 218
Braverman, Harry, 317
Bricker Building, 209
Bridge Street (Menlo Park), 107, 110, 367
Bridge Street (Newark to Harrison), 272
Britain and the British, 5, 26, 32, 51, 322
Broad Street (Newark), 64, 66, 69, 363, 367
Broadway (Newark), 123, 163
Broadway village (Warren County), 237, 239
Brook Street (Silver lake), 155, 160, 178-179, 367
Brown, Carl, 222, 251-252, 255, 265

472

Brown, Percy, 286
Bruen Street (Newark), 69-70
Brun, John, 222
Buddhism, 303
Bunker Hill, Battle of, 227
Burnett, Robert B., 157
Burroughs, John, 10, 282-283
Butchertown House, 297
Buttermilk Bridge Road, 237
Byram, 194

Caldwell College, 21
California, 77-78, 297n, 330n, 347
Cameron, Lord and Lady, 353
Canada, 5, 7, 193, 339
Cape Henlopen, 31
Cape Horn, 327
Carbolic Acid (Phenol), 148, 164, 177-180, 186, 326
Carmen('s) Pond (Menlo Park), 85, 100
Carson, Rachel, 305, 324, 337-338
Carteret Avenue, 168
Carteret, George, Sir, 31, 197, 268
Cary, Edward, 148, 176, 178
Cassandra, 344
Catholic Church, 22, 33
Cedar Grove, 163
Celluloid, 61
Cement, 10-11, 21, 24, 26, 45, 68, 79, 81, 95, 98, 110, 126-167, 171, 174, 193, 213-66, 291, 309, 319, 325, 345, 363, 365
Cenozoic Era, 30
Centenary College, 228
Centennial Exhibition (Philadelphia, 1876), 330
Center Street, 22, 33-35
Central Avenue, 35
Central Park, 38, 165
Central Railroad of New Jersey (C.R.R.N.J.), 51-53, 57, 63, 112, 215, 218, 273
Chandler, Alfred Dupont, 317
Charles Edison Foundation, 34, 221
Charles II, King, 197
Charles Street, 118
Chautauqua Institution, 365
Cheesequake State Park, 89
Chemistry, 148, 176, 304, 312, 317-321, 324, 345, 350, 356, 360
Chernobyl, 306
Chernow, Ron, 356
Cherry Street (Elizabeth), 49
Chevrolet, 330
Chicken Little, 344
China, 320, 328, 341
Christie Street (Menlo Park), 77-79, 81, 84-85, 88, 90-92, 94-96
Chrysler, 330
Cicci department store (Newark), 363
Civil War, 8, 228, 270, 355, 367
Civilization, 317-318, 320, 326, 346, 359
Clara Maass Medical Center, 155, 158, 161, 165, 174, 355, 367
Clarendon Hotel (Portland), 327
Clark Thread Works (Newark), 60, 270
Clark, N.J., 52
Class in Society, 37, 317, 339
Cletrac Tank-Type Tractor, 351
Cleveland, Grover, 21
Cliff Avenue (West Orange), 120
Cliff Walk (West Orange), 38
Cliffside Drive (Warren County), 262
Clifton Avenue (Newark), 164
Clifton Street (Newark), 123, 158
Clifton, N.J., 31, 234
Clinton, Hilary Rodham
Coal, 111, 122, 166, 199, 215-216,

473

218, 228, 248, 318, 324, 327
Coffin, Howard, 316
Cohen, Patricia, 357
Cold War, 296, 306
Cole, John, 357
Columbia (steamship), 327
Columbia River, 324, 326-327, 331
Columbia Turnpike, 234
Concrete Highway (section of Route 57 in Franklin Township), 232-233
Connecticut, 257, 278
Connell, Anne and family, 257, 259
Conot, Robert, 3
CONRAIL, 160, 182, 235, 237, 251, 265, 302
Continental Army, 237
Continental Divide, 23
Cook's Pond (West Orange), 33, 40, 120, 122, 135, 308
Coolidge, Calvin, 316
Cornell University, 148, 176
Corning Glass, 95
Cornwall, England, 196
Corporate Capitalism, 312, 317
Cottage Park (Winthrop, Mass.), 114
Courier Street (Menlo Park), 81
Cowan, Ruth Schwartz, 352
Crandall, Charles E., M.D., 222, 268
Crane, Azariah, 163
Crane, Hannah, 197
Crane, Israel, 164
Crane, Joseph, 164
Crane's Ferry (Elizabeth), 51, 197, 390
Cranetown (Bloomfield, N.J.), 163
Cranetown (Montclair, N.J.), 35
Craneville (Bloomfield, N.J.), 163
Cranford, N.J., 300
Crest Drive (Orange Valley), 18, 25-26
Cretaceous Period, 30
Crillo, Salvatore, 178-179
Crooks Pond (West Orange, N.J.), 141, 143, 290
Crystal Lake (West Orange, N.J.), 25, 38, 133, 166, 302
Cuba, 355
Cuckoo Flats (Sparta, N.J.), 192
Culture, 321, 332-333, 337, 350, 353, 417, 421, 424, 430-431, 440
Cummings, Charles F., 3, 60
Cunningham, John T., 4, 369
Curie, Marie and Pierre, 283
Curry, George, W., 137-139

Daily Advertiser Building (Newark, N.J.), 69
Dalai Lama, 303
Dally, Clarence, 285-286, 305, 349
Daly, Edward J., 147
Dams, 33, 50, 158, 163, 257, 324, 326-329, 331
Darling House (New Village, N.J.), 231, 244-245
Darwinism, 342-343
Daugherty, Lester J., 364
DaVinci, Leonardo, 318
Davis, Alexander, 38
Davis, Caleb, 163
Davis, Theodore, 96
Davy, Humphrey, Sir, 313
DDT, 305
Dead Sea scrolls, 357, 425
Deafness, 8, 54, 348, 361
Dean House (Menlo Park, N.J.), 85, 92, 94, 98
Dean, Charles, 92
Debert Site (Nova Scotia), 225
Definis, Fabio, 129
Deism, 115, 353-354, 361

Delahunty, Michael Leo, 17
Delaware Indians, 31-32, 226
Delaware River, 61, 214, 222, 226-229, 239-240, 325
Delaware Water Gap, 224, 228
Delaware, Lackawanna, and Western (D.L. & W.) Railroad, 201, 215, 239
Dellwood Road (Menlo Park, N.J.), 90
Delmonico, Charles, 36
Democrats, 9
Denville, N.J., 214, 233-234, 364
Depression, Great, 149, 296
Dethlefson, Ronald, 3
Detroit, 8, 346
Diamond Amberola Records, 351
Diamond Disc (K) phonograph records, 11, 288
Dickson, William Kennedy Laurie, 143
Digby, Nova Scotia, 5
Disney Institute and Disney World, 355
Distinguished Service Medal, 419
Dodd Street (Orange, N.J.), 33-34, 40, 122
Dodd, John M., 160
Doddtown (East Orange, N.J.), 35
Dolan, William C. "Doley," 189-191, 207
Douglas, Mary, 332-3, 335, 337-8
Dowling's coal plant (Stewartsville, N.J.), 247
DuPont de Nemours & Co., E. I., factory (Kearny, N.J.), 270, 276, 317
Dust Bowl, 342-343
Dutch settlers, 163, 191, 197, 226
Dye, 261

Eagan, R., 272
Eagan's Restaurant (Kearny), 272
Eagle Rock Avenue (Orange Valley), 39-40, 120, 130, 133
Eagle Rock Crest (Orange Valley), 16
Eagle Rock Reservation (Orange Valley), 13, 16, 18, 24-25, 303, 364
Eagle Rock Road (Orange Valley), 25, 38-39
Eagleton (Montclair), 39
Earhart, Amelia, 355
East Main Street (Denville), 234
East Newark, N.J., 60, 106-107, 268, 270, 367
EBASCO (Electric Bond and Share Company), 323
Eden, 340
Ediphone Division, 184

EDISON, Thomas A.
Edison business, residence, and work sites in New Jersey:
American Telegraph Works (Newark), 68-69
Edison Battery Factory (Glen Ridge), 170-171
Edison Battery Factory and Storage Battery Company (West Orange), 10, 118, 138, 141-142, 144-145, 149, (and Glen Ridge) 170-172, 184-185, 258, 301, 326
Edison Electric Light Co., 167
Edison General Electric Co., and General Electric Co., 9, 106-110, 276, 300, 306-308, 323-325
Edison Independent Lighting Company (Roselle), 52, 103, 112
Edison Ink Factory (Glen Ridge),

475

Edison, Thomas A. (Continued)
168-9, 302, 326
Edison Laboratory (West Orange), 10, 14, 84, 106, 117, 132, 135-149, 307
Edison Lamp Company and Lamp Works (Harrison), 84, 103-110, 276, 300, 323
Edison Manufacturing Company & Plant, and Chemical Works (Silver Lake), 11, 152, 161, 174-177, 180
Edison and Murray (also Murray & Co., and Ward Street Plant), 69-72
Edison Phonograph Works and Phonograph Company (West Orange), 11, 140, 142, 144-145, 147, (from Bloomfield) 167
Edison Portland Cement Company (also Cement Works), 95, 125-7, 193, 215-216, 219-223, 229-231, 238, 246-247, 250-251, 255-256, 259, 262, 266, 325
E-K Medical Gas Division (Silver Lake), 185
E-Mark Battery Factory (Kearny), 267-276
McGraw-Edison, 301
Newark Telegraph Works, 68
New Jersey and Pennsylvania Concentrating Works (mine), 11, 190-191, 196, 212, 218
News Reporting Telegraph Co., 69
Pope, Edison, and Co., 47-58
Thomas A. Edison, Inc., and TAE, Inc., 9, 147

Sites in New Jersey, by county:
Bergen County:
  Kingsland, 268
  Lodi, 270

Edison, Thomas A. (Continued)
  Lyndhurst, 268
  North Arlington, 268
  Rutherford, 268
  Secaucus, 268

Essex County, 9-41, 45, 51, 222, 349
  Belleville, 11, 21, 31, 122, 151 88, 193, 218, 269, 272, 302-3, 326
  Bloomfield and Silver Lake, 11, 21, 31-2, 118, 122, 149, 151-88, 193, 214, 217-9, 222, 235-6, 265, 270, 275, 300-3, 326, 332, 336, 359
  Caldwell, 21, 35, 233
  East Orange, 32, 35, 122, 156, 159, 168, 234, 298, 301
  Glen Ridge, 21, 151, 156, 164, 168-72, 270, 301-3, 326, 336
  Irvington, 32-3
  Livingston, 272
  Maplewood, 30, 32, 35, 298
  Millburn, 26, 31, 34
  Montclair, 21, 31-5, 39, 118, 120, 132-3, 164, 218, 302
  Newark, 22-3, 31-5, 47-8, 59-73, 78, 81, 98-9, 107, 110, 118, 122-3, 131, 141, 153, 156-8, 160-6, 178, 186-7, 214, 218-9, 226-7, 231-5, 265, 267-9, 272, 298, 308, 355
  Orange, 17, 22, 24, 29-40, 84, 118, 122-3, 132, 156-7, 164, 215, 218, 234-8, 259, 272, 279, 284-91, 298, 301-2
  South Orange, 25, 28, 37, 70, 234, 260, 298
  Upper Montclair, 258, 260
  Verona, 164

476

Edison, Thomas A. (Continued
West Orange, 9-41, 45, 75, 81,
  102, 106, 108, 111-49,
  152-3, 166-8, 174, 178,
  193-5, 206, 217-8, 222,
  232-7, 257-9, 265, 270,
  272, 275, 284-91, 295,
  298-311, 326, 336-8, 362

Hudson County, 22
  Bayonne, 268
  East Newark, 106-107, 268
  Harrison, 22, 103-110, 153, 265,
    268-273, 276, 300, 323
  Hoboken, 235
  Jersey City, 55-9, 61, 98-99, 165,
    214, 268-272, 298, 325
  Kearny, 22, 267-276, 325, 337

Hunterdon County,
  Clinton, 234

Middlesex County, 27
  Menlo Park, 9, 24, 45, 70, 73-
    107, 153, 193, 222, 259,
    265, 274, 298, 309, 320,
    325, 332, 340-342, 355,
    360
  Metuchen, 76, 81-83, 99
  New Brunswick, 99
  Perth Amboy, 224

Mercer County
  Princeton, 99

Morris County, 194, 228, 233
  Boonton, 214
  Dover, 194, 214, 218, 224, 235
  Denville, 214, 233-4
  Jefferson Township, 194
  Lake Hopatcong, town of, 189,
    194, 213, 218-9, 231-5

Edison, Thomas A. (Continued)
Landing, 214
Lincoln Park, 214
Montville, 214, 218
Morris Canal, 56, 58, 61-63, 70,
  122-123, 158, 162, 165-6,
  213-18, 227-8, 231, 234-
  240, 246-8, 264-5, 298
Morris Plains, 234
Morristown, 218, 224, 234-5, 237
Mount Tabor, 234
Netcong, 214
Parsippany-Troy Hills, 234
  Pompton Plains, 214
Port Morris, 214, 233
Rockaway, 214, 218
Speedwell, 234
Waterloo, 214
Wharton, 214-215, 219

Passaic County, 165
Paterson, 214, 218

Sussex County, 11, 45, 188-219,
  223, 227-231, 236-8, 242-
  243, 258, 261, 265, 339
Byram, 214
Franklin, 190, 196, 218, 303
Hopatcong, 234
Ogden mine (renamed by Edison),
  197-199, 216-8, 266, 303,
  325
Ogdensburg, 188-219, 303
Sparta, 188-219, 223, 303, 325
Stanhope, 214, 217-218

Union County, 23, 31, 222
Cranford, 300
Elizabeth, 9, 23, 31, 43, 45, 47-
  57, 98-99, 112, 153, 226,
  298, 300, 325
Linden, 300

Edison, Thomas A. (Continued)
Roselle, 52, 103-5, 111-114, 300
Roselle Park, 300
Union, 24, 26, 256-259
Westfield, 76

Warren County, 11, 45, 165, 221-66, 339-42
Asbury, 239
Belvidere, 224, 227
Broadway, 237-9
Buttermilk, 237
Franklin Township, 232-2, 237, 262, 265, 303
Hackettstown, 214, 218, 224, 228, 231, 234-7
Mount Bethel, 223
New Village, 193, 213-14, 218, 221-222, 227-231, 235-251, 258, 261-262, 303-304, 325
Oxford, 219, 226-227, 238, 246, 250-251, 262-5
Phillipsburg, 214-215, 218, 227-240, 265, 303
Pleasant Valley, 237-239
Port Colden, 214
Port Delaware, 215
Port Murray, 214
Port Warren, 214-215, 240
Rockport, 214
Stewartsville, 193, 212-223, 227-235, 238-240, 246-250, 262
Washington, 214, 223, 228, 231-232, 239, 265

Edison business, residence, and work sites in other states and countries:
California, 297
Canada, 193
England, 297, 320

Edison, Thomas A. (Continued)
Florida, 1, 9, 10, 45, 102, 236, 274, 283, 295-7, 349
France, 297
Kentucky, 297
Massachusetts, 8, 45, 103-5, 114-5, 297, 300, 308, 340-1
Michigan, 2, 8, 11, 27, 55, 82, 87, 92-3, 101, 193, 274, 295-9, 346
New Hampshire, 297
New Mexico, 193, 297
New York sites, 9-10, 14, 87, 102-103, 113, 256, 258, 300, 308, 320, 350
North Carolina, 297
Norway, 193
Ohio, 2, 7-10, 45, 115, 297, 350
Oregon, 327
Pennsylvania, 193, 297
Wisconsin, 326
Wyoming, 297

Edison's Family, 4-9
Edison, Charles "Charley" (nephew), 5
Edison, Charles (son; m. Carolyn Hawkins), 5, 9, 102, 134-135, 140, 147
(Charles Edison Foundation), 221, 236, 267-276, 279, 305, 338
Edison, Harriet Ann "Tannie" (sister), 5, 8, 115, 279
Edison, [Edeson], John "Tory John" (g-grandfather; m. Sarah Ogden), 4-5
Edison, Madeline (daughter, m. John Eyre Sloane and was mother of TAE's only grandchildren), 9, 10, 119-120, 125, 131, 236, 279
Edison, Marion (sister), 5, 8, 279
Edison, Marion "Dot" (daughter;

Edison, Thomas A. (Continued)
  m. Oscar Oeser), 9, 67, 85-7,
  100, 102, 236, 279, 299, 340-341
Edison, Mary Sharlow (step-
  mother), 5
Edison, Mary Stilwell (first wife),
  9, 47, 48, 54, 67-9, 77-8, 84-7,
  100, 102, 110, 123, 163, 279,
  299, 355
Edison, Mina Miller (second wife),
  9, 38, 40-43, 114-115, 119-125,
  129-130, 134, 170, 236, 277-279,
  297, 300-301, 340, 353
Edison, Nancy Elliott (mother), 4-
  7, 279, 353
Edison, Nancy Stimson
  (grandmother), 5
Edison, Samuel Ogden Jr. (father),
  4, 5, 7, 10, 82, 199, 279, 353
Edison, Samuel Ogden Sr.
  (grandfather), 5, 7, 199
Edison, Samuel Ogden [III]
  (brother; died young), 7
Edison, [Edeson], Sarah Ogden
  (great-grandmother), 4
Edison, Theodore Miller (son; m.
  Anna Maria Osterhout), 9, 236,
  279
Edison, Thomas A. Jr. "Dash" (son;
  m. Mary Louise Touhey), 9, 70,
  236, 279
Edison, William Leslie "Will"
  (son; m. Blanche Travers), 9,
  236, 279
Edison, William Pitt (brother), 5, 8,
  10, 70, 279
Miller, Jane (sister-in-law; sister of
  Mina), 236
Miller, Lewis (father-in-law), 355
Miller, Theodore (brother-in-law;
  brother of Mina), 236
Ogden, John (ancestor), 325

Edison, Thomas A. (Continued)
  Ogden, Swaine (ancestor), 325
  Stetsons (ancestors), 325
  Swaines (ancestors), 325

Thomas A. Edison by subject
agriculture (see botany)
analgesics and anesthetics, 185,
  345, 348-349
battery & batteries, 8, 10, 11, 83,
  138, 141, 170-171, 180, 183, 236,
  267-276, 301, 309, 325-326, 330-
  331, 345
biographies and biographers of, 3,
  4, 44, 47, 57, 75, 102, 105-6,
  109, 152, 192-3, 212, 217, 222,
  247, 273, 301, 339, 347-349,
  360-2
botany (including agriculture &
  farming), 59, 221, 228, 237, 265,
  303, 341-342, 349, 359-61
business and businessman, 54, 59,
  64-66, 102, 106-9, 111, 140,
  149, 172-173, 236, 248, 267-6,
  300, 309, 314-17, 320, 343, 350,
  362
camping trips, 10, 282-283
carbolic acid (see phenol)
cement (and concrete), 10, 11, 95,
  126-127, 130, 138, 171, 174,
  212-66, 309, 345
chemistry and chemicals, 8, 83,
  139, 173, 176-186, 207, 210, 211,
  288, 301, 304-305, 312, 320, 324,
  328, 332, 335-339, 345, 360
childhood, 5, 8, 360
education and views on education,
  8, 308, 345-347
"Edison effect," 146
electricity, electrical devices, 8-11,
  52, 57, 77, 100, 103-114, 126-7,
  132, 170, 173, 193, 210, 229-230,

Edison, Thomas A. (Continued)
312, 320, 324, 329-331, 334-336, 345, 349-352, 360
electrocution, 11
environment, environmental issues, & Department of Environmental Protection, 12, 40, 43-45, 53-59, 63-64, 73-81, 85-88, 93-94, 98-106, 110-120, 125, 129, 131-133, 135-144, 147-151, 155, 163, 171-172, 176, 180-188, 192, 198, 202-3, 206, 211-212, 219-224, 228-230, 234-240, 246-248, 252, 260-262, 267-269, 276-362
farming (see botany)
fluoroscope (see radiation)
grave, 301
health & illness, and his impact on health, 8, 85, 115, 345, 348
    bathing, 54, 280-81, 332
    deafness, 280, 348, 361
    death of, 11, 296
    dietary habits and beliefs, 54, 280-1, 304-305
dream, 43
exercise, 280-282
hearing and deafness, 8, 280
health history, 278-281
hygiene, 332
infections, 8, 279
longevity inquiry, 278-283
medical profession and
    physicians, relationships with, 277, 305, 348
memory, 144, 279
milieu interieur, 103, 277-292, 347-349, 360-361
"mind 1 and mind 2," 115, 362
    physical characteristics, 278-81, 295
safety and hazards, 86, 103, 144, 147, 151-153, 164, 173-86

Edison, Thomas A. (Continued)
207-210, 217, 266, 283-291, 338
sleep, 280
tobacco, 54, 115, 144, 281, 304, 332
honors, 11, 295, 307
human body, human environment, internal environment (milieu interieur), "human engineering," 103, 277-292, 312-317,
labor relations, 106, 110, 129, 147-9, 151, 173-174, 190, 210, 216, 240, 266, 283-291, 305, 312-317, 332, 338-339, 360-361
lamp, incandescent, electric light bulb, lighting systems, 9, 60, 77, 83-86, 94-95, 98, 100, 103-114, 172, 266, 295, 300, 308, 319-322, 327, 330, 333-334, 350-353, 362
legal issues, 178, 216
life and work, 1, 7-11
metallurgy, 151, 345
mining, iron and copper, 11, 86, 164, 188-219, 222-232, 238, 242-243, 269, 303, 309, 345
modernism (and discontinuity), 353-355, 359-361
motion pictures, kinetograph, kinetoscope, and photography, 11, 141-142, 145, 147, 236, 266, 309, 319, 345-346, 354, 362
"myth" of "Edison," 295, 309, 356, 362
nature, views on, 114-115, 340-342
Navy, U.S., 9, 11, 316, 338
Patents, inventions, 9,11,211,229
phenol (carbolic acid) and formaldehyde, plastic, 148, 164, 175-180, 186, 260, 304-307, 312, 326, 332, 345

480

Edison, Thomas A. (Continued)
phonograph, 9, 11, 77, 84-85, 95, 100, 148, 236, 266, 288, 308, 322, 334, 345, 348, 350-351, 362
plastic (see phenol)
pollution (and sewage, waste), 40, 56, 72-73, 86-87, 98, 122, 131-133, 142, 147, 151-153, 158, 164-166, 174, 178-188, 246-248, 268-269, 276, 301, 305-307, 323-326, 331-339, 345, 348
radiation – X-rays and radium, U.S. Radium Corporation and radium dial painters, fluoroscope, 11, 36, 118, 133-135, 149, 168-169, 236, 283-291, 296-297, 302, 305-306, 308-309, 326, 332, 335-336, 345, 348-349, 360-361
railroad(s) and trains, 49-72, 76-81, 85-86, 90-94, 98-100, 102, 105, 107, 110-112, 131-132, 142, 160, 164, 171-172, 176, 182-3 199-203, 209, 215-219, 224, 228-246, 250-253, 265, 268-273, 291, 299, 350
religious views and philosophy, 84, 114-115, 280, 340-341, 353-354
rubber and latex, 10-11, 274, 291, 296, 309, 345
telegrapher and telegraphy, 8, 9, 49-53, 308, 345, 348
telephone, 9, 241-5, 332-4, 352
telephone, 9, 241-245, 332-334, 352
train, electric, 59, 91-92, 99-100, 102, 132
X-rays (see radiation)

Edison Avenue (Stewartsville), 246, 262
Edison Chronology, 152, 192, 212
Edison Conference, "Interpreting Edison Conference," 152
Edison Lake (New Village, N.J.), 235, 249-250, 253, 262, 265, 365
Edison National Historic Site, 1, 14, 81, 117-18, 125, 131, 138, 146, 153, 195, 211, 255, 258, 266, 286, 289-90, 298, 301-02
Edison Papers Project, 1, 3, 106, 152, 211
Edison "Park Fast," 61, 68-69, 299
Edison Pioneers, 78, 94-95
Edison Project (charter schools), 347
Edison Road (New Village), 253, 262
Edison Road (Oxford), 262, 264
Edison Road (Sparta), 189, 205
"Edison State Park" (Menlo Park), 88, 90
Edison Street (Bloomfield), 154-5, 160, 195
Edison Tower and Tower Museum, 76, 79-81, 88-95, 98, 102, 259
Edisonia, 221
Edisonia Terrace (West Orange), 131
Edwards Dam (Maine), 329
Egbert Company, 72
Egbert, W. V., 69, 363
Eggler, Gladys, 262
Egypt, 324, 328
Einstein, Albert, 306, 354
Eisner, Michael, 355
E-K Medical Gas Division, 185
Electric Automobile, 330
Electric Light, 9, 11, 85, 100, 106-7 167, 320, 322-323, 330, 349, 353
Electric Train, 151
Electricity, 8, 95, 112, 124, 193, 210, 312, 317-321, 324, 327, 330, 332, 336, 345, 350-352, 360
Electrolier, 112-113

Elizabeth Point, 51
Elizabeth River, 22-23, 26-27, 34, 76, 156, 325
Elizabeth, N.J., 9, 23, 43, 45, 48, 50-51, 53, 55, 57, 63, 98, 112, 298, 366
Elizabethtown Gas Company, 253
Elizabethtown Water Company, 51
Elliott, Ebenezer, 5, 48
Elliott, John, 5
Elliott, Judge A. Elliott, 216, 228-232, 238, 240-3, 245
Ellis Island, 57, 366
Elm Road (Caldwell), 21, 364
Elm Street (Newark), 69-70
E-Mark Battery Company (Kearny, N.J.), 275
Emerson, Ralph Waldo, 125
Empire State Building, 14, 21, 26, 57
Engineering, 312
Enlightenment, 361-362
Environment, 1, 16, 43-45, 73, 75, 88, 98, 102, 105, 110-111, 113-5, 117, 132-3, 135, 137, 141-2, 144, 147, 149, 151, 153, 155, 163, 168, 171-2, 179-80, 187-8, 203, 208, 211-12, 219, 221-2, 247, 256, 260, 266, 276, 286, 290-3, 296-8, 302-3, 305-7, 309, 318, 324, 326, 329, 331-2, 335, 337-340, 343, 357, 359-361
Environmental Risk, 62, 178, 322, 335-338
EPICAC computer, 315
Episcopal Church, 29
Erickson, Kai, 338-339
Erie Railroad (Erie and Lackawanna), 34, 122, 142, 201, 218, 228, 235, 242, 246, 269, 273, 355, 366
Esopus Creek (Kingston, N.Y.), 226
Essex County Country Club, 25, 37
Essex County Hunt, 36
Essex County Medical Society, 118, 146, 286
Essex County Park System, 25
Essex County Toboggan Club, 37
Essex County, 4, 12-14, 16-18, 20, 23-32, 34, 36-39, 41, 45, 50, 59, 76, 118, 131, 146, 153, 156-7, 162, 164, 171, 173, 178, 186-8, 218-9, 221-2, 226, 232, 234-5, 269, 271, 284, 286, 291, 300, 303, 349, 363-7, 369
Essex Street (Harrison), 105, 107, 109
Eugene Place (Belleville), 161
Euphrates, 341
Europe and Europeans, 5, 19, 31-2, 196, 225-6, 318, 320, 343, 353
Evans Street (franklin), 190
Eve, 167
Everdell, William R., 354
Eveready, 350
Exchange Place (Jersey City), 57-8
Exxon, 365

Factories, 3, 10-12, 14, 21-4, 26, 28, 30, 34-7, 47, 51, 53, 57-8, 58, 61-4, 69-70, 73, 81, 84, 86-7, 90, 93, 98-99, 102, 105-10, 117-8, 122-4, 131-3, 135, 137-8, 140, 142-149, 152-5, 157-8, 164-174, 176, 178-179, 181-2, 184-7, 191, 193, 219, 224, 227-8, 230, 233, 236, 243-4, 250-1, 257-258, 265, 267-6, 288-90, 299-302, 307-9, 318, 320, 323-6, 328, 332, 335, 337-9, 349, 360, 361, 363-4, 366-367

Faden, William, 76
Fagin & Company (Newark), 60
Fairchild Aerial Surveys, 176
Fairmount Cemetery (Newark), 355, 364
Farms, 4, 29, 34, 50-51, 59, 115, 123, 132, 163, 194, 215, 224, 227-228, 239-240, 245, 265, 303, 325, 328, 342, 350-353, 359
Farr Street (Newark), 67
Farrand estate (Bloomfield), 167, 173
Farrand site (Bloomfield), 173
Federal Energy Regulatory Commission, 329
Felton, William H., 351
Fenn, Harry, 15, 17
Ferry Street (Newark), 68-69
Fifth Avenue (New York City), 102
Fifth Street (Harrison), 105, 107-109, 300
Finch, Katherine, Doctor, 315
Finn, Bernard, S., 3
Firestone, Harvey, 10, 274, 282-283
First National Bank (Elizabeth, N.J.), 51
First Presbyterian Church (Roselle), 112-113
First River (Essex County), 162
First Street (Newark), 165
Fish House Road (New Jersey Meadowlands), 269, 367
Fish, 84, 203, 211, 302, 324, 327-329, 342
Fisher, Irving, 278, 281, 283, 296
Flohn, Fred L., 173
Fluoroscope, 11, 236, 285-286, 305, 309, 319, 345, 349
Ford Motor Company, 257, 267-8, 270, 272-274, 322, 330
Ford, Henry, 10, 274, 282-283

Fordism, 323
Forster, E.M., 356
Fourth Street (Harrison), 107-109
Fowler, Samuel, 197-198
France, 297, 304
Frankenstein, 327
Franklin Avenue (Belleville and Newark), 155-6, 158, 160-1, 367
Franklin Mineral Museum, 196, 364, 396, 402, 440, 443
Franklin Street (Belleville), 178, 367
Franklin Township, N.J., 232-3, 237, 262, 265, 303
Franklin, Benjamin, 115, 125, 318, 354
Franklinite, 197-198, 210
Frazer, James George, Sir, 333
Frederick Street (Menlo Park), 90, 92
Freemantown (West Orange), 35
Frelinghuysen Avenue (Newark), 67
French and Indian War, 32
Friedel, Robert, 3, 106
Fritt property (New Village, N.J.), 241-242
Future, 315, 323, 326, 330, 334-5, 338, 342, 361, 382

Garden State Parkway, 23, 26, 76, 78, 123, 156-157
Gas, 112, 124, 126, 180, 253, 321, 352
Gateway Center and Hilton Hotel (Newark), 66, 72, 363
Geddes, Patrick, 318
General Electric Company, 10, 106-107, 109-110, 173, 276, 300, 306-7, 311, 313-4, 323, 325, 352
General Electric Lamp Works, 109,

276, 300
General Manufacturing Division (Edison company), 185
General Motors, 330
Geography, 1, 3, 12, 16, 24, 88, 132, 156, 226, 242, 267-268
Geology, 29
George, John, 200
Germany and Germans, 180, 296, 320-321
Geronimo, 355
Gershwin, George, 355
Gilbert Company, A. C., 369
Gillette, 350
Gilliland, Ezra, 114, 340
Glen Avenue (West Orange), 120
Glen Ridge, N.J., 168, 170, 172, 337, 367
Glenmount (West Orange), 117-135, 194, 232
Glenwood Avenue (West Orange), 122
God, 353-354
Golden Bough, The, 333
Good Springs Road (Stewartsville), 239-40, 245-6, 248, 251, 264-5
Gottlieb, Robert, 339
Gould, Jay, 9
Gould, Stephen Jay, 316
Grand Avenue (Jersey City), 57
Grand Canyon, 338
Grand Street (Newark), 58, 366
Great Fire (West Orange plant), 144-145, 178
Great Lakes, 5, 193, 308
Great Meadow Brook (Silver Lake), 160
Great Plains, 32, 351
Great Spirit, 353
Greece and Greeks, 197, 324
Green Street (Newark), 70-72
Green, Adolphus, 355

Greene Street (Jersey City), 58
Gregory Avenue (West Orange), 25, 36
Grove Street (Bloomfield), 160, 172, 302, 367

Hacknsack River, 268-270, 325
Hackettstown, N.J., 214, 219, 235
Hadonowetz, Sylvia, 196
Hadonowetz, Wasco, 195-196, 207
Halske works (Germany), 320
Halsted, Matthias Ogden, 38
Halstrom, W.I., 128-129
Hand, William H., 179-184, 184, 217
Hand's Death House (Silver Lake), 179-180
Harr, Jonathan, 337, 339
Harrison Avenue, 39, 107, 272
Harrison Fire Department, 110
Harrison Lamp Works, 106
Harrison Street (Orange), 34
Harrison, C., 120
Harrison, N.J., 84, 105-110, 276, 300, 323
Harvard College, 355
Haskell, Llewellyn, 35-36, 38-40, 120
Hatfield, Phebe, 197
Havana Cuba, 355
Hawthorne Effect, 316-317
Hawthorne Lake (Sparta), 212
Hayden Mill (Glen Ridge), 170-1
Hayden, Peter, 170
Hazards, Environmental and Occupational, 147, 180, 186, 286, 288, 291, 305, 312, 328, 337, 339
Health Issues, 37-38, 115, 118, 144, 147, 176, 178-9, 210, 277-282, 284, 286, 288, 290, 304-5, 312, 331-3, 338-9, 345, 347,

349, 360-1
Heater's Lake (Ogdensburg), 203
Heckel Street (Belleville), 160, 176, 178-179, 187, 367
Hegemeyer, Fred 49
Hendricks factories (Belleville), 158, 162
Hendricks Fields (Belleville), 158, 162
Henry Ford Museum, 4, 87
Henry Street (Orange), 33
Herpers, Henry, 187
Hicks, J. Maurice, 55, 57, 366
High Bridge Branch (New Jersey Transit), 218
High Street (Orange), 122, 235, 298
Highlands, New Jersey, 18, 184, 213, 222-4, 226-7, 261
Highlawn Pavilion (Orange Valley), 17, 38, 374
Highway 202, United States, 214
Hillside, N.J., 13, 26, 31, 62, 70, 76-77, 84, 87, 91, 119-120, 237
Hinduism, 333
Hiroshima, 306
Hoboken, N.J. 235
Holly, Henry Hudson, 41
Honda, 330

Honeysuckle Avenue (West Orange), 131
Horse Neck (Caldwell), 35
Horseshoe Cut (Sparta), 190, 202, 205, 209
Hotel Traymore (Atlantic City), 257
Hoyt house (Menlo Park), 85
Hudson County Grand Jury, 273
Hudson County, 22, 268, 276, 408, 410-411, 435
Hudson Street (Jersey City), 58

Hughes, Thomas P., 323
Human engineering, 312, 317
Hummel, Charles, 221-222
Hungarian Church (Sparta), 364
Hunt Club (Orange) 37
Hunterdon County, 227
Hurley, Andrew, 338-339
Hurrell Field (Glen Ridge), 170-1, 367
Hyatt, John Wesley, 61
Hygiene, 277-278, 280-282, 284, 286, 288, 290, 305, 332, 346

Incandescent Light, 9, 60, 77, 79, 83, 86, 94-95, 100, 105, 112, 266, 295, 308, 313, 319-20, 322, 327
Indiana, 339
Indians, 19, 29, 31-32, 37, 163, 191, 196, 225-226, 232, 315, 339, 343, 355
Industrialization and the Industrial Revolution, 24, 51, 164, 227, 246, 269, 297, 301, 304-5, 308, 311, 313, 315, 317, 320-1, 323-4, 328, 338, 348, 356, 361
Ingersoll Terrace (Union), 26, 258-260
Ingersoll, Charles, 227
Ink Factory (Glen Ridge), 168-169, 326, 367
Insull, Samuel, 108
Interstate 80 highway, 214
Iowa, 351
Iron Mining, 188-200, 202-210, 212-19, 236, 309
Ironbound section (Newark), 63, 69-70, 72, 107, 187
Iroquois, 32, 314
Irvington, N.J., 23, 32-33, 303
Iselin, N.J., 27, 76

Israel, Paul, 3
Italy and Italians, 130, 179, 180-1, 296

Jack Frost, 186
Jacksonsonburg Limestone, 223
Japan, 296
Japanese bamboo, 60
Jeanette, U.S.S., 327
Jefferson Twp, N.J., 194, 213, 364
Jefferson, Thomas, 115, 125, 353-4, 356
Jeffreys, J.T., 272
Jehl, Francis, 4, 371
Jehovah, 353
Jerome Place (Bloomfield), 166
Jersey Avenue (Menlo Park), 85
Jersey Central Railroad, 57, 366
Jersey City, N.J., 26, 47-48, 50, 52, 54-63, 66, 68, 70, 72, 98-99, 165, 201, 213-214, 218, 268-272, 298, 325, 364, 366
Jesus, 33, 353
Johnson, A. E., 287-288
Johnson, John, 213
Johnson, Mr., 288
Jordan, Sarah, 85, 92, 94
Jordan's Boarding House, Mrs. (Menlo Park), 85-86, 92, 94, 98
Josephson, Matthew, 3, 369
Joyce, James, 354
Julian Place (Elizabeth), 50
Jurassic Period, 19, 30

Kansas, 32, 224
Katyn monument (Jersey City), 58
Kawameeh Park (Union), 26
Kearny, N.J., 267-268, 276, 367
Kearny, Philip, General, 270
Keller, Helen, 355

Kennebec River, 329
Kennedy Avenue (Ogdensburg), 201
Kentucky, 297
Kiddie, Walter, 95
Kimler, Linda, 222
Kingsland (Bergen County), 268
Kingsland, Nathaniel, 270
Kingston, N.Y., 226
Kinney Building (Newark), 69, 72, 363
Kipling, Rudyard, 355
Kittatinny Mountains, 223, 226
Knoxville, Tenn., 118
Koncher, Leo, 268, 367
Koppers Coke and Gas Company, 270, 276
Korea, 296
Kruesi, John, 85, 92, 94, 98
Kuhn, Thomas, 344

Labor, 275-276, 317, 319, 342, 349-352
Laboratories, 3, 125, 138, 140-142, 144, 146-148, 295, 318, 339, 363
Lafayette Auto Parts, 9, 363-364
Lafayette Street (Newark), 67
Lake Erie, 355
Lake Hopatcong, 165, 189, 194, 196, 198, 200, 213-214, 217-219, 224, 231, 233-235, 364
Lake Street (Belleville), 155, 160
Lake Superior, 210
Lakeside Avenue (West Orange), 258, 301
Lamp Factory (Menlo Park), 81, 90, 93
Lamp Works (Harrison), 84, 105-106, 108, 110, 112, 114, 382
Laos and Laotians, 329
Lash, Scott, 338-339

Lee, James "Jim," 222, 247, 365
Lehigh Canal, 227
Lehigh River, 227, 238
Lehigh Valley Railroad, 273
Lehman, Mr., 245
Lenni Lenape, 19, 31-32, 196, 224-226
Leslie, William, 236
Liberty Island, 57
Liberty State Park (Jersey City), 55, 366
Liberty Street (Bloomfield), 164
Light, 9, 11, 34, 76, 79, 85-86, 91, 95, 100, 103, 105-110, 112-14, 122, 149, 167, 178, 197, 295, 319-20, 322-3, 326-7, 330, 334, 341-342, 349, 351-354
Limestone, 193, 212-213, 221-224, 226, 228, 230, 232, 234, 236-40, 242, 244, 246, 248, 250, 252, 254, 256-8, 260-2, 264-5, 303
Lincoln Highway (Essex-Middlesex Turnpike), 27, 77, 82, 92, 96, 99, 112
Lincoln Park (Newark), 67
Lincoln Park, N.J., 214
Lincoln, Abraham, 35
Linden, N.J., 52, 300
Livingston, N.J., 16, 24, 50, 272
Livingston, William, Governor, 50
Llewellyn Park (West Orange), 14, 37-39, 117-135, 233-4, 237, 300
Lock Street (Newark), 62
Lodi, N.J., 270
Lodygin, A. N., 322
London, 320, 379
Lopatcong Creek, 227-228
Los Angeles, 335
Louisville, Ky., 297
Lyon, David, 200

Maass, Clara, 355
Maier, Pauline, 356
Main Street (Ogdensburg), 196, 200
Main Street, 119, 123, 196, 258, 284
Maine, 38, 329
Manhattan Island, 13-14, 21, 57, 374
Mansfield (Washington, N.J.), 228
Manufacturing, 11, 34, 36, 51, 72, 107, 140, 144, 148, 152, 161, 164-165, 173, 184-185, 193, 198, 213, 216, 225, 230, 267, 273-274, 276, 303, 309, 313, 337, 345, 363-365
Maplewood, N.J., 23, 30, 32, 35, 298
Marconi, Guglielmo, 349
Market Street (Newark), 63-64, 67, 69, 72, 163, 363
Marlborough, Duke of, 108
Marmor, Milton, 125, 385, 442
Marsh, George Perkins, 344
Marshall, David Trumball, 82-84, 91
Martin, E.D., 267
Marx, Karl, 318, 343-344
Marx, Leo, 323
Marxism, 344
Massena & DuPont, 95
McCall's, 350
McCarter Highway (Newark), 63, 69, 363
McClellan, George Brinton, 35
McCullough, George P., 213
McGowan, Assemblyman, 167
McGuirk, Kathleen, 114
McLaughlin Place (West Orange), 259-260, 365

Meadowlands, 274
Meadowlands, New Jersey, 267-276, 367
Mechanic Street (Newark), 64, 363
Meddaugh, Gary, 222, 252, 254-5
Mekong River, 329
Melosi, Martin V., 3, 106, 222
Menlo Park Land Company, 77
Menlo Park Mall, 90
Menlo Park Marker Boulder, 78
Menlo Park Museum, 93
Menlo Park, 7, 9, 11, 26-27, 75-78, 80-90, 92, 94-100, 102, 106-7, 111-114, 222, 259, 299, 320, 325, 327, 332, 340, 342, 355
Merchant, Carolyn, 343
Merrill Creek (Stewartsville), 238, 240
Mesabi ore (Minnesota), 210, 303
Mesozic Era, 18-19, 30
Metro Park station (Iselin), 27, 76, 78, 80, 299
Middle Proterozoic era, 223
Middlesex Avenue (Menlo Park), 81, 88, 90-91, 98
Middlesex County, 20, 27, 73, 76, 81, 88, 90-91, 98, 365
Midland Avenue (Glen Ridge), 168, 367
Midland Railroad (New York, Susquehanna & Western), 200
Milan, Ohio, 2, 5, 7, 297, 371, 426, 432
Military Park (Newark), 61
Milk, 280-281, 304-305
Mill Street (Belleville), 158
Millard Andrè, 3, 106, 222
Millburn Avenue (Millburn), 26
Millburn, N.J., 23, 26, 32, 34
Miller, Lewis, 355
Millpond Road (New Village), 237
Milwaukee Railroad, 350

Minnesota, 210, 303
Misiur, Steve, 196
Mississippi River, 23
Missouri River, 23, 238
Model A Ford, 267-8, 270, 272-4
Model T Ford, 274, 322, 330
Modern Management, 312
Modernism and Modernity, 338, 353-355
Moffitt house (Menlo Park), 85
Monmouth Avenue (Menlo Park), 79, 85, 92, 96
Montana Road (New Village), 246
Montana, 349-353
Montclair Branch (New Jersey Transit), 171, 218
Montclair Community Hospital, 133
Montessori method, 345-346
Montgomery Street (Bloomfield), 122, 165
Montgomery Street (Jersey City), 58
Montville, 214, 218
Morgan, J.P. 313
Morris and Essex Railway Line (Morristown Line), 34, 37, 218-9, 234-235
Morris Canal Basin, 298, 366
Morris Plains, N.J., 234
Morris Turnpike, 234
Morris, B. F. 267, 275
Morristown National Historic Site, 237
Morristown, N.J., 234, 237
Morse Code, 125, 234
Moses, 333
Mother Nature, 336
Mount Bethel, N.J., 223
Mount Pleasant (Newark), 122-3, 163
Mount Pleasant (Lake Hopatcong),

233-234, 272
Mount Pleasant Cemetery (Newark), 123, 163, 384-385, 445, 447
Mount Tabor, 234
Mountain Avenue (West Orange), 206
Mountainside Hospital, 133
Mudwall Row (Sparta), 192
Mumford Lewis, 317-320, 323-329
Musconetcong River, 224-225, 234
Musconetcong Valley, 224-8
Museum of The Historical Society of Bloomfield, 118, 367
Musser, Charles, 3
Mutz, Henry A., 108
Mylod, James P., Judge, 178

Nam Theun Two project, 329
Nanina's-in-the-Park (Silver Lake), 158
National Fire Protection Association, 147
National Park Service, 62, 75, 77, 80, 82-3, 101, 117-118, 123-125, 134, 139, 141, 145-146, 148, 152, 154, 175, 191, 195, 204, 233, 244, 249, 256, 275, 282, 285, 301, 369
Native Americans, 31, 224, 226, 327
Nepal, 329
Netcong, 214
New Barbadoes, 268
New England, 114, 343
New Hampshire, 297
New Haven,, 31, 278, 296, 369
New Jersey and Pennsylvania Concentrating Works, 11, 190-1, 196, 212, 218
New Jersey Audubon Society, 211

New Jersey Bell, 276
New Jersey Department of Environmental Protection, 203, 206, 211-212
New Jersey Department of Labor, 396, 436
New Jersey Division of Fish, Game, and Wildlife (DEP), 203
New Jersey Green Acres program, 58, 298, 366
New Jersey Institute of Technology, 62
New Jersey Legislature, 167, 215, 227, 270
New Jersey state parks, 27, 55, 88-90, 214, 234, 365-366
New Jersey Superior Court, 70
New Jersey Turnpike, 23, 272
New Jersey Zinc Company, 197
New Mexico, 193, 297
New Village Road (New Village), 242, 246
New York City, 9-11, 13-14, 21, 26, 36, 38, 41, 50, 77, 87, 102-3, 110, 112-113, 164-165, 171, 173, 185, 217, 256-257, 276, 297-300, 308, 313, 320, 347, 366
New York ferry, 55
New York Times, 153, 177, 306-7. 329-330, 348, 354-355
New York, Susquehanna and Western Railroad, 200, 203, 218
Newark & Bloomfield Railroad, 164
Newark (International) Airport, 23, 26, 131
Newark Avenue (Jersey City), 269-272
Newark Avenue (Newark and Belleville), 161, 165
Newark Basin, 20, 27
Newark Bay, 23, 31, 34, 45, 107,

268, 271
Newark City Ice Company, 162
Newark City Subway, 123
Newark Museum, 20
Newark Public Library, 15
Newark Telegraph Works, 68
Newark Warehouse Company, 69
Newark, N.J., 3-4, 9, 15, 19-24, 26-27, 29, 31, 33-6, 39, 45, 47-50, 52, 54-6, 58-64, 66-70, 72-3, 78, 81, 98-99, 103, 105-107, 110, 118, 122-123, 131, 141, 152-153, 155-158, 160-166, 171, 186-187, 199, 214-5, 218-29, 226-7, 231, 234-5, 266, 286-7, 289, 299, 303, 308, 348, 355, 362-4, 366-7
Newark-Pompton Turnpike, 163, 214
News Reporting Telegraph Company, 69
Nile River, 328
Ninth Street (Newark), 161
Nishuane Park (Montclair), 32, 120
Nishuane River, 33, 133, 135, 163
Noble, David, 311-312, 314
Norfolk Avenue (Newark), 70
North Arlington, N.J., 268
North Belmont Avenue (Belleville), 161
North Broad Street (Elizabeth), 51
North Carolina, 297
North Eighth Street (Belleville and Newark), 161
North Mountain Avenue (Upper Montclair), 258, 260
North Ridgewood Avenue (South Orange), 28, 37
North Street (Elizabeth), 51
Northfield Avenue (West Orange), 24-25, 37, 131, 272
Nova Scotia, 5, 225
Nuland, Sherwin, 325

Nutley, N.J., 164

Oak Bend (Orange), 39
Oakes Wool Mill (Bloomfield), 173
Oakes, David, 164, 173
Occam's Razor, 344
Ogden Mine Railroad, 199, 209, 215, 218-219
Ogden, Aaron, 197
Ogden, Abram, 197
Ogden, Elias, 197
Ogden, John, 50, 325
Ogden, Matthias, 26, 197
Ogden, Phebe, 197
Ogden, Rebecca, 197
Ogden, Robert, III, 197
Ogden, Robert, II, 197
Ogdensburg Historical Society, 191, 195
Ogdensburg Hotel, 200
Ogdensburg Road, 195
Ohio River, 23
Ojibwa Indians, 339
Oklahoma, 32
Old Indian Road (Orange Mountain), 32, 37
Old Schoolhouse Museum (Ogdensburg), 209
Oldsmobile, 330
Oliver Street (Newark), 64, 70-72
Olmstead, Frederick Law, 38
Onsted, Walter, 200
Ontario, Canada, 5, 7
Orange Branch (Erie Railroad), 122, 160, 234, 291
Orange Heights Avenue (West Orange), 37
Orange Lawn Tennis Club, 37
Orange Mountain Cable Company (West Orange), 37

Orange Mountain, 36-37, 119, 166
Orange Park (Orange), 35
Orange Public Library, 286
Orange Street (Newark), 61, 156, 272
Orange Valley, 1, 13-14, 16, 18, 20-22, 24, 26, 28, 32, 40-41, 45, 118, 122, 125, 131-132, 135, 147, 157, 163, 288, 291, 298, 301, 303, 325, 362
Orange, N.J., 22, 24, 33-34, 38, 76, 118, 122, 131, 133, 135, 235, 259-60, 285-6, 298, 301-2, 325
Oranges, The, 4, 22-24, 32-36, 156, 218, 272, 287, 303
Oregon Railway and Navigation Company, 327
Oregon Steam Navigation Company, 327
Oser, Marion Edison, 81, 8-87, 113
Our Lady of Mount Carmel Roman Catholic Church (Orange), 22
Outcault, R. F., 79-81, 84, 88, 90-4
Overlook Road (West Orange), 259
Owen, Robert, 125
Oxford Furnace, 226-227
Oxford Quarry, 251, 263-264, 365
Oxford University, 352
Oxford, N.J., 226, 263-264, 365

Pacey, Arnold, 320-321
Paine, Thomas, 7, 115, 125, 341, 353-354
Paleozoic Era, 18, 223
Pangea, 19
Park Street (now Philips Street, Menlo Park), 81, 92
Park Way (West Orange), 120
Parrow Brook (Orange), 34, 40, 122, 132, 157, 325-326
Parrow Street, 22, 34

Passaic County, 18, 23, 32, 162-163, 165, 214
Passaic River Basin, 329
Passaic River, 4, 19, 22-24, 28, 31, 34, 39, 60, 62, 76, 103, 106-107, 122, 131, 133, 156, 162-164, 186, 214, 272, 324-326
Pasteur, Louis, 304
Paterson, N.J., 214-218
PATH (Port Authority Trans-Hudson rail line), 32, 56-57, 76, 122, 234, 298
Pathmark, 160-161, 174
Paulus Hook Battle Site, 57-58, 366
PCB's (polychlorinated biphenyls), 306-307
Pearl Street (New York City), 9, 102, 113
Pedder, Henry C., 41
Penn, William, 226
Pennsylvania Avenue (Newark), 67
Pennsylvania Railroad Station (Newark), 61, 63, 67-68, 70, 72, 83, 107, 363-364
Pennsylvania Railroad Terminal (Jersey City), 55
Pennsylvania Railroad, 51, 55, 57, 61, 63-64, 67, 70, 78, 83, 85, 107, 269, 273
Pennsylvanian period, 18
Pequest River, 227-228
Perth Amboy, N.J., 88, 224
Peters factory (Harrison), 107-108
Peters Manufacturing Company, 107-108
Peterson, Michael, 247, 255, 277
Philadelphia, 226
Philips Street (formerly Park Street, Menlo Park), 81, 92
Phillipsburg, N.J., 227
Piedmont range, 19

Pierce Papers, 118, 216, 218, 242-4
Pierce, Margaret, 118, 230, 243
Pinchot, Gifford, 327
Plato, 340
Player Piano, 314
Pleasant Valley (Orange Valley), 237-239, 248
Pleasant Valley Road (Orange Valley), 248
Pleistocene Age, 30, 157, 224
Plenge Site (Warren County), 225
Pohatcong Creek, 223, 250, 265
Pohatcong Mountain, 238-239, 245, 251
Pohatcong Railroad, 235, 250
Pohatcong Valley, 228, 230-231, 234, 237-240, 246-247, 262, 265, 303
Polish soldier, 58
Pollution, 34, 36, 73, 86, 102, 132, 144, 147, 149, 152-153, 160, 166, 174, 176, 178-179, 187, 261, 298, 305-306, 323-324, 326, 328, 331-333, 335-339, 343, 348
Pompton Avenue (Verona and Cedar Grove), 163
Pompton Plains, N.J., 214
Pompton River, 214
Pope, Frank L., 50, 52-54, 59
Pope, Franklin A., 47
Pope, Henry W., 50
Pope, Ralph, 49
Port Authority of New York and New Jersey, 56
Port Colden, 214
Port Delaware (Phillipsburg), 214-215, 227
Port Morris, 214, 233
Port Murray, 214
Port Warren, 214-215, 240
Portete Avenue (Kearny), 269, 272
Portland Cement, 10-11, 95, 126-127, 193, 212, 216, 218-219, 221-223, 229, 231, 238, 246-247, 250, 259-260, 262, 266, 325
Precambrian Era, 18, 223
Pretzer, William S., 3, 89
Princeton, N.J., 99
Prospect Avenue (West Orange), 24-25, 120, 122, 130, 122, 130, 133
Proterozoic, Middle, Era, 223
Public Service Electric and Gas Company, 95, 276, 382, 430
Pulaski Skyway (Hudson Company), 268, 271-272, 367
Purcell, David, 238, 241-242
Puritans, 19, 31-32, 107, 163
Pustay, M. R., 212

Quarries, 62, 164, 193, 206, 219, 221-2, 224, 226, 228, 230, 232, 234, 236, 238-240, 242, 244, 246, 248, 250, 252, 254, 256, 258, 260-2, 264, 266
Quarry Road, 246, 253
Quaternary Period, 30
Queen Anne architectural style, 41
Quincy's Place (West Orange), 37

Raban, Jonathan, 351, 423-436
Radiation, 283-286, 289, 291, 305-306, 360
Radio Corporation of America (R.C.A.), 109, 300
Radio Shack, 109
Radio, 109, 184, 272-3, 345-6, 364
Radioactivity, 169, 287, 290-291, 298, 331
Radiology, 286
Radium Girls, 286-287
Radium Luminous Materials

Corporation, 285
Rahway River, 22-24, 26-28, 30, 37, 76, 84, 100, 133, 166, 329
Railroad Place (Elizabeth), 50
Ramapo River, 214
Raritan Bay, 224
Raritan River, 20, 27, 224
Raritan Township, N.J., 76
Rashomon, 344
Rawlins, Wyo., 297
Raymond Boulevard (Newark), 62, 68, 70, 123, 364
Raymond Park West (Newark), 64
Raymond Plaza (Newark), 66, 363
Reed, Walter, 355
Reggae & Company, 49
Renaissance Mall (Newark), 66-67
Revolutionary War, 5, 7, 32, 50, 57-58, 163, 197
Ridge Road (Ogdensburg), 209
Ridge Road (West Orange), 38
Ridge Street (Orange), 33
Ridgewood Avenue, 170-171
Road 604, County, 234
Road 604, Warren County (Waterloo Road), 234
Road 633, County, 242, 265
Rock Spring Club (West Orange), 25, 37
Rockaway River, 214
Rockaway, N.J., 218
Rockefeller, John D., 356
Rocky Mountains, 18-19, 193, 204
Roentgen, Willhelm Conrad, 11, 283, 348
Rogers, George, 268
Rome and Romans, 22, 253, 324
Roosevelt Avenue (Belleville), 160
Roosevelt Hospital (Menlo Park), 90-91
Roosevelt, Hilbourne, 355
Roosevelt, Theodore, 353, 355

Rosanoff, M. A., 142, 144, 309, 356
Rosedale Cemetery (West Orange), 122, 134-135, 296, 365
Roselle Land Company, 111-112
Roselle, N.J., 111-114, 300
Rosenberg, Bob, 106
Rosenblatt, Roger, 100
Route 10, New Jersey, 233
Route 15, New Jersey, 194
Route 506, County, 272
Route 517, County, 195
Route 517, Sussex County, 195
Route 53, New Jersey, 234
Route 57, New Jersey, 214, 232-3
Route 615, County ("Edison Road"), 194, 213
Route 615, County, 213
Route 629, County, 214
Route 638, County, 246
Runes, Dagobert D., 345, 353
Russia, 322
Rutgers University, 1, 82, 152, 197 (also see UMDNJ)
Rutgers, Anthony, 197
Rutherford, 268

Sacred Heart Cathedral (Newark), 123, 156, 158
Salem Road (Elizabeth), 48
Salmon, 327-328
Sandford, William, 268, 270, 367
Sant' Ambroglio, Lucy, 173-174, 367
Scandia Match company, 273
Schenectady, 10, 306, 314, 325
Schuyler Avenue (Kearny), 270, 272-273, 367
Schulyer, Arent, 269-270
Scientific Management, 313, 316
Scotland and Scots, 270, 353

Scotland Road (Orange), 33-34, 235
Scotts Mountain (Stewartville), 239, 246-247, 265, 303
Secaucus, N.J., 268
Second Mountain (Orange Valley), 24, 36, 272
Sellers, Christopher C., 286
Serpentine Park (Menlo Park), 81
Seurat, Georges, 354
Shallcross, Charles, 50
Sharlow, Mary, 5
Shea, T. K., 212
Shippen, Peggy, 226
Short Hills, N.J., 26
Siberia, 31
Siemens works (Germany), 320
Silent Spring, 305, 324, 337-338
Silicon Valley, 78
Silver Lake (Bloomfield and Belleville, N.J.), 151-188
Silver Lake Chemical Works, 155, 174, 176, 179-180, 182, 184-185, 302, 306, 366
Silver Lake Church, 155-156
Silver Lake Railroad Station, 155-156, 161, 367
Silver Lake School, 156
Singer, Isaac, 51
Sir Joseph W. Swan, 322
Sixth Street (Belleville), 160
Sixth Street (Harrison), 109-110
Sloane, David Edison, Dr., 369
Sloane, Madeline Edison, 119, 125, 369
Smith, Merrit Roe, 323
Snake Rock (Kearny), 272
Snyder, Charles, 248
Society Hill (Newark), 70, 72
Solectria, 330
Somerset County, 32
Sommer, Carl August, 20-21

South America, 31
South Center Street (Orange), 22
South Mountain Reservation, 24-25, 27-28, 37, 303, 364
South Orange Avenue (Newark), 64, 363
South Orange Reservation, 26
South Orange Village, 28
South Valley Road (West Orange), 23, 28, 37, 39
Soviet Union, 296
Spano, Susan, 355
Sparta Lake, 303
Sparta Mountain Wildlife Management Area, 189, 203, 211-212, 303
Sparta Mountain, 189, 211-212, 303, 399
Sparta Mountain, 189-192, 194-196, 198, 200, 202-204, 206, 208, 210-212, 214, 216, 218-219, 223, 303, 325, 364
Sparta Township, N.J., 194, 201
Speedwell village, 234, 404
Sprague, Frank, 173
Springdale Avenue (East Orange), 159
St. Cloud Presbyterian Church (Orange Mountain), 37
St. George Avenue (Roselle), 112
St. John's Catholic Church (Orange), 33
Standish Street (West Orange), 118
Stanhope, 214, 217-218
Stanley Papers, 118, 124-125
Stanley, Jack, 118, 124-125, 286
Starr, Paul, 331, 348
Staten Island Sound, 34
Staten Island, N.Y., 23, 34, 57, 224
Sterling Hill Mining Museum, 196, 364
Sterling Hill Zinc Mine, 196, 204,

494

211
Stetson hat factory (Orange), 132, 325
Stevens, Ernest, 148
Stewartsville Road (Stewartsville), 246
Stewartsville, N.J., 212, 214, 218, 223, 229, 232, 238-239, 246, 365
Stone, Henry, 215-216, 247
Stroudsville, Pa., 201
Summerville (Sparta), 192
Sunday School (Menlo Park), 83-4
Superfund sites, 133, 135, 168-169, 289-290, 298, 301-302, 307-308, 338, 365, 367
Susquehanna River, 32
Sussex County, 11, 45, 188-219, 223, 227, 229, 231, 235-236, 238, 242, 258, 261, 266, 303, 339, 364, 366
Sussex Street (Harrison), 108-109, 366
Swaim, Ginalie, 351-352
Swan, Joseph Wilson, 320, 322
Swedenborgianism, 41
Swift, 270, 276, 327
Symington, Jim, 7
Szerszynski, Bronislaw, 338-339

Tate, Alfred O., 12, 108
Taylor, Frederick, 313, 316-319
Taylorism, 317
Technology, 209, 317, 320-323, 326
Telegraph, 8, 48-49, 51, 68-69, 308, 342, 349
Telephone, 8-9, 216-217, 222, 229, 243, 269, 311, 330, 332-334, 342, 348-349, 351-352
Tenth Street (Newark), 160
Tertiary Period, 30

Thatcher, Elisha, House (Oxford, N.J.), 264-265
Third Mountain (Orange Valley), 19
Thirds River (Yountakah River), 31
Thomas A. Edison Middle School (West Orange), 40, 133, 302
Thoreau, Henry David, 115, 125, 344, 354
Thornall Avenue (Menlo Park), 77
Thornall Estate House (Menlo Park), 85, 92
Three Mile Island, 306, 339
Tibetan Buddhist Learning Center, 303
Tobacco, 281
Toney Brook (Bloomfield), 122
Toney, W. R. R., 171
Toohey, Mary Louise, 236
Tories, 5, 58
Tory Corner (West Orange), 33, 39, 133, 135
Tower Avenue (Menlo Park), 88
Tower Street (formerly Woodbridge Avenue, Menlo Park), 79, 85, 92, 94-95
Toxic chemicals, 168, 181, 186, 276, 297, 305, 307, 312, 331-332, 338, 348
Toyota, 330
Transcendentalism, 115
Traxel, David, 354-355
Treat, Robert, 31, 69
Triassic Period, 19, 29-30
Tselos, George, 3, 286
Tuberculosis, 38, 279

U. S. Radium Corporation, 36, 40, 118, 133, 169, 285-291, 298, 301-302, 308, 365
Underwood Typewriter Building (Conn.), 257

495

Unger, William, 68
Union Army, 35
Union County Historical Society, 50
United Hatter's Association of North America, 37
United Kingdom, 333-334
United States Army, 35, 237, 316, 318, 355
United States Congress, 11, 314
United States Council of National Defense, 316
United States Environmental Protection Agency (EPA), 133, 168-169, 290, 298, 302, 338
United States Naval Consulting Board, 11, 316
United States Navy, 10, 338
United States War Department, 316
United States War Industries Board, 316
University of Medicine and Dentistry of New Jersey (UMDNJ), 70, 118, 286-287, 289, 323
Upper Montclair, N.J., 258, 260, 365
Upton house (Menlo Park), 81, 85, 92, 94, 98, 112
Upton house (New Village), 244-5
Upton, Francis R., 85, 94, 106, 108, 244-245, 321

Valley Avenue, 23-24
Vanderbilt, Byron M., 3
Veblen, Thorstein, 318
Vermont, 344
Verona, N.J., 163-164
Victaulic Company, 250-251, 258
Vietnam, 296
Villard, Henry, 327

Vincent, John, Bishop, 355
Voicewriter, 85
Von Helmholtz, H.L.F., 321
Vonnegut, Kurt, 314

Wachhorst, Wyn, 3
Wacker, Peter O., 194
Walden, 344
Walker Road (West Orange), 37
Wallkill River, 190, 194, 196, 218, 325
Wallkill Valley, 190, 194, 197-198, 218
Walnut Street (Bloomfield), 165
Ward Place (Newark), 107
Ward Street (Newark), 64, 69, 363
Wardesson (Bloomfield), 163
Warne, George K., 222, 252-253, 262
Warren County, 221-266, 339
Warren, Joseph, 227
Washington Avenue (Warren County), 239, 248
Washington Rock (Orange Valley), 24-26, 28, 364
Washington Street (West Orange), 34, 39-40, 57, 70
Washington, George, 26
Watchung Mountains, 19, 118, 224,
Watchung Reservation, 18
Watchung Street (West Orange), 118, 149, 161
Waterloo Road (Warren County), 234
Watsessing Avenue (Bloomfield), 32, 172, 176, 302
Watsessing Lake, 122
Watsessing Park, 32, 122, 162, 393
Watt, James, 318
Wellesley College, 82
West Orange Chronicle, 302

496

West Orange Public Library, 286
West Orange, N.J., 27, 117-149, 166, 194, 216, 219, 228, 232, 234, 237, 329, 365
Western Electric Company, 270, 276, 316
Westfield Avenue (Roselle), 112
Westfield, N.J., 76
Westinghouse, 173, 311, 313-314
Weston, Edward, 60-61
Wharton, 214-215, 219
Wheeler, Nathaniel, 29
White Bridge (New Village), 242
White Tar Company, 273
White, Richard, 324, 327-328
Whitman, Walt, 115, 125, 354
Whitney Creek, Mont., 349-351, 353
Whitney, Eli, 318, 321
Whittle, Christopher, 347
Wickes, Stephan, 4, 13, 29
Wiener, Norbert, 311
Wigwam Brook (West Brook), 29, 32-34, 36, 39-40, 120, 122, 132, 135, 142, 149, 157, 162, 168, 171, 284-286, 290-291, 298, 301, 308, 326
Wile, Raymond R., 3
Will, George, 317
Williamstown (Essex County), 35
Willow Grove Mill Road (New Village), 246
Wilton, Conn., 85
Winding Way (West Orange), 37
Wisconsin, 326
Woburn, Mass., 337-338
Wood Avenue (Menlo Park), 78-79, 81, 90
Wood, Leonard, 355
Woodbridge Avenue (Menlo Park), 79, 85, 92, 94
Woodland Period, 226

Woodside Villa (Winthrop, Mass.), 114, 340-341
World Bank, 329
World Trade Center, 14, 22, 57
World War I, 10-11, 173, 283, 287, 316, 318, 338, 351
World War II, 273-274, 296, 306
Worster, Donald, 343-344
Wright Street (Newark), 64, 67-68, 70, 72, 299, 363
Wright, Orville and Wilbur, 321
Wynne, Brian, 339
Wyoming Avenue (South Orange), 25
Wyoming, 297

X-rays (see Radiation)

Yankee Stadium, 256-258
Yellowstone National Park, 338
Yellowstone River, 350, 353
Yerkes, Robert M., 313, 316
York, Duke of, 197
Yosemite, 189, 204-206, 219
Yountakah River (Third River), 31

Zinc, 60, 83, 190-191, 193, 196-198, 200, 204, 210-211
Zincite, 197

Some Other Publications by George J. Hill

Books
Leprosy in Five Young Men
Clinical Oncology (three editions) and Spanish translation, *Cirurgia Menor* (two editions)
Outpatient Surgery (with John Horton)
Liberia and the U.S., 1917-1947 (two editions)
John Saxe, Loyalist
Hill: The Ferry Keeper's Family
Proceed to Peshawar
Western Pilgrims (2 vols.)
Quakers and Puritans (2 vols.)
Fundy to Chesapeake (2 vols.)
American Dreams (1 vol.; it is also the title of a 7-volume tetralogy comprised of the last four books)

Papers on Edson and the Environment
"Thomas Alva Edison: Health, Medicine, and the Great Inventor," *New Jersey Medicine*
"When the 'Wizard' Left Menlo Park," *New Jersey Heritage*
"Assessing Accountability for Natural Resource Damage: The Limits of History," *New Jersey Reporter*

Papers on the Environment and Toxicology
"…and Some Will Have It Cold," *Proceedings, U.S. Naval Institute*
"Blood cyanide levels in mice after administration of amygdalin," *Biopharmaceutics and Drug Disposition* (with H. Z. Hill)
"Lead Poisoning due to Hai Ge Fen," *Journal of the American Medical Association* (with Sarah Hill)

Diplomatic History
"Intimate Relationships: Secret Affairs of Church and State in the U.S. and Liberia, 1925-1947, *Diplomatic History*

About the Author

Dr. George J. Hill was born in 1932 in Cedar Rapids, Iowa. He is a fifth generation Iowan, the son of a small town banker and a college teacher. After graduation from high school in Sac City, Iowa, he received scholarships to study at Yale College and the Harvard Medical School, where he received the M.D. degree in 1957. Dr. Hill began a career in surgery by training at the New York Hospital-Cornell Medical Center and the Peter Bent Brigham Hospital in Boston. He joined the faculty of the University of Colorado in 1966 as an Instructor in Surgery. He later was a Professor of Surgery at Washington University in St. Louis, Missouri; at Marshall University in Huntington, West Virginia; and at the New Jersey Medical School in Newark, New Jersey. He is also an alumnus of the Harvard Business School, as a participant in the Program for Health Systems Management V in 1976. He retired from surgery in 1996 and was appointed Emeritus Professor of Surgery at the UMDNJ-New Jersey Medical School (now Rutgers University). He was Interim President of Sterling College in 1996. In 1999 he earned the M.A. in history from Rutgers University, Newark, N.J., and in 2005 he received the D.Litt. in history from Drew University, Madison, N.J. In 2000-01, Dr. Hill was an Adjunct Professor of History at Kean University in Union, N.J. He is currently an Adjunct Professor of Surgery at the Hébert Medical School of the Uniformed Services University of the Health Sciences, Bethesda, Maryland. He is a retired Captain in the U.S. Navy Medical Corps.

A life-long member of the Boy Scouts of America, Dr. Hill is currently a member of the Executive Board of the Northern New Jersey Council, BSA. He has been a ranch hand in Montana, a military parachutist, and a marathon runner. His biography appears in *Who's Who in America*. Dr. Hill is married to Helene Zimmermann Hill, Ph.D., who is Professor of Radiology Emerita at the New Jersey Medical School – Rutgers University. They live in West Orange, N.J., and they have a certified Tree Farm in New Hampshire. The Hills have four children and three grandchildren.

Heritage Books by the author:

American Dreams: Ancestors and Descendants of John Zimmermann and Eva Katherine Kellenbenz Who Were Married in Philadelphia in 1885

Edison's Environment: The Great Inventor Was Also a Great Polluter

Fundy to Chesapeake; The Thompson, Rundall and Allied Families: Ancestors and Descendants of William Henry Thompson and Sarah D. Rundall, Who Were Married in Linn County, Iowa, in 1889

Hill: The Ferry Keeper's Family, Luke Hill and Mary Hout, Who were Married in Windsor, Connecticut, in 1651 and Fourteen Generations of Their Known and Possible Descendants

John Saxe, Loyalist (1732–1808) and His Descendants for Five Generations

Quakers and Puritans: The Shoemaker, Warren and Allied Families; Ancestors and Descendants of William Toy Shoemaker and Mabel Warren, Who Were Married in Philadelphia in 1895

Western Pilgrims: The Hill, Stockwell and Allied Families; Ancestors and Descendants of George J. Hill and Jessie Fidelia Stockwell, Who Were Married in Wright County, Iowa, in 1882

www.ingramcontent.com/pod-product-compliance
Lightning Source LLC
Chambersburg PA
CBHW060909300426
44112CB00011B/1394